AMERICAN DIPLOMACY

POLICIES AND PRACTICE

AMERICAN DIPLOMACY

POLICIES AND PRACTICE

BY

BENJAMIN H. WILLIAMS

Professor of Political Science
University of Pittsburgh

FIRST EDITION
SECOND IMPRESSION

McGRAW-HILL BOOK COMPANY, INC.

NEW YORK AND LONDON

1936

THE MAPLE PRESS COMPANY, YORK, PA.

To

WILLIAM GWIN WILLIAMS

PREFACE

In the following pages the subject of American foreign relations is discussed from the point of view of political science rather than of history. The principal aim has been to describe and analyze existing policies and institutions rather than to trace the diplomatic narrative, although historical material has been used in order to prepare the proper backgrounds. No claim to finality in treatment is made. Principles arrived at regarding the changing subject of international relations at any given moment must be to some extent tentative. Subsequent discovery of additional data will necessitate a reexamination of present conclusions. Increased use of the resources and methodologies of the related social sciences will improve our understanding of the vast material and psychic forces which bear upon the problem. Thus every era will bring a fresh challenge to scholarship. The present work represents an effort to collect a considerable body of significant data upon an immensely important subject and to organize it according to principles now believed to be valid.

The obligations of the author are many and they extend over a number of years. A general expression of sincere gratitude must suffice for their recognition except in a few salient cases. The great debt to other writers in the field is only partially expressed by footnote references. Certain individuals have been of special service in directing me to sources of current information. Wallace McClure of the Department of State, whose writings on economic diplomacy are well known, was very gracious in making suggestions as to the finding of certain recent material of a technical character. William A. Manger was kind enough to throw light on several matters concerning the significant work of the Pan American Union. Benjamin Gerig and other members of the League of Nations Secretariat courteously placed me in touch with data regarding subjects of American cooperation at Geneva. Concerning the larger movements of the cycle of civilization, with which the subject of American policy should be correlated, I have had the benefit of various discussions with Arnold J. Toynbee, whose expositions of the trends of history as they affect modern international relations are unsurpassed. My colleagues in the Political Science Department of the University of Pittsburgh have made valuable suggestions. Those who have read portions of the manuscript are: Elmer D. Graper, James C. Charlesworth, Roger V. Shumate, Rosalind L. Branning, Louis W. H. Johnston, and Eugene E. Koch. My wife has rendered very great assistance in preparing the manuscript and in making the index. The mention of any individuals will not, I hope, cast upon them any blame for such errors or unwarranted conclusions as may be found in the book.

Benjamin H. Williams.

Pittsburgh, Pennsylvania,
    April, 1936.

CONTENTS

PART II

ECONOMIC DIPLOMACY

PART III

POLICIES OF PEACE AND WORLD ORGANIZATION

AMERICAN DIPLOMACY

CHAPTER I

INTRODUCTION: FROM SECLUSION TO IMPERIALISM OR INTERNATIONALISM

THE QUESTION OF DIRECTION

The World Changes though Opinion Lags. The foreign policy of the United States, the most powerful industrial and social unit which history has yet evolved, must be judged in part by the direction of the world currents in which our destiny is set. If we first consider the trends of those phenomena which affect fundamentally the relationships between nations, it may then be possible to anticipate somewhat the necessities which will beset the American diplomat and to predict in a rough way the drift of events. Failing in the precarious task of prediction, however, the student will at least be fortified against that greatest of intellectual errors: the illusion of permanency in a world of change.

After the fall of the Roman Empire the process of disintegration continued for several centuries. Splendidly paved highways fell into ruin, grass-grown and earth-covered. Pirates intercepted commerce upon the Mediterranean. Cities, centers of ancient commerce, were depopulated; and the shifting sands of oblivion covered much of the work of the Roman. Political adjustments were made to place the world in harmony with localized life. The imperial system of control vanished. Kingdoms replaced the empire and these in time gave way to a feudalism in which, concurrently with an incredibly low standard of living, the manor frequently became self-sufficient to a degree that approached diminutive autarchy. It was a period of exhausted rest following activity, of disintegration after unity. It was the conquest of nature over man, of the forest and creeping vine over the temple and forum. But deeply rooted dogmas remain after facts have changed, and the magnificent imagery of a world state lingered long after the physical and governmental facts had disappeared. For centuries

1

there existed the shell of a Holy Roman Empire which became, as Voltaire said, neither holy nor Roman nor an empire.

But even before the ceremonials of the older world unity had disappeared, the groundwork of a new period had been laid. In the two-beat rhythm of history a day of action followed after a night of slumber. The dynamic condition followed the static, and man began pushing back the jungle in accordance with a spirit of social triumph which we cannot understand but can only observe in its manifestations. The movement, at least in its mechanical aspects, has proceeded most rapidly in the last century and a half, a period which corresponds to the independent existence of the United States. In this age there has also been a great lag in the transition of thought patterns. Widely held theories of localism, state rights, and national isolation have remained long after the processes of national and international unification have made them, in their older sense, grossly inapplicable to the realities about us.

The Future of World-unifying Civilization. As we stand on the slope of the machine age, possessed of a capacity for overcoming nature and for self-destruction unknown to any previous people, the question must necessarily be asked: What is the future of Western civilization? The answer to that question must profoundly affect America's relation to the world. European writers, facing the probability of suicidal wars, are disposed to pessimism. Spengler, in *The Decline of the West*, gloomily predicts that Western society has passed from what he calls the "culture" period to an era of artificiality characterized by the world-city proletariat. We face, he affirms, a twentieth century of wars of annihilation and a period of imperialism. We are to see the spectacle of force-politics coupled with internal decline. Arnold J. Toynbee, author of a stimulating work of scholarship involving the movements of twenty-one civilizations,[1] although less pessimistic than Spengler, casts some doubts likewise upon the value of the achievements of the machine age. Mechanical proficiency and territorial expansion may be symptoms of decay rather than of progress. But he feels that the processes of destruction may still be stayed by intelligent international cooperation if world sentiment can be inspired by a fervent change of heart. American writers, looking at life in a younger society in which conditions portending disaster are less pronounced, generally take a more optimistic view. In that outstanding work by Charles and Mary Beard, *The Rise of American*

[1] *A Study of History* (3 vols. thus far published), Oxford University Press, London, 1934.

Civilization, the authors feel that there is some justification for hope in viewing a civilization that has broken down the outworn patterns of the past to provide a fuller supply of goods and services. The common opinion of the American public, based upon persuasive evidence, is that our civilization is still in the process of achievement. The authors conclude their work with the comment that if this opinion is true, "it is the dawn, not the dusk, of the Gods."

Whichever of these views one may take, it seems fairly evident that a permanent swing backward toward localism will not occur in our time. Even if the gloomy views of Spengler should prove to be justified, the momentum of the machine age will doubtless carry on far beyond the life expectancy of this generation. Whether we face a future of progressive world unification through advancing civilization or are to take a part in a world drama of Caesarism, the isolated and provincial position of the United States has been to a large extent destroyed.

The greatest field of worth-while political adventure lies in the attempt to reshape government to bring it into line with economic and social progress—a progress which in a material sense has been as great during the last century and a half as it had been during the previous millennium. Within each country the state is blindly groping after new systems of business control and after new principles for the distribution of the increasing flood of consumption goods. Governments are tardily seeking to prevent the heartless waste of human resources and to raise standards of living to a point in keeping with the vast growth of production. In the realm of international affairs there has arisen the task of adjusting political machinery to meet the needs of a new world—a world in which the volume of commerce is a hundred times greater and in which the speed of communication is a thousand times faster than in the quiet sphere with which George Washington was familiar.

THE CRESCENDO OF INTERNATIONAL PARTICIPATION

Shipping. It is yet impossible to grasp the full political meaning of the changes in shipping and communication of the last hundred and fifty years. The thirteen colonies were connected with Europe by tiny sailing vessels of 200 or 300 tons which rolled and pitched uncertainly along the slopes of mountainous waves. The *Mayflower* of 180 tons made the voyage from Plymouth to the New England coast in 61 days, which was nine days shorter than the time consumed in the voyage of Columbus from Palos to the Bahamas. When the British Post Office attempted to establish a regular

schedule with the colonies in 1710, the *Royal Anne* on the first trip
made the westward run in 50 days and the return voyage in the fast
time of 28 days.[1] But this was exceptional. Estimating for waits
between boats and for land transportation at either end of the
voyage, one would be forced, even under favorable conditions, to
allow three or four months for the sending of a message and the
receipt of a reply. Under unfavorable conditions the time was much
longer. Only two or three messages could thus be exchanged in the
course of a year. There was no close physical bond of union
between the two worlds. The Declaration of Independence was
long foreshadowed by a growing economic self-reliance and a
cultural independence as the proportion of American-born and
American-educated persons in the colonies increased.

In 1776 the political tie that bound the colonies to the remote
government of Great Britain was formally severed. To achieve this
freedom, however, the Continental Congress was forced to seek the
cooperation of the strongest British rival in Europe; and the French
alliance of 1778 became another form of political union with the
Old World. The association was based on a merely temporary
community of interest. In 1793, when France and England went to
war, the disadvantages of this involvement in the military system
of Europe became apparent. Neutrality was proclaimed and the
French alliance was abrogated. American policies were for a considerable period to be directed mainly toward the ordering of conditions in the Western Hemisphere. The doctrines of isolation and
nonintervention arose. Thus the center of political gravity for the
United States came to coincide much more nearly with the point at
which the lines of American life converged. In 1823 the Monroe
Doctrine was proclaimed to prevent the European powers from
acquiring territories on the American continents and thus to keep
the ocean barrier between the United States and the dreaded
European system.

Changes in transportation, commerce, and communication were,
however, already setting in; and these, in time, were to destroy much
of the factual foundation for isolation. We can measure the progress of material unification by changes in sailing schedules, tonnage, and knots per hour. Sailing packet service was established
across the Atlantic following the War of 1812. Regularity and
greater speed of communication were attained. The chug of the
steamer presaged a new day in transportation. The *Savannah*,

[1] BOWEN, FRANK C., *A Century of Atlantic Travel*, p. 3, Little, Brown &
Company, Boston, 1930.

350 tons, equipped with auxiliary engines, crossed in 1819. For one or two decades the "teakettles" were scoffed at by sailing ship masters, but soon they demonstrated their superiority for speed and regularity over ships propelled solely by the winds just as the sailing vessel had previously surpassed the galley. In 1840 the Cunard Line inaugurated its steamship service; and the *Britannia*, 1,150 tons, made its first run from Liverpool to Boston in 14 days and 8 hours. When the first issue of *The New York Times* was published in 1851, the editors were able to print dispatches from England which were about two weeks old. The period between the date of issue and the date of the news dispatch from Vienna was 22 days, and from Constantinople, 33 days.

Kaleidoscopic changes followed each other in rapid succession. The paddle boat gave way to the screw liner. In 1867 the *City of Paris*, 3,086 tons, made the westward run in 8 days and 4 hours; and in 1889 another vessel of the same name was the first to cross in less than six days. In 1909 the ill-fated *Lusitania*, of 30,696 tons, crossed in 4 days and 11 hours from Queenstown to New York, a distance of 2,870 miles. Since the World War the records for the Atlantic voyage have been broken successively by a number of gigantic liners, including the *Bremen*, 51,656 tons, the *Rex*, 50,100 tons, and the *Normandie*, 79,280 tons. These magnificent floating palaces, equipped with the luxury of a metropolitan hotel, have made of the ocean passage a swift pleasure. The time for transatlantic travel has been reduced to about one-eighth or one-tenth of the fastest eighteenth-century time, and the size of the largest liner has grown to more than 200 times that of the colonial ship.

Air Traffic. In keeping with the fast tempo of modern life has come the airplane, zooming above land boundaries and across wide stretches of water to add further intimacies and complications to international affairs. The Department of Commerce lists nineteen United States foreign air transport routes with a total length of 22,284 miles and a daily average of 13,605 scheduled plane miles.[1] Streamlined flying boats connect the air center of Miami with Cuba, Panama, the northern coast of South America, and, farther south, with Rio de Janeiro, Montevideo, and Buenos Aires. Planes also leave for foreign destinations from such ports as Brownsville, El Paso, Los Angeles, New York, and Seattle. In progress of completion is the transpacific route of the Pan American Airways. Giant clipper ships departing from San Francisco travel to Hawaii,

[1] Bureau of Air Commerce, *Air Commerce Bulletin*, Vol. VII, No. 1 (July 15, 1935), pp. 24–25.

Midway Island, Wake Island, Guam, Manila, and will eventually proceed further to Canton on the Asiatic mainland, a total distance of well over 8,000 miles. Comparable intercontinental air systems operated by European powers are the Imperial Airways, Air France, the Deutsche Lufthansa, the Royal Dutch Airlines, and the Soviet Air Trust. Lines spread outward from Europe to Africa, South America, Asia, and Australia. Already the potentialities of the airplane with regard to our foreign relations may be seen in the inaugurating of closer relations with Latin America and in projecting American enterprise into the Pacific where air bases have a strategic as well as commercial importance. In seeking to prognosticate the future we see the shadowy hands of the great powers reaching out for positions in mid-ocean which can serve as harbors for air commerce or as military air bases.

Communication. The development of transatlantic communication ran for a time parallel with that of shipping. Then with the coming of the cable it pursued an independent course, a course more revolutionary even than that of the transformation of ships. Altogether the facilities for the exchange of intelligence have brought about magical alterations in the conditions of international life. The Jay Treaty was signed in London on November 19, 1794. President Washington did not receive a copy of the document until March 7, 1795, or three and a half months after the signature, owing to the fact that winds from the west had impeded the vessel which carried the treaty back to the United States. The negotiations in Paris in 1803 regarding Louisiana were carried on largely without the knowledge of the President. Four months elapsed between the departure of Mr. Monroe from Washington and the receipt of the treaty which informed Mr. Jefferson that a great empire had been acquired. The negotiators, as is well known, went beyond their instructions in making the purchase. The United States commissioners who went to Ghent in 1814 to make peace with Great Britain were out of touch with military conditions in the United States as well as with the opinion of the Department of State. A period of 132 days elapsed between the last instruction to the commissioners and the receipt of the signed treaty in Washington. During this period the commissioners had been frequently in doubt. Neither group of diplomats at Ghent was informed at any given time of the situation in the zone of war during the previous several months. The opposing forces at the Battle of New Orleans, January 8, 1815, were unaware that the treaty of peace had been signed fifteen days before the engagement. Under early nineteenth-century conditions crises arose which might have made international action desirable, but such crises were reached and passed before governments could be notified. It was impossible for diplomats representing distant countries in that day to deal intelligently with changing situations.

But the world moved on. Despite the jeers of the conservative and unimaginative, a successful transatlantic cable was put into operation in 1866. Dispatches from Europe could now be printed in the newspapers within a day of the occurrence of the events. The effect of the cable in diplomatic communication is shown by the daily exchange of instructions and dispatches between the Department of State and the American peace commissioners in Paris in 1898. The striking difference between the departmental control over the Paris negotiators of 1898 and the Paris negotiators of 1803 or the Ghent negotiators of 1814 reflects the rapid improvement in the conveying of political intelligence throughout the world during a century which had seen the greatest progress in communication in world history.

In 1901 the letters S.O.S. were faintly transmitted across the Atlantic over the Marconi instruments and the wireless had come to add to the facility of transatlantic communication. At the Paris conference of 1919 from 70,000 to 80,000 words were sent home daily to the American papers through the combined facilities of communication which included the wireless tower at Lyons and eight heavily loaded cables connecting France with America.[1] The sending of the summary of the Treaty of Versailles, a 14,000-word dispatch, was considered a notable achievement; but this was eclipsed five years later by the transmission of the Dawes Report of 40,000 words over three cables. In 1915 words spoken over the wireless telephone were first heard across the Atlantic. Loans, stock orders, and Parisian styles soon came to be matters of intercontinental conversation. By 1931 the transatlantic telephone had become such an important agency for the conduct of relations with Europe that Secretary of State Stimson installed a special apparatus with ten receivers in the Department of State to permit as many departmental officials to listen-in on the conversations with Geneva, London, or Paris.[2]

Communication with the continent of Asia shows even a more spectacular contrast between present and early intercourse. In

[1] BAKER, RAY STANNARD, *Woodrow Wilson and World Settlement*, I: 123–124, Doubleday, Page & Company, Garden City, N.Y., 1922.

[2] *N.Y. Times*, Nov. 8, 1931.

1784 the *Empress of China* made the voyage to Canton in 6 months and 6 days and returned in 5 months and 13 days. The whole voyage, counting the stop at Canton, occupied 1 year, 2 months, and 19 days. The words "Japan" and the "Far East" were probably not in the official vocabulary of George Washington, and no mention of China appears in Richardson's *Messages and Papers of the Presidents* until the administration of Andrew Jackson.[1] If, in 1784, the Japanese had sought to extend their military power in Manchuria, the news could have reached New York in about six or seven months; but in that period of American history Manchurian events would not have been regarded as news. An attack upon Shanghai of five weeks duration, similar to that of January, 1932, would doubtless have been deemed worthy of mention; but the information regarding it would not have arrived in the United States until several months after the affair had terminated.

The shortest period for the New York-Shanghai mail transmission, by air across the continent to Seattle and thence by steamer, has been cut to about 18 days, while that for the San Francisco-Manila air route is somewhat under 60 flying hours. Regular communication by cable and wireless is maintained. In 1931 and 1932 most of the dramatic Far Eastern events were regularly reported in the United States within twenty-four hours of their occurrence and they had an immediate and stirring effect upon American public opinion. The rapidity of world communication is well illustrated by the progress of a single negotiation during these difficulties. On February 1, 1932, before breakfast in Washington, a dispatch from Tokyo confirmed previous reports that the Japanese government would welcome the good offices of the powers to extricate it from the embarrassing hostilities at Shanghai. At 9 A.M. President Hoover and Secretary Stimson conferred together and planned a proposal for joint mediation in concert with other governments. At 10 A.M. Secretary of State Stimson broached the matter to the British government over the transatlantic telephone. At 11 A.M. another telephone conversation took place during which the attitude of Great Britain was definitely made known. By noon the two governments had agreed upon the outlines of the plan and cables were sent asking the views of the French and Italian governments. The next day before the sun had risen over the city of Washington, the American and British ambassadors in far-off Tokyo were submitting the plan to the Japanese government, and before they had left the Foreign Office the French ambassador was entering to sup-

[1] See Vol. II, p. 114.

port the proposals. On the same day at Geneva the British representative in the Council of the League of Nations informed that body of the contemplated mediation. The French and Italian representatives then arose to state that their governments were taking action to back the plan, and the President of the Council announced the association of the authority of that body with the scheme.[1] Within the space of thirty-six hours the tentative negotiation which involved the interchange of dispatches and telephonic communications between a half dozen governments on three continents was completed and the newsboys of every American city were shouting the headlines.

Today the telephone connects Washington and the Far East. On December 7, 1934, Secretary of State Hull inaugurated the service by conversing with Koki Hirota, Japanese Foreign Minister, in Tokyo. Mr. Hull during the ceremony referred to the voyage of Perry to Japan in 1853, a journey of many months. Eighty-one intervening years, he said, have seen such a conquest of space by science as permits peoples to talk with one another across the world. Mr. Hirota in reply prophesied the coming of television for the further enhancement of intimacy between nations. The conversation was full of suggestions of unknown and unpredictable political changes which may be expected in some fashion to come straggling after the march of science.[2]

FOREIGN TRADE AND THE CREDITOR BALANCE

A Remarkable Commercial Expansion. Commerce, partly cause and partly effect of improved shipping and communication, has increased likewise during American history to give highly practical reasons for international political development. In 1790 the combined imports and exports of the United States amounted to $43,000,000. Owing in large measure to the Napoleonic Wars these rose swiftly. In 1810 they totaled $152,000,000. Following the destructions of the War of 1812 and the return to normalcy of European competitors, American commerce was restored but slowly. In 1830 it amounted to but $134,000,000. With the development of the cotton industry and the settlement of new lands the total trade rose rapidly to $317,000,000 by 1850. Following the Civil War the increase was swifter still. Railroads, canals, and industries were built and national development had its effect in

[1] *N.Y. Times*, Feb. 3, 1932.
[2] Dept. of State, *Press Releases*, Dec. 8, 1934, pp. 335–336.

greater commerce. The figures were $847,000,000 in 1870 and
$1,647,000,000 in 1890. The commercial stimulation and rising
prices of the early twentieth century carried the value of American
foreign trade by 1910 to $3,429,000,000. The World War saw an
enormous expansion of American commerce which amounted to
more than thirteen billions in 1920. Notwithstanding the postwar
fall in trade the figures stood at $9,640,000,000 in 1929 or over 220
times those of 1790. The rise in commerce was, of course, largely
due to the increase in population. But the value of trade has risen
more rapidly than has the number of people. The per capita trade
in 1790 amounted to $11.00. In 1810 it had risen to $21.00. For
some time after the War of 1812 the per capita commerce receded,
being $10.46 in 1830 and $13.66 in 1850. These were years when
the American people were devoting their energies to the work of
internal improvement and the center of population was shifting
away from the Atlantic seaboard. After the Civil War, however,
foreign trade became more important than ever to the citizen,
reaching $21.96 in 1870, $26.17 in 1890, $37.29 in 1910, and $79.20
in 1929. Thus the per capita foreign trade of 1929 was some seven
times that of 1790.

Diminuendo—the Depression and Foreign Trade. With the
coming of the depression in 1929 the strong international commercial
and investment forces were dealt a heavy blow. Trade fell rapidly.[1]
Combined imports and exports, which were $9,640,000,000 in 1929,
declined to $2,935,000,000 by 1932. The balance of exports over
imports dropped from $841,000,000 to $289,000,000 during the
same years. If rising trade and investment have the effect of
creating influences for programs of international expansion through
force or cooperation, then the effect of a drop in the figures may be
expected to have a contrary result because of the bankruptcy and
humiliation of many groups engaged in foreign enterprise. Apparently the depression had this effect. International bankers were
vigorously assailed in Congress and in public discussion. Financiers
interested in foreign investments were almost entirely ignored as,
e.g., in the debates from 1932 to 1935 over the independence of the
Philippines. A trend back to nationalism and localism seemed
under way. Some persons alleged that the rise of Western civilization had come to an end in 1929 and that a collapse comparable
to the fall of the Roman Empire was under way. There was much
talk of the desirability of autarchy or national self-sufficiency. In

---

[1] For a world-wide picture of the depression see League of Nations, *World
Economic Survey*, 1931–1932, and the same publication for 1932–1933.

America Self-contained,[1] a book circulated by the Chemical Foundation, Samuel Crowther declared that the United States should close its markets to all foreign commodities except those that are essential. He then proceeded to show that there are practically no essential imports which could not be supplied in the United States either directly or by substitution through chemical processes. His ultranationalist attitude was well indicated by the declaration: "Fortunately we need no friends; fortunately we need fear no enemies."[2] During this time Mr. Hearst's "Buy American!" was echoed in the commercial club of the small town: "Buy Bingville!" The proponents of autarchy were shortsightedly attempting to appraise a long-time movement only by its failures and to evaluate the rise of a world unity only by its cyclical depressions.

On the other hand, there were writers who believed that the making of governmental adjustments for a permanent world collapse where there was no such collapse would be nothing short of an attempt to force the fall of a civilization which was still ascending toward its zenith. What agonies would attend such a ruthless disruption can be partially imagined. Secretary of Agriculture Henry A. Wallace pictured the violent effects which isolation would have upon the American population. Many United States industries, too well developed to be satisfied by the local market, would necessarily be severely curtailed and the policy would occasion enormous distress. The government would be forced, Mr. Wallace explained, to make permanent the retirement from cultivation of from 40,000,000 to 100,000,000 acres of crop land to reduce the immense annual exports of agriculture. It might be necessary to shift part of the population from the cotton lands of the South. To find occupations for the dispossessed farmers would be a responsibility of no small proportions. The same problems on a somewhat smaller scale would be encountered in the corn and wheat belts.[3] But while the debate raged the fallen figures of international trade started once more to rise. Prophecies of a return to a national or local economy had been premature. In 1935 the United States had a total trade of $4,280,633,142 although the surplus of exports over imports amounted to but $203,357,282.

The volume of American foreign trade has had a strong relation to American policy in that it has created large exporting and import-

---

[1] Doubleday, Doran & Company, Garden City, N.Y., 1933.

[2] P. 1.

[3] *America Must Choose*, World Affairs Pamphlets, No. 3, pp. 10–11. See also TIPPETTS, CHARLES S., *Autarchy: National Self-sufficiency*, Public Policy Pamphlets, No. 5, University of Chicago Press, Chicago, 1933.

ing groups whose welfare is vitally affected by conditions of world business. The individual may not be conscious that materials in his fountain pen or watch come from abroad or that the wheat, cotton, electrical goods, or automobiles which he helps to produce are sold abroad; but somewhere in Washington are located lobbyist organizations which are aware of these facts and know precisely what changes in policy are necessary to protect or to stimulate the particular economic activity in question.

The Favorable Balance and the Outward Pressure. Aside from the volume of trade there is an important factor, the creditor or debtor balance, which profoundly affects political action. So long as the import and export items, visible and invisible, in a country's international account are evenly matched without requiring loans or gold movements to balance, there is a minimum pressure of international economics upon national institutions. But if there is a so-called favorable relationship of items, *i.e.*, one which requires loans or investments abroad or inward gold movements to reach a balance, an outward political pressure is generated. If we can imagine that nations are like compartments separated from each other by movable walls and that international business transactions involve a flow from compartment to compartment over these walls, we can see that, when the movements are strongly outward from one compartment, the tendency is to push back its walls and to move those of other compartments inward. But if in each case the outward pressures are exactly equal to the inward pressures, there is no stress placed upon the walls. When a country has a so-called favorable balance in the international account over a long period of time, gold movements will not suffice and the balance must be accounted for by foreign loans and investments. The resulting tendency toward political expansion of strong nations has thus far been irresistible. Contrariwise, when there has been a sudden excess of inward pressures over outward pressures, such as came in many countries with the depression, the detrimental effect upon national institutions has rendered the situation critical. Thus, for example, when an excess of imports has drained gold from beneath the national currency the whole economic and governmental structure has been imperiled. Many desperate nations have accordingly been engaged in the last few years in building supports to their compartmental walls by means of higher tariffs, quotas, and exchange restrictions.

The United States is the chief center of outward economic pressures in the modern world. During the period from 1896 to

1933 inclusive this country had a favorable balance of trade amounting to $36,646,000,000. When items visible and invisible are set off against each other for this period, a creditor balance is shown of approximately $25,000,000,000 which is accounted for by loans, investments, and gold movements.[1] A tremendous outward force of these proportions if continued in the future is certain to result in enormous political stress upon existing institutions, and it hardly seems possible that recurring creditor balances can be avoided by the United States. There are certain concepts concerned in the inevitable process of readjustment which must be discussed at this point. Chief among these concepts are nationalism, imperialism, and internationalism.

NATIONALISM, IMPERIALISM, INTERNATIONALISM

Nationalism. Nationalism is the sense of unity within an area among at least a majority of the inhabitants who have similar racial, linguistic, or religious characteristics or unifying community experiences. A people seized with a national sentiment have a feeling for independence from the domination of other peoples, aspiring to achieve such freedom if it is not yet attained; and, if it is already accomplished, they are determined to maintain it against the incoming internationalistic or imperialistic tendencies of the times.

The radius along which the individual can feel a fellowship with other human beings about him is limited. Modern ethnological research, education, improved communication, and the increased sweep of business have lengthened the radius and have thus enlarged the area in which a community consciousness is possible. In a period of rising materialist civilization the unit of political fellowship changes from the manor to the principality and then to the nation-state. In one lifetime the primary allegiance of the Japanese subject swung from the local daimio to the Emperor. In an area which presents particularly favorable conditions for the spread of a common social consciousness, as in the United States, it has now become possible to create a sensitive feeling of oneness among a people on almost a continental scale. In some areas which are backward industrially and where also psychological obstacles of a historical nature block the spread of nationalism, the nation area is small indeed, as it is in Eastern and Southern Europe. Here it is

---

[1] PEEK, GEORGE N., *Letter to the President on Foreign Trade* (May 23, 1934), p. 4, Govt. Printing Office, Washington, 1934.

that the individual suffers most in the conflict between economics and politics.

The circles of nationalism move outward slowly. Far as the mind is now able to reach through the human mass to seek national companionship, it cannot keep pace with the economic and materialistic influences which easily shoot out beyond the confines set by mass mentality. Thus nationalism can be seen as a lag in the distance of unification (social psychology falling short of economics) as conservatism is a lag in the time of adjustment. A fundamental conflict arises between international material forces—which may be represented by trade routes, lines of communication, and threads of foreign investments—and the existing nation-state system graphically symbolized by boundary lines drawn upon a map. It is morally certain that political forms will be continually modified in the future as in the past. The pressures for change come from private groups which look for profits in international projects, and they also take the form of public movements for participation in wider activities for reasons of national interest. Frequently the private and public aspects are closely intertwined. As the changes in national boundaries come through conquests by strong nations, we have the phenomenon of imperialism. As national institutions are adjusted to the new economic order through the cooperative and voluntary action of states, we have internationalism. We must expect one or the other or both, mixed together in varying proportions. If there is to be no cooperative method of rechannelizing new forces, then such provisions for maintaining the political *status quo* as Article X of the Covenant of the League of Nations are futile.

Imperialism. As a nation-state becomes the center of superior economic radiations, the general tendency is for it to expand politically. The small empire of Japan is the center of the most vigorous economic life in Eastern Asia. Without the territory to support their industries the Japanese have pushed outward their political boundaries. The lines of least resistance to imperialism lead into backward areas which, not yet affected by the quickening influences of modern life, have developed no great psychological or military defense. Imperialism may also extend into territory occupied by other nation-states, striking against the national boundaries and attempting to destroy the national institutions. In such cases the resistance is greater and the conflict more bloody.

Imperialism is in one sense the outgrowth of nationalism, but the two must be distinguished. When imperialistic interests sweep outward into another territory and build up an economic life which in turn sends its disturbing waves rolling backward into the parent country, the difference between nationalism and imperialism becomes evident. The economic nationalists of the mother country then protest this invasion from the annexed region and a conflict is staged between nationalistic and imperialistic economic interests. Thus the grape growers of southern France are pitted against those of Algeria, the farmers and coal miners of Japan against those of Manchuria, and the sugar beet growers of Colorado against the cane planters of the Philippines.

Internationalism. Internationalism signifies the adjustment of national institutions to modern world influences through the voluntary cooperation of nation-states. It is an intermediate position between strict nationalism and the doctrine of a world state. It seeks to conduct the rising voltage of international economics by safe and insulated transmission lines across national boundaries. Legislative conferences for the development of law, judicial machinery for the settlement of disputes, and administrative bodies for the application of international treaties are the means of cooperative internationalism. One of the most difficult problems of internationalism is thus far unsolved, *i.e.*, the necessity of cooperative change in national rights and institutions when development in world conditions makes the existing legal setup no longer adequate.

When a strong nation, like the United States, enters into cooperative internationalism with other nations, such as in the Pan American Union, the strong power must be prepared to make concessions as well as to receive benefits. Some pressure groups in the stronger country will oppose such concessions with great vigor. But certainly the weaker nations will not be prepared to receive voluntarily the economic invasions from the stronger nation without guarantees in return. The new situation must be made palatable to both. Another difficulty in internationalism is to bring about a voluntary cooperation between a large number of jealous nationalisms. The attempt to reach agreements between numerous political units runs athwart of a multiplicity of objections which appear important to the particular nations. The task of appeasing these objections is one of great delicacy requiring infinite patience. Imperialism has no such complicated adjustments to make. It operates more definitely and more ruthlessly behind powerful emotions that are not embarrassed by the mental conflicts that arise in rational thinking. And it will not wait forever on the tiresome debates of hair-splitting nationalists who place impossible barriers to the formation of international agreements. On the other hand, the great advantage of internationalism over imperialism is in the conservation of human resources and productive capacities by the cooperative method. Imperialism, leading to war, is enormously destructive of the resources of the conqueror and of the conquered. Rome brought about unification with Carthaginia after the terrific campaigns of the Punic Wars that devastated the industry and drained the resources of both countries and left the greatest commercial city of antiquity a jumble of blackened stones.

The Alternatives. As the United States continues its economic progress the outward pressures, as measured in so-called favorable balances of visible and invisible items, will probably force this country to adopt one of the two alternatives of imperialism or internationalism or both in mixture. There seem to be only two possibilities that this will not occur. One is that by periodic defaults the world will wipe out its indebtedness to the United States and thus relieve the political pressures. The other is that by a system of internal distribution for use and not for profit the United States may be able to turn surplus productive power inward to the raising of the American standard of living, bringing about a possibility of balancing the international account without outward pressure.[1] Assuming for the time being that neither of these possibilities is a probability, which, then, will be emphasized in our policy: imperialism or internationalism? The evidence of the intentions of the government cannot be read entirely from current policies. For it may be that great forces are now being mobilized which are not yet translated into diplomacy but which will later sweep us into political action contrary to any present official intention. The indications of imperialism and of internationalism in American policy will be traced in the following chapters.

The primary forces making for internationalism and imperialism are not composed of lecturers and writers on peace and world cooperation or speculators, concessionaires, and proponents of expansion urging us on to conquest. These are only staff correspondents and camp followers in a campaign in which the army of modern tech-

---

[1] Charles A. Beard, in *The Open Door at Home* (The Macmillan Company, New York, 1935), believes that the difficulties in which we become involved by foreign trade might well be solved by turning the forces of American wealth and energy to the task of raising the standard of living at home. Exports, he believes, should be made only in such quantities as are required to purchase imports that are necessary for this purpose. Whether this excellent aim can be reached under a capitalistic system of production, however, is a matter of serious doubt.

nology is slowly but ruthlessly pushing back the horizons of
human life. The great enlisted strength of the army is made up of
men of steel—tireless, mechanically moving robots. In the hier-
archy of command are machine tenders, mechanics, electricians,
draftsmen, chemists, engineers, captains of industry. The successive triumphs of this powerful force are not immediately or fully
appreciated. Battles are won and positions are taken long before
the indifferent and preoccupied public is aware of the trend of the
campaign. But even before the public is informed of the significance of the new movement, political action has been taken to
adjust government to its wider scope of operation. The United
States is a part of this procession of facts. It is the first nation to
apply the power of machinery, chemistry, electricity, and radioactivity upon a modern scale to the development of a large and
homogeneous population. But the American people interpret their
political role in accordance with an ideology, part of which was
derived from simple preindustrial conditions. In the attempt to
understand the changing world, to anticipate the political alternatives, and perhaps to play a part in making the governmental
adjustments, the serious student will find a fascinating field for
study and work.

PART I
REGIONAL POLICIES

CHAPTER II

POLICY VARIATIONS BY AREAS

THE DEPARTURE FROM ISOLATION

Noncooperation and Nonintervention, the Original Bases of American Policy. The oft-quoted warning in Washington's Farewell Address with regard to entangling our peace in the toils of European ambition was directed against a particular type of obligation, *i.e.*, a permanent political compact such as the embarrassing French alliance of 1778 which had then been but recently ruptured.[1] Washington left room for entrance into temporary alliances. He also at other times suggested that international consultations for the common advantage of nations might in time be advisable. In the decades after 1796, however, the major emphasis was placed upon the isolation features of Washington's advice. In time two precepts of peacetime seclusion came to stand forth: (*a*) nonparticipation in cooperative action with a group of governments or with the whole community of nations and (*b*) nonintervention in the internal affairs of other single nations. While there were instances in early relations which cast doubt upon the complete acceptance of these twin principles of isolation, they may be regarded as the bases of early American diplomacy. They were appropriate foundation stones in the policy of a weak nation. The variation from the first of these precepts in more recent years represents the American trend toward internationalism, and the departure from the second is characteristic of imperialism.

The Trend toward Cooperation and Intervention. For one hundred years after independence the conditions making for isola-

---

[1] As a matter of fact the alliance of 1778 was a departure from a previously formed resolution not to become involved in the politics of Europe. BEMIS, SAMUEL FLAGG, *The Diplomacy of the American Revolution*, pp. 12, 46, 48, D. Appleton-Century Company, Inc., New York, 1935.

tion remained dominant. Most of the national energy was exerted in internal development. It is true that foreign commerce was gradually increasing in value and that improved communications made the American public more alert as to conditions abroad. But for about a century, during which time the United States was a debtor country, the reasons for positive policies abroad were not sufficiently strong to overcome the well-developed inhibitions against such policies. By about 1880 the forces making for international political action could no longer be denied. Cautiously, and often against domestic opposition, the United States began to cooperate in international legislation with regard to nonpolitical matters. Until 1884 the United States had participated officially in but two international conferences. In the next three decades this country was represented in twenty-eight such conferences.[1] And today the number is sometimes as high as forty or fifty per year.[2]

Until the time of the World War the United States lacked a certain driving force in the international field owing to the fact that this country was still debtor to the world at large. The Universal Postal Union, the Brussels Convention regarding the slave trade in Africa, and the conventions of the Hague Conferences are typical of the projects in which the United States was willing to participate. Representation in the Algeciras Conference of 1906, regarding the highly charged Moroccan situation, was exceptional for that period. While the United States was still borrowing from Europe, American capital was moving into the Caribbean region; and American marines and warships began to play a part in Caribbean politics. The Panama affair, the "Big Stick" policy in the Dominican Republic, and the Platt Amendment in Cuba indicated that the

[1] BLAKESLEE, GEORGE H., *The Recent Foreign Policy of the United States*, p. 20, Abingdon Press, New York, 1925.

[2] The United States participated in 48 international conferences and congresses in 1929, in 61 during 1930, in 50 during 1931, and in 23 during 1932. Dept. of State, *The Department of State of the United States*, p. 17, Govt. Printing Office, Washington, 1933. The Division of Protocol and Conferences supplies the information that the government participated in 51 conferences, congresses, or international meetings in 1933 and in 59 during 1934. In addition this country participates in the work of a considerable number of international bureaus and commissions. Dept. of State, *American Delegations to International Conferences, Congresses and Expositions and American Representation on International Institutions and Commissions with Relevant Data* (annual publication). Twenty-nine organizations to which the United States belongs are described in SCHMECKEBIER, LAURENCE F., *International Organizations in Which the United States Participates*, Brookings Institution, Washington, 1935.

doctrine of nonintervention was on the wane. Philander C. Knox, Secretary of State from 1909 to 1913, was seeking to derive the greatest possible political influence from the export of capital; but his ambitions for dollar diplomacy ran far ahead of the financial support which he could obtain from American bankers.

With the coming of the World War a vast stream of merchandise flowed outward to make all continents debtor to this country. From July 1, 1914, until the end of 1922, a term of years which has been called the war period of American commerce, the world at large was placed in the debt of the United States to the extent of about $19,000,000,000. Such powerful forces moving like a mighty flood played havoc with old American ideals of isolation. Washington's warnings against becoming embroiled in the conflicts of Europe were suddenly ignored, and in 1917 the United States plunged headlong into the greatest of all European wars. This country spent its wealth and energies profusely in the settlement of matters which were largely European in character. Was it democracy, a zeal for peace, trade protection, banker influence, national defense, or a desire to rectify the balance of power in Europe by preventing the domination of Germany that caused America to leap into the center of the European turmoil? When the psychoanalysis of the nation as it existed in April, 1917, is finally achieved, great weight will probably be placed on subconscious prejudices which were not acknowledged in presidential messages. It will probably be shown that submerged desires running with strong economic tides swept the United States all unaware toward the cause of the Allies. Social psychology may one day reveal that when President Wilson was being elected in 1916 on the slogan: "He Kept Us Out of War," at that very time the hum of industry and the departure of cargoes were making it impossible that the promise implied in the campaign could be carried out.

Following the World War the United States repudiated the League of Nations which it had helped to create. Notwithstanding this action, the American government participated in an increasing measure in world conferences both political and nonpolitical. It here becomes necessary to emphasize a differentiation between participation in the creation of world organization and law, on the one hand, and the attempt to control the political and economic life of special areas, on the other. The first type of cooperation is dealt with in Part III of this volume. The second class of action is the subject of the following pages, which deal with regional policies in Europe, the Far East, and Latin America.

VARIATIONS IN THE APPLICATION OF POLICIES BY CONTINENTS

Factors to Be Considered. The new policies of cooperation and intervention, as they have been used to adjust the life of particular areas to our greater advantage, have found varying degrees of attraction and repulsion in the different continents. Originally the doctrine of isolation was promulgated with reference to Europe, for it was only from that continent that temptations to entanglements seemed to come. The doctrine was frequently expressed, however, in universal language as if it included the whole world. Its strength has differed widely as it has been applied to the major areas. A brief résumé of the distinctive factors affecting American diplomacy in each of the continents will demonstrate the contrasts in conditions which have brought about a differentiation of policies. While a large number of considerations must enter into the regional diplomacy of a country, in the present comparison only the principal factors will be considered. The positive factors which tempt this country to leave its isolation and to enter into active guardianship in other lands are the strategic and the economic. Strategic factors are: (1) primary, those relating to positions connected with the actual defense of the American people, such as the Panama Canal, and (2) secondary, those relating to positions connected with the advancement of trade or imperialism, such as the Island of Guam. Of these, it is plain, the primary strategic positions are of far greater importance in the policy of a country such as the United States whose vital interests are located at home. The economic factors are connected mainly with trade and investments. Their strength depends upon the amounts involved and the possibility that political action in the particular region is an effective means to improve the prospects of American businessmen. On the negative side the strongest restraining influence tending to keep the United States true to its early policies of noncooperation and nonintervention is the fear of military involvement. War looms in the background as a threat to those who assume active responsibility in other regions.

Europe. There are in Europe no points of strategic value to the United States. American economic interests have been of great importance in that continent but they have not been such as could be favorably affected by policies energetically exerted upon European affairs. Resentments created by American interference would undoubtedly have done more harm than good to American business. Furthermore, during the greater part of the period in which our policy was being formed, this country was a debtor to Europe; and from our standpoint the economic pressures were thrusting inward rather than outward. The fear of military entanglement has been keen with regard to ventures in Europe where a balance of power has divided strongly armed nations into hostile camps. The factors which have affected our diplomacy in Europe thus far have accordingly been strongly conducive to isolation. The United States has dealt with European powers with regard to Asia, Africa, and America, but not, in any serious way, except in the World War period, with regard to matters in Europe. Perhaps a time will come when, due to the increase of American investments and the debacle of continental militarism, the United States will feel strong enough to attempt the dangerous task of acting as guardian to the estate of an incapacitated Europe. Or perhaps a reform of the European system or the rise of Soviet Russia will place such a development completely out of the realm of possibility. At any rate a responsibility for strictly European affairs is not in the contemplation of this generation of Americans. The questions as to whether we should settle our problems with Europe by regular judicial or conciliatory processes and as to whether we should act with them in building up world institutions for the development of law—these are entirely different matters. They should not be construed to be a regional policy for the adjustment of European affairs. In fact it may well be argued that, should the United States support the institutions of world law, war in Europe might be made less likely and the probability of American involvement in that region might be correspondingly reduced.

Asia. Asia possesses no primary strategic interest for this country. The Philippines and Guam are strategic positions of a secondary character. The principal incentive for seeking to order the affairs of the Far East has been the hope of trade. Expectancy of a new era in which the world's commercial center is to shift from the Atlantic to the Pacific has made it impossible to dismiss the Far East from consideration in Washington. Diplomatic positions have been taken from time to time with regard to the open door in China and the maintenance of war vessels in Far Eastern waters for the purpose of guarding business interests. Until comparatively recent years the progress of American policy in Asia ran unhindered by the prospect of serious military entanglements. China presented no threat; and, during a large part of the period of policy-incubation, Japan was not an important power. Distance, the lack of primary strategic interests, and the slowness of development of trade and investments have been influences for moderation in policy. The fact that about half of the Americans resident in China are connected with missions has been a restraining influence. The progress of missionary work might well be impeded by strong policies of intervention by the United States in China. Altogether the American government has not been willing to exert much force or pressure in the Orient. Among the policies of the great powers that of the United States has been distinguished by a restraint which has been approved at home but which has at times been denounced as weakness by impatient Americans resident in Asia.

Africa. The United States can hardly be said to have a policy in Africa. This country has possessed no strategic interests in the Dark Continent; and, since the abandonment of the slave trade, the economic relations have been of slight consequence. Rubber investments in Liberia have given the United States an interest in that republic in recent years, but the amounts involved seem to be too small to call for any emphatic commitments. The slave trade and a desire for its suppression have in turn aroused American interest in Africa. There has been nothing to fear from the military strength of African countries, but there has been a potential danger from the possible clash of aims with those of European powers which have acquired practically the whole of the continent.

Latin America. Latin America remains the one area in which the development of an important regional policy has seemed justified. Primary and vital strategic reasons have given us a great concern in Central America and the Caribbean while investments and trade have added to this interest. No fear of military disaster has existed with regard to the relations between the United States and other American republics. In fact the proper adjustment by this country of the politics of Latin America has always appeared to hold out the hope of reducing the military threat from Europe. Accordingly the regional policies of the United States in Latin America as a whole and particularly in the Caribbean region have been stronger than similar American policies in any other part of the world. The United States has gone further both in international cooperation and in intervention in these regions than in any others. The following table is a rough attempt to appraise the various factors affecting American policy in each of the great regions. The table is presented as a summary—an effort to show at one glance the main forces working for and against American initiative in regional policies; and no precision is claimed for the values assigned.

ROUGH ESTIMATE OF POSITIVE AND NEGATIVE FACTORS IN THE FORMATION OF
UNITED STATES REGIONAL POLICIES
(1, slight; 2, considerable; 3, very great)

Factors	Europe	Asia	Africa	Latin America
Positive:				
Strategic............	0	1	0	3
Economic...........	3	2	1	2
Miscellaneous......	...	....	0.5(racial)	
Negative:				
Military danger....	−3	−1.5	−1	−1
Miscellaneous......	...	−0.5(missionary)		
Total or index of forces making for positive regional policies....	0	1	0.5	4

With this brief sketch of the major factors shaping American
policies for the adjustment of the affairs of the various continents,
it is now appropriate to take up the principal regional policies in
detail.

CHAPTER III

NONPARTICIPATION IN THE AFFAIRS OF EUROPE: NEUTRALITY, NONCOOPERATION, NONINTERVENTION

There are three possible methods by which the United States might attempt to enforce regional policies in Europe:

1. By participation in a European war, throwing our weight on one side or the other and determining the balance of power.

2. By peaceful cooperation with a group of countries in Europe to change political or economic conditions on that continent.

3. By single intervention to control the policies of a particular European government in order to serve certain of our own interests.

The purpose of this chapter is to consider the general American aversion to all of these types of action and to set forth the conditions which, despite this disinclination, have tempted the United States at various times to leave its isolation and to participate in the regional politics of Europe. It should be reiterated that policies to control peculiarly European affairs must be distinguished from cooperation in a world-wide movement to maintain a regime of peace or to improve conditions in all nations, including our own, through international legislation and administration. The unwillingness of the United States at times to participate in the world movement is not discussed here but is considered in later chapters.

OUR NEUTRALITY POLICY— ITS SUCCESSES, FAILURES, AND PRESENT STATUS

Because our neutrality policy first grew out of a particular European situation and because its chief applications have been with regard to Europe, it seems desirable to treat the subject in connection with our policy concerning that continent. The neutrality policy has been an important part of the European policy of the United States.

The Abrogation of the French Alliance. Under the Treaty of Alliance with France of 1778 the United States agreed to guarantee forever the French possessions in America. Under the Treaty of Commerce and Amity of the same year French prizes taken in war were permitted to be brought into American ports. When, in 1793, war broke out between France and a European coalition consisting of England, Prussia, Austria, and the Netherlands, the French did not make an open demand upon the United States for full compliance with the Treaty of Alliance. They did, however, claim that the privilege of bringing prizes into American harbors included the right to arm the prizes in port for the purposes of raiding the commerce of their enemies. Citizen Gênet, who came to the United States as French minister, set up prize courts under French consuls in this country and issued commissions to privateers to prey upon British trade. The situation was critical for the American government. If the French practices had been condoned, the United States would probably have become involved in a war with Great Britain and other strong powers. To have been dragged into a destructive conflict over a purely European question would have been highly disastrous to the young nation which was just then struggling to its feet. The French alliance had ceased to be of value from the American point of view.

Economic reasons also dictated abrogation. American foreign trade was conducted largely with Great Britain. France had tried energetically to develop commerce with the United States, but American customs and language proved to be powerful influences in throwing the business to England. British merchants had also been better able to extend credit than had their French rivals. American naval stores and other products found a considerable market in England. In 1790 the Americans exported $20,194,794 worth of goods of which $9,246,526 went to England. In the same year the total of imports paying ad valorem duties was $15,388,409 of which $13,798,168 came from England. American vessels furnished more than 40 per cent of the tonnage engaged in this trade.[1] Professor Bemis describes the value of the British commerce to the United States at about this time as follows:

If Anglo-American commerce was indispensable to British prosperity in 1789 it was vitally necessary for the national existence of the United States. By that year a complete recovery had been made from the collapse of commerce that accompanied the Revolution, and the new Government was heavily dependent on that prosperity in making the experiment of Nationalism in the Constitution. Ninety per cent of American imports came from Great Britain and the American revenue came mostly from tariff on imports. Suddenly to have upset commercial relations with Great Britain, no matter how unfair and humiliating the British discriminations against American commerce, would have meant the destruc-

[1] For a discussion of Anglo-American commerce of this period see BEMIS, SAMUEL FLAGG, *Jay's Treaty, A Study in Commerce and Diplomacy*, Chap. II, The Macmillan Company, New York, 1923.

tion of three-fourths of American foreign commerce. To use a later expression of Alexander Hamilton, it would have cut out credit by the roots. Without financial credit the new national government must have reverted to the pitiful impotency of the old Confederation. The experiment of the Constitution would have ended in failure. It is this very real fact which dominated the foreign policy of the United States. . . . [1]

There was, however, a large element in the United States which, remembering with gratitude the part of France in the Revolutionary War and exulting over the downfall of the Bourbon monarchy, desired that the American government should take up the French cause. This group came into conflict with the wealthier New England merchants and Federalist leaders who stanchly opposed any assistance to France and who regarded the French alliance as destructive of their interests.

The Proclamation of 1793. The decision to remain neutral, which was made by President Washington in consultation with his cabinet, inaugurated the new policy of the United States. The proclamation of April 22, 1793, putting the policy into effect, avoided the use of the term "neutrality"; but the absence of the word did not affect the character of the pronouncement. In the proclamation the President recited the existence of war between France and the opposing coalition and stated that the duty and interests of the United States required a friendly and impartial conduct toward the belligerents. He exhorted and warned American citizens to avoid all acts which were contrary to such a course and declared that the protection of the United States would not be extended to any citizens who should violate the law of nations by committing, aiding, or abetting hostilities or by carrying contraband. He announced that he had given instructions to prosecute any who should violate the law of nations in giving assistance to either of the parties to the conflict. In the following year Congress passed the first neutrality act which made more specific the obligations of American citizens and imposed penalties upon all who should violate the statute. The law forbade the performance of a number of acts within the United States against any power with which this country should be at peace. Among these acts were the acceptance and exercise of military commissions, the enlistment of soldiers, the fitting out and arming of vessels, and the organization of military expeditions.[2]

[1] *Ibid.*, pp. 35–36.
[2] For a study of our neutrality system see Fenwick, Charles G., *The Neutrality Laws of the United States*, Carnegie Endowment for International Peace, Washington, 1913.

Benefits of Neutrality. The policy framed in 1793 by Washington and his cabinet suggested itself naturally to a New World government. It was a break with the past, but the wisdom of the declaration is beyond dispute. The United States avoided for a considerable time the military expenditures and commercial devastation which war would have entailed. Neutrality brought returns in increased prosperity which had not been entirely anticipated. So long as the United States remained out of the struggle, American shipbuilding, commerce, and finance enjoyed a phenomenal increase due to the heavy demands of the belligerents for American vessels and goods. American shipping expanded from 478,377 tons in 1790 to 1,424,783 tons in 1810. American foreign trade, which amounted to $62,253,000 in 1792, the year before the war, rose to $246,843,000 in the peak year of 1807. Receipts from customs duties were multiplied more than four times. These were the gratifying dividends which were yielded by the policy of remaining aloof from the quarrels of Europe.

When President Washington came to deliver his Farewell Address in 1796, he already had had some opportunity to observe the blessings of neutrality. It was this advantage which he had in mind when he made the following statement, often taken as the text for sermons on the gospel of isolation:

Europe has a set of primary interests which to us have none or a very remote relation. Hence she must be engaged in frequent controversies, the causes of which are essentially foreign to our concerns. Hence, therefore, it must be unwise in us to implicate ourselves by artificial ties in the ordinary vicissitudes of her politics or the ordinary combinations and collisions of her friendships or enmities.

For the same reasons President Jefferson, in his first inaugural address delivered in 1801, advocated: "peace, commerce, and honest friendship with all nations, entangling alliances with none." The term "entangling alliances," which has become famous in the literature of isolation, was used with reference to the French alliance and similar special agreements.[1]

When the next great European war broke out in 1914, the power to proclaim neutrality had been long vested by practice in the Executive. President Wilson accordingly issued a proclamation on August 4, 1914. Abstinence from the war coupled with the oppor-

---

[1] "This expression, now become proverbial, was unquestionably used by Mr. Jefferson in reference to the alliance with France of 1778." From a note of Edward Everett, Secretary of State in 1852, *Moore's Digest*, VI: 463.

tunity to profit because of the increased needs and reduced production of Europe again brought a lucrative neutral trade to the United States. This country was swept by a tidal wave of prosperity. American exports jumped from $2,329,684,025 for the year ending June 30, 1914, to $6,227,164,050 for the year ending June 30, 1917. The so-called favorable balance of trade was multiplied eight times during neutrality, rising from $435,758,368 to $3,567,808,865. The United States now for the first time in its history showed a heavy favorable balance of accounts considering both visible and invisible items. If there is any validity to the theory of the outward pressures resulting from a favorable balance, the United States was about to be shoved abruptly from its isolation. At any rate the American people enjoyed for a short time a period of unprecedented business stimulation. By 1917, however, the purchasing power of the Allies was reaching a state of exhaustion. President Wilson on March 5, 1917, received an amazing telegram from Walter Hines Page suggesting that perhaps the only method of preventing a panic in the United States was to enter the war and lend the Allies the funds with which to buy American goods.[1] By this action, said Ambassador Page, the United States could "reap the profit of an uninterrupted and perhaps an enlarging trade over a number of years." The dread of a panic and the love of prosperity have always been powerful motivations to political action. Who can estimate their proportionate influence in the decisions of 1917?

The Failure of American Neutrality. In the two major European struggles in which American neutrality has been proclaimed, the policy has ultimately failed to keep this country out of war. The attempt to protect an inflated neutral commerce under a claim of neutral rights has in both cases led us into armed conflict. During the Napoleonic Wars the United States waged an undeclared naval war with France in 1798 and a formally declared war with Great Britain in 1812. In the World War the United States was able to maintain neutrality for almost three years; but, after serious conflicts with both parties over the doctrine of neutral rights, this country finally entered the struggle in 1917. The American government as an "associated power" became virtually a member of an alliance with European governments. At the end our statesmen were engaged in helping to adjust boundaries in Europe and in deciding a multitude of strictly European questions. The present political system of Europe was determined in no small part by the

[1] HENDRICK, BURTON J., *The Life and Letters of Walter H. Page*, II: 269–271, Doubleday, Page & Company, Garden City, N.Y., 1922.

United States. This country expended and incurred obligations
sometimes estimated as high as $100,000,000,000 for the privilege of
making these decisions. Probably the strongest of all American
policies, that of keeping out of European politics, was disregarded on
account of so-called neutral rights.

Belligerents, fighting for their existence, are certain to attempt
to shut off trade with their enemies. The concepts of blockade and
contraband have been created to explain and legalize their activities.
They seek to expand these doctrines as far as possible. In both the
Napoleonic Wars and the World War each set of belligerents refused
to abide by traditional practices. Protesting this disregard of
so-called law, American diplomats have vainly sought to procure the
observance of a strict construction of blockade, contraband, and
visit and search.[1] During the World War the United States
declared that the sinking by German submarines without warning
of merchant ships bound for England constituted a violation of
American rights. This doctrine was pressed so far as almost to
commit the United States to enter the war because of the destruction of the Lusitania, a British ship carrying passengers and supplies,
including munitions, to Great Britain. In the note of May 13, 1915,
regarding the Lusitania, the following language was used by Secretary Bryan:

The Imperial German Government will not expect the Government of
the United States to omit any word or any act necessary to the performance
of its sacred duty of maintaining the rights of the United States and its
citizens and of safeguarding their free exercise and enjoyment.

When this telegram reached Ambassador Gerard he requested that
he be given full instructions as to all possible contingencies in view of
what seemed to him to be the inevitable consequences of the note.[2]
It thus seems that claims of rights which have not been fully
recognized by the community of nations have involved this country
in two European wars.[3] The great cost of sentimentalizing upon
contentions as if they were unquestioned law has created a considerable opinion for the abandonment of so-called rights connected with
the commercial profits of exporters. Charles Warren, who was

[1] For an exposition of the American attitude generally, see SAVAGE,
CARLTON, Policy of the United States toward Maritime Commerce in War, Govt.
Printing Office, Washington, 1934.

[2] Foreign Relations, 1915 (Supplement), p. 396.

[3] See the author's chapter on "The Doctrine of Neutral Rights," The
United States and Disarmament, Whittlesey House, McGraw-Hill Book Company, New York, 1931, where much of the foregoing material is found.

assistant attorney general of the United States during the period of
American neutrality in the World War, has said regarding the
freedom-of-the-seas diplomacy: "There is too much talk in international affairs about rights and too little about adjustments.
Harping on rights leads to arrival at positions from which a nation
cannot withdraw or yield; it leads to ultimatums which eventually
lead to war."[1]

The Neutrality Resolution of 1935. In 1935 Congress made
significant changes in the American neutrality code. The traffic in
war supplies had been under severe attack, and a chief point of
controversy in the enactment of the new legislation was whether
an embargo on munitions should apply as against both belligerents
in a war in which this country remained a neutral or whether the
President should have discretion in applying the embargo. If the
President were given an option in the matter, he could refuse arms
to an aggressor while supplying them to the victim of the aggression.
Such discrimination was considered necessary in some quarters if
harmony with the peace effort of League members under Article XVI
of the Covenant was to be maintained. It had been proposed in
the Capper Resolution which had been placed before the Senate in
1930 and 1932.[2] The administration desired the discretionary
embargo, but Congress refused to grant any option to the President
in the matter. Instead, the Neutrality Resolution of 1935 made
provision for an absolute embargo on shipments of munitions to
both belligerents. Other important amendments to the neutrality
system were incorporated. Further provisions (Secs. 1(a) and
1(b)) were enacted in February, 1936, the chief addition being an
embargo on loans and credits for belligerent purposes. The principal features of the resolution of 1935 as amended in 1936 are:

Sec. 1. In case of war between two or more foreign states the President
shall proclaim the fact. It shall thereafter be unlawful to export "arms,

[1] "Troubles of a Neutral," *Foreign Affairs*, April, 1934, p. 390. On this
problem see also BRADLEY, PHILLIPS, *Can We Stay Out of War?* W. W. Norton
& Company, Inc., New York, 1936; BRIGGS, HERBERT W., and R. L. BUELL,
"American Neutrality in a Future War," *Foreign Policy Reports*, Vol. XI, No. 3
(Apr. 10, 1935); DULLES, ALLEN W., and HAMILTON FISH ARMSTRONG, *Can We Be
Neutral?* Council on Foreign Relations, New York, 1936; and WRIGHT, QUINCY,
"The United States and Neutrality," *Public Policy Pamphlet* No. 17, University
of Chicago Press, 1935. A mine of material on war influences affecting the
United States, 1914–1917, is found in *Munitions Industry*, Hearings before the
Special Committee Investigating the Munitions Industry, U.S. Senate, 1934–
1936, Gov. Printing Office, Washington, 1934–1936. The hearings were
completed in February, 1936.

[2] See p. 335.

ammunition, or implements of war" to the ports of either belligerent or to any neutral port for transshipment to or for the use of either belligerent. The President shall by proclamation definitely enumerate the arms, ammunition, or implements of war which are to be prohibited under the act.

Sec. 1(a). After the President has proclaimed the existence of war, it shall be unlawful within the United States to purchase or sell securities of any belligerent government or of any political subdivision thereof, issued after the date of the proclamation, or to make any loan or extend any credit to such government, provided that if the President deems wise he may make exceptions in case of ordinary commercial credits and short-time obligations in aid of legal transactions and those of a normal peacetime character. The prohibitions mentioned shall not apply to renewals or adjustments of existing indebtedness.

Sec. 1(b). This act shall not apply to an American republic engaged in war against a non-American state, provided the American republic is not cooperating with a non-American state in such war. (Sec. 1 and all proclamations issued under it shall expire on May 1, 1937.)

Sec. 2. A National Munitions Control Board is created. Registration of firms engaged in trade in arms, ammunition, or implements of war is required and licenses are made necessary for the importation or exportation of these articles.[1]

Sec. 3. After the President has proclaimed the existence of war, American vessels are prohibited from carrying arms, ammunition, or implements of war to any belligerent port or to any neutral port for transshipment to or for the use of a belligerent country.

Sec. 4. Whenever during a war in which the United States is neutral the President shall have cause to believe that any vessel is about to carry men or supplies to a belligerent warship from an American port but the evidence is not sufficient to hold the vessel under the existing laws, the President may, if he deems such action advisable, require a bond to guarantee that the vessel will not deliver such men or supplies.

Sec. 5. The President, should he find it advisable, can prohibit belligerent submarines from entering American ports or territorial waters except under such conditions as he may prescribe.

Sec. 6. Should the President consider it advisable that American citizens should refrain from traveling as passengers on the vessels of any belligerent nation, he may proclaim that fact; and thereafter no citizen shall so travel except at his own risk, unless in accordance with such regulations as the President may prescribe.

Sec. 7. The penalty for the violation of the act is a fine of not more than $10,000 or imprisonment of not more than five years or both.

The President signed the resolution but expressed fears that the absolute embargo feature might defeat its own purpose by dragging this country into war. He said:

The policy of the Government is definitely committed to the maintenance of peace and the avoidance of any entanglements which would lead us into conflict. At the same time it is the policy of the Government by

[1] See pp. 384–385 for details as to this feature.

every peaceful means and without entanglements to cooperate with other similarly minded governments to promote peace.[1]

On October 5, 1935, several days after the beginning of the Italian invasion of Ethiopia, President Roosevelt issued a proclamation placing into effect an embargo upon the export of arms, ammunition, and implements of war to the belligerents. At the same time, acting under Section 6 of the resolution, he admonished all citizens of the United States to abstain from traveling on the vessels of the belligerents.

The Warning Regarding Transactions with Either Belligerent. In addition to the two above-mentioned proclamations the President made an unusual announcement the authority for which was not derived from the terms of the resolution. He declared:

> In these specific circumstances I desire it to be understood that any of our people who voluntarily engage in transactions of any character with either of the belligerents do so at their own risk.

The President was evidently announcing as a new policy the principle that the United States does not intend to be dragged into war through diplomatic activity in protecting American businessmen in their war trade. While not based on statute, the announcement was well within the constitutional powers of the President to give or withhold protection and to announce in advance his intentions with regard to such matters.[2]

NONCOOPERATION IN PEACE

The Concert of Europe. From the time of the Napoleonic Wars until the World War the great powers of Europe, fearing the threat of another fierce conflict, made sporadic attempts to work in unison for the maintenance of peace. The beginnings of the concert are traced to the plan of Alexander I of 1804 and to the treaty of 1815 between the nations composing the Quadruple Alliance against Napoleon. The four governments agreed to meet at intervals to examine measures for the prosperity of the nations and for the peace of Europe. The occasional meetings which followed constitute the beginning of the concert of Europe, the work of which has been praised by students of international government.[3]

[1] Dept. of State, *Press Releases*, Aug. 31, 1935, p. 163.

[2] For the attempt of the Executive to cut down the export of such war supplies as are not covered by the 1935 resolution, see DULLES and ARMSTRONG, *op. cit.*, pp. 70*ff*.

[3] See WOLF, L. S., *International Government*, p. 25, George Allen & Unwin, Ltd., London, 1916; and an article by FAY, SIDNEY B., "Concert of Powers,"

The attitude of the United States toward the concert was fixed to a large extent by the unfavorable reactions to the Holy Alliance, which was one aspect of European organization. The so-called Holy Alliance originated in a joint pledge taken in 1816 by the Czar of Russia, the Emperor of Austria, and the King of Prussia, promising that the monarchs would be guided in their relations by the principles of friendship, peace, and the Christian religion. Other sovereigns in Europe, except the Sultan and the Pope, were invited to join. Great Britain refused but the others eventually adhered. The United States was approached informally upon the subject of subscribing to the declaration. At least one advocate of international friendship, Rev. Noah Worcester, Secretary of the Massachusetts Peace Society, favored adherence to "the pacific alliance."[1] The government, however, had no hesitation in refusing to associate with the movement on the ground that the promotion of peace in both Europe and America demanded that "the European and American political system [sic] should be kept as separate and distinct from each other as possible."[2]

The American attitude of unwillingness to join the alliance soon developed into one of positive antagonism and alarm. At the Congresses of Troppau and Laibach, 1820–1821, Russia, Prussia, and Austria affirmed their faith in the divine right of kings and declared their intention to suppress revolutionary movements aimed at legitimate sovereigns. The three were joined by France at Verona in 1822 in an agreement to use every endeavor to bring an end to the system of representative government in Europe. England dissented and for a time withdrew from cooperation with the powers. Resentment in the United States against such doctrines was heightened by evidence of the intentions of the Holy Alliance to restore the revolted Spanish colonies to Spain. Hostility to such a plan gave rise to the Monroe Doctrine. These suspicions had their influence against American cooperation with Europe even down to the years 1919 and 1920 when the Holy Alliance was paraded through the United States Senate chamber as a warning against membership in the League of Nations.

Encyclopaedia of the Social Sciences, IV: 153. A full description is found in PHILLIPS, WALTER ALISON, *The Confederation of Europe*, Longmans, Green & Co., London, 1920; and MOWAT, R. B., *The Concert of Europe*, Macmillan & Co., London, 1930.

[1] CURTI, MERLE EUGENE, *The American Peace Crusade*, 1815–1860, p. 27, Duke University Press, Durham, N.C., 1929.

[2] John Quincy Adams, Secretary of State, to Mr. Middleton, Minister to Russia, July 5, 1820, *Moore's Digest*, VI: 379.

The first European confederation, established in 1815, broke up in 1822; but the powers continued from time to time to cooperate for the settlement of questions which threatened the peace of the Continent. The policies of the concert were not always opposed to liberalism. In 1827, during the Greek struggle for freedom, a joint naval force from the Russian, British, and French fleets sank the Turkish-Egyptian fleet at Navarino, thus making possible the independence of Greece.

The United States, the Concert, and the Persecution of Jews in Rumania. In 1872 the American consul in Bucharest participated with representatives of Austria-Hungary, France, Germany, Great Britain, Greece, and Italy in protesting to Turkey against the harsh treatment of Rumanian Jews.[1] Secretary of State Fish also intimated that these governments should act to end the persecutions under the provisions of the treaty made in 1859 between the European powers and Turkey. In 1878 the Congress of Berlin, called to prevent war between Great Britain and Austria, on the one hand, and Russia, on the other, considered the Balkan question. Among other things the freedom of Rumania was recognized with the stipulation that liberty of religion should be granted and that no religious beliefs should be made the basis of civil or political discrimination. The United States, of course, was not represented at the conference; but more than two decades later, in 1902, Secretary Hay made an appeal based on the 1878 treaty and alleged that the clause relating to freedom of religion had been ignored by the Rumanian government. The persecutions had been so severe that many of the Jews had fled to the United States. Secretary Hay, therefore, appealed to the Rumanian government to end this condition. He also made representations to the European powers who were signatory to the treaty. The reasons for this deviation from the ordinary policy of isolation were that Jewish societies had interceded with the Department of State and that the persecutions had affected the United States by driving numbers of impoverished outcasts to our shores, thus placing an undue burden upon this country.[2] The American protests, however, were without avail.[3]

The Danish Sound Dues. An illustration of the refusal of the United States to participate in a conference to regulate a European

[1] *Moore's Digest*, VI: 360.

[2] *Ibid.*, VI: 362–367. In 1863 the United States refused to join with Great Britain, France, and Austria in asking the Czar to show greater leniency in dealing with the people of Russian Poland. *Ibid.*, VI: 22.

[3] DENNIS, ALFRED L. P., *Adventures in American Diplomacy*, 1896–1906, p. 432, E. P. Dutton & Co., New York, 1928.

situation even though our interests were affected is found in the case of the Danish Sound dues. For centuries previous to 1855 the Danish government had collected dues on vessels passing through the sound and the two belts which form a passage from the North Sea into the Baltic. The collections had been recognized as legal in a number of treaties, one agreement, that with the Hanseatic Republics, dating back to 1368. The United States objected to the dues in 1848 and again in 1853. The Secretary of State alleged that the tariffs operated as a discrimination against American products, particularly raw cotton. The charges levied upon raw cotton amounted to 3 per cent while those upon cotton twist from Great Britain were but 1 per cent.[1] In 1855 the United States gave notice of the abrogation of a commercial treaty with Denmark, one clause of which might have been interpreted as acquiescing in the dues. The Danish government then arranged for an international conference and invited the United States to send representatives. The invitation urged that the matter should not be treated as merely an affair of commerce or finance, but that it should be dealt with as a political matter so that the solution might serve to complement the European treaties of peace and the balance of power upon the Continent.[2] The invitation could not have been more appropriately worded for insuring a rejection. The fact that the conference was to deal with the political affairs of Europe was the chief reason for the refusal of the United States to attend.[3] The conference met and arranged for the discontinuance of the dues and the payment of a lump sum to Denmark for the upkeep of lights and buoys. The United States then joined in the movement by making a separate treaty with Denmark by which the sum of $393,011 was paid in exchange for freedom of passage and the maintenance of navigation guides.[4]

Refusal to Participate in a Joint Mediation in 1870. In the various actions of the European concert during the nineteenth century to prevent war or to bring about an early termination of wars the United States took no part. At the present date it may be of some interest to look back upon the political tendencies that were later to result in the World War and to observe how blissfully unaware the United States remained regarding the relationship of these developments to its own future. In 1870 the United States

[1] House Executive Document No. 108, 33d Cong., 1st Sess., p. 56.

[2] Text in *British and Foreign State Papers*, 1855–1856, XLVI: 655.

[3] Annual Message of President Pierce, Dec. 31, 1855, Richardson's *Messages and Papers of the Presidents*, VII: 2868.

[4] *Treaties, etc., of the U.S.*, I: 380; *Moore's Digest*, I: 659–664.

was informed that France desired the American government to act with the European powers in an effort to end the war with Prussia. The provisional French government, struggling to avoid the cession of territory to the Germans, made the plea that a durable and just peace would benefit Europe and that a disgraceful peace would be followed by a war of extermination.[1] The United States was unwilling to join with European powers in such a mediation. Secretary of State Fish instructed the American minister at Paris: "It is not the policy or interest of the United States to act jointly with European powers in European questions."[2] In 1918, after enormous expenditures in the World War, a war which arose partially from the 1871 settlement, President Wilson demanded in Point VIII of his famous Fourteen Points that "the wrong done to France by Prussia in 1871 in the matter of Alsace-Lorraine, which has unsettled the peace of the world for nearly fifty years, should be righted, in order that peace may once more be made secure in the interests of all." It would be folly to argue that Secretary Fish in 1870 could have foreseen the vital interest which the United States was one day to have in a durable European peace. The forces of mechanics, industry, and politics were slowly but surely propelling the ship of state in a manner which was beyond the power of statesmen to predict.

Noncooperation with the League of Nations in European Regional Disputes. In its cooperation with the League of Nations the United States has taken great care to steer clear of projects which involve the settlement of disputes in Europe. This country has associated itself in varying degrees with the League regarding regional matters in Asia, Africa, and Latin America; but in no case has the American government dealt with the League concerning affairs which are limited to Europe. This abstention is to be noticed particularly when it is remembered that many of the bitter regional disputes to be considered at Geneva are European in character. When the Aaland Islands case, the Polish-Lithuanian dispute, the Corfu affair, and the Greco-Bulgarian controversy were brought up in the League Council, the United States showed no desire to participate in the work of conciliation.

NONINTERVENTION

If it has ordinarily not seemed advisable for the United States to cooperate with other countries in the settlement of European dis-

---

[1] *Foreign Relations*, 1870, p. 140.

[2] *Ibid.*, pp. 68–69; *Moore's Digest*, VII: 11–13. It was intimated that this country might act as sole mediator if requested by both parties.

putes, it has appeared even less desirable that this country should intervene singly by force or diplomatic representation to determine the affairs of any of the European nations.   For cooperation carries with it the strength and aid of associated nations, but single intervention may well expose the unsupported intruder to the wrath of the nation which is the victim of intervention as well as of its allies and friends.   Intervention in Europe would involve far greater dangers than a similar action in the Caribbean.   There have, however, been certain influences making for intervention by the United States in the affairs of Europe.   In the early history of this country the sympathy of Americans for those peoples in Europe who were seeking to set up republican forms of government was very strong.   Demands were made by some leading Americans, particularly in the case of Greece and Hungary, that the United States should recognize the revolting communities.   In the last few decades the great growth of American investments in Europe has supplied another motive.   Thus far, however, the powerful influences against intervention have been in almost all cases stronger than those making for intervention.

Movements for Premature Recognition of Revolting Communities in Europe.   The revolution of the Greek people against the rule of the Sultan, beginning in 1822, aroused some enthusiasm in the United States and memorials were presented to Congress requesting the recognition of the Greek state.   In 1824 Daniel Webster made a celebrated speech supporting a resolution introduced by himself for the appointment of an agent or commissioner to Greece whenever the President should deem it expedient to make such an appointment.   Webster's resolution, had it been passed and had the President acted, would have resulted in a premature recognition amounting to intervention.   The resolution failed, however, and so cautious was the United States in this matter that recognition was not extended to Greece until 1837, ten years after the joint naval forces of England, France, and Russia had destroyed the Turkish-Egyptian fleet at Navarino.

The Hungarian revolution of 1848 also evoked American sympathy.   In 1848 and 1849 Hungarian patriots came to the United States and asked the President to grant recognition to Hungary.   In view of these requests the United States at this time took an unusual step, one which might conceivably have involved this country in difficulties in Europe had the Hungarian revolution been temporarily successful.   An American agent, A. Dudley Mann, was instructed by the Department of State to secure information regarding the probable outcome of the struggle and the possibilities of obtaining favorable commercial agreements with Hungary. The instructions showed a strong sympathy for Hungary. They mentioned the anxiety which had been felt in the United States as to the fate of the revolution and expressed a desire to be the first to recognize the Hungarian government were it able to maintain the independence which it had declared. The revolution, however, was promptly suppressed; and Mr. Mann did not reach Hungary. The publication of these instructions in 1850 was followed by a bitter protest by the Austrian chargé regarding what he termed our interference in the internal affairs of Austria. Daniel Webster, who had meanwhile become Secretary of State, then made a flamboyant reply.[1] When Kossuth, the spectacular Hungarian revolutionist, visited the United States in 1851 he was received with courtesy but with firm refusals of assistance. The attitude of the American government had by this time become cautious. It was well represented in the statement made by Henry Clay in a private interview with Kossuth:

Far better is it for ourselves, for Hungary and for the cause of liberty, that, adhering to our wise pacific system and avoiding the distant wars of Europe, we should keep our lamp burning brightly on this western shore, as a light to all nations, than to hazard its utter extinction, amid the ruins of fallen and falling republics in Europe.[2]

No Protest Made Concerning Treatment of Jews by Hitler Regime in Germany. When Hitler came into power in Germany in March, 1933, a period of Jewish persecution ensued. Representatives of Jewish organizations visited the Department of State, but no diplomatic protests were sent to the German government except in such cases as the victims were American citizens. The Secretary of State, however, informed the Jewish organizations that he would "continue to watch the situation closely, with a sympathetic interest and with a desire to be helpful in whatever way possible."[3] While a large part of the American people condemned the policy of the Hitler regime in failing to put an end to the persecutions, the Department of State considered that it was beyond its province to make any attempts to reform the policy of the German government.

The Economic Pressures for Intervention. The private investments of Americans in Europe amount to $4,000,000,000 or more. The accumulation of these interests has created influences tending

[1] *Moore's Digest*, I: 218–234.
[2] *Moore's Digest*, VI: 52.
[3] Dept. of State, *Press Releases*, Apr. 1, 1933, p. 202.

to break down the inhibitions against intervention in Europe. At the present time there is little indication in the operations of policies that the United States will succumb to these new influences. But possibly the running of subsurface currents of economic forces may prove stronger than the intentions of departmental officials or political parties. The vigorous protests of the United States to the Spanish government in 1932 regarding the passage of a law for the nationalization of the telephone system of Spain amounted to intervention upon a matter of considerable interest to the International Telephone and Telegraph Company, a powerful American corporation.[1] While one instance of this sort cannot be said to constitute a policy, the continued increase of American investments in Europe will bring up such issues recurrently in the future. Should a disastrous European war reduce further the relative strength of the nations of Europe as compared with the United States, it is not inconceivable that the American government will feel emboldened to intervene from time to time to affect the domestic policies of European countries to the advantage of American capitalist interests.

[1] See pp. 218–219.

CHAPTER IV

THE MONROE DOCTRINE

Areas Forbidden to Imperialism. The creation of a sanctuary in a backward or politically weak region which is to be kept free of rival imperialistic poachers has been resorted to in modern times by more than one great power. The motives behind the establishment of such a protected area are ordinarily national or imperial defense and the prevention of exploitation by economic competitors. Great Britain has at various times striven to preserve the integrity of Turkey against Russian attack. The entry of Russia into the Sultan's territories, it was contended, would have threatened the British position in India. The British government also accepted the Pact of Paris subject to the following understanding:

there are certain regions of the world the welfare and integrity of which constitute a special and vital interest for our peace and safety. His Majesty's Government have been at pains to make it clear in times past that interference with these regions cannot be suffered. Their protection against attack is to the British Empire a measure of self-defense.

The regions alluded to in this interpretation have been understood to mean Afghanistan and Egypt. Japan has for more than thirty years viewed with apprehension and displeasure the encroachments of European powers in China. The Mikado's government has sought on several occasions to remove the alleged dangers to its safety by force of arms. Thus, in 1904, the Japanese ejected Russia from Manchuria and Korea; and in 1914 they displaced Germany in Shantung. Viscount Ishii informs the American public that the Japanese in defending China against the aggressions of third powers have been "actuated by the same principle incorporated in the Monroe Doctrine."[1] In recent years the attempted guardianship of Japan over the affairs of China has been explained as an effort to maintain the peace of Asia.

[1] Ishii, Viscount Kikujiro, "The Permanent Bases of Japanese Foreign Policy," *Foreign Affairs*, XI: 227 (January, 1933). See also Blakeslee, George H., "The Japanese Monroe Doctrine," *Foreign Affairs*, XI: 671 (July, 1933).

41

An inevitable problem arises when the excluding power, after righteously prohibiting others from entering the protected zone, proceeds to seize for itself some portions of the forbidden territory. A country in this position must speak and act both the opposing roles of protector and aggressor, of defender of virtue and libidinous ravisher.   Thus Great Britain has encroached upon Tibet, Persia, and Afghanistan and has brought under its control important portions of the Turkish Empire, the integrity of which it once sought to maintain.   Japanese officials protested at one time that their Asiatic doctrine was not imperialism, but later Japan proceeded to lay hands on Manchuria.   Such opposite action necessarily places a heavy burden upon the rhetoricians of diplomacy who must search for the terminology which will make it clear to their own public, if not to the world, that both actions are motivated by the highest moral considerations.

The Monroe Doctrine is probably the best known of these policies of forbidden imperialism.   It has involved both the negative defensive policy of prohibiting the annexation of territories in the Western Hemisphere by European powers and the aggressive defensive policy of seizing imperialistic controls for ourselves in the Caribbean.   Although variously understood and interpreted, it has probably the greatest hold on the minds of the American people of any of our foreign policy dogmas.

THE ORIGIN OF THE DOCTRINE

The Monroe Doctrine was brought forth in 1823 following the revolt of the Spanish colonies in America.   Its origin was due to the apprehension that European powers would join with Spain in a reconquest of the colonies.   The colonial revolt had begun in 1806 and by 1822 independence was well established in most parts of Spanish America.   In that year Monroe had obtained an appropriation from Congress with which to send a diplomatic mission to those countries which should be deemed ready for *de jure* relationships.   Recognition of the major countries followed shortly.   The opposition of the Holy Alliance to the system of representative government, the intervention of the alliance in Spain to restore the power of the Spanish king, and the possibility that it would aid in the reconquest of the Spanish possessions in America caused misgivings in both England and the United States.   The British were primarily interested in trade.   Spain had prohibited her colonies from dealing with the outside world, but the commercial barriers were lifted as independence was established.   Reconquest of the colonies would probably have put an end to the newly established commerce. The interest of the United States was one of self-defense, for this country feared the further entrance of European military powers into the Western Hemisphere.

When in 1823 it seemed possible that the countries of the Holy Alliance might aid Spain in retaking the colonies, the British government decided to try a countermove. Great Britain feared particularly that France might acquire large portions of the old Spanish territories. Accordingly George Canning, British foreign minister, proposed to Mr. Rush, the American minister in London, that the two countries should agree, among other things, to a joint declaration of opposition to the transfer of any portion of the colonies to any country other than Spain. The United States shared the fears of Great Britain. John Quincy Adams warned in a cabinet meeting that the European allies might partition the Spanish possessions among themselves. Russia might take California, Peru, and Chile; France might seize Mexico and Buenos Aires; and Great Britain, if she could not stop the scramble for possessions, might take Cuba. With France in Mexico and Great Britain in Cuba, what would be the situation of the United States?[1] The advisers of President Monroe disagreed as to the acceptance of the British proposal. Jefferson and Madison, ex-presidents who were asked for their opinions, were favorably inclined. In the cabinet discussions, however, Secretary of State John Quincy Adams opposed a joint declaration with Great Britain and advocated a unilateral doctrine sponsored by the United States. His advice prevailed.

Monroe's Message of December 2, 1823. In his message to Congress of December 2, 1823, President Monroe set forth the declaration which in the course of events was to be known as the Monroe Doctrine. At the time of its promulgation the doctrine consisted of two parts, the first opposing further colonization by European powers in the Western Hemisphere and the second placing a prohibition on the reconquest of the revolted Spanish colonies by the European powers or the extension of the European political system to the Americas.

The part which dealt with noncolonization was aimed to stop the efforts of Russia to establish colonies along the northern Pacific coast. This part of the message read:

the American continents, by the free and independent condition which they have assumed and maintain, are henceforth not to be considered as subjects for future colonization by any European powers.[2]

[1] Moores' *Digest*, VI: 400.

[2] Richardson's *Messages and Papers of the Presidents*, II: 778.

The passage forbade the practice of obtaining title to new and unoccupied lands in the Americas by settlement. In this sense the words have long ago lost their significance because the areas open to colonization have been legally occupied. The terms used, however, have been given a great extension beyond their original meaning. President Polk in 1845 declared it to be our settled policy that no future European colony or *dominion* should be established in North America. The word dominion apparently included any kind of extension of territory whether by voluntary cession or otherwise.[1] In this greatly enlarged sense the first part of the message has by some writers been fused with the second part in a general doctrine of opposition to the transfer of American territory to European nations.

The more important part of the doctrine, that directed against reconquest of the Spanish colonies by the Holy Alliance, read as follows:

We owe it, therefore, to candor and to amicable relations existing between the United States and those powers to declare that we should consider any attempt on their part to extend their system to any portion of this hemisphere as dangerous to our peace and safety. With the existing colonies and dependencies of any European power we have not interfered and shall not interfere. But with the Governments who have declared their independence and maintained it, and whose independence we have, on great consideration and just principles, acknowledged, we could not view any interposition for the purpose of oppressing them, or controlling in any other manner their destiny, by any European power in any other light than as a manifestation of an unfriendly disposition toward the United States.[2]

In the course of time all schemes for the reconquest of the Spanish colonies were abandoned. It is probable that the Monroe message had little part in bringing about the relinquishment of the European plans.[3] But the general notion underlying the doctrine, *i.e.*, that any extension of European holdings in the Western Hemisphere would be dangerous to our peace and safety, grew in the following decades to become a major American policy. Other declarations were made in succeeding administrations. Eventually it became difficult to say just what the doctrine involved.

---

[1] MOORE, JOHN BASSETT, *The Principles of American Diplomacy*, pp. 245–246, Harper & Brothers, New York, 1918.

[2] Richardson's *Messages and Papers of the Presidents*, II: 787.

[3] PERKINS, DEXTER, *The Monroe Doctrine*, 1823–1826, p. 255, Harvard University Press, Cambridge, 1927.

WHY THE DEFINITION OF THE MONROE DOCTRINE IS IMPORTANT

One might inquire as to what, after all, is the importance of ascribing an exact meaning to the doctrine. Would not, for example, various actions taken by the United States to control smaller republics in the Caribbean smell as sweet if classified under "the Caribbean policy" of the United States as if they were labeled "the Roosevelt corollary of the Monroe Doctrine"? There are two specific reasons why a definition of terms in this particular is important.

In the first place, the Monroe Doctrine is suffused with emotion in the American mind. Citizens who know but little of the content of the doctrine grow patriotically indignant whenever anyone suggests that it should be diminished or abandoned. Those who desire a strong foreign policy toward Latin America accordingly wish to define the doctrine so as to include their imperialistic designs. Thus they can mobilize behind their projects all the emotions associated with the doctrine. On the other hand, persons desiring a nonintervention policy in Latin America seek to define the doctrine in the narrower terms of self-defense. In this way they can detach imperialism from the name of Monroe and deal with it separately, avoiding the sacrilege which is attached to an attack on the doctrine.

In the second place, the doctrine should be defined as accurately as possible because of the fact that it has become a legal term embedded in a considerable number of treaties, conventions, and interpretations of treaties and conventions. The United States has on several occasions thought fit to attach to its signature an interpretation that nothing in the convention in contradiction to the Monroe Doctrine or in conflict with the traditional position of the United States on American affairs shall be binding upon the United States. The doctrine is specifically safeguarded in the Covenant of the League of Nations. A clause excepting disputes which depend upon or involve the maintaining of the Monroe Doctrine is found in some twenty-eight arbitration treaties negotiated in 1928 and thereafter. An interpretation of the Pact of Paris was made in 1928 by the Senate Committee on Foreign Relations to the effect that the Monroe Doctrine was a policy of national security and defense; and, therefore, by implication, the right to go to war in support of the doctrine was not abrogated by the pact. With the Monroe Doctrine appearing in connection with these various treaties and conventions, it seems important in order to construe them properly that there should be, so far as possible, a precise understanding of the meaning of the term.

EVOLUTION OF THE DOCTRINE

The Monroe Doctrine, as has been intimated, cannot be defined in the words of Monroe alone.   Like an original sacred writing, its terms have been enlarged upon and interpreted by latter-day secretaries of state and presidents.   Three variable factors which have reacted upon its meaning have been the power of the United States, the danger of European expansion in this hemisphere, and the desire of the United States to strengthen the world's peace machinery.

Three different periods in the history of the doctrine indicate its flexibility and conformity to the spirit of the particular period in which the interpretations are made.   (1) In the early history of the country down almost to the Spanish-American War, the United States was weak and stressed the purely defensive side of the doctrine.   (2) From the time of the Spanish-American War to the end of the World War, the United States was inclined toward imperialistic ventures, while, with the increase of European financing in Latin America, the dangers of European interference increased. The fear of European expansion was exaggerated in the nervous atmosphere which came with the early years of the World War. During the period from 1898 to 1920 the doctrine grew in vigor and was interpreted as giving to the United States the right to intervene for purposes of protection in the affairs of Latin-American countries. (3) Following the war, when Europe was relatively weak and had ceased to threaten the territorial integrity of Latin America, the urge to expand the doctrine was greatly reduced.   When the United States began to participate more actively in the world peace movement, an agressive Monroe Doctrine became an embarrassment.   Beginning in 1928, accordingly, the doctrine was contracted to something like its mid-nineteenth-century form.

I. MEANING ACQUIRED DURING THE EARLY OR DEFENSIVE PERIOD

The Doctrine Has Probably Prevented European Seizures of Territory in Latin America.   The doctrine has been a strong deterrent against the seizure of territory in the Western Hemisphere by European governments.   During the latter part of the nineteenth century the greater European powers began to acquire lands on a large scale in Africa and to extend their controls with speed and energy in Asia.   Latin America furnished a more fertile field in many respects than Asia or Africa, and the fact that it escaped the ambitious expansion of the powers during this period was doubtless due in no small measure to the Monroe Doctrine.

The Doctrine Is Opposed to the Establishment of Monarchical Institutions on This Hemisphere through European Intervention. The United States has not opposed the establishment of monarchical institutions in Latin America by domestic factions. The Emperor Dom Pedro of Brazil was recognized by Monroe in 1824, and the creation of a monarchy in Haiti in 1857 was not regarded as hostile to the doctrine. The establishment of an Emperor in Mexico by the aid of French troops was, however, stanchly opposed by the United States. In 1862 France, England, and Spain sent a joint expedition into Mexico for the collection of claims. England and Spain eventually dropped out, but France continued the expedition and occupied Mexico City. The French had for several years considered the advantage of assisting the conservative and clerical elements in Mexico in setting up a monarchy which might adequately resist the encroachments of Yankee imperialism.[1] The opportunity now presented itself. A provisional government was set up and later an empire was proclaimed with Ferdinand Maximilian, Archduke of Austria, as Emperor. When the Civil War was concluded and the United States was free to act, Secretary Seward instructed the American minister in France that, unless the French government should withdraw its support from the monarchy, which had been established upon the ruins of republican institutions, the friendly relations between the two countries would be imminently jeopardized. Partly because of the power of the United States at the end of the Civil War and partly because of the growing strength of Prussia,[2] France decided to withdraw her troops. The empire fell and Maximilian was executed. Although in the Mexican case the Monroe Doctrine was not specifically mentioned and no reference was made to the part of the text involved, presumably the action of France was regarded as an attempt to extend the European system to this hemisphere.

[1] PERKINS, DEXTER, *The Monroe Doctrine*, 1826–1867, pp. 312–367, Johns Hopkins Press, Baltimore, 1933.

[2] According to Professor C. A. Duniway, who made a study of the occupation from French sources, there were four reasons for withdrawal. These were: dissatisfaction with the slow and costly process of pacifying Mexico, financial difficulties in France which made the expense of the expedition a considerable burden, the aggressive policy of Prussia, and the attitude of the United States. "Reasons for the Withdrawal of the French from Mexico," *Annual Report of the American Historical Association*, 1902, I: 315.

The Doctrine Is Opposed to Voluntary Cessions of Territory by American Governments to European Powers. When, in 1848, the Mexican authorities offered to cede Yucatan to the United States, Great Britain, or Spain because of an Indian revolution in that state, President Polk announced that the doctrines of Monroe prohibited a transfer to any European power.[1]   In 1884 rumors reached the United States that the Haitian government had proposed to cede the peninsula of the Mole of St. Nicholas or the Island of Tortuga to France.   The American minister at Paris was instructed to inform the French government that such a cession would conflict with the Monroe Doctrine.[2]   The opposition to voluntary cession appears to have been a reasonable extension of the original doctrine.   The proximity of a strong European power to the United States might well be as dangerous if its new position were acquired by voluntary transfer as if it were obtained by conquest.   Furthermore, it is difficult to draw a line in all cases between peaceful cession and forcible annexation.   A weaker government may be manipulated so as to give the appearance of willingness to dispose of territory although the transaction may not represent in any sense the desire of the population.

The Doctrine Is Opposed to the Transfer of an American Possession from One European Power to Another. President Monroe specifically stated that he did not intend to interfere with the possessions already held in the Americas by European powers.   When later, however, a possession was to be ceded by one European power to another, the doctrine was extended to prevent the transfer.   The extension appears altogether logical.   At first thought it might appear to be of no consequence whether an area should be in the possession of this European power or that.   Certainly by such a transfer no Latin-American republic would be robbed of its territories.   The security of the United States, however, might well be diminished by the exchange of one European owner for another.   In the more usual case of a transfer of territory the area passes from an older imperialistic nation whose activities are diminishing to a younger, more virile and, from our standpoint, more dangerous power.   Thus the net result of a number of such transfers would be to exchange harmless neighbors for more aggressive ones.   In 1825 a French squadron maneuvered in the vicinity of Cuba. Henry Clay, Secretary of State, fearing the cession of Cuba and Puerto Rico by Spain to France, instructed the American minister at

[1] *Moore's Digest*, VI: 423.
[2] *Ibid.*, VI: 432.

Paris that the United States could not consent to the occupation of those islands "by any other European power than Spain under any contingency whatever."[1] President Grant, in 1869, stated in his annual message to Congress with regard to European possessions in the Americas that they were "no longer regarded as subject to transfer from one European power to another."[2] In 1870, after the Italian government had made an offer to Sweden for the Island of St. Bartholomew, Secretary of State Fish informed the Swedish and Norwegian minister that he hoped the disposition of the subject would be postponed as the United States would prefer to avoid a controversy with a friendly power.[3] The Italian offer was not accepted.

The Doctrine Is Interpreted to Mean that Disputes Between European Powers and Latin-American Republics Cannot Be Settled by Force when such a Settlement Might Mean Territorial Gains or Political Control by the European Power. In Some Cases the United States Has Insisted on Settlement by Arbitration. One of the most serious situations to arise in connection with the Monroe Doctrine was that of the Venezuelan boundary dispute. From the latter part of the Spanish colonial period until 1895 the boundary line between Venezuela and British Guiana was the subject of dispute. The British claims to the boundary were from time to time extended farther into the territory claimed by Venezuela. In 1882 Venezuela proposed arbitration but Great Britain was willing to arbitrate with regard to only a small part of the disputed area. Venezuela appealed to the United States in 1881 and this country offered its good offices, but without avail. In 1887 Venezuela suspended diplomatic relations with Great Britain. In 1895 Secretary of State Olney remonstrated vigorously with Great Britain in the name of the Monroe Doctrine and demanded arbitration. The language of Secretary Olney was at times highly bombastic. At one point he said:

Today the United States is practically sovereign on this continent, and its fiat is law upon the subjects to which it confines its interposition.[4]

The British government refused the American demand. President Cleveland thereupon sent a message to Congress setting forth the

---

[1] *Ibid.*, VI: 447.

[2] Richardson's *Messages and Papers of the Presidents*, IX: 3986.

[3] *Moore's Digest*, VI: 428. A few years later, however, the island was sold to France without objection by the United States. Thomas, David Y., *One Hundred Years of the Monroe Doctrine*, p. 555, The Macmillan Company, New York, 1923.

[4] *Moore's Digest*, VI: 553.

correspondence and recommending that Congress should appropriate money for the expenses of a commission which should investigate the dispute on the spot and report as to a proper boundary. It should then be the duty of the United States to resist the seizure by Great Britain of territory on the Venezuelan side of this boundary. The message created an excited state of international feeling, and war became a possibility. The British government, fortunately, yielded in the matter and agreed to arbitrate the dispute. The arbitration tribunal awarded a large part of the disputed territory to Great Britain.[1]

The United States has on various occasions admitted that the Monroe Doctrine does not prevent the collection of honest debts in Latin America by the creditor nations of Europe. Even collection by force was at one time recognized as unobjectionable. Where force is used, however, a most embarrassing situation is likely to result. Military intervention for the primary purpose of debt collection has sometimes threatened to lead to permanent political or financial control. In such cases the United States has vigorously objected.

In 1861, when France, Spain, and Great Britain agreed to push the collection of claims in Mexico by military force, those governments communicated their intentions to the United States. As American citizens likewise held claims against Mexico, the three powers requested the assistance of the American government. The United States had already become apprehensive about the whole matter and, in order to prevent intervention, had attempted to negotiate a treaty with Mexico by which the United States should assume the interest on the debts. The treaty failed and, in answering the communication of the three powers, Secretary of State Seward said:

the President does not feel himself at liberty to question, and does not question, that the sovereigns represented have undoubted right to decide for themselves the fact whether they have sustained grievances, and to resort to war against Mexico for the redress thereof, and have a right also to levy the war severally or jointly.[2]

While admitting the right of the powers to go to war for the collection of claims in this instance the United States, as has been pointed out, made objections when the French forces proceeded to overthrow the Mexican government and to set up in its place a pup-

---

[1] *Ibid.*, VI: 533–583; LATANÉ, JOHN HOLLADAY, *The United States and Latin America*, pp. 238–249, Doubleday, Page & Company, Garden City, N. Y., 1921.

[2] *Moore's Digest*, VI: 486.

pet state with Maximilian as Emperor. It was not the use of force in the collection of claims but the imposition of the European monarchical system upon Mexico which was the basis for the protests of the United States. The situation was cleared when the French government withdrew its troops and the Maximilian government fell.

A somewhat similar situation arose with regard to the intervention of Germany, Great Britain, and Italy in Venezuela in 1902 to collect claims owed to their nationals. Having been previously made aware of the contemplated use of force, President Roosevelt stated in his message to Congress of December 3, 1901: "We do not guarantee any state against punishment if it misconducts itself, provided that punishment does not take the form of the acquisition of territory by any non-American power."[1] A year later the powers, being unable to collect the debts by peaceful means, established a blockade of Venezuelan ports and seized Venezuelan gunboats. German ships bombarded Puerto Cabello. It was the intention of Germany as a last resort to take temporary charge of Venezuelan customhouses. The United States now desired that the matter should be arbitrated. Great Britain and Italy agreed, but Germany refused. President Roosevelt made vigorous protests to Germany coupled, it has been alleged, with a secret threat of force. Germany then withdrew its objections and the arbitration took place.[2]

Following this incident, the United States took a more definite stand against the unqualified use of force in the collection of contract claims. The government of Argentina suggested that the American government should support the principle of the Drago doctrine, *i.e.*, that armed intervention or the occupation of territory could not be admitted as a method for obtaining the payment of a contract debt. The United States proposed a convention which embodied a modified form of the Drago doctrine at the Second Hague Conference of 1907. This agreement, known as the Porter Resolution from the fact that it was introduced and defended by General Horace Porter of the American delegation, provided:

[1] *Moore's Digest*, VI: 590.
[2] *Moore's Digest*, VI: 586–592; for President Roosevelt's alleged threat of force see THAYER, WILLIAM ROSCOE, *The Life and Letters of John Hay*, II: 286–288, Houghton Mifflin Company, Boston, 1915. Serious doubt is thrown upon the story, however, in HILL, HOWARD C., *Roosevelt and the Caribbean*, pp. 125*ff*., University of Chicago Press, Chicago, 1927, and PRINGLE, HENRY F., *Theodore Roosevelt, A Biography*, pp. 284*ff*., Harcourt, Brace & Company, New York, 1931.

Force should not be used for the recovery of contract debts unless

a. The debtor state refuses or neglects to reply to an offer of arbitration, or

b. Having accepted an offer of arbitration prevents any *compromis* from being agreed on, or, after the arbitration, fails to submit to the award.[1]

II. THE IMPERIALISTIC PERIOD

Early Plans for Repelling European Influence by Controlling the Affairs of Latin-American States. In order to prevent European nations from intervening with force to collect claims and to protect their nationals in Latin-American countries, the United States has frequently been tempted to take steps to provide for a greater measure of order and financial stability in the delinquent countries. Mention has already been made of the attempt to avoid intervention by France, Great Britain, and Spain in Mexico by a treaty which would permit the United States to assume the payment of the interest of the debts of Mexico. Mr. Seward sought to include in the treaty a mortgage in favor of the United States on the public lands and minerals of several Mexican states, the title to become absolute in the United States if Mexico did not reimburse this country within six years.[2] These were amazingly hard terms. Before the treaty was negotiated the United States Senate passed a resolution opposing the plan which put an end to further efforts. In 1881 Secretary of State Evarts considered favorably a proposal that the United States should act as agent for distributing payments due from Venezuela to European creditors. Shortly afterward Secretary Blaine suggested that in case of default in the Venezuelan debt for more than three months an American agent should collect the duties at two customhouses and pay the debts from the proceeds. The opposition of France caused the failure of this proposal.[3] In 1901 the United States established its first definite control of the affairs of a Latin-American country by imposing the Platt Amendment upon Cuba. The purpose of this amendment was to give to the United States such a hand in the affairs of Cuba as to make intervention by European countries impossible. The Cuban government promised not to impair its independence. The United States further obtained a control over the Cuban debt and a right of intervention in order to preserve Cuban independence and to

[1] *The Proceedings of the Hague Peace Conferences, The Conference of* 1907; I: 616, Oxford University Press, New York, 1920; *Treaties etc., of the U.S.,* II: 2248.

[2] Latané, *The United States and Latin America,* p. 200.

[3] Thomas, *op. cit.,* pp. 207–209.

maintain a government adequate for the protection of life, property, and individual liberty. "This clause," Secretary of State Root is reported to have said, "is simply an extension of the Monroe Doctrine."[1]

The Roosevelt Corollary. Following the Spanish-American War the United States became increasingly conscious of its strength. Meanwhile European capital had been invading the Caribbean. Claims for defaulted debts were becoming more numerous, and demands by European governments for customs control were expected. The time was ripe for an expansion of the Monroe Doctrine.

The Roosevelt corollary was announced with regard to Santo Domingo in 1905. In that year a protocol was drawn up with the Dominican government providing that the United States should name officials to take charge of the collection of the Dominican customs. President Roosevelt placed this protocol before the Senate with a message in which he attempted to show that financial control by the United States in this case was a logical derivation from the Monroe Doctrine. The public debt of the Dominican Republic amounted to $32,000,000, of which $22,000,000 was owed to Europeans. The public revenues, said President Roosevelt, were inadequate to meet both the expense of government and the charges of the debt. The San Domingo Improvement Company, an American corporation, had obtained a lien on certain customhouse receipts to satisfy debts due it. European creditors would soon clamor for similar privileges. Thus, to prevent action by European governments which would give them control of Dominican customhouses, a plan providing for American customs control and the payment of Dominican creditors was deemed necessary. "It has for some time been obvious," said the President, "that those who profit by the Monroe Doctrine must accept certain responsibilities along with the rights which it confers; and that the same statement applies to those who uphold the doctrine."[2] The Senate failed to approve the protocol, but President Roosevelt put the system into effect by an executive agreement. In 1907 a convention authorizing customs control was formally adopted as between the two countries. The details of this system are described elsewhere.[3]

One of the principal reasons for the American intervention in Haiti in 1915 and for the imposition upon the little republic of the

[1] BUELL, RAYMOND LESLIE, "Cuba and the Platt Amendment," Foreign Policy Association, *Information Service*, Vol. V, No. 3 (Apr. 17, 1929), p. 48.

[2] *Moore's Digest*, VI: 521.

[3] See pp. 235ff.

treaty of the same year was the fear that European nations might obtain financial and territorial control in that country. Just prior to the World War, France and Germany were anxious to obtain some kind of customs receivership in Haiti which would protect the investments of their nationals. A plan was proposed which would have given joint customs control to France, Germany, and the United States, each to be represented in the personnel of the control in proportion to the amount of the claims held by its nationals. Such a plan would have left the United States a very small participation and was opposed by this country.[1] At that time, it seems, Germany was contemplating armed action in Haiti. Secretary Lansing later told a story of the landing of German sailors from the cruiser *Karlsruhe* at Port au Prince on the evening of July 31, 1914. The sailors proceeded halfway down the wharf, turned round, and went back to their ship.   Mr. Lansing believed that the reembarkation was due to orders cabled from Germany to the German legation ordering the *Karlsruhe* from Port au Prince because of the anticipated outbreak of the European war.[2] If the story is accurate, it provides another instance in which the quarrels of Europe prevented imperialistic aggression—this time checking the invading troops at the very gates of the city. In the next year the United States intervened with armed forces which were to remain in the Haitian Republic for nineteen years. Mr. Lansing stated that the purpose of the occupation was to prevent a European government from obtaining a foothold in Haiti through the seizure of customs control, a coaling station, or a naval base. Such extensions of European power, he believed, would have been "in flagrant defiance of the Monroe Doctrine."[3] Diplomatic and armed interventions in Cuba and Nicaragua have likewise been based in part, at least, on the desire to eliminate reasons for European interference in those countries.[4]

The Roosevelt corollary was not based on the strict language of the Monroe Doctrine. The doctrine was proclaimed in 1823 at a time when the United States accepted nonintervention as a foremost principle of our foreign policy. The opposition to the Holy Alliance, which gave rise to the doctrine, was accompanied in the United States by a denunciation of intervention by one country in

[1] *N.Y. Times*, May 14, 1914.

[2] *Congressional Record*, 62: 6487 (May 8, 1922).

[3] *Ibid.*, p. 6488.

[4] For a vigorous criticism of the Monroe Doctrine and the interventions made in its name see NERVAL, GASTON, *Autopsy of the Monroe Doctrine*, The Macmillan Company, New York, 1934.

the affairs of another. The twisting of the doctrine into an excuse for intervention did much violence to the words and intention of President Monroe.

III. REDEFINING THE MONROE DOCTRINE

The Roosevelt Corollary Disowned. Following the World War the term "Monroe Doctrine," as has been stated, was written into a number of treaties and conventions connected with the machinery of peace. After the year 1927 the United States was especially interested in promoting and strengthening certain agreements for arbitration and for the renunciation of war. Exceptions in favor of the Monroe Doctrine, with their imperialistic implications, became a source of embarrassment to the Department of State. Latin-American statesmen and governments made protests at Geneva and elsewhere against the formal recognition of a doctrine which, they feared, gave the United States the right to invade their territories.

At the same time the World War had so reduced the strength of the European powers as compared with that of the United States and Latin America that it became an open question as to whether the doctrine was any longer necessary. Germany, which had been deemed an aggressor to reckon with in the Caribbean in 1914, had been rendered impotent. France was now vitally interested in security and in maintaining the *status quo* in Europe. She did not care to jeopardize these policies by creating troublous situations in America. Great Britain was confronted by an American navy almost equal to her own and had no desire to test the new rivalry by operations in American waters. New financing in Latin America was carried on for the most part in New York. Certainly the fears of former years had passed away with the shift in national power brought about by the World War.[1]

The movement for the contraction of the Monroe Doctrine began shortly after the war. In 1923 Secretary of State Hughes defined the doctrine in narrow terms. "The policy of the Monroe Doctrine," he said, "does not infringe upon the independence and sovereignty of other American states."[2] In 1928, when the pressure for the narrower definition had become stronger, Secretary of State Stimson directed Undersecretary of State J. Rueben Clark to pre-

[1] "Henceforth, both European and Asiatic powers are hardly more likely to attempt imperialistic adventures in the Americas than in the moon." SIMONDS, FRANK H., and BROOKS EMENY, *The Great Powers in World Politics*, p. 357, American Book Company, New York, 1935.

[2] ALVAREZ, ALEJANDRO, *The Monroe Doctrine*, p. 421, Oxford University Press, New York, 1924.

pare a memorandum on the meaning of the doctrine. Mr. Clark's scholarly researches, reported to the Secretary during the same year, cover some 238 printed pages and are a careful consideration of the history of the doctrine and of the interpretations attached to it. In this memorandum Mr. Clark stated that the doctrine did not legitimately include the Roosevelt corollary and similar expansive interpretations. "The doctrine states a case of the United States *vs.* Europe, and not of the United States *vs.* Latin America."[1] While the Clark memorandum purported to give only the personal view of its author, the strict interpretation thus set forth was evidently adopted by the Department of State. In 1931 W. R. Castle, Jr., acting secretary of state, in a public address stated that the doctrine "does not give our Republic any warrant to interfere in the internal affairs of an American state. It has no taint of imperialism."[2]

The foregoing interpretations do not deny that the right of intervention in Latin-American affairs may exist under some other kind of doctrine, such as that of self-defense, Panama Canal protection, or Caribbean policy. For clarity's sake, however, the name of Monroe should not be dragged into such transactions. Nor should the treaties which contain reservations in favor of the Monroe Doctrine be given the onus of protecting the legality of our Latin-American interventions.

THE MONROE DOCTRINE AND THE LEAGUE OF NATIONS

The origin of Article XXI of the Covenant of the League of Nations, which states that nothing in the Covenant shall be deemed to affect the validity of regional understandings like the Monroe Doctrine, is discussed elsewhere.[3] When the article was considered at Paris there was much discussion as to the meaning of the Monroe Doctrine and, consequently, as to the effect of the provision under discussion. To Latin-American countries the question immediately occurred: Did this stipulation permit the United States to seize control of weaker Latin-American countries under the guise of carrying out the Monroe Doctrine and did it prohibit the League from taking action in such cases? Strict definition of the doctrine was, therefore, demanded. Señor Bonnilla of Honduras unsuc-

---

[1] CLARK, J. RUEBEN, *Memorandum on the Monroe Doctrine*, xxiv, Govt. Printing Office, Washington, 1930.

[2] Dept. of State, *Press Releases*, July 4, 1931, p. 30. See also a news story in the *N.Y. Times*, June 24, 1930, to the effect that the Department had adopted the Clark interpretation.

[3] See p. 258.

cessfully proposed an amendment providing a definition.[1] The demand for a definition has been raised from time to time since the Peace Conference. The most dramatic instance of such a request came in 1928. The Council of the League had made advances to Costa Rica, hoping to induce that government to reconsider its action of withdrawal from the League, which had become effective the year previous. Costa Rica, which had long been suspicious of the aggressive intention of the United States, then asked to know the interpretation placed by the League upon the Monroe Doctrine and the scope of the doctrine when included in Article XXI. The Council replied that the doctrines referred to in Article XXI could have no validity beyond that which they possessed at the time of the inclusion of the article in the Covenant. The meaning of these engagements was not for the framers of the Covenant to determine, but was of concern only to those states which accepted the understandings as among themselves.[2] The answer of the Council was necessarily somewhat elusive. However the later redefinition of the doctrine in the United States along the lines of the Clark memorandum gave additional reassurance to Latin-American countries that the United States receives no warrant for imperialism under Article XXI.

Another serious question arose in Paris as to whether the Monroe Doctrine would operate to prevent the League from settling disputes between two Latin-American countries. M. Kramar of Czechoslovakia asked in the League of Nations Commission whether the Monroe Doctrine would prohibit the League from supporting a Latin-American state which was the victim of aggression on the part of another Latin-American state. President Wilson replied that it would not.[3] There is no doubt, however, that if the League in the first years of its existence had attempted to intervene in such a conflict there would have been a clamor among nationalists in the United States to resist its action as an infringement of the Monroe Doctrine. League settlement of American controversies might well be held to conflict with the extreme statement of Secretary Olney that "the United States is practically sovereign on this continent, and its fiat is law upon the subjects to which it confines its interposition." Opponents of the League stated in the United States Senate debates that the intervention of the League to settle Ameri-

[1] MORLEY, FELIX, A Society of Nations, p. 207, Brookings Institution, Washington, 1932.
[2] Ibid., pp. 329ff.
[3] Ibid., p. 195.

can disputes would clearly be in conflict with the Monroe Doctrine. No controversy between the United States and the League on this point has occurred. With the contraction of the Monroe Doctrine and the improvement of American feeling toward the League it has been officially accepted in this country that there is no conflict between League settlement of American controversies and the Monroe Doctrine.

The Leticia affair provided the first instance of American approval of League action. When on February 25, 1933, the Council of the League made a proposal for a settlement of that controversy, Secretary Stimson made haste to telegraph the Peruvian and Colombian governments urging acceptance of the League proposal. The League plan, he said, was most straightforward and helpful. "In giving my fullest support to this proposal," he concluded, "I have the honor to express the hope that your Government will see its way clear to accepting it."[1] The United States continued thereafter to support the work of the League in adjusting this controversy.

In the Chaco case the road to League settlement was not so free from obstruction by rival plans. In 1928, when hostilities broke out between Paraguay and Bolivia, the Council cabled the parties expressing confidence that they would settle the matter in accordance with their international obligations.[2] At the same time the International Conference of American States on Conciliation and Arbitration, in session in Washington, ignored the League and proceeded to seek a separate method of conciliation.[3] The United States was a member of the so-called neutral commission which was set up in 1929. The efforts of the commission were long, patient, but disappointing. The commission finally decided to withdraw from the dispute and to leave the parties free to accept a settlement through the League if they should so choose.[4] This action, concurred in by the representative of the United States, was the second instance in which it was made clear that conciliation set up by the League in American disputes was not objectionable to this country. Although the efforts of the League broke down and the problem was again turned back to American governments for a solution, the failure of Geneva was not due to objections by the United States.

[1] Dept. of State, *Press Releases*, Mar. 4, 1933, p. 159.
[2] League of Nations, *Official Journal*, January, 1929, p. 21.
[3] See p. 107.
[4] Dept. of State, *Press Releases*, July 1, 1933, p. 1.

THE MONROE DOCTRINE IS THE UNILATERAL POLICY OF THE UNITED STATES

From the beginning our government has taken the position that the Monroe Doctrine is distinctly the policy of the United States; and this country reserves the right to define, interpret, and apply it. In the World Court debates in the Senate in 1926 Senator James Reed proposed that the Monroe Doctrine should be acknowledged by the members of the court to be a rule of international law. Senator Swanson objected on the ground that the doctrine was the unilateral policy of this country. If it should be acknowledged as law it would become a proper matter for interpretation by an international judicial body.[1]

Many Latin Americans resent the maintenance of the doctrine by the United States alone. The stronger nations of South America feel that the assumption of their protection by the United States is humiliating to them, and they believe that the doctrine should be made the multilateral policy of all the American republics. A proposal to this effect was made at the Fifth International Conference of American States at Santiago in 1923, but it was opposed by the United States and failed to carry. Presidents Theodore Roosevelt and Taft and Secretary of State Olney, however, had previously advocated that the doctrine should be made multilateral.[2]

A wise suggestion for a compromise between unilateral and multilateral enforcement was made in 1925 by Secretary Hughes. He proposed that each of the American republics should announce the Monroe Doctrine as its individual policy. This would keep for the United States the right of singleness of action in case our safety should be jeopardized by the aggressive imperialism of a European power. On the other hand, it would satisfy Latin-American dignity and give to the doctrine the weight of universal American support.[3] In recent years the contracted interpretation of the doctrine by the Department of State has robbed this question of much of its importance. With the growth of Pan-American organization, however, discussions of the matter may be expected to take place in the conferences of American republics.

[1] GARNER, JAMES WILFORD, "The Recrudescence of the Monroe Doctrine," *Political Science Quarterly*, XVL: 249 (June, 1930).

[2] BLAKESLEE, GEORGE H., *The Recent Foreign Policy of the United States*, p. 93.

[3] *Ibid.*, pp. 95–97.

CHAPTER V

THE CARIBBEAN POLICY OF THE UNITED STATES

Reasons for a Special Policy. Between the Greater Antilles and the northern coast of South America is the Caribbean, a tropical sea, washing the white beaches of palm-decked islands. To the east its waves touch the shores of the Lesser Antilles. Central America lies along the southwestern border narrowing at its lower extremity to a thin line of land curving in a moderated gooseneck pattern. Here engineering genius has cleft the isthmus and by means of great dams has built a raised interoceanic waterway. Through the ponderous locks of this elevated canal towing engines conduct heavily laden steamers bearing cargoes destined to all continents. In the policies of the United States this has been the most important spot in the world outside our own borders. For the protection of the canal it is necessary that the Caribbean area shall not come under the influence of any strong foreign power. This country dominates the commerce and finance of the Caribbean. The nearness of the United States and the distance of Europe allow the American government a large degree of freedom from imperialistic competition; and the weakness of the nine small Caribbean republics permits our government to pursue its policies with relatively slight opposition from the native population. Here then is one of the lines of least resistance along which the outward pressures promoted by economic forces are certain to find an outlet in the setting up of regional policies through intervention or cooperation. Additional interest in this region has been created by the fact that Caribbean ports are bases for the violation of United States revenue and immigration laws and a possible source of tropical disease.[1]

The American government has ordinarily sought to promote and protect its interests in the Caribbean by unilateral policies rather than by the development of international organization. Reasons exist, however, which have inclined this country toward certain broader policies of cooperation. These reasons are the desire for

[1] JONES, CHESTER LLOYD, HENRY KITTREDGE NORTON, and PARKER THOMAS MOON, *The United States and the Caribbean*, p. 92, University of Chicago Press, Chicago, 1929.

Latin-American trade and friendship and an ambition by a territorially satisfied nation to bring about a world-wide renunciation of war as an instrument of national policy.   There is also the traditional sentiment of nonintervention, fragments of which survive from the days when this country was a debtor nation and had practical reasons for sympathizing with the Latin-American victims of European intervention.   The United States Caribbean policy has been a resultant of all of these conflicting motives and has varied with conditions which emphasize now one and now another.

STRATEGIC CONSIDERATIONS: THE TWO CANAL ROUTES

The Anglo-American Diplomatic Game.   When the United States came into existence as an independent nation, it possessed no territories bordering on the Gulf of Mexico or on the Caribbean. Great Britain, on the other hand, had already pushed its influence into the region.   Besides insular possessions in the West Indies, the British government had established some uncertain claims to territory in British Honduras or Belize, which claims were later to ripen into a recognized title.   The British had also long asserted a protectorate over the Mosquito Coast of Nicaragua, a control which was finally abandoned under pressure from this country.   Although the position of the United States in the beginning was quite inferior to that of the mother country, the growth in American resources and population gradually permitted this government to displace Great Britain as the dominating power in that section.   The result was the more readily obtainable since the proximity of the American base provided a near-by fulcrum which permitted a more effective exertion of force than could be applied from across the Atlantic.

Two important treaties have registered the change in the Caribbean influence of the two countries, adjusting the legal situation to fit the facts.   In the game of Central American canal diplomacy the first principal move was the Clayton-Bulwer Treaty of 1850 which raised the United States from a position of inferiority to one of approximate equality.   The treaty provided that neither the United States nor Great Britain should maintain control over a ship canal through Nicaragua and that neither should assume or exercise dominion over any part of Central America.[1]   Positions on the political chessboard were altered a half century later when the second great move, the Hay-Pauncefote Treaty of 1901, changed the American status from one of equality to one of predominance.

[1] *Treaties, etc., of the U.S.*, I: 659.

The Hay-Pauncefote Treaty abrogated the Clayton-Bulwer Treaty and gave to the United States the right to build a canal under its own control. It authorized the United States to maintain such military police along the canal as might be necessary to protect it against lawlessness and disorder. In return the United States became obligated to keep the canal free and open to the vessels of commerce and war of all nations observing the rules on terms of entire equality.[1]

Acquiring the Canal Zone. After completion of the Hay-Pauncefote Treaty the United States took steps to obtain a canal right of way. The two best routes proposed were across the Isthmus of Panama, which was at that time the territory of the Republic of Colombia, and through Nicaragua by the San Juan River and Lake Nicaragua. President Roosevelt approved the Panama route. Congress authorized the President to proceed to deal with Colombia for a right of way and to pay not more than $40,000,000 for the rights of a French company which had made considerable excavations on the isthmus. The President was instructed to deal with Nicaragua in case of failure to obtain either the French title or a right of way from Colombia on reasonable terms. The Hay-Herran Treaty was then negotiated with Colombia under which the United States agreed to pay $10,000,000 and an annuity of $250,000 for the lease of a strip of land six miles wide. The United States Senate approved the treaty, but the Colombian Senate refused to consent. Reasons for the refusal were alleged to be: the desire for a larger payment from the United States, possibly $15,000,000; the hope of retaining a greater degree of sovereignty over the canal zone; and the desire to obtain a part, if not all, of the $40,000,000 which was to be paid to the French company.[2] The rights of the French company were soon to expire and the title to their concession would shortly revert to the Colombian government. The identity of the stockholders of the French company was not known; but their interests were represented by two exceedingly active lobbyists in the United States, Bunau-Varilla, a French engineer, and W. N. Cromwell, a New York attorney and a heavy contributor to the Republican campaign fund. Cromwell later claimed $800,000 from the French company for his services. These men had done much to influence the choice of the government in favor of Panama as opposed to Nicaragua and they labored to point

[1] *Ibid.*, I: 782.

[2] *Foreign Relations*, 1903, pp. 163*ff.*; HILL, HOWARD C., *Roosevelt and the Caribbean*, pp. 47–48.

out the injustices of Colombia's demands.[1]   Representatives of the company, fearing that they might lose all payment for their holdings either through expiration of their concession or through the action of the United States in turning to Nicaragua, became desperate and fomented a revolution in Panama.   The S.S. *Nashville* was conveniently on the scene, and the commanding officer acted with dispatch to prevent Colombian troops from leaving Colon for the scene of the uprising.   The order for this action came from Washington.   The revolutionists, being virtually unopposed, were successful; and a provisional government was set up which the United States recognized in three days.   Fifteen days after the uprising the United States had signed a treaty with the new Republic of Panama acquiring a perpetual lease of a canal right of way ten miles wide. The compensation was $10,000,000 and, in addition, an annual payment of $250,000.[2]

The Panama episode represented a collapse of the diplomatic method.   Tyler Dennett, who has written a restrained but penetrating account of the affair, remarks: "The saddest aspect of the episode was that it had all been so unnecessary."[3]   Since the United States had two routes from which to choose and since it held practically all the high cards of diplomacy, it seems that a little patience might have brought about the desired result.   But patience with senatorial haggling either foreign or domestic was not a virtue of Theodore Roosevelt.   Although apologists have sought to uphold the American action by defending it in legal terminology, President Roosevelt in later years disdained such pretexts and announced in a public address: "I took the Canal Zone and let the Congress debate."[4]   There is little wonder that Mr. Roosevelt, at other times an advocate of judicial settlement, refused to arbitrate the question.   Eventually, to appease Colombia, the United States paid to that republic the sum of $25,000,000.[5]

Importance of the Canal.   After the treaty of 1903 with the newly created Republic of Panama had been concluded, the way was clear for the building of the canal.   Actual construction work was

[1] PRINGLE, *Theodore Roosevelt, A Biography*, pp. 302ff.

[2] For an account of this incident see HILL, HOWARD C., *op. cit.*, Chapter III; PRINGLE, *op. cit.*, pp. 301ff.; STUART, GRAHAM H., *Latin America and the United States*, pp. 97ff., Century Company, New York, 2d ed., 1928.

[3] *John Hay*, p. 382.

[4] NEARING, SCOTT, and JOSEPH FREEMAN, *Dollar Diplomacy*, p. 83, B. W. Huebsch and the Viking Press, New York, 1925.

[5] The indemnifying treaty was signed in 1914 and ratified in 1922. *Treaties, etc., of the U.S.*, III: 2538.

begun in 1907 and the canal was opened to navigation in 1914. In ten years the tonnage traversing the new waterway was approximately equal to the traffic through the Suez Canal. The importance of the Panama Canal to American commerce can be seen by the following table of distances saved by the use of the canal in preference to the routes that were available before its construction:

TRADE ROUTE DISTANCES THROUGH THE PANAMA CANAL AS COMPARED WITH ALTERNATIVE ROUTES[1]

	By Straits of Magellan, miles	By Panama Canal, miles	Savings by use of canal route, miles
New York to San Francisco......	13,135	5,262	7,873
New Orleans to San Francisco....	13,551	4,683	8,868
Liverpool to San Francisco.......	13,502	7,836	5,666
Iquique to New York............	9,143	4,004	5,139
	By Suez Canal		
New York to Yokohama.........	13,566	9,798	3,768
New York to Shanghai...........	12,525	10,649	1,876

[1] See JOHNSON, EMORY R., *The Panama Canal and Commerce*, Chapter III, D. Appleton & Company, New York, 1916.

From the standpoint of naval strategy the canal has an important service to perform. In case of war the short cut by the isthmian route would permit a more rapid assembly of certain needed supplies and materials and it would also make possible a much speedier mobilization of naval strength. War, coming suddenly, might find the bulk of the American fleet in the Pacific when it would be imperatively needed in the Atlantic, or vice versa. Before the construction of the canal the transfer of vessels was made by way of the Straits of Magellan. The canal saves something like 7,000 or 8,000 miles in fleet transfer.

In order to protect the canal, strong fortifications have been built at both ends of the waterway, and some 10,000 officers and men are regularly stationed in the Canal Zone. In addition both army and navy maintain airfields in the zone.

The Nicaraguan Route. In 1912 the Nicaraguan government, which was in financial difficulty, approached the United States with regard to the sale of a canal route through Nicaraguan territory. The advantages for the United States in such a transaction were listed in *Foreign Relations* as: the acquisition of facilities for further growth of coastwise commerce, elimination of foreign political influence in Nicaragua, prevention of canal concessions to European or Asiatic powers, an additional defense of the Panama Canal, and an effective means for guaranteeing the Washington Conventions,[1] this last evidently meaning that the United States would have additional power to prevent revolutions in Central America. The agreement, known as the Bryan-Chamorro Treaty, was finally negotiated in 1914 and was ratified in 1916. The provisions were as follows:

1. The United States received a perpetual grant of a right to construct and operate a canal by way of the San Juan River and Lake Nicaragua or by any other route over Nicaraguan territory.

2. The United States received leases to the Little Corn and Great Corn Islands and also the right to establish a naval base in Nicaraguan territory on the Gulf of Fonseca. The term of the leases was ninety-nine years with the privilege of renewal at expiration for another term of ninety-nine years.

3. For these rights the United States became obligated to pay $3,000,000 but this sum could be spent by Nicaragua only with the approval of the Secretary of State of the United States.[2]

Naval Bases. The rights to establish a naval base on the Gulf of Fonseca and to utilize the Great Corn and Little Corn islands, which lie off the Caribbean coast of Nicaragua, have not thus far been exercised. When the Nicaragua Canal is finally built, the question of developing these strategic points will arise. At the present time the United States has a series of naval stations and bases extending in a long line from the Gulf of Mexico to the Virgin Islands. Stations are maintained at New Orleans and Pensacola. A defended base at Key West controls the straits of Florida. Guantánamo, a naval station located on leased territory at the eastern end of Cuba, is situated strategically near to the commercially important Windward Passage. For an annual rental of $2,000 the United States holds a lease of land and water in this excellent harbor. The base has fuel storage facilities, wharves, docks, and a marine barracks. Equipment for minor naval repairs has been installed.[3] Farther to the east, in the harbor of St. Thomas in the Virgin Islands, the

---

[1] *Foreign Relations*, 1913, p. 1021.

[2] *Treaties, etc., of the U.S.*, III: 2740.

[3] The Commission on Cuban Affairs in 1935 raised the question as to whether the surrender of this base would not improve political relations with Cuba. *Problems of the New Cuba*, pp. 499–500, Foreign Policy Association, New York, 1935.

United States maintains a naval anchorage with facilities for commercial fuel oil and minor repairs. In the Canal Zone a great deal of money and effort has been expended to prepare land, air, and naval defenses. The naval base includes an oil depot, commercial drydocks, a submarine base, a torpedo depot, marine barracks, and an airfield.[1]

INVESTMENTS

The following table shows the extent of the investments of United States citizens in the Caribbean:

AMERICAN INVESTMENTS IN THE NINE CARIBBEAN REPUBLICS AS OF DEC. 31, 1933

(In millions of dollars)[1]

Costa Rica.............	32	Honduras...............	66
Cuba...................	951	Nicaragua..............	13
Dominican Republic.......	85	Panama.................	42
Guatemala..............	72	Salvador...............	33
Haiti..................	25		
		Total.................	1,319

[1] *The Balance of International Payments of the United States in 1933*, p. 56.

The rising importance of American investments is a phenomenon of the last three or four decades. Formerly British capitalists occupied the first place. Since the Spanish-American War, however, the increase in American holdings has been so great as to bring them far above British investments.[2] Thus in the realm of finance, as in that of naval power, the United States has taken the leading place formerly held in this section by Great Britain.

Owing to the inability of the small republics to observe consistently the mores of capitalism with regard to their governmental obligations, loans have sometimes brought with them political control. Investments have been both cause and effect of the American Caribbean policies. Secretaries of State have at times promoted loans in that section in order to give an excuse for intervention and to shut out foreign influence.[3] There has been no very definite connection,

[1] STONE, WILLIAM T., "Outlying Naval Bases," Foreign Policy Association, *Information Service*, Vol. V, No. 15 (Oct. 2, 1929), contains general information concerning Caribbean defenses.

[2] JONES, CHESTER LLOYD, *Caribbean Backgrounds and Prospects*, p. 295, D. Appleton & Company, New York, 1931. Dr. Jones estimated the investments in 1928 to be: American, $1,683,000,000; British, $273,000,000; and all others, $37,000,000.

[3] See pp. 190–192.

however, between the size of the investments and the amount of control exercised in the different countries. Nicaragua, where the amount invested is relatively small, has been brought under much closer political control than Guatemala and Honduras where investments are much larger.[1] Greater strategic interests in Nicaragua, due to the canal right of way, go far to explain why this situation exists.

NONRECOGNITION OF REVOLUTIONARIES AS A CENTRAL AMERICAN DOCTRINE

Antirevolutionism. Governmental instability in the Caribbean region has been regarded as detrimental to American interests because in the past it has created conditions favorable to European intervention and it has also been injurious to American trade and investment. Furthermore, the policy of promotion of United States policies through the maintenance of controlled governments, as has at times occurred in Haiti and Nicaragua, would naturally be defeated if favored presidents should be ejected from office.

The opposition to Central American disorders as a general program was first manifested when, in 1907, the five republics were convened at Washington in response to invitations by the governments of the United States and Mexico. The purpose of the conference was to draw up an agreement which would put an end to wars, revolutions, and the meddling by one government in the affairs of another. A general treaty of peace and amity was signed. In an additional convention the five governments agreed not to recognize any government which should come into power in any of the five republics by revolution against the recognized government so long as the freely elected representatives of the people had not constitutionally reorganized the country. During the administration of Woodrow Wilson the doctrine of nonrecognition of revolutionary governments was proclaimed as the policy of the United States toward all of Latin America. This country desired security in the American republics and had little sympathy with self-seeking revolutionists.[2] The doctrine was applied as against Huerta in Mexico, Cespedes in the Dominican Republic, and Tinoco in Costa Rica.

In 1923 a second Central American conference was held in Washington at which the five governments signed another convention opposing revolution. The signatories repeated their 1907 pledge against the recognition of revolutionary governments and

---

[1] JONES, *Caribbean Backgrounds and Prospects*, p. 299.
[2] *Foreign Relations*, 1913, p. 7; 1914, p. 443.

added that, even if the freely elected representatives of the people should have constitutionally reorganized the government, the new administration would not be recognized if the president, vice-president, or chief of state should be a person who was leader of a *coup d'état* or revolution or a close relative of such a leader. The United States was not a party to this agreement and was, therefore, not legally bound by it. The Department of State, nevertheless, based its nonrecognition policy in Central America for about a decade upon the 1923 convention.

Antirevolutionism Becomes a Difficult Policy. The Wilsonian principle of refusal to recognize revolutionary governments throughout Latin America proved to be entirely unrealistic. Such a policy can be made effective only with regard to small countries which are under American influence and which can be manipulated without creating undue antagonisms. Even in such cases it is not an easy policy to pursue. The impracticability of the general policy was made entirely clear when the depression of 1929 blossomed into the revolutions of 1930 in South America. When revolutionary governments came into power in such countries as Argentina and Brazil, the United States, for commercial reasons, could not withhold recognition. In Argentina, for example, recognition followed shortly on the heels of the successful revolution. On September 8, Provisional President Uriburu, who had overthrown the legally elected President Irigoyen, was inaugurated. The leading commercial nations almost immediately began laying plans for recognition, and on September 18 the United States recognized the new government.

Antirevolutionism Contracted into a Central American Policy. The position of the United States then required some new explanation. Secretary of State Stimson accordingly acknowledged that the American government had departed from the Wilsonian principle,[1] and was applying the policy of nonrecognition only to the five Central American republics which had signed the 1923 treaty. Since 1923, he said, no revolutionary government had been able to maintain itself in Central America because of the attitude of the United States. The denial of recognition had in each case compelled the revolutionary president to resign on account of his inability to borrow money in the international market.[2]

[1] In a speech of Feb. 6, 1931, "The United States and the Other American Republics," Dept. of State, *Latin American Series*, No. 4, p. 8.

[2] There is some question whether under the treaty the United States should have recognized the Diaz government in Nicaragua in 1926, as Diaz was said

Costa Rica and Salvador Object to Nonrecognition of Revolutionaries. The policy of refusal to recognize revolutionary governments is often regarded in Latin America as a serious infringement upon the sovereignty of the nations concerned. It constitutes a refusal to permit the Central American countries to change administrations in a manner which is sometimes considered as normal to that region. It is an attempt to foist Anglo-Saxon constitutional methods upon a Latin-American community. Much opposition has, therefore, been shown to the 1923 convention. Costa Rica gave notice of denunciation of the agreement in December, 1932, and this action was shortly afterward followed by a similar notice on the part of Salvador. The denunciations became effective on January 1, 1934. A revolutionary government which had been in power in Salvador since December, 1931, was recognized by the other four governments of Central America. The United States then recognized Salvador on January 26, 1934.[1] The nonrecognition policy accordingly has been greatly weakened in that it no longer applies to either Salvador or Costa Rica, although the treaty is evidently still binding on Guatemala, Honduras, and Nicaragua.

SUMMARY OF UNITED STATES RELATIONS WITH EACH OF THE NINE REPUBLICS

While the general attitude of the United States in the Caribbean can be described as one of great interest in the local political situations and of comparatively little regard for the sovereignty of the various governments, the particular policies pursued from time to time have varied in each of the countries concerned. The American government has exercised particularly strong control in five of the republics—Cuba, the Dominican Republic, Haiti, Panama, and Nicaragua. All these governments have on occasion been subjected to political manipulation, and the use of American marines for the maintenance of order or the assistance of a favored president has been relatively frequent. Several years ago Parker Thomas Moon described our relation to these five countries by stating that they "may be classed as 'wards', 'virtual protectorates,' or 'quasi-protectorates,' as you will, for they are nominally sovereign but actually dependent client states."[2] In the other countries the relationship of the United States has been somewhat nearer to that

---

to have been associated with Chamorro, who had upset the former legal government by a *coup d'état.*

[1] Dept. of State, *Press Releases*, Jan. 27, 1934, p. 51.

[2] JONES, NORTON, MOON, *The United States and the Caribbean*, p. 153.

standard of equal treatment which is usually extended under international law. Two of these countries, Costa Rica and Salvador, have shown a considerable independence of spirit.

Cuba. The special interest of the United States in Cuba was maintained for a century previous to Cuban independence. Situated in the central Caribbean and commanding the trade routes of that region, the Pearl of the Antilles was from the beginning an object of particular regard by the United States, a regard which was increased with the acquisition of Louisiana and the development of commerce between the Gulf and Atlantic ports. Spanish policies in Cuba were closely watched in Washington throughout the nineteenth century.

The Spanish-American War and the terms set down by the Platt Amendment at the end of that war as a condition for the withdrawal of American troops fixed for over thirty years a new relationship with Cuba. The principal provisions of the Platt Amendment were:

1. Cuba shall not enter into any treaty with a foreign power which shall impair its independence nor permit any foreign power to obtain control over any portion of the island.

2. Cuba shall not contract any public debt to pay the interest upon which and to make reasonable sinking-fund provisions for the ultimate discharge of which the ordinary revenues, after defraying the expenses of government, shall be inadequate.

3. The United States may intervene for the preservation of Cuban independence and the maintenance of a government adequate for the protection of life, property, and individual liberty.

. . . .

7. Cuba agrees to sell or lease to the United States lands necessary for coaling or naval stations at points to be agreed upon.[1]

The chief motive behind the Platt Amendment was the desire to maintain the independence of Cuba from European control. Following the World War, however, the probability of European invasion greatly decreased while huge sums were invested in the island by Americans. Economic considerations increased relatively in importance. The control over indebtedness was used at times to bring about "reforms" in the government. Under the Platt Amendment there were three occasions on which troops were landed for the maintenance of order, *i.e.*, in 1906, 1912, and 1917. After the notorious Machado government had maintained itself during 1932 and part of 1933 by the use of the most oppressive methods, the American government finally employed diplomatic pressure to

[1] *Treaties, etc., of the U.S.*, I: 362.

force the resignation of the President.[1]   When a student and radical government was set up under Grau San Martin in 1933, the United States refused recognition on the grounds that it was not representative of the Cuban people.   The fear that American investments might suffer under a labor government doubtless was an influence shaping the attitude at Washington.   The refusal of the United States to recognize the government made it impossible for Dr. Grau to obtain credit.   The government collapsed and the fallen president stated: "I fell because Washington willed it."[2]   The Mendieta government, which was conservative and had business support, was recognized by the United States within five days. Credits and an arrangement for a sugar quota followed.   The Commission on Cuban Affairs, organized by the Foreign Policy Association to investigate the situation, found in 1934 that the fundamental obstacle to good Cuban-American relations was the widespread belief that the United States had attempted to control Cuba through the making and unmaking of governments.[3]

The fact that the United States did not land troops during the troublous times of 1933–1934, however, indicated a growing opposition in this country to armed intervention.   Demands of Cuba for the withdrawal of the Platt Amendment were finally answered in 1934 by a treaty with the United States abrogating the distasteful provisions.[4]   The supplanting of the Commercial Treaty of 1902 by the Trade Agreement of 1934 likewise led to better feeling between the two countries.

The Dominican Republic.   In 1905 the United States assumed the collection of Dominican customs duties under an executive agreement.   In 1907 this arrangement was written into a formal convention.   For the next nine years our diplomacy in Santo Domingo was based upon customs control which gave to the United States considerable power in forcing measures and policies upon the Dominican government.   In 1916 this country intervened with military force and took over the governmental functions of the republic.   In 1924 the United States withdrew its armed forces and returned the government to the Dominican officials, retaining,

[1] THOMSON, CHARLES A., "The Cuban Revolution: Fall of Machado," *Foreign Policy Reports*, Vol. XI, No. 21 (Dec. 18, 1935).

[2] HERRING, HUBERT, "Another Chance for Cuba," *Current History*, XXXIX: 657 (March, 1934).

[3] *Problems of the New Cuba*, p. 497.

[4] *U.S. Treaty Series*, No. 866; FITZGIBBON, RUSSELL H., *Cuba and the United States*, 1905–1935, p. 200, George Banta Publishing Company, Menasha, Wis., 1935.

however, the right of customs collection. A convention drawn up in 1924 authorized the continuation of American customs control until the retirement of all bonds secured under the agreement.[1]

Haiti. The Haitian Republic came to have a new importance in the diplomacy of the United States in the years just preceding the World War. The prospects of German and French intervention to protect business interests in Haiti caused apprehension in Washington. In 1910 Secretary of State Knox, through urgent representations, opened an opportunity for American capital to purchase shares in the National Bank of the Republic of Haiti, the official depository of Haitian funds. From that time on the United States sought to influence Haiti regarding financial questions. In 1915 a bloody revolution was followed by the landing of American troops. A favorably inclined Haitian leader, Sudre Dartiguenave, was elected to the office of president through American influence; and the Treaty of 1915 was forced upon Haiti by various forms of pressure.

The principal provisions of the Treaty of 1915 were as follows:

1. The supervision of Haitian customs collections by a General Receiver and the installation in the Ministry of Finance of a Financial Adviser were provided for, both officials to be appointed by the President of Haiti upon nomination of the President of the United States.

2. Haiti promised not to increase her public debt nor to modify the custom duties in a manner to reduce the revenues without the consent of the United States.

3. A Haitian constabulary, organized and officered by Americans, was provided for, the American officers to be replaced by Haitians as soon as the latter were found to be qualified.

4. Haiti promised not to surrender any territory by sale, lease, or otherwise to any foreign power nor to enter into any treaty with any foreign power which would tend to impair her independence.[2]

The Haitian legislature was dissolved in 1917 and the government was conducted by the President and the appointed Council of State. In 1922 Louis Borno, who was even more amenable to American control than Dartiguenave, was selected as president. The American regime maintained itself unyieldingly until 1930. During this period sanitation and education were improved and public works were built.[3] Because of popular dissatisfaction in Haiti in 1929, however, President Hoover sent to that country an

[1] *U.S. Treaty Series*, No. 726.

[2] *Treaties, etc., of the U.S.*, III: 2673.

[3] MILLSPAUGH, ARTHUR C., *Haiti under American Control*, 1915–1930, pp. 138, 158, 162, World Peace Foundation, Boston, 1931.

investigating body known as the Forbes Commission. Following the recommendations of the commission the legislature was restored. Parliamentary elections were held in October, 1930. Stenio Vincent, who was opposed to the American occupation, was elected president. Further agreements for the relinquishment of certain American fiscal controls and the withdrawal of American marines were made. The power of the American financial adviser to visa expenditures was relinquished and the collection of internal revenues was given back to Haiti. The command of the Haitian *Garde* was turned over to native officers on August 1, 1934; and the marines were withdrawn on August 15. The work of the general receiver and financial adviser was continued by an official similarly chosen, called the fiscal representative.[1]

Panama. The 1903 treaty between the United States and Panama contains a guarantee of the independence of Panama by the United States. The treaty gives to the United States the use, occupation, and control of a zone across the isthmus which is ten miles wide and which extends three miles into the ocean at either end. In addition the United States is given the use, occupation, and control of any other lands and waters outside the zone which may be necessary and convenient for the construction, maintenance, operation, sanitation, and protection of the canal. The cities of Colón and Panama, which lie in the zone, are not included in the lease. Over the zone and the necessary auxiliary lands and waters the United States is granted the rights, power, and authority which it would possess and exercise if it were the sovereign of the territory.[2] In order to combat disease in the formerly unhealthful isthmus, the United States is authorized to construct sanitary works in the cities of Colón and Panama and to enforce health regulations. The Health Officer of the Canal Zone has supervised the public health administration of these cities. The canal area has accordingly been freed from the scourge of yellow fever while other tropical diseases have been greatly reduced.[3] This country is authorized to maintain public order in the cities of Panama and Colón when it deems that the government of Panama is unable to do so. It is to be especially noted that the United States has the right of control over any part of Panama which is necessary and convenient for

[1] *Executive Agreement Series*, Nos. 22 and 46. See also Dept. of State, *Press Releases*, Aug. 15, 1931, p. 145; Aug. 19, 1933, p. 103; Aug. 18, 1934, p. 103.

[2] *Treaties, etc., of the U.S.*, II: 1349.

[3] MUNRO, DANA G., *The United States and the Caribbean Area*, p. 81, World Peace Foundation, Boston, 1934.

the protection of the canal. Under conditions of modern large-scale warfare this could easily be interpreted to mean the whole of the territory of Panama.

The United States under the treaty has intervened on three occasions to keep order in Colón and Panama.[1] The Department of State has maintained that this country has also a general right to intervene in other parts of Panama to suppress disorder where the Panamanian government is unable to do so. This general right, it is claimed, is derived from the guarantee of the independence of Panama. An intervention under this interpretation occurred in 1918; but in 1931, when a revolution took place, the United States did not intervene. The failure to intervene, according to Raymond Leslie Buell, was apparently in line with the new Hoover policy of moderation.[2]

Nicaragua. The modern relations with Nicaragua date from 1910 when the Zelayan government, which had incurred the enmity of Secretary of State Knox, was overthrown by revolutionists supported by the policies of the United States.[3] In 1911 the new revolutionary government was recognized. Soon afterwards Adolfo Diaz, who sympathized with American aims, became president; and for years this official and his successors were able to stay in office because of the presence of American marines. Financial control was established through an agreement between American bankers and the Nicaraguan government. In 1926 Diaz, who had been out of office for a few years, was selected in an emergency as president by the Nicaraguan Congress. The office had been vacant because of the resignation of the President and because Juan Sacasa, the Vice-President, had been forced to flee from the country. Upon Sacasa's return Diaz clung to the presidency under a dubious constitutional interpretation. The United States upheld Diaz and took action to bring about the defeat of Sacasa. More than 5,000 marines were sent into the country. Colonel Henry L. Stimson, who went to Nicaragua as special agent of the United States, soon obtained the acceptance of a plan of peace between the two factions; but Augusto

[1] BUELL, RAYMOND LESLIE, "Panama and the United States," *Foreign Policy Reports*, Vol. VII, No. 23 (Jan. 20, 1932), p. 412.

[2] *Ibid.*, p. 415. For the incidents of the revolution and the attitude of the United States see Dept. of State, *Press Releases*, Jan. 3, 1931, p. 8; Jan. 17, 1931, p. 33. A new treaty between the two governments was signed on March 2, 1936. When ratified, it will replace much of the 1903 treaty.

[3] For a discussion of the part played by American concessionaries in upsetting Zelaya see BEARD, CHARLES A., *The Idea of National Interest*, pp. 174*ff.*, The Macmillan Company, New York, 1934.

Sandino, a former Sacasa general, refused to agree and continued open warfare for some years. The United States marines and the National Guard of Nicaragua, which was organized under American supervision, made desperate attempts to suppress Sandino and finally drove him from the country. Moncada, a Sacasa leader, was elected president in 1928; and in 1932 Sacasa himself was chosen to that office. The Department of State announced the complete evacuation of marines from Nicaragua as of January 2, 1933.[1]

A feature of American relations with Nicaragua for some years previous to the evacuation was the supervision of Nicaraguan elections by the United States. In 1922 Dr. Harold W. Dodds was appointed by the Nicaraguan government on the recommendation of the Department of State to draft an electoral law. The 1924 elections were held under this law and were regarded as relatively honest and free from violence. After American occupation three elections were supervised by Americans. In 1928 General Frank R. McCoy was appointed chairman of the National Board of Elections. In 1930 Captain Alfred W. Johnson, U.S.N., served in that capacity, and in 1932 Rear Admiral Clark H. Woodward was chosen. An American electoral commission with the assistance of several hundred sailors and marines conducted the supervision.[2]

Guatemala. Guatemala is the most populous of the Central American states and has the largest foreign trade. Coffee planting is the leading occupation. The International Railways of Central America and the United Fruit Company, both of which are Keith interests, constitute the chief American investments. Guatemala has been relatively free from domination by the United States. Philander C. Knox, when secretary of state, sought to impose a control upon Guatemalan finances but failed because British investors, who held the debt of the country, refused to cooperate in the Knox refunding plan.

Honduras. Honduras has suffered more than its neighbors from financial and political instability. The foreign debt due to loans of 1867–1870 mounted far above the capacity of the country to pay and was later refunded at a mere fraction of its face value, being reduced from about $123,000,000 to $6,000,000. The backwardness of the

[1] Dept. of State, *Press Releases*, Jan. 7, 1933. Sandino reached an agreement with President Sacasa in 1933 but was treacherously shot by members of the National Guard in 1934.

[2] For a description of the machinery of supervision see BUELL, RAYMOND LESLIE, "American Supervision of Elections in Nicaragua," Foreign Policy Association, *Information Service*, Vol. VI, No. 21 (Dec. 24, 1930). See also MUNRO, *The United States and the Caribbean Area*, pp. 242, 260, 266.

population and the interference of the neighboring countries have caused many revolutions. The United States intervened with military force on six occasions between 1907 and 1925.[1] Secretary Knox in 1912 negotiated a treaty with Honduras for the control of Honduran finances, but the agreement failed of ratification in both countries. The chief American interests are railways and fruit investments on the eastern coast.

El Salvador. Salvador, with an area of 1,183 square miles, is the smallest of the five Central American countries, but it ranks well toward the top in population and trade. The governing class of Salvador is able and progressive. The International Railways of Central America constitute the largest American investment in the country although there are also important steamship, mining, and banking interests.[2] Salvador has been outstanding because of its independent attitude toward the United States. In 1912 the Salvadoran government objected to the landing of American marines in Nicaragua. In 1913 and in 1916 it protested against the grant to the United States of the right to establish a naval base in the Gulf of Fonseca.[3] Salvador was the only Central American republic to refuse to follow the leadership of the United States in declaring war on Germany. In 1919 it openly demanded that the United States should define the Monroe Doctrine. It followed the lead of Costa Rica in 1932 in bringing about the downfall of the nonrecognition treaty of 1923. In opposition to the Hoover-Stimson Doctrine, Salvador, in 1934, recognized the government of Manchukuo. It thus defied one of the principal policies of the United States in the Far East.

Costa Rica. The population of Costa Rica contains a greater proportion of white blood than that of any other Central American republic. A large percentage of the people own their own homes and the interest in education is proverbial. The Costa Rican government is characterized by peace, stability, and relative democracy.[4] The United Fruit Company, however, is an important factor in the affairs of the country; and in certain sections along the east coast,

---

[1] RIPPY, J. FRED, *Historical Evolution of Hispanic America*, pp. 532-533, F. S. Crofts & Company, New York, 1932.

[2] For the loan contract with Minor C. Keith of 1922 which imposes financial control upon the country and for the tolerant attitude of the United States in the case of the 1932 default see p. 235.

[3] See *Foreign Relations*, 1913, p. 1027.

[4] MUNRO, DANA G., *The Five Republics of Central America*, pp. 143, 148, Oxford University Press, New York, 1918.

even the police duties of the central government are to a great extent exercised through the agents of the company.[1]

The attitude of Costa Rica, like that of Salvador, has been one of independence and of resistance against the influence of the United States. The refusal of the United States to recognize the revolutionary Tinoco government in 1917 and the succeeding Quiros government in 1919, coupled with the recommendation of the Department of State that Aguilar should be chosen president, gave rise to protests in Costa Rica. The United States was denounced for meddling unduly in the affairs of the republic.[2] Costa Rica objected to the grant by Nicaragua to the United States of a canal route along the San Juan River. Because of the opposition of the United States, Costa Rica, although a belligerent against Germany, was not invited to the peace conference in Paris in 1919 and was not given the opportunity to become an original member of the League of Nations.[3] The name of Costa Rica was intentionally omitted from those named in the annex to the Covenant who were invited to accede to the Covenant. Later Costa Rica joined the League and then withdrew, giving as a reason her inability to meet the required League contributions. When urged to reconsider this action, the Costa Rican government attracted considerable international attention by requesting from the League Council a definition of the Monroe Doctrine.[4] Felix Morley suggests that possibly Costa Rica joined the League in order to be in a better position to raise this issue in an international forum.[5] As has been mentioned, in 1932 Costa Rica again opposed an American policy by leading the movement to break down the nonrecognition treaty of 1923.

INTERNATIONAL ORGANIZATION IN THE CARIBBEAN

No regional organization has been created for the Caribbean region as such. The movement for Central American cooperation, which touches a part of the area, has received support from the United States; but our efforts have been seriously retarded by the attempt to pursue our own single national policies in contradiction to the aim of solidarity and cooperative organization in the region. Central America was at one time united in a federal republic which

---

[1] *Ibid.*, p. 161.

[2] BUELL, RAYMOND LESLIE, "The United States and Central American Stability," *Foreign Policy Reports*, Vol. VII. No. 9 (July 8, 1931), pp. 177*ff.*

[3] See *Foreign Relations*, 1919, p. 852.

[4] See p. 57.

[5] *The Society of Nations*, p. 330.

was recognized by the United States in 1824. By 1839, however, the federation had been split into the five present republics. Several attempts to establish unity among these governments have been made from time to time by leaders in the various countries. After acquiring the right to the Panama Canal Zone in 1903, the United States took a deeper interest in Central American peace and stability. Wars between the republics and revolutions supported by international intrigues were regarded as a menace to economic development and to the safety of our canal interests. It is this very instability, however, which has made difficult, if not impossible, the policy of cooperation by the United States.

In 1907 this country joined with Mexico in inviting the representatives of the five republics to a conference in Washington. The principal agreements reached at this meeting were a Treaty of Peace and Amity, a convention to set up a Central American Court of Justice, and an agreement not to recognize revolutionary governments.[1] The Central American Court of Justice was short-lived, expiring shortly after it rendered a decision which declared illegal certain privileges granted to the United States in the Bryan-Chamorro Treaty. Furthermore, after promoting the movement against revolution, the United States intervened to assist a revolution in Nicaragua in 1910 and then recognized the revolutionary government.

In 1923 another conference was held in Washington to further the movement for Central American stability and unity. A new court, the International Central American Tribunal, was established. The tribunal is modeled upon the Permanent Court of Arbitration at The Hague. A panel is created consisting of thirty jurists, six designated by each government. In case of a dispute a tribunal of three judges is to be chosen from the panel. A new treaty forbidding the recognition of revolutionary governments was also concluded at the 1923 conference. Other conventions drawn up at this time included one for the limitation of armaments and another for the establishment of Central American commissions to study the common problems of finance and communications.[2] While the conditions in Central America have improved during the years since

[1] For a report of the conference see *Foreign Relations*, 1907, Part 2, pp. 665*ff.*

[2] *Conference on Central American Affairs, Washington, December* 4, 1922–*February* 7, 1923, Govt. Printing Office, Washington, 1923. A Treaty of Central American Fraternity between the five Central American governments was signed at Guatemala City on Apr. 12, 1934. When ratified this treaty will replace, in some respects, the 1923 treaties.

1907, there has been considerable skepticism regarding the sincerity of the efforts of the United States to establish peace and order on a basis of law and equality. The interference of this country in Nicaragua in 1926–1927 added to the feeling of cynicism.

If the United States has not played an entirely consistent role in bringing about international organization in the Caribbean region, this country has nevertheless in recent years thrown some enthusiasm into the promotion of Pan-American organization, a movement which necessarily includes the Caribbean in its scope. The work of the United States with regard to this program is described in the next two chapters.

OUTLINE OF CARIBBEAN POLICY

The policy of the United States in the Caribbean area is difficult to summarize since it has been differently pursued in different countries and since also it has changed with the pressures of the times. In the following outline the attempt is made to give a rough perspective of the political activity of the United States in this region.

I. Unilateral action by the United States.
   A. Obtaining titles to or rights in territories.
      1. Annexations.
         a. By conquest—Puerto Rico.
         b. By purchase—the Virgin Islands.
      2. Leases and easements.
         a. Canal routes—Panama Canal Zone (perpetual lease) and Nicaraguan canal rights (perpetual grant of right of way).
         b. Defensive positions.
            (1) Naval base rights—Guantánamo (lease at will of United States); treaty right to establish naval base in Nicaraguan territory on Fonseca Bay for 99 years.
            (2) Territory for fortifications—Great Corn and Little Corn islands (lease for 99 years).
   B. Military intervention.
      1. Permitted by treaty—Haiti (right to give aid and protection to customs receivership and to give aid for the maintenance of stable government); Dominican Republic (right to give aid and protection to customs receivership); cities of Colón and Panama (right to intervene to compel observance of sanitary regulations and to maintain public order); right of intervention in Cuba formerly granted under the Platt Amendment but now abandoned.
      2. Right of intervention claimed under treaty guarantee of territorial integrity—Republic of Panama outside the cities of Colón and Panama.
      3. Interventions not based on treaty—interventions for political purposes and for the protection of life and property. (Interventions

for the latter reason are sometimes called "interpositions." The two reasons have in recent years become difficult to dissociate.[1] There have been probably thirty interventions in the Caribbean under this heading but the United States has now repudiated the policy of armed intervention.)

C. Manipulation, *i.e.*, controlling of Caribbean governments in order to obtain from them apparently voluntary actions favorable to the United States.

    1. Through granting or withholding of recognition—Haiti, the Dominican Republic, Nicaragua, and Cuba.

    2. Through control of arms traffic—Nicaragua.

    3. Through armed support to favored government in defeating revolutionists—Haiti and Nicaragua.

D. Control of finances and investments.

    1. Through financial supervision conducted by or assented to by the United States government—Dominican Republic, Haiti, Panama, Nicaragua, and Salvador. (The formal system of controlling the debt of Cuba was abandoned with the abrogation of the Platt Amendment.)

    2. Through diplomatic encouragement to American investments or through action to discourage European investments—Cuba, Haiti, Nicaragua, Panama, Guatemala, and Honduras.

II. International cooperation.

A. Through promotion of action by the five republics of Central America in the Washington conferences of 1907 and 1923.

    1. By promoting the doctrine of antirevolutionism—now partially abandoned.

    2. By promoting the peaceful settlement of disputes among the five republics.

        a. Through aiding in the creation of the Central American Court of Justice, which later fell because the United States failed to recognize and support its decisions regarding the Bryan-Chamorro treaty.

        b. Through aiding in the creation of an International Central American Tribunal.

    3. By the development of Pan-Americanism.[2]

THE RETREAT FROM IMPERIALISM

Beginning at about the year 1928 the general policy of the United States toward interventions underwent a considerable change. Imperialism came into disfavor and the policies of international cooperation with Latin-American countries were given greater emphasis. Various reasons to which this change may be ascribed are: the desire of the United States to promote world peace; the

[1] See p. 226.

[2] The foregoing outline follows to a considerable extent the treatment of MOON, PARKER THOMAS, in *The United States and the Caribbean*, pp. 148*ff.*

desire to encourage Pan-Americanism; the increase in strength and stability of Latin-American countries;[1] the growth of nationalistic feeling in those countries; the depression of 1929 and the consequent rise of nationalism in the United States as opposed to imperialism; the subsidence of military fears and suspicions which existed in the World War and which contributed to the unprecedented imperialism in the American diplomacy of that period. Some of the evidences of this change are as follows:

The redefinition of the Monroe Doctrine in accordance with the Clark memorandum of 1928.

The limitation of the doctrine of the protection of American citizens in Central America as outlined in the statements of Secretary Stimson in 1931.

The withdrawal of marines from Nicaragua which was completed at the beginning of 1933.

The renunciation of armed intervention as made at the Seventh International Conference of American States in 1933.

The increase in enthusiasm for Pan-Americanism as shown by Secretary Hull's attitude at the above-mentioned conference.

The abrogation of the Platt Amendment in 1934.

The relinquishment of certain financial controls in Haiti and the withdrawal of marines from that country which was completed in 1934.

The curve of imperialism has for the time definitely turned downward. Whether this is to mark the permanent direction of American policy or whether it will be followed by a reversion to the imperialisms of Theodore Roosevelt, Philander C. Knox, and Woodrow Wilson it would be perilous to prophesy. Certain economic, psychological, and military transitions going on at the present time may be setting the stage for a revival of foreign intervention on a grand scale. Whatever the result may be, the contest in American governmental circles between a cooperative Pan-Americanism and imperialism is certain to require decisions of the utmost importance in shaping the future of the Western Hemisphere.

MEXICO

Although Mexico is not strictly a part of the Caribbean area, its situation, state of economic development, people, and institutions have made the problems of American diplomacy at Mexico City somewhat comparable to those in Central America and the Caribbean islands. There has been, however, less consideration for

---

[1] "It may take several years for the people of the Central American Republics to establish permanently stable political institutions, but the progress which has already been made toward this end has been sufficient materially to affect the basic factors governing the Central American policy of the United States." MUNRO, *The United States and the Caribbean Area*, p. 226.

strategy and more for protection of citizens in regard to their persons and property. The value of American holdings in Mexico has been far greater than in any of the Caribbean countries, with the exception of Cuba;[1] and proximity has added its temptations to intervention. Mexico is, however, more populous than all of the Caribbean republics combined. Greater nationalism and greater political strength have made possible more resistance to interference by the United States than can be shown by the governments of the smaller republics. Twentieth-century relations between the United States and Mexico have been strongly affected by two movements: the investment in Mexican enterprises by American citizens of large amounts of capital—at one time estimated at about a billion dollars—and the Mexican revolution.

The revolution, which began in 1910, ended the period of encouragement to foreign capitalists and started the downfall of the system of large estates which had flourished under Porfirio Diaz. It was the protest of the peon class voiced through its leaders against a system of ruthless exploitation by the great landholders. It was the demand of the agricultural workers for land. About three-fifths of the people of Mexico consisted of agricultural laborers and their families bound to the great estates. Large governmental landholdings had gradually been alienated and consolidated in the enormous haciendas. The revolution against this system has been one of the most hopeful political developments of recent times, but in its early stages it created disorders involving foreign life and property. The attempts of the revolutionists to exert the power of the state over land and mineral resources, much of which was held by foreigners, provoked acute diplomatic crises. And thus a number of troublesome issues were raised between Mexico and the United States. Perhaps these disputes are indicative of the problems that are still to arise in vaster form in the diplomacy of the United States—a great creditor nation in a world of ferment. Several of the controversies with Mexico have been referred to elsewhere in this volume. The principal ones were concerned with oil and land,[2] claims,[3] protection of citizens against violence,[4] arms embargoes,[5]

---

[1] Investments of American citizens in Mexico at the end of 1933 were estimated at $635,000,000. *Balance of International Payments of the United States in* 1933, p. 56.

[2] See pp. 216*ff.*

[3] See p. 220.

[4] See *Foreign Relations* for the year 1912 and thereafter.

[5] See pp. 224–225.

and recognition.[1] In the beginning of 1927 these disputes seemed well-nigh insoluble by peaceful means. But a moderation of the stand of the Mexican government, concurrent with the sending of an intelligent and sympathetic ambassador by the United States in the person of Dwight W. Morrow and with the general contraction of imperialistic plans at Washington, restored cordial relations between the two governments.

[1] Merely referred to on pp. 67 and 222.

CHAPTER VI

PAN-AMERICANISM

THE QUESTION OF REGIONAL ORGANIZATION

International organizations are of two kinds: systems which seek to be world-wide, such as the League of Nations or the Universal Postal Union, and more limited associations located in one geographical region, such as the former concert of Europe or the organization of Central American states. There are certain problems arising within special areas which more vitally affect the immediately neighboring nations than they do those situated across oceans and at great distances. As a result of the limitations of political thinking, furthermore, distance often gives important international questions the appearance of unreality to far-off countries and makes such matters less susceptible of organized treatment on a world basis. Thus from the purely psychological standpoint regional organization may be a more practical matter in some respects than world organization.

Regionalism and War Prevention. In disputes which threaten to result in war in a specific area the adjacent nations are particularly concerned because they are frequently in danger of being drawn into the struggle. To avert disaster their governments have a seemingly greater justification for intervening in the quarrel in order to obtain a peaceful settlement than do those of nations situated on other continents. Even in the years since the World War, during which period the theory that wars are apt to be world-wide has gained much credence, regional organization has been employed as a supplement to world organization. The Draft Treaty of Mutual Assistance, presented to the League of Nations Assembly in 1923, anticipated that military aid against an aggressor would be furnished by countries located on the same continent. In the Geneva Protocol for Arbitration, Security, and Disarmament of the following year, the giving of assistance against aggression was to be performed by each signatory state in the degree which its geographical position and armament should allow. These draft treaties, which represented the best thought of the times on the question of security, failed of ratification; but the regional plan was adopted in the Locarno agreement of 1925. One of the conditions for the taking effect of the Locarno agreement was that Germany should become a member of the League of Nations. Germany's entrance as a permanent member of the Council was temporarily blocked by several nations, among them Brazil. It was strikingly incongruous that Brazil should have had the power to interfere with such an important matter affecting the peace of Europe. The situation brought out strongly that world organization has a serious weakness where a regional matter is under discussion and where the controls of the machinery for the solution of the problem have been placed in the hands of a distant and somewhat indifferent government. The earnestness shown by European nations, in dealing through the League of Nations with the threat of war in Europe, as compared with their relative indifference regarding disputes in Asia or Latin America, illustrates the vitality of the regional method.

As European nations have discovered that they have a greater stake in the peace of their own continent than in the tranquillity of other regions, so American nations may also find that to work out an effective system against war in these continents will require the giving of serious guarantees by governments in the Western Hemisphere. Whether the principle will be carried out even further by the formation of special regional groups within the Pan-American area, as in South America or Central America, is something which the future must decide. Up to the present time, however, such special groupings seem to be less promising than the Pan-American movement.

Economic Regionalism. Economic matters sometimes possess a distinctly regional character. Several economic problems considered by the League of Nations have been handled with special reference to the European situation. Thus such questions as those of railways, road traffic, commercial motor transportation, and freedom of transit have been dealt with very largely as European problems, for it is among European nations that the difficulties of international rail and motor transportation have arisen in their most acute form. The Pan-European plan of M. Briand provided for a closer economic cooperation among the countries of Europe. In fact the opinion is widely held that without such cooperation Europe will find itself under an impossible handicap in production and commerce as compared with large units within which there is unrestricted trade, such as the United States and Russia. It is a contention in commercial bargaining that contiguous countries frequently have such strong reasons for closer economic relations that they are justified in exchanging valuable trade concessions which are not extended to other countries. Whatever validity there may be in this reasoning adds strength to the case for regional organization.[1]

The Codification of Law as a Regional Project. A number of peculiarly American legal disputes justify the devotion of considerable effort to the work of codification of international law in the Western Hemisphere. The important controversies over legal principles in the Americas touch upon the difference in views between a strong, stable, common law, creditor country and twenty other nations, many of which are weak and unstable and all of which are civil law and debtor countries. Concerning such matters as diplomatic protection, recognition, asylum, and treatment of private property of foreigners, there are serious differences in attitudes as between the United States and the twenty Latin-American republics.

Certain so-called legal principles set forth by European writers and by the orthodox jurists of the United States are emphatically spurned by most of the Latin-American writers and statesmen. Any doctrine which is opposed by such an important bloc of states does not receive that support of the world community which is necessary before it can be truly christened international law. If this is not clear to European writers, it should nevertheless be obvious in North and South America where the United States has been decidedly in the minority. If there is to be any worth-while Pan-Americanism, the United States must be prepared to concede to the Latin-American states a substantial proportion of their contentions in this field. Doubtless it is preferable to provide a regional forum which can specialize upon the reconciliation of views on such questions rather than to rely upon a world movement for codification. A world conference would give but little attention to these particular problems and, if it did deal with them, would attempt to solve many of them in such a manner as would be entirely unacceptable to most American countries. Latin America will demand a greater voice in the legal system of any Pan-American organization than it could have in that of a world movement.

A Balance between World and Regional Organizations Is Desirable. Set off against the advantages of regional organization,

---

[1] See COLEGROVE, KENNETH W., *International Control of Aviation*, p. 93, World Peace Foundation, Boston, 1930, for a consideration of the question of regional versus world regulation in the field of aviation control.

there are undisputed merits in world organization. Where problems are world-wide they cannot be adequately dealt with by a few nations separately. Problems of oversea colonies, transoceanic trade, international health, the law of navigation, safety at sea, and the adjudication of intercontinental disputes cannot be held within regional boundaries. There is also much prestige attached to numbers. The World Court holds a position of dignity and influence which cannot be approached by any other international judicial tribunal. No adequate demarcation has yet been made between the functions of regional and world organizations. Ideally both should survive and be integrated in a system which would allocate regional matters to one and world-wide matters to the other while a number of intermediate problems would be attacked cooperatively by both.

FORCES FOR AND AGAINST PAN-AMERICANISM

Common Political Origins. In the early days of their independence Latin Americans felt a certain amount of friendship for the United States owing to their common revolutionary origins and because of the intercontinental influence of American revolutionary writers, such as Paine and Jefferson. The militaristic European system which threatened the independence of the Latin-American countries aroused a feeling of common hostility toward the oversea danger. The Monroe Doctrine was at first regarded with gratitude by Latin Americans. The constitutions of the new governments were quite generally modeled on that of the United States. This early moral leadership of the United States has been largely relinquished. The imperialistic tendencies of the "colossus of the North" have awakened resentment. European systems of law and administration seem to be on the whole better fitted to Latin-American needs than are those of the United States. The tradition of common revolutionary origin still exists, however, in ceremonial oratory and in spectacles reminiscent of the past such as the gallery of patriots in the Pan American Building in Washington. The common heritage of republicanism and the feeling of uncongeniality with the war system of Europe are still factors of some consequence in the varied catalogue of sentiments that go to make up Pan-Americanism.

Proximity. It has been argued that the area of Pan-Americanism is not of such a compact nature as to promote a close organization. The region consists of twenty-one republics extending from the northern boundaries of the United States to Cape Horn, covering 15,200,000 square miles, and inhabited by some 250,000,000 people, about one-half of which reside in the United States. As vessels bound from the United States must sail more than half of the distance across the Atlantic to round the coast of Brazil, the important southeastern coast of South America is as close to Europe as it is to the northern Atlantic ports of the United States. If Argentina, Uruguay, Paraguay, and a large part of Brazil are as close to Europe as they are to the United States, the argument for political organization due to proximity would at first glance seem to apply to a union with Europe as well as to one with this country. Such a contention would have been particularly true in the days before the World War when the steamship connections between Europe and South America were much superior to those between the United States and South American ports. The countries on the southeastern coast are still bound by strong economic ties to Europe. Thus Argentina, by a commercial treaty in 1933, entered into closer economic relations with Great Britain than it held with other American countries.

Despite their distance from the United States such countries as Argentina and Uruguay are parts of the Latin-American system, held to the others by ties of language, religion, culture, and a common political origin. And to the Latin-American system as a whole, the United States is in intimate proximity. With Mexico this country has a common boundary 1,744 miles in length. The island republics of the Caribbean lie at varying distance within a radius of a few hundred miles from the coast of Florida. Planes from Miami wing their way daily across the blue waters of the Caribbean. Our coastwise commerce between Atlantic and Gulf ports and the Pacific coast passes near to Caribbean islands and traverses the Panama Canal, cut through the heart of a Latin-American republic. Since the construction of the canal, points along the west coast of South America are about 2,500 miles nearer to New York and 3,100 miles nearer to New Orleans than they are to Liverpool.[1] The installation of direct steamship lines and the advent of the automobile and the airplane, together with the improvement of rail facilities, have tended to draw parts of Latin America much closer to the United States than to Europe.

Economic Ties. As will be shown later, the chief object of the United States in promoting Pan-American organization has been to reduce economic barriers in order that this country may have certain trade and investment advantages over European rivals in Latin-

[1] For some distances on this route see JOHNSON, EMORY, *op. cit.*, p. 34.

American territory. For many years after the independence of the Latin-American counties was recognized, their chief commercial relationships were with Europe. To Europe they sold raw materials and from Europe they purchased manufactured goods. Gradually in the decades following the Civil War, the United States began to compete with Europe as a source of manufactured products and as a market for raw materials. When world commerce reached its high peak in 1929, 36.7 per cent of the foreign trade of Latin-American countries, amounting to $1,981,401,000, was with the United States. Latin America purchased in that year $946,991,000 in goods from the United States and sold to us products valued at $1,034,410,000.[1] While the amount of trade with Europe was still high, no single country on that continent approached these figures. A considerable volume of inter-American commerce does not in itself prove that there should be political organization in order to promote more trade. In fact Latin Americans have at times stated positively that they do not wish to give the United States preferences that will cut them off from Europe.[2] Dr. Wallace McClure, in analyzing the trade policies of the American republics, has shown that Pan-Americanism has not been able to affect greatly the economic systems of countries in this hemisphere. They have had their commercial treaties with European nations and have also subscribed to international trade conventions of the world-wide variety. There has been little intra-American reciprocity.[3]

A latent but important reason which may some day cause American nations to adjust their trade to meet the maximum of their needs within the Western Hemisphere is the undependability of Europe due to the war system of that continent. For a considerable period of time following August, 1914, the World War shut off Europe as a source of manufactured goods and capital and interfered with the export of raw materials from American countries across the Atlantic. Much of the shipping from Europe to Latin-American ports was withdrawn in 1914. The First Pan American Financial Conference was called in Washington in May, 1915, to find a remedy

[1] ZIER, JULIAN G., "Commercial Interdependence of the Americas," *Bulletin of the Pan American Union*, 67: 198–199 (March, 1933).

[2] There were speeches to this effect in the First International Conference of American States. See *International American Conference*, I: 124, Govt. Printing Office, Washington, 1890.

[3] "The Development of Commercial Treaties in the Americas," *Bulletin of the Pan American Union*, 65: 991 (October, 1931). Of the ten existing reciprocity agreements since made between the United States and other countries, however, five are with Latin-American governments and one with Canada.

for the desperate situation by a readjustment of American affairs which would make this hemisphere, for the time being and so far as possible, an independent economic unit. Practically all of the nineteen delegations present at the conference spoke of the new need. Luis Izquierdo, a delegate from Chile, remarked upon it as follows:

. . . the war in Europe is hindering and in some cases is paralyzing and stopping the commercial intercourse of Latin America with its European markets, and this is not only on account of the troubles in the production and industrial life in Europe, but principally on account of the sudden lack of shipping, which was universally the first consequence of the war.[1]

Shipping facilities improved later on, but European goods were to a large extent displaced in Latin-American markets. The exports of the United States to Latin America trebled in value from 1914 to 1919. Rapidly increasing trade during this period placed a great deal of additional work upon the Pan American Union, increasing its influence and usefulness and making necessary a growth in its size.[2] Although the World War brought an end to the fear of European aggression in the Western Hemisphere, it also dealt a heavy blow to European economic supremacy. The gloomy prospects for peace in Europe in the last two or three years have made it questionable whether or not another cataclysm will descend upon that continent, causing a further decrease in the influence of those countries in American affairs. If, on the other hand, the United States should become involved in a great war, say, in Asia, while Europe is at peace, we must expect a reverse tendency. The United States would then doubtless lose its markets and its investment preeminence in Latin America while Pan-Americanism would be largely displaced by some form of union among the Latin-American countries or by a combination in which Europe would play a far greater part. At the present time, however, the trend is toward closer commercial relations between Latin America and the United States. The moderation in the imperialism of the United States and the diplomacy of Secretary of State Hull at the Seventh International Conference of American States in 1933 have been followed by a stronger trend toward reciprocity between American countries than previously prevailed.

[1] *Proceedings of the First Pan American Financial Conference, Washington, May 24 to 29*, 1915, p. 97, Govt. Printing Office, Washington, 1915.

[2] KELCHNER, WARREN H., "The Development of the Pan American Union," *Bulletin of the Pan American Union*, 64: 341 (April, 1930).

Race, Religion, Language. In most of the "Pan" movements (German, Slavic, Islamic, etc.) there have been strong cementing ties of race, religion, or culture. None of these bonds exist in Pan-Americanism. In Latin America there are the following diverse racial elements: (1) the native Indians; (2) the descendants of the conquering Spaniards (or Portuguese, in the case of Brazil); (3) negroes descended from imported slaves; (4) recent European immigrants; (5) mestizos, or persons of mixed Indian and white strains; (6) mulattoes, descended from negroes and whites; and (7) zambos, or persons of negro and Indian blood. There is little sympathetic feeling between these racial groups and the Anglo-Saxon. Religiously the United States finds almost no ties binding it to Latin America, this country being chiefly Protestant, while Latin-American peoples adhere to Roman Catholicism. The dominant culture of Latin America is derived from Europe, particularly from France and Spain. Language constitutes something of an obstacle. Four languages are spoken in the Pan-American area, French in Haiti, Portuguese in Brazil, English in the United States, and Spanish in the eighteen other countries. These cultural differences make it impossible to draw upon some of the emotions for political solidarity which are present in most of the "Pan" movements. They stand in the way of the development of a strong Pan-American organization.

Fear of American Imperialism. Suspicion of the motives of the United States pervades Latin America[1] and is strongest among the intellectuals who resent American imperialism most keenly. Political leaders of the United States have sensed this feeling and have tried to counteract it by public statements to the effect that the United States has no imperialistic aims in the countries to the south. Latin Americans, however, have not failed to note the gulf frequently existing between such idealistic public utterances and the acts of the United States government. At Rio de Janeiro in 1906 Secretary of State Elihu Root informed the Third International Conference of American States:

> We deem the independence and equal rights of the smallest and weakest member of the family of nations entitled to as much respect as those of the greatest empire.[2]

Yet Root had helped to draft the Platt Amendment. He had been a member of the Roosevelt cabinet when Panama was torn from

[1] See MOON, PARKER THOMAS, *Imperialism and World Politics*, p. 455, The Macmillan Company, New York, 1926, for a typical evaluation of this sentiment.

[2] *Foreign Relations*, 1906, Part I, p. 129.

Colombia and when the "Big Stick" policy was developed in the Caribbean. Some years later Secretary of State Philander C. Knox, in a Caribbean tour, informed a Haitian audience:

The tide of world sentiment is setting strongly toward the accommodation of international controversies by processes of reason and justice; not by defiance and the sword. That tide is sweeping over my own country, where the ideal of universal peace with justice is dear to every heart. Should not we, of the common brotherhood of all the Americas, share alike in the devotion to that ideal, and stand mutually helpful toward whatever may assure, by pacific means, peace and good will among brethern?[1]

Knox, however, was the great dollar diplomat. His aim was financial control of the Caribbean; and, if we judge from his official acts, the tides of his own mind were strongly set against arbitration and equal treatment. He, it was, who introduced the marines to his "brethern" in Nicaragua. Even Woodrow Wilson, one of the most idealistic of presidents, showed wide contrasts between the rhetoric of his speeches on conciliation and the acts of his administration. In his famous Mobile speech of 1913 with regard to his policy in the Latin-American countries he exalted the ideal of liberty and announced: "We must prove ourselves their friends and champions upon terms of equality and honor."[2] Yet within three years his administration had occupied the Dominican Republic by armed force and several thousand Haitians had been shot down by United States troops. In some cases prisoners were executed without trial, and wounded Haitian *cacos* were dispatched upon the battlefield. There should be little wonder that Latin-American intellectuals have ceased to hold a great deal of respect for the speeches of American officials regarding liberty, justice, and equality.

As an offset to this suspicion it is still remembered that the United States has on certain occasions protected Latin-American countries against European aggression. The ebbing of American imperialism during the administrations of Herbert Hoover and Franklin D. Roosevelt furthermore has helped to allay fears and has constituted one of the most practical movements making for Pan-Americanism. When Cordell Hull gave vent to idealistic statements at the Seventh International Conference of American States

---

[1] *Speeches Incident to the Visit of Philander Chase Knox to the Countries of the Caribbean*, p. 170, Govt. Printing Office, Washington, 1913.

[2] *The Public Papers of Woodrow Wilson, The New Democracy*, edited by BAKER, RAY STANNARD, and WILLIAM E. DODD, I: 67, Harper & Brothers, New York, 1926.

at Montevideo in 1933, and when it appeared that his declarations were being borne out in American policy, a new enthusiasm toward Pan-Americanism was noticeable in many quarters of Latin America.

THE DEVELOPMENT OF PAN-AMERICANISM

Early Conferences. In the early years of the nineteenth century various schemes were proposed for union among the American countries which were struggling to be free from the control of Spain. Just as the unity of the thirteen colonies in North America was forced by common opposition to the government of Great Britain, so the tendency to unity among the struggling revolutionary countries of Latin America resulted from a similar need for the combination of their forces against Spain and other European powers. The struggle for freedom was largely carried on by common campaigns. Thus San Martín with an army organized in Argentina crossed the Andes to free Chile and to give battle for liberty in Peru. Bolivar, a native of Caracas, served in New Granada, Venezuela, Ecuador, Peru, and Upper Peru, which was called Bolivia in his honor. He dreamed of a common organization of all Spanish America.

During the struggle of the Spanish colonies for independence the sympathy of the people of the United States was, generally speaking, with the colonies. The United States government attempted to maintain impartiality, particularly since the policy of acquiring Florida necessitated the maintenance of friendly relations with Spain; but our neutrality laws were not always well enforced. In addition private plans for an alliance or union between the United States and the revolting colonies were proposed on both sides. In 1820 Henry Clay, in arguing for the recognition of the new governments, declared: "It is in our power to create a system of which we shall be the center, and in which all South America will act with us."[1] Various projects had likewise developed in South America for more limited confederations, and treaties of alliance were signed between several of the new governments.[2]

In December, 1824, Bolivar dispatched a circular letter inviting the countries of Spanish America to send representatives to an "assembly of plenipotentiaries" to meet at Panama. Later Brazil, the United States, and Great Britain received invitations.

---

[1] *Annals of Congress*, XXXVI: 2226, (May 10, 1820), quoted in LOCKEY, JOSEPH BYRNE, *Pan Americanism, Its Beginnings*, p. 282, The Macmillan Company, New York, 1926.

[2] LOCKEY, *op. cit.*, pp. 292*ff.*

The congress met in 1826.   The United States appointed delegates;
but, owing to a long debate in the Senate which delayed their confirmation, these were sent too late.   One delegate fell ill en route and
died.   The other left the United States after the congress had
adjourned.   The United States was not represented at any inter-
American conferences until 1889.   The instructions of Secretary of
State Clay to the delegates to the 1826 conference, however, show
how far the United States was willing to go at that time in participation in a Pan-American organization.   The delegates were not to
enter fully into the movement and were not to discuss subjects
relating to the war with Spain.   They were to propose a declaration
by each country that no European colonies were to be established
within its territory and that the republican form of government was
preferred.   They were instructed that benefits in an isthmian canal
ought not to be exclusive to any one nation and they were asked to
bring back any plans that might be made for joint construction and
any information which might be obtained regarding the costs of
construction.   There were various other instructions concerning
such matters as the nonrecognition of Haiti, the maintenance of the
status quo in Cuba, and the security of private property and non-
combatants at sea during war.   The United States was, therefore,
ready at that time to cooperate in a rather weak organization to
obtain certain aims held in common with Latin America; but we
were not willing to enter into the defensive union which Bolivar had
in mind.[1]

With the establishment of independence, the waning of the Holy
Alliance, and the greater security of the South American republics,
the feeling of internationalism diminished and a strong nationalism
took its place.   A growing localism was evidenced by the partition
of some of the existing countries to form new states.   Uruguay,
which had been under the control of Buenos Aires and then Brazil,
became independent in 1830.   The Republic of Colombia, consisting
of the present Colombia, Venezuela, and Ecuador, was broken up,
Venezuela withdrawing in 1829 and Ecuador in 1830.   The Republic
of the United States of Central America was dissolved in 1839
to become the five separate republics of Central America.   Nevertheless, Latin-American conferences for common defense continued
to meet until 1864, at which time the fear of reconquest was drawing

[1] For the text of the instructions see *International American Conference*,
IV: 113, Govt. Printing Office, Washington, 1890; and also CLEVEN,
N. ANDREW N., *Readings in Hispanic American History*, p. 618, Ginn & Com-
pany, Boston, 1927.

to an end. Other Latin-American conferences were held during the next few decades, particularly the conferences on private international law at Lima in 1877 and at Montevideo in 1888–1889.[1] The work of these two conferences became the basis for much that was done in this field in the International Conferences of American States.

The Beginnings of the International Conferences of American States. During the 1880's the United States began to take an active interest in promoting international conferences in the Western Hemisphere. This country was becoming strong enough economically to cherish ambitions to supplant the European nations in the trade of Latin America. James G. Blaine, who was interested in the extension of American trade, became the apostle of Pan-Americanism in order to procure trade advantages for the United States and also to maintain peace in the Western Hemisphere. In 1881, while secretary of state, he issued a call for a conference to meet in Washington for the purpose of preventing war in the Americas; but as the War of the Pacific, then in progress, did not abate, the conference was not held. A few years later, in 1888, Congress passed an act authorizing the President to invite the Latin-American nations to Washington for the discussion of economic matters and arbitration. The conference was called under the Cleveland administration, but by the time it assembled a Republican president had moved into the White House. James G. Blaine was again secretary of state; and, in that capacity, he presided over the deliberations of the conference. With the meeting of 1889–1890 a regular series of International Conferences of American States was inaugurated. The second was held in Mexico City in 1901–1902, the third in Rio de Janeiro in 1906, the fourth in Buenos Aires in 1910, the fifth in Santiago in 1923, the sixth in Havana in 1928, and the seventh in Montevideo in 1933. These conferences have been the central forum for the discussion of Pan-American affairs.

THE ORGANS OF PAN-AMERICANISM

The Functions of the International Conferences of American States. If we omit the period between the first and second conferences and also that of the World War, the International Conferences of American States have met at intervals of about five years.

[1] An account of the various conferences is found in ROBERTSON, WILLIAM SPENCE, *Hispanic-American Relations with the United States*, pp. 383*ff.*, Oxford University Press, New York, 1923.

The programs of the conferences are prepared in advance by the Governing Board of the Pan American Union and the delegations are given ample notice of the matters to be discussed. New questions cannot be raised in the conference except by a two-thirds vote. The predetermination of the agenda emphasizes the diplomatic as distinguished from the legislative character of the gathering. Each government is ordinarily given full opportunity to instruct its delegation regarding the desired position to be taken on each item. The conferences cannot legislate except for the internal organization of the union. They have power to draw up and sign conventions which must then be ratified by the governments. They may also pass resolutions which are of two kinds. In the first class are resolutions recommending a particular legislative or administrative policy to the member states. These have no legal effect but are intended to result in action by the legislatures or executive departments of the various governments. Another kind of resolution concerns the internal administration of the Pan American Union either through changing the form of organization or through directing the Governing Board to take a particular kind of action. The conference is thus a legislative body for the union. In the Sixth Conference in 1928, however, a convention was drawn up providing for the organization of the union. When, and if, this is ratified by all the governments, it will place the union upon a treaty basis and will, perhaps unfortunately, make it impossible to alter its constitution by mere resolution.

The principle of equality is observed at the conferences. Although the delegations vary from one to ten or more members, each government is entitled to one vote. The rule of unanimity does not exist for most acts. Resolutions are passed by a majority vote.[1] Conventions, except in rare instances, do not require unanimous signature or ratification. Some conventions become operative between such countries as may ratify them and others require that a certain minimum number shall ratify before the convention becomes effective. It is customary for each conference to decide upon the place of meeting of the following conference.[2] The decision as to

[1] For the set of regulations passed by the Governing Board for the government of the Sixth Conference, see SCOTT, JAMES BROWN, *International Conferences of American States, 1889–1928*, p. 299, Oxford University Press, New York, 1931. Similar regulations for the Seventh Conference are found in *Report of the Delegates of the United States of America to the Seventh International Conference of American States*, p. 69, Govt. Printing Office, Washington, 1934.

[2] Thus the Seventh Conference designated Lima as the meeting place for the Eighth Conference.

the time of meeting is left to the Governing Board and the government of the country at which the conference is to be held. Frequently the conference has recommended that the following conference shall be held within five years. The unratified convention of 1928 for the organization of the Pan American Union (Article 2) provides that not more than five years shall elapse between conferences except in case of *force majeure*.

Governing Board of the Pan American Union. The Governing Board of the Pan American Union is composed of representatives appointed by the member governments. The diplomatic representatives of the member states at Washington may be, and in fact almost invariably are, designated to act on the board. The president and vice-president of the board are elected by that body. At one time the Secretary of State of the United States was *ex officio* president and the board was constituted only of diplomats accredited to the government of the United States. At the Fifth Conference the constitution of the board came under criticism for two reasons. Objection was made to the fact that the Secretary of State was always the president of the board, thus giving a predominant position to the United States. Accordingly the principle of election was introduced.[1] Various governments also complained that it was possible to disfranchise a Latin-American country by the withdrawal of recognition of that country by the United States. Such a breach in relations would leave the unrecognized government without a diplomatic representative in Washington and consequently without a member on the board. It was, accordingly, provided by the conference that each government might appoint a special representative on the board in the absence of a diplomatic representative in Washington.[2] It was further provided that each government should enjoy "as of right" membership in the union. The Sixth Conference resolved that the union should be composed "of the representatives that the American governments may appoint."[3]

The board directs the work of the Pan American Union. It appoints the director general and the assistant director. Other officers of the union are appointed by the director general subject to the approval of the board. The board approves the budget and the regulations for the various services of the union. It fixes the dates of the International Conferences of American States, and it is

[1] It is the practice, however, to elect the Secretary of State to this office.

[2] SCOTT, *op. cit.*, p. 270.

[3] *Ibid.*, p. 397. The member from Salvador during 1932 and 1933 was not a diplomatic representative as in those years the Salvadoran government was not recognized by the United States.

frequently called upon by resolutions of these conferences to provide for the assembling of other conferences on special subjects.[1] According to a resolution of the Sixth Conference, the board is prohibited from exercising functions of a political character. The resolution, if observed, would prevent the board from assuming a position of any great importance in the Pan-American movement. This rather unnatural provision was, however, seemingly ignored when on July 30, 1934, the Governing Board passed a resolution calling upon the governments which were neutral in the Chaco dispute to indicate their attitude upon a joint move to bring about arbitration or conciliation between the disputants.[2]

Special Conferences. The International Conferences of American States, like the Assemblies of the League of Nations, have found it impossible to deal adequately with all the pressing international problems that are presented for solution. Accordingly the conferences have frequently passed resolutions asking that the Governing Board of the Pan American Union shall call special conferences or assemble commissions to go more thoroughly into the various subjects and, in many cases, to draft conventions for the ratification of the governments. Conferences of this kind have been called to deal with arbitration and conciliation, commerce, finance, trademarks, codification of international law, sanitation, highways, cultural relations, and numerous other subjects.

The Pan American Union. The title Pan American Union is given particularly to the secretariat of the Pan-American organization. The first conference in 1889–1890 created the Commercial Bureau of the American Republics to be located in Washington as the permanent organ of the union. In the Second Conference in 1902 this became the International Bureau of the American Republics and, in the Fourth Conference in 1910, the name was again changed to the present one, the Pan American Union. The chief officers of the union are a director general, an assistant director, a counselor, a foreign trade adviser, and chiefs of the divisions of statistics, financial information, intellectual cooperation, and agricultural cooperation. In addition there are staff members who deal with editing of publications, translating, supervising the library, mailing, and with general clerical work. The increase in the numbers of staff members shows a rapid rate of growth. In 1890 there

---

[1] The constitution of the Governing Board is provided for in resolutions of the Fifth and Sixth Conferences, SCOTT, *op. cit.*, pp. 268, 397.

[2] *N.Y. Times*, July 31, 1934.

were five employees attached to the organization. This had increased to twenty-four in 1906 and by 1930 had grown to eighty-six, counting twenty-two persons engaged in caring for the buildings and grounds.[1]

The functions of the union are in the main the education of the public in matters connected with the American republics and the performance of duties dealing with the International Conferences of American States and such special conferences as may be held. The union is given the task of compiling information and reports on the commercial, industrial, agricultural, and educational development of American states. It is charged with maintaining complete information regarding the treaties concluded among American states as well as the legislation enacted by each. Information connected with all these subjects is published in the valuable periodical, the *Bulletin of the Pan American Union.* The duties of the union with regard to the conferences consist in providing documentary material for the use of the delegates in advance of the conferences dealing with the projects to be considered, drafting conventions for the consideration of the conference, keeping the archives, assisting in obtaining ratifications of the treaties and conventions, and receiving the deposit of ratifications of the conventions when it is provided that they should be deposited with the union. Ordinarily at international conferences ratifications are deposited with the government of the country in which the conference is held. The practice of the League of Nations has been that the ratifications are deposited with the Secretariat. A similar practice has developed with regard to the Pan American Union. In the Sixth Conference it was provided in nine of the eleven conventions that ratifications should be deposited with the union, and a like provision was made for all the conventions of the Seventh Conference. In conferences which are held in Washington the union makes the necessary preparations for the holding of the sessions.[2]

The budget of the union is drawn up by the director general and submitted to the Governing Board at its November session. After

[1] KELCHNER, WARREN H., "The Development of the Pan American Union," *Bulletin of the Pan American Union,* 64: 344 (April, 1930).

[2] For the duties of the union see the resolution of the Fifth Conference on the organization of the union, SCOTT, *op. cit.,* p. 268; and also MANGER, WILLIAM, "The Pan American Union and the Pan American Conferences," *Bulletin of the Pan American Union,* 65: 367 (April, 1931) and "The Pan American Union as the Permanent Organ of the International American Conferences," *Bulletin of the Pan American Union,* 66: 261 (April, 1932).

approval of the budget the board submits it to the member nations with an indication of the quota which each is to pay. The quota is fixed in proportion to population.

The character of the building in which the Pan American Union is housed has done much to enhance the dignity of the organization. The edifice is built of white marble and is surrounded by beautiful grounds. The architectural features are mainly Spanish. The building was made possible largely through a gift of Andrew Carnegie.

Ad Hoc Organizations of a Research and Administrative Character. In addition to the union a number of commissions, committees, bureaus, and institutes have been set up in accordance with resolutions of the conferences to deal with particular problems. There is space here only to name some of the more important of these, *i.e.*, the Inter-American Trade Mark Bureau at Havana; the Pan American Sanitary Bureau at Washington; the Inter-American Commission of Women at Washington; the Pan American Institute of Geography and History at Mexico City; the American Academy of International Law at Havana; the International American Institute for the Protection of Children at Montevideo; and Headquarters of the Pan American Confederation for Highway Education at Washington.

CHAPTER VII

POLICIES OF THE UNITED STATES WITH RELATION TO PAN-AMERICANISM

WAR PREVENTION

The Movement for Arbitration. While the United States has generally maintained a policy of promoting peace in the Western Hemisphere, it must bear its share of the blame for the failure of Pan-Americanism to build up institutions for the prevention of war. The main purposes of the United States in working for peace among American nations seem to have been: the promotion of commerce and investment in a tranquil American area and the elimination of any excuses for European intervention because of Latin-American disorders. Secretary of State Blaine's call for a conference in 1881, which conference never met, stated that the meeting was to be for the purpose of "considering and discussing the methods of preventing war between the nations of America." The Act of Congress of 1888, which authorized the calling of the First International Conference of American States, included as the first subject on the agenda "measures that shall tend to preserve the peace and promote the prosperity of the several American States"; and a later item called for a definite plan for arbitration.[1] Owing largely to the discussions of arbitration in the Second International Conference of American States in 1901–1902, the United States was instrumental in obtaining a place for Latin-American countries in the Second Hague Conference in 1907. All but two of these countries subsequently became members of the Permanent Court of Arbitration.[2]

The United States has until recently, however, been generally antagonistic to a compulsory system of arbitration. President Theodore Roosevelt in 1901, previous to the Second Conference (1901–1902), instructed the Secretary of State that all arbitration

[1] Scott, *op. cit.*, pp. 3, 4.

[2] For a list of the countries that are parties to the Hague Conventions see DE WOLF, FRANCIS COLT, *General Synopsis of Treaties of Arbitration, Conciliation, Judicial Settlement, Security and Disarmament, Actually in Force between Countries Invited to the Disarmament Conference*, p. 175, Carnegie Endowment for International Peace, Washington, 1933.

should be voluntary.[1] A treaty for compulsory arbitration of all disputes not affecting the independence or national honor of the parties was signed by nine states at that conference[2] but the United States refused to join in the agreement. Previous to the Third Conference (1906) Secretary of State Root instructed the United States delegation that proposals for compulsory arbitration were premature until the Latin-American states were more disposed toward signing an agreement to arbitrate pecuniary claims.[3] The United States, as a creditor nation, was particularly interested in the collection of the debts of its citizens while the Latin-American nations were more interested in a convention to arbitrate political disputes.

The strengthening of United States policies on cooperation for world peace, together with the moderation of imperialism, brought about a change in the attitude of the Department of State with reference to a Pan-American compulsory arbitration treaty. The Inter-American Arbitration Treaty, which was drawn up by the conference on conciliation and arbitration in Washington in 1929, provided for compulsory arbitration of juridical questions. The United States delegation at the conference supported the principle of the new treaty and Charles Evans Hughes declared: "We are all anxious to further this cause of obligatory arbitration to the furthest possible extent."[4] When the treaty first reached the Senate, however, that body so emasculated the instrument as to alter its essential character. Two reservations were attached. The first provided that in each case of arbitration a special agreement should be drawn up which must have the approval of the Senate. The second reservation provided that the treaty should not be applicable to disputes which were pending or which should arise in the future from acts which had occurred previous to the taking effect of the treaty or from other treaties which had been negotiated previous to the arbitration treaty. Disputes over some 105 treaties between the United States and Latin-American governments would thus have been placed outside the arbitration provisions.[5] The President refused to ratify the treaty after these contrary amendments. Upon request of the President three years later the Senate acted upon the treaty again.

[1] *Foreign Relations*, 1906, Part II, p. 1575.

[2] Scott, *op. cit.*, p. 100.

[3] *Foreign Relations*, 1906, Part II, p. 1569.

[4] *Proceedings of the International Conference of American States on Conciliation and Arbitration, Washington, December 10, 1928–January 5, 1929*, p. 488, Govt. Printing Office, Washington, 1929.

[5] *Congressional Record*, 75: 2243 (Jan. 19, 1932).

This time it dropped the second reservation and included only that requiring the Senate's concurrence to the special arbitration agreements. The President, thereupon, ratified the convention.

The Collection of Claims. The United States has strongly upheld compulsory arbitration with regard to a particular type of dispute, *i.e.*, that arising from pecuniary claims. A creditor to Latin America, this country has advocated collection machinery with the same conviction that a banker would support the debt collection activities of domestic courts. In the Second Conference (1901–1902) a treaty was concluded for the compulsory submission of such claims either to the Permanent Court of Arbitration or to a special tribunal constituted by the parties. The United States and eight other governments ratified the treaty.[1] Later this country attempted to obtain ratifications by additional governments. When the duration of the treaty was extended at the Third and Fourth conferences (1906 and 1910),[2] the United States sought to prevent any restriction of the right to invoke arbitration. An amendment proposed at the Fourth Conference provided that if there were any question of the propriety of diplomatic intervention by the creditor country to obtain arbitration of claims the point should be settled by the arbitration tribunal. The amendment on being considered in committee was stanchly resisted by the United States member on the grounds that it would limit the freedom of diplomatic action and would invite denials of the propriety of invoking arbitration.[3] The United States thus pushed the principle of compulsory adjudication of claims despite the suspicions of Latin Americans who were fearful that arbitration might be resorted to in cases which should properly be decided by the national courts.

Inquiry and Conciliation. During the period when little was accomplished in securing a general treaty of compulsory arbitration, greater strides were being made in provisions for inquiry and conciliation. The principle of compulsory inquiry was advocated by Secretary of State Bryan and incorporated in a large number of bilateral treaties. In the Fifth Conference (1923) the Paraguayan jurist, Manuel Gondra, introduced a treaty of inquiry providing for

---

[1] SCOTT, *op. cit.*, p. 104.

[2] The treaty as drawn at the Fourth Conference in 1910 is now in effect as between twelve countries including the United States. Figures relating to the ratifications of inter-American conventions in this chapter are taken from *Status of the Treaties and Conventions Signed at the International Conferences of American States and at Other Pan American Conferences*, Pan American Union, Washington, July 1, 1935.

[3] *Foreign Relations*, 1910, pp. 42–45.

the investigation of international disputes. The Gondra treaty has received general acceptance among American states. The feature of conciliation was added to the plan in 1929 by the General Convention of Inter-American Conciliation. A great need still exists for a strong and influential body which can perform the function of conciliation as has sometimes been done by the Council of the League of Nations. The Governing Board of the Pan American Union is the logical body for this purpose. The United States in the Fifth Conference opposed the development of the board as a body separate from the diplomatic representatives, fearing that one purpose of the proposal was to create "the nucleus of a possible future council of an American League of Nations." The delegation thought it "unwise and impracticable to set up in Washington a separate political body to deal with Pan-American affairs."[1] In the Sixth Conference (1928) a resolution was passed declaring that the Governing Board should not exercise functions of a political character.[2]

Existing Pan-American Treaties for the Avoidance of War. The principal conventions of Pan-Americanism for the settlement of international disputes are as follows:

1. The Claims Convention of 1910, previously referred to.
2. The Gondra Treaty to Avoid or Prevent Conflicts between the American States of 1923. The treaty provides that all controversies which cannot be settled by diplomatic means or by arbitration are to be submitted to inquiry except disputes which affect constitutional provisions or which involve questions already settled by other treaties. Two permanent commissions of diplomats are constituted for the purpose of putting the machinery of inquiry into motion. They are situated at Washington and Montevideo and are composed of the three American diplomats longest accredited at these capitals. A request for an inquiry can be made to one of the commissions by either party to a dispute. The commission shall immediately notify the other party. Steps are then taken to constitute a special commission of inquiry which shall consist of five persons. Each party shall appoint two, only one of whom shall be a national of the appointing country. The four shall then appoint a fifth who shall not be of the same nationality as any of the others. The commission shall investigate the dispute and report its findings within one year. The parties agree not to mobilize or concentrate troops on the frontier from the time steps are taken to convene the commission of inquiry until six months after the report.[3]
3. The General Convention of Inter-American Conciliation of 1929. The convention, drawn up at the Washington conference of 1929, goes further

[1] *Report of the Delegates of the United States of America to the Fifth International Conference of American States*, p. 4, Govt. Printing Office, Washington, 1924.

[2] Scott, *op. cit.*, p. 398. See p. 98.

[3] For the text of the treaty see Scott, *op. cit.*, p. 285.

than the Gondra treaty by specifically adding conciliation to inquiry. That is, the convention provides for a friendly effort to bring about settlement of the dispute. The permanent commissions of diplomats at Washington and Montevideo are obligated to exercise conciliatory functions when there is danger of a disturbance of peaceful relations or when they are requested to do so by a party to a dispute. The efforts of the commission shall continue until the special commission of inquiry is organized. The latter commission shall then have the power of attempting conciliation in addition to the function of inquiry.[1]

4. The Inter-American Arbitration Treaty of 1929. The treaty binds the parties to arbitrate all disputes of a juridical nature and mentions among the matters falling in that category the following questions (which correspond to those in Article XIII of the Covenant of the League of Nations and in Article XXXVI of the statute of the Permanent Court of International Justice):

   a. The interpretation of a treaty.

   b. Any question of international law.

   c. The existence of any fact which, if established, would constitute a breach of an international obligation.

   d. The nature and extent of the reparation to be made for the breach of an international obligation.

Two types of juridical questions are excepted. Parties are not bound to arbitrate either domestic questions or those which affect the interest or refer to the action of a state not a party to the treaty.[2]

5. The Argentine Anti-War Treaty of 1933. This treaty condemns wars of aggression and pledges the parties to settle their disputes by pacific means established by international law. The parties agree to recognize no territorial arrangement not obtained through pacific means. If any power fails to comply with these obligations, the parties agree to make every effort for the maintenance of peace and to adopt a common and solidary attitude using political, juridical, and economic means authorized by international law; but in no case shall they resort to either diplomatic or armed intervention. The latter prohibition is, however, subject to the obligations imposed upon the signatories by other collective treaties.[3]

Shortcomings of the Peace Machinery—the Leticia Affair. The inadequacy of the Pan-American peace machinery was amply demonstrated in the Leticia and Chaco disputes. In the Leticia affair between Peru and Colombia both nations were parties to the Gondra treaty of inquiry, and Peru at the outset took steps to

---

[1] Scott, *op. cit.*, p. 455. For a discussion of the treaty see *Proceedings of the International Conference of American States on Conciliation and Arbitration*, pp. 282ff.

[2] *U.S. Treaty Series*, No. 886; Scott, *op. cit.*, p. 458.

[3] For the text and an explanation of the treaty by the Argentine government, see "The Anti-War Treaty Proposed by the Argentine Government, and the Brazilian Reply," *Bulletin of the Pan American Union*, 67: 320 (April, 1933); text also in Dept. of State, *Press Releases*, Apr. 28, 1934, p. 234; and *Report of the Delegates of the U.S.A. to the Seventh Conference*, p. 184.

SUMMARY OF PAN-AMERICAN CONVENTIONS FOR PEACEFUL SETTLEMENT
ALL OF WHICH HAVE BEEN RATIFIED BY THE UNITED STATES

Treaty	Provisions	Number of ratifications or adherences
Claims Convention of 1910.	Compulsory submission of claims to the Permanent Court of Arbitration or to a special tribunal.	12
Gondra Treaty of 1923.	Inquiry to be made by special commission of five. Initiative in constituting commission to be taken by permanent commission of diplomats at Washington or Montevideo.	20
General Convention of Inter-American Conciliation of 1929.	Addition of the function of conciliation to that of inquiry by the permanent commission of diplomats and the special commission of five constituted under the Gondra treaty.	14
Inter-American Arbitration Treaty of 1929.	Compulsory arbitration of juridical disputes excepting domestic questions or those affecting a state not a party to the treaty.	14
Argentine Anti-War Treaty of 1933.	Condemnation of wars of aggression, settlement of disputes by pacific means, and nonrecognition of any territorial arrangement not made through pacific means.	16

invoke the action of the permanent commission of diplomats at Washington. Colombia refused to submit to inquiry, claiming that its case came under the exceptions in the Gondra treaty, *i.e.*, constitutional questions and those already settled by other treaties. In this case the boundary between Peru and Colombia had been fixed by the Salomon-Lozano treaty of 1922. The Colombian government stated also that the question was a domestic one. The Brazilian government attempted to reconcile the parties, but Peru demanded unacceptable terms as a condition of mediation and the plan failed. The Council of the League of Nations then sought to deal with the matter, first under its general powers and later under Article XV which was invoked by Colombia. After considerable effort by the Council a plan was agreed to by which the troops of both parties withdrew from the disputed corridor. A commission consisting of a citizen of the United States, a Brazilian, and a Spaniard was appointed to administer the territory. A detachment of Colombian troops was used by the commission as an international force to maintain order. The parties were then encouraged to negotiate; and a settlement was arranged by the signature of a treaty on May 24, 1934, which was based on respect for existing treaties, the demilitarization of the Leticia area, free navigation of the Amazon and Putumayo, and a pledge of nonaggression. Ratifications of the treaty were exchanged on September 27, 1935.

The Chaco Dispute. In the Chaco controversy between Bolivia and Paraguay there was no American treaty of conciliation to be invoked. Bolivia had not approved the Gondra treaty of inquiry and the other treaties of arbitration and conciliation had not as yet been concluded. In fact when the border clash took place on December 7, 1928, the International Conference of American States on Conciliation and Arbitration was in session in Washington engaged in drawing up these conventions. The conference, alarmed by the Chaco dispute, attempted to set up *ad hoc* machinery for mediation. A commission of nine, consisting of five neutral members and two from each of the disputants, was appointed.[1] The commission obtained an agreement between the parties to restore the *status quo ante* in the Chaco and to resume diplomatic relations. The territorial question was still unsettled, however, and threatened to result in a renewal of hostilities. The work of the commission of nine was then continued by the five neutral members who were thereafter referred to as the neutral commission. The commission presented various plans for the settlement of the dispute but none was accepted by the parties. One action suggested by the commission is worthy of note. A joint declaration was drawn up and signed by representatives in Washington of all the countries in the Pan American Union excepting Paraguay and Bolivia, declaring that the signatories would not recognize any territorial arrangement of the controversy which had not been obtained by peaceful means nor the validity of territorial acquisitions which were obtained through occupation or conquest by force of arms.[2]

In addition a more limited group of Latin-American states, consisting of Argentina, Brazil, Chile, and Peru, who shunned the

---

[1] For the text of the protocol providing for the commission see *Proceedings of the International Conference of American States on Conciliation and Arbitration*, Washington, 1929, p. 162.

[2] Dept. of State, *Press Releases*, Aug. 6, 1932, p. 100.

neutral commission, attempted mediation but without success. The League of Nations, to which both parties belonged, was meanwhile seeking a settlement through a committee of three, appointed by the Council. Both American groups temporarily abandoned the field in favor of the League. The neutral commission, in announcing its relinquishment on June 27, 1933, declared: "Experience has shown that if there is more than one center of negotiation confusion and lack of agreement are the inevitable results. The Commission therefore feels that it can best contribute to peace on this continent by withdrawing from the negotiations."[1] At the Seventh International Conference of American States at Montevideo in December, 1933, an ovation was given to the League committee. The League, however, had little success in seeking an adjustment. The weakness of the League was due partly to the fact that it was distracted by more serious troubles in Europe and partly to resentment in South America regarding outside interference. On November 24, 1934, the Council proposed a plan for peace which included the suspension of hostilities, the demilitarization of a 100-kilometer zone, and conciliation or adjudication of all claims. Paraguay rejected the plan and Bolivia accepted. The Chaco committee proposed to brand Paraguay as an aggressor nation by lifting the arms embargo on Bolivia while retaining it on Paraguay. Paraguay then gave notice of withdrawal from the League. Several South American governments under the leadership of Argentina, which was sympathetic to Paraguay, protested against a League embargo. On March 15, 1935, the League in turn suspended its efforts, to permit a settlement through the mediation of American nations.

Under the leadership of Foreign Minister Carlos Saavedra Lamas of Argentina, the governments of Argentina and Chile then made another attempt to bring about mediation upon the basis of the plan of the Council of November 24, 1934. The attempt met with success. A mediatory group consisting of Argentina, Brazil, Chile, Peru, the United States, and Uruguay met with representatives of the belligerents at Buenos Aires in June, 1935. The United States was represented by Hugh Gibson, ambassador to Brazil, while the other mediatory governments were represented by their foreign ministers. A twelve-day truce was arranged to begin on June 14. A peace conference, consisting of representatives of the above-mentioned mediatory nations and of the belligerents, was then convoked in Buenos Aires on June 30. The truce was extended

[1] Dept. of State, *Press Releases*, July 1, 1933, p. 1.

and it was agreed to demobilize the fighting forces within ninety days. The armies were to be reduced to a strength of 5,000 men each. The conference then proceeded to the attempt to settle the Chaco difficulty and to establish permanent peace. On October 28 the conference declared that the war had terminated. Meanwhile a neutral commission had already entered the war zone and had begun to fix the positions to be maintained by the belligerents and to supervise the work of demobilization.[1] While the League gave valuable assistance in the work of settlement, the actual conclusion of the armistice and peace in this case was brought about by the countries of the American continent.[2]

Up to the present time the Pan-American peace machinery has left much to be desired. Perhaps no machinery could operate with success without the solid opinion of the American republics behind it. The desirability of strong regional machinery, however, is evident. Ratification by all of the twenty-one republics of the existing treaties for inquiry, conciliation, arbitration, and peace would go far to remedy existing defects. The Governing Board should also be developed as an organ of conciliation. A greater consolidation of opinion against war and the realization of the necessity of some common action by the American countries would give the necessary psychological support to strengthen these measures. Secretary of State Hull made notable progress toward this end when, at the Seventh Conference (1933), he used his influence to bring the Argentine government to the support of the various treaties. Up to that time Argentina had stood aloof, partly because of suspicions of the United States. To obtain Argentine cooperation, Secretary Hull agreed to sign the Argentine Anti-War Treaty; and in return the Argentine government declared its readiness to ratify the Gondra treaty, the treaties of 1929 on conciliation and arbitration, and the Pact of Paris.[3] A resolution was passed inviting all the countries represented at the conference which had not already done so, to adhere to the five treaties. At the end of the Seventh Conference the Pan-American peace treaties seemed to be

---

[1] At the date of writing, a permanent settlement is still under negotiation.

[2] For a discussion of the Chaco and Leticia controversies see COOPER, RUSSELL M., *American Consultation in World Affairs*, pp. 109, 285, The Macmillan Company, New York, 1934; DE WILDE, JOHN C., "South American Conflicts, the Chaco and Leticia," *Foreign Policy Reports*, Vol. IX, No. 5 (May 24, 1933).

[3] See GRUENING, ERNEST, "Pan-Americanism Reborn," *Current History*, XXXIX: 529 (February, 1934).

in process of evolution toward a more effective system for the settlement of disputes.[1]

THE CODIFICATION OF INTERNATIONAL LAW

One of the most persistent movements in Pan-Americanism has been that for the codification of public and private international law. The United States has frequently declared its support of the movement. Secretary of State Root said in his instructions to the American delegation to the Third Conference (1906):

It is important in the interests of peace that the rules, especially of public international law, should be understood and that they should be understood alike by the governments and peoples of different countries. Nothing can contribute more usefully to this among the American States than the creation of a standard to which all will give assent, because all the States have united in establishing it.[2]

Whether the codification of international law as a world-wide matter is a practical aim or not is a debatable question; but at least the movement in Pan-Americanism has brought reconciliation on a few points in some important controversies. Some of the issues which have been subject to dispute have been concerned with: the legality of armed intervention; the status of aliens; recognition; asylum; and the rights of women.

Intervention. Because of numerous armed interferences by the United States in Latin-American countries, the question of intervention has been present whenever Pan-Americanism has been considered. Latin-American leaders have sought a convention declaring intervention to be contrary to international law. In 1927 a commission of American jurists met in Rio de Janeiro to draw up projects of law to be considered at the Sixth International Conference of American States, which was to meet at Havana the following year. One of the principles prepared by the commission was that "no State may interfere in the internal affairs of another." At the Sixth Conference in Havana (1928) delegates representing a

---

[1] For descriptions of Pan-American peace machinery see KELCHNER, WARREN H., "Inter-American Peace Machinery," Dept. of State, *Press Releases*, July 7, 1934, p. 11; STONE, WILLIAM T., "The Pan-American Arbitration Treaty," Foreign Policy Association, *Information Service*, Vol. V, No. 18 (Nov. 13, 1929).

As this book goes to press, plans for a conference to consolidate the Pan-American peace machinery are under way. The proposal for a conference was initiated by the United States.

[2] *Foreign Relations*, 1906, Part II, p. 1569.

majority of the Latin-American countries arose one after another to support the proposal. A representative of Argentina vigorously condemned intervention as an attempt against the independence of nations. A Colombian delegate foresaw that unless the conference complied with the wishes of the people of the entire continent and abolished the right of intervention there might be an end to Pan-American conferences.[1] With American marines in Nicaragua and with President Coolidge making extreme public statements justifying intervention, the United States delegation was prepared to contest the principle proposed by the commission of jurists. Charles Evans Hughes, chief of the delegation, took the floor and, in a vigorous speech, upheld the right of intervention. He blamed the internal conditions of weaker governments for making intervention necessary and eloquently asked: "What are we to do when government breaks down and American citizens are in danger of their lives?"[2] Delegates from Peru and the controlled governments of Nicaragua and Cuba supported Mr. Hughes, and several other delegations were willing to postpone the matter for the sake of harmony. It was then decided to leave the question in abeyance until the next conference, but the debate left its traces of bitterness in the minds of many Latin Americans.

When the Seventh Conference met at Montevideo in 1933, conditions had changed. The United States was by that time well on its way in the retreat from imperialism which had begun a few years before. Secretary of State Hull, leader of the United States delegation, was a strong opponent of intervention and was sympathetic with Latin-American proposals to abolish it. Article VIII of the Convention on the Rights and Duties of States which was proposed at Montevideo read: "No state has the right to intervene in the internal or external affairs of another." In the general debate on the convention the opposition to intervention was reaffirmed by Latin-American delegates. Secretary Hull then gave the support of the United States to the convention with a reservation which seemed to confine the policy of renouncing intervention to the Roosevelt administration. He declared, among other things: "I feel safe in undertaking to say that under our support of the general principle of nonintervention, as has been suggested, no government need fear any intervention on the part of the United States under the Roose-

---

[1] "The Sixth Pan American Conference," Part I, Foreign Policy Association, *Information Service*, Vol. IV, No. 4 (Apr. 27, 1928), p. 68.

[2] Protection of American lives, however, has had little to do with most of the principal interventions of the United States in Latin America.

velt administration." The convention was unanimously adopted, on December 26, 1933, the vote of the United States being subject to the above reservation. Two days later President Roosevelt, in a notable address before the Woodrow Wilson Foundation, announced: "The definite policy of the United States from now on is one opposed to armed intervention."[1] On June 29, 1934, the Montevideo convention was ratified by the President with a reservation embodying the explanatory remarks of Secretary Hull.[2] This change in policy by the United States created great satisfaction among Latin-American delegations and went far to remove the unpleasant feeling that had been brought about by the Hughes speech of five years before. The foundations of Pan-Americanism had been in a large measure repaired.[3]

The Rights of Aliens. The United States has in the past differed with the traditional view of Latin America regarding the position of foreigners under the law. This country, being a creditor nation, has desired stronger protection for its citizens residing in and owning property in Latin America than the Latin-American governments have, in many cases, been able to give. The United States has subscribed to the doctrine of the international standard of protection evolved by creditor nations which asserts that in unstable countries the alien is entitled to the protection accorded in advanced countries even if that standard necessitates a higher degree of protection than the government affords its own citizens.[4] Latin Americans charge that, in attempting to maintain this doctrine, the United States has sought to place its citizens upon a preferred basis in Latin-American countries, raising them above the natives in the administration of the law. The celebrated Argentine jurist, Calvo, was the foremost expounder of the doctrine that the alien must be judged by the same standards as the citizen. At the First International Conference of American States (1889–1890) a resolution was adopted to the effect that foreigners are entitled to all civil rights provided by law but that the nation has no further obligations toward them than toward its own citizens.[5] The majority report of the committee on this matter opposed "the pretension that the foreigner should be superior to the native; that he should be a

---

[1] Dept. of State, *Press Releases*, Dec. 30, 1933, p. 381.

[2] *Treaty Information Bulletin*, June, 1934, p. 4.

[3] HERRING, HUBERT, "Pan Americanism, New Style?" *Harper's Magazine*, CLXVIII: 692 (May, 1934).

[4] See pp. 213–214.

[5] SCOTT, *op. cit.*, p. 45.

perpetual menace to the territory whose protection he seeks and whose advantages he enjoys."[1]   The United States member of the committee presented a minority report and the United States delegation voted against the resolution when it reached the floor.   A convention in line with the resolution of the First Conference was subscribed to by fifteen states at the Second Conference (1901–1902), but the United States refused to sign.   At the Seventh Conference (1933), however, the Convention on Rights and Duties of States contained in Article IX the following statement:

> Nationals and foreigners are under the same protection of the law and the national authorities and the foreigners may not claim rights other or more extensive than those of the nationals.

Since the United States has ratified this convention it would appear that the doctrine of the international standard of protection has been abandoned so far as Latin America is concerned.

Recognition.   The policy of recognition which developed in the United States just previous to the World War continually placed revolutionary governments in Latin America in an inferior position.[2] The United States has on various occasions driven bargains with the governments of some of those countries before extending recognition.   Woodrow Wilson inaugurated an idealistic but untenable policy that revolutionary governments, being unlawful, should not be recognized by the United States.   The Coolidge-Hoover administrations applied this doctrine to the five Central American republics and based it upon the General Treaty of Peace and Amity signed by the Central American States in 1923.[3]   The policy has been a standing cause of grievance against the United States on the part of many Latin-American governments who regard it as an unwarranted assumption of superiority.   At the Fifth Conference (1923) the United States policy was particularly under consideration.   The Mexican government had been disfranchised in Pan-American affairs because, being unrecognized at that time by the United States, it had no diplomatic representative in Washington to sit upon the Governing Board of the Pan American Union.   It was this situation that brought about the amendment by the Fifth Conference to the rules of the Governing Board to make it possible for a government to have a special representative on the board

[1] *International American Conference*, II: 934.
[2] See p. 69.
[3] See pp. 67–68.

during such time as it had no diplomatic representative at Washington.

The United States has gradually modified its policy of non-recognition of revolutionary governments until few remnants are now left. At the Seventh Conference (1933), however, the United States was criticized by the Cuban delegation for not recognizing the Grau government. The convention on the Rights and Duties of States, adopted at that conference, included some rather general provisions on recognition which do not appear to affect the specific problem. Among other things the convention provided that the political existence of a state is independent of recognition by other states,[1] that states are equal juridically,[2] and that recognition is unconditional and irrevocable.[3]

Asylum. A contrast in views on the international law of asylum between the United States and Latin-American countries has arisen because of a considerable difference in governmental stability. Government officials in unstable countries regard the practice of giving asylum in embassies and legations to political fugitives as a convenient protection against the excesses of revolutionary movements. This custom, which was once common, has been largely abandoned in Europe but still persists in Latin America.[4] The United States has ceased to recognize the general practice although asylum is sometimes extended in case of political refugees fleeing from mob violence. At the Sixth Conference (1928) a convention was adopted regarding the restrictions to be observed in granting asylum.[5] The delegation from this country signed with the reservation "that the United States does not recognize or subscribe to as part of international law, the so-called doctrine of asylum."[6]

The Right of Women. The placing of issues concerning women's rights upon the agenda of Pan-American conferences was to a large extent due to the activities of certain women's organizations in the United States. In the Fifth and Sixth conferences (1923 and 1928) action was taken to prepare a program for consideration of the legal rights of women.[7] At the Seventh Conference (1933) a convention

---

[1] Article III.

[2] Article IV.

[3] Article VI.

[4] FENWICK, CHARLES G., *International Law* (rev. ed.), p. 374, D. Appleton-Century Company, New York, 1934.

[5] SCOTT, *op. cit.*, p. 434.

[6] Even with this reservation, the United States has not ratified the convention.

[7] SCOTT, *op. cit.*, pp. 244, 324, 408, 494.

was signed for the removal of all discriminations in law and practice between the sexes with regard to nationality. A resolution was also passed recommending to the governments the establishment of the maximum equality possible between men and women in civil and political rights. The National Women's party in the United States had been the leading organization in obtaining a hearing on questions connected with equal rights, and Miss Doris Stevens of New York was chairman of the commission appointed to bring these matters before the Seventh Conference. Certain other women's organizations in this country were opposed to urging the question through Pan-American channels. The United States delegation at the Seventh Conference was evidently moved more by the latter group than the former and at first opposed the nationality treaty. A storm of protest from women's organizations in the United States, however, displayed such an unexpected force of feminine enthusiasm for the project that the delegation reversed its stand and approved the treaty.[1] The convention was ratified by the United States the following year.

SANITATION

The bringing of Latin-American ports into closer touch with ports of the United States through increased traffic and the establishment of direct steamship lines has made acute the problem of the spread of tropical diseases. The question of quarantine and sanitary regulations had been taken up by the Latin-American nations previous to 1889. The matter was discussed at the First International Conference of American States (1889–1890) and again at the Second Conference (1901–1902). Adoption of the existing Latin-American sanitary conventions was recommended; and a new convention was also drafted by a conference called by the Governing Board which met in Washington in 1905. This latter agreement was based on the Paris convention of 1903 and contained additional provisions relating to the dread Caribbean disease, yellow fever, which had played such havoc in ports touched by ships from the West Indies. The convention provided notification by each party to the other governments of the existence of plague, cholera, or yellow fever, the publication of defensive measures against departures from an infected region, and set forth rules for

[1] THOMSON, CHARLES A., "The Seventh Pan-American Conference, Montevideo," pp. 88–89, *Foreign Policy Reports*, Vol. X, No. 7 (June 6, 1934); DÁVILA, CARLOS, "The Montevideo Conference, Antecedents and Accomplishments," *International Conciliation*, No. 300 (May, 1934), pp. 152*ff.*

the regulation of infected ships as well as recommendations regarding inspection at land frontiers.[1] In planning for the Third Conference (1906), Secretary of State Root instructed the United States delegation that they should urge a general acceptance of the convention so that quarantine procedure might be improved. Secretary Root urged also an international agreement to eradicate epidemic disease in the country in which it first occurs. He declared:

> The injury done to the states of Central and South America by yellow fever alone, and the fear of yellow fever, is incalculable; yet the science and self-devotion of the medical officers of the American army ascertained how yellow fever is communicated and completely extirpated the disease in Cuba. It seems now that the same thing has been accomplished in Panama and Colon and in the Canal Zone of the Isthmus. Manifestly, the same thing can be done everywhere so that this dread disease will no longer exist.[2]

The Third Conference recommended the adoption by the governments of measures for better sanitation in cities. A code for maritime sanitary law, drawn up at the Seventh Pan American Sanitary Conference at Havana in 1924, has been ratified or adhered to by twenty countries including the United States and has been placed in force by decree in the remaining country.[3]

ECONOMIC AIMS

Probably the strongest motive which the United States has had in promoting and supporting Pan-Americanism has been the desire to outsell European nations in the Latin-American markets. The interest of the United States in Pan-Americanism began to rise at the time that this country, changing to an industrial economy, desired assistance and special privilege in competing against established European rivals. President Theodore Roosevelt aptly phrased this economic stimulus in his instructions to the Secretary of State just previous to the Second Conference (1901–1902), when he said:

> If our manufactures are successfully competing with European industries by their increasing sale in the home markets of the latter, it would seem to be a foregone conclusion that they will also compete with them successfully in distant markets, such as South America; and we may assume that, if the proper means are provided, the volume of our trade

[1] *Treaties, etc., of the U.S.*, II: 2144.

[2] *Foreign Relations*, 1906, Part II, p. 1571.

[3] Scott, *op. cit.*, p. 235, note 1. For text of convention and additional protocol see *U.S. Treaty Series*, Nos. 714, 763.

with South America will soon grow to large proportions.   These measures are: Adequate transportation facilities, such as steamship lines, railroads, and an isthmian canal; reciprocal trade relations; participation in the business of banking; and a corps of commercial travelers specially equipped for the Latin American trade.[1]

The Plan for a Customs Union.   The boldest stroke which the United States has made for closer commercial relations with Latin America came at the First Conference (1889–1890) when Secretary of State Blaine, acting in accordance with the instructions of Congress, proposed a customs union for all the member states.   Such a plan was designed to bring Latin-American markets into a common confine with the producers of the United States while shutting out the goods of Europe.   The Latin-American countries were unwilling to enter such a restrictive enclosure.   They did not wish to be shut off from the Old World which was the source of their culture and which contributed in large measure to their business life.   A customs union would have alienated Europe and, in the words of an Argentine delegate, would have precipitated "the war of one continent against another."[2]   The customs union plan was defeated and in its place the conference recommended, to such governments as might be interested, the conclusion of bilateral treaties providing for partial reciprocity.[3]

After thirty-eight years the question of tariff reduction was raised again at the Sixth Conference (1928), but the views of the United States and Argentina were then reversed.   Argentina had come to feel the need of commercial advantages to be gained through a customs union while, at that particular time, the United States was under a high tariff administration and was firmly committed to the equal treatment and unconditional most-favored-nation theory of tariffs.   Mr. Pueyrredón of Argentina reminded the delegates that the act of the United States Congress calling for the First Conference had set forth as a desirable objective the formation of a customs union.   The terms of the invitation, he alleged, constituted a gentlemen's agreement which had not been revoked and should still be regarded as the foundation of Pan-Americanism.   He, therefore, proposed that the preamble of the convention of the Pan American Union should contain a declaration for the mutual reduction of excessive tariff barriers.   Secretary of State Hughes opposed

[1] *Foreign Relations*, 1906, Part II, p. 1574.
[2] *International American Conference*, I: 124.
[3] *Ibid.*, p. 105; SCOTT, *op. cit.*, p. 35.   For the tariff bargains obtained by the United States following this recommendation, see pp. 168–169.

the plan on the ground that it would interfere with the sovereignty of nations. "The right to protect the people of a country," he said, "in determining what goods shall enter a country, what duties shall be imposed, or what export taxes shall be imposed is of the essence of sovereignty."[1] He asked that the conference should not destroy the union by trying to make of it "a tariff commission, or a tax commission, for the purpose of impinging upon our respective authority as independent States."[2] The Argentine proposal was defeated.

In the Seventh Conference (1933), however, the policy of the United States was again changed. The administration of Franklin D. Roosevelt was pledged to the lowering of tariffs through reciprocity agreements. Secretary Hull, accordingly, proposed a resolution for the reduction of high duties through bilateral or multilateral reciprocity treaties, the elimination of duties which retard trade most seriously, the unconditional most-favored-nation clause, and the establishment of a permanent international agency to observe and to furnish information regarding the progress achieved in the reduction of tariff barriers.[2] The Hull resolution was unanimously adopted. The resolution has perhaps had the effect of stimulating the negotiation of bilateral trade agreements.

The Removal of Miscellaneous Trade Obstructions. In addition to the resolution for the mutual lowering of customs duties, many proposals have been presented to the conferences for the removal of other barriers to commerce, such as those arising from oppressive customs formalities, from lack of uniformity in the nomenclature of merchandise in tariff laws, from port dues, and from the lack of transportation facilities. In his instructions to the delegates which represented the United States at the Third Conference (1906), Secretary of State Root expressed a wish that they might awaken an interest in the subject of customs nomenclature and of the methods of dealing with vessels and merchandise by port authorities. "It is hardly necessary to say," read the instructions, "that the successful treatment of this subject will greatly decrease one of the most serious hindrances to commercial intercourse."[4]

---

[1] "The Sixth Pan American Conference," Part I, Foreign Policy Association, *Information Service*, Vol. IX, No. 4 (Apr. 27, 1928), p. 59.

[2] *Ibid.*

[3] For text see *Report of the Delegates of the U.S.A. to the Seventh Conference*, p. 196. See also THOMSON, *loc. cit.*, pp. 89–90; DÁVILA, *loc. cit.*, p. 146.

[4] *Foreign Relations,* 1906, Part II, p. 1571.

The United States delegation has concerned itself in various conferences with obtaining resolutions and conventions for uniformity of practice with regard to such matters. In the Fifth Conference (1923) the delegation secured the adoption of a resolution making certain provisions for the uniformity of customs regulations and procedure.[1] They were also able to obtain the passage of a convention adopting the Brussels nomenclature of 1913 for statistics of international commerce.[2] Partly due to the initiative of the United States, action has also been taken to bring about uniformity in shipping papers and consular practices.[3]

Pan-American Railway and Highway. The United States has been chief sponsor of the project to construct a Pan-American railway, a subject which has been frequently considered in Pan-American conferences. The first conference (1889–1890) adopted a resolution approving the plan for a railway and making provision for a commission of engineers, consisting of three from each country, to ascertain the possible routes, the length, and the costs of construction.[4] The commission investigated and made reports at the second and subsequent conferences. Secretary of State Root was a hearty supporter of the idea both for the direct trade which it would bring to the United States and also for the political stabilization which he believed would follow railway construction. "Nothing polices a country," he said, "like a railroad. Nothing material so surely discourages revolution and unites a people as adequate railroad communication."[5]

About three-fourths of the line has now been constructed by the governments and private companies within the various countries, the main plan of the commission of engineers being followed. A great deal of attention has been given to transverse lines which will connect the countries lying off the main route with the trunk line. When completed the main line will run from Ottawa to Buenos Aires, the total length of the route being approximately 10,650 miles.[6]

[1] SCOTT, *op. cit.*, p. 263; *Report of the Delegates of the U.S.A. to the Fifth Conference*, pp. 17, 177.

[2] SCOTT, *op. cit.*, p. 233; *Report of Delegates of the U.S.A. to the Fifth Conference*, pp. 18, 104.

[3] SCOTT, *op. cit.*, pp. 21, 194, 250, 378.

[4] SCOTT, *op. cit.*, p. 11.

[5] *Foreign Relations*, 1906, Part II, p. 1570.

[6] "The Pan American Railway," *Bulletin of the Pan American Union*, 67: 58 (January, 1933).

With the coming of automobiles and the need for hard-surfaced roads, a new channel for passenger transportation was proposed, *i.e.*, an inter-American highway. At the suggestion of the United States delegation the Fifth Conference (1923) recommended to the governments that highways be established between the important cities and also between the national capitals.[1] The conference also requested that a highway conference should be convened by the Governing Board. The First Pan American Highway Congress, meeting in 1925, formulated a plan for a Pan American Highway, which was approved by the Sixth Conference (1928). The interest of the United States government in this project was sufficiently great that Congress appropriated $50,000 in 1930 to enable the Secretary of State to cooperate with the several governments of the Pan American Union in reconnaissance surveys. Shortly afterward a group of highway engineers from the United States Bureau of Public Roads of the Department of Agriculture made surveys in Panama and Central America.[2] In 1934 Congress authorized the expenditure of a further sum of $75,000 to continue the reconnaissance work. In addition $1,000,000 was appropriated to enable the United States to cooperate in the work of survey and construction.[3] The line tentatively agreed upon from the United States to Panama is of remarkable interest for the wealth of archaeological remains and the unusual scenic beauty along the route.[4]

For a similar purpose of improving communication and transportation, resolutions for the installation of direct steamship lines,[5] as well as recommendations intended to stimulate the development of commercial aviation,[6] have been passed. At the Sixth Conference (1928) a Convention on Commercial Aviation was agreed upon which has now been ratified by ten governments including the United States. The convention follows the usual legal principle in recognizing the sovereignty of each state over the air space above its territory and provides for the freedom of innocent passage in time of peace of the aircraft of the other contracting states under various

[1] *Report of Delegates of the U.S.A. to the Fifth Conference*, p. 14; SCOTT, *op. cit.*, p. 276.

[2] *Report of the Delegates of the U.S.A. to the Seventh Conference*, p. 286.

[3] Dept. of State, *Press Releases*, June 23, 1934, p. 424.

[4] ROWE, L. S., "The Larger Significance of a Pan American Highway," *Bulletin of the Pan American Union*, 64: 221 (March, 1930); JAMES, E. W., "Present Status of the Inter-American Highway," *Bulletin of the Pan American Union*, 65: 719 (July, 1931).

[5] See SCOTT, *op. cit.*, pp. 15, 16, 18, 186, 274, 383, 393.

[6] *Ibid.*, p. 277.

rules and regulations. The proclamation of prohibited zones and the fixing of routes to be followed in its air spaces are permitted to each state. Customs airdromes for landing upon entering a state and points of departure at which clearances must be obtained are provided for. Each aircraft must be registered, but registration can take place in only one state. A certificate of air worthiness from the government of the craft's nationality is required for each aircraft operating under the convention. Certificates of competency for pilots and members of operating crews are also issued by the state in which the aircraft is registered. Such a certificate must set forth that the holder has passed satisfactory examinations with regard to the traffic rules existing in the other contracting states over which he desires to fly.[1] The convention does not set up a system of international machinery for the transmission of information as to the rules and regulations of the contracting states. In this respect the convention clings to the old-fashioned and cumbersome method of communication by each state with all the other contracting states and does not take advantage of the arrangements for international administration that have proved so advantageous in various conventions devised at Geneva, and in the case of the International Commission for Air Navigation (C.I.N.A.) in Paris.[2]

Trademarks, Patents, and Copyrights. In a period of increasing international commerce certain serious questions are bound to arise regarding the titles to industrial and literary property. In order to prevent the unauthorized use in Latin-American countries of the trademarks and patents of United States citizens and to guard against the pirating of books published in this country, our government has taken the lead in advocating Pan-American agreements for the protection of the rights of inventors, manufacturers, and authors. Action on these questions was proposed in the agenda for the First Conference (1889–1890) set forth in the Act of Congress of 1888 and has been discussed in one form or another at almost every conference since.

Difficulties sometimes arise because of national differences in the law of trademarks. They become the property of the manufacturer in this country merely through use, while in Latin-American countries the property is acquired through legal registration. That is, if a citizen of the United States manufactures a "Z" brand of condensed milk, he becomes the legal owner of the mark in this country through use. If the fame of this brand should spread

---

[1] *U.S. Treaty Series*, No. 840.

[2] Colegrove, *International Control of Aviation*, p. 92.

throughout the world, some enterprising person might register the brand in a Latin-American country. The owner in this country would then be unable to ship his product under the "Z" brand to the Latin-American country without making himself liable to suit by the registrant. In 1927 an individual from South America, after a visit in the United States, returned to his own country and registered some forty trademarks used here in connection with radio apparatus.[1]

An Inter-American Trademark Bureau is located at Havana. The owner of a trademark registered in one of the contracting states who wishes to register it in any of the other contracting states makes application in the proper office in the country of original registration. This office forwards the application to the Havana bureau. The cost of the registration is $50 plus the fees required in the country or countries for which the registration is to be made.[2]

The problem of patent protection, as in the case of trademarks, is largely one of guarding the products of the United States. The nonindustrialized countries of Latin America are not particularly interested in international protection inasmuch as they import a far greater number of patented articles than they export. The United States has taken an active interest in securing Pan-American patent agreements, and the United States Commissioner of Patents was sent to the Fourth Conference (1910) in order to assist in drafting a technically correct convention.[3] The convention drawn up at that conference provides that any person obtaining a patent in one of the countries shall enjoy such protection in any one of the other states as its laws concede to the holders of patents, provided the holder shall file his application in such other states and shall comply with its laws. This is the principle of national treatment. After he has made application for a patent in one state he enjoys for a period of twelve months a right of priority for the purpose of making application in the other states.[4]

The great increase in the publication in the United States of books in the Spanish language, following the acquisition of Spanish-speaking territories in 1898, resulted in a rise in the export of such

[1] BROWN, JAMES L., "Misappropriation of American Trademarks Abroad," *Commerce Reports*, June 4, 1928, p. 572.

[2] Convention of 1929 and protocol, SCOTT, *op. cit.*, pp. 469, 476. The convention has been ratified by eight governments including the United States.

[3] *Foreign Relations*, 1910, pp. 38–39.

[4] SCOTT, *op. cit.*, p. 191. The convention has been ratified or adhered to by fourteen governments including the United States.

books to the Latin-American countries.[1]   Accordingly the United States delegations to several of the conferences have been instructed to urge a convention granting reciprocal protecton for copyrights on the basis of national treatment.   By conventions drawn up in the Fourth and Sixth conferences (1910 and 1928), it has been provided that the acknowledgment of a copyright in one state shall automatically give protection in all the other states which have ratified the convention, providing that there shall appear in the book a statement indicating a reservation of the property right.[2]

[1] *Foreign Relations*, 1906, Part II, p. 1572.
[2] SCOTT, *op. cit.*, pp. 180, 409.   The 1910 convention has been ratified or adhered to by fourteen governments, and the 1928 convention, by four.   The United States has ratified the convention of 1910 but not that of 1928.

CHAPTER VIII

THE FAR EAST—CHINA

GENERAL CONSIDERATIONS OF ORIENTAL POLICY

Relative Unimportance of Material Interests. China has long occupied a greater place in American thought and policy than its contemporary material interest to the American citizen would seem to justify. The American shipping in Chinese commerce was once of some consequence but it declined at about the time of the Civil War. During the greater part of our relations with that populous country, which contains almost one-fourth of the human race, the Chinese trade has amounted to only 1 or 2 per cent of our total foreign commerce. The rise in commercial importance of China during the last two or three decades has not brought the proportion up to more than 3 or 4 per cent. American investments in China have always been comparatively small. A 1933 estimate places them at $132,000,000[1] which represents a little less than 1 per cent of all American foreign holdings and roughly about one-seventh of American investments in Cuba.

Prospects of Future Markets. Despite this paucity of commerce and investment China has always exercised a potent influence over American businessmen, missionaries, travelers, and officials. Added to the charm of the East there is the prospect that the sleeping populations of China will one day awaken to new methods of life and will acquire new power to purchase Western goods. The rise in American exports to Japan from less than $3,000,000 in 1880 to $228,000,000 in 1928[2] may suggest a forecast of the alluring markets that will be opened and the new riches that will accrue through commerce when the slumberers of Cathay become fully aroused under the energizing influences of industrialism.

---

[1] *The Balance of International Payments of the United States in 1933*, p. 57. Another estimate gives the sum of $196,800,000 in 1930. REMER, C. F., *Foreign Investments in China*, p. 333, The Macmillan Company, New York, 1933. In addition to the latter figure, the value of American mission property was estimated at $43,100,000.

[2] They amounted to $202,589,000 in 1935.

The transition of Japan may also indicate the line of change in policy that may be expected.   For some decades after the isolated and backward little island empire was opened to trade by a bold stroke of gunboat diplomacy, special policies were applied to that country.   The Japanese customs were controlled by treaty and the nationals of the Western powers enjoyed the privilege of extra-territoriality.   Forceful methods were used to promote business profits.   Then Japan was transferred by the industrial revolution to the ranks of the strong powers and became an equal member of the community of nations.   Today the United States can have no profitable policy in Japan outside of that of legal and equal treatment.

The Chinese are passing through a slower and more massive transition than did the Japanese, and their future is a subject of the utmost importance in international politics.   They have been in many respects the world's most remarkable and successful people.   China was an established nation before the time of Rome, and the Chinese have endured as an organized society while the Western empires of antiquity have long been but memories.   No other people can point to a similar record of long-time social stability and attainment.   Hemmed about by the possessions of four encroaching nations—Japan, Russia, Great Britain, and France—China is undergoing a partial disintegration.   Outlying territories, such as Manchuria, Outer Mongolia, and Outer Tibet, have fallen under foreign control.   Inner Mongolia, Inner Tibet, and Sinkiang are in process of being alienated.   The French have developed a sphere of interest in South China, which is particularly strong in the Province of Yünnan where the most important economic outlet is provided by a railway which leads through French Indo-China.[1] The loss of these territories, temporarily or permanently, can hardly be a great disaster to China.   In one sense it may well prove to be an aid through the removal of an excess load of administration over populations mostly non-Chinese at a time when all available energies are urgently needed for the regeneration of China proper.   Of far greater significance, however, are the Japanese encroachments in North China where an area containing a population of approximately 100,000,000 Chinese is in danger of being alienated.

In the light of the present as well as of the past the capacities of the Chinese for future achievement are evident.   Their commercial ability is proverbial and has been demonstrated in competition with

[1] BISSON, T. A., "The Dismemberment of China," *Foreign Policy Reports*, Vol. X, No. 4 (Apr. 25, 1934).

foreigners in China, the Philippines, and Malaysia. The younger Chinese are intelligent, adaptable, and willing to learn from the West. Add these factors to the social solidarity of 400,000,000 people and the possibilities contained in the renaissance of the Oriental nation become impressive. Their rise will necessarily be slow but it will doubtless have the steadiness that is characteristic of great momentum. It is necessary to review briefly in this way the probabilities of Chinese evolution for the Far Eastern policies of the United States in general have been based on faith in China while those of certain other powers have been predicated on Chinese weakness and inferiority. The exact line of Chinese political development is not, of course, predictable. Probably the Chinese of the next few decades will not be satisfied with the forms of government known to the West. Whether China will adhere to bourgeois republicanism, however, or drift into a form of modified communism or originate a political type for which we have no nomenclature should not be the principal concern of Western powers. The domestic political affairs of China can be dealt with more wisely by the Chinese than by others who have extrinsic interests to serve,[1] but they will doubtless present questions of a diplomatic character as matters of property and investment rights become entangled with changing theories of the state.[2]

Imperialism versus Equal Treatment. In approaching the problem of American relations with China there are two main attitudes which from the first have been shown by various groups of Americans, *i.e.*, those of domination and friendship. The policy of domination, which has been for four centuries a traditional European method of dealing with Asia, has sometimes been advocated by American commercial groups in China. Many American business-men, in common with the tradespeople of other countries, have assumed a feeling of superiority toward the Chinese. The factor of prestige or "face" looms large in their minds. Accordingly they have demanded a program of strong action and have advocated cooperation with the imperialistically inclined nations of Europe in

---

[1] " . . . there is no policy more promising in the long run for the tranquillity of the Far East and the peace of the world than the exercise of the necessary patience and forbearance by the Powers while the Chinese themselves set their own house in order." HOLCOMBE, ARTHUR N., *The Chinese Revolution*, p. 347, Harvard University Press, Cambridge, 1931.

[2] For a sympathetic description of China's problems see QUIGLEY, HAROLD S., "Chinese Politics Today," University of Minnesota, *The Day and Hour Series*, No. 8, 1934.

forcing this policy on China. It is only military power, according to this view, which can exact respect from the Oriental mind.

Most Americans who have studied the Far Eastern problem from the standpoint of continental United States as distinguished from that of the small American community in Asia have come to the conclusion that the policy best adapted to the resources at the command of the government and best fitted to the commercial objects to be attained is that of friendly cooperation with China. This attitude arises from confidence in the future of the Chinese. It also springs from an aversion to entanglements in the Far East which would probably involve dangers and expense far out of proportion to any material advantages to be attained. This view has been adopted, particularly in recent years, by the missionaries in China who realize that the success of their efforts is possible only while a friendly feeling exists on the part of the Chinese. They fear that imperialistic action and a resulting antiforeign feeling would result in a sharp fall in conversions of Chinese to Christianity or might cause the loss to the missions of a share of the already converted native Christian community. The American missionary interests in China have been relatively important, about one-half of the Americans in that country being connected with missions. As between the two attitudes, the Department of State has ordinarily adhered to the second or more pacific approach,[1] although at times it has swung over temporarily to the policy of firmness and military action.

COMMERCIAL POLICIES—OPEN PORTS AND TARIFFS

The hope of commerce has been the chief reason for American diplomacy concerning China. At present the Chinese have a low purchasing power. Even a slight improvement in the economic status of their vast population is certain, however, to have great effects in the world of commerce. As has been suggested, the rise in importance of Japanese commerce with the industrialization of Japan may be an indication of what will happen with regard to China. In 1880 about 1 per cent of American foreign trade was with Japan. This rose to 2.7 per cent in 1900 and to over 8 per cent in 1935. The industrialization of China will presumably open rich markets to Western nations. China will demand huge quan-

---

[1] HORNBECK, STANLEY K., *China To-Day: Political*, pp. 480*ff.*, World Peace Foundation, Boston, 1927; BLAKESLEE, GEORGE H., *The Pacific Area*, p. 67, World Peace Foundation, Boston, 1929.

tities of Western consumption goods as well as large shipments of machinery for production. In return vast consignments of Oriental goods will be exported to enrich the life of the West. This alluring prospect of trade, dangling ever uncertainly before the eyes of American diplomats, has kept their attention fixed upon the Orient; and American trading groups in both the Far East and the United States have aided in keeping the official interest at a high level.

The Treaty of 1844. In 1784 the *Empress of China* was the first ship to carry the flag of the newly created United States to China. The vessel sailed home the following year; and upon the settlement of the affairs of the enterprise a profit of $30,727 was declared upon an investment of $120,000, a return of slightly over 25 per cent.[1] From that time forward American ships participated to a considerable extent in the limited trade permitted to foreigners. A number of American vessels reported rich earnings which amounted in some cases to several hundred per cent on the investment. Foreigners in those days were permitted to go only to Canton, and their stay in that city was restricted to certain months of the year. The general rendezvous for foreign shipping was Macao, a Portugese settlement on an island in the estuary of the Pearl River.

The taste of rich profits on this limited trade caused the American merchants to yearn for increased opportunities. At the conclusion of the so-called Opium War in 1842 the British gained new privileges in the Treaty of Nanking. Five Chinese ports were opened to the trade and residence of British subjects. These were Canton, Amoy, Foochow, Ningpo, and Shanghai. In the following year the tariff which was to be charged on British goods was fixed by treaty at specific rates amounting to about 5 per cent ad valorem. The prospects that the British were to obtain a treaty had at the beginning of the war created a demand among American merchants for trade advantages. In 1839 they petitioned Congress to send a commercial agent to negotiate a trade agreement. In 1843, at the request of the President, Congress appropriated $40,000 to send an American diplomatic expedition to China. Caleb Cushing was appointed special commissioner to negotiate a treaty. He departed for China in 1843 accompanied by a squadron of war vessels. The Treaty of 1844, which was the result of his labors, obtained for the United States the same commercial advantages as had been granted to Great Britain, *i.e.*, the right of residence and trade at the five ports and the limitation of Chinese duties on American goods to

[1] *The Journals of Major Samuel Shaw*, p. 218, Wm. Crosby and H. P. Nichols, Boston, 1847.

specific rates which amounted to about 5 per cent ad valorem. It was also provided that Americans should in no case be subject to the payment of other or higher duties than should be required of any other nation.[1] The most-favored-nation clause, thus set forth in the treaty, became the basis of the American trade policy in China, later to be called the open door.[2] Other commercial advantages in the treaty were the fixing of tonnage dues to be charged on American ships and the granting of permission for Americans to carry on business without the intermediation of the Hong merchants or Chinese commercial guilds through which all trading had formerly been conducted.

Ports and Concessions. After 1844 the United States joined its influence with that of other foreign powers in extending the trade area by obtaining from China additional treaty ports or open ports for foreign trade and residence.[3] Exclusive of Manchuria, there are 43 cities which are open as treaty ports, marts, and customs stations; 16 others are opened to trade; and 26 are ports of call on the Yangtze and the West River.[4] In some of the ports, concessions have been set aside for foreigners where they may reside and where they may, in some cases, establish their own governments. With regard to this matter the ports may be classified as follows:

(1) Ports in which no area is set aside for foreigners.

(2) Ports containing areas set aside for foreigners in which land is bought or leased from native owners and in which the foreigners live under the Chinese municipal government.

(3) Ports in which international settlements have been created. There are two of these, one at Shanghai and the other at Amoy. The municipal governments are under the control of the representatives of the foreign residents although there are now five Chinese among the fourteen members of the council in the International Settlement at Shanghai.

(4) Ports in which perpetual leases of certain areas have been granted to single powers for the establishment of settlements under the control of the

---

[1] For the text of the treaty see, *Treaties, etc., of the U.S.,* I: 196.

[2] Commodore Kearny had previously made a request to the Governor of Canton for most-favored-nation treatment for Americans and had been told that it would not be permitted that American merchants should come "to have merely a dry stick." Dennett states, however, that the origin of the most-favored-nation policy on the part of China was a voluntary act of the Chinese government which had come of its own accord to see the advantage of treating the foreign nations upon an equal basis. See DENNETT, TYLER, *Americans in Eastern Asia,* p. 110, The Macmillan Company, New York, 1922.

[3] Some ports have been declared open by decree of the Chinese government and are, therefore, not strictly speaking treaty ports.

[4] *The China Year Book,* 1933, p. 156, The North-China News and Herald, Ltd., Shanghai.

lessee power.   Exclusive of Manchuria, there are now nine of these "concessions," as they are called.   They are located in five Chinese cities.[1]

(5) Ports in leased territories as, for example, Kowloon.   Here the lessee power exercises what amounts to sovereignty over the entire area.

Chinese nationalists have waged a campaign for the rendition or return to China of the concessions, particularly in class 4.   The holding of such areas by foreign powers is regarded as a serious infringement of the sovereignty of China.   In recent years about a dozen such settlements have been returned to Chinese control under pressure.   Thus Germany, Austria, and Russia have lost their settlements and the British have returned their settlements in Hankow, Amoy, Kiukiang, and Chinkiang.   The Belgians have rendered their settlement in Tientsin.[2]   The United States has not been active in pressing the policy of building foreign settlements in Chinese cities.   This country has had three leased concessions, at Amoy, Shanghai, and Tientsin.   The concession at Amoy was returned to China and the concession in Tientsin was merged with that of the British.   At Shanghai the American concession was also merged with the British to become the International Settlement in the government of which the United States has participated.

Treaty Tariffs and their Abolition.   Chinese tariffs, as has been stated, were early fixed in treaties between China and the powers and were originally placed at specific rates which amounted to about 5 per cent ad valorem.   The Chinese had two objections to the treaty tariff system.   In the first place, the embedding of the tariff rates in treaties so that they could not be changed without the consent of foreign governments was regarded as a restriction of the right of China to regulate domestic affairs.   The unanimous consent of the powers was necessary for revision since no one of them would agree to raise the tariff rates on its own goods so long as its competitors were enjoying the low rates.   In the second place, the rate was too low for the necessities of the government with regard to both revenue and the protection of Chinese production.   As the prices of goods rose, the specific rates, which at first equaled 5 per cent, came to represent even a lower percentage.

One of the principles espoused by the young nationalists of China was the abolition of tariff control.[3]   The demand for abolition was

---

[1] *The China Year Book*, 1933, pp. 105–107.

[2] WARE, EDITH E., *Business and Politics in the Far East*, p. 98, Yale University Press, New Haven, 1932.

[3] The situation was more complicated than has been indicated.   The duties were collected by the Maritime Customs Service which has been largely in the

made at the Paris Conference in 1919 and at the Washington Conference in 1921–1922. On several occasions the powers agreed to a modification of the tariff treaties to the extent of permitting an upward revision to an effective 5 per cent. Such a revision was accomplished in 1902 to meet the indemnity placed upon China by the powers following the Boxer uprising. Another was effected in 1918 because of the rise in prices due to the World War. In this latter case the Chinese claimed that the revision was not sufficient and that it raised the yield to only 3½ per cent.[1] In accordance with the Treaty Relating to the Chinese Customs Tariff signed at the Washington Conference, another revision occurred in 1922.

The customs tariff treaty above referred to provided for the assemblage of a special conference to arrange for the abolition of likin, or internal transit taxation, which had been levied in various parts of China for many years. The conference did not meet until 1925–1926; but it compensated for its delay by adopting a resolution recommending that tariff autonomy should be granted to China on January 1, 1929.[2] The United States was the first of the powers to conclude a treaty with China agreeing to relinquish control in accordance with this recommendation, retaining, however, the rights accorded the most-favored nation.[3] The other powers followed.[4] On February 1, 1929, before ratifications of the treaties were exchanged, the first autonomous Chinese tariff was placed in operation. One goal of Chinese nationalism had been attained.

THE OPEN DOOR

When in 1844 the United States obtained from China a treaty granting most-favored-nation treatment, the principle of equal opportunity was established. Later on it became necessary to make representations to the other powers to dissuade them from seizing advantages in China in which the United States would not be permitted to share. This course of action was called the policy of the open door. In order to realize the distinctiveness of the open-door program, it should be contrasted, in the first place, with the aims of

---

hands of foreigners since 1854, and the proceeds from the customs were mortgaged to pay off foreign indebtedness.

[1] WILLOUGHBY, WESTEL W., *Foreign Rights and Interests in China* (rev. ed.), II: 789, Johns Hopkins Press, Baltimore, 1927.

[2] TREAT, PAYSON J., *The Far East*, p. 475, Harper & Brothers, New York, 1928.

[3] *U.S. Treaty Series*, No. 773.

[4] Japan did not sign a treaty but was forced by circumstances to acquiesce.

the other great powers in obtaining special privileges in China. In the second place, it should be compared with the policy of the United States in the Caribbean where this country has sought unusual advantages for itself and has said nothing about the open door. The open-door policy in China has been manifested principally by making representations opposing the grant by China and the seizure by the powers of special concessions of a commercial nature. As a corollary, however, this country has also asked for the preservation of Chinese territorial integrity. So long as Chinese territorial integrity is maintained, the United States has the right through the most-favored-nation clause to ask for equal treatment. But if portions of China should be annexed by the powers, this treaty right would be lost; and the seized territories would probably be incorporated in the tariff systems of the annexing governments.

The Hay Notes of 1899. In 1898 it appeared to many political observers that China was to be broken up. Four of the great powers—Great Britain, France, Germany, and Russia—had forced China to grant them leases of ports and spheres of interest in large interior areas. In addition Japan had also claimed a sphere of interest in one Chinese province. In the leased territories China practically yielded her sovereignty to the lessee power for periods of 25 or 99 years. In the spheres of interest the acquiring powers gained certain preferential investment privileges. Should the Chinese government seek to borrow foreign capital for the building of railways or public works within a sphere, it must apply first to the power claiming the sphere. In 1898 Germany acquired a lease of Kiaochow Bay in Shantung for 99 years and claimed a sphere of interest throughout Shantung. Russia gained a lease of Port Arthur and Dalny at the southern tip of the Liaotung peninsula in Manchuria for 25 years and claimed a sphere of interest in Manchuria and northern China. Great Britain obtained leases of Kowloon for 99 years and of Weihaiwei for so long as Russia should hold Port Arthur, and claimed a sphere of interest in the Yangtze Valley. France obtained a lease of Kwangchowan for 99 years and asserted title to a sphere of interest over the southern provinces and the Island of Hainan. Japan claimed a sphere in the Province of Fukien.[1] At this time the Chinese were fearful that their ancient empire was to be torn to pieces. American businessmen appre-

---

[1] Japan gained the Russian lease of Port Arthur in 1905 and seized the German leasehold at Kiaochow Bay in 1914. She made claim to spheres of interest in Southern Manchuria and Shantung as a consequence of these acquisitions.

hended that the future markets of China would be monopolized by the powers.

There were two reasons why the United States did not acquire a lease or claim a sphere of interest in China. In the first place, this country was not prepared psychologically to make territorial demands in China. American energies had been absorbed in internal development and no general sentiment for oversea expansion had made itself felt. In the second place, during the 1898 scramble in China, the attention of the United States was diverted by the Spanish-American War.

Because of the fact that the United States held no leases or spheres of interest in China, the American government was particularly anxious to place limits on the acquisitions of the other powers and to retain, so far as possible, equality of commercial opportunity. At this point the policy of the open door was given new life. W. W. Rockhill, formerly secretary of the American legation in Peking, was in the United States in 1899 and submitted to Secretary of State John Hay a memorandum regarding the pledges which it was desirable to obtain from the powers. Hay then sent instructions to the American diplomatic representatives at the capitals of the interested governments to present notes asking that equality of opportunity should be retained in the spheres of interest and leased territories. These are known as the Hay open-door notes. They asked assurance that, in the territories referred to, the powers would not interfere with equality of trade by placing higher charges on foreign commerce than on their own with respect to tariffs, harbor dues, or railway rates. Mr. Hay requested that the Chinese tariff should continue to apply and that there should be no interference with any treaty port or vested interest.[1] Some of the powers, such as Great Britain and Japan, were already largely convinced that the open-door policy was preferable to a general system of discriminatory tariffs. Others, such as Russia, were more reluctant to adopt the American point of view. In the end, however, all the powers gave their assent to the principles set forth in the notes.

The Territorial Integrity of China. In 1900, after the Boxer uprising, some of the incensed allies desired to wreak stern punishment upon China. Secretary Hay then sent forth another set of notes in which he said, among other things, that the United States desired to preserve the territorial and administrative integrity of

[1] *Foreign Relations*, 1899, pp. 129*ff*. For a general treatment of the open-door question, see BAU, MINGCHIEN JOSHUA, *The Open Door Doctrine*, The Macmillan Company, New York, 1923.

China and the principle of equal and impartial trade with all parts of the Chinese Empire.   During the negotiations for a settlement with China the United States also declared for lower reparations than the other powers were willing to accept, feeling that a crushing indemnity might permanently weaken the Chinese government. The influence of the United States at this point was strongly exerted to prevent the disruption of China.

Attempts to Maintain the Open Door and Territorial Integrity of China.   The American government has made diplomatic representations subsequently on various occasions in behalf of the principle of the open door.   In the course of time a type of unequal treatment not mentioned in the Hay notes of 1899 was protested, *i.e.*, discrimination against American investors due to the spheres of interest claimed by most of the great powers.   In 1902 a complaint was made to Russia because of certain monopolistic advantages about to be granted in Manchurian investments in favor of the Russo-Chinese bank.[1]   In 1915 the United States insisted upon the modification of the twenty-one demands made by Japan upon China which, in their original form, had included a preference for Japanese capital in the Province of Fukien.[2]   Again in 1915 objections were made to the Japanese policy in Manchuria of regulating the freight rates on Manchurian railways so that they would favor Japanese goods.[3]   This policy, it was alleged, was a direct violation of the Hay open-door notes of 1899.   In 1916 and 1917 the Department of State was engaged in making ineffective representations to protect the rights of the Siems-Carey Company, which had signed contracts with the Chinese government for the construction of 1,500 miles of railways in various parts of China.[4]

The desire of the United States to maintain the territorial integrity of China as one of the fundamentals of its Far Eastern policy was shown by the incidents of the World War and the Peace Conference.   Partly to rid itself of German territorial rights and influence, China followed the suggestions of the United States in severing diplomatic relations with Germany on March 12, 1917, and in declaring war upon Germany on August 14, 1917.   But Japan had early in the war taken possession of the German leasehold at Kiaochow Bay and the German railroad in the interior of

[1] *Foreign Relations*, 1902, p. 928.
[2] *Ibid.*, 1915, pp. 108–109.
[3] *Ibid.*, 1915, p. 594; 1916, p. 446.
[4] See p. 195.   For a further discussion of the open door for capital through a system of joint investments see pp. 196*ff.*

Shantung. At the Paris Peace Conference in 1919 Japan insisted strongly upon a treaty clause which would cede to her these rights. Great Britain, France, and Italy were bound by promises to support the Japanese claims. The American delegation sided with the Chinese, protested against the transfer, and offered an alternative plan to cede the former German holdings to the Allied and Associated Powers which were to make the proper disposition of them later. President Wilson was not able to hold out against the Japanese demands, and a clause was included in the Treaty of Versailles by which Germany renounced in favor of Japan her rights in Shantung.[1] China thereupon refused to sign the treaty. The matter was, however, not to rest with the Treaty of Versailles. At the Washington Conference in 1921–1922 the Chinese and Japanese delegates met with British and American observers to consider the problem. As a result of these discussions Japan agreed to return to China the leased territory at Kiaochow Bay in Shantung and also to permit China to purchase the railway which had been acquired from Germany.[2]

The Nine-Power Treaty. The principle of the open door has been reaffirmed from time to time in various treaties and agreements. The United States was a party to the Root-Takahira agreement of 1908 and the Lansing-Ishii agreement of 1917, both of which were with Japan.[3] The outstanding expression of the doctrine came in the Nine-Power Treaty which was framed at the Washington Conference. Because of the subsequent importance of the treaty, Article I and most of Article III are worthy of quotation.

Art. I. The Contracting Powers, other than China, agree:

(1) To respect the sovereignty, the independence, and the territorial and administrative integrity of China;

(2) To provide the fullest and most unembarrassed opportunity to China to develop and maintain for herself an effective and stable government;

---

[1] Article CLVI.

[2] WILLIAMS, EDWARD THOMAS, *China Yesterday and Today*, pp. 510–521, Thomas Y. Crowell Company, New York, 1923; VINACKE, HAROLD M., *A History of the Far East in Modern Times*, p. 434, Alfred A. Knopf, New York, 1928.

[3] The Lansing-Ishii agreement gave lip service to the principle of the open door but was really somewhat in conflict with that principle since it recognized the special interests of Japan in China.

(3) To use their influence for the purpose of effectually establishing and maintaining the principle of equal opportunity for the commerce and industry of all nations throughout the territory of China;

(4) To refrain from taking advantage of conditions in China in order to seek special rights or privileges which would abridge the rights of subjects or citizens of friendly States, and from countenancing action inimical to the security of such States.

. . . .

Art. III. With a view to applying more effectually the principles of the Open Door or equality of opportunity in China for the trade and industry of all nations, the Contracting Powers, other than China, agree that they will not seek, nor support their respective nationals in seeking

(*a*) any arrangement which might purport to establish in favour of their interests any general superiority of rights with respect to commercial or economic development in any designated region of China;

(*b*) any such monopoly or preference as would deprive the nationals of any other Power of the right of undertaking any legitimate trade or industry in China, or of participating with the Chinese Government, or with any local authority, in any category of public enterprise, or which by reason of its scope, duration or geographical extent is calculated to frustrate the practical application of the principle of equal opportunity.[1]

The treaty was to a large extent formulated by the American delegation at the conference. It embodies the principal points for which the United States has contended: equal opportunity for trade, equal opportunity for investments, and the territorial integrity of China. Article III was intended to nullify the spheres of interest claimed by the various powers. Japan was a party to the treaty, a fact which has been of particular interest because of the violation of the first clause in Article I by the Japanese policy in Manchuria. The Japanese aggressions were protested by the United States because of the violation of the Nine-Power Treaty as well as on the grounds of the violation of the Pact of Paris.[2]

Japan's Right of Veto over China's Borrowing. Japan nevertheless proceeded with the Manchurian venture and erected the State of Manchukuo, which operates under the control of Japanese

---

[1] *Treaties, etc., of the U.S.*, III: 3122.

[2] See p. 325. See also the memorandum delivered by the American ambassador in Tokyo to the Japanese Foreign Office on Nov. 5, 1931, the public statement of Secretary Stimson on Dec. 10, 1931, and the identic note sent to the governments of Japan and China on Jan. 7, 1932, published in *Conditions in Manchuria*, Senate Document No. 55, 72d Cong., 1st Sess.

advisers.[1] The long-time prospects for Japan, with Russian opposition and with the certainty that eventually a greatly strengthened China will oppose her, are, however, none too bright. Japanese officials plan that their government by assuming the role of "guardian of the peace of Asia" shall maintain an increasing control over China. On April 17, 1934, the chief of the intelligence division of the Japanese Foreign Office gave verbally to the press a statement of a proposed Japanese policy. The statement declared that technical or financial aid to China almost invariably became military or political in character and that Japan would reserve the right to make objections to the extension of such aid. Specifically Japan would claim the right to object to the supplying of military airplanes, the building of airdromes, the furnishing of military advisers and instructors, and the granting of political loans.[2] The issuance of the statement to the press by a high official raised the supposition that it was intended as a trial balloon to determine what the sentiment of the other powers would be with regard to such a policy. The reaction of the press in the United States and Great Britain to the proposed policy was quite critical. The British Foreign Office answered the Japanese statement with a note which was not published but which was described by Sir John Simon in the House of Commons as having the object of clarifying the position of the British government.[3]

The United States informed the Japanese government that the treaty rights of this country could not be ignored. "In the opinion of the American people and the American Government," said the communication, "no nation can, without the assent of the other nations concerned, rightfully endeavor to make conclusive its will in situations where there are involved the rights, the obligations, and the legitimate interests of other sovereign states."[4] Meanwhile, evidently convinced of the hazards of attempting to defy so abruptly the Western powers, the Japanese government had revised the statement and had issued a declaration much more moderate in character which merely asserted: "Japan bears the responsibility for maintenance of peace and order in Eastern Asia with other Asiatic powers, particularly China."[5]

[1] BISSON, T. A., "Japan and Manchoukuo," *Foreign Policy Reports*, Vol. VIII, No. 8 (June 22, 1932); DORFMAN, BEN, "Two Years of the Manchoukuo Regime," *ibid.*, Vol. X, No. 14 (Sept. 12, 1934).

[2] For text see *Parliamentary Debates—Commons*, 288: 1368 (Apr. 24, 1934).

[3] *Parliamentary Debates—Commons*, 288: 1367 (Apr. 24, 1934).

[4] Dept. of State, *Press Releases*, May 5, 1934, p. 245.

[5] *N.Y. Times*, Apr. 28, 1934.

Mr. Hull's Statement Regarding North China. On December 5, 1935, when it had become evident that the Japanese military authorities were active in supporting the movement to separate the northern provinces of China under the guise of an autonomy movement, Secretary of State Hull issued a statement to the press in which he reminded Japan by indirect language of the obligations assumed under the Nine-Power Treaty. He said apropos of the North China situation:

This government adheres to the provisions of the treaties to which it is a party and continues to bespeak respect by all nations for the provisions of treaties solemnly entered into for the purpose of facilitating and regulating, to reciprocal and common advantage, the contracts between and among the countries signatory.[1]

THE PROTECTION OF CITIZENS IN CHINA

While the subject of diplomatic protection is discussed elsewhere, it may appropriately be referred to in this place to indicate its special application to China and to bring out the distinctive policy of the United States. Over a long period of time the protection activity of the United States in China had exceeded in amount the similar activity of our government in any other part of the world with the possible exception of Mexico. American missionaries in the early days were subject to attack for a variety of reasons which included resentment on the part of the literati and others toward a foreign religion and the alleged interference of missionary buildings with the *fêng-shui* or the influences of wind and water. The coming of new industries brought down upon the heads of the Westerners the wrath of those who had suffered from business dislocation, while the political aggressions of Western powers added to the native indignation. In recent times banditry and revolutionary disturbances have given rise to many pleas for protection.

Without going into detail regarding cases, the protection policy of the United States in China may be briefly summarized under four main headings:

1. This government has made strong demands upon China for indemnities, for punishment of rioters, and at times for the infliction of penalties upon Chinese officials. The United States in so doing has imposed upon China a high doctrine of responsibility, much higher than it would be willing to admit with regard to itself.

2. The Department of State has not been willing to go so far as the business community of Americans in China has demanded. Business groups have asked for a more generous use of armed force than has been employed and have also

[1] *N.Y. Times*, Dec. 6, 1935.

requested that the United States should join with other foreign powers in attempting a complete pacification of China. The United States has ordinarily rejected military cooperation with the powers and has sometimes refused to extend protection in the interior. Americans have frequently been asked to leave interior cities and proceed to places more accessible to the United States naval forces.

3. The American government has on occasion resorted to arms for the protection of its nationals and has maintained military and naval forces in China as a regular policy. A regiment has been stationed at Tientsin and a legation guard at Peking since the Boxer uprising of 1900. A Far Eastern squadron has its winter base at Manila and its summer base at Chefoo. Gunboats patrol the Yangtze for protection purposes.

4. This country has, however, been much more moderate in protection policies than have the other great powers. France has made the protection of Catholic missionaries a principal method for acquiring territory and economic rights in the Far East. Germany presented her famous demands for a leased port at Kiaochow Bay and for a sphere of interest in Shantung following the killing of two German priests by bandits in Shantung. The Japanese made the destructive attack on Shanghai in 1932 because of a boycott of Japanese goods. The United States has acquired no territory or economic rights in this manner. The distinctive feature of American policy is that it has been limited to gaining security for American citizens and to obtaining compensation for their injuries. This distinction is due largely to the fact that because of lack of military tradition and because of internal preoccupation the United States has not been prepared for a campaign of aggression in Asia, such, for example, as it has waged in the Caribbean.

Some of the most fundamental problems of protection now rising on the Far Eastern horizon are those involved in the clash between communistic factions of China and the Nationalist government. Communism, so called, is entrenched in a large area in western China and may extend itself in time to a much larger part of the country. While the doctrines practiced by the alleged communists are a considerable modification of the Marxian brand,[1] there is sufficient socialization in the plan to bring it into conflict with American business interests wherever it is extended. Furthermore the banditlike operations of communist military forces increase the possibilities of conflicts with the institutions of capitalism. Here will probably arise a question of protection of business and capital against a creed that is antagonistic to the American conception of the rights of private property.[2]

[1] George E. Sokolsky defines communism in China as largely an agrarian protest against centralization and he describes the Chinese Soviet Republic as "a moderate socialist revolutionary organization." "Political Movements in China," *The Annals of the American Academy of Political and Social Science*, CLXV: 21 (July, 1933).

[2] For a description of communism in China see YAKHONTOFF, VICTOR A., *The Chinese Soviets*, Coward-McCann, Inc., New York, 1934; BISSON, T. A.,

EXTRATERRITORIALITY

Origin of Extraterritoriality in China. When Westerners first went to China, they found themselves under Chinese jurisdiction. In the celebrated Terra Nova case of 1821 a sailor on an American ship, the *Emily*, in the river at Canton, killed a Chinese woman. After some protest he was given over to the Chinese authorities by whom he was strangled to death. A group of American merchants are reported to have said during the controversy over the surrender of the sailor: "We are bound to submit to your laws while we are in your waters, be they ever so unjust."[1] The foreign community, however, disliked to place itself under Chinese jurisdiction for several reasons. Chinese punishments, from death by slicing to whipping by the bamboo, were regarded as cruel and unusual. Chinese prisons were horrible in their lack of sanitation, overcrowding, and high death rates. Justice was administered by executive officers whose efficiency records apparently depended upon the certainty of conviction of accused persons. Witnesses as well as suspected criminals were subjected to torture. Under the Chinese doctrine of responsibility the family was held liable for the acts of the individual members. The Chinese, moreover, were prejudiced against foreigners who were regarded as barbarians of low status.

In the Treaty of Nanking in 1842 the British obtained a clause granting to them the right of extraterritoriality, that is, the jurisdiction of British authorities over British subjects in judicial matters in China. In the first treaty between the United States and China, in 1844, the same right was obtained with some additions to the British provisions. The 1844 treaty provided that cases arising in China should be tried as follows:

1. American citizens accused of crime should be tried and punished by the authorities of the United States.
2. Civil suits between American citizens should be tried by the United States authorities.
3. Suits between American citizens and Chinese subjects should be tried in the court of the defendant's nationality.
4. The trial of civil suits between Americans and the nationals of other foreign states should be regulated by agreement between the United States and the foreign governments in question.

"The Communist Movement in China," *Foreign Policy Reports*, Vol. IX, No. 4 (Apr. 26, 1933); QUIGLEY, *loc. cit.*, p. 15.

[1] *North American Review*, XL: 66 (January, 1835). The account in the *Review* was attributed to the owner and the captain of the *Emily*.

From 1844 until 1906 the jurisdiction over American cases in China lay with the United States consular officials. In 1906 the United States Court for China was created in order to provide a judicial tribunal to try the more serious cases and also to provide a court to hear appeals from the consular decisions. Under the provisions of the 1906 act the United States Court for China has jurisdiction over civil cases involving more than $500 and over criminal cases in which the penalty exceeds $100 or sixty days' imprisonment. Consular courts retain their jurisdiction over the minor offenses and have the power of preliminary hearing and commitment to the United States court in the more serious cases. Appeals may be made from the consular courts to the United States Court for China. From this court, in turn, appeals may be made to the Circuit Court of Appeals in the Ninth Judicial District at San Francisco.

Abuses of Extraterritoriality. Extraterritoriality was eventually granted to some eighteen foreign powers in China; but has been yielded by three—Austria, Germany, and Russia. Chinese nationalists have pointed out grave abuses of the system and have made demands that it be abolished. Extraterritoriality is to them a humiliating infringement of their nation's sovereignty. One of the most serious defects in the system has been the complacent manner with which foreign tribunals have regarded offenses against the Chinese. Serious crimes committed against coolies and other Chinese have gone without adequate punishment. As early as 1865 Samuel Wells Williams, United States chargé d'affaires, wrote from Peking:

Cases have already occurred in China of aggravated manslaughter and even of deliberate killing of the natives by foreigners, whose crimes have been punished by simple fines or mere deportation or short imprisonment; while foreigners strenuously insist on full justice when life is taken by the natives, or maiming with intent to kill.[1]

Some of the cases before the American consular courts have revealed the most extravagant leniency. An American, who entered a Chinese tailor shop, knocked down a boy, seized some clothing, and fired a shot at the protesting tailor, was fined $5 and told to leave Shanghai.[2] Two American sailors, who entered a Chinese dwelling and terrified the occupants, were fined $15 each. The consul

---

[1] *Foreign Relations*, 1865, Part 2, p. 454.
[2] U.S. People *vs*. Nash, *North-China Herald*, May 14, 1903.

severely told the defendants that they must behave themselves.[1]
The Demenil case in 1907 arose over an American who unlawfully
seized a gun from a Chinese soldier and fired in his direction in order,
as alleged, to frighten him.   The shot killed a near-by Tibetan lama.
The accused was acquitted by the United States Court for China
on the grounds that there was no criminal intent.[2]   The Chinese
Foreign Office protested in this case:

> After thus taking human life he is not convicted of any crime, and is
> not even fined.   The great wrong done the murdered man is not in the
> least atoned for.   When the people of Ssu-ch'uan and Yünnan hear of this
> the hair will rise on their heads.[3]

Leniency of this kind is to be contrasted with the strong demands
for the execution of Chinese leaders of riots against foreigners and
even, in some cases, for the execution of Chinese officials who have
failed to maintain order.[4]

Movements for Abolition of Extraterritoriality.   With the rise of
the new nationalism in China efforts have been made to abolish
extraterritoriality.[5]   At the Paris Conference of 1919 and again at
the Washington Conference of 1921–1922 China asked for its
termination.   The abolition of extraterritoriality has been a
principal plank in the program of Kuomintang.   Great Britain in
1902, the United States in 1903, and several other powers in succeeding years have agreed to the eventual abrogation of the system.
Article XV of the American treaty of 1903 provides:

> The Government of China having expressed a strong desire to reform
> its judicial system and to bring it into accord with that of Western nations,
> the United States agrees to give every assistance to such reform and will
> also be prepared to relinquish extra-territorial rights when satisfied that
> the state of the Chinese laws, the arrangements for their administration,
> and other considerations warrant it in so doing.[3]

At the Washington Conference it was decided that a commission
should inquire into the matter of extraterritoriality.   In 1926 the

---

[1] U.S. People *vs.* McCoy and Tyler, *North-China Herald*, July 14, 1905,
p. 100.

[2] U.S. *vs.* Henry N. Demenil, *North-China Herald*, Dec. 6, 1907, p. 606.

[3] *Foreign Relations*, 1909, p. 56.

[4] For a full statement of other Chinese objections to extraterritoriality, see
WILLOUGHBY, *op. cit.*, II: 660–668.

[5] HORNBECK, *China Today: Political*, pp. 452–456; BLAKESLEE, *The Pacific
Area*, pp. 20–33.

[6] *Treaties, etc., of the U.S.*, I: 269.

commission met under the chairmanship of Silas Strawn, an American lawyer. After some investigation it asked for the elimination of specific evils that have grown up under extraterritoriality and recommended further reforms in Chinese judicial administration. Among other things it suggested that the Chinese judiciary be made independent of coercion by the other branches of the government; that certain enumerated modernized codes of law should be completed and placed in operation; that the system of modern courts,[1] prisons, and detention houses should be extended; and that adequate financial provision should be made for the maintenance of the machinery of justice. The commission declared that when these reforms should be carried out the relinquishment of extraterritoriality by the powers would be warranted.[2]

On December 28, 1929, the Nationalist government issued a declaration abolishing extraterritoriality as of January 1, 1930; but it was not strong enough to put the decree into effect. The United States, following the lead of Great Britian, stated that it was willing to consider the date of January 1, 1930, as that on which the gradual abolition of extraterritoriality "should be regarded as having commenced in principle."[3] The United States declared on two occasions at about this time that it would be willing to negotiate for the gradual abolition of extraterritoriality in China either as to particular areas or as to particular kinds of jurisdiction or both "provided that such gradual relinquishment proceeds at the same time as steps are taken and improvements are achieved by the Chinese Government in the enactment and effective enforcement of laws based on modern concepts of jurisprudence."[4]

THE QUESTION OF JOINT ACTION WITH OTHER POWERS

From the time of the first treaty with China in 1844 the United States has been confronted with the question as to whether it should pursue a lone policy in the advancement of American interests or should join with a concert of powers in enforcing its policies against the Chinese government. The interests of the United States have been in some respects identical with those of the other powers. On the other hand, the methods used by the European governments,

---

[1] For a list of the existing modern courts see *The China Year Book*, 1933, pp. 700–704.

[2] *Report of the Commission on Extraterritoriality in China*, pp. 107–108, Govt. Printing Office, Washington, 1926.

[3] MORSE, HOSEA BALLOU, and HARLEY FARNSWORTH MCNAIR, *Far Eastern International Relations*, p. 754, Houghton Mifflin Company, Boston, 1931.

[4] Dept. of State, *Press Releases*, Nov. 16, 1929, p. 62; Nov. 15, 1930, p. 327.

which have long been accustomed to oversea imperialism, have not
been suited to the requirements of American policy.

Influences Making For and Against a Joint Policy.   In company
with the commercially ambitious nations of Europe the United
States has at various times sought open ports in China; the maintenance of a treaty tariff; the abolition of likin, or internal transit
taxes; the right of diplomatic representation at Peking; and the
abolition of the humiliating kowtow, a form of prostration which was
at first required of foreign diplomats at audiences with the Emperor.
Citizens and subjects of all of the powers have been victims of
mob violence and the demands for protection and redress have been
common to all.   The foreign business and diplomatic community
in China long ago developed a common psychological approach to
the Chinese problem.   The Chinese were regarded as inferior to the
peoples of the West.   The American business group has sometimes
desired joint action with militaristically inclined powers.   Thus
in 1927 the American Chamber of Commerce in Shanghai declared:

> We believe that immediate concerted action by the powers to restore a
> condition of security for foreign lives and property in all the treaty ports
> and to recover all foreign properties which have been destroyed or con-
> fiscated will have a far-reaching influence throughout China to the ultimate
> benefit of the Chinese people.   This result should not be difficult to attain
> with the naval forces now in Chinese waters.[1]

But the Department of State has rather consistently ignored the
demands for joint military action although it has been willing to
cooperate in many instances where the use of force has not been
involved.   The department, in contrast with some European foreign
offices, has banked heavily upon Chinese good will.

Refusals to Join a Concert of Powers for Military Action.   The
circumstances at the time of the first American treaty with China
were such as to bring out strongly the difference in methods between
the United States and Great Britain.   The British had just forced a
humiliating peace at the end of a war waged for dubious reasons.
The British treaty of 1842 contained a clause providing for an
indemnity of $6,000,000 for opium taken by the Chinese officials
from British subjects in Canton, and no amount of explanation on
the part of English writers or parliamentarians was able to efface
this condemning clause.   The American special commissioner,
Caleb Cushing, was instructed to make clear to China that the aims
of the United States were those of peace and that we did not seek

[1] *N.Y. Times*, Apr. 4, 1927.

territorial gain.[1] It was expected that by a peaceful approach the United States might obtain the same advantages as had been accorded to Great Britain without the financial burden or ill-feeling entailed in an expensive war. And this, indeed, proved to be the case. Again, in 1857, the United States emphasized its singleness of method. In that year war was being waged against China by Great Britain and France. The British provocation was provided by the incident of the Lorcha *Arrow*, a Chinese-owned schooner, once registered under the British flag and whose registry had expired when the boat was seized by the Chinese at Canton for piracy. Great Britain made a formal request that the United States should join with the two European allies and give at least moral support to the war which was conducted partially to redress commercial and diplomatic grievances. The United States refused to join and Secretary of State Marcy urged upon the American legation the most punctilious neutrality. The sympathies of the American colony in Canton were with their British colleagues; and under the influence of this sentiment, Dr. Parker, the American chargé, recommended American participation. He even suggested a plan, which originated with some American businessmen, that Formosa be seized as a pledge of a satisfactory settlement. Parker was instructed from Washington, however, that "the British Government evidently have objects beyond those contemplated by the United States, and we ought not be drawn along with it, however anxious it may be for our cooperation."[2] Tyler Dennett points out that it would have been impossible to procure authorization from Congress for military action in China. "Public opinion," he said, "would have seen in them only a trick by which England was seeking the aid of the United States in her efforts to secure the legalization of the opium trade."[3] William B. Reed, who was sent as minister about this time, was instructed to cooperate with the other powers only by means of peaceful representations. He reported that the French and British were disappointed at the American decision and that the British were "especially irritable . . . at their inability to involve the United States in their unworthy quarrel."[4]

Instances of Military Cooperation. It was not until 1900 that the United States participated in a joint military action in China;

[1] FOSTER, JOHN W., *American Diplomacy in the Orient*, p. 80, Houghton Mifflin Company, Boston, 1903.

[2] *Ibid.*, p. 229; CALLAHAN, JAMES MORTON, *American Relations in the Pacific and the Far East*, 1784–1900, p. 99, Johns Hopkins Press, Baltimore, 1901.

[3] *Op. cit.*, p. 304.

[4] Quoted in FOSTER, *op. cit.*, p. 233.

and then our cooperation was given under the provocation of an unusual emergency, the Boxer uprising.[1] In that year the increase of hostility toward foreigners on the part of the Chinese resulted in a number of antiforeign demonstrations and riots, culminating in the attack upon the legations in Peking. In the effort to clear the way for relief the Chinese forts at Taku were taken by the foreign vessels on June 17, 1900. The United States, however, did not join in the assault. In the next month American troops cooperated in the capture of Tientsin, and United States soldiers brought from Manila marched in the relief expedition to Peking. The legations were relieved on August 17. The American forces did not take part in any of the subsequent punitive expeditions, but the United States was a party to the Protocol of 1901 which arranged the terms of settlement. This country has in later years participated in joint representations for the enforcement of the protocol, as it did in March, 1926, when the powers protested to China regarding fortifications and impediments to commerce at the mouth of the Pei River.[2]

The general policy of refusal to be drawn into the various military operations of the powers has had its beneficial results. In recent years it has come to be understood that policies of force are ordinarily not productive of commercial profit in the face of rising Chinese nationalism. In 1925 and 1926 the United States was fortunately not connected with such incidents as the Shameen massacre and the Wanhsien bombardment and was not therefore a principal victim of the anti-British boycott movement which proved so disastrous to the trade of English merchants. In 1927, however, American destroyers joined with British vessels in shelling a portion of Nanking during antiforeign depredations by Nationalist troops.

Instances of Nonmilitary Cooperation. Aside from military expeditions the United States has cooperated with the powers in China in a number of ways. Joint representations have been made regarding antiforeign violence. Thus at Tientsin in 1870, after the killing of some nineteen foreigners, mostly French missionaries, the United States united with the other powers in making severe

[1] There had been one precedent for a joint military expedition in the Far East, that in Japan in 1864 to coerce the Prince of Nagato who had interfered with commerce passing through the Straits of Shimonoseki. In that case the United States joined in a naval expedition with Great Britain, France, and Holland, this country contributing one vessel among seventeen in the expedition.

[2] *Current History*, XXIV: 311 (May, 1926).

demands for the punishment of the rioters and the officials. Eighteen alleged culprits were eventually decapitated and twenty-three others were deported.[1] The joint representations did not go as far, however, as the demand of the French chargé d'affaires that two of the Chinese officials should be decapitated.[2] Another instance of a joint demand for reparation occurred following the Nanking incident of 1927 when the United States in unison with the governments of Great Britain, France, Italy, and Japan demanded adequate punishment of the responsible troops, an apology from the commander in chief of the Nationalist forces, and adequate financial reparation.[3]

The cooperation of the United States in the government of the International Settlement at Shanghai is worthy of mention. The American consul at Shanghai joined with the other members of the consular body in that city in 1854 in drawing up land regulations regarding foreign property in the foreign concessions. In 1863 the American settlement of Hongkew was merged with the British settlement to form the International Settlement. In 1864 and 1869 the American minister agreed to regulations drawn up by the diplomatic corps which became a sort of constitution for the government of the new municipality and which excluded the Chinese within the area from a share in the government. The United States has thus been associated in the government of this strange, little, semiautonomous political unit, established in the commercial heart of China. American sentiment with regard to the settlement seems, however, to have diverged at times from that of the British. American consuls in the 1850's argued against British opposition that the sovereignty of the concession was Chinese, that land titles should be conferred by the Chinese, and that Chinese subjects should be permitted to hold property in the area.[4] In more recent years the American sentiment has been more sympathetic to the Chinese than has that of the British or Japanese. An international commission, consisting of judges of American, British, and Japanese nationality, in 1925 investigated the shootings which had occurred during that year in Shanghai. The British and Japanese judges found that the settlement officials were not at fault; but the Ameri-

[1] WILLIAMS, S. WELLS, *The Middle Kingdom*, II: 704–705, Charles Scribner's Sons, New York, 1898.

[2] For this incident see *Foreign Relations*, 1871–1872, pp. 69, 358, 377.

[3] MORSE and McNAIR, *op. cit.*, p. 737.

[4] MONROE, PAUL, *China: A Nation in Evolution*, pp. 247–248, The Macmillan Company, New York, 1928.

can member, Judge E. F. Johnson of the Philippine Supreme Court, placed a certain amount of blame upon the authorities for not adequately estimating the danger and for not taking the proper precautions. The municipal council permitted the police commissioner and inspector to resign and eventually paid to the Chinese the sum of $150,000 silver.[1] Mr. Fessenden, an American member of the municipal council, presented a resolution to the Shanghai rate-payers on April 14, 1926, recommending Chinese representation upon the council. Today the Chinese have five council members as compared with five for the British residents, two for the Japanese, and two for the Americans.[2]

Cooperation Through International Organization. The pressure of events in a unifying world has been almost everywhere toward cooperation rather than singleness of action; and a new type of common consultation has been gradually developing. Action through international conferences and through the League of Nations has been resorted to with regard to the Far East as it has been in connection with other regions. In the Washington Conference of 1921–1922 and the Peking Tariff Conference of 1926 the powers discussed their common problems regarding China. Conference and consultation by many powers are to be clearly distinguished from the older policy of military alliances. In the Washington Conference the Anglo-Japanese alliance was terminated and in its place the Four-Power Treaty was substituted. This treaty, agreed to by the United States, Great Britain, France, and Japan, provides that if a controversy shall arise between two of these powers relating to their insular possessions in the Pacific, the parties shall invite the other High Contracting Parties to a joint conference to which the whole matter shall be referred for adjustment. If the territories of any one of the parties shall be affected by the action of an outside party, the four shall communicate with one another in order to arrive at an understanding as to the most effective measures to be taken to meet the situation. The Four-Power Treaty does not apply to China and there are many who believe that it can have little effect in case of difficulties over the Pacific possessions. But even if it has done nothing more than to terminate the alliance between Japan and Great Britain, it marks a triumph for the newer diplomacy. In more recent years the work

[1] MORSE and McNAIR, *op. cit.*, p. 726.

[2] For a survey of the problems of the International Settlement see LOCKWOOD, WILLIAM W., JR., "The International Settlement at Shanghai, 1924–34," *American Political Science Review*, XXVIII: 1030 (December, 1934).

of the League of Nations for the improvement of Chinese sanitary and economic conditions and for the maintenance of peace illustrates the trend of cooperative action in the East.[1] The United States has been associated with the League agencies to a certain degree in attempts to settle the Manchurian affair and in the disposition of the Shanghai question in 1932.[2] The advantages to the United States of cooperation through international conferences or through the institutions of international organization are that common problems are thus dealt with by common action. But such cooperation is not apt to draw this country into a joint imperialistic aggression, which, by its threats to Chinese sovereignty, would be likely to defeat the fundamental policies of the United States in the Far East. The danger of involvement in expensive military operations has grown with the rise of Japan. For this reason the attempt to adjust the affairs of Eastern Asia by joint action with world organization may provide a surer method of avoiding a costly entanglement or war than policies pursued by the United States alone.

[1] For the beginning of American participation, see "The United States and the League of Nations during 1933," *Geneva Special Studies*, pp. 14–15.

[2] See pp. 236*ff.*

CHAPTER IX

THE PHILIPPINES: A STUDY IN IMPERIALISM AND RELINQUISHMENT

THE PROBLEM

The Conquistadores Are Challenged by the Domestic Lobby.
The experiment of governing the distant and alien people of the
Philippines has been an education in the effects of imperialistic
adventure; and it offers a curiously interesting demonstration of the
manner in which influential factions within a ruling nation act and
react to give a resultant direction to national policies. It is almost
predictable that particular groups will show certain definite reactions
to the imperialistic situation. Investors and officials who have
gone forth to reside in the conquered land ordinarily manifest
satisfaction with the results of the occupation. Forced into a
compact community by the pressure of surrounding aliens, they
develop a stubborn imperialistic psychology, more extreme than
anything of its kind that can possibly exist in the home country.[1]
Shipowners desire the maintenance of a control which may bring
them aid through navigation laws. Groups which dream of military power are reluctant to yield colonial conquests. Domestic
producers who feel the competition of colonial products brought into
the home market become nationalistic and sometimes anti-imperialistic. All these have performed their roles in the drama of the
Philippines but with an emphasis by the domestic producers which
is new in history.

The vote of Congress to give freedom to the Philippines is a
unique act in modern times. In no other case has a rising power
reached a voluntary decision to give independence to a fully annexed
territory of such importance. The novel features which have
distinguished this situation have been:

1. The United States as the first of the well-developed large-
land nation-states possesses an internal economic domain and

[1] For example Stuart Chase reports such an attitude of Americans in
Mexico where Ambassador Morrow's intelligent and sympathetic policy was
resented in the American colony. *Mexico, A Study of Two Americas*, pp.
270, 278, The Macmillan Company, New York, 1931.

market which dwarfs in comparison the resources and purchasing power of even such a considerable territory as that of the Philippine Islands. The groups attached to our continental economic enterprises have shown a power in Congressional lobbying considerably greater than that manifested by those attached to the development of the Philippines. When strong domestic interests finally came into a well-defined conflict with those of the islands, the home forces triumphed. Economic nationalism in this conflict was too strong for economic imperialism. Such a situation is distinctly in contrast with that which has existed in certain small-land nation-states which have developed huge colonial domains through sea power. In such countries as Great Britain and Holland, trade, investment, shipping, and civil service oversea activities have been of great consequence as compared with those interests which produce for the domestic market. A few decades hence when the economic pressures moving outward from the United States will probably have created much larger investments abroad, the balance of interests will be different; and in such a conflict other results might conceivably be expected.

2. The period of history in which the Philippines were acquired by the United States was relatively unfavorable to the long-time expansion of a Western power in the East. By 1898 the trend toward European domination of Asia, which had lasted for some four centuries, had reached its furthest point. Japan had become a strong power and was casting off Western controls. In other Eastern countries the sentiment of nationality was beginning to stir. During the early years of the twentieth century Asiatic nationalism increased. At the Washington Conference of 1921–1922 the United States agreed not to increase fortifications in the Philippines. The possibility of a Far Eastern war due to our possessions, which would cost the United States hundreds of times as much as any profits which might be derived from Asiatic exploitation, hung like a pall over our imperialism. In fact the Philippine account of the United States is already in the red by much more than a half billion dollars without counting the greater liability of a possible Far Eastern war which may accrue because of our connection with the islands.

3. The United States still retains to some extent that sympathetic regard for the independence of small countries which began with the American Revolution and was later sustained by suspicions of European imperialism in Latin America. The importance of the independence fixation in its bearings on the Phillippine question is

difficult to appraise but it has doubtless been considerable. The
1900 presidential campaign placed imperialism on the defensive.
From the time of McKinley all presidents have been forced to
explain the Philippine policy of the United States in terms of ultimate independence. When finally certain powerful domestic
economic interests became anxious to shut out Philippine competition by granting independence, they found in American tradition
the emotional fanfare which they could sound in answer to the
patriots who spoke of the onward destiny of the flag or as a rebuttal
to the owners of Philippine investments who talked about the sacred
duty we owe to our brother Filipinos.

The Physical and Social Background. The Philippines are an
archipelago of some 7,083 islands, the chief of which are Luzon and
Mindanao. The total land area of the islands is 114,000 square
miles and the population numbers almost 13,000,000. From the
standpoint of population the Philippines occupy a prominent place
among American territories, being far greater than all the other
insular possessions together and almost equal to the nine republics
of the Caribbean region in which the United States has shown such a
warm interest. The Filipinos, with the exception of some few
thousand aborigines or Negritos, are of Malay stock[1] and migrated
to the islands from the south. They had established a culture of
their own, including written languages, before the time of Magellan.
The Spaniards brought their institutions and language to the islands,
but native dialects are still spoken by the great majority of the
Filipinos. The early native literature was almost entirely destroyed
under Spanish rule. Eight major dialects and some seventy-nine or
eighty minor dialects are spoken. The educated Filipino under-
stands Spanish, English, and at least one native dialect. The basis
of the Philippine law is Spanish except that business law and, to a
large extent, procedural law are from American sources.

GOVERNMENTAL AND ECONOMIC DEVELOPMENTS UNDER AMERICAN RULE

Recent Political History. In 1896 the decadence of Spain as a
colonial power was manifested by revolutions in Cuba and the
Philippines. In the latter, José Rizal, gifted author and Philippine
national hero, was executed. The revolt was suspended on the
understanding that Aguinaldo and thirty-five of his principal

---

[1] BARROWS, DAVID P., *A History of the Philippines*, Chap. II, American
Book Company, New York, 1905; HAWES, HARRY B., *Philippine Uncertainty*,
pp. 32*ff.*, D. Appleton-Century Company, Inc., New York, 1932.

followers should leave the islands for Hong Kong. With the coming of the Spanish-American War and the defeat of the Spanish fleet in Manila Bay on May 1, 1898, Aguinaldo and his followers returned. The Aguinaldo forces were supplied with arms by the United States and they cooperated with the American troops in driving Spain from the islands. The Philippine Republic, proclaimed in 1898, was not recognized by the United States; and open warfare between Filipinos and Americans broke out in February, 1899. This one-sided conflict lasted until the capture of Aguinaldo on March 23, 1901. The military government set up by the United States after the capture of Manila was gradually liberalized by successive stages as follows:[1]

1. In 1900 the legislative function was transferred from the military forces to a civil commission under the headship of William Howard Taft. In 1901 the executive power was handed over to the head of the commission, who acted as civil governor.

2. In 1907 a legislative assembly elected by the natives was set up and became the lower house of the legislature, acting in conjunction with the civil commission which was the upper house.

3. In 1913 Filipinos were appointed to the commission in sufficient numbers to give them control of that body and thus of both houses of the legislature.

4. In 1916 the Jones Act provided for an elective Senate and House of Representatives and an appointive Governor General. Two senators and nine members of the lower house were appointed by the Governor General to represent non-Christian districts. The act announced the policy of freeing the islands as soon as a stable form of government should be established.

Filipinization of the civil service followed the liberalization of the form of government. In 1913 there were more than 2,600 Americans holding civil service positions. By 1930 the number had been reduced to 456 of which 282 were employed in education.[2] The policy of Filipinization was opposed by the American community in the islands;[3] but the opposition of officials and investors could not stay the movement which was directed from Washington.

[1] FORBES, W. CAMERON, *The Philippine Islands*, Houghton Mifflin Company, Boston, 1928 (2 vols.); WORCESTER, DEAN C., *The Philippines, Past and Present*, The Macmillan Company, New York, 1914 (2 vols.); HARRISON, FRANCIS BURTON, *The Corner-Stone of Philippine Independence*, Century Company, New York, 1922.

[2] *Independence for the Philippine Islands*, Hearings before the Committee on Insular Affairs, House of Representatives, 72d Cong., 1st Sess., p. 39, Govt. Printing Office, Washington, 1932 (cited hereafter as *House Hearings*); FORBES, *The Philippine Islands*, II: 467.

[3] HARRISON, *The Corner-Stone of Philippine Independence*, p. 85.

Political liberalization was accompanied by striking developments in many other respects. The promotion of education in the islands constituted one of the most brilliant colonial achievements in modern times. In 1898 there were some 2,000 schools in the islands. By 1930 this number had been increased to 7,821 public schools and 621 private schools.[1] In the school year 1899–1900 the enrollment in the public schools was 6,900 and in 1932–1933 the number was 1,204,375. In addition there were 93,502 in the private schools and colleges, making a total of 1,297,877.[2] A contrast between the Philippines and other similarly located colonial peoples made a few years ago showed the following percentages of the entire populations in school attendance: The Philippines, 9.26; the Dutch East Indies, 3; Korea, 2.7; and French Indo-China, 1. The Philippines in 1930 expended about 28 per cent of their total budget for education as compared with an expenditure in colonies of other powers approximating 4 or 5 per cent.[3] In addition to progress in politics and education, an interesting story could also be told about the revolutionary achievements made from 1898 to 1935 in the field of public health.

Economic Ties Created. Meanwhile tariff legislation at Washington had been giving a contrary direction to the destiny of the islands by making them more and more dependent upon the United States. When the Philippines were acquired from Spain, it was the avowed intention of the American government to maintain equal commercial opportunities to all nations. "Asking only the open door for ourselves, we are ready to accord the open door to others," said President McKinley in instructing the peace commissioners in 1898.[4] For some time the open door was nominally maintained. A stipulation of the 1898 treaty gave to Spain equal tariff treatment for ten years, and the same equality was extended to all other nations. Even during this decade, however, the trade was partially closed to foreigners through the practice of giving products which were peculiar to the United States a lower tariff rating. In 1909, when the ten-year agreement with Spain expired, the door was slammed shut. A tariff law was passed giving American goods free entry into the islands while a protective tariff was

---

[1] *House Hearings*, p. 33.

[2] *Annual Report of the Governor General of the Philippines Islands*, 1933, House Document No. 32, 74th Cong., 1st Sess., pp. 47, 55.

[3] Buell, Raymond Leslie, *Philippine Independence*, Foreign Policy Association, *Information Service*, Vol. VI, Nos. 3 and 4 (Apr. 30, 1930), p. 43.

[4] *Foreign Relations*, 1898, p. 907.

erected against goods coming in from foreign countries. Philippine products, with some exceptions, were given free entry into the United States; and in 1913 all barriers to Philippine exports to this country were removed. The effect of this policy has been to give an artificial stimulus to Philippine-American trade and thus to bind the islands to the United States by strong commercial ties that cannot be broken without considerable disruption in Philippine economic life.

The effects of the legislation can be traced in the commercial statistics of this period. Before the occupation of the islands the trade of the United States with the Philippines was negligible. In 1893 this country sold to the Philippines merchandise valued at $956,706, or 6 per cent of the imports of the islands.[1] In 1933 imports from the United States amounted to $43,540,000, or 58.3 per cent of the total. The share of the United States in the Philippine exports is even greater. In 1933 we received $91,314,000, or 86.3 per cent of the goods shipped from the islands. Philippine agriculture has been developed in large part for the purpose of supplying the American market. Sugar, coconut products, Manila hemp, and tobacco are the main exports to the United States. Two of these products are worthy of brief consideration in order to illustrate the economic forces which have entered into the political problem.

Sugar. For the five years previous to the overthrow of Spanish rule the exportation of sugar from the Philippines to all countries had averaged 230,000 long tons per annum. Free access to the American market gave Philippine sugar an advantage over Cuban sugar, which paid a tariff. Production was stimulated; and by 1930 the exportation had risen to 744,000 tons, of which 671,000 tons was sent to the United States. A radical increase in sugar acreage in the islands resulted. In 1910 the sugar plantations included 205,425 acres, which acreage was tripled by 1930 when 639,804 acres were planted.[2] Large importations of Philippine sugar finally caused the beet and cane sugar industry in the United States to favor independence for the islands in order to place the Philippines in a position where their products would be forced to pay the regular American tariff. The existence of the new industry in the Philippines, however, creates a situation which will result in economic suffering when sugar exports are subjected to tariffs in the United States.

[1] *Monthly Summary of the Commerce of the Philippine Islands, July, August, and September*, 1899, p. 26, Govt. Printing Office, Washington, 1900.
[2] *Ibid.*, p. 259.

Coconut Oil. Coconut oil, derived from copra or the kernel of the coconut, is used for the manufacture of soap and oleomargarine. To a much less extent it is used in candy making.[1] Free entry of Philippine oil, coupled with a duty of 2 cents per pound on the foreign product, gave to the insular industry such an advantage in the United States that it captured the American market. In 1929 the Philippines exported 420,019,000 pounds of coconut oil, of which 415,981,000, or 99.04 per cent, came to the United States. In addition they sold to us 285,756,000 pounds of copra, from which 181,855,000 pounds of oil was obtainable.[2] The American market created planting and crushing industries in the islands and these were opposed to independence. Vegetable oil and animal fat producers in the United States, however, became converts to the independence movement.

THE CLASH OF INTERESTS OVER THE PHILIPPINE QUESTION— THE OPPOSITION TO INDEPENDENCE

American Investors in the Philippines. American investors in the Philippines have constituted a body which in the past has opposed the liberalization of American rule. When independence measures were before Congress from 1932 until 1934, investing interests advised strongly against any policy of freeing the islands within a short period of time. One witness, representing this opposition before the House committee, possessed investments in Philippine sugar and rubber and had previously been president of the Philippine-American Chamber of Commerce of New York. Another was president of the Manila Electric Company and the Philippine Railway Company. A third represented coconut oil interests in the Philippines and alleged that the granting of independence would ruin the industry.[3] American investments in the islands have been variously estimated from $150,000,000 to $250,000,000, rather small sums as compared with the domestic investments affected.

Exporting Interests. Exporters have looked to the Philippines as a market and have seen in the city of Manila a possible distributing center for the vast quantities of goods which they hope to sell on the continent of Asia. The export idea was in the mind of President McKinley when the decision to hold the islands was being made following the Spanish-American War; and it played its part in

[1] *Ibid.*, p. 318.
[2] *Ibid.*, p. 65.
[3] *Ibid.*, pp. 201, 239, 329.

the campaign of 1900, which was largely devoted to the issue of the Philippines. Senator Marcus A. Hanna, chairman of the Republican National Committee, favored retaining the Philippines as a base for commercial operations in China. "If it is commercialism," he said, "to want the possession of a strategic point giving the American people an opportunity to maintain a foothold in the markets of that great Eastern country, for God's sake let us have commercialism."[1] Exporters have from time to time demanded that the tariff be framed in such a way as to give them considerable advantages in the Philippine market over foreign producers. In the fight over independence in 1932, however, they seem not to have mobilized any great strength. Like the investors they were dwarfed by the larger interests which favored independence.

Americans Resident in Asia—Advocates of a Policy for Prestige. The feeling that relinquishment of the islands would be a blow to the international standing or "face" of Americans in the Orient, whether investors, officials, or military officers, is strongly held by many who have served or resided in the Far East. Secretary of State Stimson, who once filled the position of governor general of the islands and was, therefore, in a position to understand the feelings of the American community, said that relinquishment of the Philippines would appear to every foreign eye as "a demonstration of selfish cowardice and futility on our part."[2] Nicholas Roosevelt, one-time vice-governor of the Philippines, who served also as newspaper representative in the East and was in touch with American opinion in Asia, declared that the loss of the Philippines would injure the prestige of the United States in the Orient. Respect for all things American would decrease and the actual protection of the lives and property of United States citizens would become more difficult.[3] The prestige or "face" of the small number of Americans living in Asia has, however, been subordinated to other considerations in

[1] REYES, JOSÉ S., *Legislative History of America's Economic Policy toward the Philippines*, p. 38, Columbia University Studies in History, Economics, and Public Law, Vol. 106, No. 2.

[2] Quoted in *House Hearings*, p. 388. "A great many people, especially the 'old hands' of the Orient, believe the United States would not only antagonize the European powers holding colonies in the Orient if she granted independence to the Philippines, but that she would lose 'face' with Asiatic peoples and would have much difficulty in maintaining her position in that part of the world." VEATCH, ROY, "Strategic Position in the Far East," *Current History*, XXXV: 767–768 (March, 1932).

[3] "Philippine Independence and Peace in the Pacific," *Foreign Affairs*, VIII: 413 (April, 1930).

Congress. The attention of congressmen, for political reasons, has
naturally been centered upon the great domestic interests whose
lobbies in Washington have favored independence.

The Military Influence. Military officers and War Department
officials have usually presented a group view which has been opposed
to independence. Perhaps this view can be traced to the attitude
of military officers toward the Filipinos during the campaigns for
the suppression of the insurrection of 1899–1901. Soldiers, who
face death constantly in an alien jungle, are forced to harden their
hearts toward the enemy. When William Howard Taft went to
the islands in 1900 at the head of the Second Philippine Commission and announced the policy of "the Philippines for the
Filipino," he came into many serious clashes with the military
command, which did not look favorably upon the policy.[1] A later
military view is expressed in an article written in 1930 by Major
General Henry T. Allen, who had seen seven years of service in the
islands. General Allen declared that naval bases and distributing
centers are essential to the future of the United States in the
Pacific and that our moral obligations to the Filipinos should
prompt us to retain control.[2] In 1932, when a proposal for independence was before Congress, Secretary of War Hurley testified:
"The War Department believes that the enactment of the bill in
question, or of any similar legislation, would be highly inexpedient."
He stated that to relinquish the Philippines in accordance with the
bill would be to "break faith with those who died" in the military
service in the islands.[3]

INTERESTS FAVORING INDEPENDENCE

Agriculture. The domestic groups which bore the brunt of the
fight for Philippine independence during the recent contest were
nothing less than the combined lobbies of agriculture and labor.
Agricultural products which American farmers have sold in the
islands have been far less in value than those which have been
imported from the islands. Agricultural organizations presenting
their views to the House Committee on Insular Affairs in favor of
the independence measure in 1932 included: the National Grange,
the National Farmers' Union, the American Farm Bureau Feder-

[1] HARRISON, *op. cit.*, pp. 36, 37.

[2] "The Philippines: America's Duty to Retain Control," *Current History*,
XXXII: 283 (May, 1930).

[3] *House Hearings*, pp. 394, 407. The Hare bill then under consideration
would have provided for independence after a five-year period of transition.

ation, the National Cooperative Milk Producers' Federation, the National Dairy Union, the National Beet Growers' Association, the Texas Cottonseed Crushers' Association, the Oklahoma Cottonseed Crushers' Association, and the *American Agriculturist*. A representative of the sugar beet industry declared that some 800,000 tons of sugar was imported annually from the Philippine Islands free of duty and in competition with the beet sugar products of American high-priced labor. The beet sugar industry, which was thus threatened with annihilation, employed more than 200,000 people.[1] Senator Broussard of Louisiana appeared before the committee urging independence on behalf of the cane sugar growers of his state.[2] The dairy interests favored independence so that the regular duty of 3 cents per pound might be placed upon Philippine coconut oil which goes into the making of oleomargarine. The cottonseed crushing industry desired protection against coconut oil which competes with cottonseed oil in soap manufacture and oleomargarine production. Thus the dairy industry and its old rival the cottonseed industry joined hands to exclude from the American dinner table their common enemy from across the Pacific.

Labor. The legislative representative of the American Federation of Labor urged independence before the committee and cited resolutions passed at the annual convention of the federation favoring this action.[3] The A. F. of L. desired to shut out from the American market certain articles manufactured by cheap labor in the Philippines (this attitude being largely due to the influence of the cigarmakers) and also wished to exclude the competition of Filipino immigrants. Filipino competition was said to exist in railway section work and in hotel labor. It was contended that it would be unconstitutional to shut out Filipino labor so long as the Philippines were an American territory. The right of immigration, it was urged, was one of the fundamental rights guaranteed by the Constitution to the inhabitants of the territories according to the decisions in the Insular Cases. Furthermore, restriction was not politically practicable without a guarantee of independence. Labor was heartily joined by civic organizations on the Pacific coast in seeking restriction of immigration through independence. The whole California congressional delegation was for the measure.

Party Politics and Independence. The Democratic party has been strongly behind the movement for Philippine independence for

[1] *House Hearings*, pp. 158*ff*.
[2] *Ibid.*, p. 425.
[3] *Ibid.*, pp. 233*ff*.

a number of reasons. The doctrines of Thomas Jefferson give a theoretical basis for independence. The Democratic party has been largely the party of agriculture, and agriculture has lobbied for independence. Also in 1898 and 1900 the party was placed in the position of opposing the Republican annexation of the islands. At that time the Democrats adopted an anti-imperialist position with regard to the Philippines. The Democrats passed the Jones Act of 1916. In 1933, when the Hawes-Cutting Act was passed, only one Democratic vote was recorded against the measure in each house.

CONGRESS VOTES FOR INDEPENDENCE

The anti-imperialist forces in the United States, being supported by the powerful lobbies of agriculture and labor, swept the legions of imperialism from the field. In 1933 the principal victory was won when the Hawes-Cutting bill was passed over the veto of President Hoover. The Philippine legislature refused to accept the terms of the act, however, and it became void. Under the recommendations of Franklin D. Roosevelt, Congress passed the Tydings-McDuffie bill in the following year. This act, which was accepted by the Philippine legislature, provided for the adoption of a constitution by the Philippine people. After the acceptance of the constitution by the President of the United States an election was held and a president was inaugurated. Thereupon an intermediate period of ten years commenced. During these ten years, known as the commonwealth period, the United States is represented at Manila by a high commissioner instead of a governor general. On the first Fourth of July after the conclusion of the ten-year period, the islands are to become independent. Military bases in the Philippines are to be given up by the United States and the question of the maintenance of naval bases is to be left to negotiation between the two governments.

The Economic Arrangements for the Commonwealth Period. The tariff provisions for the ten-year period have been widely criticized as unequal and unfair. In the beginning the United States admits annually free of duty from the Philippines 850,000 long tons of sugar, 200,000 tons of coconut oil, and 3,000,000 pounds of cordage and similar fibers. Shipments above these quotas are subjected to the regular American duties. From the sixth to the tenth years of the period the Philippine government is required to assess an export tax on products sent to the United States, beginning with 5 per cent of the American tariff and reaching 25 per cent in the tenth year. After that time, unless a contrary agreement is reached, the entire American tariff will apply against Philippine goods. Meanwhile, during the ten years, American goods are to be shipped into the Philippines free of duty. The inequality of these conditions testifies to the one-sidedness of commercial pressures brought to bear upon the American Congress. As to Philippine immigration, it is provided that the number of Filipinos entering this country during the commonwealth period should be limited to fifty per year.

The Processing Tax on Coconut Oil. Subsequent to the passage of the act and a few days after its acceptance by the Philippine legislature, Congress struck an additional blow at the industry of the islands by imposing a processing tax of 3 cents per pound on coconut oil in the United States. This tax, which operates in the same way as a protective duty, has only added to the injustice of the economic arrangements between the two countries during the commonwealth period. President Roosevelt reluctantly signed the revenue bill containing the tax but later made an unsuccessful attempt through a message to Congress to obtain a repeal of the particular item. The President stated that the coconut oil levy was directly contrary to the intent of the Tydings-McDuffie Independence Act and that it would produce a serious condition among thousands of families in the Philippine Islands.[1]

THE COMMONWEALTH OF THE PHILIPPINES

The Constitution of February 8, 1935. A constitution drawn up by a convention in Manila was completed on February 8, 1935. The document was approved by President Roosevelt and ratified by an overwhelming vote of the Philippine electorate. The constitution, including a Bill of Rights, is modeled largely on that of the United States although the federal system is lacking. There appear also several constitutional modernizations, some of them being taken from American state constitutions. The legislature, or National Assembly, is unicameral, and the membership shall not exceed 120. The assemblymen are chosen every three years; they are apportioned according to population and are elected by popular vote except in the provinces of Sulu, Lanao, and Cotabato, where they are selected "as may be determined by law." The President is elected by direct vote for six years and may not be elected for the following term. He presents a budget to the National Assembly the appropriations of which shall not be increased except as they pertain to the National Assembly and the

[1] Dept. of State, *Press Releases*, June 2, 1934, p. 326.

Judicial Department. He possesses the item veto with regard to appropriation and revenue bills. He nominates and, with the consent of the Commission on Appointments of the National Assembly, appoints the important executive and military officers; but the National Assembly may by law vest the appointment of inferior officers in the President alone, in the courts, or in the heads of departments. A Civil Service shall be provided for; and appointments in that service, except to such positions as are policy-determining, primarily confidential, or highly technical, shall be made only according to merit and fitness to be determined, so far as practicable, by competitive examination. While the form of government is presidential, a feature is embodied which has often been recommended in the United States, *i.e.*, the right of the heads of departments upon their own initiative or upon the request of the National Assembly to appear before and to be heard by the assembly on any matter pertaining to their departments. The Supreme Court possesses the power to pass upon the constitutionality of laws and treaties, but these measures may not be declared unconstitutional without the concurrence of two-thirds of all members of the court.[1]

The Relationship of the Commonwealth to the United States. An ordinance appended to the constitution sets forth the details of the relationship between the Commonwealth and the American government. All citizens of the Philippines owe allegiance to the United States, and the officials of the Commonwealth are required to take an oath to maintain such allegiance.

The United States retains a strong financial control. Trade and tariff relations between the two countries are fixed by the Tydings-McDuffie Act. The public debt of the Commonwealth shall not exceed the limits set by the Congress of the United States. The President of the United States must approve all foreign loans. He has the authority to suspend the taking effect of laws and contracts which, in his judgment, will result in a failure of the Philippine government to fulfill its contracts or to meet the obligations of its public debt. His approval is also necessary for all acts affecting currency, coinage, imports, and exports, as well as immigration.

Foreign affairs are under the direct supervision and control of the United States. This country may also intervene for the preservation of the government of the Philippines, for the protection of life,

---

[1] For a discussion of the constitution see, KALAW, MAXIMO M., "The New Constitution of the Philippine Commonwealth," *Foreign Affairs*, XIII: 687 (July, 1935).

property, and individual liberty, and for the discharge of governmental obligations under the Philippine constitution. The right of the United States is recognized to expropriate property for public uses, to maintain military and other reservations and armed forces in the Philippines, and to call into the service of such armed forces all military organizations of the Commonwealth.

The United States retains some rights of review over the governmental acts of the Philippines. In addition to the previously mentioned right of approval on all acts affecting currency, coinage, imports, exports, and immigration, the President of the United States has a similar right regarding amendments to the Philippine constitution. All acts passed by the National Assembly must be reported to Congress; and all decisions of the courts of the Philippines, including cases involving the constitution of the Philippines, shall be subject to review by the Supreme Court of the United States. The authority of the United States High Commissioner is specifically recognized in the ordinance.

On November 15, 1935, Manuel Quezon, the elected president of the new government, took office. The powers of administration were turned over to the Philippine officials by the United States; and the government of the Commonwealth of the Philippines, which is to prepare for ultimate independence under the Republic of the Philippines on July 4, 1946, was inaugurated.

PART II
ECONOMIC DIPLOMACY

CHAPTER X

EXPORT PROMOTION

PART I. NATIONAL ACTION

THE FAVORABLE BALANCE OF TRADE DOGMA AND THE DEPRESSION

The promotion of sales and the discouragement of purchases, for the purpose of enjoying an excess of exports over imports, have long been popular international trade policies in the Western world. There was a time, during the Middle Ages, when an opposite theory prevailed and it was considered that the restriction of exports and the stimulation of imports would best add to the community wealth. The preference for exports rather than imports, which came to characterize commercial policy under the mercantilist system, was, for obvious reasons, increased by the growing activity of producers. Governmental classes accepted it because it resulted in the importation of gold which was desirable for political reasons. In modern times the increase in industrialization, which is brought about when a nation expands its manufacturing plant to produce for export, has added to national power; and the military superiority of an industrialized nation over an agricultural community has been frequently demonstrated. The stimulation of prosperity by sales abroad has also been a chief reason for attempting to expand exports. Under the profit system the inevitably recurring excess of goods over purchasing power within a community results in a clogging of distribution, the condition being orthodoxically referred to as overproduction. A speeding-up of production through export orders results in freer internal distribution because of larger payments for wages and materials, and this stimulation would be temporarily promoted even if the goods were taken out to sea and dropped overboard. At the time of the entrance of the United States into the World War there was much enthusiasm for loans to the Allies. Part of the lending zeal sprang from the desire to continue huge sales of American goods to the Allied countries and thus to maintain the

164

unprecedented pay rolls and enormous profits which then characterized American industry. The question whether the goods could be ultimately paid for was given little intelligent thought. The ill-fated loans did, however, prevent a slump in American business in 1917 by maintaining our stupendous exports.

As trade grows to large proportions, creditor balances cannot be met by the debtor countries with gold, and this fact leads eventually to the conversion of such balances into foreign loans and investments by the exporting countries. The income from foreign investments, however, together with the income from services rendered to foreigners, such as shipping and banking, finally in well-advanced capitalist countries tends to bring an end to the excess of merchandise exports. Creditor countries must eventually receive payment for various items, such as interest on loans, merchant marine earnings, and banking commissions; and such payments over a period of years can best be made in goods. Previous to the World War some outstanding creditor nations were receiving more goods than they were sending abroad. Great Britain and Holland were examples of creditor-importing nations. Creditor balances continued, but the principal items in these cases were sums due for interest and services.

In the United States, on the other hand, popular opinion clung to the theory that an excess of exports was desirable, even when this country had become a great world creditor. The tariff was raised to the high level of the Smoot-Hawley Act of 1930. Exports were encouraged through diplomacy and through the efforts of the Department of Commerce. Partly because of these governmental efforts but mostly because of the great productive power of the United States, a large excess of exports was maintained; and debtor countries were, in the main, able to pay the balances due to Americans only through additional borrowing. Economists vainly contended that high tariffs and a creditor-nation status were incompatible. A critical British view regarding these policies was expressed by W. T. Layton, editor of the *Economist* of London and a delegate of the British Empire to the World Economic Conference of 1927. Speaking of the large loans abroad by the United States, he said:

But what are the consequences of this phenomenon? The conditions under which this export of capital has taken place are unlike any to which we have hitherto been accustomed. Great Britain, it is true, has previously been a lender on an even greater scale; but Great Britain bought and transported the products of the countries she developed with her capital. Throughout the last fifty years, when she has been so freely developing the distant countries of the world, her trade balance has shown a large visible surplus of imports. The United States, on the other hand, shows to-day a surplus of exports, and, so far at all events as European trade is concerned, she is taking steps to keep out the products of the countries which her capital is developing or restoring.[1]

A Persistent Creditor Balance Conflicts with the Nation-State System. The independence and equality of nation-states is not consistent with the indefinite extension of exports financed through loans by great creditor powers. Such an extension leads to one or more of the following results:

1. Internationalism, or the cooperative action of nations to guard capital interests and to supervise the affairs of the debtor nation, as, for example, in the case of Austria under the protocols of 1922. While this would seem to be a rational method of dealing with the subject, the nationalist sentiment in both creditor and debtor nations does not permit of its wide extension at the present time.

2. Imperialism, or the extension by the creditor nation of its political power in the supervision of its foreign investments. This is the forcible and unilateral method of international unification. The imperialistic country is more self-seeking and less rational in its consideration of the interests of the debtor countries than are the institutions of international organization.

3. Defaults on the part of the debtor nations in order to redress the economic balance, as in the case of the war debts. This is the protest of nationalism against international economic forces. By 1932 internationalism was impractical, American imperialism with regard to the strong states of Europe was impossible, the sentiment of nationalism was strong, and defaults came as the only method of protecting currencies and national systems of economy. A financial crisis was necessary before the United States could be brought to realize the serious difficulties of indefinitely continuing export balances under the present regime of nation-states.

The United States Seeks an Even Exchange of Goods. During the depression which began in 1929 foreign lending was temporarily suspended. Many foreign issues went into default and a reaction in sentiment set in against international loans. The international banker was subjected to much public criticism. The inter-Allied debts, which represented for the most part exports of war supplies, were defaulted by the debtor countries; and it became evident that they would not be paid. They came to represent only the memory of an unwilling gift of vast quantities of American products which

---

[1] League of Nations, *Reports and Proceedings of the World Economic Conference, Held at Geneva, May 4th to 23rd,* 1927 (C. 356. M. 129. 1927. II), I:107. Comparisons with Great Britain regarding merchandise balances, however, are partly misleading because the British put a much larger share of their business energy into shipping which results in large invisible exports.

the debtor countries, under the present system of national tariffs and currencies, could not return without grave economic and political trouble. Out of the resultant pessimism came much discussion of the futility of a great excess of exports.

The Roosevelt administration, groping for a commercial policy which would guide a chastened country into a more healthful state of foreign trade, was confronted by three factors: the desire for exports in order to improve American business, the embarrassment to a creditor nation of export balances over a long period of time, and a strong objection to the importation of goods which would compete with American products. From all this conflict of opposing interests a new commercial policy was formed, a policy which was intended to open foreign markets to American producers through reciprocity but which was not to promote large export balances. In his message to Congress on January 3, 1934, President Roosevelt said:

> Furthermore, all of us are seeking the restoration of commerce in ways which will preclude the building up of large favorable trade balances by any one nation at the expense of trade debits on the part of other nations.

Francis B. Sayre, assistant secretary of state and chairman of the Executive Commercial Policy Committee, a short time later put the matter in the following words:

> Clearly the only way in which America can sell her surplus goods in foreign markets is to trade them for other goods or services. No other course is possible; for we have learned the evil during the past decade of sending American goods abroad and receiving in return nothing but promises to pay.[1]

It is doubtful, however, if such fundamental commercial and financial movements can be made to respond to the will of governments under a capitalistic system of production. It would probably be easier for the leopard to change his spots than for the United States to give up its annually recurring creditor balance.

Before discussing the policies of the Roosevelt administration, it is necessary to set forth previous American tariff-bargaining policies by way of comparison and contrast.

Preliminary Classification of Tariff-Bargaining Policies. The recent history of American tariff bargaining may be divided into three consecutive policies:

---

[1] Address of Mar. 26, 1934, on "Tariff Bargaining," pp. 5–6, Govt. Printing Office, Washington, 1934.

1. The policy which was pursued previous to the World War of seeking special favors for exports and of adhering to a conditional interpretation of the most-favored-nation clause in commercial treaties.

2. The policy which was pursued during the twelve Republican years following the World War of giving and demanding equal treatment and of promoting unconditional most-favored-nation treatment while maintaining a high tariff.

3. The policy ushered in by the Roosevelt administration in 1933 of seeking reciprocity agreements with special nations while at the same time adhering to the unconditional most-favored-nation policy. The terminology above used requires some explanation.[1]

THE SPECIAL BARGAINING PERIOD BEFORE THE WORLD WAR

Penalties and Concessions for Bargaining Purposes. In the eighties and nineties of the past century a commercial policy of extending export trade by obtaining special concessions which would give to American goods the greatest obtainable advantage over competitors in foreign markets was developed. Such special favors were deemed necessary to overcome the advantages which European competitors held because of their lower production and distribution costs. As has been already stated, the United States proposed a plan at the First International Conference of American States (1889–1890) for a customs union which would include the entire Pan-American territory. The scheme, which would have been a gift from the gods to American exporters in the Central and South American fields, was unequivocally rejected by the Latin-American delegates, who were not desirous of shutting themselves off from Europe or of tying themselves economically to the United States.

After the failure of the customs union proposal a provision to force special concessions from other countries was incorporated in the Tariff Act of 1890. Sugar, molasses, coffee, tea, and hides were admitted free; but the President was authorized to place a penalty tariff upon these articles when they were imported from countries whose duties on American products appeared to be unequal and unreasonable in view of the free admission of the above-mentioned products into the United States. From the nature of the articles, which were referred to as the tropical list, it was intended that the President should use diplomatic pressure to force breaches in the tariff walls of Latin-American republics or

[1] In addition to tariffs, there are other factors which have been dealt with through diplomatic channels, such as import and export prohibitions and restrictions and currency stabilization. These will be considered later.

Latin-American colonies of European states. Armed with this power, the President through his agents was able to obtain ten agreements for tariff reductions on American goods, eight of them dealing with countries and colonies in Latin America. Penalties were placed by the President upon the products of three Latin-American countries which failed to reduce their tariffs to American goods.[1]

The penalty clause of 1890 was repealed in the Tariff Act of 1894. Another provision of similar import but with a somewhat different list of bargaining articles was enacted in 1897. Acting under the 1897 law, President Theodore Roosevelt threatened a penalty tariff on coffee imported from Brazil. With disaster looming in the principal market of its greatest export product, the Brazilian government capitulated to the American demands and, in 1904, made substantial concessions in tariffs collected on certain kinds of American merchandise.[2]

A slightly different and a more conciliatory kind of tariff-bargaining provision was also incorporated in the Tariff Act of 1897, by which concessions were offered in the American tariff on certain articles, mostly wines and liquors, in return for concessions to American goods. This provision was intended to promote American trade with the wine-producing countries of Europe. It is significant that, while waving the big stick of penalty tariffs at the countries of Latin America, the United States was offering the olive branch of concessions to European countries. Under the concession clause a number of arrangements were entered into with European countries which were called the "argol agreements." Certain American products were given the minimum tariff rates in Switzerland, France, Germany, Spain, Portugal, and Bulgaria. Minor concessions were obtained in Great Britain, Italy, and the Netherlands.[3]

Formal Reciprocity Treaties. The making of reciprocity treaties is more difficult under the American system than the conclusion of special agreements, such as those just referred to under the acts of 1890 and 1897. Special agreements of that type require only a previous general authorization by Congress and do not call for a subsequent two-thirds vote by the Senate. For a considerable period of time, corresponding roughly with the last half of the nineteenth century, the Department of State sought to follow the

---

[1] For the negotiations under this law see U.S. Tariff Commission, *Reciprocity and Commercial Treaties*, pp. 145ff., Govt. Printing Office, Washington, 1919.

[2] *Ibid.*, pp. 285ff.

[3] *Ibid.*, p. 213.

more difficult course of entering into reciprocity treaties. Three treaties were actually completed, one with Great Britain regarding Canada in 1854, one with the Hawaiian government in 1875, and the third with Cuba in 1902. The Canadian treaty was abrogated by the United States in 1865, the Hawaiian treaty came to an end with the annexation of the islands in 1898, while the treaty with Cuba was suspended by the trade agreement with that country in 1934. In addition some thirteen treaties were negotiated but failed of final ratification,[1] principally because of the inability to obtain a two-thirds approval in the Senate. The failure of these treaties constituted a valuable object lesson in the futility of attempting to conduct commercial diplomacy by means of treaties.

The Conditional Most-Favored-Nation Policy. During the period of special concessions, which has been described, the United States clung to the conditional theory of the most-favored-nation clause. In fact the conditional theory had been maintained since the days of the Articles of Confederation, and it fitted in well with the American conception of special bargaining of the nineteenth century. A concession given to a particular country for reciprocal advantage was not, under the conditional interpretation, given to countries with which we had most-favored-nation treaties unless they were willing to give to the United States a value similar to that which was given by the reciprocating country. Frequently the most-favored-nation treaty countries were unable or were not permitted to enter into a bargain with the United States for the concession and were thus effectively excluded from sharing in the lowered tariff rates or other favors involved. Thus, under the conditional interpretation, the United States was able to exchange concessions with third countries and to prevent the extension of the American tariff reductions to treaty countries. This was in sharp contrast with the unconditional theory, then generally accepted by European governments, under which a concession given to a third nation must be immediately, unconditionally, and without consideration extended to most-favored-nation treaty countries.

The Twelve Postwar Republican Years of Equal Treatment and Unconditional Most-Favored-Nation Treaties

Equal Treatment Advocated. Following the World War the United States suddenly found itself in the forefront of exporting nations owing largely to mass production and the stoppage of

[1] WILLIAMS, BENJAMIN H., *Economic Foreign Policy of the United States,* p. 285, McGraw-Hill Book Company, Inc., New York, 1929.

European industries by the war. There were many commodities, characteristic of the later machine age, which could be manufactured in this country more cheaply and with better quality than elsewhere. Against American trade, however, such obstacles as tariff discriminations and import prohibitions began to rise. This country had, it is true, long maintained a formidable tariff wall which tended to go higher rather than lower. But by the time of the World War the policy of exchanging special concessions had been abandoned. In 1922 it was decided to terminate the policy of demanding special concessions from others. Brazil was released from the 1904 arrangement which had provided for especially low rates in that country to certain American products. Aside from the reciprocity treaty with Cuba, equality of treatment was extended to all nations and none was asked to give special treatment to the United States. The intent of the new policy was to place such emphasis upon equality of treatment as to prevent the building up of discriminations against the United States in foreign markets. The American government demanded equality of treatment for American products everywhere.[1]

The Penalty Clause of 1922 as a Weapon against Discriminations. In the Tariff Act of 1922 the President was empowered to impose penalties upon the goods of any country which should treat American products in an unequal and unfavorable manner. If after negotiation the offending country should refuse to remove its discriminations, the President was authorized to raise the duties upon any or all of the products of that country by as much as 50 per cent ad valorem. If the discriminations should still be maintained, the President could place a complete bar upon the entry into the United States of any or all goods from that country.[2] The clause was repeated in the Tariff Act of 1930.

The penalties above described have never been applied although there have been numerous discriminations against American commerce. On one occasion, at least, the Secretary of State threatened

---

[1] The policy of demanding equal treatment abroad, which bloomed in the postwar period, had been preceded by a provision of the Tariff Act of 1909 which was similar in intent. That act provided a two-schedule tariff. The minimum rates were to be applied generally and the maximum rates were to be applied as penalties upon the products of countries which should discriminate against American trade. The maximum rates were never applied although some countries did practice discrimination.

[2] For a discussion of this clause see McCLURE, WALLACE, *A New American Commercial Policy as Evidenced by Section 317 of the Tariff Act of 1922*, Columbia University Studies in History, Economics and Public Law, Vol. 114, No. 2.

that the clause might be invoked against France. In 1927 the French government entered into a commercial agreement with Germany in which certain kinds of goods were given the minimum rates of the French tariff while the same goods coming from the United States were charged the maximum duties. In several classes of commodities the rates paid by American exporters were four times the rates charged upon German goods. For a time German commercial firms did a thriving business in France at the expense of Americans. In the protests made to France regarding these unequal tariffs, the Secretary of State declared that the United States was "very loath" to invoke the provisions of the law as against French goods and had refrained from so doing because it had hoped that France would remove the discriminations. Probably because of the veiled menace in these words the French government then restored some of the more favorable duties on American imports, and the discriminations were to a large extent removed.[1]

An Unconditional Most-Favored-Nation Clause. While the United States was protesting discriminations, it was also urging the twin policy of *unconditional* most-favored-nation treatment. If other nations could be induced to pledge to the United States as good treatment under all circumstances as they accorded the most-favored-nation, there would be no discriminations against American commerce. The first of the commercial treaties following the war to incorporate this revolutionary change in policy was that with Germany signed in 1923 which was ratified in 1925. Article VII of the treaty reads in part:

Any advantage of whatsoever kind which either High Contracting Party may extend to any article, the growth, produce or manufacture of any foreign country shall simultaneously and unconditionally without request and without compensation, be extended to the like article the growth, produce, or manufacture of the other High Contracting Party.[2]

Special tariff rates given to Cuba were excepted from the operation of this and other similar treaties and agreements.

High Tariffs in the United States Were a Hindrance to Republican Tariff Bargaining. The United States found little encourage-

---

[1] See Dept. of State, *Press Releases*, Oct. 3, 1927, p. 6; Taussig, F. W., "The Tariff Controversy with France," *Foreign Affairs*, VI: 177 (January, 1928).

[2] *U.S. Treaty Series*, No. 725. In 1934 Germany gave notice in accordance with provisions in the treaty of intention to abrogate parts of Article VII including the above-quoted provision. Dept. of State, *Press Releases*, Oct. 13, 1934, p. 249. This partial abrogation of the treaty was agreed to in 1935. *U.S. Treaty Series*, No. 897.

ment in obtaining unconditional most-favored-nation treaties so long as the American tariffs were maintained at a high level and so long as no concessions were made to any countries. Little inducement could be held out unless favors were given by the United States in which the most-favored-nation could participate. Thus Germany negotiated some eleven commercial treaties in the decade following 1923 and in each case was obligated to extend to the United States the favors granted under the treaties.[1] In return Germany received no special concessions from the United States, for none had been extended to other countries. Germany gave much but got nothing in return except equal treatment, which would doubtless have been received without the most-favored-nation treaty. The other great commercial nations, seeing no profit in such a system, were cool to American solicitations. Great Britain, Canada, France, Italy, and Japan did not sign most-favored-nation agreements with this country. Eleven countries, however, entered into such treaties in addition to five with which treaties had already been made. Seventeen others signed executive agreements to the same effect.[2]

TARIFF BARGAINING UNDER THE NEW DEAL

A Revival of Reciprocity. With the coming of the Roosevelt administration in 1933 the American commercial program was again altered. The Democratic platform of 1932 had advocated "reciprocal tariff agreements with other nations." The policy of demanding equal treatment and of threatening to penalize countries which practiced discrimination against American commerce had been of little assistance to American exporters who, after 1929, were confronted by rising tariff walls, discriminatory treatment, quota provisions, exchange restrictions, depreciated exchanges, and embargoes. From 1929 to 1932 American exports were cut by more than two-thirds in value, falling from $5,241,000,000 to

[1] WALLACE, BENJAMIN B., "Tariff Bargaining," *Foreign Affairs*, XI: 628 (July, 1933).

[2] The list of nations with which the United States concluded unconditional most-favored-nation treaties between 1922 and 1934 was as follows: Austria, China, Estonia, Germany, Honduras, Hungary, Latvia, Norway, Poland, Salvador, and Turkey. Treaties previously made are still in effect with Morocco, Muscat, Siam, Yugoslavia, and Zanzibar. Executive agreements were concluded with Albania, Brazil, Bulgaria, Chile, Czechoslovakia, Dominican Republic, Egypt, Finland, Greece, Guatemala, Haiti, Lithuania, Nicaragua, Persia, Rumania, Saudi Arabia, and Spain. Dept. of State, *Treaty Information Bulletin*, January, 1934, p. 24.

$1,611,016,000. Bilateral agreements for tariff reduction now appeared to offer the best chance of success of any of the alternative procedures. Attempts to lower American tariffs by act of Congress have always been met by such organized opposition and by such exaggerated tales of anticipated woe from the representatives of domestic producers that congressmen have ordinarily been paralyzed by apprehension and rendered incapable of acting favorably to reduction. Under the New Deal the method of lowering tariffs by executive agreements with other countries was adopted.

The Unconditional Most-Favored-Nation Clause and Reciprocity. In one respect the new reciprocity policy is different from any that has previously been used by the American government: the unconditional most-favored-nation clause is joined with a system of special bargaining. This clause was used in the policy of the twelve years of Republican postwar administrations; but, as no concessions were made, no advantages could be generalized under the treaties. Under the New Deal, however, the tariff reductions given to special governments must be extended to all countries with which we have unconditional most-favored-nation treaties. The consideration for this extension is that the United States shares in all concessions which may be granted by such countries. It has been proposed by this government, however, that reductions of tariffs under certain kinds of multilateral treaties which create a freer trade area of considerable size and which are open to the accession of all countries shall not be generalized under the unconditional most-favored-nation treaties to countries which refuse to join in the treaty.[1] The general policy of asking for bilateral tariff agreements and of generalizing any concessions given under such agreements through the unconditional most-favored-nations clause, although not tried in the United States previous to the Roosevelt administration, had for many years been tested in European tariff diplomacy.[2] Whether it can be made to work as a practical method for wholesale tariff reductions is still doubtful, because of the heavy pressure of domes-

---

[1] The policy was outlined in the American suggestions to the London World Economic Conference of 1933 regarding a program on commercial policy, Dept. of State, *Press Releases*, Aug. 12, 1933, pp. 91–92. Secretary of State Hull at the Seventh International Conference of American States (1933) introduced a proposition to the same effect which was recommended for study by the conference. The proposition, as redrafted in agreement form by the Pan American Union, is open to signature by the various governments at the offices of the union. See *U.S. Treaty Series*, No. 898.

[2] WALLACE, *loc. cit.*, p. 622.

tic producers who are anxious that any concessions granted in the American tariffs shall be narrowly applied. Our trade diplomats will doubtless keep in mind a formula generally asociated with this type of tariff bargaining: *"ordinarily no concession is made to any country except in respect of articles imported chiefly from that country."*[1] As will be seen, however, the policy has been vigorously pushed and a considerable number of agreements are already in effect.

The Trade Agreements Act. In 1934 Congress passed the Trade Agreements Act which gives to the President for three years the power to enter into agreements with foreign governments for the promotion of commerce. He is empowered in so doing to alter the tariff rates by as much as 50 per cent. Thus he may make substantial reductions in certain duties in order to obtain concessions from another country for the benefit of American goods. The agreements so made are subject to termination on due notice at the end of three years from the dates upon which they come into force. The reductions given to one government are extended not only to all countries with which we have most-favored-nation agreements but to all other countries, except that the President may refuse to apply them to the goods of nations which discriminate against American commerce. The purpose of the law was thus twofold: (a) to maintain and increase the interchange of goods, and (b) to assure equitable treatment to American commerce.[2] Under the law exclusive agreements may be made with Cuba, the reductions under which do not need to be generalized, that is, they need not be extended to other countries.[3]

The Roosevelt administration has made sincere efforts to apply the new policy. An interdepartmental organization, known as the Committee on Foreign Trade Agreements, has been set up for the purpose of making studies and advising with reference to the selection of countries for negotiations. A Committee for Reciprocity Information, likewise interdepartmental in character, has also been established to receive information and views from American

[1] *Ibid.*, p. 624. Alonzo Taylor in *The New Deal and Foreign Trade* (pp. 220–221, The Macmillan Company, New York, 1935) expresses the opinion that most-favored-nation treaties will render the operation of the bilateral agreements nugatory. For an authoritative defense of the existing policy see SAYRE, FRANCIS BOWES, *America Must Act*, World Peace Foundation, Boston, 1936.

[2] FEIS, HERBERT, "Seven Mildly Controversial Comments on International Trade," Dept. of State, *Press Releases*, Feb. 16, 1935, p. 91.

[3] *U.S. Statutes at Large*, 48: 943.

businessmen regarding the agreements. Supplementary oral views may also be presented to this committee.[1]

The Cuban Agreement. A little more than two months after the passage of the act the first of the agreements, that with Cuba, was announced. The agreement provided for sweeping reductions of duties by each country upon certain imports from the other. The United States tariff on sugar from Cuba was previously 1.5 cents per pound, the rate being a reduction of 20 per cent below the general rate of 1.875.[2] Under the trade agreement the rate was reduced to 0.9 cents per pound.[3] The duty on Cuban rum was dropped from $4.00 to $2.50 per gallon. A quota for tobacco importations from Cuba was fixed at 18 per cent of American domestic consumption and within this quota the rates were substantially reduced. Cuban fresh fruits and vegetables were permitted to enter the United States at reduced rates during the early season before most fruits and vegetables in the United States come upon the market. Cuba in turn reduced her tariffs upon American foodstuffs. American hog lard, which had been charged the almost prohibitive duty of $9.18 per hundred pounds, was admitted into Cuba at $2.73. Vegetable oils from cottonseed, corn, and soya beans were reduced from $4.36 per hundred pounds to $0.88. The duty on American automobiles priced at less than $750 was cut from 24 per cent to 12 per cent ad valorem. Other American products which received the benefit of reductions in the Cuban tariffs are wheat, flour, textiles, iron, steel, and copper. Tobacco, which under the Treaty of 1902 was not entitled to any preference in Cuban rates, was given a reduction below the general Cuban duty.[4] By this trade agreement the President hoped to restore some of the Cuban-American trade which had fallen from a high point of $493,936,000 in 1924 to $79,786,000 in 1933. It was one of the first practical signs of reaction against the rising tide of tariffs to be shown by the United States. The agreement became effective on September 3, 1934, and the American ambassador to Cuba reported that consignments of

[1] Dept. of State, *Press Releases*, June 30, 1934, pp. 458–459, and July 7, 1934, p. 7. These committees are subordinate to a third interdepartmental committee, the Executive Commitee on Commercial Policy. For the establishment of this body see Dept. of State, *Press Releases*, Nov. 25, 1933, p. 283. See also SAYRE, *op. cit.*, p. 52.

[2] A previous presidential order had brought about a reduction to these figures from a general rate of 2.5 cents and a rate on Cuban sugar of 2 cents.

[3] This did not, however, affect the quota allotment to Cuban sugar of 1,902,000 tons per year under the Jones-Costigan Act.

[4] *Executive Agreement Series*, No. 67.

lard amounting to 1,000,000 pounds were waiting in the custom-houses of Havana to be cleared as soon as the new schedule should go into force. Large shipments of other goods, also, were either in the customhouses or on the way.[1] During the first nine months the agreement was in effect the trade between the two countries increased 76 per cent over that of the corresponding period of the previous year.[2] Part of the increase was due to general recovery and part to the agreement.

The Cuban agreement is not, however, to be taken as a representative test of the new policy. Since a specific exception of Cuban preferences has been made in the most-favored-nation treaties and agreements entered into by the United States, and since the 1934 law permits an exclusive agreement with Cuba, the reductions in this case were not generalized. Other trade agreements are being constructed with much care because of the necessity of applying their reductions to the goods of third countries. Under the terms of the law, previously described, it is the policy of the administration to extend the reduced rates not only to those countries with which we have most-favored-nation treaties but also to all countries which do not discriminate substantially against American goods.[3] With regard to the goods of certain countries which practice discrimination, the reduced rates have in some cases been applied temporarily, pending the making of agreements to withdraw the discriminations against American commerce. Certain other countries are given the benefit of the lowered duties until thirty days from the termination of most-favored-nation agreements with the United States.[4] At the present time agreements are in effect with Belgium, Brazil, Canada, Colombia, Cuba, Haiti, Honduras, the Netherlands, Sweden, and Switzerland. Following an agreement with Brazil in which the duty on manganese was reduced 50 per cent, the United States made a special agreement with Russia assuring that country the benefits of this and other reductions in the various trade agreements excepting that with Cuba. Russia in return for these benefits agreed to take steps to increase substantially its purchases in the United States. The Soviet government gave assurances of its

---

[1] Dept. of State, *Press Releases*, Sept. 8, 1934, p. 180.

[2] Address of Henry F. Grady, Dept. of State, *Press Releases*, July 6, 1935, p. 12.

[3] Dept. of State, *Press Releases*, Apr. 6, 1935, p. 212.

[4] See *ibid.*, pp. 217–218, for a list of countries in the various classes with regard to the Belgian agreement of Feb. 27, 1935.

intention to buy American goods to the value of $30,000,000 during the year succeeding the making of the agreement.[1]

PART II. INTERNATIONAL ACTION

TARIFFS

The League of Nations. With the coming of the League of Nations an attempt was made through international cooperation to reduce the recently raised tariff walls and to modify the increasing number of trade restrictions. Some conference action had been taken prior to the war, particularly in the limitation of sugar duties brought about by the International Sugar Convention signed in Brussels in 1902;[2] but in the prewar world the question of tariffs had been generally regarded as outside the sphere of international politics. The League, however, came to look upon the high tariffs and other commercial restrictions of the postwar period as matters of world concern.

The United States was represented in the International Economic Conference of 1927, which was called under the auspices of the League. The delegates were designated by their governments but were not empowered to draw up a treaty. Their action consisted in making recommendations to the Council of the League. The American delegation signed the report of the conference which recommended the lowering of tariffs. The conference resolution stated that "the time has come to put an end to the increase in tariffs and to move in the opposite direction." The methods suggested for accomplishing this object were:

1. Action by each state in the reduction of its tariff barriers.
2. Commercial treaties accomplishing mutual reductions.
3. Abandonment of practice of putting excessive duties into effect in advance of negotiations for bargaining purposes.
4. Collective action for elimination or reduction of obstructions undertaken after inquiry through the Economic Organization of the League.[3]

The conference also resolved in favor of the unconditional most-favored-nation clause in commercial treaties, an action which was in line with the policy of the United States. The recommendations of

[1] Dept. of State, *Press Releases*, July 13, 1935, p. 45. *Executive Agreement Series*, No. 81.

[2] McClure, Wallace, *World Prosperity as Sought through the Economic Work of the League of Nations*, p. 49, The Macmillan Company, New York, 1933.

[3] League of Nations, *Report and Proceedings of the World Economic Conference, Held at Geneva, May 4th to 23rd*, 1927 (C. 356. M. 129. 1927. II), I: 41.

the conference had no perceptible effect in checking the rise of commercial barriers.

Preliminaries to the London Conference of 1933. The Roosevelt administration, which took office in 1933, was in sympathy with the attempts to lower tariffs by international agreement. The Democratic platform of the previous year had advocated lower tariffs and "an international economic conference to restore international trade and facilitate exchange." It was significant as bearing on the trend of the times that the United States was now committed to the consideration of tariff problems in conference with other nations. The International Economic Conference of 1933 was arranged through the League of Nations to meet in June, 1933. Previous to the conference President Roosevelt invited the representatives of some fifty-three governments to meet him separately in Washington during April and May for preliminary conversations regarding the aims of the conference. Typical of the declarations issuing from these individual conferences was the joint statement made by President Roosevelt and Prime Minister Bennett of Canada in which it was declared: "Economic and monetary policies must be adjusted to permit a freer international exchange of commodities."[1]

While preparing for the conference, the United States took the initiative in bringing about a tariff truce. A plan for a truce had been recommended by the Assembly of the League of Nations in 1929, but a general acceptance was then impossible. A separate truce, however, had been agreed to by five customs units in Europe.[2] In May, 1933, the United States proposed a truce to last at least during the proceedings of the London conference. The plan was approved by the organizing committee of the conference and was accepted by sixty-two governments.[3] Each reserved the right to withdraw from the truce after July 31 upon giving one month's notice.[4]

Secretary Hull Urges the Removal of Trade Barriers. When the conference convened, the American delegation, headed by Secretary of State Hull, gave its enthusiastic support to the move-

---

[1] Dept. of State, *Press Releases*, May 6, 1933, p. 303.

[2] McCLURE, *op. cit.*, pp. 377–382.

[3] *Treaty Information Bulletin*, August, 1933, pp. 11–12, and September, 1933, p. 11.

[4] For the text see League of Nations, *Journal of the Monetary and Economic Conference, London*, 1933, July 28, 1933, p. 225, and *Treaty Information Bulletin*, No. 44, May, 1933, p. 15. The truce was generally abandoned by the various countries in October, November, and December, 1933.

ment to reduce the obstacles to international trade. On June 14 Secretary Hull made an address to the conference in which he stated:

Economic nationalism as practiced since the war comprised every known method of obstructing international capital and trade, such as high tariffs, quotas, embargoes, exchange restrictions and depreciated currencies. Many governments by manifesto are constantly changing their tariff and other obstructions so that their utter lack of stability is seriously destructive of business. These trade barriers inevitably caused a disastrous reaction upon production, employment, prices, and distribution within the confines of every nation. Under the ravages of these combined methods of extremism uncounted millions of people are starving in some parts of the world while other parts are glutted with vast surpluses. Raw materials are fenced off from factories, factories from consumers, and consumers from foodstuffs.

Secretary Hull did not urge a complete removal of trade barriers but rather moderate and progressive action. He said:

The gradual and careful readjustment of the excesses of tariff and other trade barriers to a moderate level would not contemplate either unreasonable or excessive competitive imports against efficient domestic industry operated under normal conditions on the one hand nor monopolistic price advantages at home on the other. This policy, if practiced generally among the nations, would insure healthier and more prosperous conditions in all industries at all efficient in every country.

Mr. Hull went on to recommend that all excesses in the structure of trade barriers should be removed, that all unfair trade methods and practices should be abandoned, that in the monetary field suitable measures should be taken for an immediate policy which would give the greatest measure of stability during the period of reform, that the problem of a permanent international monetary standard must then be faced, and that coincidently measures should be taken for the removal of restrictions upon foreign exchange dealings. The United States, he said, was prepared to offer concrete suggestions with regard to all these matters.[1]

The American Currency and the London Conference. To the administration in Washington, however, domestic recovery through the raising of the price level seemed far more important than the problems being considered at London. When President Roosevelt began his preliminary talks with the representatives of other govern-

[1] Secretary Hull's speech is given in Dept. of State, *Press Releases*, June 17, 1933, pp. 445–450. The same, slightly abridged, is found in *Journal of the Monetary and Economic Conference*, June 15, 1933, pp. 26–27.

ments in Washington, the United States was apparently agreed that currency stabilization and tariff agreements must be considered together. In a joint statement with M. Herriot of France, President Roosevelt had declared that world recovery was to be brought about by diminishing the impediments to international trade and "by the reestablishment of a normal financial and monetary situation."[1] These factors, trade freedom and currency stabilization, according to the statement, "constitute the separate elements of a single problem." The joint statement, which thus acknowledged the interdependence of the currency and tariff questions, was, according to the French view, repudiated a few weeks later by President Roosevelt. The President became convinced that the depreciation of the dollar was necessary for American domestic recovery. Already at the time of the joint statement above referred to, the dollar had begun its spectacular decline. In order to prevent a drain on the American gold supply through withdrawals of short-term loans and through the flight of American capital, as well as to raise domestic prices to stimulate recovery, the President on April 19 had placed an embargo on the shipment of gold. When the dollar was no longer maintained in the international market by exports of gold, it fell rapidly in terms of other currencies. The fall of the dollar awakened apprehension among our commercial rivals because of the advantage which it gave to American export trade. Certain nations, including France, felt that this development called for further increases in customs duties in order to maintain the *status quo*. French officials feared that otherwise an excess of imports over exports might drain gold from their country and force the franc off the gold standard. The French people lived in dread of another inflation like that of the years following the war which wiped out four-fifths of the value of obligations payable in francs.

By June, 1933, President Roosevelt could not well agree to the stabilization of currencies for political reasons. The fall of the dollar had been accompanied by a rise in the value of stocks. A temporary feeling of prosperity was in the air. Had the President agreed to currency stabilization and had the promise of prosperity vanished, the rebound against the administration's policy of stabilization would have been powerful and disconcerting. Mr. Roosevelt turned against currency stabilization with some vehemence. On July 3 Secretary Hull made public a message from the President which took the conference roundly to task for failure to consider tariffs and other trade obstructions before currency stabilization

[1] Dept. of State, *Press Releases*, Apr. 29, 1933, p. 276.

could be agreed to. "I do not relish the thought," it read, "that insistence on such action should be made an excuse for the continuance of the basic economic errors that underlie so much of the present worldwide depression."[1] The message was unfortunate in that the President was denouncing as folly the coupling of monetary stabilization with tariffs to which union he had apparently given his approval only two months before. Had he explained in more diplomatic language that conditions had now arisen which made currency stabilization impossible in the United States, his explanation would probably have been accepted with good grace, though with regret. As it was, the message produced a most unpleasant effect. A few weeks after this bombshell had exploded, the conference adjourned, having failed to arrive at any agreement regarding the main questions on the agenda.[2]

IMPORT AND EXPORT PROHIBITIONS AND RESTRICTIONS

The League Calls a Conference on Trade Restrictions. During the World War international commerce was checked to a considerable extent by prohibitions and restrictions designed to keep certain valuable raw materials at home and to prevent the upset of currencies by an excess of imports. These restrictions took the form of embargoes, quotas, and other trade impediments. They are to be distinguished from protective tariffs, although the effect is somewhat similar. Following 1918 the wartime restrictions were maintained in many cases while numerous new ones were added. Some countries prohibited the export of various minerals, some of particular foodstuffs, and some of plant specimens. Governments placed their ban upon the import of commodities that jeopardized industries important in plans for national defense. General restrictions were, in some cases, placed upon imports in order to protect currencies.

The movement for the abolition of trade prohibitions and restrictions was promptly taken up and sponsored in many conferences held under the auspices of the League, including the Brussels Conference of 1919, the regional conference in Portorose in 1921, the International Economic Conference at Genoa, in 1922, and the Geneva Conference on Customs Formalities in 1923. In 1924 the Economic Committee of the League was directed by the Assembly to consider the expediency of an agreement to remove these

---

[1] Dept. of State, *Press Releases*, July 8, 1933, p. 15.

[2] For the agreement on silver policy, concluded during the conference between eight governments including the United States, see *Executive Agreement Series*, No. 63.

commercial barriers, and the committee spent two and one-half years preparing for a conference on the subject.[1] Information was assembled and a preliminary draft agreement was drawn up. In 1927 the International Economic Conference strongly urged the abolition of these restrictions and the Assembly in September of that year made a similar declaration. In October, 1927, the Conference on Import and Export Prohibitions and Restrictions met in Geneva.

United States Exporters Favor a Convention. Reactions of American export businesses to the efforts of the conference at this time indicate the forces that were propelling the Department of State toward international action. The automobile and motion-picture industries were foremost in raising objections to the prohibitions and restrictions imposed by European countries. Senator Vandenberg of the automobile-producing state of Michigan declared that the placing in effect of a general convention would open markets for thousands of American-made automobiles in Europe.[2] The motion-picture film exporters had for some years been fighting against the quota provisions of various European countries which had been principally designed to diminish the use of American films and to build up the domestic film industries. At their instance the Department of State protested in 1929 as follows:

There have been persistent and substantial demands for American pictures on the part of foreign exhibitors, and this has created an extensive foreign market for this American product. The building up of this market has involved an investment of large proportions, and it is felt that this investment is jeopardized by certain governmental measures arbitrarily restricting the distribution of American films . . . It [the American government] believes firmly that the interests of the motion picture industry in all countries are best promoted by the freest possible interchange of films based solely on the quality of the product.[3]

The American government maintained only a few prohibitions on commerce, such as the export prohibition on helium gas and the import prohibition on wines and liquors for beverage purposes. By covering such special prohibitions with reservations, the United States would have nothing to lose by entering into a convention for

[1] For a list of the League pronouncements see League of Nations, *Proceedings of the International Conference for the Abolition of Import and Export Prohibitions and Restrictions, Geneva, October 17th to November 8th*, 1927 (C. 21. M. 12. 1928. II), p. 53.

[2] *N.Y. Times*, Sept. 19, 1929.

[3] Dept. of State, *Press Releases*, Apr. 12, 1929. The representation was made to the governments of France, Germany, Czechoslovakia, Austria, Hungary, Italy, and Spain.

the general abolition of export and import prohibitions and restrictions; and it would have much to gain by the elimination of such restrictions as interfered with American exports.

The United States at the Conference. When the League conference met in 1927, the United States was represented by Hugh Wilson, the American minister to Switzerland, who strongly supported the plan for a convention. Because of the American high-tariff policy, however, it was necessary for the United States to maintain a complete separation in the Geneva discussions between tariffs, on the one hand, and commercial prohibitions and restrictions, on the other. Various governments took a contrary view. The Dutch delegate stated that it made no difference whether a country had a protective tariff or an import prohibition against a particular article. If prohibitions and restrictions were abolished without taking any action on tariffs, he said, Holland would lose a means of defense against high-tariff countries.[1] A clause was included in the general act of the conference to maintain a relationship between the two subjects. It provided that if products were to be freed from trade restrictions a corresponding obligation was placed upon the parties to maintain an equitable tariff regime, particularly with regard to import duties on articles manufactured from raw materials for which free exportation had been provided under the convention. Mr. Wilson opposed the provision;[2] and he finally signed the agreement with a reservation exempting the tariff system, among other things, from the operation of the convention.[3] The convention gave to each contracting party the right to name in the annex certain excepted commodities with regard to which it might maintain restrictions of import and export. The United States made exception to helium gas, the export of which from the United States is prohibited by law. The convention provided for the abolition of import and export prohibitions and restrictions aside from such as were excepted in the annex and also from such as related to vital matters, as health, morals, and security. Two additional conferences were held before the convention could be brought into effect on January 1, 1930; and then the treaty applied to but six countries.

The United States Turns toward Restriction. The failure to obtain wide acceptance of the Geneva agreement was the occasion

---

[1] *Proceedings of the International Conference* (above cited), p. 64.

[2] *Ibid.*, pp. 141, 144.

[3] For the text of the convention see *U.S. Treaty Series*, No. 811. The reservation is on p. 16.

for a change in American policy; and on June 29, 1933, the United States gave notice of withdrawal from the convention. The Department of State expressed the hope that another treaty could be agreed upon which would be more widely accepted.[1] The United States then adopted the quota system with regard to certain commodities. The repeal of prohibition created new markets for foreign wines and liquors. These were allotted upon a quota basis through a system of bargaining which opened up further markets for American products abroad. Thus, for 1934, France was given a quota of 1,568,000 gallons of wine, which was double that previously allowed, in return for an increased quota of 20,000 long tons of American apples and pears in France, which was about four times the former amount.[2] Great Britain was given a quota of 1,214,000 gallons of wines and liquor under a four months' arrangement in return for a 7.6 per cent minimum allotment of pork products in the British market. This was an increase from 6.3 per cent or a gain to American exports at the rate of about $1,000,000 per year over the allotment formerly proposed[3]—a neat bargain in "pig and liquor" diplomacy, as it was called. In the Jones-Costigan law of 1934 sugar importation into the United States was placed upon a quota basis. The allotment for Cuba was fixed under this law at 1,902,-000 tons. Another quota provision is found in the United States-Cuban trade agreement of 1934 in which the Cuban exports of tobacco to the United States are limited to 18 per cent of United States domestic consumption. The quota system has been included as a limitation upon goods which can come in under reduced rates in other recent trade agreements. Thus the American government, having withdrawn from the convention, has adopted to some extent the quota system. The United States is, however, by the nature of its powerful producing system, an exporting country. Our economic system and national institutions have not been threatened by adverse balances of trade. For this reason the American government in addition to its high tariff is not apt to adopt the rigid systems of commercial controls that have been used in Europe and Latin America. As can be seen, some of the quota provisions already adopted have been included in trade agreements the net effect of which, however, has been the stimulation of commerce.

[1] Dept. of State, *Press Releases*, July 8, 1933, p. 18.

[2] *N.Y. Times*, Dec. 22, 1933.

[3] Dept. of State, *Press Releases*, Jan. 13, 1934, pp. 8–9. Because of high liquor prices in the United States the quota system on liquor importations was abandoned on May 1, 1934, subject to reimposition on sixty days' notice.

CHAPTER XI

THE DIPLOMACY OF CAPITAL EXPORTS

POLITICAL CONSEQUENCES OF THE RISE TO THE CREDITOR POSITION

The United States came into existence as an impoverished revolutionary country, pleading with the political enemies of Great Britain for financial aid. Some valuable loans were obtained in addition to gifts of money during the crisis of the Revolution, but additional requests for financial assistance prompted by the acute distress of the American troops were in some cases warmly rebuked. On one occasion, when Congress asked the French government to carry the burden of interest on previous loans, the French reply was an emphatic refusal with the admonition that if the Americans did not like it their dissatisfaction would be regarded as an evidence of ingratitude. Certainly, in a financial sense, the American nation had a humble beginning.

A century and a half later this country had become the world's richest nation and the foremost exporter of capital. The interesting incidents of this remarkable evolution, including defaults upon state debts, heavy borrowings for railway and industrial development, an idealistic tendency to reproach Europe for economic imperialism, and the gradual accumulation of financial strength cannot be described here. Probably the most spectacular changes came during the World War. Previous to that struggle the United States was still a debtor nation. American industries were obligated to Europeans in a sum of from $4,500,000,000 to $5,000,000,000 while Americans had, on the other hand, invested some $2,500,000,000 in territory outside of the United States. Huge exports during the war gave to the United States the capacity to buy back the securities of American industries that were held in Europe.[1] Substantial sums were lent abroad and, after the war, the lending process continued. By 1930, exclusive of the inter-Allied debts, Americans had placed about $15,000,000,000 in long-term investments abroad, whereas there was probably $4,700,000,000 of foreign long-term

[1] NOYES, ALEXANDER D., *The War Period of American Finance*, 1908–1925, G. P. Putnam's Sons, New York, 1926.

capital in the United States.[1] The fever of finance previous to the stock market crash of 1929 brought into being high-powered security-selling organizations which in turn encouraged some unsound investments. The long-term investments held abroad at the end of 1933 had shrunk by an undetermined amount owing to the depreciation of the depression and to repurchases of securities by foreigners because of their low price. As estimated by the Bureau of Foreign and Domestic Commerce, the par and book values of these investments by geographical regions were:

Canada and Newfoundland................	$ 3,950,000,000
Europe................................	4,132,000,000
Central America and Mexico...............	893,000,000
West Indies............................	1,112,000,000
South America.........................	2,920,000,000
Asia.................................	978,000,000
Africa................................	131,000,000
Oceania: Australia and New Zealand........	413,000,000
Total.............................	14,529,000,000
Add: Bank capital....................	125,000,000
Deduct: Estimated net repurchases by foreigners (mostly European bonds)..	855,000,000
Net total............................	$13,799,000,000*

* *The Balance of International Payments of the United States in* 1933, pp. 53–58.

The colorless figures of loans and investments shown above represent largely the accounting transactions in the export of vast cargoes of goods and materials—the triumphant march of American technology. Power plants, factories, railroads, meat-packing establishments, road systems, automobiles, aeronautical equipment, mining and oil-field installations, motion-picture paraphernalia, have all spread outward to other countries mostly in the American hemisphere. Jungles have been transformed. The lives of other peoples have been enriched by industrial processes. The two questions of policy that accompany industrial expansion are: How far should the United States through its own strength seek to order the governmental institutions of those who employ American capital in order to assure favorable treatment of investors

[1] U.S. Department of Commerce, *The Balance of International Payments of the United States in* 1930, pp. 35–36, 40, Govt. Printing Office, 1931. Dr. Max Winkler gives the figure of $17,528,254,000 for American investments abroad at the end of 1930, "American Foreign Investments in 1931," *Foreign Policy Reports*, Vol. VII, No. 24 (Feb. 3, 1932), p. 428.

and how far should this country encourage the purely cooperative organization of the nations for the same purpose? In studying the political effects of the vast financial changes which took place in the transition from a debtor to a creditor nation we find that the attitude of the United States toward the world has been altered in two different ways depending upon whether the countries in which the investments have been made are weak or strong.

Our Relation to the Weak and Backward Debtor. When American capital has flowed into weak and undeveloped countries, particularly those in the vicinity of the United States, lobbies of investors have sometimes demanded strong action to coerce the debtor nation into the adoption of policies favorable to their interests. The attorneys for powerful financial groups have emphasized the virtues of order and stability and have contended that the use of marines to suppress riots and to maintain a proper attitude toward investments is a profitable procedure. In the Caribbean, political and military considerations have combined with stern business practice to bring a number of the governments under American control.

Native political leaders frequently claim that these republics have become mere appendages to great banking institutions. Thus Haitian nationalists came to feel that Haiti was a "territory of the National City Bank,"[1] and Nicaragua was once referred to as "The Republic of Brown Brothers."[2] That such allegations are something more than the idle accusations of irresponsible native politicians may be gathered from highly respectable evidence, such as the testimony of Frederick Strauss of J. & W. Seligman & Co., which firm was associated with Brown Brothers in Nicaragua. Mr. Strauss stated before the Senate Finance Committee in 1932:

In the Nicaraguan case, if I may revert to it for a moment, there was a case where we undertook at the request of [sic] instigation or at the suggestion of the State Department the running of internal affairs of that country. We collected the customs, we ran the railroads, we ordered the currency, we undertook the tutelage of that country of a kind that has never been undertaken before. We did, if I may be permitted to say so, a successful job, and then withdrew from it after many years; but there has been constant criticism of the Nicaraguan experiment, and I can see perfectly well why, from a certain point of view, they are justified in saying

[1] *Sale of Foreign Bonds or Securities in the United States*, Hearings before the Senate Committee on Finance, p. 2159, Govt. Printing Office, Washington, 1931.

[2] *The Nation*, 114: 667 (June 7, 1922).

that we have no business, no matter how good the work that was done, to be in business there, to undertake to run the country.[1]

As has been previously suggested, it is not yet certain whether this policy of strong control in the Caribbean is to be a permanent feature of American policy or whether it is an early manifestation of financial domination which is even now undergoing modification.

Our Relation to the Politically Strong Debtor. In the dealings of the United States arising from investments in strong countries it seems that the arguments for friendship and tolerance have been stronger and more apparent than in the case of our relations with weaker countries. The effect of capital exports has been to create within this country certain groups that have an interest in the promotion of the cause of international organization. Such factions realize that a war between the United States and a strong power or combination of powers would wipe out valuable American investments. The fact that hundreds of thousands of American citizens now hold titles to property located in foreign countries and are dependent for their incomes upon uninterrupted production abroad is an argument for international cooperation in the solution of world-wide economic and political questions. The international capitalistic influences making for peace may, however, be easily overestimated. In times of rising nationalism financial leaders frequently lack the strength to resist the power of mass psychology. Also there are some domestic economic interests which favor international misunderstanding because of the expectancy of war profits. For these reasons predictions of the abolition of war based upon the rise of international finance, such as the prophecies made previous to the World War, have thus far proved to be fallacious.

I. OFFICIAL PROMOTION OF CAPITAL EXPORTS

The work of the American government with relation to capital exports has been of two opposite kinds, encouragement and discouragement. Coming first to the specific policies that have been adopted in stimulating foreign investments we find that this task has brought the Department of State into contact with three different types of institutions: (1) governments of the countries in which the investments are to be made, (2) American banking houses and American investors, and (3) the governments of other capital-exporting nations whose bankers are competing in the making of loans or investments.

[1] *Sale of Foreign Bonds or Securities in the United States*, p. 1323.

1. Relations with Countries in Which the Investment Is to Be Made

Presenting the Case of the American Investor. One of the functions of the diplomatic service is to see that applications of American businessmen for contracts and concessions abroad are duly presented to the proper officials of the foreign government and that they receive a fair hearing in competition with proposals presented from third countries. Advice is given in drawing up the terms of the proposed contract so that future difficulties may be avoided.[1] An illustration of such assistance is shown by the diplomatic correspondence in obtaining a concession from the Brazilian government on behalf of the Western Union Telegraph Company for a cable from Brazil to the West Indies. The president of the company advised the Secretary of State of the project and requested the good offices and assistance of the department. The American ambassador in Brazil was then instructed from Washington to give "any proper assistance consistent with the instructions of the Department." When an unsatisfactory concession was offered by the Brazilian government, which was evidently influenced by a British company, the ambassador was instructed to give aid in obtaining amendments to the concession. Communications from the president of the company to his agent in Brazil were forwarded through the Department of State and the American ambassador.[2] When another American firm, the Central and South American Telegraph Company, sought a concession from Brazil for a cable to Brazilian ports from Buenos Aires, the president of the corporation acknowledged "the powerful influence of the Department of State and the American Ambassador to Brazil" in advocating this concession.[3]

Pressing the Backward Country to Accept Loans. In the Central American and Caribbean region the Department of State has sometimes proceeded on the theory that the introduction of American capital is necessary to provide an excuse for political control in a region of great strategic importance to the United States. In such cases the department has at times brought pressure upon the governments concerned to accept the loan. The

---

[1] *Foreign Service of the United States*, Hearings before the Committee on Foreign Affairs, House of Representatives, pp. 42–43, Govt. Printing Office, Washington, 1924.

[2] See *Foreign Relations*, 1918, pp. 47–48, 71.

[3] *Ibid.*, p. 35.

existence of European capital in the area and the fear that European nations might make use of their investments to extend their political influence have been largely responsible for these unusual activities of the American government.

American capital was once pumped into Nicaragua by political force. In 1910, when Secretary Knox was attempting to extend American control in Nicaragua, he obtained from the new revolutionary government, previous to its recognition, an agreement to solicit the good offices of the United States in obtaining a loan to be guaranteed by a certain percentage of the customs receipts.[1] He had in mind a loan of $15,000,000, one of the purposes of which was to refund the British-owned public debt. The United States Senate refused to advise the ratification of the treaty partly because of the plan for customs control. The bankers then went ahead with a much smaller loan of $1,500,000. When the agreements regarding these loans were pending, the Department of State and the American legation at Managua made every effort to procure favorable action on the part of the Nicaraguan government. At one time the American minister advised the Department of State:

Rumors have been current that the Liberals are organizing a concerted uprising all over the country with the declared object of defeating the loan. It is difficult to estimate how serious a measure this might be if well organized and led, as the Liberals are in such a majority over the Conservatives. I therefore hasten to repeat my suggestion as to the advisability of stationing permanently, at least until the loan has been put through, a war vessel at Corinto.[2]

A war vessel soon appeared at Corinto. The legation at Managua was thereafter repeatedly instructed that favorable action upon the loan was a matter of primary importance; and the subject was brought emphatically to the attention of President Diaz until the proper ratification of the loan of $1,500,000 was obtained.

After the occupation of Haiti in 1915 the American financial adviser and the Department of State requested that the Haitian government should contract a loan in New York, one of the purposes of which was to refund previous French loans. In February, 1917, the American financial adviser wrote a strong letter to the Haitian government insisting upon the loan. In the following month an agreement was signed between the American minister extending the

[1] *Ibid.*, 1911, p. 653.
[2] *Ibid.*, 1911, pp. 661–662.

duration of the Treaty of 1915 containing customs control provisions until the year 1936 in order to protect the proposed loan.[1] On several occasions between 1917 and 1922 the American government renewed its suggestion concerning the loan.[2] After President Dartiguenave, who had failed to sign the loan agreement, had been replaced by Louis Borno, who was more susceptible to American influences, the loan was made. Georges N. Leger, a Haitian, testifying before the Finance Committee of the Senate, stated that he regarded the transaction as a political loan pushed through by the domination of the Department of State.[3]

The policy of influencing Caribbean countries to accept loans from United States bankers may well be a phase of financial diplomacy which belongs to the past. It would seem to have been characteristic of a period in which the United States was fearful of the encroaching imperialism of Europe in the Caribbean region.

Removing Local Restrictions against American Capital. Backward countries, fearing the loss of independence which comes with a flood of foreign investments, have sometimes set up restrictions for the purpose of impeding or altogether preventing such investments. In Haiti, for more than a century previous to American occupation, a clause had existed in the constitution forbidding foreigners from owning land. After the establishment of control in 1915 the United States sought to remove this restriction which kept American corporations from purchasing the exceedingly fertile agricultural land of Haiti. In 1917 the President was induced to summon the National Assembly for the purpose of approving a new constitution which was to contain no such prohibition. The assembly refused to comply. The unwilling President was then persuaded to sign an order for the dissolution of that obstinate body. General Butler of the United States Marine Corps took the order to the meeting hall and evicted the assembly. The occupation officials provided for a referendum on the new constitution in 1918 and the American marines threw their influence toward obtaining a favorable vote. The ballots were cast under the supervision of the Haitian constabu-

---

[1] For the text of this agreement, see *Treaties, etc., of the U.S.*, III: 2677.

[2] *Sale of Foreign Bonds or Securities in the United States*, pp. 2131*ff*.

[3] *Ibid.*, pp. 2129, 2147. Secretary Stimson testified with regard to the loan: "This Government assisted Haiti to obtain such a loan to straighten out the financial chaos that then existed and its efforts since that time have been directed solely to helping Haiti and to doing what appeared to be to the best interests of the Haitian people." *Ibid.*, p. 2174.

lary which was under the control of the marines. The constitution carrying the desired changes received an overwhelmingly favorable vote in a light election.[1] Following this amendment a few American corporations acquired real estate holdings in Haiti.[2]

Financial and Political Controls Stimulate American Capital Exports. The fact that investments have been afforded protection abroad and the expectation that such protection will continue are inducements to American bankers to make other investments. Particularly has this been true when the United States has set up a formal system of control which has given to this country a regularized and intimate relationship with the backward country for the maintenance of stable government. The Platt Amendment, which from 1904 to 1934 granted to the United States the treaty right to suppress disorders under certain circumstances in Cuba, was responsible for a great increase in American investments. The customs control system in Haiti, Santo Domingo, and Nicaragua has been associated with strong protection policies and has helped to attract American capital to those countries. The comparatively high prices of the bonds of the controlled governments are evidences of the readiness of capitalists to invest in such securities.

The financial control system also influences the debtor countries to seek American capital in preference to that from other investing countries. In Cuba the United States maintained until 1934 the power of passing upon foreign loans. New York bankers were accordingly favored. In Haiti and Liberia, American financial advisers have naturally turned to New York when questions of borrowing have arisen. American officials attached to other governments have influenced those governments to resort to American bankers for loans or to prefer American concessionaires. Dr. James W. Angell remarks concerning these tendencies:

Particularly in Cuba and the Dominican Republic, and to a less extent in most of the other countries [in the sphere of American influence], the political actions of the United States government created situations which promised order and security; and which in fact if not in law gave pre-

---

[1] WILLIAMS, *Economic Foreign Policy of the United States*, pp. 34ff. The constitution also carried clauses ratifying the acts of the American occupation. The text of the constitution is found in *Foreign Relations*, 1918, p. 487.

[2] Other examples of objections to local restriction upon capital are those against Mexican land regulations in 1879, *Foreign Relations*, 1913, p. 647, and the complaints against Chinese mining regulations which impeded the investment of foreign capital contrary to the stipulations of the Treaty of 1903. See *Foreign Relations*, 1908, pp. 152, 173, and *ibid.*, 1914, p. 134.

ferential treatment to Americans, as against the citizens of other foreign countries. Behind the wall of protection thus created, American capital and business enterprise made haste to flow in.[1]

2. REQUESTING AMERICAN BANKERS TO MAKE LOANS

The Department of State has found that in carrying out certain of its policies the assistance of American capital has been indispensable.[2] For this reason the department has sometimes requested that American bankers should make loans in cases where the invested dollar can be expected to be an ally of diplomacy. In answer to a question about loans made by his company at the request of the Department of State in Nicaragua, the representative of J. & W. Seligman, testifying before the Senate Finance Committee, in 1932, said: "As long as we were the bankers for Nicaragua in any shape I will say that we did nothing that was not either approved by the State Department or at its suggestion."[3] In 1909 the Department of State was keenly interested in Honduran finance because of the difficulties between Honduras and British bondholders. The department made efforts to interest American bankers in taking over the public debt. In various cases when bankers visited the Department of State on other matters, the question of Honduran financing was placed before them by departmental officials.[4] When Secretary Knox desired to introduce American capital into the National Bank of the Republic of Haiti in 1910, he requested that several bankers from New York should meet with him in Washington to discuss the matter. The subsequent purchase of the bank is referred to later in this chapter.[5] Various loans to China have also been discussed with American bankers by the Secretary of State.[6]

[1] *Financial Foreign Policy of the United States*, p. 38, a report to the Second International Studies Conference on The State and Economic Life, London, May 29 to June 2, 1933, published in New York, 1933.

[2] For an examination of the ways in which investments serve diplomacy see STALEY, EUGENE, *War and the Private Investor*, Chapter IV, Doubleday, Doran & Company, Garden City, N.Y., 1935. See also Chapter X of the same work for the methods used by governments in influencing investors.

[3] *Sale of Foreign Bonds or Securities in the United States*, p. 1316.

[4] *Foreign Relations*, 1912, p. 551.

[5] See pp. 199–200.

[6] See, for example, the preliminary discussions leading to the consortium of 1920, *Foreign Relations*, 1918, p. 172. Another illustration is found in the influence brought to bear upon the National City Bank to extend credit to Colombia in 1931. See pp. 223–224.

3. MEETING THE COMPETITION OF OTHER CAPITAL-EXPORTING POWERS

Probably the greatest danger to peace from the export of capital into backward areas comes not from friction with the backward nations but from collisions with other great powers which are supporting the policy of their investors in those regions. The United States has adopted a double set of policies in meeting this competition. In the far-off continent of Asia, where with the exception of the Philippines the United States has no territorial interests and no great military power, this country has adopted the unaggressive policy of the open door. In the Caribbean region the United States possesses important strategic interests and has been easily able to apply armed force to support its policies. The open door has not been stressed in that section; but a modified sphere of interest has existed in which American enterprises have been encouraged and European enterprises sometimes discouraged.

The Open Door. The pressure upon the Department of State for the open-door policy in Asia has come from merchants seeking equality in trade opportunities[1] and from bankers who have looked across the Pacific at the exceptional possibilities for capital in the development of China. A huge population, latent resources, and a scarcity of capital has offered hopes for a higher rate of interest than could be obtained at home. But before Americans had come to the point where they were able to furnish capital in any considerable quantities, China had been divided into spheres of interest by other capitalist powers. Thus North Manchuria was claimed as a region for economic development by Russia, South Manchuria by Japan, Shantung by Germany until 1915 and then by Japan, the Yangtze Valley by Great Britain, Fukien by Japan, a portion of South China and the Island of Hainan by France. In each of these areas the power claiming the sphere demanded for its nationals the right to supply capital, if foreign financial assistance should be needed, for the construction of railways and public works. In some places a monopoly for the furnishing of foreign capital for mining development was also claimed.

The Department of State found that this system of spheres of interest was destructive of American investment opportunities. In 1916 the Siems-Carey Company, financially supported by the International Corporation, obtained contracts from the Chinese government for the construction of railway lines totaling about

---

[1] For the commercial side of the open-door policy see pp. 131*ff.*

1,500 miles to be located in various parts of China. The contract rights were, however, almost entirely nullified by the opposition of powers claiming spheres of interest in the provinces where the different roads were to be built. The United States combated the claims of spheres of interest and sought to clear away the objections to the proposed railroad construction, but with little success.[1] The Nine-Power Treaty, drawn up during the Washington conference of 1921–1922, contained provisions which were intended to destroy the system of spheres of interest. These provisions were proposed by Secretary of State Hughes,[2] and were an amplification of the American policy.

The open-door policy of the United States in Asia has had the effect at times of making China and other Asiatic governments disposed to favor American capital as opposed to that from countries which have been more aggressively inclined. This sentiment, however, has not been evidenced in Latin-American countries where the opinion has sometimes been expressed that American capital is more dangerous to the independence of the borrowing country than would be that from European countries.

Joint Investments as a Means of Introducing American Capital. As a positive means of obtaining equal participation for American financiers in foreign enterprises, the United States has, on occasion, demanded that American capital be admitted into specific investments jointly with that of other creditor powers. Thus, in 1909, Secretary of State Knox demanded for certain New York banks the right to participate in the promising Hukuang Railways enterprise, an ambitious project, designed to connect the populous areas of Canton, Hankow, and the Upper Yangtze. The enterprise had been organized by British, German, and French capitalists; and their governments attempted earnestly in Peking to block American entry into the group. Finally, in pressing the embarrassed Chinese government for a favorable decision, President Taft sent a telegram direct to the Prince Regent of China, stating that he was "disturbed" at the opposition to American capital; while Secretary Knox informed the Chinese Foreign Office that the refusal of the request would be an act of "singular unfriendliness." The Chinese govern-

[1] *Foreign Relations*, 1916, pp. 183*ff.*; *ibid.*, 1917, pp. 160*ff.* See also WILLOUGHBY, *Foreign Rights and Interests in China*, II: 1083; WILLIAMS, E. T., *China Yesterday and Today*, p. 425, Thomas Y. Crowell Company, New York, 1923.

[2] *Conference on the Limitation of Armament, Washington, November 12, 1921–February 6, 1922*, p. 1214, Govt. Printing Office, Washington, 1922. See also pp. 135–136.

ment finally yielded and the New York bankers were admitted to the project.[1]

Secretary Knox was not so successful in his efforts, begun in November, 1909, to obtain American participation in the financing of the Manchurian Railways. He suggested that an impartial administration of the railroads might be created with the ownership vested in China and the funds furnished by the interested powers. China, Russia, Japan, Great Britain, France, and Germany were approached. Russia and Japan, because of their interests in the Chinese Eastern and South Manchurian railways respectively, refused to agree; and the plan was dropped.[2]

With the coming of the Wilson administration in 1913 the United States for a time abandoned the policy of seeking joint investments with European capitalists. When the Wilson administration took office, certain American bankers were considering a plan for participating in a joint enterprise. The four-power group which had entered the Hukuang Railways venture had been increased by the addition of Japan and Russia to a six-power consortium; and the new group was contemplating a loan of $125,000,000 to the Chinese government for reorganization purposes. To make certain of the support of the new administration, a letter of inquiry was written to Secretary Bryan stating that the group had entered the loan at the request of the Department of State and asking to know the wishes of the new administration as to the future conduct of the negotiations. Shortly afterwards President Wilson answered the inquiry by a statement to the press in which he declined to request the continuance of the American group in the undertaking because the conditions of the loan in mortgaging some of the taxes of China seemed to touch very nearly the administrative independence of that country.[3]

In 1918, however, the American government reversed its policy again. Criticisms had been made that the idealism of Wilson rendered impossible the introduction of American capital into China. The United States had begun to view investment matters from the standpoint of a creditor nation. Furthermore, because of war conditions, Chinese financing was coming under the domination of Japan. In 1918, therefore, Secretary of State Lansing proposed to Great Britain, France, and Japan that the four governments should

---

[1] See *Foreign Relations*, 1909, pp. 144*ff.*; 1910, pp. 269*ff.*; 1912, p. 87.

[2] *Ibid.*, 1910, pp. 231*ff.*; CROLY, HERBERT, *Willard Straight*, pp. 238*ff.*, The Macmillan Company, New York, 1925.

[3] See *Foreign Relations*, 1913, p. 170.

support a new four-power consortium which should make all public loans to China.[1] Banking groups were accordingly designated in the four countries and on October 15, 1920, their representatives, with the acquiescence and support of their governments, signed the consortium agreement.[2] Public loans to the Chinese national or provincial governments or agencies were thereafter to be made jointly by the four groups. The groups were given a monopoly of governmental support in each of the countries concerned. Although there was no legal provision to prevent bankers outside the groups from lending money to China, the realization that they would receive no governmental support was expected to discourage the public flotation of the bonds by nonconsortium bankers. Thus far the political disorders of China have made the matter of loans impossible. Defaults in previous loans and the fact that nationalistic Chinese have been antagonistic to the consortium have made the situation unfavorable. Some of the Chinese allege that the consortium is an attempt to monopolize the business of lending to China, to dictate money terms, and to bring China more completely under foreign domination.[3] The consortium by its terms was to expire in five years. The agreement was continued by common consent among the banking groups, each one retaining the right to withdraw upon one year's notice. No notice has thus far been given. Early in 1935, however, it was reported that the Japanese government was attempting to make a large loan directly to China without the cooperation of the other powers. The British government at the same time was seeking to block the Japanese plan by promoting a joint loan by the four consortium powers.[4] Until this matter is settled, the fate of the system of joint investment in China is hanging in the balance.

The opposition of the United States to the recent Japanese program of controlling commercial investments in China has already been alluded to.[5] Perhaps this subject opens up a controversy over investment opportunities in the Far East which will prove to be much more serious than have any disputes of the past.

---

[1] *Foreign Relations*, 1918, pp. 169*ff.*; 1919, I: 420*ff.*

[2] For the text see *Treaties, etc., of the U.S.*, III: 3822.

[3] CLARK, GROVER, *Economic Rivalries in China*, p. 70, Yale University Press, New Haven, 1932; T'ANG LEANG-LI, *China in Revolt*, pp. 93–96, Noel Douglas, London, 1927.

[4] CLARK, GROVER, "Japanese Pressure on China," *Current History*, XLII: 108 (April, 1935).

[5] See p. 136.

The American Sphere. In the region of American influence in the Caribbean and in Central America, the United States has possessed vital strategic interests, and has, at the same time, been in a position to exercise its military strength with comparatively little effort and danger. This country has, therefore, not demanded the open door. The policy has rather been to stimulate the introduction of American capital and at times to place obstacles in the way of European investors. When Secretary of State Philander C. Knox sought to refund with American dollars the British-held public debt of Guatemala in 1913, he referred pointedly to this section as "a sphere in which this government is preeminently interested."[1]

American views as to the political importance of investments and as to the desirability of obtaining financial control in the Caribbean area were well demonstrated by the action of the Department of State in introducing American capital into Haiti. Prior to the World War the strongest financial interests in Haiti were French. The National Bank of the Republic of Haiti was for the most part in the hands of French bankers and the public debt of Haiti was likewise owed, for the most part, to French bondholders. German financiers also held interests in Haiti. In 1913 and 1914 reports reached Washington that French and German warships had been instrumental in collecting sums due their respective nationals. The French government had conceived a plan for taking control of the Haitian customhouses in cooperation with Germany and the United States. The fact that participation by each government in this plan was to be in proportion to the holdings of its nationals emphasized the political importance of investments.

The United States had already taken action to replace French capital in the bank. In 1910 Secretary Knox had complained about a project for the reorganization of the National Bank of the Republic of Haiti because it gave too much power to the bank; and he advised the Haitian government against a plan "so prejudicial to American interests, so disastrous to the sovereignty of Haiti and so unjust in its operations in regard to the people and government of Haiti."[2] Furthermore, he insisted that American bankers should be allowed to participate in the ownership of the institution. The reorganization was blocked and four New York banking houses were then

[1] *Foreign Relations*, 1913, p. 559.

[2] BUELL, RAYMOND LESLIE, "The American Occupation of Haiti," Foreign Policy Association, *Information Service*, Vol. V, Nos. 19 and 20 (Nov. 27–Dec. 12, 1929), p. 334.

permitted to buy 8,000 of the 40,000 shares of the bank. After the World War began, Secretary Bryan suggested on several occasions that it would be advantageous to the United States if American bankers should own the whole of the bank. Acting on departmental advice, the National City Bank in 1917 purchased the 8,000 shares owned by the New York banks; and in 1920 the same institution acquired the remaining shares of the bank.[1] Considering the importance which the French government had attached to the domination of French capital in Haiti, it must be assumed that the Haitian bank was not given up lightly. It is probable that the desperate financial condition of France following the World War and the heavy obligations to the United States for financial and military assistance caused the French government to advise the sale of the bank to conform to the wishes of the Department of State. From the time when American bankers first obtained a share in the bank, that institution became a valuable agency to advance American political control in Haiti.

Obstacles have in many cases been placed in the way of British and European investors in the Caribbean. In Cuba the Department of State once opposed concessions to companies which it believed to be owned by British subjects. In the case of the Caibarién-Nuevitas railway project, the Department of State instructed the American minister as follows:

Information received by Department forecasts an attempt to renew a project of British capitalists to rush through Cuban Congress concession for railroad from Nuevitas to Caibarién.

You will earnestly urge upon the President the desirability of postponing final action on this bill sufficiently to allow the fullest investigation and consideration, emphasizing the burden it would impose on the Cuban Treasury in favor of capital which is neither American nor Cuban.[2]

Likewise in Panama the United States has opposed foreign investments of certain kinds because of our strategic interests in the Panama Canal. In 1912 the Dziuk railway concession to British and German businessmen was canceled by Panama after objections

---

[1] See *Inquiry into Occupation and Administration of Haiti and Santo Domingo*, I: 105–106, 119; and Buell, above cited, pp. 343, 368. The bank was sold in 1935 to the Haitian government. See *N.Y. Times*, July 10, 1935.

[2] *Foreign Relations*, 1913, p. 381. See also the objection to the contract between Cuba and the Cuban Ports Company, a British concern, *Foreign Relations*, 1917, pp. 431*ff*.

from Washington.[1] In 1914 the United States government, after some insistence, obtained the right to a complete and permanent control over radio communication in Panama.[2] Foreign companies were thus barred from Panama.

Perhaps nothing more clearly demonstrates the contrast between our policies in the Caribbean and those maintained in the Far East than the insistence upon the creation of an American radio monopoly in Panama during such time as we were asking for the open door in China. In 1921 Secretary of State Hughes argued energetically that the Federal Telegraph Company of California should not be excluded from China by monopolies which were claimed by the Mitsui Company of Japan and by the British Marconi Company. Mr. Hughes made it clear to China that we made no claims in that country for special rights and privileges and would not acquiesce in any arrangement giving such privileges to other foreign countries.[3] The protection of the Panama Canal, on the other hand, appeared to the United States to be a sufficient reason for actively seeking a complete radio control in the Republic of Panama.

OIL DIPLOMACY AS ILLUSTRATIVE OF CAPITAL-EXPORT POLICIES

The activities of the Department of State in behalf of American oil interests exemplify in a general way the policy of the open door and of the American sphere. In Asia the United States has asked for equal treatment for American interests, but in the area of the Caribbean non-American capital has been discouraged.

Oil diplomacy was a natural aftermath of the World War. The motorization of army transportation by the use on a large scale of trucks, tractors, motorcycles, and airplanes, and the introduction of oil-burning engines in naval and merchant shipping emphasized the importance of petroleum in connection with military power. A nervous state of mind regarding future supplies was inevitable, and a contest for the world's oil began among the leading nations. In the forefront of the fight were huge petroleum companies searching for fabulous riches of "black gold." The Standard Oil and the Royal Dutch-Shell were chief among the economic giants, but there were other large concerns in England and America which collided fiercely with each other. Behind these companies were the Department of State and the British Foreign Office each supporting its own capitalists with the rhetoric of diplomacy.

[1] *Foreign Relations*, 1912, pp. 1167*ff.*

[2] *Ibid.*, 1914, pp. 1036–1052.

[3] WILLOUGHBY, WESTEL W., *Foreign Rights and Interests in China*, I: 103; II: 961.

The Demand for the Open Door in Asia. In requesting the open door for the investment of American capital in distant oil fields, probably the most important controversy took place concerning Iraq. The Mesopotamian oil resources were well known previous to the World War. In order to develop them, the Turkish Petroleum Company had been formed and a promise of a concession had been obtained by joint British and German representations to the Turkish government. The company was owned by the Anglo-Persian (50 per cent), the Royal Dutch-Shell (25 per cent), and the Deutsche Bank (25 per cent). Following the war the British government sought this area, now known as Iraq, as a mandate and received a favorable decision at the San Remo Conference in 1920.[1] In a secret agreement the share of the Deutsche Bank in the Turkish Petroleum Company, which had been expropriated by Great Britain, was awarded to French interests in return for the promise of a right of way for a pipe line to the Mediterranean across the French mandate of Syria.

When the agreement was published, American oil interests were alarmed to see a rich oil field fully preempted by rival companies. The United States, having contributed to the victory in the war, then claimed the right to participate in discussions affecting the mandates. The Department of State made representations to the British government for the inclusion of American interests and urged that a policy of equality of treatment in the matter of concessions in the mandates should be adopted. The controversy was finally settled by an adjustment permitting certain American companies to acquire an interest amounting to 21.25 per cent in the project. Standard Oil officials in the United States regarded this outcome as in conformity with a practical open-door policy.

In addition to the expostulations in Iraq, demands for the open door for American capital were made upon the Dutch government with regard to Djambi and upon Persia with regard to the North Persian fields. Protests were also made to Great Britain concerning the interference of British officials with the exploratory work of the Standard Oil Company in Palestine.[2]

[1] Iraq, however, was never actually placed under mandate.

[2] Regarding these oil controversies consult DAVENPORT, E. H., and SIDNEY RUSSELL COOKE, *The Oil Trusts and Anglo-American Relations*, The Macmillan Company, New York, 1924; FISCHER, LOUIS, *Oil Imperialism*, International Publishers, New York, 1926; DENNY, LUDWELL, *We Fight for Oil*, Alfred A. Knopf, New York, 1928; ISE, JOHN, *The United States Oil Policy*, Yale University Press, New Haven, 1926; DE LA TRAMERYE, PIERRE L'ESPAGNOL, *The World-Struggle for Oil*, Alfred A. Knopf, New York, 1924.

The Veto of the Ethiopean Oil Concession of 1935. An illustration of a reverse position of the Department of State is shown in the unfavorable attitude taken toward an oil concession granted to an American company in Ethiopia before the invasion of that country by Italy in 1935. On August 29, 1935, the Ethiopian government granted to the African Exploration & Development Corporation, a subsidiary of the Standard Vacuum Oil Company, an extensive petroleum concession. The press was immediately filled with comments as to the possibility of the United States being drawn into a dispute with Italy over the validity of the American concession. Officials of the Standard Vacuum Oil Company visited the offices of the Department of State and were advised by Secretary Hull to drop the concession. The company then notified the Ethiopian government of the abandonment of the project.[1]

The Attempt to Keep Foreign Oil Companies Out of the Caribbean. In the American sphere the task of acquiring oil concessions for American companies in competition with those of Great Britain has been regarded as a serious task for diplomacy. In several cases the Department of State has opposed the granting of concessions to foreigners in this area. Negotiations for concessions in Colombia to the British Pearson interests were abandoned in 1913 after the opposition of President Wilson. In the same year the United States also opposed the granting of a concession to the Pearson group in Costa Rica. The Pearson request was refused by the Costa Rican government following the American protest, and a contract was then given to an American concern.[2]

Another concession-seeking company, John Amory and Son of New York, came under suspicion as being actually British in character. An American oil promoter, Lincoln J. Valentine, through some sort of espionage produced evidence to convince the American chargé that the company had strong British affiliations. The Secretary of State, on being informed of the evidence, sent the following instructions to the chargé:

[1] Dept. of State, *Press Releases*, Sept. 7, 1935, pp. 165–167.

[2] BUELL, RAYMOND LESLIE, "The United States and Central American Stability," *Foreign Policy Reports*, Vol. VII, No. 9 (July 8, 1931), p. 178. See also RIPPY, J. FRED, *The Capitalists and Colombia*, pp. 107ff., The Vanguard Press, New York, 1931. Even in the case of the American concessionaire, Dr. Greulich of New York, departmental officials were skeptical. The Teutonic name of the concessionaire and the fact that investigation showed that he had spent a large part of his life outside the United States caused the department to withdraw its support. He was, however, granted the concession. *Foreign Relations*, 1919, I: 869–871.

Department is most dissatisfied with the Amory concession as it cannot but feel that no oil properties in the neighborhood of the Panama Canal should be owned by other than Americans.[1]

The treaty for the payment of $25,000,000 to Colombia, which was negotiated during the Wilson administration to make amends for the Panama affair, was for some years held up in the United States Senate by the opposition of friends of Theodore Roosevelt. When it became known, however, that there were rich petroleum lands in Colombia and that American companies were having difficulty in obtaining concessions in competition with British companies, there was a definite change in senatorial attitude. With the senatorial runways well lubricated with oil, the treaty was easily passed.[2]

II. CAPITAL EMBARGOES

The Nature of the American Policy. Thus far we have discussed positive influences exerted by the Department of State on the export of American capital, influences which have had for their object the stimulation of the outward flow of capital. Negative influences have also been exerted at various times to prevent the making of American investments abroad when for some reason the department has either desired to penalize the foreign government by refusing it the privilege of borrowing in the United States or has wished to discourage the particular sort of enterprise for which the money has been sought.

The formal statement of American policy is found in a State Department announcement of March 3, 1922, and in subsequent explanations. Banking firms in this country which are contemplating making loans abroad by public flotation are asked to inform the Department of State. The department will then be in a position to say whether it has any objections to the loans from the standpoint of national policy. Should the department object to any loan, the firm will still be at liberty so far as the law is concerned to float a bond issue. The American system of capital embargo contrasts in this respect with the system used in France and some other countries where the consent of the government is a legal requirement for the public flotation of a bond issue. Despite its purely extralegal character, however, the American policy of departmental advice is undoubtedly effective. Should the banker proceed with the loan

[1] *Foreign Relations*, 1919, I: 874. The Amory concession was granted in 1918 but it was later annulled after the United States had expressed its dissatisfaction.

[2] WILLIAMS, *Economic Foreign Policy of the United States*, pp. 74–77; RIPPY, *The Capitalists and Colombia*, pp. 115ff.

against the objections of the department, it is more than likely that public knowledge of the official disapproval would so interfere with the sale of the bonds as to bring losses upon the firms connected with the flotation. Bankers have, therefore, been willing to respect departmental wishes.

Officials of the department have stated on numerous occasions that they do not pretend to pass upon the soundness of the loans as business propositions. The form of the departmental reply where there are no objections to the loan is illustrated in the following case. A firm informed the department in 1930 of a proposal for an issue by the Cuban government of $80,000,000 of 5½ per cent gold bonds for the construction of public works. The department answered as follows:

> In reply to your request to be advised of the attitude of the State Department with respect to this proposed financing, the Department desires to confirm the notification made to you by telephone to the effect that the Government of the United States does not perceive occasion for raising any objection to the proposal in question.[1]

Officials have repeatedly pointed out that the failure to object to a bond issue is not to be construed as an approval of the loan and they do not wish that the bankers should refer to the position of the department upon the loan. An additional requirement has been added since the notorious Peruvian loans of 1927 and 1928, when Juan Leguia, son of the President of Peru, received an "introductory commission" of $415,000 for his service in obtaining the business for the bankers. The department has adopted a rule that bankers should state with regard to any loan that no commissions are being paid to any government officials or persons connected with such officials.[2]

The Application of the American Policy. The principal reason for the department's pronouncement in 1922 seems to have been the necessity of bringing pressure against countries which had refused to fund their war debts owed to the United States. France was the particular country in mind. In 1925 a dramatic speech in the Chamber of Deputies by Louis Marin had voiced the sentiment of opposition to the debts. M. Marin said:

> While war still raged, statesmen in every country appealed in the common cause. Some gave their ships, some munitions, some the lives of their sons, some money, and today only those who gave money come saying to us: "Give back what we loaned."

[1] *Sale of Foreign Bonds or Securities in the United States*, p. 1966.
[2] *Ibid.*, p. 1909.

Yet during the war money was munitions. It was not more valuable than the lives given by 1,450,000 Frenchmen who died on the field and 300,000 who died of their wounds.

Enthusiastic cheers broke from all parts of the chamber. Such evidence of the attitude of France regarding the debts caused Washington to advise against further loans to France until the debt should be funded.[1] The embargo was a severe blow to France. The fall of the franc in 1926 made it highly desirable that the government should obtain large loans to support its currency but these could not be procured. Bitter sentiment was for a time evoked against Americans. The embargo was raised by degrees. In 1927 the ban was lifted with regard to refunding of existing loans. In 1928 industrial loans were permitted; and finally, in 1929, when the French parliament had acted favorably upon the Mellon-Berenger funding agreement, the embargo was terminated.[2]

An embargo was placed on loans to Russia after 1922 because of the fact that the Soviet government had repudiated its loans to the United States and had expropriated without compensation property belonging to American citizens. The department also extended its objections to include some loans to Russia not publicly floated. Thus, in 1928, the department objected to the sale of Russian bonds directly through the mail to American investors.[3]

Embargoes set up because of disapproval of the purpose of the particular loans are illustrated in the cases of the potash and coffee loans of 1925. The State of São Paulo in Brazil sought capital for the valorization of coffee, and the German Potash Syndicate desired a loan to support the potash monopoly. Both these loans were disapproved because of the objections of Herbert Hoover, then Secretary of Commerce and the outstanding foe of raw material monopolies. Secretary Hoover took the position that American bankers should not participate in enterprises which would injure American consumers by creating an artificial rise in prices.[4] An objection was made in 1927 to a loan to establish a brewery in Czechoslovakia, a purpose which did not appear justifiable to the officials of the then-dry United States.[5]

[1] See WILLIAMS, *Economic Foreign Policy of the United States*, pp. 89–92.

[2] See, however, p. 207 for the embargo on public loans set up by the Johnson Act.

[3] WILLIAMS, *op. cit.*, p. 93.

[4] *Ibid.*, pp. 94–95.

[5] EDWARDS, GEORGE W., "Government Control of Foreign Investments," *American Economic Review*, 18: 699 (December, 1928). An outline of the

The Johnson Act Prohibiting Loans to Defaulting States. By 1928 the policy of advising against loans to countries which had defaulted in their payments to the American government remained effective only against Russia. The other war debtors whose intentions had been under suspicion had by this time funded their indebtedness. The epidemic of defaults which began in December, 1932, however, reopened the question; and nationalists in Congress took the matter into their own hands. In 1934 a Congressional act was passed placing an embargo upon loans to countries in default in the payment of debts to the United States government.[1] The act makes it a criminal offense to sell in the United States the securities of defaulting governments or political subdivisions issued after the passage of the act or to make loans to such governments or subdivisions except by way of renewal or adjustment of existing indebtedness. The securities of foreign private corporations and of governmental subdivisions not themselves in default are not affected.[2]

The Neutrality Act and Capital Embargoes. The lending of money to belligerents for war purposes has come under fire in the United States for a number of reasons. Such assistance has been considered by some to be contrary to the proper neutral spirit. The use of American funds for destructive purposes has been regarded as antisocial. There is the possibility that capitalists who have invested their money in supporting one set of belligerents will seek to involve the United States in war on the side of their customers in order to protect their investments. There is the further possibility that even victorious countries at the end of a disastrous war will be unable to repay the loans and that American capital will be thereby lost. On August 15, 1914, Secretary of State Bryan opposed loans to belligerent governments in a letter to J. P. Morgan and Company. He said: " . . . in the judgment of this Government, loans by American bankers to any foreign nation which is at war are inconsistent with the true spirit of neutrality."[3] The reasons behind Mr. Bryan's attitude are found in a letter of August 10, 1914, to President Wilson. The Secretary of State

principal grounds on which the United States has objected to foreign loans or on which it has contemplated objecting is found in ANGELL, *Financial Foreign Policy of the United States*, pp. 106–107.

[1] *U.S. Statutes at Large*, 48: 574.

[2] For a consideration of the effect of the act see the opinion of the Attorney General which was concurred in by the Department of State, Dept. of State, *Press Releases*, May 5, 1934, p. 259.

[3] *Foreign Relations*, 1914 (Supplement), p. 580.

declared that money was the worst of all contrabands because it commanded everything else and that the powerful financial interests would attempt to use their influence in behalf of the borrowing government. It would thus become more difficult for the United States to maintain its neutrality.[1] The embargo applied only to loans, and credit arrangements with American bankers were not disapproved.[2] Great financial forces soon set about to reverse the policy regarding loans. The pressure for exports became difficult to resist, and after Mr. Bryan retired from the Department of State in 1915 the embargo was withdrawn. President Wilson informed Secretary Lansing that the United States should take no stand either for or against such transactions.[3] This decision left the gate wide open, and shortly afterward loans to Great Britain and France were publicly floated in the United States.

That the financial aid to the Allies rendered by American bankers together with the consequent commercial relations played a considerable part in drawing the United States into the World War has become a popular belief in this country and is supported by much evidence. Revelations of banker influence by the Senate munitions investigation of 1934–1936 created a considerable sentiment against loans of this character. Accordingly, when amendments to the Neutrality Resolution of 1935 were passed in 1936, the making of loans and the extension of credits for belligerent purposes in times of neutrality were included in the list of proscribed acts.[4]

The Securities Act. The Department of State assumes no general responsibility for passing upon the soundness of loans as business propositions. Some of the reasons for advising unfavorably upon loans deal with capacity to pay and other factors connected with soundness. With the unfortunate experience of American bondholders during the depression there developed a feeling in Congress that the investing public was entitled to additional protection. In 1933 and 1934 Congress passed legislation which provides that certain information regarding security issues must be filed with the Securities and Exchange Commission before such securities can be sold in this country. The law applies to both foreign and domestic securities. With regard to foreign govern-

---

[1] The letter was uncovered in the Senate munitions investigation in 1936. See *N.Y. Times*, Jan. 8, 1936.

[2] *Foreign Relations*, 1915 (Supplement), p. 820.

[3] *N.Y. Times*, Jan. 10, 1936. See also *Foreign Relations*, 1916 (Supplement), p. 8.

[4] For a more detailed statement of the provisions of the act see pp. 31–32.

mental issues it is required that the information to be filed must set forth among other things the purpose of the issue, a description of the existing indebtedness of the government, a statement of any defaults that may have occurred within twenty years, and an itemization of governmental receipts and expenditures. A prospectus containing similar information must be used in connection with the sale of the securities. Unless these provisions are complied with, it is unlawful to use the mails or the instrumentalities of interstate commerce for the purpose of sale or transportation of the securities.[1] The purchaser thus receives some additional protection against false prospectuses and is given some facts upon which he can form a judgment as to the soundness of the investment.

[1] *U.S. Statutes at Large*, 48: 74, 905.

CHAPTER XII

PROTECTION OF LOANS AND INVESTMENTS

In an unorganized world there is a tendency for debtor nations to disregard somewhat the rights of their foreign creditors. The local government responds to political pressure from its own population whose interests are frequently opposed to those of nonresident investors. The age-old struggle between debtor and creditor classes thus becomes an international conflict with the local government on the side of the debtor. If there were not some compensating factors, the development of backward nations through imported capital would indeed be a precarious procedure. The foreign investors have, however, some redress through their right to refuse additional funds and through the intervention of their own government. Thus the foreign offices of creditor nations have been pressed to make representations and to impose diplomatic and military sanctions in behalf of their citizens who have investments abroad.

There are two reasons, however, why the protective activities of the creditor government may sometimes lead to international misunderstandings and injustices. In the first place, the doctrine of the security of property, which the creditor nation is forced to advocate, frequently comes into conflict with the right of the debtor government to control business for the social welfare. In the second place, the principle of the sanctity of contracts, which is the backbone of capitalistic morality, is sometimes difficult to apply in dealings across national boundaries because of the implacable obstacles created by international exchange.

With the above considerations in mind, it seems that in the present disorganized state of international dealings the creditor nation cannot well avoid a certain amount of diplomatic concern in seeing that debtor nations do not ruthlessly disregard the rights of investors. The duty of supervision over investment interests should, however, be subjected to at least three qualifications. (1) The remedies should not involve a cost in money and good will which would amount to more than a very modest proportion of the investments which are to be protected or which may be beneficially affected by the establishment of the particular protection principle.

(2) Ample allowance should be made for the rights of the debtor government to apply a reasonable police power in the interests of its own people even if such legislation should reduce the profits of the investment. (3) The creditor government should take into consideration the difficulties if not the impossibility of making international payments against an adverse exchange.

No great creditor nation has ever reached the above-outlined standards of moderation in its protection policies. The ex parte character of the evidence presented to foreign offices and the complete lack of any political responsibility to the people of the debtor nation have made it highly improbable in any given case that a fair and objective view will be taken. Many students of the protection problem have advised that institutions of international organization should be created to deal with such matters. Perhaps the creditor nation would benefit most of all if it were able to shift the well-nigh impossible task of maintaining a wise and moderate protection policy to the shoulders of regional or world commissions and tribunals.

TENDENCIES IN THE UNITED STATES REGARDING PROTECTION POLICIES

New interest groups created in the United States by the sudden rise in foreign investments have solicited the government to extend its protective activity. Influential and capable lawyers, some of them former diplomatic officials, have been employed to represent investors before the Department of State. Senators have been asked to communicate to the department requests for protection for the property of their constituents. Chambers of commerce, composed of American businessmen residing in other countries, have protested against threats to the enterprises of their members. American corporations of many descriptions have invoked the assistance of the department. Woodcutting and mining companies in Nicaragua have asked for warship and marine protection during riotous times. Sugar corporations in Cuba, petroleum owners in Mexico, and trading companies in China have called for diplomatic intervention or for the display of force in their behalf.[1] The United States has often ignored these requests, asking the investors to seek their remedies from the foreign government. Nevertheless, the multiplication in the years from 1914 to 1929 of the numbers and enthusiasm of citizens holding property abroad unquestionably made substantial alterations in the character of American policies.

[1] See STALEY, *op. cit.*, pp.204 *ff.*, as to methods by which investors influence their governments.

Perhaps American protection policies received their fullest expression in the pronouncements of Calvin Coolidge. President Coolidge idealized the constitutional principles of property protection that have been developed under the Americanized common law. The American guarantees which protect the individual and his business against the interference of the government were, he erroneously believed, usually accepted in principle if not in practice by all civilized countries. He declared that the right to governmental protection accompanied the American businessman wherever he might travel. For, he said, "the person and property of the citizen are part of the general domain of the nation, even when abroad."[1] Such an audacious formula would have given the United States the right to intervene in the political affairs of every section of the earth into which the vast, outflowing tide of American capital might find its way. But even President Coolidge did not attempt to put the doctrine fully into practice. Its implications were too vast and too full of potential world-wide trouble to be applied. The Coolidge administration contented itself with strong protection efforts in the region of Mexico and the Caribbean where the risk was relatively small and the stakes were relatively large.

The depression, with its devastating effects upon international economic enterprises, weakened the American creditor group. Their fervor receded and their lobby pressure was lowered in comparison with the influence of powerful factions which made appeals in behalf of domestic interests. The moderation of American protection policies, which is one of the most striking phenomena of recent American diplomacy, was largely coincident with the depression

LAW AND POLICY

An important part of the work of the Department of State is concerned with the advocacy of the rights of Americans who have legal claims to present against foreign governments. A considerable body of international law is devoted to defining the liability of states for injuries done to foreigners. One of the duties of the legal adviser and his assistants in the Department of State is to determine whether demands for diplomatic assistance are well founded in law or are justified under some particular treaty. The subject belongs to a treatise on law rather than to a consideration of policy.[2] A large

---

[1] *N.Y. Times*, Apr. 26, 1927.

[2] See particularly BORCHARD, EDWIN H., *The Diplomatic Protection of Citizens Abroad*, Banks Law Publishing Company, New York, 1915.

part of protection activity, however, lies outside the field of juris-prudence. There are many points on which the law is not clear. Diametrically opposite rules are sometimes advanced by different classes of countries with countrary interests, as, for example, the debtor and creditor countries. Each group contends for the legal correctness of its position. Even where the law appears to be clear, the strong political influence of interested individuals may sometimes cause a government to act in a manner which is contrary to the established legal principle. Foreign offices, for purposes of more effective diplomatic representation, frequently deal with doubtful matters in precise legal terminology to convey the impression that the contentions of the government are merely a statement of well-recognized and fully accepted principles. Such a practice gives rise to an illusion that the field of protection activity is well covered by law.

Creditor-Nation Attitude of the United States in Controversies on International Law. In some of the diplomatic controversies in which this country has engaged we can see the tendency of the United States to associate itself in legal doctrine with the stronger, capital-exporting countries as opposed to the less powerful, capital-importing nations. Jurists of creditor nations have sought to make a differentiation as between the legal principles applied to the stronger and weaker countries. The generally acknowledged responsibility of strong and well-ordered countries is that they must give to foreigners the same standards of protection that they apply to their own citizens. With regard to weaker and less stable governments, such as in China and the countries of the Caribbean, a different doctrine has been applied. It has been argued that, since these governments are incompetent to maintain a proper and civilized condition of order within the country and since they cannot measure up to what has been called an international standard of justice, the guarantees which they give to their own citizens are not adequate. They must, therefore, bestow upon the foreigners a higher degree of protection than they give to their own citizens. Their efforts to afford protection must be judged by the so-called international standard. Elihu Root, who had been Secretary of State at a time when large American investments were being made in Mexico and the Caribbean, explained the doctrine in 1910 in these words:

There is a standard of justice, very simple, very fundamental, and of such general acceptance by all civilized countries as to form a part of the international law of the world. The condition upon which any country is entitled to measure the justice due from it to an alien by the justice which it accords to its own citizens is that its system of law and administration shall conform to this general standard.[1]

Mr. Root cited certain remarks of Lord Palmerston, an aggressive creditor-nation foreign minister, to support his point.

This doctrine has been repudiated by writers and foreign offices of many debtor countries. Since international law is presumed to consist of a body of rules accepted by the family of nations, it would appear to be incorrect to refer to any doctrine as law upon which the nations are divided into two camps.[2] Nevertheless, writers and officials of the United States frequently treat of the doctrine as if it were established law.[3]

There has also been a warm difference of opinion upon the legal right of the creditor to protest against the internal legislation of debtor states which injuriously affects investments. Such diplomatic intervention has been objected to by debtor nations as an interference with domestic affairs and, therefore, as an infringement of sovereignty. The United States, on the other hand, has claimed ample right to intervene for the protection of the property of its nationals from confiscation or unfair treatment where no adequate redress is provided in the local courts. There seems to be no possibility that the family of nations can agree on any precise principles concerning such matters.

The Calvo clause has frequently been used by Latin-American nations to shut off diplomatic protection. This clause, which appears in Latin-American constitutions, statutes, or in concession contracts, provides that a foreigner must accept contract rights or make investments subject to the understanding that he is not to

---

[1] *Proceedings of the American Society of International Law*, 1910, p. 21.

[2] See LAUTERPACHT, H., *The Function of Law in the International Community*, pp. 121–122, Oxford University Press, London, 1933.

[3] The record of crimes committed against foreigners in this country in past times casts serious doubts upon our former claims of a superior standard of law enforcement. Professor MacNair writes of the American treatment of the Chinese as follows: "From the time that the Chinese began to arrive in large numbers in the United States, during the sixth decade of the nineteenth century almost to the present day, individually and by groups, they have suffered bodily assault, robbery, and murder in hundreds of cases. No aliens in America have suffered as have the Chinese; compared with the treatment meted out to them in the United States the illtreatment of foreigners in China prior to 1900 was almost mild. Beating, stabbing, and shooting were practiced upon them with almost monotonous regularity for twenty years between 1855 and 1876." MACNAIR, HARLEY FARNSWORTH, *The Chinese Abroad*, pp. 278–279, The Commercial Press, Shanghai, 1925.

invoke the diplomatic protection of his government in any dispute relating to the concession or the investment. The United States has opposed the validity of such clauses on the theory that a citizen has no capacity to contract away the protection of his government. The right of protection, it is claimed, does not belong to the individual but rather to the state. The individual cannot waive the right. Legal tribunals have divided upon the legality of the Calvo clause.[1]

THE DUE PROCESS DOCTRINE

In protecting American property located abroad from confiscation, the United States government has at times resorted to a doctrine somewhat resembling that applied by the American courts under the provisions of the Fifth and Fourteenth amendments of the United States Constitution, which forbid the national government and the states respectively from depriving persons of property without due process of law. The Department of State has protested against various rules and regulations affecting property on the ground that they conflict with certain concepts of the Americanized common law. President Coolidge stated in a public address:

We have set up our institutions, established our ideals, and adopted our social standards. We believe that they are consistent with right and truth and justice. We live under a system that guarantees the sanctity of life and liberty through public order and protects the rights of private property under the principle of due process of law. . . . The fundamental laws of justice are universal in their application. These rights go with the citizen. Wherever he goes, these duties of our government must follow him.[2]

The Necessity of Court Review. At various times the Department of State has raised objection to the procedure adopted in other countries for determining questions affecting property rights by executive action without court review. Thus where the matter of compensation in cases of the expropriation of private property for public use has been in controversy, the department has emphasized that both the question as to whether the expropriation is for a public use and the question of the amount of compensation to be paid to the owner should be determined by an impartial tribunal after opportunity for a hearing. The department has felt that "this principle is

[1] For a general statement regarding such clauses see *Moore's Digest*, VI: 293*ff.*; BORCHARD, *op. cit.*, pp. 792*ff.*; RALSTON, JACKSON H., *The Law and Procedure of International Arbitration*, pp. 58–72, Stanford University Press, Stanford University, Calif.

[2] *N.Y. Times*, Apr. 26, 1927.

followed generally throughout the world as in accordance with the general idea of justice and equity."[1] The determination of such matters by executive action alone, in the eyes of the department, has violated this common principle. On various other occasions the United States has pointed out to Spanish countries the necessity of a final appeal to the courts in matters affecting property, such, for example, as the cancellation of concessions, and the determination of the amount of land necessary for the commercial purposes of American corporations.[2]

Objections to Allegedly Confiscatory Action—Oil in Mexico. Probably the outstanding dispute over legislation of a foreign state and, according to Secretary Lansing, "one of the most serious international questions that ever confronted this government,"[3] arose in connection with the oil legislation of Mexico. The Mexican constitution of 1917 stated in Article XXVII: "In the Nation is vested direct ownership of all minerals or substances which in veins, layers, masses, or beds, constitute deposits whose nature is different from the components of the land, such as minerals . . . petroleum and all hydrocarbons—solid, liquid or gaseous." While the ownership of the nation was said to be inalienable, concessions for exploitation could be granted by the government under certain conditions. The effect of these provisions was to restate the principle of separation of the subsoil from the surface and to retain in the government the title to the subsoil. Such had been the rule under the old Spanish law. During the Diaz regime the old principle of national ownership of the subsoil had been revoked in order to encourage the investment of capital. Such revocation had been made by the laws of 1884, 1892, and 1909, which legalized the transfer of subsoil titles to the individuals who purchased the surface title. Under this encouragement Americans had come into Mexico and had bought large tracts of oil lands. When Article XXVII of the new constitution went into effect, the Department of State, urged on by well-organized oil interests, took up with the Mexican government the matter of obtaining a nonretroactive interpretation in order to safeguard American petroleum titles already vested. The Mexican government seemed at times to have agreed to this interpretation.

---

[1] *Investigation of Mexican Affairs*, Hearings of the Committee on Foreign Relations of the United States Senate, II: 3178, Govt. Printing Office, Washington, 1920. See also *ibid.*, pp. 3121–3122, and *Foreign Relations*, 1917, p. 947.

[2] WILLIAMS, *Economic Foreign Policy of the United States*, p. 131.

[3] *Foreign Relations*, 1919, I: 773.

In 1925, however, a law was passed by the Mexican Congress on this subject which, in the opinion of the Department of State, was retroactive in its application. The law placed the petroleum properties in two classes:

1. The first class included those in which "positive acts" had been performed prior to May, 1, 1917, which was the date when the constitution had taken effect. By the term "positive acts" was meant an open declaration or act of exploitation which indicated an intent to take the oil from the ground. If there was not actual exploitation of the oil property, there must have been a lease or a contract which expressed in its terms the purpose of oil exploitation. Where positive acts had been performed, the oil rights could be exchanged for a concession of not more than fifty years. The concession might be renewed after its expiration. Thus the unlimited property right which had been previously held was reduced to a fifty-year concession from the government.

2. The second class included those properties with regard to which "positive acts" had not been performed. In these cases no concession to extract petroleum could be obtained as a matter of right. The law seems to have been based on the theory that the subsoil titles, granted to the property owner during the Diaz regime, were gifts from the state and that they must have been possessed by open act in order to have been fixed as property rights. In the eyes of the legislature no substantial injustice would have been done if a landowner had petroleum under his property and had simply held it for speculation or had been in entire ignorance of the existence of the petroleum prior to May 1, 1917.[1]

The United States contended that the doctrine of "positive acts" was unjust and that, after the property to the subsoil had been once granted, there was no need of "positive acts" to perfect the title. Such would undoubtedly have been the case under the laws of the United States, but Mexican officials cited civil law authorities to support the legality of the positive acts provision under the Mexican system of jurisprudence.

The United States further contended that in the case of those who had performed "positive acts" the reduction of their titles to fifty-year concessions was the exchange of a greater for a lesser estate in the land and was to that extent a confiscation of property. The Mexican officials argued that the owners would have ample time to extract the oil under a fifty-year concession and that if they could not exhaust the supply in that time the concession could be extended. Therefore, they affirmed, no injustice was done by this provision.

In 1927 the Mexican Supreme Court declared unconstitutional that portion of the law which had reduced the "positive act" titles to fifty-year concessions. These titles, it was declared, vested the

---

[1] For a discussion of the origin and character of the "positive acts" doctrine, see DUNN, FREDERICK SHERWOOD, *The Diplomatic Protection of Americans in Mexico*, pp. 347*ff.*, Columbia University Press, New York, 1933.

owners with permanent rights in the subsoil. Following the decision, a law, approved January 3, 1928, provided for the confirmation without limitation of time of concessions for petroleum exploitation of those properties where "positive acts" had been performed prior to May 1, 1917. Owners of properties with regard to which "positive acts" had not been performed were, however, unable to obtain satisfaction.[1]

Protest against Spanish Project for Nationalizing American Telephone Monopoly. A forecast of the kind of conflict which may arise between a strong capitalist creditor nation, such as the United States, and the new type of socialistically inclined government, now becoming prevalent in different parts of the world, may be seen in the controversy in 1932 with the Spanish Republic on the question of the nationalization of the telephone service which was largely American owned. During the dictatorship of Primo de Rivera, under the monarchy in 1924, the Spanish National Telephone Company was created and was given a monopoly for twenty years of the telephone service in Spain. The controlling interest in the company, to the extent of $65,000,000, was owned by the International Telephone and Telegraph Company, an American corporation. There were also some 20,000 Spanish security holders.

On December 10, 1931, the very day on which the first constitutional president for Spain was elected, the Minister of Communications placed before the Cortes a project declaring that the monopoly of the National Telephone Company was illegal and that the system should be nationalized. He also proposed that within six months a bill should be introduced providing for the idemnification of the shareholders. One of the reasons alleged by the

---

[1] Another important contest took place over the rights of foreigners in lands in Mexico. For a discussion of the land and oil questions see HACKETT, CHARLES WILSON, *The Mexican Revolution and the United States*, 1910–1926, World Peace Foundation, Boston, 1926; DUNN, *op. cit.*, pp. 332–381; CALLAHAN, JAMES MORTON, *American Foreign Policy in Mexican Relations*, pp. 584*ff.*, The Macmillan Company, New York, 1932; Dept. of State, *Proceedings of the United States—Mexican Commission Convened in Mexico City, May* 14, 1923, Govt. Printing Office, Washington, 1925; *Rights of American Citizens in Certain Oil Lands in Mexico*, Senate Document No. 96, 69th Cong., 1st Sess.; *American Property Rights in Mexico*, Govt. Printing Office, Washington, 1926; TANNENBAUM, FRANK, *The Mexican Agrarian Revolution*, pp. 370*ff.*, The Macmillan Company, New York, 1929; GRUENING, ERNEST, *Mexico and Its Heritage*, pp. 111*ff.*, 600*ff.*, Century Company, New York, 1928. For objections to an oil decree in Colombia in 1919 see *Foreign Relations*, 1919, pp. 771*ff.* For objections to Colombian legislation in 1928 see RIPPY, J. FRED, *The Capitalists and Colombia*, pp. 142*ff.*

Spanish government for the illegality of the concession was that it had been granted by the nonrepresentative Spanish monarchy. Another allegation was that representatives of the company had paid 500,000 pesetas in bribes to a high personage in order to obtain the monopoly.

The bill lay before the Cortes for almost a year during which time consideration was urged by the deputies of the Left. In November, 1932, the government was finally prepared to consider the measure and the company was ordered to make a formal defense. At this point the United States entered objections to the bill. The American ambassador protested against the unilateral destruction of the contract and alleged that a confiscation of property rights might result. The United States seemed to feel that the Spanish government would set a bad example for the Latin-American countries who look to Spain for cultural leadership. If the Spanish government could successfully set aside a contract duly granted under a previous government, all American investments in Latin America might be jeopardized. The Spanish Foreign Office replied that the matter was a domestic issue between the Spanish government and a Spanish company. At this time dispatches from Washington carried the news that the controversy had reached an acute state and that the American ambassador might be withdrawn should the Cortes pass the bill. Feeling that the opposition of the American government might endanger the very existence of the new republic, the Spanish leaders decided to adjust the matter without bringing the bill up for a vote before the nationalistic Cortes. The Cortes then authorized a settlement between the government and the company on the basis of an amended contract without complete abrogation. The United States government acquiesced in this decision.[1]

MEANS OF PROTECTION—NONMILITARY METHODS

Diplomatic Protests. The usual and routine method of protection is through diplomatic representation. The department asks that the American citizen who wishes to present a claim will first exhaust his remedies before such judicial or administrative tribunals of the foreign state as may have jurisdiction over the matter. If there is then a denial of justice attributable to the foreign government or if the remedies prove to be inadequate or inapplicable, the

[1] *N.Y. Times,* Dec. 11, 1931; Nov. 19, 26, 30, 1932; and Dec. 1, 3, 4, 6, 7, 8, 1932. SURRIDGE, ROBERT G., "Prevention of Injury to American Investments Abroad," *Cumulative Digest of International Law Relations,* American University Graduate School, Vol. 2, Bulletin 48 (Dec. 17, 1932).

department will examine the claim with a view to ascertaining whether it may be properly urged through diplomatic channels.[1] A diplomatic request is frequently insufficient to procure the remedy sought by the American claimant. The other government may feel that the claim is unjustified or it may resist the demand for reasons of national feeling. The Department of State may then feel that other methods should be used. Methods sometimes used have included the submission of the claim to arbitration, the use of auxiliary methods of diplomatic pressure, and the employment of armed force.

Arbitration of Claims. The United States has taken a leading part in the movement for the arbitration of claims. This country has been much more insistent upon arbitration in such matters than it has upon the judicial settlement of other types of controversies. Being a creditor nation and feeling that most cases of claims in which this country is likely to become involved will be presented on behalf of the United States rather than against it, the American government has sought to obtain agreements in Pan-American conferences for the compulsory arbitration of pecuniary disputes.[2] This country has made a number of particular agreements with other governments to provide for submission of claims to mixed commissions. Some agreements have dealt with the claims of certain persons or companies.[3] Other agreements have included all outstanding claims between the countries. The convention of 1868 with Mexico provided for the submission to a mixed commission of the whole list of claims which had been presented to either government for interposition since the Treaty of Guadalupe Hidalgo in 1848. Each government appointed a commissioner. An umpire was selected by the two to cast the deciding vote in cases of disagreement. The General Claims Convention of 1923 with Mexico[4] provided for the arbitral settlement of all claims arising on either side since the convention of 1868 except claims resulting from the revolution which began in 1910. Arbitration of the revolutionary claims was provided for in the Special Claims Convention of 1923.[5] The decision of claims by a mixed commission

---

[1] Dept. of State, *General Instructions for Claimants*, Oct. 1, 1924 (rev.).

[2] See p. 103.

[3] See, for example, the executive agreement to arbitrate the claims of Pelletier and Lazare against Haiti in 1884. *Treaties, etc., of the U.S.*, I: 932.

[4] *U.S. Treaty Series*, No. 678. This was modified by a protocol of 1934, *U.S. Treaty Series, No.* 883.

[5] *Ibid.*, No. 676. See also No. 878 in which an adjustment was reached by convention apart from the claims commission previously provided.

between the United States and Panama was provided for by the General Claims Convention of 1926 and a supplemental convention of 1932.[1] The commission in this instance sat for four months and passed upon twenty-three cases involving fifty separate claims.[2] Of the 23 awards, 19 were in favor of American citizens and totaled $114,396.25, while four were in favor of citizens of Panama and amounted to $3,150.[3]

The settlement of claims by arbitration is a notable step in the direction of international government. The method has produced excellent results and has eliminated a large amount of irritating controversy. It is questionable, however, whether the mixed claims commission of three members is an entirely satisfactory device for settlement. Each party has a representative and the umpire casts the decision in cases of dispute. Much depends upon whether the umpire is a jurist of a creditor or debtor nation and upon his personal attitude toward the problems of international law. A larger and more representative permanent tribunal would appear to offer greater hope of satisfactory judicial settlement. A permanent international court of claims has been advocated by a number of authorities in this field. An essential feature as proposed by some writers would be the provision for the direct access of individuals and corporations to the court. Such a tribunal would relieve the foreign offices of creditor nations of much disagreeable work and would make possible a settlement of claims without relation to political controversies pending between the debtor and creditor nations.[4]

Withholding Recognition to Force Protection. In some cases a new government has been refused recognition by the United States until after alteration of particular policies that affect Americans or until certain disputes with American firms have been settled in accordance with American contentions. The policy has been described by a sympathetic writer as requiring that the new government must show an ability and willingness to discharge international

---

[1] *Ibid.*, Nos. 842 and 860.

[2] HUNT, BERT L., "The United States-Panama General Claims Commission," *American Journal of International Law*, XXVIII: 61 (January, 1934).

[3] *American and Panamanian General Claims Arbitration under Conventions of July* 28, 1926, *and December* 17, 1932, Govt. Printing Office, Washington, 1934.

[4] See BORCHARD, *op. cit.*, p. 861; STALEY, *op. cit.*, pp. 502, 540; and *An American Foreign Policy toward International Stability* (a memorandum drawn up by a committee of faculty members of the University of Chicago), p. 48, University of Chicago Press, Chicago, 1934.

obligations and responsibilities.[1]   Following the revolution of 1910 in Nicaragua, the United States drove a bargain with the new government by which certain promises of economic "reforms" were obtained in exchange for recognition.   One of these pledges was that the system of monopolies, opposed by American businessmen, would be abolished.   The new regime promised that all unsettled claims arising from canceled contracts and concessions would be examined by a mixed commission appointed by the government of Nicaragua in agreement with the United States.[2]   In 1914 when a new president had been elected in the Dominican Republic, the United States obtained from the incoming executive certain agreements to increase American control in Santo Domingo, *i.e.*, that the position of the American comptroller should be strengthened and that the collection of Dominican internal revenues should be placed in the hands of Americans.   After the promises were obtained in writing, the United States recognized the new administration.[3]   When Dr. Henriquez was chosen Dominican president in 1916, Secretary Lansing instructed the American minister as follows:

> Provisional government will not be recognized until it shows itself to be favorable to our interpretation of convention as to control, constabulary and other reforms and proves itself free from dominion of Arias.[4]

Some of these American interpretations of the convention with the Dominican Republic were hardly justifiable from a strictly legal point of view.   Nevertheless, when Dr. Henriquez refused to accede, recognition was refused.   The United States has entered into agreements favorable to American economic interests in exchange for recognition in Haiti and Mexico, while the making of a favorable bargain was part and parcel of the American policy in the recognition of Soviet Russia.

The Power of Finance : The Barco Concession.   A complicated case of protection, involving several types of relationship between American business and diplomacy, was that of the Barco oil concession in Colombia.   The safeguarding of a valuable speculation in petroleum in this affair led the United States government to make use of the power of finance to produce the proper diplomatic effects.

[1] HUGHES, CHARLES EVANS, *Our Relations to the Nations of the Western Hemisphere*, p. 41, Princeton University Press, Princeton, 1928.

[2] *Foreign Relations*, 1911, p. 653.   The commission was constituted by appointing two Americans to one Nicaraguan in order "to assure the justice and impartiality of the tribunal."   *Ibid.*, p. 640.

[3] *Ibid.*, 1914, pp. 255–261.

[4] *Ibid.*, 1916, p. 235.

In 1926 the Colombian government canceled the Barco concession which had been held by the Carib syndicate, an American oil concern. The concession, which had carried the right of exploitation in a rich petroleum region near the Venezuelan boundary, was set aside on the claim that the company had not fulfilled its contract. Two weeks after the cancellation a 75 per cent interest in the syndicate was purchased by the Gulf Oil Company, a Mellon corporation. After two years of unsuccessful effort to obtain a regrant of the concession, the company secured the assistance of the Department of State. The Colombian government, however, refused to recognize the right of political intervention. In 1928 the United States Department of Commerce issued a warning to bankers that Colombian bonds were a questionable investment.[1] The Colombian government then had difficulty in obtaining credits from abroad.

In 1930 when President-elect Olaya Herrera visited the United States, he was guest of honor at a dinner given by the Secretary of State and was seated next to Secretary of the Treasury Andrew W. Mellon. Matters affecting Colombia's economic recovery were naturally discussed. President Olaya later declared in a message to his Congress that the American officials showed him "great kindness." Secretary Mellon advised him: "Settle your pending question on petroleum; decide fairly and justly the difficulties which have been presented in this respect; and once you have adopted a policy which gives stability to the industrial activities in this branch, there will be opened for Colombia no doubt, ample ways for its economic progress and for its financial restoration."[2] After his inauguration President Olaya recommended on June 9, 1931, that the Colombian Congress should regrant the Barco concession. He felt that the action would have a good effect on the progress of Colombian financing in the United States.

The only question of financing open at the time was the matter of a $4,000,000 credit with the National City Bank of New York. The

---

[1] For the diplomatic negotiations up to this time no information can be obtained through published diplomatic correspondence. The account given here is taken from testimony before the Senate Finance Committee. See *Sale of Foreign Bonds or Securities in the United States*, pp. 1623*ff.*, 1798*ff.*, 1850*ff.* See also RIPPY, *The Capitalists and Colombia*, pp. 143*ff.*, for an account of the controversy taken largely from Colombian sources. Dr. Rippy states that circumstantial evidence points strongly to the conclusion that the Department of Commerce action was an attempt to exert pressure in behalf of the *Petroleros*. *Ibid.*, p. 148. The matter of the Barco concession, however, was only one of the oil disputes current at this time.

[2] *Sale of Foreign Bonds or Securities in the United States*, p. 1921.

Colombian Congress regranted the Barco concession on June 18, 1931. At the same time the Department of State was busy trying to persuade the National City Bank to extend the credit in question, an action which was evidently against the bank's judgment.[1] The activities of the department before and after the regrant included telephone conversations with the bankers and a visit from the Secretary of State. The official files were searched for instances in which the bank had been assisted by the department so that the bankers might be reminded of their dependence upon Washington. On June 30 the bank granted the credit. The circle of diplomatic and financial manipulation was then complete.

The Arms Embargo as a Sanction. The United States has since 1912 maintained a policy of discouraging revolutions in Latin America through stopping the shipment of arms to countries in which disorders occur which might be stimulated by the importation of arms. The arms embargo has sometimes been used to sustain the Latin-American government against domestic violence by supplying it with arms while refusing them to the revolutionists.[2] The arms embargo thus becomes an instrument of antirevolutionism. In the case of Mexico at least the arms embargo has been used as a weapon to obtain more favorable treatment for American investors. Early in 1919 the Mexican government was in dire need of arms to protect itself against threatened revolution. Arms shipments were permitted by the United States in January and February. In March, however, the two governments were engaged in controversy over the question of American oil rights under Article XXVII of the Mexican Constitution. The Mexican government issued orders to stop drilling for oil without a governmental permit. It was the intention of Mexico to grant the permits upon the understanding that the licensee would recognize the right of the government to property in the oil under Article XXVII. On April 11 Acting Secretary of State Polk instructed the American chargé in Mexico City that he had been endeavoring to secure more liberal treatment for Mexico with regard to the shipment of arms but that the refusal of Mexico to permit oil exploitation would seriously interfere with his efforts. He advised the chargé to take the matter up informally with the Mexican Foreign Office and to obtain at least provisional permits. "Should the Mexican Government prove obdurate," he said, "it will encounter difficulty in securing

[1] There was at that time a controversy between the bank and Colombia over the balancing of the Colombian budget.

[2] See p. 386.

further shipments of arms and munitions."[1] On July 12 President
Wilson formally proclaimed an arms embargo against Mexico.
The Mexican government made eleven different applications for
permission to import arms between July 7 and November 22, but no
answer was received. On January 2, 1920, the Mexican ambassador
asked for an answer and was told by Secretary of State Lansing that
"after mature deliberation, it appears to me inexpedient to permit
the issuance of licenses to ship arms and munitions of war to Mexico
at the present time."[2] Again in 1927, when the controversy over
oil rights had flamed anew, President Coolidge announced the
termination of a convention with Mexico which had required each
government to inform the other of all shipments of merchandise
across the border.[3] The action was regarded as a veiled warning
that the United States might be contemplating the lifting of the
arms embargo then existing so that Mexican rebels might obtain
weapons. The lifting of the embargo would have been ineffective
for this purpose so long as the United States was obliged to inform
the Mexican government of arms shipments.[4] It is impossible to
determine whether this action had any effect in bringing about a
favorable settlement of the oil problem about eight months later.

THE USE OF ARMED FORCES IN PROTECTION

The United States at various times in the past has made use of
warships and landing parties for the protection of American lives
and property. Naval patrols are maintained in the Caribbean and
the Far East. The presence of American war vessels has sometimes
caused the cessation of disorders. At various times of insurrection
neutral zones have been established in areas where American property is located. In zones thus formed no fighting has been permitted
as between revolutionaries and governmental forces. In a memorandum of the Solicitor for the Department of State, written in 1912,
a large number of reasons are set forth for the use of armed forces
for protective purposes. The instances are classified under the
following chief headings:

a. Simple protection of American citizens located in disturbed areas.

b. Destruction of pirates infesting certain areas, whether nationals of
the disturbed areas or otherwise.

c. Punishment for murder of American citizens.

[1] *Foreign Relations*, 1919, II: 594.
[2] *Ibid.*, II: 555.
[3] Dept. of State, *Press Releases*, Mar. 22, 1927.
[4] *N.Y. Times*, Mar. 23, 1927.

d. Punishment for insults or injuries to American citizens or American officers, such injuries not resulting in death.

e. Reestablishment of American legation, collection of indemnities, and protection of minister.

f. Suppression of local riots.

g. Preservation of order during interregnum between control of regular government and revolutionary government.

h. Establishment of presumed regular government.

i. Protection of customhouse at the instance of regular local officials.

j. Securing of indemnity.

k. Invasion of foreign territory for protection of American citizens and American territory.[1]

The memorandum above quoted goes to considerable length to argue the right under international law to interpose by force for protective purposes. The distinction is emphasized between mere protection or *interposition*, on the one hand, and *intervention* in the political affairs of the foreign country, on the other.

Many writers on international law deny that there is a legal right to *interpose* by armed force for protection purposes. Certainly the United States would be the last to acknowledge the right of a foreign government to make use of troops or warships to protect aliens in this country. Furthermore, the distinction between interposition where force is used and intervention is frequently not at all clear. The landing of armed troops for a strictly protective purpose often sets up a variety of influences which may cause the interposing country to proceed with its troop movement to other objectives than those originally contemplated. Thus the memorandum above cited gives as an illustration of interposition the landing of forces to protect American interests in Nicaragua in 1910, 1912, and 1926–1927.[2] But these interpositions had important political results. In each case the use or threat of force by the United States determined the party which was to govern Nicaragua. In times of growing nationalism it is impossible to separate interposition from intervention. As soon as troops land, a wave of resentment running through the invaded country may submerge all other political issues. Under such circumstances the allegation that the troops are landed for purely protective purposes and that no political intentions are involved becomes exceedingly unreal and unconvincing. Altogether the difficulties of considering the use of armed force as a

[1] *Right to Protect Citizens in Foreign Countries by Landing Forces* (Third Revised Edition with Supplemental Appendix up to 1933), pp. 34–35, Govt. Printing Office, Washington, 1934.

[2] *Ibid.*, pp. 75, 119, 122.

well-defined legal right are so great that it would appear to be more satisfactory to regard the matter as not covered by law.

MODIFICATION OF THE POLICY OF ARMED PROTECTION

Aside from legal considerations, the policy of sending armed forces into the interior of other countries in order to protect American investments has sometimes produced results of a most unsatisfactory character. American troops operate at a disadvantage in an unfamiliar terrain as against small bands of elusive native soldiers. The expense of sending expeditions into broken and jungle country is exceedingly high, in both life and money, while the advantages accrue only to a few investors. The cost of the Nicaraguan intervention, beginning in 1926, has been estimated at $8,000,000,[1] a sum equal to about 60 per cent of the American investments in that country. It is practically impossible for soldiers of one country, no matter how well disciplined, to be billeted among another people of a different race and color without doing injury to noncombatants and thus arousing intense international dislikes and prejudices. Finally the commitment of the United States to the Pact of Paris has made it highly undesirable that this country should be laid open to the accusations that come from the use of force in other countries. American good faith would now be questioned if this country should use force to pursue its objects. It would then become difficult for this country to remonstrate with others for violating the pact, as, for example, with Japan regarding Manchuria.

Secretary Stimson's Policy of Limiting Protection to Coast Towns. For these various reasons the Department of State has come to doubt the advisability of armed interposition in Latin America. On April 1, 1931, during a period of Sandino attacks in Nicaragua, Secretary Stimson announced a policy, which had already been used to a considerable extent in China, that of limiting armed protection to Americans situated in coast towns. The Secretary declared that the United States could not undertake the protection of citizens throughout Nicaragua. Those in the interior who felt insecure were advised to withdraw from the country or at least to move for the time being to the coast towns. Here they could be more easily protected or, if necessary, evacuated. "Those who remain," said Mr. Stimson, "do so at their own risk and must not expect American forces to be sent inland to their aid."[2] At the

---

[1] BUELL, RAYMOND LESLIE, "Reconstruction in Nicaragua," Foreign Policy Association, *Information Service*, Vol. VI, No. 18 (Nov. 12, 1930), p. 342.

[2] Dept. of State, *Press Releases*, Apr. 18, 1931, p. 284.

same time a similar policy was applied in Honduras where revolutionary activities had brought complaints from American citizens. The department announced: "The American forces will limit themselves to making provisions for the safety of American lives and property in the coast towns."[1]

Under the changed policy the hazards and difficulties of the service of supplies in jungle campaigns were eliminated. The less expensive system of water transportation and cruiser protection was retained. The danger of arousing antagonisms among the native populations was diminished. The matter of interposition was thus simplified just as it had previously been in the Far East where in 1927 protection behind the sandbagged fortifications of the International Settlement in Shanghai had been found a much easier matter than the attempt to prevent disorders in the treaty ports of the vast interior of China.

The Renunciation of Armed Intervention. Finally, in 1933, came the striking departure in the policy of the United States regarding armed intervention which has already been referred to.[2] By the public statements of Secretary Hull and President Roosevelt and by the ratification of the Montevideo Convention on Rights and Duties of States the American government definitely renounced the practice of armed intervention. While it may still be possible to examine the meaning of the word "intervention" and to argue that its renunciation does not include the abandonment of "interposition" for protective purposes, the spirit and context of the Hull and Roosevelt declarations indicate that the word "intervention" was not used in any narrow sense.

DEFAULT DIPLOMACY

One of the most baffling problems that has confronted American diplomacy is that with regard to the remittance of payments to the United States by debtor countries. The United States is an industrial high-pressure area from which the economic forces tend to flow outward. Normally each year the world is more in the debt of this country than it was in the previous year. It is impossible under these circumstances that any net payments can be transferred to the United States from abroad. Certain obligations may be paid, it is true, but there must at the same time be loans from the United States to other countries to offset not only the payments that are made but also the so-called favorable balance of items in the inter-

[1] *Ibid.*, Apr. 25, 1931, p. 312.
[2] See pp. 111–112.

national account generally.[1]   Without a reversal of economic trends
payments to this country can only be made coincident with loans.
But when in times of depression the capital market is such that no
further loans can be made, it becomes impossible, because of the
exchange situation, for many countries to meet their debts to the
United States.   Some of the funds due which cannot be transferred
to the United States can be reinvested abroad.   Where it has been
impractical to reinvest, no method has been devised for satisfying
the obligation.   Default has, therefore, been common.   Thus the
irreducible obstacles of international exchange have come into direct
opposition to the capitalistic dogma of the sanctity of contract.
The United States government has sometimes ignored the difficulties
of the situation and has in some cases regarded the inability of
nations to make payments to this country as evidence of moral
delinquency.   American default diplomacy has had two aspects:
(1) with regard to the intergovernmental debts arising from the
World War and (2) with regard to defaults on private investments.

The War Debts.   After the United States entered the World
War it was necessary to continue and even to increase the supply of
goods and munitions to the Allies.   The war debts are the record of
these exports.   They represent an accounting for vast cargoes which
were carried from the United States to the allied European countries.   In round figures the debts amounted to slightly more than
$10,000,000,000.[2]   They could have been paid only by the reversal
of trade, *i.e.*, the return to the United States of a similar value of
goods or by the performance to the United States of enormous
services.   The United States was unwilling as well as unable to
accept a surplus of goods and services.   After the war the tariff was
twice raised by general act.   Economic groups contended that
services, such as shipping, should be performed by Americans rather
than by foreigners.   The international account continued to favor
the United States.   In such an economic setting payments on the
war debts could be made to this country only through heavy lending
by the United States.   Large private loans were made from 1919 to
1930; but, following the depression, the loans stopped.   The world
faced a crisis in the summer of 1931 because of the inability of
governments to make international payments.   The crisis was
focused in Germany which had previously been able to pay repara-

---

[1] Shipments of gold to this country may be made but they cannot be relied
on for a very large percentage of the payments over a period of years.

[2] For details see MOULTON, HAROLD G., and LEO PASVOLSKY, *War Debts
and World Prosperity*, Brookings Institution, Washington, 1932.

tions because of borrowing. An international one-year moratorium was declared on July 1, 1931, under the leadership of President Hoover.[1] Following the moratorium, reparation payments were not renewed, being dropped in accordance with the spirit of the Lausanne agreement of June, 1932. The United States, however, insisted that war debt payments be resumed. On December 15, 1932, the first payments following the moratorium were due. The European debtor countries then for the first time faced the necessity of making large payments to this country without the aid of loans from the United States. Six countries, including France and Belgium, defaulted. The war debt payments, which had exceeded $200,000,000 before the depression, fell to $20,000,000 in 1933. In 1934 all governments but Finland ceased payment. Most of the debtor countries felt that they must choose between either default or the destruction of their currencies by the draining of gold from the country. They accordingly chose default.

The Attitude of the United States Regarding War Debt Defaults. In 1923 President Harding declared with regard to the war debts: "The call of the world today is for integrity of agreements, the sanctity of covenants, the validity of contracts." No sympathy was shown for the demand for cancellation. As time passed, the executive branch of the government doubtless became aware of the economic impossibility of the fulfillment of its demands; but, hampered as it was with a stern and uncomprehending Congress, it found great difficulty in making concessions. Nevertheless, the debts were revised and greatly reduced by funding arrangements with each country which provided for payment over a period of 62 years. In December, 1932, the Department of State further indicated to the debtor governments that after the December payments were made it would be willing to consider additional revision. The promise came too late and the inevitable defaults occurred. The Department of State has since continued to send statements to the debtor countries and in addition has sometimes made declarations similar to the following, which was included in the correspondence of November, 1934, with regard to the payments which were due December 15:

I wish to take this occasion to assure you that this Government is fully disposed to discuss, through diplomatic channels, any proposals your Government may desire to put forward in regard to the payment of this

[1] For the events before and after the inauguration of the moratorium see TOYNBEE, ARNOLD J., *Survey of International Affairs*, 1932, pp. 97*ff*., Oxford University Press, London, 1933.

indebtedness, and to assure you that such proposals would receive careful consideration with a view to eventual submission to the American Congress.[1]

The Department of State, bound by the laws of Congress, must thus continue to make a pretense of collection. Without some unexpected change in the international situation, however, the debts are uncollectible.

Defaults of Debts to American Citizens. It was in 1931 that international lending by the United States ceased. In that year the moratorium on intergovernmental debts was declared and in the same year the defaults on obligations to private citizens began. Eventually total or partial suspensions of payment were declared on some or all of the national obligations of Bolivia, Brazil, Bulgaria, Chile, China (predepression default), Colombia, Costa Rica, Germany, Greece, Guatemala, Hungary, Mexico (predepression default), Panama, Peru, Rumania, Russia (pre-Soviet loans), Salvador, Uruguay, and Yugoslavia.[2] Some of the defaults were total. Others, however, were partial, *i.e.*, payments were made in local currency, scrip, or refunding bonds. By 1934 it was reported that 32 per cent of American-held foreign bonds were in default, 14 per cent total and 18 per cent partial.[3]

Against such a flood of defaults diplomacy was futile. Secretary of State Hull at one time declared that the matter was not one for diplomatic action. The government rather sponsored the creation of a private bondholders' commission, the Foreign Bondholders' Protective Council, representing the investors, which was set up to deal directly with the debtor governments and corporations. "In this way," said Mr. Hull, "a separation or divorce is also obtained both from the international bankers or distributing houses and from the Federal Government itself."[4] The Depart-

[1] The texts of a number of these notes are found in the Dept. of State, *Press Releases*, Dec. 15, 1934, pp. 356ff.

[2] Foreign Bondholders' Protective Council, Inc., *Annual Report*, 1934. See also SCROGGS, WILLIAM O., "Foreign Treatment of American Creditors," *Foreign Affairs*, XIV: 345 (January, 1936).

[3] *The Balance of the International Payments of the United States in 1933*, p. 60.

[4] *Report of the Delegates of the United States of America to the Seventh International Conference of American States*, pp. 27–28. The Foreign Bondholders' Protective Council was incorporated under the laws of Maryland in 1933 for the purpose of looking after the interests of holders of defaulted foreign bonds. LAVES, WALTER H. C., "Toward a Consistent Foreign Loan Policy," *American Political Science Review*, XXVIII: 1047 (December, 1934). For an instance in which a settlement was made by this organization with the Dominican Republic, see Dept. of State, *Press Releases*, Aug. 18, 1934, p. 105; Foreign Bondholders' Protective Council, *Annual Report*, 1934, pp. 57–67.

ment of State, however, in some cases has used its good offices to bring about an increase in interest payments to American citizens. Representations have been made on occasion where the arrangements for the payment of coupons have been more favorable to bondholders residing in other foreign countries than to those in the United States.

The German Discriminations. In one particular instance the United States engaged in a serious protest against the terms of the default which seemed to discriminate unduly against American citizens. During the first half of 1934 the German government in paying the coupons on medium and long-term foreign bonds other than the Dawes and Young loans drew distinctions between the holders located in different countries according to the following system. Interest on some of the bonds was to be paid 30 per cent in foreign exchange and 70 per cent in scrip convertible at 67 per cent of its face value. Dutch and Swiss bondholders were paid in full, the specially favorable treatment being due to trade arrangements with the two countries. American bondholders, however, were unable to obtain even their scrip payments promptly because of the failure of the German government to complete the necessary arrangements. Other discriminations against Americans were practiced in connection with the Dawes and Young loans, British holders being preferred over those in the United States.[1]

Germany upheld the discriminations against the United States as necessary to protect her economic system by limiting payments to a country with which she had an unfavorable balance of trade. Practically all of the gold reserve and foreign currency reserve of the Reichsbank had been sacrificed, the amount having diminished from approximately 3,000,000,000 Reichsmarks at the close of 1930 to 108,900,000 Reichsmarks by June 12, 1934. The note coverage had fallen from 56.2 per cent to 3.1 per cent during this period. It was impossible, according to the German statement, to make further payments without obtaining additional trade opportunities for German exports. Any attempt to do so would result in a disruption of the German currency system.[2]

The objections of the United States to the discriminations were principally that the trade between two particular countries should

---

[1] Note to Germany of Nov. 23, 1934, set forth in Dept. of State, *Press Releases*, Dec. 1, 1934, p. 325. For 1933 discriminations see *The United States in World Affairs*, 1933, Council on Foreign Relations, pp. 113ff., Harper & Brothers, New York, 1934.

[2] German memorandum delivered to the Secretary of State June 15, 1934, Dept. of State, *Press Releases*, June 30, 1934, p. 436.

not be used as the basis for determining the matter of payments between them. If the proper exchange to make the payments could not be obtained by exports to the particular creditor, it could be secured through triangular arrangements. Furthermore, while Germany had refused to make full payments to American bondholders, German citizens had been able to obtain the exchange with which to purchase in New York large amounts of depreciated German bonds. These in turn had been sold to the German government. Thus American citizens who had in good faith lent money to Germany lost their property while the German government profited through this device which had driven down the price of the bonds to a point where they could be advantageously repatriated. The German government had also used foreign exchange, which might have been employed to pay coupons, for the purchase abroad of materials susceptible of military use.[1] Altogether the affair was a most puzzling financial tangle due to the difficulties of making international payments in a period of depression and to the belief of German leaders that the very existence of the Reich depended upon taking unorthodox measures to protect German exchange. The United States naturally objected to measures of discrimination which involved financial losses to large numbers of American investors; but it is doubtful if such problems are susceptible of satisfactory solution in a world of nationalistic currencies.

FINANCIAL CONTROL

When investors place their money in the bonds of backward countries they often demand a wise supervision of the funds so as to make the investment secure and productive of a liberal return. Such an expectation is frequently not realized. The people of the backward country do not always have the same standards of financial integrity that prevail among the people of more advanced capitalistic nations. Revolutionary uprisings add to the uncertainty. And corruption in politics sometimes eats into the public revenues to such an extent as to interfere with the prompt and full payment of obligations. None of the backward countries, of course, can surpass the worst of the American cities in the extent of their corruption. Here also the business group is often at war with the politicians. But American politicians show a certain respect for big business on which they rely for campaign contributions. The conflict between the businessman and the politician is accentuated

---

[1] See the note of June 27, 1934, Dept. of State, *Press Releases*, June 30, 1934, p. 444, and the note of Nov. 23, 1934, *Press Releases*, Dec. 1, 1934, p. 325.

when differences of race and color exist. For these various reasons investors are often desirous of forcing advanced business standards upon backward countries through the imposition of political or financial control.

The American policy of establishing financial control in other countries was a development of the first three decades of the twentieth century.[1] Previous to that time such policies were frequently denounced as unjustifiable imperialism. Little capital was invested by Americans in other countries. The fear that European governments would deal with Latin America as they had with Egypt and China made it natural to denounce such controls. Following the Spanish-American War the United States felt more confident of its strength. It then appeared that an effective way of keeping European countries out of the Caribbean was through the imposition of controls by the United States which would prevent troublesome defaults. Finally the growing investments of the United States, clamoring loudly for protection, became a force for intervention. Panama (1903), Cuba (1904), the Dominican Republic (1905), Nicaragua (1911), Haiti (1915), Bolivia (1922), and Salvador (1923) came under one form or another of financial control in the Caribbean, while upon the African continent financiers from the United States began to order the life of the Liberian Republic (1912 and 1926). The various forms of financial control one or more of which have been tried in all of these countries may be classified as follows:

> Customs collection.
> Internal revenue collection.
> Veto over new indebtedness.
> Supervision of the framing of the budget.
> Preaudit of expenditures.[2]

In the retreat from imperialism which came with the depression a few of these devices were abandoned. Some forms of control still exist, however, in all of the above-mentioned countries excepting Cuba.

Customs Collection. Customs collection generally involves the mortgaging of all or a part of the customs revenues for the payment of certain debts. The collections are administered by an agent of the bankers or by an official appointed or approved by the American government. After providing for the cost of collection and the

---

[1] It had, however, been suggested much earlier. See p. 52.

[2] The various systems of control as they existed in 1929 are described in WILLIAMS, *Economic Foreign Policy of the United States*, Chapters X and XI.

service of the debt, the supervising official turns the remainder of the receipts over to the native government.   To insure that an adequate collection will be received, it is ordinarily provided that the tariff rates cannot be changed without the consent of the United States.   In the Dominican Republic in 1933 five of the chief officers, out of a total of 172 employes, were Americans.   These five held the positions of general receiver, deputy general receiver, auditor, special inspector, and purchasing agent in New York.[1]   The general receiver in the Dominican Republic is appointed by the President of the United States.   The same officer in Haiti, under the title of fiscal representative, is appointed by the President of Haiti upon the nomination of the President of the United States.   In Liberia, according to the contract of 1926 with the bankers, the financial adviser is the collecting officer.   He is appointed by the President of Liberia upon the nomination of the President of the United States. In Nicaragua the collector is nominated by the bankers and approved by the Department of State.   In Bolivia supervision is under a permanent Fiscal Commission of three members of which two are recommended by the American bankers.   In Salvador a fiscal representative of the bankers inspects the collection service.[2]

Internal Revenue Collection.   Because of native inefficiency in the collection of internal revenues American officials and financiers have at times wished to include this source of revenue in the system of control.   Internal revenue collectorships existed at one time in the Dominican Republic and Haiti but have been discontinued.[3] Internal revenue collectorships are supervised by the American financial adviser in Liberia.[4]   In Bolivia the Permanent Fiscal

[1] *Report of the 27th Fiscal Period Dominican Customs Receivership* (*Calendar Year* 1933), p. 120, Govt. Printing Office, Washington, 1934.

[2] JONES, CHESTER LLOYD, *Caribbean Backgrounds and Prospects*, pp. 271–273, D. Appleton & Company, New York, 1931.   A clause in the Salvadoran agreement provides that in case of default a collector general shall be appointed to take charge of the customs service.   He is to be selected from two men named by the fiscal agent with the concurrence of the Secretary of State.   In 1932, however, when a default occurred, the Secretary of State declined to participate in the establishment of an American collectorship, giving the reason that it had not recognized the existing government of Salvador.   THOMSON, CHARLES A., "The Caribbean Situation: Nicaragua and Salvador," *Foreign Policy Reports*, Vol. IX, No. 13 (Aug. 30, 1933), p. 148.

[3] In Haiti the American Fiscal Representative has power to inspect the Internal Revenue Service and make recommendations as to its proper operation. Article VIII, *Executive Agreement Series*, No. 46.

[4] Loan agreement of 1926.   The enforcement of this agreement has, however, been uncertain during the past two or three years.

Commission has supervision.   In Nicaragua, if the internal revenues for any three consecutive months shall be less than $200,000, the American collector general shall take over the function of collection.[1]

Veto over New Indebtedness. Under the Platt Amendment, which until 1934 governed the relations of the United States and Cuba, the Cuban government was prohibited from contracting any public debt unless the ordinary revenues of the island, after deducting the current expenses of government, were adequate to provide for the interest and sinking funds.   Since the question as to whether the provisions were complied with could be raised in the case of any contemplated loan, the United States claimed the right to be consulted regarding Cuban borrowing.   At times reforms in the internal administration of the Cuban government were demanded before loans would be agreed to.[2]   The Platt Amendment, however, was abrogated by mutual agreement in 1934.

A similar type of debt restriction, that in Article III of the Dominican Convention of 1924,[3] gives the United States the right to be consulted in more explicit terms.   This provision, copied verbatim from the 1907 convention, reads:

Until the Dominican Republic has paid the whole amount of the bonds of the debt, its public debt shall not be increased except by previous agreement between the Dominican Government and the United States.

In 1914 a controversy occurred between the two governments as to whether the term "public debt" meant only a bonded indebtedness, as claimed by the Dominican officials, or included floating expenditures as contended by the United States.   In 1916, when American troops entered Santo Domingo, the legal reason alleged for the occupation was that, by incurring a considerable floating indebtedness without the consent of the United States, the Dominican government had violated Article III.[4]

---

[1] Internal revenues, however, should normally show a considerable margin over this sum.   CUMBERLAND, W. W., *Nicaragua, an Economic and Financial Survey*, p. 78, Govt. Printing Office, Washington, 1928.

[2] See General Crowder's memorandum on "Conditions Previous to the Approval of a Loan," delivered to the Cuban government previous to the loan of 1923.   Text is given in DUNN, ROBERT W., *American Foreign Investments*, p. 287, B. W. Huebsch and the Viking Press, New York, 1926.

[3] *U.S. Treaty Series*, No. 726.

[4] *Foreign Relations*, 1916, pp. 246–247.   The Haitian agreement of Aug. 7, 1933, requires that there shall be no new loans without the consent of the fiscal representative "unless the ordinary revenues of the Republic, after defraying

Supervision of the Framing of the Budget. In order that the debtor nation may not appropriate sums in excess of its revenues and thus bring about financial instability, the United States has sought in various cases to advise economy at the time of drawing up the budget. In 1914 it was agreed that a financial adviser should be sent to theDominican Republic. His activities in the control of the budget brought forth such objections from the Dominican officials that his office was abolished and some of his powers were transferred to the general receiver.[1] In Haiti the American financial adviser, provided for in the Convention of 1915, exercised for some time the power to veto items in the Haitian budget. In 1931 this right was withdrawn, but the United States specifically retained the power to present diplomatic protest against any law which should be deemed inconsistent with American treaty rights.[2] The only case in which the right of budget control is now formally exercised by an American control officer is in Liberia where the financial adviser may insist that all the expenditures provided for in the loan agreement of 1926 shall be included in the budget and that the appropriations as a whole shall not exceed the resources of the government. The agreement has, on various occasions, been disregarded by the Liberian government.

Preaudit of Expenditures. Even after a governmental budget is correctly drawn up and passed, funds may be diverted from the purpose for which they were appropriated. Because of unfortunate experiences, the office of auditor with the right of preaudit of expenditures has become a common fixture in American state, local, and national governments. The auditor is commonly given the power to examine an account before it is paid to make certain that it comes within the authorization of valid appropriation. His signature to the warrant is necessary to the disbursement of funds. In order to make certain that native officials shall not raid the treasury through a system of illegal expenditures, the United States has on several occasions asked that an American financial adviser should be given the power of preaudit over governmental expenditures. Such a power was given to the American financial adviser in the Dominican Republic in 1914 but it was discontinued the following year after protest by Dominican officials. In Haiti the Ameri-

---

the expenses of the Government, shall be adequate to assure the final discharge of such obligation." Art. XVII, *Executive Agreement Series*, No. 46.

[1] See *Foreign Relations*, 1915, p. 311.

[2] Art. V, *Executive Agreement Series*, No. 22; Dept. of State, *Press Releases*, Aug. 15, 1931, p. 147.

can financial adviser exercised this power from 1918 to 1931.[1] Under the Liberian loan contract of 1926 an auditor is appointed by the President of Liberia in agreement with the fiscal agent of the loan which is the National City Bank of New York. The auditor's approval, according to the contract, is necessary for governmental expenditures.[2]   In Nicaragua the High Commission, of which two members are American, can supervise extra expenditures up to $26,666 per month when the ordinary budget exceeds $115,000 per month.

The right of exerting control over the expenditure of certain funds of the Republic of Panama has been claimed and exercised to some extent by the United States. The funds in question are the $250,-000 annual payment upon the canal lease and the income from a certain part of the $10,000,000 paid for the lease in 1903 which was invested as an endowment for the government. There is no warrant in the treaty of 1903 for control over these funds by the United States, but this government has claimed the right of supervision on the grounds that the purpose of the payment of the sums was to maintain government stability through an assured revenue.[3]   A fiscal agent is appointed by Panama through the good offices of the United States, and an American has been consistently appointed to the post. He has powers of disapproving orders of payment when contrary to the law, but his decisions are subject to the approval of the President and to review by the Supreme Court. His office is created by Panamanian statute.[4]

Effects of Financial Control. Financial control has ordinarily given to the supervised governments greater fiscal security and a higher credit rating than they would have otherwise possessed.[5] The control system was successful in eliminating temptations to European intervention in the Caribbean by the establishment of financial stability. The replacement of European capital by American in that region and the relative political weakness of Old World countries since the World War have aided in relieving the fears of European intervention.

[1] This power was taken away in the Haitianization Agreement of Aug. 5, 1931, Art. VI, *Executive Agreement Series*, No. 22.

[2] This provision has also been disregarded by Liberia on some occasions.

[3] *Foreign Relations*, 1913, pp. 1100–1104.

[4] MUNRO, DANA G., *The United States and the Caribbean*, p. 100, World Peace Foundation, Boston, 1934.

[5] It has not, however, prevented defaults in interest payments by Bolivia, Liberia, Panama, and Salvador. Cuba has also had one loan in default.

Latin-American countries have, however, looked askance at the system of control as being a menace to the sovereignty of the controlled country and as leading to further intervention and imperialism. Through the control of finance the United States has gained a powerful supervision over the internal affairs of some of the countries. When the regulated country is in need of additional funds the United States has been able to say that these would be supplied from the moneys in the hands of the collector of customs provided certain internal reforms should be made. In some cases these "reforms" have meant the granting of additional powers to United States officials. Such instances have occurred in our relations with the Dominican Republic, Haiti, and Nicaragua. Demands of this sort have helped to create a strong Latin-American prejudice against financial control. Partly to appease this prejudice the United States has modified its control system in recent years in the Dominican Republic and Haiti while such control as existed under the Platt Amendment in Cuba has been withdrawn.

PART III

POLICIES OF PEACE AND WORLD ORGANIZATION

CHAPTER XIII

BUILDING AND REJECTING THE LEAGUE

I. UNITED STATES COOPERATION IN PLANNING THE COVENANT

The part of the United States in the construction of the League of Nations and in the subsequent work of that organization must be considered as among the most important indexes of the drifts in American foreign policy. In 1793 the declaration of neutrality and the abrogation of the French alliance represented the natural responses of a physically isolated, young, and comparatively weak nation to the involved and militaristic politics of Europe. Today a somewhat more confident attitude toward the League of Nations represents the reaction of a greatly strengthened and commercially active America to the efforts of a more unified but a more dangerous world to find peace in cooperation. During the World War, American sentiment for international organization increased swiftly. American contributions to the construction of the League at the end of the war were of great significance. American entry into the League was blocked in 1920 by a reviving fear of European entanglements, by internal politics, and by the difficulties of the treaty-making process. A resulting period of antipathy to the League was short-lived. The United States cooperation with Geneva then began slowly and gained momentum gradually. The story of these events shows the forces of tradition in conflict with those of aspiration. The resulting compromise position is not permanently fixed but shifts with American opinion and the necessities of American interests as determined in Washington.

NATAL AND PRENATAL CONTRIBUTIONS TO THE COVENANT

The antecedents and sources of the League of Nations Covenant may be classified as: (1) the remote ancestry, including all important previous efforts at international cooperation down to the outbreak of the war in 1914; (2) the private proposals for world organization

240

brought out during the World War; (3) the official plans drawn up at the end of the World War; and (4) the work of the Paris Conference.

Remote Ancestry. The whole previous evolution of international law and of diplomatic relations was contributory to the formation of the League. The concert of Europe, the increasing number of international conferences in the latter half of the nineteenth century, the development of administrative unions, and the work of the Permanent Court of Arbitration all helped to prepare the way. The United States cannot be said to have been a leader in this growing internationalism which preceded the World War, and the major credit must be given to the great powers of Europe which under the necessities of their politics were quicker to acquire the habit of cooperative action. In one particular, however, the United States demonstrated leadership, that is, in the continual efforts made to bring about the creation of a world court. American citizens became prominent in this movement before the Civil War and the United States government made serious efforts to create such a court during the Hague Conferences. Machinery for the settlement of justiciable disputes was the special ideal of the American people although this country reacted emphatically against the cooperative settlement of nonjusticiable disputes by political groups.

Private Proposals Brought Out by the World War. The World War in dramatic style focused attention upon the problem of strengthening international organization. Appalling casualty lists and unprecedented expenditures by belligerent governments during 1914, 1915, and 1916 caused a widespread search on the part of neutral Americans for new formulas to strengthen the world's political structure. During these neutral years Americans were freer to engage in speculation regarding war prevention than were the peoples of the fiercely beset belligerent countries. In the first months of 1915 a large number of plans were in process of formation.[1] The most noteworthy of the organizations to propose a program was the League to Enforce Peace which was started by a small group of men including Theodore Marburg, Hamilton Holt, and William Howland. The matter was talked over at periodical dinners early in 1915.[2] The plans discussed were considered at an organization

---

[1] See *Towards an Enduring Peace, A Symposium of Peace Proposals and Programs*, 1914–1916, compiled by Randolph S. Bourne, American Association for International Conciliation, New York.

[2] *Development of the League of Nations Idea, Documents and Correspondence of Theodore Marburg*, edited by John H. Latané (2 vols.), II: 703*ff.*, The Macmillan Company, New York, 1932.

meeting in Philadelphia in June, 1915. In his opening address the chairman, William Howard Taft, forecast a league which would use force to insure security against aggression. The exhaustion and horrors of the war, he said, would cause the peoples of the world to look with much more favor upon leagues for the preservation of peace than ever before.[1] Resolutions were adopted in favor of membership of the United States in a league which would require judicial settlement of justiciable questions and which would prescribe investigation by a conciliation commission for all other controversies not amicably settled by the parties. This alternative provision for either judicial decision or conciliation was later embodied in Article XII of the League of Nations Covenant. In the 1915 plan military and economic sanctions were recommended to enforce these provisions and the codification of international law was proposed.

Numerous projects of this kind were worked out by private societies in the United States during the period of 1914–1917. Peace organizations, churches, and business groups participated in the movement. In November, 1915, the Board of Directors of the Chamber of Commerce of the United States asked for a referendum on various questions connected with the proposals of the League to Enforce Peace. Ninety-six per cent of the local chambers agreed that the United States should take the initiative in forming a league of nations binding the members to submit justiciable questions to an international court and nonjusticiable questions to conciliation. Seventy-seven per cent agreed that these decisions should be enforced by economic pressure, and 64 per cent felt that military force might also be used when necessary. From this return, R. G. Rhett, national president of the chamber, concluded:

It may therefore be safely said that the business men of this country are heartily in accord with all the proposals of the League [to Enforce Peace] save that providing for the use of military force in the event of the failure of economic pressure. With reference to this the majority of the business men seem to be in favor of it, but the Chamber of Commerce of the United States of America, under its constitution and by-laws, is not committed to its endorsement or support [a two-thirds vote being required].[2]

[1] League to Enforce Peace, American Branch, p. 14, published by the League to Enforce Peace, New York.

[2] Enforced Peace, p. 96, published by the League to Enforce Peace, New York. Of course, during this same time plans were being developed by private societies in Great Britain, France, Germany, Holland, and other countries. As it is the purpose of this volume to set forth American policy, however, the treatment must necessarily be mainly from the American viewpoint.

Official Plans at the End of the World War. The official plans which became the basis of the work of the Paris Conference were for the most part English and American and they were intimately interwoven. The Phillimore draft, drawn up by a British commission under Sir Walter Phillimore, was the first of the official plans. The commission was influenced to some extent by the work of the American League to Enforce Peace.[1] The Phillimore report of March 20, 1918, contained a provision for the prevention of war and for the pacific settlement of international disputes. A copy was sent to President Wilson who turned it over to Colonel House for examination. Colonel House then drafted a plan for Mr. Wilson's consideration. With this as a guide the President in July, 1918, prepared the first Wilson draft. This paper he took with him to the Peace Conference. When he arrived in Paris he was furnished with copies of two additional drafts which had been constructed by General Smuts and Lord Robert Cecil. After studying these documents, President Wilson wrote his second draft, drawing somewhat from General Smuts and also incorporating additional provisions the need of which had been brought to his attention since the writing of the first draft. After some criticisms, notably by General Bliss, who was a member of the American delegation, and by David Hunter Miller, the legal adviser to the delegation, President Wilson prepared his third draft. At about the same time, January 20, 1919, the British delegation completed the formation of a plan which combined the previously mentioned British proposals. The problem of reconciling this plan with the third Wilson draft was submitted to a joint conference of the legal advisers of the two delegations, C. J. B. Hurst for Great Britain and David Hunter Miller for the United States. The result was a composite creation known as the Hurst-Miller draft which became the basis for discussion in the League of Nations Commission of the conference.[2]

At the Paris Conference. President Wilson made his greatest contribution to the creation of the League when he insisted that the Covenant should be made an integral part of the treaty of peace. Representatives of the other principal allied and associated powers

[1] MORLEY, *The Society of Nations*, p. 10.

[2] BAKER, RAY STANNARD, *Woodrow Wilson and World Settlement*, Chapter XIII, Doubleday, Page & Company, Garden City, N. Y., 1922 (3 vols.), contains an account of the various preliminary drafts. MILLER, DAVID HUNTER, *The Drafting of the Covenant*, Chapters I to VI, G. P. Putnam's Sons, New York, 1928 (2 vols.), contains a fuller and slightly different account. Texts of the drafts can be found in BAKER, Vol. III, and MILLER, Vol. II. MORLEY, *op. cit.*, Chapters I and II, also contains an account of the preliminary plans.

expected to obtain a large share of the spoils of war. The United States had no territorial aims and was placed in an independent position to advocate a plan for the solution of the more fundamental problems of the war. Had President Wilson failed to insist that the League should be a part of the treaty, it is quite likely that it would have been pushed aside and forgotten during the time which was most propitious for its formation.[1] On January 25, 1919, the President in the second plenary session delivered a strong speech in favor of a league as "the central object of our meeting." The matter of drafting the Covenant was referred to a Commission on the League of Nations which was composed of nineteen members. Two were selected from each of the principal allied and associated powers and one was chosen from each of nine smaller powers. President Wilson was the chairman of the commission.

The commission held ten meetings and by February 14 had agreed upon a draft of the Covenant. President Wilson then made a hurried visit to the United States with this draft and placed it before various American groups for criticism. He discussed the matter before a joint meeting of the members of the Senate Committee on Foreign Relations and the House Committee on Foreign Affairs at which meeting definite amendments were suggested. All these were subsequently incorporated in the Covenant after the President's return to the conference. Other amendments were proposed by the press and by leaders of opinion.

Upon returning to Paris on March 14, President Wilson found that in his absence there had been a strong sentiment in the Council of Ten for setting aside the League and proceeding to fix at once the military and territorial terms of the peace. The President, however, was stubborn in his insistence that the Covenant should be an integral party of the treaty. After some effort he won a favorable decision. The Commission on the League of Nations continued its work. Revisions were made; and eventually, by April 28, the Covenant was completed and ready to be incorporated in the general peace treaty.

Summary of American Activities in the Creation of the Covenant. To recapitulate, in the long period before the World War the United States played a relatively minor role; but in one movement, the attempt to set up an international court, this country took the leading part. During the World War, when private societies in

[1] For the conflict of views see NOBLE, GEORGE BERNARD, *Politics and Opinions at Paris*, 1919, pp. 104–110, 121–133, The Macmillan Company, New York, 1935.

many countries were thinking in terms of world organization, various American groups, particularly the League to Enforce Peace, were busy drawing up plans. During the period of preliminary planning for a league at the end of the war, most of the effective contributions were made by British and American statesmen, the brunt of the work in the United States being borne by President Wilson. In the Peace Conference, numerous American ideas found their way into the Covenant. It was due to the stubborn insistence of President Wilson that the League was included in the terms of peace. There is much reason, therefore, for the inscription on the plaque erected by the City of Geneva which describes Woodrow Wilson as *Fondateur de la Société des Nations.*

The specific contributions to the text of the Covenant from American sources may be classified as follows:

1. Plans and suggestions regarding the form of the peace machinery.
2. Democratic and antimilitaristic safeguards.
3. Opposition to a strong central organization.

Plans and Suggestions Regarding the Form of the Peace Machinery

Article X. Article X, which is a guarantee of the territorial integrity of member states as against external aggression, was regarded by President Wilson as the extension to the whole world of the Monroe Doctrine. During the period of American neutrality the Department of State had outlined a program for a stronger Monroe Doctrine to be enforced by the American republics in cooperation.[1] Among other things the department had proposed that "the United States and all other nations of this hemisphere mutually agree to guarantee the territorial integrity of the countries of this hemisphere." When the time came to suggest plans for a League of Nations, this proposal was made world-wide. The provision for a mutual guarantee of the territories of all the members of the League appears in the American plans from the beginning, having been a part of Colonel House's draft and of President Wilson's three drafts.

An important part of Article X was suggested by General Bliss. As the clause stood in President Wilson's first two drafts it was a simple guarantee of territorial integrity of the member states. To General Bliss it appeared that this would be taken as a guarantee against revolution. Such an idea would have been opposed in the

---

[1] Communication to the press of Jan. 5, 1916.

United States where the right of revolution, at least on the part of the dependencies of European powers, is highly regarded. He therefore proposed that the guarantee of territorial integrity should be modified by the phrase "as against external aggression."[1] This amendment was accepted by the President. The wisdom of making the change was well proved when in the treaty debates in the United States the opponents of the Covenant attacked Article X on the grounds that it would compel the League to suppress revolution and would guarantee forever the territories of the British and Japanese empires. In the Bliss amendment the friends of the treaty then had an answer to the charge that Article X was a guarantee of empire, an answer which was logically satisfactory even if it did not entirely convince the opposition.

President Wilson considered that Article X was "the heart of the Covenant." He alleged that the principal cause of the recent war was an absolute disregard of the territorial integrity and political independence of the smaller nations. "Article Ten," he said, "cuts at the very heart, and is the only instrument that will cut at the very heart, of the old system."[2]

Article XI. A frequently used provision for war prevention in the Covenant is Article XI which provides that any war or threat of war is a matter of concern to the League and that the Secretary-General shall, on the request of any member of the League, forthwith summon a meeting of the Council. This article appears to have been entirely an American creation, all of the provisions coming from the House and Wilson drafts. Under this clause the League has taken action on several occasions to prevent war. Great Britain brought to the attention of the League Council the dispute between Sweden and Finland over the Aaland Islands. Poland brought before the Council the dispute with Lithuania; Greece, her dispute with Italy, *i.e.*, the Corfu affair; Bulgaria, the affair with Greece in 1925; China, the aggressions of Japan in 1931; and Ethiopia, the Ual Ual boundary dispute with Italy in 1935.

President Wilson declared that Article XI was his favorite article, because it made it possible for the smallest nation in the League to bring before the Council the provocative action of the greatest power. "The weak and oppressed and wronged peoples of the world have never before had a forum made for them in which

[1] See memorandum of General Bliss, Point 4, BAKER, III: 112; MILLER, II: 94.

[2] FOLEY, HAMILTON, *Woodrow Wilson's Case for the League of Nations*, p. 81, Princeton University Press, 1923.

they can summon their enemies into the presence of the judgment of mankind, and if there is one tribunal that the wrongdoer ought to dread more than another, it is that tribunal of the opinion of mankind." The tribunal of opinion, he alleged, was one for which the United States had had a traditional regard, the Declaration of Independence having been published "out of respect to the opinion of mankind."[1]

Article XII. Article XII is a pledge of the members of the League that if there should arise between them any dispute likely to lead to a rupture, they will submit the matter either to arbitration,[2] or to inquiry by the Council. This article makes compulsory as between the members an attempt to use some method of pacific settlement before resorting to war. The intention, as gathered from this and succeeding articles, is that justiciable questions shall be submitted to arbitration and nonjusticiable questions to inquiry by the Council.

The distinction between justiciable and nonjusticiable questions had been partially worked out by international lawyers prior to the war. In the Root arbitration treaties negotiated by the United States in 1908–1909, provision was made for arbitrating differences "of a legal nature, or relating to the interpretation of treaties" subject, however, to the exception that they should not affect the vital interests, etc., of the parties. In the ill-fated general arbitration treaties of 1911 negotiated with France and Great Britain, the designation of questions to be arbitrated was that they should be "justiciable in their nature by reason of being susceptible of decision by the application of the principles of law or equity."

A number of plans drawn up by private associations during the war provided for the arbitration of justiciable questions and the settlement of other questions by some process less binding and more flexible than arbitration. The proposal of the League to Enforce Peace to provide a court to try justiciable questions was, according to William Howard Taft, drawn from the arbitration treaties submitted to the Senate during his own administration. Mr. Taft traced the idea further to the method of settling disputes between the states in the United States Supreme Court. The court had on several occasions drawn the distinction between justiciable and nonjusticiable cases. The legal method of settlement was appropriate for the justiciable cases. Nonjusticiable disputes could be

---

[1] FOLEY, *op. cit.*, pp. 102–103.
[2] The words "or judicial settlement" have since been added by amendment.

settled by compromise agreement with the consent of Congress, but not by war.[1]

Article XVI. The provision of Article XVI for sanctions to be imposed upon any member which shall go to war in disregard of Article XII, XIII, or XV, of the Covenant is partially, at least, of American origin. The plan of the League to Enforce Peace had provided for the use of economic and military sanctions against recalcitrant powers.

DEMOCRATIC AND LIBERAL SAFEGUARDS

Publicity for Treaties. The plan for the publicity of treaties occupied the highly conspicuous place of Point One in President Wilson's Fourteen Points. The President demanded as a condition of the peace: "Open covenants of peace openly arrived at, after which there shall be no private international understandings of any kind but diplomacy shall proceed always frankly in the public view." The principle of publicity of treaties was, of course, not new with President Wilson, but had been frequently favored in the United States and England. In America, where treaties need the approval of the Senate and where it is manifestly impossible to conclude them without their contents being known to all factions in that body, secret treaties are regarded as a European vice. Executive agreements of a secret character are, however, sometimes concluded by the United States with foreign governments. A proposal for the registration of treaties with an international court was made by the Fabian Society in London in 1915.[2]

General Bliss suggested to President Wilson that there should be a declaration against secret treaties, and David Hunter Miller proposed publicity for all treaties and international agreements. Mr. Miller formulated the provision. It was copied into the Hurst-Miller draft and thus became the basis of the discussion in the Commission on the League of Nations. The plan called for registration of treaties with the Secretariat and for their publication. In the seventh meeting of the commission Mr. Wilson moved the amendment that a treaty should not be operative until so registered.[3] President Wilson believed that by these provisions, which became

[1] *Taft Papers on League of Nations*, edited by Theodore Marburg and Horace E. Flack, pp. 33*ff*., The Macmillan Company, New York, 1920. The distinction may also be traced to various European sources. See LAUTERPACHT, H., *The Function of Law in the International Community*, pp. 9*ff*.

[2] *Towards an Enduring Peace*, p. 292.

[3] MILLER, I: 198; WILSON, FLORENCE, *The Origins of the League Covenant*, p. 73, Hogarth Press, London, 1928.

Article XVIII of the Covenant, the commission had eliminated "the most dangerous thing and the most embarrassing thing that has hitherto existed in international politics."[1]

Mandates. The consideration shown in the Covenant for the peoples of the conquered territories was to no small extent due to American influences. Among the facts which constitute the American background of the mandates principle may be mentioned: the Declaration of Independence, Bryan's anti-imperialistic campaign of 1900, the liberal colonial policy of the United States as expressed in the Jones Act of 1916 regarding the Philippine Islands, and the utterances of President Wilson pertaining to the self-determination of nationalities. Sentiments favorable to the ultimate self-determination of backward peoples, of course, had from time to time been expressed by factions in every colonial power, particularly Great Britain. A number of the plans drawn up by private British organizations had included the idea of self-determination[2] which principle was, as is well known, strongly favored before the Armistice by the Allied powers with regard to the territories of their enemies.

General Smuts, himself a member of a conquered nationality and therefore filled with sympathy for the peoples of defeated territories, set forth in his plan for a league concrete recommendations for a system of mandates for the peoples and territories formerly belonging to Russia, Austria-Hungary, and Turkey. It may be significant that he failed to mention the German colonies and, therefore, omitted German Southwest Africa, a territory which was greatly desired by the Union of South Africa.

President Wilson had previously declared in the fifth of his Fourteen Points for an adjustment of colonial claims with an eye to the interests of the populations concerned. Previous to the Smuts plan, he had also asked that "the German colonies should be declared the common property of the League of Nations and administered by small nations," with a view to making the resources of each colony available to all members of the League.[3] Since he had already developed the idea of trusteeship, Mr. Wilson immediately became a stanch advocate of the Smuts proposal. In his second draft he incorporated the mandates principle and went

[1] FOLEY, *op. cit.*, 109.

[2] See also the memorandum on War Aims of the Inter-Allied Labour and Socialist Conference in London, Feb. 22, 1918, *London Times*, Feb. 25, 1918, set forth in PHELPS, EDITH M., *Selected Articles on a League of Nations*, p. 139, H. W. Wilson Company, New York, 1919.

[3] MILLER, DAVID HUNTER, "The Origin of the Mandates System," *Foreign Affairs*, VI: 281 (January, 1928).

further than General Smuts to include former German territories. In the Commission on the League of Nations and in the Council of Ten, the President became the outstanding champion of this provision. He faced powerful opposition. The British prime minister, the prime ministers of the Dominions, the French minister of colonies, and the Japanese delegates, all had direct annexations of coveted territories in mind.

On January 27, 1919, in the Council of Ten, President Wilson made a speech in favor of the mandate system. The Paris press thereupon attacked him for his allegedly impractical ideas. The fight became bitter, but finally a compromise was reached. The plan of the mandate system was placed in the Covenant (Article XXII), but the British dominions and the Japanese obtained the classification of their coveted territories as Class C mandates which are administered as integral portions of the territory of the mandatory state. When the territorial ambitions of the various powers are considered, it seems certain that had it not been for President Wilson's insistence the whole mandatory system would have been forgotten.[1]

The Representation of Small Powers upon the Council. The United States, by its unique position in world politics, has frequently been placed in the position of advocating the rights of small nations. Through the Monroe Doctrine this country has defended Latin-American states against the encroachments of the powerful European governments. The great powers of Europe have formed a concert to which we have not been a party. The American government has, therefore, found its friends frequently to be among the smaller states.

The proposal to admit small powers to the Council of the League was made by General Smuts, and he outlined a plan for a council in which the great powers would have a bare majority. President Wilson was immediately impressed by the plan and incorporated it in his second draft. Opposition to this type of council was expressed by Lord Robert Cecil who proposed a body on which only the great powers would have representation. The contest between the advocates of these two plans in the Commission on the League of Nations was quite warm. President Wilson became the leader of the fight to admit the small states to membership, and the contest in the commission revolved around the principal features of his draft.[2] The final decision was that the Council should be made up

---

[1] See BAKER, I: 252*ff.*; WILSON, FLORENCE, *op. cit.*, pp. 87*ff.*
[2] MILLER, *The Drafting of the Covenant*, I: 140*ff.*

of five great powers and four others elected by the Assembly from time to time in its discretion.   This was regarded as a victory for the small states.

Labor.   President Wilson in his second draft (Supplementary Agreements, Article V) brought the question of better standards for labor into the League of Nations discussions by the following provisions:

> The Powers signatory or adherent to this Covenant agree that they will themselves seek to establish and maintain fair hours and humane conditions of labour for all those within their several jurisdictions who are engaged in manual labour and that they will exert their influence in favour of the adoption and maintenance of a similar policy and like safeguards wherever their industrial and commercial relations extend.

This provision, with some modifications, became Section (a) of Article XXIII of the Covenant.   Here again President Wilson did not originate the idea.   He merely gave expression to the demands of labor organizations that labor should be considered in framing the peace.   Labor has, of course, important international aspects. Matters which are primarily domestic, such as hours and conditions of labor, have, because of the growth of international trade, come to affect the industrial conditions in other countries.   The pledge to establish fair hours and conditions for labor resulted in the creation of the International Labor Organization[1] which was referred to by President Wilson as "the great charter, the new constitutional charter of labor."[2]   The part which Americans played in the draft of the provisions for the International Labor Organization will be referred to later.[3]

THE QUESTION OF ARMS

Disarmament.   Article VIII of the Covenant regarding disarmament arose out of the general dissatisfaction throughout the world with the top-heavy military establishments which had played a part in bringing on the war.   Germany was the most heavily armed nation in the world in 1914 and much of the war propaganda of the Allies had emphasized that fact.   The war had been aimed against militarism.   World opinion toward the end of the war was favorable to a drastic reduction of armaments.   In no country was there a

---

[1] This is not provided for in the Covenant but in Part XIII of the Treaty of Versailles.

[2] FOLEY, p. 43.

[3] See pp. 284–285.

stronger sentiment against armaments than in the United States where, in addition to the antimilitaristic spirit of the moment, tradition was on the side of a relatively small army and navy.

In Point Four of his Fourteen Points President Wilson set forth as a peace aim: "adequate guarantees given and taken that national armament will be reduced to the lowest point consistent with domestic safety." This clause was embodied in the President's drafts of a covenant with the further clause that in addition to the standard of domestic safety there should be sufficient armaments for "the enforcement by common action of international obligations." With the standards of national armaments thus set upon the double basis of domestic safety and international action, this clause survived the various drafts and redrafts and came before the Commission on the League of Nations at the Peace Conference. In the commission the Japanese delegate moved to amend by striking out the term "domestic safety" and substituting the expression "national safety." With this rather considerable change, the clause became the aim of the League as expressed in Article VIII of the Covenant.

Publicity of Armaments. The United States was in an excellent position to urge the publicity of armaments at Paris. This country had developed no large land armaments. The military strategists of the United States were not in a continual state of anxiety regarding sudden land attacks across our borders, and they did not feel the necessity of maintaining large secret stocks of materials for the purpose of arming conscript troops in sudden emergencies. The principle of publicity for armaments was contained in Colonel House's draft and was continued in all of President Wilson's drafts. It found its way into the Covenant in Article VIII in the words: "The Members of the League of Nations undertake to exchange full and frank information as to the scale of their armaments, their military, naval and air programs, and the condition of such of their industries as are adaptable to warlike purposes." This clause is the basis for the League's publication of the *Armaments Year Book* in which a fair degree of publicity is given to the armaments of all nations, whether members of the League or not. The publishing of more complete material based on this clause was later the subject of discussion in the Preparatory Commission for a Disarmament Conference; and in this commission the United States continued to give support to the publicity principle.

The Private Manufacture of Arms. During American neutrality the powder and armament firms of this country had made enormous profits by selling their wares to the Allies.[1] The refusal of the American government to stop this practice was perfectly in accord with traditional international law but was regarded by many people as inconsistent with neutrality in a realistic sense. The President was evidently convinced of the essential evil of the practice, and the House and Wilson plans for a league carried a prohibition of the private manufacture of arms.[2] General Smuts' draft contained a similar provision. No such clause, however, appeared in the British or in the Hurst-Miller draft. In the fourth meeting of the Commission on the League of Nations, President Wilson caused the insertion of a clause which was somewhat less peremptory than that which had appeared in his own drafts. The suggestion was that of Wilson, though the wording was evidently that of Cecil. It read as follows:

The High Contracting Parties further agree that munitions and implements of war should not be manufactured by private enterprise, and direct the Executive Council to advise how this practice can be dispensed with.[3]

The British Admiralty objected to the prohibition. In a memorandum to Lord Robert Cecil, they made the comment: "If it had not been for the factories of the United States, the position of the Allies would have been excessively difficult, if not impossible, before the entry of America into the war."[4] Further modifications were made in the clause and in the final Covenant it appears in a diluted form as follows:

The Members of the League agree that the manufacture by private enterprise of munitions and implements of war is open to grave objections. The Council shall advise how the evil effects attendant upon such manufacture can be prevented, due regard being had to the necessities of those Members of the League which are not able to manufacture the munitions and implements of war necessary for their safety.

The latter part regarding the nonmanufacturing nations was inserted at the request of Portugal and Rumania.[5]

OPPOSITION TO A SUPERSTATE

Despite ardent American sentiment for cooperation in 1919, isolationist tradition was still a factor of considerable importance.

---

[1] The war orders of the Du Pont de Nemours Powder Company were estimated at $1,245,000,000. *Munitions Industry* (Senate Hearings), p. 1023.

[2] The House draft, Article XXI; Wilson's drafts, Article IV.

[3] MILLER, *The Drafting of the Covenant*, I: 172.

[4] *Ibid.*, I: 288.

[5] WILSON, FLORENCE, *op. cit.*, p. 46.

The fact that the United States was not threatened by a strong enemy near its frontiers explains the absence of any urge for a powerful international organization with sufficient energy to deal promptly with a threat of war. Nations situated like France, which had suffered from disastrous invasions, were willing to yield some of their independence in return for greater security. Also the nations which had gained by the war desired an energetic organization to protect their newly acquired position. The need of a vigorous league was not, however, so strongly felt in the United States. While it was truly argued that a war in Europe might be a very expensive matter to this country, such reasoning was not as convincing or moving as the more direct dangers which confronted European nations. The American delegates were not, therefore, willing to support a plan for a superstate. National independence was a more important consideration. The delegation realized also that the opponents of the League in the United States would make great capital out of any provisions for yielding independence of action. During President Wilson's meeting with the members of the Senate Committee on Foreign Relations and the House Committee on Foreign Affairs in Washington in March, 1919, many suggestions were made to him for the purpose of weakening the Covenant and for making stronger the guarantees of national independence of the member states. These suggestions were taken by the President back to the Paris Conference.

The Word "Constitution." A relatively unimportant matter, which nevertheless showed the trend of opinion in the United States, was the elimination of the word "constitution" from the preamble of the Covenant. The draft of February 14, which was brought to the United States by President Wilson during his mid-conference visit, contained in the preamble the expression: "the Powers signatory to this Covenant adopt this constitution of the League of Nations." After the President's return to Paris, a cable from America in summarizing newspaper and current opinion suggested that the word constitution should be stricken from the Covenant. The reason given was that "the word constitution to American students of law and history connotes the formation of a new world state."[1] The term Covenant was accordingly substituted by the drafting committee.

Opposition to a General Staff for the League. Probably the most notable suggestion for giving strength and power to the new organization was the French plan for an international military force

[1] MILLER, I: 387, 389.

which should be supplied by the various member states and should be at the disposal of the League. This scheme provided for a permanent general staff which should be charged with inspecting the international forces and armaments and with suggesting improvements.[1]

The American delegation was from the beginning strongly opposed to the French plan. President Wilson objected that to hand over the control of American troops to an international body would conflict with the Constitution of the United States.[2] Although opposing the plan, he sought to reassure the anxious French delegation by promising: "When danger comes, we too will come, and we will help you, but you must trust us. We must all depend on our mutual good faith."[3] Lord Robert Cecil cautioned the French not to insist upon their plan against the opposition of the American delegation. He warned them that in case of failure to form a league Great Britain intended to seek an alliance with the United States.[4] In place of the international general staff of the French proposal the commission finally adopted a plan for a permanent commission to advise the Council regarding military, naval, and air questions.[5]

Opposition to Compulsory Process for Enforcing Awards. The United States delegation, while favorable to the principle of peaceful settlement of international disputes, opposed a grant of power to the League to carry out the decisions of the Council. M. Venizelos proposed that in case of a unanimous decision of the Council under Article XV, that body "should have some right to secure the satisfaction of the claims of the injured party."[6] Mr. Miller, the legal adviser to the American delegation, argued against the plan as giving to a unanimous decision of the Council the effect of an arbitral award. This, he thought, would raise great opposition in the United States. As the members of the League have agreed in Article XII to submit their disputes either to arbitration or inquiry by the Council, the Venizelos proposal would have meant that the decision in both cases would be binding, which would have amounted to a system of compulsory arbitration. The clause was accordingly weakened in the preliminary draft of February 14 to read that in

[1] See Part III on Military Sanctions in the Official French Plan for a League of Nations.
[2] MILLER, I: 210.
[3] *Ibid.*, II: 297.
[4] *Ibid.*, I: 216–217.
[5] Art. IX of the Covenant.
[6] MILLER, I: 193.

case of refusal to comply with a unanimous recommendation under Article XV, the "Council shall propose the measures necessary to give effect to the recommendation."[1]

The clause as thus stated was still too strong for American opinion. When President Wilson visited the United States in February he found opposition to it among the members of the Senate Committee on Foreign Relations. A hypothetical case was suggested as follows: Suppose the Japanese should acquire a harbor for a naval base in Magdalena Bay and that the United States should contest that action. The dispute might be referred to the Council which might decide in favor of the propriety of the Japanese action on the grounds that it was merely a commercial transaction. If the United States should refuse to accept the decision, the Council might propose action against the United States. As a result of American objections, the Council was granted no power in the matter. In the final Covenant, the members merely agree that they will not go to war with any party to the dispute which complies with the recommendations of the Council's report.

Matters of Domestic Jurisdiction. The clause in Article XV which provides that the Council shall make no report in a case in which the dispute is found to be solely within the domestic jurisdiction of a party was placed in the Covenant because of the demands made in the United States. These demands came from members of the Committee on Foreign Relations of the United States Senate and of the Foreign Affairs Committee of the House of Representatives,[2] from William Howard Taft,[3] and from Senator Hitchcock, who was anxious to appease opposition sentiment.[4] Many Americans appeared fearful that unless there were such a provision, the anti-Japanese land laws of California and similar questions would be investigated by the League. A safeguarding clause eliminating domestic questions from the jurisdiction of the Council was prepared as an amendment to Article XV by President Wilson and was accepted by the Commission on the League of Nations.[5]

Restricting the League to an Advisory Organ. American influence was further exerted to prevent the League from making decisions in its own right without referring the matter to the member

[1] Text of February 14, Art. XV.
[2] HOUSTON, DAVID F., *Eight Years with Wilson's Cabinet*, II: 9, Doubleday, Page & Company, Garden City, N.Y., 1926.
[3] MILLER, I: 277.
[4] *Ibid.*, I: 276.
[5] *Ibid.*, I: 331.

states.   In two instances the American delegates introduced amendments to make certain that decisions must be adopted by the member governments before becoming effective.

As an antidote to the stereotyping of existing boundaries in Article X, the British draft of the Covenant contained a clause to the effect that the Body of Delegates (the Assembly) should make provision for the periodic revision of treaties.   Mr. Miller, legal adviser to the American delegation, was critical of this clause which might be interpreted to mean that the body would have the power to revise treaties by its own action.   It would, therefore, be in conflict with the constitutions of such states as required treaty changes to be made with the consent of the national legislative body.[1]   In the eighth meeting of the commission President Wilson moved to amend the article to read that the Body of Delegates would have power merely to "advise the reconsideration" of inapplicable treaties by the member states.[2]   Such is the provision of Article XIX as it now stands.

The clause providing for the amendment of the Covenant, as first introduced, read that amendments should take effect when made "by an unanimous vote of the Executive Council confirmed by a majority of the Body of Delegates."   Mr. Miller considered that this clause was contrary to the Constitution of the United States under which the Senate must approve treaties.   Because of this objection the article was finally altered to read that the amendments should take effect when *ratified* by the member states whose representatives composed the Council and by a majority of the states whose representatives compose the Assembly.[3]

Unanimity.   Ex-President Taft in a telegram of March 18, 1919, urged an express provision for unanimity of action in the Council in order to satisfy American opinion.   The Covenant was then changed to include a clause requiring unanimity except in matters of procedure and in certain cases otherwise provided for.   The text of the amendment was evidently proposed by Lord Robert Cecil. Lord Cecil explained that this was nothing more than the Covenant would mean even if it were not expressly stated, but the amendment was introduced to satisfy criticism.[4]

Withdrawal.   The right of a member to withdraw from the League was placed in Article I in response to objections raised by

---

[1] *Ibid.*, I: 202.

[2] *Ibid.*, I: 203, 205.

[3] *Ibid.*, I: 203–204; II: 290.

[4] *Ibid.*, I: 285.

members of the Senate Committee on Foreign Relations and the
House Committee on Foreign Affairs. Senator Hitchcock also
urged that such a clause would make easier the passage of
the treaty.[1]

The Monroe Doctrine. One of the strongest objections to the
League of Nations on the part of Senate members arose out of the
fear that the new organization would interfere with and possibly
destroy the Monroe Doctrine by admitting European nations into
the consideration of problems of the Western Hemisphere. There
was no possibility that the Covenant would actually destroy the
doctrine in its original sense which forbade European nations to
seize the territory of American republics. There was good reason,
however, for believing that the Covenant would not be consistent
with the greatly expanded interpretation of the doctrine which
elevated the United States to the position of supreme arbiter upon
the American continents.

When President Wilson made his visit to the United States in
February, 1919, he was confronted with a demand for an amendment to safeguard the doctrine.[2]   Senator Hitchcock and ex-President Taft also impressed upon him the necessity for such a provision. Upon his return to Paris an attempt was made to satisfy this
demand.   Article XXI was created to make sure that nothing in
the Covenant would be deemed to affect the validity of international
engagements, such as treaties of arbitration or regional understandings like the Monroe Doctrine, for securing the maintenance of
peace.   The first draft was evidently prepared by Sir William
Wiseman who was attached to the British delegation.[3]   President
Wilson, in explaining the Covenant to the American people, made
much of Article XXI and contended that the recognition in the
Covenant of the doctrine, which had formerly been disliked in
Europe, "constitutes nothing less than a moral revolution in the
attitude of the rest of the world toward America."[4]

**All of the Suggestions of the Congressional Committee Members
Were Incorporated in the Covenant.** From the foregoing discussion
of the framing of the Covenant, it can be seen that influence of the
United States was strong. The Paris Conference went far to
embody American ideas.   Well might President Wilson state to the
Senate Committee on Foreign Relations with regard to the former

[1] HOUSTON, op. cit., II: 9–11; MILLER, I: 277, 344.
[2] MILLER, I: 277, 322.
[3] Ibid., I: 336.
[4] FOLEY, op. cit., p. 91.

suggestions of committee members: "On my return to Paris, all these matters were taken up again by the Commission on the League of Nations, and every suggestion of the United States was accepted."[1] The League is thus a structure built to no small extent upon American plans with American materials. In no other instance have the efforts of American statesmen had such a profound effect upon the machinery of world organization.

II. THE DEFEAT OF THE TREATY

Relation of the United States to Europe Reconsidered. In a changing period of history it is inevitable that the relations of this country with world movements must be periodically revised. Minor decisions for policy readjustment are made from day to day by the Department of State without attracting much attention. The recurrence of world crises, showing in a catastrophic way the lack of harmony between nationalism and the growth of international social and economic forces, will doubtless in the future from time to time compel a general review of American policy. The debates of 1919 and 1920 with regard to American entry into the League of Nations are thus far the most thorough reexamination of the general question. It is doubtful if the debates were the principal determining factor in the decision against ratification of the Versailles Treaty. It is probable that political and emotional factors were of more importance. But the student attempting to arrive at a rational judgment on American policies cannot neglect the multitude of arguments brought forth at that time bearing directly upon American relationship to world cooperation.

The Treaty of Versailles, including the Covenant of the League of Nations, was brought back from Paris by President Wilson and submitted to the Senate on July 10, 1919. From that time until November, 1920, a gigantic debate took place in the United States. The controversy was carried on from the floor of the Senate, on the lecture platform, in the Pullman smoking car, in the corner grocery store, at the boisterous political conventions, and in the party rallies of the 1920 presidential campaign. Only a few of the arguments, mostly drawn from the Senate debate, can be summarized here.[2]

American Traditional Policy and the New Economic Era. The most effective senatorial contention against League membership was that it would have represented a drastic departure from the time-

---

[1] HOUSTON, *op. cit.*, II: 9.

[2] A full account of the controversy over the League is found in FLEMING, DENNA FRANK, *The United States and the League of Nations*, 1918–1920, G. P. Putnam's Sons, New York, 1932.

honored policy of isolation. Washington's Farewell Address was quoted on numerous occasions and the old fears of militaristic Europe were revived. Senator James Reed stated in characteristically forceful language:

. . . it is proposed that we shall abandon our ancient and traditional peace and shall become entangled in every broil of Europe as these broils may now or as they may hereafter exist. It is the most monstrous doctrine ever proposed in this Republic.[1]

The friends of the League urged that the abandonment of isolation had become advisable because of the radical change in conditions since the time of Washington. American exports had passed the seven billion dollar mark and had made this country dependent upon the outside world for markets. Peace had become essential to American welfare. Senator Jones of New Mexico put the argument as follows:

We must have world peace; we must have stable conditions in all countries with which we deal. We need the products of other countries, and those countries need our products. Our personal comfort as well as our prosperity depend upon the relationship which we shall establish with foreign nations. Peace is a prime essential. Without it all else fails.[2]

Striking increases in the speed of communication and in the mass of commerce had rendered it impossible for the United States to keep out of world disputes. The epidemic character of war in an economically unified world made neutrality impossible.

"Suppose," said Senator Ransdell, "a world war should happen between any two important countries, no matter which, would it not interfere greatly with our commerce, would it not step hard on the toes of many of our manufacturers and bankers and agriculturists and shippers? How could we avoid being drawn, sooner or later, into the war to protect our own interests?"[3]

Senator McCumber referred to the murder at Sarajevo which ultimately cost the lives of 50,000 American soldiers and brought a financial charge to the American people which, he said, would eventually reach $100,000,000,000. He inquired: "Is a conflict in Europe which compels us to load that enormous debt upon the American people for a century a conflict which does not concern us?"[4]

[1] *Congressional Record*, 56: 11,622 (Nov. 21, 1918).
[2] *Ibid.*, 58: 5399 (Sept. 15, 1919).
[3] *Ibid.*, 58: 3399–3400 (July 31, 1919).
[4] *Ibid.*, 58: 1264 (June 18, 1919).

The argument that the expansion of American business had made entrance into the League necessary was construed by the opposition to spring from the demand of capitalists that their international profits should be insured by American participation in a League army. After reciting the names of a large number of successful American financiers who were supporting the movement to enter the League, Senator Borah suggested that the businessmen who held the "wider view" might be those who owned foreign securities and properties which they hoped were to be guaranteed by American soldiers.[1] Senator Sherman referred to identic letters which he had received from persons connected with insurance and bond organizations advocating the ratification of the treaty. These, he claimed, were evidence that international bankers had organized a lobby to back the League movement.[2]

Would the League Keep Us Out of War? War prevention was the foremost purpose of the League. Previous to the Armistice it had been commonly taken for granted that the "war to end wars" would be followed by the creation of machinery to maintain world peace. The League was about the only attempt to carry out this expectation. President Wilson predicted that unless some such machinery as the League should be provided the next world war would come within a generation. Such a war would be made terrible by gases of increased destructive power and great self-guiding projectiles that would travel hundreds of miles and throw tons of explosives upon defenseless cities.[3] The Covenant, it was alleged, was the promise of peace for which the war-torn peoples had patiently waited. The articles which contain the bulwarks against war are those from X to XVII, inclusive, and XIX. Many of their provisions have already been discussed.

The opponents of the treaty contended that the League would not prevent wars but that the necessity of participating in military sanctions would involve this country in more frequent conflicts. Henry Cabot Lodge pointed to the allegedly peaceful history of the United States as distinguished from the warlike experiences of Europe. "If we join a League, therefore," he said, "it must be with a view to maintaining peace in Europe, where all the greatest wars have originated, and where there is always danger of war, and in Asia, where serious conflicts may arise at any moment."[4]

[1] *Ibid.*, 58: 2063 (June 30, 1919).
[2] *Ibid.*, 58: 5497 (Sept. 16, 1919).
[3] FOLEY, *op. cit.*, pp. 202–203.
[4] *Congressional Record*, 57: 4527 (Feb. 28, 1919).

Senator Borah supposed a situation in which the Council of the League, acting in an emergency, might advise that the United States should send "100,000 or 250,000 or 300,000 troops to Russia or to Japan or to the Balkans." The United States, he contended, would be under moral obligation to comply.[1] Several of the opposition senators warned that this country would be forced to engage in war with China to defend Japanese rights in Shantung. The question at issue was as to whether the obligation to assist in coercing an aggressor would not involve this country in greater trouble than would be avoided by the attempt to prevent war.

League or Superstate? Various senators attacked the League as a superstate which would exercise some of the powers normally reserved for the sovereign nations. Senator Fall referred to his oath of office to support the Constitution of the United States. The Covenant infringed the Constitution, robbing Congress of certain of its rightful powers. His conscience, therefore, prevented him from voting for the treaty.[2] Under Article X the Council has the duty to recommend the means of fulfilling the obligations of the members in certain emergencies; and under Article XVI, the Council is to recommend what effective military, naval, or air forces the members shall contribute to protect the covenants of the League in case of the violation of Article XII, XIII, or XV. Some of the opponents of the League contended that the power to declare war was taken from Congress by these articles and given to the League. Senator Borah declared that even if the League had only the power to advise, the obligation should, nevertheless, be regarded as morally binding.[1] Senator Fall went further and claimed that the United States would be obliged to comply with recommendations of the Council with regard to furnishing military, naval, or air forces and that refusal would be "an act of rebellion against the league government and would justify war upon us."[3] In vain was it pointed out that due to the unanimity necessary for Council action on most substantive matters and due to membership of the United States on the Council it would be impossible for that body to act without American consent.[4] Senator Walsh of Montana explained that the League had no army and no independent treasury and no

---

[1] *Ibid.*, 58: 2735 (July 17, 1919).

[2] *Ibid.*, 58: 2062 (June 30, 1919).

[3] *Ibid.*, 58: 3496 (Aug. 1, 1919). See also the opinion of Senator Poindexter, *ibid.*, 56: 11,565–11,566 (Nov. 15, 1918).

[4] This was repeatedly explained. See, for example, the statement of Senator Swanson, *Congressional Record*, 58: 2534 (July 14, 1919).

means of securing either. "It is idle," he said, "to assert that an organization thus equipped is a government at all."[1] But the fears of the opposition senators could not be allayed.

Objections to Article X. The guarantee of the territorial integrity of members of the League was the center of attack by the treaty opponents. This pledge, they asserted, would involve the United States in difficulties all over the world. Although the safeguarding amendment suggested by General Bliss limited the article to cases of external aggression, the opposition refused to consider the matter in that light and continually alleged that the provision would make the United States a guarantor for the territories of Great Britain and other empires as against revolution. The picture of the League as a suppressor of revolutions stirred the antagonism of the Irish nationalists. These men were bitter toward the President for failing to support their cause at Paris, and they now appeared before the Senate Committee on Foreign Relations to denounce the League as an attempt to trample upon and destroy the rights of the weak.[2]

The Monroe Doctrine. The various interpretations of the Monroe Doctrine played a conspicuous part in the treaty debate. Senator Poindexter asked: "How can the President honestly tell the people that a world league founded on the principle that Europe shall participate in the control of American affairs, and that America shall participate in the control of European affairs, does not abrogate the Monroe Doctrine?"[3] President Lowell of Harvard contended that the view of the Monroe Doctrine which attempted to maintain Latin America as a game preserve for the United States ought to be rejected.[4] He pointed out, as did many others, that the true doctrine was designed to keep European governments from seizing the territories of American republics and that the League only strengthened it by guaranteeing the territorial integrity of League members. But to make the matter doubly sure, the doctrine was expressly safeguarded in Article XXI of the Covenant. The imperialistic interpretation of the doctrine in subsequent years has been rejected by the Department of State and the League has without American objection sought to aid in the settlement of Latin-American wars. It seems now, therefore, to be rather well demonstrated that the League is an additional support to the ideas of President Monroe.

---

[1] *Ibid.*, 58: 961 (June 11, 1919).
[2] *Ibid.*, 58: 4654*ff.* (Sept. 3, 1919).
[3] *Ibid.*, 58: 5027 (Sept. 8, 1919).
[4] *N.Y. Times*, Mar. 20, 1919.

The Defeat in the Senate.   The question of League membership was determined more by the ebb and flow of emotions, by the raising of party issues in the Senate, and by the difficult nature of the treaty machinery than by the rationality of the argumentation as to the meaning of the Covenant.   The psychological ebb was attested by the change in opinions of numerous senators who were from 1915 to 1918 ardently in favor of a league and who by 1920 turned vigorously upon the only practical proposal for a league that was presented. Henry Cabot Lodge in 1916 praised the work of the League to Enforce Peace and eloquently declaimed regarding world peace organization: "Not failure, but low aim is the crime."[1]   But by 1919 he had experienced a radical change of mind.   Philander C. Knox and Warren G. Harding likewise turned from advocacy of a league to become opponents of *the* League of 1919.   The leaders of the fight against the treaty were well aware of the psychological ebb and realized that time was on their side.   Senator Lodge reported a conversation during the latter part of April, 1919, in which he told Senator Borah that any attempt to defeat the League by a straight vote at that time would be hopeless.[2]   The dilatory tactics of amendment and reservation were, therefore, adopted; and the discussion dragged out until well into the year 1920.   By that time the sentiment for a league had so far cooled that failure by the Senate to approve the treaty would no longer bring public rebuke.

The various votes in the Senate on the League showed that at first a majority of the senators were favorable to the treaty with mild reservations.   In November, 1919, a majority of 53 to 38 was against it without reservations.   The treaty was finally put to a vote in March, 1920, with fifteen reservations attached, some of which were directly in contradiction to the spirit of the Covenant.   The treaty was then rejected by a vote of 49 for and 35 against because some twenty friends of the League, following the advice of President Wilson, voted in the negative.   They preferred that the treaty should fail rather than that it should be adopted with embarrassing reservations.[3]

---

[1] *Enforced Peace*, p. 166.

[2] LODGE, HENRY CABOT, *The Senate and the League of Nations*, p. 147, Charles Scribner's Sons, New York, 1925.

[3] For an analysis of the vote see HOLT, W. STULL, *Treaties Defeated by the Senate*, pp. 295*ff.*, Johns Hopkins Press, Baltimore, 1933; FINCH, GEORGE A., "The Treaty of Peace with Germany in the United States Senate," *International Conciliation*, No. 153 (August, 1920).

CHAPTER XIV

COOPERATION WITH THE LEAGUE OF NATIONS

THE GENERAL CHARACTER OF COOPERATION

The Change from Isolation to Cooperation. For some time after the inauguration of President Harding in 1921 American officialdom was influenced by the desire for isolation and by antagonism to the League. As Elihu Root observed: "it came to be a common thing that we could read in newspapers and hear in speeches and in conversation expressions of expectation that the League would fail, and evident pleasure when it seemed that it might fail."[1] The administration evidently regarded the 1920 election as a mandate to leave the League strictly alone. Participation in the activities of the League, which had occurred in two instances in the Wilson administration,[2] was immediately abandoned. President Harding, in his first message to Congress in April, 1921, stated that the United States would "have no part" in the League. Intimations that official correspondence from the League was not desired were conveyed to Geneva through the American embassy in London.[3] The Secretary-General nevertheless deemed it advisable to send notes to Washington regarding matters of interest to this country. At first these were filed away in the Department of State and remained unanswered. In fact the American consul at Geneva called upon the Secretary-General to inform him that the United States had no relations with the League and would not reply to certain notes that had recently been received.[4]

From this time on, however, the attitude of the United States gradually changed as the force of onrushing facts played havoc with the affirmations of the Republican leaders. When the nations of the

---

[1] Quoted in HOWLAND, CHARLES P., *Survey of American Foreign Relations*, 1928, p. 303, Council on Foreign Relations, New York, 1928.

[2] The United States had designated a member of the Committee of Rapporteurs in the Aaland Islands case, and a representative from this country had participated "unofficially" in the Brussels Financial Conference of 1920.

[3] HOWLAND, *op. cit.*, p. 303.

[4] GARNER, JAMES WILFORD, *American Foreign Policies*, p. 195, note 22; BERDAHL, CLARENCE A., *The Policy of the United States with Respect to the League of Nations*, p. 98, Publications of the Graduate Institute of International Studies, Geneva, 1932.

world gathered with increasing frequency in conferences upon matters in which this country had a deep interest, it became difficult to remain away from the meetings. As each advance toward cooperation was made by the United States, the administration sought to pacify isolationist sentiment by publicly setting limits to its participation at Geneva. As soon as the necessities of diplomacy made it advisable to overstep these boundaries, further limits were set.[1] The process of pushing back the frontiers of American cooperation are briefly described in the following paragraphs.

About six months after Mr. Harding's inauguration formal notes were sent from Washington acknowledging receipt of communications from the Secretariat. In 1923 the cooperation proceeded a step further when representatives were sent to Geneva to participate in an unofficial and consultative capacity in the consideration of several social and economic subjects. It was declared that this country was not to participate officially and that its observations were to be limited to social and humanitarian matters. Late in 1924 the United States went beyond this position and sent official delegates to the Second Opium Conference at Geneva; and, in 1925, another official delegation journeyed to the seat of the League to participate in the Conference on the Traffic in Arms. Official delegates have gone since then to take part in practically all of the important League conferences whether they have dealt with humanitarian matters or with politically tinged subjects such as the arms traffic and disarmament. The United States has also participated in the consideration of the highly political Manchurian and Liberian situations.

In the matter of the form of participation the United States did not stop after it had proceeded from unofficial observation to official participation in League conferences. It was affirmed stanchly for some years that this country would not appoint members to the boards, commissions, or committees of the League.

---

[1] For a general discussion of American cooperation at Geneva see HUBBARD, URSULA P., "The Cooperation of the United States with the League of Nations and with the International Labour Organization," *International Conciliation*, No. 274 (November, 1931); HUDSON, MANLEY O., "America's Role in the League of Nations," *American Political Science Review*, XXIII: 17 (February, 1929); HOUGHTON, N. D., "The Present Status of the League of Nations," *International Conciliation*, No. 317 (February, 1936). See also two articles by BERDAHL, CLARENCE A., "Relations of the United States with the Assembly of the League of Nations" and "Relations of the United States with the Council of the League of Nations," *American Political Science Review*, XXVI: 99, 497 (February and June, 1932).

In 1926 the United States refused to deal with the Permanent Advisory Commission regarding armaments and it was necessary to set up the same body under another name (Sub-Commission A of the Preparatory Commission for the Disarmament Conference) before an American member could participate in the deliberations. In 1931 an American Foreign Service officer, Samuel J. Reber, Jr., was designated to sit as official American representative upon the Council's committee to draft reforms with regard to Liberia.   In the following year General McCoy went to the Far East as a member of the Lytton Commission, his selection having been made in collaboration with the Department of State and his participation having been made possible by act of the American government in relieving him from current military assignments.   Likewise in 1932 Americans sat with the Organizing Committee of the Council to prepare for the International Economic Conference of 1933.   The United States has even joined to a limited degree in the work of the Council.   Active correspondence with that body was kept up by the Department of State during the Far Eastern crisis of 1931– 1932.   At one session in Geneva in 1932, the American consul, Prentiss Gilbert, sat at the Council's horseshoe table, participating in an advisory capacity.   In 1933 the American minister to Switzerland acted with the Council in the election of members to the Permanent Central Opium Board.[1]

Characteristics of Participation Summarized.   *In general, American participation has been more active in conferences held under the auspices of the League than in the boards, commissions, and constitutional organs of the League itself.   This country has taken part more consistently in humanitarian and welfare activities than in political controversies.   In the consideration of politics the cooperation of the United States has been greater with regard to matters of universal regulation, such as disarmament and arms traffic, than with regard to regional disputes.   Concerning the latter this country has shown some interest in the settlement of problems in Asia, South America, and Africa but has abstained from aiding the League in the adjustment of the dangerous political controversies of Europe.*

FURTHER DESCRIPTION OF AMERICAN ACTIVITIES AT GENEVA

Participation of Private Citizens and Public Officials in League Work.   There are now more Americans in Geneva dealing with the

---

[1] All the proposals for membership in the World Court have anticipated that American representatives would eventually sit with both the Council and the Assembly for the purpose of electing the judges of the court.

League in various public and private capacities than there are
nationals of many of the League members. Aside from those who
represent private associations, the following types of American
representatives have participated in League work:

1. Private American citizens serving in the League Secretariat and on
various League boards and commissions without any connection with the
American government. Illustrations of this type of collaborator are Arthur
Sweetser and Benjamin Gerig in the Information Section of the Secretariat,
and Dr. F. G. Boudreau in the Health Section. Norman Davis was for several
years a member, in a private capacity, of the Financial Committee of the
League.

2. United States officials serving on boards and commissions but not on
nomination of the United States government. Participation of this kind is
designed to keep American officials in touch with important developments in
their fields of work. Various officers of the United States Public Health
Service have attended meetings of the League Health Committee and conferences called to deal with health matters. Treasury officials have attended
fiscal committee meetings.

3. United States officials representing this country as observers at conferences and League committee meetings.

4. Representatives of the United States serving on advisory and preparatory
commissions and at conferences in a full official capacity. In the year ending
June 30, 1934, American observers or advisers were present at the sessions of
five committees while official delegates represented this country in four conferences and one committee of the Council. An American was also officially
named to participate in the Governing Body of the High Commission for
Assistance to Refugees from Germany, which was created by the Council but
was not responsible to it.[1]

**Discussions of International Legislative Policy in League Com-
missions and Conferences.** Probably the greatest efforts of the
United States in connection with League work have been in the
attempt to formulate treaties of an international legislative character such as those regarding the drug traffic, disarmament, and the
arms traffic. Ordinarily when the League seeks to advance a
particular idea in world organization, it adopts a sequence of procedures about as follows: An advisory or preparatory commission is
created to perform the initial work. Discussions in the commission
ensue. With the help of Secretariat officials an effort is made to
reduce the various national views on the subject to compromise form
in a draft convention. A conference of plenipotentiaries of the

---

[1] Dept. of State, *American Delegations to International Conferences, Congresses and Expositions*, Govt. Printing Office, Washington, 1935. For a list
of Americans who served in various capacities from 1919 to 1931, see "American
Cooperation with the League of Nations, 1919–1931," *Geneva Special Studies*,
Geneva Research Information Committee, Vol. II, No. 7 (July, 1931).

governments is then called to agree to the convention with or without modifications. If the convention is signed at the conference, it is sent to the various governments for ratification after which it takes its place as international legislation.

American official representatives or observers have sometimes been counted among the outstanding personalities in League conference diplomacy. One of the most forceful of the American diplomat-orators at Geneva was Stephen G. Porter who was an observer at the meetings of the Permanent Advisory Committee on Opium and represented this country officially at the Second Opium Conference of 1924–1925. Mr. Porter had borne an important part in the Congressional discussion of the drug traffic and was a sincere worker for the abolition of the illicit trade. He did not have, however, a particularly broad international outlook nor much confidence in the motives of the representatives of foreign governments when they disagreed with his particular formula for the solution of the problem. In the conference he urged the restriction of the production of raw opium to the amount necessary for medical and scientific purposes and created considerable enthusiasm among the representatives of the smaller states. His controversy with Lord Robert Cecil over the method of opium control was the most dramatic point of the conference. When it seemed impossible to obtain the adoption of the American views, he led the United States delegation from the conference. In the 1931 conference on the same subject the American delegation, headed by John K. Caldwell of the Department of State, was more inclined to compromise. Representatives of other governments had also moderated their attitudes, and the 1931 treaty was signed and ratified by the United States.

Hugh Gibson, then American minister to Switzerland, represented the United States for several years in the Preparatory Commission of the Disarmament Conference where he established himself as one of the best informed men at Geneva with regard to disarmament problems. Mr. Gibson was spokesman for the Hoover administration in making certain important contributions to the disarmament discussions, including the proposal of a naval yardstick and a plan for qualitative and quantitative disarmament. He was also a member of the American delegation at the Disarmament Conference in 1932. For many years Norman Davis has been a representative of the United States in League discussions. He had previous diplomatic experience as undersecretary of state and was active at the Paris Conference of 1919. In 1923–1924 he served in a private capacity as president of the League Commission on the Memel Dispute. In 1927 he went as a member of the American delegation to the International Economic Conference in Geneva. In 1931 he was appointed in his private capacity as a member of the League Financial Committee. Beginning in 1933 he became the chief American representative in Geneva with regard to disarmament and also with regard to general political subjects. He was sometimes referred to as our "ambassador at large." During this latter period, as the spokesman for Secretary of State Hull, Mr. Davis voiced the official American sentiment which favored greater participation by the United States in the world peace machinery.

It would not be feasible to attempt here a survey of the course followed by this country in the commissions and conferences of the League. At other places in this volume the policies of the United States in League meetings are treated in greater detail. Some conception of the subject can be obtained by referring to the following topics:

Commerce, tariffs, import and export prohibitions and restrictions, Chapter X.
War Prevention, Chapter XVII.
Disarmament, Chapter XXI.
Drug traffic, pp. 273*ff.*
Slavery, pp. 279*ff.*
International Labor Organization, pp. 284*ff.*

Among other matters regarding which the United States has participated officially, but which are not discussed in this volume, are the codification of international law, the buoyage and lighting of coasts, press relations, and educational films.

The Ratification of Treaties Resulting from League Conferences. Not all the conferences attended by American delegates have resulted in the formulation of treaties and not all the treaties so formulated have been ratified by the United States. Some of the more important which have been ratified by this country are: The Traffic in Arms Convention of 1925, the Slavery Convention of 1926,[1] the Convention for the Abolition of Import and Export Prohibitions and Restrictions of 1927, the Traffic in Drugs Convention of 1931, and the Educational Films Convention of 1933. Agreements which have been made but which have not required ratification have been the Armaments Truce of 1931, the Wheat Agreement of 1933,

---

[1] The convention was drawn up in the Assembly and was adhered to by the United States in 1929.

and the Silver Agreement of 1933. The changing attitude of the Senate with regard to advising ratification has been striking. In the beginning of the Harding administration it was obvious that no treaty which arranged for the administration of the provisions through the League would be acceptable to the Senate. In 1932, however, the Senate advised the ratification of three treaties which contained provisions for administration through the League. In the Traffic in Drugs Treaty of 1931, for example, the parties accepted the Permanent Central Opium Board for purposes of administration. Not only did the Senate advise ratification of the treaty, but as has been previously stated, the United States has since designated a representative to sit with the Council in electing the members of the board.

The Transmission of Information to the League Secretariat. In response to requests from the League Secretariat and sometimes in accordance with the provisions of treaties, the United States has cooperated to provide Geneva with a considerable mass of information on American conditions affecting certain international problems. Material thus sent has covered such subjects as the drug traffic, armaments, health, traffic in women, American legislation on the nationality of women, and industrial labor conditions. The United States has also sent answers to League questionnaires regarding the attitude of this country upon such subjects as the codification of international law and the organization of international statistics.

Treaty Registration. Until 1934 the United States did not register its treaties with the League. Most of the treaties to which this country was a party were registered by the other parties and the remainder were "communicated" to the Secretariat but not registered. These "communicated" treaties were published but were not included in the regular treaty series. They were given a separate numbering and their publication was delayed until all interested League members had been notified. In 1934 the United States agreed with the Secretariat to register all treaties and other international agreements to which we should be a party. The treaties are now published without delay in the *League of Nations Treaty Series*. The new policy of registration does not commit the United States to the Covenant requirement that treaties shall not be binding until registered.[1]

[1] *Executive Agreement Series*, No. 70; Dept. of State, *Press Releases*, Feb. 3, 1934, p. 62. For a discussion of the question of registration see HUDSON, MANLEY, O., *Progress in International Organization*, p. 109, Stanford University Press, Stanford University, Calif., 1932.

The Payment to the League of the American Share of Expenses of Activities in Which This Country Participates. In 1923 the United States paid about $70 to the League for the share of the United States in compensating for the loan of League staff members to the meeting of the International Committee of Jurists at The Hague. From that date it became the policy of the United States to contribute a part of the extraordinary expenses of each undertaking in which this country officially participated. The share paid was on the same basis as that of Great Britain. It did not, of course, include the overhead expenses of maintaining the permanent staffs of the League. The payments were usually made through executive action, Congress having voted a lump sum to defray the costs of American participation in the particular conference, including the expenses of delegates. In 1932, however, an item in the appropriation bill for attendance at the Disarmament Conference was specifically earmarked for the payment of the United States share in the League expenditure for the conference. Congress, by voting this item, gave its approval to the general policy.[1] Up to July, 1935, the United States had paid approximately $70,000 into the League treasury. Since that time the annual contributions of the United States have increased because of membership in the International Labor Organization. For the fiscal year 1935–1936 Congress has appropriated $174,630 for the share of the United States in the I.L.O. In addition to these various contributions private individuals in this country have paid large sums for the support of different League enterprises.

Channels of American Communication with the League. The United States has frequently used the diplomatic method of communication with the League, sending its messages to the Secretariat through the American minister in Berne. In 1928 Secretary of State Kellogg explained that this system was used for the more dramatic matters and that less important affairs were conducted through the United States consul in Geneva.[2] Owing to the increase in American business with the League, the consulate in Geneva was enlarged in 1928 and several Foreign Service officers were assigned to duty at that post for the specific purpose of keeping watch on League activities and maintaining the necessary contacts. When Prentiss Gilbert, formerly assistant chief of the Division of Western Euro-

[1] "The United States and the League of Nations during 1932," p. 14, *Geneva Special Studies*, Geneva Research Center, Vol. III, No. 12, 1932.
[2] BERDAHL, *op. cit.*, p. 113.

pean Affairs, was assigned to the Geneva post as consul in 1930, he was referred to journalistically as our "consul to the League."[1] At present there are eight Foreign Service officers at Geneva of which five devote their time to observing the work of the League. In 1932 special offices were established in Geneva for the United States delegation to the Disarmament Conference, and for awhile another office was maintained for the American economic experts.[2] Telephonic communications exist between Washington and the Geneva offices, thus placing the Department of State in intimate touch with affairs at the seat of the League.

COOPERATION WITH THE LEAGUE IN LIMITING THE DRUG TRAFFIC

The Nature of the American Problem. Of the three evil practices in connection with opium—the eating of raw opium, the smoking of prepared opium, and the habitual use of narcotic drugs—only the last-named practice has been sufficiently prevalent in the United States to provoke nation-wide demands for legislative action. Smoking, it is true, was introduced with the immigration of Chinese. In 1909 it was estimated that of 118,000 Chinese in the United States, 17,700 were heavy smokers, 23,600 were light smokers, and 11,800 were "social" smokers.[3] There has also been some smoking in the Philippine Islands although it has been forbidden by law since 1908. Opium smoking is not practiced by the general American population and is not regarded in this country as a great social menace. Drug addiction has, however, a much more sinister aspect. Morphine, heroin, and other derivatives of opium, and cocaine, which is the product of the coca leaf, are powerful habit-forming drugs, and result in the moral and mental degradation of their victims. Addicts frequently are driven by their unsatisfied desires to commit the most serious crimes in order to obtain the drugs which will gratify their craving. Only in comparatively recent years, *i.e.*, since the chemical revolution, has the evil reached large-scale proportions. In the United States the number of

[1] JAMES, EDWIN L., "Our 'Consul to the League,'" *N.Y. Times*, Aug. 26, 1930, referred to in BERDAHL, *op. cit.*, p. 115.

[2] "The United States and the League of Nations during 1932," pp. 13–14. See also POTTER, PITMAN B., "Permanent Delegations to the League of Nations," *American Political Science Review*, XXV: 29–30 (February, 1931).

[3] Statement of American Delegation, *Report of the International Opium Commission, Shanghai, China, February 1 to February 26, 1909*, II:8, published by the North China Daily News and Herald, Ltd., Shanghai, 1909.

addicts has been variously estimated from 100,000 to more than 1,000,000.[1]

Because habit-forming drugs are insignificant in volume, their importation into the United States is a comparatively easy matter. Drugs have been smuggled in belts worn under the clothing of sailors, in quilted jackets, in holes bored in furniture, in the soles of shoes, in tins immersed in barrels of olive oil, behind secret panels in staterooms, in false bottoms of trunks, in the earth of potted plants, in the air tanks of lifeboats, and in numerous other ways. Smuggling prevention remains the primary problem in attacking the drug evil in the United States.[2] The best organized system of detection at the seaport cannot block the efforts of the international drug dealers. The United States as the richest of the "victim" countries has been the ultimate market for much of the drugs produced in factories in Istanbul or Basle and distributed by drug rings frequently financed by American capital, which have been operated from Vienna, Berlin, or Paris. Under the incentive of enormous profits, several thousand per cent in some cases, the dealers operating in the illicit drug trade have put forth every effort to outwit the agents of the American government.

The United States, caught between the horrors of the spreading narcotic evil and the impossibility of preventing the bootlegging of drugs, has taken the position that the narcotic evil should be stopped at the source, *i.e.*, in the poppy fields and in the areas where the coca shrub is grown. This policy of limitation at the source of the raw material found its official expression in the Porter Resolution of March, 1923, in which Congress requested the President to urge upon the producing governments the necessity of limiting the growth of poppies and coca leaves to the amounts required for medicinal and scientific purposes. The resolution alleged that the world's medicinal and scientific needs for opium could be taken care of by the production of 100 tons per year, whereas 1,500 tons was actually produced. This left 1,400 tons to find its way into the illicit traffic.[3]

The Hague Convention of 1912 Fails to Provide International Machinery for Enforcement. Previous to the formation of the

---

[1] For a discussion of estimates see TERRY, CHARLES E., and MILDRED PELLENS, *The Opium Problem*, pp. 1*ff*., published by the Committee on Drug Addictions in Collaboration with the Bureau of Social Hygiene, New York, 1928.

[2] *Traffic in Opium and Other Dangerous Drugs*, p. 22, Report by the Government of the United States for 1931, Govt. Printing Office, Washington, 1932.

[3] H.J. Resolution No. 453, 67th Cong.

League of Nations, there had been several attempts to bring about international action for the suppression of the illicit traffic in narcotics.   Largely due to the efforts of the United States, an international commission representing thirteen countries met in Shanghai in 1909 and passed resolutions urging the further control of the traffic.   In 1911 President Taft, desiring to give legal force to the resolutions of the Shanghai Commission, proposed an international conference; and such a meeting was called by the Dutch government.   The conference met at The Hague in December, 1911; and an international opium convention was adopted in January, 1912.

The Hague convention provided: (1) With regard to raw opium the powers should prohibit its export to countries which prohibited its import and control its export to countries which restricted its entry.   This latter provision was a praiseworthy attempt but was exceedingly difficult to enforce as it stood.   Most countries permitted the import of raw opium for manufacture in the legitimate trade.   The matter of controlling the trade to those countries which restricted it could not be accomplished without some machinery for international concert as to the amount of shipments.   Such machinery was not provided.   (2) With regard to prepared opium, which was used for smoking, it was declared that measures should be taken for the gradual and efficacious prohibition of its manufacture.   The internal traffic in and the use of prepared opium were to be suppressed "in so far as the different conditions peculiar to each nation shall allow of this."   The mere expression of a pious hope for better conditions provided no cooperative method by which the legislation of the different countries was to be brought about nor any standards by which the accomplishments of the countries could be measured.   (3) With regard to narcotic drugs the convention contained an agreement of the parties to enact laws to confine to "medical and legitimate" uses the manufacture, sale, and use of morphine, cocaine, and their respective salts.   The term "legitimate" did not add anything to the convention as, of course, anything not prohibited by law is legitimate.   Nor was any machinery set up in this case for carrying the agreement into effect.   (4) The parties agreed to send information regarding their laws and administrative regulations and statistics as to the extent of their drug traffic to the government of the Netherlands.   This was the only semblance of an enforcing system contained in the treaty.   The convention was thus an example of the old-fashioned method of attempting to solve an international problem by an agreement for the independent action of sovereign states unsupported by any international administrative machinery. The convention had not received a sufficient number of ratifications to become effective at the beginning of the World War. At the close of the war the various peace treaties provided that the ratification of those treaties should constitute ratification of the Hague Opium Convention. By 1924 forty-eight governments were parties to the instrument.

The League Takes Over the Problem.   In Article 23 (*c*) of the Covenant of the League of Nations it was provided that the execution of agreements with regard to traffic in opium and other dangerous drugs should be under the supervision of the League. Thus the matter passed into the sphere of international government. The Secretariat of the League was designated to receive the communications of the governments which under the Hague Convention were to go to the government of the Netherlands. The United States, however, objected to this procedure and continued to send its communications to The Hague. The Dutch government then transmitted the American information to the Secretariat. For a time the United States refused entirely to recognize the new position of the League in the suppression of the opium traffic. Because of the impotence of the Federal authorities to stop importations, however, the United States was unable to make satisfactory progress by reliance solely on domestic action.

In 1923 the United States sent representatives in an "unofficial and consultative" capacity to the Permanent Advisory Committee on Opium and to the Fifth Committee of the Fourth Assembly. The American representatives sought to gain acceptance for the American policy as expressed in the Porter Resolution. In November, 1924, a strong delegation represented this country in full official capacity at the Second Opium Conference and there asked for the adoption of the American principle of the restriction of the production of the poppy and coca leaf to the amount necessary for scientific and medicinal purposes. One of the most heated discussions in the history of League conferences occurred at this meeting.[1] Representatives of governments with Far Eastern possessions resisted the American proposal upon the ground that it was not on the agenda. They also opposed it on its merits. The suppression of the production and traffic, they argued, would mean smuggling upon a large scale. This would mean greater abuses and the loss of revenues. They piously asserted, however, that the revenue side

[1] For the debates see League of Nations, *Records of the Second Opium Conferences, Geneva, Nov. 17, 1924–Feb. 19, 1925* (C. 760. M. 260. 1924. XI).

had no bearing upon their attitude. They argued that if they should agree to restrict production, countries which were outside the convention or which could not control their production and traffic would continue to sell and would monopolize the trade. Furthermore, it was pointed out that there was no relationship between the poppies grown in India and China and the traffic in harmful drugs, inasmuch as these drugs were not manufactured from the low-grade opium product of Indian or Chinese poppies but from high-grade opium produced in the Near Eastern countries, Turkey, Persia, and Yugoslavia. Angered by the combined and in some cases highly irritating opposition and seeing no prospect of the adoption of the American proposal, the United States delegation left Geneva. This conference represented an immature flag-waving stage in the attempts to secure international cooperation. In future meetings a saner attitude was to be taken.[1]

The Convention of 1925. The second conference of 1924–1925 did, however, produce a convention which was much in advance of the Hague Convention of 1912. It incorporated a practical method for controlling the commerce in opium and drugs by providing that each importing country should require an import authorization for each importation of drugs stating the quantity of drugs and the names and addresses of importer and exporter. Each exporting country should allow the export of the substances only upon special permit which should be issued after the exporter had produced an import certificate from the government of the importing country. This practical piece of mechanism had previously been suggested by the League's Advisory Committee on the Traffic in Opium and Other Dangerous Drugs.[2] Drug production, traffic, and uses were more specifically to be limited to "medicinal and scientific" purposes. While there is again no method of compelling the nations to comply with the agreement, a stronger force of persuasion than any that had hitherto existed was set up by the convention. A Permanent Central Opium Board was provided for. The creation of this new organ of international government probably represented the most valuable contribution of the 1925 convention. The board

---

[1] For a general account of the conference see WILLOUGHBY, WESTEL WOODBURY, *Opium as an International Problem, the Geneva Conferences*, Johns Hopkins Press, Baltimore, 1925; BUELL, RAYMOND LESLIE, *The International Opium Conferences*, World Peace Foundation, Boston, 1925.

[2] EISENLOHR, L. E. S., *International Narcotics Control*, p. 76, George Allen and Unwin, London, 1934. This volume presents a complete picture of the control system at Geneva.

consists of eight persons elected by the Council of the League. The United States was invited to nominate one person to assist in the election but for several years declined to do so. An American, Herbert L. May, was chosen as a member of the board by the Council. The board receives statistics from the parties regarding production, traffic, consumption, and confiscations, and publishes them in its annual report. If the figures lead the board to believe that any country is in danger of becoming a center of illicit traffic, it may ask, through the Secretary-General, for an explanation. If no explanation is forthcoming or if an unsatisfactory one is given, the board may call the attention of the parties and the Council of the League to the matter,[1] and may recommend that no further exports of opium or narcotic drugs shall be made to the country concerned until the board is satisfied with the situation in that country. While the United States failed to sign the convention, it has complied with the terms of the treaty and has regularly sent all required information to the Secretary-General of the League through the American legation at Berne.

The Convention of 1931. In 1931 another conference was held at Geneva under the auspices of the League.[2] The United States participated in the conference and signed and ratified the convention which issued from it.[3] This convention requires each party to furnish to the Permanent Central Opium Board estimates of its drug requirements for medical and scientific purposes for the following year. The parties agree to limit imports and production to the figures thus presented. The estimates are examined by a Supervisory Body consisting of one member appointed by each of the following: the Advisory Committee on the Traffic in Opium, the

---

[1] The board has called attention to the danger of the illicit traffic in opium in Turkey and of the excessive manufacture of heroin in Bulgaria. MOORHEAD, HELEN HOWELL, "International Administration of Narcotic Drugs, 1928–1934," *Foreign Policy Reports*, Vol. X, No. 26 (Feb. 27, 1935), pp. 339–340. Action in such cases is taken in collaboration with the Advisory Committee. In its report to the Council in 1934 (C. 390. M. 176. 1934. XI), p. 14, the board called attention to excessive exports of narcotics to Honduras during the previous year; and in the report on the work of its twentieth session in 1935 (C. 253. M. 125. 1935. XI), p. 25, the Advisory Committee stated that information pointed to the fact "that all Central American countries south of the Mexican border are used as bases for illicit traffic, except Panama and Guatemala." For some other findings of the board see EISENLOHR, *op. cit.*, p. 191.

[2] See League of Nations, *Records of the Conference for the Limitations of the Manufacture of Narcotic Drugs, Geneva, May 27th to July 13th*, 1931 (C. 509. M. 214. 1931. XI).

[3] *U.S. Treaty Series*, No. 863.

Permanent Central Opium Board, the Health Committee of the League, and the International Public Health Office. The Supervisory Body may request explanations and will furnish, so far as possible, estimates for countries failing to make an estimate. Mr. May is also a member of this body as a representative of the Permanent Central Opium Board. The principle of limitation of trade and production to medical and scientific purposes which the United States has so consistently striven for has thus been adopted so far as habit-forming narcotic drugs are concerned although it has yet to be adopted for raw and prepared opium. The convention, which replaces for the most part the Hague Convention of 1912, provides that the Secretariat of the League shall be the channel for communication regarding the convention.[1] The older policy of the United States of refusal to communicate data to Geneva and of insistence upon sending the material to the Dutch government has thus been entirely abandoned. Furthermore this country has made nominations for members of the Permanent Central Opium Board and has participated with the Council in the election of the members.

THE QUESTION OF SLAVERY

The American Interest in Abolishing Slavery. The Civil War placed the stamp of antislavery ideology upon American foreign policy and raised this country to an equal place with Great Britain in the movement to uproot the slave traffic. In the Berlin Congress of 1884–1885 American delegates advocated the abolition of the slave trade in Africa and signed a convention for that purpose. Following a change of administrations, however, the incoming president, Mr. Cleveland, refused to submit the convention to the United States Senate. The United States participated in the Brussels Conference of 1890 and ratified the resulting convention in which the signatories agreed to forbid the slave trade in Africa and to take measures for preventing it. In 1919 the United States signed a convention concluded at Saint-Germain revising the general acts of Berlin and Brussels.[2] This convention went beyond the previous two in pledging the suppression of slavery as well as of the slave trade. No international means of enforcement were provided.

The League of Nations soon after its founding assumed the leadership of the antislavery movement. Certain provisions in the

---

[1] Fifty-four governments have ratified the convention.

[2] *U.S. Treaty Series*, No. 877. The United States did not ratify the convention until 1934.

mandate agreements were aimed at eliminating slavery and the slave trade. Under the terms of the B and C mandates, the mandatories agreed to abolish the slave trade. Mandatory powers of Class B mandates also pledged themselves to suppress slavery. Mandatory powers of A and B mandates were obliged to adhere on behalf of the mandates to any general conventions regarding the slave trade that were in existence or that might be concluded.[1] The League also has been interested in the extinction of slavery outside of the mandates. In 1924 the Temporary Commission on Slavery was appointed to gather information with regard to the charges that there had been a revival of slavery and slave trading. The committee reported that slave trading and slave raiding existed in various parts of Africa and Asia.[2] A general convention for the suppression of the slave trade and the progressive abolition of slavery in all its forms *"as soon as possible"* was drafted in the Assembly of 1926. The convention stipulated that compulsory or forced labor could be exacted only for public purposes. The parties agreed to communicate to the Secretariat of the League any laws and regulations which they might enact in applying the provisions of the conventions. The convention failed to provide an international commission to watch over the execution of treaty obligations but left the matter to the good faith of the parties. A plan for a Permanent Slavery Commission to strengthen the convention at this point was brought forth in the Eleventh Assembly by the British delegation but was not adopted. In this respect the convention fell below the level of recent international legislation. The United States government acceded to the convention in 1929 but refused by reservation to adhere to the clause by which forced labor is to be abolished except for public purposes. The United States Senate, opposing everything that smacked of servitude, refused to give even an implied approval to forced labor for public purposes.[3]

The Liberian Situation.   The greatest cooperation between the United States and the League of Nations with regard to slavery has

[1] See "The Suppression of Slavery," *Geneva Special Studies*, Vol. II. No. 4 (April, 1931), pp. 5–6; WRIGHT, QUINCY, *Mandates under the League of Nations*, University of Chicago Press, 1930, which gives the texts of typical mandates in the appendices; MARGALITH, AARON M., *The International Mandates*, pp. 111–112, Johns Hopkins Press, Baltimore, 1930.

[2] League of Nations, *Report of the Temporary Slavery Commission* (A.19. 1925. VI), p. 6.

[3] For text of convention see *League of Nations Treaty Series*, No. 1414, LX: 253; *U.S. Treaty Series*, No. 778. For a general discussion see "The Suppression of Slavery," *Geneva Special Studies*, previously cited.

come with reference to the conditions of labor in Liberia. For some years previous to 1929 there had been suggestions from various writers that certain forms of slavery and forced labor existed in that African republic. The United States government has a three-fold reason for interest in the subject. In the first place, the United States was largely responsible for the establishment of the Liberian Republic and the consequent foisting of the rule of some 20,000 Afro-Americans upon some 1,500,000 primitive African people. When this ruling class becomes flagrantly delinquent in its duties to protect the population against injurious practices and more particularly when public officials actively participate in and profit from labor exploitation, it is difficult for the United States to disclaim all responsibility. In the second place, the antislavery sympathies of the American people, expressed through resolutions and petitions, have forced the government to take notice of the question. In the third place, there are important American economic interests in Liberia, particularly the Firestone Plantations Company, which has extensive rubber plantations, and the Finance Corporation of America, which holds the Liberian public debt. These interests are certain to be affected by any thoroughgoing reforms instituted to abolish slavery.

Moved by these various considerations, the United States brought the matter directly to the attention of the Liberian government. On June 8, 1929, a note was presented in Monrovia stating that the United States had received reliable evidence that the export of Liberian labor to the Spanish island of Fernando Po had resulted in a system of labor recruiting "which seems hardly distinguishable from organized slave trade" and that the Liberian Frontier Force and certain high governmental officials had aided in the traffic. In reply the Liberian government denied the existence of such conditions and declared that it would have no objections to an investigation of the question by a commission on the spot. The Liberian government also presented the matter to the Council of the League and suggested that the proposed inquiry commission should be composed of one member appointed by the government of the United States, one appointed by the Council of the League, and one appointed by the Liberian government. This commission was duly constituted. It visited Liberia and, in 1930, rendered a report of great importance regarding conditions of labor in that country.

The commission found that the forcible raiding of villages along the southeastern coast of Liberia for the Fernando Po labor supply had depopulated large areas. At one village, Kordor, there had been forty-one huts but all had been abandoned. The townsite was overgrown with weeds and vines. The thatched roofs and mud-covered sides were crumbled in, leaving a scene of complete desolation. These raids had been directed in part by a high Liberian official named Yancy, formerly a local administrator in this section, who, in 1928, had been elected vice-president of the Republic. The soldiers of the Frontier Force had assisted in the raids.

The commission found other labor abuses. Cases of pawning of human beings as guarantees for the payment of debts were discovered. It was understood in some instances that the pawn was never to be redeemed. In one case a man forty years of age had been pawned when a child. The pawner was dead and there was no hope of redemption. In another case, a man, who had been fined by the government for road delinquencies, pawned his wife and child for £7. At the time of the investigation they had been in pawn for five years. There were also many cases of abuses connected with forced labor for both public and private purposes. None of these practices constituted slavery in the strict sense, that is, a status of ownership in which the human being is sold or bequeathed at will under recognized legal procedure. The condition was, nevertheless, sufficiently deplorable to warrant an international protest and a demand for the institution of reforms by international action.

The commission found that the solution of the Liberian labor question could not be brought about by legal action on the part of the Liberian government without some assistance which would eliminate political and economic difficulties. Slavery, after all, is a social condition associated with a backward stage of economic development. It has been abolished by all industrially advanced countries. The commission, in recommending plans for the abolishment of oppressive labor conditions, included a broad program for administrative reform, financial reorganization, health improvement, and the extension of education to all alike.[1]

American Cooperation with the League Fails to Solve Liberian Problem. Following the report of the commission the American government was faced with the alternatives of individual action to check abuses in Liberia and cooperation with the League in establishing a sort of international guardianship. The prospect of individual action, which would probably have necessitated the use of marines in far-off Africa, was not a pleasant one for the United States which was

---

[1] League of Nations, *Report of the International Commission of Enquiry in Liberia* (C. 658. M. 272. 1930. VI). This document was printed by the Department of State, Govt. Printing Office, Washington, 1931.

sponsoring the Pact of Paris and which was already well along the road in the retreat from imperialism. Cooperation with the League seemed to be the less objectionable course of action and was the one which was adopted. The fact that powerful American economic interests were apt to oppose any statesmanlike proposal which might issue from an international body was, however, an impediment to the plan of joint action with the League.

In 1931 the Council of the League formed a committee to advise it with regard to the administrative and financial reforms necessary in Liberia. The United States, upon the Council's invitation, named Samuel J. Reber, Jr., who was then serving as chargé d'affaires at Monrovia, to be the American representative upon the committee. Two sets of opposite interests influenced the work of the committee. On the one hand, the Firestone companies, sometimes backed by the American government, demanded a firm system of control by foreign administrators and sought to preserve as much of their existing contract rights as possible. The Finance Corporation of America went so far at one time as to contend that the chief adviser in the new administrative scheme should be an American. As the financial adviser under the existing fiscal system was an American, the company's suggestion would have brought the Liberian government largely under American control. On the other hand, the Liberian government opposed the grant of strong administrative powers to the proposed foreign advisers and desired to restrict their functions, so far as possible, to the giving of advice to Liberian officials. Drastic modifications of the existing contracts, such as the reduction of interest on the debt and the increase in the annual rental on the plantation company's holdings, were likewise desired. The financial experts of the League agreed that modification of the contracts to some degree was necessary.

The first plan drawn up by the League committee in May, 1932, provided for a corps of foreign officials to assist the government of Liberia. The principal officials were to be three provincial commissioners and a chief adviser. These were to cooperate with the American advisers who supervised finances under the loan agreement of 1926 between Liberia and the Finance Corporation of America. The plan was first weakened to meet objections from Liberia and then strengthened somewhat to appease the United States. The American government then forwarded it to the Finance Corporation as a basis for negotiations between the company and Liberia for the readjustment of the contract and for extending further financial aid. The corporation was not satisfied with the plan and undertook independent negotiations with Liberia. This move seemed to make matters worse, for Liberia then suspended payment of interest on the corporation's bonds. A second plan was later drawn up by the committee and endorsed by the Council in October, 1933. The new scheme gave greater powers to the foreign officials and dealt more lightly with the contracts of the American companies. Liberia made so many reservations to the plan that the Council considered it useless to proceed with the matter further. Thus this most important attempt at collaboration between the United States and the League failed because of the impossibility of reconciling the claims of the American corporations with the views of the Liberian government.[1] It is probable that the only method by which this impasse could have been avoided would have been the refusal of the United States government to be influenced unduly by the Firestone interests and to demand that the corporations should accept some such solution as the amended first plan upon pain of withdrawal of American diplomatic support.

THE UNITED STATES AND THE INTERNATIONAL LABOR ORGANIZATION

The Formation of the International Labor Organization.   Samuel Gompers, President of the American Federation of Labor, was president of the Commission on International Labor Legislation at the Paris Conference of 1919 in which the plan for the I.L.O. was produced. Mr. Gompers, H. M. Robinson, another American member of the commission, and Professor James T. Shotwell, who attended some of the meetings, were instrumental in modifying the project to meet American objections. They explained that in a federal system of government such as ours the matter of labor legislation came within the scope of the states and could not be modified by such conventions as were contemplated in the International Labor Conferences. The plan was accordingly altered so that the decisions of the conferences were to take the form of either (1) recommendations to the members that might be given effect

---

[1] A summary of the matter is found in KOREN, WILLIAM, JR., "Liberia, the League and the United States," *Foreign Policy Reports*, Vol. X, No. 19 (Nov. 21, 1934). Many of the documents are published in the *Official Journal of the League of Nations*. The League publication C. 595. M. 277. 1933. VII, regarding the second plan, is reprinted by the Department of State in the publication *Liberia, Documents Relating to the Plan of Assistance Proposed by the League of Nations*, Govt. Printing Office, Washington, 1933. See also YOUNG, JAMES C., *Liberia Rediscovered*, Doubleday, Doran & Company, Garden City, N.Y., 1934.

by national legislation or otherwise or (2) draft conventions for ratification by the members.[1]   It was further made optional for federal states to treat draft conventions as recommendations only. The probability that labor legislation standards might be higher in the United States than those adopted by the conference led to the inclusion of a provision that in no case should any member be asked or required to lessen its standards of labor protection as a result of the adoption of the recommendations or conventions of the International Labor Conferences.   The particular reason for the clause was the belief that any international standards applying to seamen would be below those of the United States as found in the La Follette Seamen's Act of 1917.[2]   Andrew Furuseth, president of the International Seamen's Union of America was, however, not satisfied with this safeguard and became the outstanding opponent of the I.L.O. in American labor circles.[3]   Altogether the influence of the American members of the commission was, in a large measure, a negative and weakening one; and the credit for the greater part of the constructive work must go to the British.[4]   Perhaps, however, the modifications brought about by the American delegation in 1919 made possible the entrance of the United States into the organization without notable opposition from American isolationists in 1934.

   American Isolation Weakens the Work of the I.L.O.   In the first conference of the new organization, Americans took an active part.   Secretary of Labor William B. Wilson presided and Mr. Gompers addressed the meeting on the subject of the eight-hour day.   Thereafter the question of representation arose on several occasions but the United States did not send delegates to the annual conferences again for fourteen years.   In several cases Americans were officially appointed to commissions of the organization and in a much larger number of instances they participated privately in its work.   A branch office was established in Washington to keep the League informed regarding the social and economic tendencies in this country and to contribute accounts of American conditions in the various world-wide studies of the I.L.O.

---

   [1] Article 405 of the Treaty of Versailles.   For the discussions see *The Origins of the International Labor Organization*, edited by James T. Shotwell, I: 145–162, Columbia University Press, New York, 1934 (2 vols.).
   [2] *Ibid.*, I: 163.
   [3] *Ibid.*, II: 421.
   [4] WILSON, FRANCIS GRAHAM, *Labor in the League System*, pp. 52–53, Stanford University Press, Stanford University, Calif., 1934.

During this period of American nonmembership the absence of the United States was deplored at Geneva. Representatives of European employers frequently raised objections to the control of industry through treaties on the ground that they did not dare to accept severe regulations unless the United States should be similarly bound. European motion-picture producers, for example, objected to restrictions upon child labor in the film industry unless similar regulations would be imposed upon American companies. Albert Thomas, the director who guided the I.L.O. during the important years of its formative period, summarized the matter in his 1930 report as follows:

. . . when the Office endeavours to secure ratification of its international labour Conventions by the States of Europe, Asia or South America or to overcome the opposition of employers preoccupied by the fear of foreign competition, it is constantly being told that all its efforts are negatived by the fact that the most powerful industrial country in the world not only cannot subscribe to any of its Conventions but does not even interest itself in its work. The difficulties of the Office's position are, indeed, being aggravated by the fact that during the last few years employers in a considerable number of countries have been seriously concerned by what they are sometimes apt to call American economic imperialism. Surely there are some grounds for thinking that, if some representatives or observers from the United States were to meet some European employers or workers in conference, whether officially or unofficially at a session of the International Labour Conference or otherwise, in an endeavour to ascertain in all sincerity and objectivity what might be the real consequences of their economic policy on the labour conditions of the rest of the world, many prejudices might be dispelled, many possibly unfounded apprehensions allayed, and perhaps a clearer idea obtained in their own interest of the possible repercussions and reactions on their own country.[1]

The American objections to association with the International Labor Organization, in addition to the general disapproval of the isolationists, were that the I.L.O. was under socialistic influences and that the labor standards provided by the treaties framed at the conferences were not as high as those existing in the United States. The first point had no intrinsic merit inasmuch as the recommendations arising from the I.L.O. had merely sought to establish regulations of labor in line with moderate bourgeois idealism. The second objection was unfounded for two reasons. In the first place, if American standards should happen to be higher

---

[1] *International Labour Conference, Fourteenth Session, Geneva,* 1930, p. 11.

than those of the conventions, there would be no necessity for lowering those standards through the adoption of the recommendations of the conferences. In the second place, American standards were frequently far below those recommended by the conferences in such matters as regulation of hours, child labor, and social insurance.[1]

The United States Joins the I.L.O. The coming of the New Deal brought with it a much greater enthusiasm for the improvement of labor than had previously existed in American governmental circles, and with it there developed a more friendly feeling toward the I.L.O. A delegation of four official observers was sent to Geneva to attend the seventeenth conference in June, 1933. The delegation on its return recommended adherence to the I.L.O. for the reason that the economic and social questions that are considered in Geneva are interwoven with the problems of the American industrial system. Social insurance, maximum hours of labor, and methods of increasing wages and purchasing power have become of primary interests in the United States. According to the delegation, this country should be in a position to discuss such matters internationally upon a basis of equality with the other members of the I.L.O.[2] The Roosevelt administration was now ready to take the significant step of joining the organization. By a joint Congressional resolution of June, 1934, the President was authorized to accept membership. The International Labor Conference in Geneva a few days later invited the United States to become a member. In August, 1934, the invitation was accepted and the United States entered the organization.[3] Membership on the part of the United States entails a financial contribution to the League treasury for the support of the I.L.O., the sending of a complete delegation to the annual conferences, and the submission of the action of the conferences to the competent authorities in the United States.[4] Perhaps the joining of the I.L.O. is the most significant

[1] See CHENEY, ALICE S., "International Labor Standards and American Legislation," *Geneva Special Studies*, Vol. II, No. 8 (August, 1931).

[2] *Report of United States Delegation at the International Labor Conference, Geneva, June, 1933, to the Secretary of Labor*, pp. 8–9, Gov. Printing Office, Washington, 1934.

[3] For the communications see Dept. of State, *Press Releases*, Aug. 25, 1934, p. 109, and *U.S. Treaty Series*, No. 874. See also an explanation of the Department of State attitude in the address by Wallace McClure, Dept. of State, *Press Releases*, July 14, 1934, pp. 49–52.

[4] WILSON, FRANCIS G., "Internationalism in Current American Labor Policy," *American Political Science Review*, XXVIII: 915 (October, 1934).

step thus far taken by the United States toward cooperation at Geneva.

Some indication of the type of aims to be pursued by the United States in the I.L.O. may be gleaned from the President's message to the American delegates to the Nineteenth International Labor Conference in 1935. President Roosevelt placed stress on two subjects for consideration, the forty-hour week in certain industries and the problem of unemployment among the young. The movement for a forty-hour week, he said, represented on an international scale what the United States had done through the NIRA and local legislation. The President hoped that the American delegation would earnestly contend for this proposal. The problem of unemployment among the young had been approached in this country through the Civilian Conservation Corps, which accomplishment should be something of a guide to the American delegates. He likewise asked that the delegation should learn from European experience by making careful inquiries into such aspects of economic security, old-age pensions, and unemployment insurance as might come up for discussion at the conference.[1]

[1] For the text of the message see *N.Y. Times*, May 23, 1935.

CHAPTER XV

THE PACIFIC SETTLEMENT OF INTERNATIONAL DISPUTES

Influences Affecting American Policy. The present system of pacific settlement of international disputes is a development of the last 140 years, the rise of modern arbitration being ordinarily traced from the Jay Treaty of 1794. The economic and social integration of the world has since that time been followed, somewhat belatedly, by progress in the invention and application of processes of good offices, inquiry, conciliation, arbitration, and judicial settlement. During the same period the strength of nationalism has increased and the occasions for international dispute have multiplied. History has in this respect revealed a race between the development of the processes of peace, on the one hand, and the growth of nationalistic aggravations coupled with preparations for war, on the other, with the martial system somewhat in the lead.

The behavior of the United States with regard to the peaceful settlement of international controversies has been conditioned by several important and sometimes divergent circumstances. The factors inclining this country toward the use of pacific settlement have been: (1) the early peaceful disposition of Americans due to weakness and the absence of dangerous neighbors; (2) the economic stake of this country in the avoidance of war because of business relations with the nationals of strong countries; and (3) territorial satisfaction. The factors which have caused this country to act with indifference toward or in opposition to peaceful settlement have been: (1) the imperialistic attitude of the United States which has at times developed as American business has come into contact with weaker countries in Latin America, an attitude which has weakened during recent years; (2) the isolationist sentiment which was originally caused by a fear of becoming involved in European wars and which in turn has brought about a reluctance to participate in world organization for peace; and (3) our difficult treaty machinery which has placed heavy odds against the adoption of thorough-going arbitration agreements.

With these contrary influences operating against each other, the actions of the United States with regard to pacific settlement have been anything but consistent. Glowing praise of arbitration and one-time leadership in the movement to create a world court have been followed by an unwillingness from time to time to adopt thoroughgoing arbitration treaties and by a refusal to accept the World Court. This attitude, in turn, must be set off against the sponsorship of the Pact of Paris which binds the signatories not to seek the settlement of disputes by other than peaceful means. A willingness to submit important controversies with Great Britain to arbitration must be contrasted with an occasional refusal to arbitrate matters with countries in the Caribbean region. The desire for peaceful procedure shown in the creation of the Central American Court of Justice in 1907 must be compared with an attitude of nonsupport which contributed to the death of the tribunal ten years later when the court rendered a decision adversely affecting American interests. The policy of this country has been one pursued through changing conditions, in dissimilar situations, dominated now by the Executive and again by the Senate or by a Senate minority. The attitude of the United States toward the pacific settlement of international disputes cannot, therefore, be dismissed, as has sometimes been done, by simple expressions of eulogy or condemnation.

THE PROCEDURES OF PEACEFUL SETTLEMENT DEFINED

When a dispute becomes too difficult to be adjusted by the unaided diplomatic efforts of the parties, there are various well-recognized procedures for peaceful settlement which necessitate the employment of outside agencies. In good offices and mediation, as the terms are usually employed, the outside agency is one or more friendly powers. In the other methods to be described, an international commission or tribunal is set up to perform the work of peaceful settlement in accordance with the more formal methods of international organization. While the usage by different writers of the terms involved is not always in agreement, the different procedures may be defined for our purposes as follows:

Good offices means the tender of assistance by a power friendly to both disputants in aiding the direct settlement between the parties by promoting communication between them or in furnishing them a common meeting place.

Mediation is a term used to denote the efforts of a third state or states in proposing a solution which, it is hoped, will be acceptable to the two parties.

Inquiry includes an investigation and report regarding the causes of the dispute by an international commission. Pure inquiry does not involve a recommendation as to a solution. A plain statement of facts, however, will sometimes clearly suggest a just settlement. Ordinarily bodies of inquiry go further and assume the function of conciliation.

Conciliation is a term used to designate an investigation and proposal of a settlement by an international commission. The parties are not obliged to accept the proposal.

Arbitration is the method by which the parties agree to submit the dispute to a tribunal of their own choosing which is to settle the question "on the basis of respect for law," to use the words of the Hague Convention.[1] The tribunal is *ad hoc* in character and is set up after the dispute has arisen. The parties agree in advance to accept the judgment of the tribunal.

Judicial settlement means the adjudication of a dispute by a permanent tribunal in accordance with international law, the judgment being binding on the parties.

Disputes of a legal character are best dealt with by arbitration or judicial settlement. Disputes of a nonlegal character, which cannot be satisfactorily settled on the basis of the existing law, are best disposed of through inquiry and conciliation. Therefore, the distinction between justiciable and nonjusticiable disputes becomes important in considering the method of settlement to be employed.[2]

THE AMERICAN RECORD OF ARBITRATION

The Jay Treaty. In the year 1794 a cumulation of controversies between Great Britain and the United States had produced a critical situation. British creditors clamored for the payment of debts from Americans and denounced the legal obstacles which had in some states been set up to prevent the use of the courts for collection. British soldiers still held the frontier posts which they

---

[1] Article XXXVII of the Convention for the Pacific Settlement of International Conflicts of the Second Hague Conference.

[2] For definitions of the various methods see *Arbitration and the United States*, pp. 451–452, World Peace Foundation, Boston, 1926; POTTER, PITMAN B., *An Introduction to the Study of International Organization* (rev. ed.), pp. 193*ff.*, Century Company, New York, 1925; MOWER, EDMUND C., *International Government*, pp. 293*ff.*, D. C. Heath & Company, Boston, 1931; VINACKE, HAROLD M., *International Organization*, pp. 281*ff.*, F. S. Crofts & Company, New York, 1934; FENWICK, CHARLES G., *International Law* (rev. ed.), pp. 405*ff.*, D. Appleton-Century Company, New York, 1934; STOWELL, ELLERY C., *International Law*, pp. 603*ff.*, Henry Holt & Company, New York, 1931; EAGLETON, CLYDE, *International Government*, pp. 315*ff.*, Ronald Press Company, New York, 1932; WILSON, GEORGE GRAFTON, *International Law* (9th ed.), pp. 228*ff.*, Silver, Burdett and Company, New York, 1935.

had promised to evacuate in the Treaty of 1783. Americans pressed claims against the British for slaves which had fled into the British lines during the Revolution and which had been taken to England. American merchants demanded payments for losses on account of seizures by the British in the European war which had begun the year before. British merchants had claims for losses from seizures by French privateers which had been commissioned in American ports. Because of these legal disputes and the fact that a large part of the American public was sympathetic to France, it seemed not unlikely that war between the two countries might result. Another cause for ill feeling was the barring of American goods from the British West Indies.[1]

The merchants of New England, who conducted a considerable transatlantic business, were, in the main, anxious to dispose of these grievances by treaty.[2] Their swollen profits derived from neutral trade were dependent upon continued peace with Great Britain.[3] John Jay, a fitting representative of the Federalist group, was accordingly sent to London to negotiate an agreement, and the Jay Treaty of 1794 was the result. Briefly summarized it contained provisions for the withdrawal of the British soldiers from the frontier posts without compensation for their allegedly illegal occupation. It omitted any provision for compensation for the slaves but secured closely restricted rights of trade in the British West Indies. Articles of arbitration provided for the adjudication of the Northeastern boundary, the debts owed to British merchants by Americans which were uncollectible owing to legal impediments, the losses of Americans due to illegal captures by British ships in the current war, and the damages done to British commerce by the French privateers proceeding from American ports in violation of American neutral obligations.

In the storm of objection to the treaty which swept the United States, principally in the South and West, the chief complaints were not made against the arbitration provisions.[4] Nevertheless, these provisions did not entirely escape criticism. Objections of unconstitutionality were raised against the submission to arbitration of

[1] BEMIS, SAMUEL FLAGG, Jay's Treaty, A Study in Commerce and Diplomacy, p. 23, The Macmillan Company, New York, 1923.

[2] ADAMS, RANDOLPH GREENFIELD, A History of the Foreign Policy of the United States, p. 102, The Macmillan Company, New York, 1924.

[3] For the importance of Anglo-American trade to both countries see BEMIS, op. cit., pp. 33ff.

[4] Indignation was aroused particularly regarding the commercial clauses.

matters concerning the obstacles raised in this country to British debt collection. It was claimed that such questions could be settled only by the tribunals of the United States. The method of selecting the tribunal was condemned. The tribunal in one instance was to be chosen as follows: two members were to be named by each party and the fifth was to be chosen by unanimous agreement of the four. If they could not agree, the fifth commissioner was to be selected by lot. This meant, said one congressman, that the decision was practically to be made by lot. He complained against the anticipated loss of the decision under such a system and asked: "Why is this solemn mockery of our rights?"[1] The choice-by-lot system of selecting the odd member was a weak point in an immature method and was subject to criticism in later times. Some of the enemies of the treaty, however, conceded the value of the arbitration clauses. Albert Gallatin, who because of his political affiliations was not a supporter of the treaty, declared that "when a weak nation had to contend with a powerful one, it was gaining a great deal if the national honor was saved even by the shadow of an indemnification, and by an apparent concession on the part of the aggressor."[2] Although during the debate comparatively little attention was paid to the arbitration clauses, the treaty has, in later years, received much commendation for the wise provision for the adjustment of disputes and has been regarded as the inauguration of modern arbitration.

As we might expect where little precedent for international adjudication existed, these first arbitrations were not automatically or easily carried out. An award was made in 1798 with regard to the principal question in the Northeastern boundary dispute, the identity of the St. Croix River; but the decision was not brought into effect. After various attempts at an agreement, the boundary question was finally settled in 1847.[3] In the matter of the British debts, the attempt at arbitration failed due to the withdrawal of the American members of the commission. The question was later disposed of in the Treaty of 1802 which provided for the payment by the United States of £600,000.[4] The commercial losses of

[1] *Annals of Congress*, IV: 1011 (Apr. 16, 1796).

[2] *Ibid.*, p. 1187.

[3] *Arbitration and the United States*, p. 482. For the agreements and the award of 1798, see MOORE, JOHN BASSETT, *International Adjudications*, Modern Series, Vols. I and II, Oxford University Press, New York, 1929, 1930.

[4] The arbitration is set forth in MOORE, *International Adjudication*, Modern Series, Vol. III.

British and Americans in the existing war, due to violations of international obligations by the two governments, were finally adjudicated by a mixed commission in 1804. Under the decisions, Americans recovered sums amounting to $11,650,000 while British subjects were awarded $143,428.14.[1]

The arbitration record of the United States since the time of the Jay Treaty is a long one and cannot be set forth in detail. One of the most important of the controversies submitted to arbitration is herewith discussed, however, for purposes of illustration.

The Alabama Claims. During the Civil War a number of cruisers were built for the Confederacy by English firms. The armaments for these ships were also purchased in England but were not installed in that country. They were exported and placed upon the ships at foreign ports. This method was adopted as a legalistic device to prevent the accusation that fully armed ships had been fitted out for a belligerent within a neutral country. The *Alabama*, built in Liverpool by a British firm under contract with a Confederate agent, was the most noted of the British-built cruisers. The British government was amply warned of the character of the ship by Charles Francis Adams, the American minister. The *Alabama* put out to sea partly equipped, received the rest of its arms and supplies as well as its crew in the Azores, and proceeded to prey upon the shipping of the United States. This cruiser destroyed fifty-seven prizes and released others under ransom bond.[2] Opinion in the United States ran high against Great Britain for failure to prevent the construction of these commerce destroyers in her ports, and damages were demanded. The British government at first resisted the American claims, stating that they were not based upon any principle of international law. It was admitted that the law imposed upon the neutral the obligation of preventing armed expeditions from setting forth from its ports. But the British contended that there was nothing to prevent the sailing of an unarmed ship and the export of its equipment on a different vessel. The United States proposed arbitration as early as 1863, but the offer was refused. Other issues, such as those arising from the recognition of the belligerency of the Confederacy by Great Britain, from the Fenian movement in the United States, from the aid which the Confederates had received from persons in Canada, and from the abrogation of the Canadian Reciprocity and Fisheries Convention, added fuel to the growing antagonism between the two English-

---

[1] *Ibid.*, IV: 160–161.

[2] LATANÉ, *American Foreign Policy*, p. 429.

speaking countries. Charles Sumner, chairman of the Senate Committee on Foreign Relations, eloquent but somewhat irresponsible, urged extreme claims against Great Britain in a pseudo-patriotic manner. Calmer counsels prevailed, however; and after the removal of Sumner from the chairmanship of the Committee on Foreign Relations, the Treaty of Washington was signed on May 8, 1871, and approved by the Senate on May 24. It dealt with a large number of subjects, the first eleven articles being devoted to the arbitration of claims arising from the losses suffered from the British-built cruisers. Under this treaty an arbitration commission met in Geneva from December, 1871, until June, 1872. The tribunal was composed of five persons, one member being appointed by each of the following: the President of the United States, the Queen of Great Britain, the King of Italy, the President of Switzerland, and the Emperor of Brazil.[1] This method of composing the tribunal was an improvement over that used in Article VII of the Jay Treaty, above described, for it eliminated the selection of the umpire by lot, a principle which had been ridiculed in the United States.

The treaty set forth certain principles to govern the award, the main one being that it is the duty of a neutral state to use due diligence to prevent the fitting out within its jurisdiction of any vessel intended to carry on war with a country with which the neutral is at peace. The British government agreed to this principle while at the same time stating that it could not assent to it as a statement of the existing law. The American agent presented huge claims for indirect damages, such, for example, as those due to the rise in insurance rates during the operations of the cruisers. These had been strongly demanded by Sumner. They were overruled by the commission. Direct damages amounting to $15,500,-000 were, however, awarded to the United States.[2] The settlement of the Alabama claims has been regarded as one of the greatest achievements in the record of arbitration. In Geneva, Switzerland, the enthusiastic guide in pointing out the features of the Alabama Room in the old *Hotel de Ville* may remark, at least to American tourists, that it is the most famous room in the city.

It is impossible in short space to go further into detail with regard to the numerous arbitrations of the United States. The

---

[1] Article I of the treaty, *Treaties, etc., of the U.S.*, I: 701.

[2] MOORE, JOHN BASSETT, *History and Digest of the International Arbitrations to Which the United States Has Been a Party*, I: 658, Govt. Printing Office, Washington, 1898.

great wealth of documentary material upon the subject down to 1896 has been assembled in Moore's *International Arbitrations*, a set of six volumes, and in *International Adjudications, Modern Series,* compiled likewise by Professor Moore.[1] Garner stated a few years ago that the United States had been a party to some eighty-five arbitrations with twenty-five different countries.[2]

CASES IN WHICH THE UNITED STATES HAS REFUSED ARBITRATION

The excellent record made in submitting important matters to arbitration must not be taken as representing the entire and consistent attitude of the United States.   Particularly in the Caribbean region, where this country has dealt with weaker governments and where American interests have been regarded as of vital importance, the United States has been at times unwilling to consider arbitration as a method of settling disputes.   In a few of these cases the United States has even used military force as a preferred method of securing national aims.   The American government refused to arbitrate the questions with Spain growing out of the destruction of the *Maine*, the issues with Colombia arising from the Panama affair of 1903, and the dispute with the Huerta government in Mexico following the Tampico incident of 1914.   Arbitration was not considered as a satisfactory method of settling the differences with Costa Rica, Honduras, and Salvador which grew out of the Bryan-Chamorro Treaty of 1914 between the United States and Nicaragua, although the suggestion of arbitration was made by the American Peace Society.[3] In 1914 the Haitian government, during a dispute with the United States over the National Bank of the Republic of Haiti, pointed out that the charter of the corporation provided that such disputes should be settled by arbitration between the Haitian government and the bank.[4] No attention appears to have been paid to this clause by the United States.   In 1916, when the United States occupied Santo Domingo alleging rights under the Treaty of 1907, the Dominican government complained that the dispute over the treaty should have been decided by legal suit and not by military force.[5]

In an affair in Panama in 1915 the rejection of arbitration was accompanied by an attitude of extreme righteousness.   During that

---

[1] Of this later series, six volumes have thus far been published.

[2] *American Foreign Policies*, p. 144.

[3] GARNER, *op. cit.*, p. 150.

[4] *Foreign Relations*, 1915, p. 502.

[5] *Ibid.*, 1916, p. 244.

year an incident in Colón between the local police and American soldiers, who were attending a ball game in the city, resulted in the killing of an American soldier. The United States thereupon demanded that the rifles of the police should be taken away and declared that refusal to give them up might result in intervention by this country to maintain order in the cities of Colón and Panama under Article VII of the Treaty of 1903. When the Panama government suggested submitting the matter to the arbitration of the A.B.C. powers, the American minister replied that the world would regard that the United States had been more than fair in its dealings with Panama. The question of submission of the matter to arbitration was, however, unworthy of serious consideration because the rights of the United States were clearly and definitely granted in a treaty of recent date for which full consideration had been paid.[1] In other words, the United States was so clearly in the right that it could not consider submitting the matter to the judgment of others.[2]

Three factors appear to have prompted the attitude of the United States in these Caribbean cases: a doubt as to whether arbitration would uphold the justice of the American contention, particularly if Latin-American jurists should be on the tribunal; anxiety regarding the possibility of threats arising in the Caribbean to American defense; and a lack of conviction concerning the material value of establishing the principle of arbitration. The value of arbitration was easily recognized when it prevented disastrous conflicts with Great Britain, but there seemed to be no similar material advantage to be derived from the arbitration principle in relationships with weaker countries. The situation has, however, changed considerably in these regards since the World War. There no longer seems to be any probability of European entrenchment in the Caribbean area and, therefore, American anxiety has been somewhat relaxed. The United States has come to regard the system of world peace in general and the creation of Latin-American good will in particular as a material interest of the highest consequence. A resulting trend toward arbitration has been evinced by the ratification of the Inter-American Arbitration Treaty of 1929 which incorporates the principle of compulsory arbitration of justiciable disputes.[3]

[1] *Ibid.*, 1915, p. 1236.

[2] In 1912, also, the United States had advised the elimination from a private contract with the government of Panama of a clause calling for the renunciation by the American contractor of diplomatic protection and the submission to arbitration of disputes regarding the contract. *Foreign Relations*, 1912, pp. 1202–1203.

[3] See p. 102.

GENERAL TREATIES

A first stage in the historical development of arbitration was that in which *ad hoc* agreements were made to submit specific disputes to arbitration. A later development has been the making of general treaties to submit all disputes of a certain character which may thereafter arise. When a case occurs under the general treaty, however, a special agreement or *compromis* is necessary in order to fix the particular terms of submission to arbitration. General treaties have come into existence largely since 1850.[1] Two different questions have arisen with regard to agreements of this character: (1) what disputes are to be excluded from the terms of the treaty and (2) what will be the power of the Senate in passing upon the *compromis* in each dispute as it comes up? In other words, shall each separate dispute require senatorial concurrence in a special treaty or shall an executive agreement be sufficient?

A popular movement for peaceful settlement began on a small scale immediately after the War of 1812. Many petitions for arbitration were presented to Congress and many resolutions in favor of such a policy were passed by private societies in the decades preceding the Civil War. The movement was revived in the late 1880's, and further pressure was brought upon Congress. In 1890 Congress passed a resolution introduced by Senator Sherman calling upon the President to undertake negotiations with other governments for the purpose of effecting arbitration agreements.

The British Negotiations of 1895–1897. Negotiations began with Great Britain in 1895, and in 1897 a treaty was signed. When the document came before the Senate, however, that body, which has been the graveyard of many arbitration treaties, cut the agreement to pieces with drastic amendments. By these changes questions were withdrawn from arbitration which affected the honor, territorial integrity, and the foreign or domestic policy of the United States. Questions as to the present effectiveness of any treaty which was once in force and claims against any state of the United States (meaning the defaulted state debts) were not to be submitted. Each agreement to submit a particular matter to arbitration was to be negotiated as a separate treaty, and thus the two-thirds approval of the Senate was to be required in each case. Even with these amendments it was impossible to secure the necessary two-thirds vote of the Senate and the treaty failed. From that

[1] HUDSON, MANLEY O., *The Permanent Court of International Justice*, p. 3, The Macmillan Company, New York, 1934.

date to this the Senate has in one or more cases blocked the plans of each administration for agreements to promote the pacific settlement of disputes. McKinley, Theodore Roosevelt, Taft, Wilson, Harding, Coolidge, Hoover, and Franklin D. Roosevelt have all found their policies for the settlement of disputes hampered in some respect by the Senate.

The British Treaty of 1904. In 1904 a limited arbitration treaty was signed with Great Britain. When it came before the Senate in 1905, that body amended it to require a new treaty on each submission. This requirement was unsatisfactory to President Roosevelt who described it as a step backward. Previously it had been possible to submit matters to arbitration by an executive agreement. The result of the Senate's amendment would have been to make arbitration more difficult than it had been before. The treaty was dropped.

The Root Treaties. In 1908 and 1909 the general arbitrations commonly referred to as the Root treaties were successfully negotiated. Differences of a legal nature or questions relating to the interpretation of treaties between the parties which could not be settled by diplomacy were to be referred to the Permanent Court of Arbitration at The Hague. The demands of the Senate, however, were to some extent met. Disputes affecting "the vital interests, the independence, or the honor of two contracting states" and those which concerned the interests of third parties were excepted from arbitration. A special treaty necessitating a two-thirds vote of the Senate was made a requirement of each arbitration. These treaties have since been superseded by the Kellogg arbitration treaties which will be described later.

President Taft's Efforts in 1910. In 1910 President Taft made an effort to obtain a more satisfactory arbitration arrangement by negotiating treaties with Great Britain and France which were to apply to "justiciable" disputes arising under a claim of right by one party, and no exceptions were made in case of national honor. If there should be a dispute as to whether a certain case came within the treaty, the matter was to be decided by a joint high commission of inquiry. The Senate made particular objection to this latter provision. The right of the Senate to concur in each *ad hoc* agreement had been set forth in the treaty, but by placing in the hands of a joint commission the question of the obligation to submit a particular dispute the hands of the Senate were somewhat tied in advance. There are many questions which should not be submitted to arbitration, said the Senate Committee on Foreign Relations in a report presented by Henry Cabot Lodge. The Senate struck out the clause for reference of the question of justiciability and added an amendment enumerating a number of cases to which the treaty would not apply. These exceptions included immigration, the admission of aliens to schools, territorial integrity of the United States, state debts, and questions connected with the Monroe Doctrine. President Taft then allowed the mangled treaties to die without resubmitting them to the other parties. Referring later to the action of the Senate upon the treaties, he said: "That august body truncated them and amended them and qualified them in such a way that their own father could not recognize them."[1]

The Bryan Treaties. In 1913–1914 William Jennings Bryan successfully negotiated some thirty peace treaties of a different character. Under the treaties all disputes between the parties which cannot be adjusted by diplomacy or by other existing agreements shall be referred for investigation and report to a permanent international commission. Thus the scope of the treaty, dropping as it does all exceptions on grounds of national honor, is much broader than was that of the Root arbitration treaties.[2] The function of the commission, however, is not arbitration but inquiry and report. The report of such a commission in any case will doubtless contain suggestions for the solution of the controversy; and the treaties, therefore, are commonly referred to as conciliation treaties. The treaties provide that the report of the commission is to be made within one year from the date on which it shall declare its investigation to have begun, unless the parties limit or extend the time by mutual consent. The parties agree not to declare war or to begin hostilities before the report is submitted. A waiting period is thus provided during which it is expected that the disputing countries will "cool off." The commission is in each case composed of five members chosen as follows: one by each government from among its own nationals, one by each government from the nationals of third countries, and one chosen by common agreement between the two governments, it being understood that the fifth member is not to be a citizen of either country. It is intended that the commissions shall be permanent in character. The treaty does not require that a new treaty shall be made in each case of dispute and the two-thirds vote of the Senate is thus avoided. Germany

---

[1] *Arbitration and the United States*, World Peace Foundation, p. 534.

[2] For a discussion of the origin of the treaties see CURTI, MERLE EUGENE, *Bryan and World Peace*, pp. 143*ff*., Smith College Studies in History, Vol. XVI, Nos. 3 and 4, Northampton, Mass., 1931.

was one of the governments with which a treaty could not be completed. Colonel House quotes the Kaiser as saying with regard to it:

> Germany will never sign such a treaty. Our strength lies in being always prepared for war at a second's notice. We will not resign that advantage and give our enemies time to prepare.[1]

What effect this attitude had upon the subsequent history of Germany and the entry of America into the war must always be a matter of speculation. Beginning in 1928 the Department of State renewed its efforts in negotiation of treaties on the Bryan plan. In the new treaties when a dispute arises the permanent commission may spontaneously offer its services of investigation and report and may request the cooperation of the two governments concerned in conducting the inquiry.

The Kellogg Arbitration Treaties. The Root arbitration treaties of 1908–1909 were not considered by the Executive as satisfactory. The exceptions of cases affecting the vital interests, independence, and honor of the parties were regarded as impairing the value of the treaties; and in 1928 and 1929 the Department of State began to negotiate new agreements which would eliminate these phrases. The first of the new treaties was negotiated with France during the time that the Pact of Paris was under consideration and was signed on February 6, 1928. This type of treaty deals with arbitration in the case of justiciable disputes not otherwise adjusted. The arbitrations shall in each case require a special agreement with Senate concurrence and shall be submitted to the Permanent Court of Arbitration at The Hague or to some other competent tribunal. The exceptions to arbitration are made specific. Arbitration need not be used when the subject matter of the dispute:

(*a*) is within the domestic jurisdiction of either party,
(*b*) involves the interests of third parties,
(*c*) involves the Monroe Doctrine, or
(*d*) involves the obligations of France under the Covenant of the League of Nations.[2]

Thus the sweeping exceptions of the Root treaties were reduced to four specific categories.

---

[1] SEYMOUR, CHARLES, *Intimate Papers of Colonel House*, I: 256, note 1, quoted in *Arbitration and the United States*, p. 546.

[2] *U.S. Treaty Series*, No. 785. This type of treaty has been concluded with twenty-eight governments.

Article II of the Pact of Paris. The subject of treaties for the pacific settlement of international disputes cannot be dismissed without reference again to the Pact of Paris which in Article II provides that the settlement of international disputes shall never be sought except by pacific means. Accordingly with the Kellogg arbitration treaties, the Bryan treaties, and the Pact of Paris, the United States has entered into a comprehensive set of agreements not to use war as an instrument of national policy, not to settle disputes except by pacific means, and specifically that justiciable disputes, with certain exceptions, shall be referred to arbitration, and that others which cannot be settled by diplomacy shall be referred to a permanent commission for investigation and report.[1]

INTERNATIONAL TRIBUNALS

The Permanent Court of Arbitration (The Hague Court). At the first Hague Conference in 1899 a convention was signed creating the Permanent Court of International Justice. This "court" continued until the World War to be the principal institution for the settlement of international disputes. Its chief features are as follows:

The Panel. Each signatory power is entitled to select four persons of known competency in the field of international law whose names are submitted to the Bureau of the Court at The Hague. All of these persons, totaling 152 in 1933,[2] constitute a panel from which members of tribunals of arbitration can be selected when the occasion arises.

The Tribunal. When a controversy arises and the parties desire to have recourse to the court for its settlement, they sign a *compromis* arranging the details of settlement including the size of the tribunal and the method of drawing the judges from the court panel. The United States has been a party in five cases in which members of the panel were selected for the arbitration.[3]

---

[1] For a description of the treaties for pacific settlement which refer only to inter-American disputes see pp. 101–106.

[2] Hudson, *Permanent Court of International Justice*, p. 7, note 22. If all the contracting parties availed themselves of the right to name four members and there were no duplications, the number of the judges on the panel would be 180.

[3] The cases are: The Pious Fund Case with Mexico, 1902; The North Atlantic Fisheries Case with Great Britain, 1910; the Orinoco Steamship Company Case with Venezuela, 1910; the Island of Palmas Case with the Netherlands, 1928; and the *Kronprinz Gustav Adolph* Case with Sweden in 1932. Another case, that with Norway over the seizure of ships, was arranged through

The chief mechanical defects of the Permanent Court of Arbitration are: (1) The tribunal is made up after the dispute has arisen and it is not unlikely that in each case some of the arbitrators will be chosen with regard to their views on the principles in dispute. (2) The number of partisans on each tribunal will be relatively high as compared with the neutrals. If three are chosen, two will be selected by the parties in dispute and may be nationals of those parties. A tribunal which is two-thirds partisan cannot be judicial in temperament. (3) The tribunal is not permanent and is dissolved after the dispute is settled. The members will probably never meet again upon a similar tribunal. Such a temporary set of arbitrators can accumulate no prestige; their members can gain no great practice in arbitration; and, finally, the precedents handed down will naturally not be binding upon other such tribunals in the degree that a permanent tribunal will be obligated to follow its own decisions.

The Permanent Court of International Justice (The World Court). No sooner had the Permanent Court of Arbitration been established than its deficiencies became apparent and the movement to create a more perfect organ in the form of a permanent tribunal was renewed. A campaign among private societies in the United States for a world court had been started in the early nineteenth century and had been called "the American plan" in international peace circles.[1] The American delegates to the First Hague Conference had been instructed to introduce a plan for a permanent court. This was done, but opposition on the part of such countries as Germany and Austria made its adoption impossible. A compromise plan along lines suggested by Great Britain was agreed to and became the Permanent Court of Arbitration above described. When the American delegates went to the Second Hague Conference in 1907, they carried instructions from Secretary of State Root which emphasized the weakness of arbitration under such a system as that which had been established. "It should be your effort,"

---

the secretary-general of the court but the arbitrators were chosen outside the panel. Descriptions of cases of the court are found in *The Hague Court Reports*, James Brown Scott, Editor, Oxford University Press, New York, 1916, and a second series of the same published in 1932. See also HUDSON, *Permanent Court of International Justice*, pp. 12ff.

[1] See CURTI, MERLE EUGENE, *The American Peace Crusade, 1815–1860*, p. 55, Duke University Press, Durham, N. C., 1929; PHELPS, CHRISTINA, *The Anglo-American Peace Movement in the Mid-nineteenth Century*, pp. 103–107, Columbia University Press, New York, 1930.

the instructions read, "to bring about in the Second Conference a development of the Hague Tribunal into a permanent tribunal composed of judges who are judicial officers and nothing else, who are paid adequate salaries, who have no other occupation, and who will devote their entire time to the trial and decision of international causes by judicial methods and under a sense of judicial responsibility."[1]   At the conference a plan for a Permanent Court of Arbitral Justice was adopted.   The plan left the actual inauguration of the court in abeyance until a method for the election of judges could be worked out.   The difficulty regarding election was that no acceptable compromise could be found as between the large and the small states.   The small states insisted upon equality, but a court with one representative from each state would have been too large. The great powers desired to have one judge each, but a system which would insure that result and scatter the remaining judgeships among the small powers was difficult to invent.   Before the World War no satisfactory system could be agreed to.

The next great step in the development of a world court came with the creation of the League of Nations.   Article XIV made it incumbent upon the Council to formulate and submit to the members of the League plans for the establishment of a Permanent Court of International Justice.   This article did not come from the American drafts but was suggested in the proposals of several other countries.   President Wilson, while in complete accord with the idea, did not regard it as appropriate to insert matters of such detail in his plan.   The American delegation did, however, support the clause at Paris, and Article XIV has become the foundation for one of the League's greatest achievements.

Early in 1920 the Council of the League created an advisory committee to draft plans for the court.   Elihu Root, former Secretary of State of the United States, was a member of the committee. Root's greatest contribution to the framing of the court statute was his suggestion for the selection of judges.   He proposed nomination by the national groups in the Permanent Court of Arbitration, *i.e.*, by the judges named by each member state upon the panel of that court,[2] and election by the Council and Assembly of the League sitting separately.   This system gives the small powers an equal voice in one body but gives the great powers a voice out of proportion to their numbers in the other.   As it works out in practice a

[1] *Foreign Relations*, 1907, Part 2, p. 1135.
[2] The method of nomination was suggested simultaneously by M. Loder of the Netherlands.   HUDSON, *Permanent Court of International Justice*, p. 131.

national of each of the great powers sits upon the court and the other places are distributed among the nationals of the smaller powers.

On the Permanent Court of International Justice are fifteen judges elected for nine years. Four deputy judgships originally provided for have been abolished by an amendment. Judges are nominated by the national groups of the Permanent Court of Arbitration. They are elected by the Assembly and Council of the League sitting separately. Any nominee receiving a majority in both bodies is declared elected. If two candidates of the same nationality should receive a majority, the older would be declared elected. In case all seats are not filled in the first election, a second, and, if necessary, a third, election takes place. If there are still vacancies, a conference committee is provided for; and, if this fails, the members of the court already elected will choose judges for the unfilled positions. An American was continuously upon the court until 1935. The first American judge was John Bassett Moore, famous compiler of the *Digest of International Law, International Arbitrations of the United States,* and later of *International Adjudications.* The place of Judge Moore was taken in 1928 by Charles Evans Hughes, who had already served as associate justice of the United States Supreme Court. In 1930 the place of Judge Hughes was taken by Frank B. Kellogg, who had served as United States Senator, Ambassador to Great Britain, and Secretary of State. He had negotiated the Pact of Paris with France and the Kellogg treaties of arbitration and inquiry. Mr. Kellogg resigned in 1935, but his place has not as yet been filled.

The jurisdiction of the court comprises all cases which the parties refer to it and all matters specifically provided for in treaties and conventions.[1] Numerous treaties since the creation of the court have included clauses requiring that if any dispute shall arise over the meaning of the treaty it shall be referred to the court. Certain kinds of cases are specified in the Covenant of the League as generally suitable for submission to arbitration or judicial settlement. These cases include disputes as to:

1. The interpretation of a treaty.
2. Any question of international law.

[1] Article XXXVI of the Statute of the Permanent Court of International Justice. For a detailed consideration of jurisdiction see DE BUSTAMANTE, ANTONIO SANCHEZ, *The World Court,* Chapter XI, The Macmillan Company, New York, 1925.

3. The existence of any fact which, if established, would constitute a breach of any international obligation.

4. The nature or extent of the reparation to be made for any such breach.

A clause is included in the World Court statute (Article 36) which makes it possible for any member of the court to declare that it recognizes the jurisdiction of the court to be compulsory, *ipso facto* and without special agreement, in any of the four cases above mentioned if it should arise with any member of the court which accepts the same obligation. This is called the optional clause and is accepted by forty-one of the forty-nine members of the court.[1]

In addition to rendering judgments in cases between parties, the World Court is also authorized to give advisory opinions upon disputes or questions referred to it by the Council or the Assembly. Thus the tribunal is endowed with a function which most American courts do not exercise, for the Supreme Court of the United States and the majority of state courts refuse to give such opinions. Some American state courts, however, and many foreign courts render advisory opinions. The giving of advisory opinions by such a respected tribunal as the World Court has proved useful in stopping international controversies before they arrive at the stage of formal litigation.

THE AMERICAN POLICY REGARDING THE WORLD COURT

On February 24, 1923, President Harding sent the protocol of signature of the World Court statute to the United States Senate, asking that that body consent to ratification of the instrument.[2] On January 27, 1926, the Senate advised adherence to the court with five reservations, which may be summarized as follows:

1. Such adherence should not be taken to involve any legal relation on the part of the United States to the League of Nations.

2. American representatives should sit in the Council and the Assembly for the purpose of the election of judges.

3. The United States should pay a fair share of the expenses of the court as determined by Congress.

4. The United States should be able to withdraw from the court at any time and the statute of the court should not be amended without the consent of the United States.

5. Advisory opinions should be rendered publicly and after public hearing; and the court should not, without the consent of the United States, entertain

---

[1] HUDSON, *Permanent Court of International Justice*, p. 629.

[2] The attitudes of the administration and the Senate are set forth in JONES, ROBERT L., *History of the Foreign Policy of the United States*, Chapter XXV, G. P. Putnam's Sons, New York, 1933.

any request for an advisory opinion touching any dispute or question in which the United States has or claims an interest.

The other members of the court were willing to accept these qualifications with the exception of the last half of the fifth reservation which would give the United States a veto on advisory opinions touching questions in which the United States has or claims an interest. In the Eastern Carelia case the World Court had decided that it would not render an opinion when such action was opposed by a party in the case. There remained, however, the possible veto of the United States in a case in which it was not a party but in which it claimed an interest. It is possible that such a reservation, if accepted, would give the United States a greater power in blocking advisory opinions than that possessed by any member of the Council. Inasmuch as the vote in requesting advisory opinions has in each case been unanimous, it is still uncertain whether a mere majority of the Council will suffice for this purpose. If a unanimous vote is found necessary, any member of the Council will possess an absolute veto upon Council requests. In such a case the reservation of the Senate would not prove to be unreasonable. If it should be found that a majority of the Council is sufficient, no one member would be able to prevent the request. The demands of the United States for an absolute veto would then be regarded as seeking a position of special power possessed by no member of the Council.

In 1929 a committee of jurists was assembled in Geneva to consider the revision of the World Court statute. Elihu Root, a member of the committee, presented a plan which was designed to avoid the objections of the United States Senate and at the same time to satisfy the members of the court. The Root proposal was approved by the committee after some additions by the British jurist, Sir Cecil Hurst. The Hurst-Root plan was then incorporated in the form of a protocol to be adopted by the members of the court and by the United States. Most of the members of the court approved the protocol and it was signed by the United States on December 9, 1929.[1]

With regard to advisory opinions the Hurst-Root plan provided that when a proposal should come before the Council or Assembly of the League to request such an opinion of the World Court, the Secretary-General would inform the United States; and, if desired,

[1] For the evolution of the Root plan see HUDSON, *Permanent Court of International Justice*, pp. 217*ff.*; JESSUP, PHILIP C., "The United States and the Permanent Court of International Justice," *International Conciliation*, No. 273 (October, 1931).

an exchange of views as to whether an interest of the United States is affected would take place between the Council or Assembly and the United States. In order to give a double opportunity for the United States to enter objections, it was further provided that when a request for an advisory opinion should come to the court, the registrar would notify the United States. If no opportunity for an exchange of views had previously been given and if the United States advised the court that the question affected the interests of the United States, proceedings would be stayed to permit of an exchange of views between the United States and the Council or Assembly. An objection of the United States would have as much weight in blocking the opinion as a negative vote of a member of the Council or Assembly. In other words, if it should be decided that a unanimous vote of these bodies in requesting an opinion was necessary, the United States objection would stop proceedings, just as the vote of any one member of the Council or Assembly would stop them. If, however, it were decided that only a majority of these bodies should be necessary, the objections of the United States would not be a bar.[1] If after an exchange of views it became apparent that no agreement could be reached, and the United States was not prepared to forgo its objection, then the United States could withdraw from the court without any imputation of unfriendliness or unwillingness to cooperate generally for peace and good will.

The 1935 Defeat of the Court. In January, 1935, the Hurst-Root plan was placed before the Senate subject to a reservation proposed in the Committee on Foreign Relations which provided that "the Permanent Court of International Justice shall not, over an objection by the United States, entertain any request for an advisory opinion touching any dispute or question in which the United States has or claims an interest." The reservation, as can be seen, was somewhat weaker than the fifth reservation previously proposed. In this form the protocol received 52 affirmative votes to 36 negative votes, thus failing to receive the requisite majority of two-thirds. Since this defeat the subject of membership in the court has not been reopened.

Summary of Treaties to Which the United States Is a Party. In addition to being a party to the Hague Conventions of 1899 and

---

[1] For a discussion of the question of the vote necessary in the Assembly or Council, see HUDSON, *Permanent Court of International Justice*, p. 437; RICHES, CROMWELL A., *The Unanimity Rule and the League of Nations*, pp. 69*ff.*, Johns Hopkins Press, Baltimore, 1933.

1907, the Pact of Paris, and all the principal Pan-American peace treaties, the United States is a party to the following bilateral treaties for the settlement of disputes:[1]

Arbitration Treaties.
Root treaties (1908 and 1909) with six countries as follows:
Brazil, Ecuador, Haiti, Liberia, Peru, and Uruguay.
Kellogg treaties (1928 and after) with twenty-eight countries as follows:
Albania, Austria, Belgium, Bulgaria, China, Czechoslovakia, Denmark, Egypt, Estonia, Ethiopia, Finland, France, Germany, Greece, Hungary, Iceland, Italy, Latvia, Lithuania, Luxemburg, Netherlands, Norway, Poland, Portugal, Rumania, Sweden, Switzerland,[2] and Yugoslavia.
Inquiry and Conciliation.
Bryan treaties (1913 and 1914) with nineteen countries as follows:
Bolivia, Brazil, Chile, China, Denmark and Iceland, Ecuador, France, Great Britain, Italy, Netherlands, Norway, Paraguay, Peru, Portugal, Russia, Spain, Sweden, Uruguay, and Venezuela.
Treaties on Bryan plan, slightly amended (1928 and after) with seventeen countries as follows:
Albania, Austria, Belgium, Bulgaria, Czechoslovakia, Estonia, Ethiopia, Finland, Germany, Greece, Hungary, Latvia, Lithuania, Luxemburg, Poland, Rumania, and Yugoslavia.

The chief treaties of a world-wide scope for the peaceful settlement of international disputes to which the United States is not a party are the Covenant of the League of Nations and the Protocol of the World Court.

[1] As of Dec. 31, 1934.
[2] The Swiss treaty provides for both arbitration and conciliation.

CHAPTER XVI

THE RENUNCIATION OF WAR

WAR IN THE MODERN WORLD

The Seriousness of the Problem of Maintaining Peace. The avoidance of war has during the last few decades become the world's outstanding diplomatic problem. In the rise of industrial civilization much of man's creative genius has been turned to perfecting the means of mass slaughter. Dreadnaughts, submarines, quick-firing artillery, time shrapnel, machine guns, armored tanks, military chemistry, and aerial warfare have all been developed within the last few decades. The implements of social unification—rapid communication and transportation—which enable a vast population to give an instantaneous response to orders of mobilization, bring the whole momentum of man power, woman power, industry, and finance into modern warfare with horrifying impact. Whatever may be said of the growth of methods of national defense to offset the weapons of offense, there has been one factor which has been left unprotected, *i.e.*, human life. The casualty curve has swung upward with alarming rapidity in the wars of nationalism. The 10,000,000 wooden crosses of the last war testify forcefully that there is no defense for the individual in industrialized combat. The economic dislocations of war are also catastrophic in their consequences. They seem unimportant as compared with the direct loss of life, but their agonizing aftermaths prolong distress among the masses for years after the echo of the last salvo has died away. Every reconstruction period is a Tragic Era.

Paradoxically enough, war, which is so destructive to society as a whole, is economically beneficial to a considerable number of individuals. When processes of distribution under the profit motive bog down, war brings the power of the state to stimulate artificially and to readjust temporarily the dispersion of the national income. A reserve officer who may be unemployed and destitute knows that upon the declaration of war he will be immediately placed in a well-remunerated position of honor. To the impoverished victim of the depression, dragging out a miserable existence upon the dole, the assurance of high wages in a munitions factory or a shipyard comes like manna from heaven; and for him even compulsory service in the military forces holds no terrors. The state calls private corporations to its assistance in promoting vast military preparations at great expense, and thus it aids the stockholders of the present at the expense of the taxpayers of the future. What matters it if the youth of the country, the product of modern culture and education, are to be mowed down like wheat? Such disasters are contingent and uncertain as to particular individuals, while dividends in the hand are realistic and satisfying to the despairing holders of depressed stocks. These war-profit phenomena are, from the social standpoint, temporary and special illusions; but they help to beguile the public mind into an acceptance of war.[1]

Conflicting Views as to the Inevitability of War. Two gloomy dogmas have been persistently reiterated since the World War: (1) war is inevitable, and (2) the next great war will destroy civilization. If both of these are true, it is obvious that the present industrialism will speedily destroy itself. Archaeologists, then, in future eras will study the evidences of the great age of mechanics, electricity, chemistry, and radioactivity which received its death blow some time during the twentieth century. Data will be uncovered to show the character of the power apparatus which so greatly amplified man's energies, and perhaps testimony will be found of the unparalleled human misery which accompanied the great debacle of this ill-fated system.

There are various factions which accept each of the above-mentioned dogmas. Many radicals believe thoroughly in the unavoidability of war under the capitalist system but deny that it will mean the end of civilization. The inevitability of war between nations which operate under the profit system, according to the followers of Marx and Lenin, arises from the clashes of expanding imperialisms. Under capitalism, in its well-developed stages, capital is exported into the backward regions until the weaker peoples come under the domination of the industrial powers. For a time spheres of influence are mapped out and an equilibrium is maintained by agreement between governments. But a time comes when a rapidly rising power finds that the backward regions are already controlled by others. Only through force can the economic energies of the industrialized newcomer find an outlet, and war is the inevitable result.

[1] "Wars and revolutions are avenues of discharge for collective insecurities," LASWELL, HAROLD D., *World Politics and Personal Insecurity*, p. 25, Whittlesey House, McGraw-Hill Book Company, Inc., New York, 1935.

A great many peace workers feel that Western civilization cannot survive another world war, but they do not accept the inevitability of such a conflict. They place much emphasis upon the increased strength of certain economic forces making for peace. The most successful producers and financiers have risen to places of power with the expansion of world trade and finance. These business leaders realize that old-fashioned nationalism is in many respects exactly contrary to their own interests. Persons who hold these views have supported the peace machinery of the League of Nations and have relied upon the ultimate effectiveness of such agreements as the Pact of Paris. They deny that war is an economic institution since it is so uneconomic and wasteful in character. The cost of the World War to the United States is roughly estimated at considerably more than $100,000,000 for each day of our participation in that conflict. The peace policies of this country have been prompted by some such reasoning as that just described. As the most successful capitalistic nation in the world, with more to lose by war than any other country and with a relatively pacific situation in the Western Hemisphere, the United States has developed a widespread and highly organized movement for peace which extends through millions of members of churches and peace societies to the Capitol itself.

The Epidemic Character of War. The United States views the possibility of war from a special position. This country has no military rival upon the American continents and cannot well visualize a war waged against an enemy in Europe or Asia on account of a direct quarrel. But dangers of wars between other powers exist in both Europe and Asia. War is contagious in character; and, should a struggle break forth on another continent, the incidents and temptations which would stir the martial spirit in the United States would be immediately multiplied. On two occasions the United States has been drawn into a general European war through causes which arose from and did not exist previous to the outbreak of the conflict in Europe. Just as it is to the interests of the resident of a crowded city to aid in keeping healthful conditions throughout the municipality lest members of his own family should be infected, so each member of the community of nations has an interest in preventing wars among others because of the danger of becoming involved. Even if all wars cannot be eliminated, if only a few hundred thousand lives and a few billions of dollars can be saved, the task is still worthy of the utmost skill of the world's foreign offices. In comparison with this work such efforts as the protection of a tourist, the collection of a debt, and the demanding of the open door for an oil company pale into insignificance as matters of national interest.

THE PACT OF PARIS

American versus French Views on Peace Methods. The greatest diplomatic enterprise launched by the United States for the maintenance of peace is the Multilateral Treaty for the Renunciation of War, more commonly referred to as the Pact of Paris. The negotiation of the treaty was for the most part a clash and a reconciliation between the negative peace policies of the United States and the positive policies of France. The plan favored in Washington for a general but unimplemented convention for the renunciation of war was eventually modified to avoid conflicting with the various military guarantees which were a part of the system for keeping the peace developed in Europe.

To most Americans war is an academic matter. No foreign militaristic establishments loom threateningly across our borders. Americans are in favor of peace as a general principle but are not willing to restrict the freedom of action of their government by giving strong guarantees against a war danger which seems remote. Characteristic of the views of a large body of American peace advocates is the plan for the outlawry of war proposed some years ago in which the sanction against warmakers was to be the power of national and international public opinion.[1] The French, on the other hand, have been reared amidst a military setting. The casualties of each generation give to war a reality in the French mind. During the World War Allied armies fought alongside of the French on French soil in defense of the institutions and territory of the Republic. International cooperation and mutual guarantees against an aggressor are to them, therefore, naturally suggested as a means of keeping the peace. At various conferences since the World War, including particularly the Paris Conference of 1919 and the League of Nations Assemblies, French representatives have advocated a strong international organization capable of using force to maintain world order.

Briand's Proposal. The treaty which was to be known as the Pact of Paris was first broached informally when on the tenth anni-

[1] See MORRISON, CHARLES CLAYTON, *The Outlawry of War*, Willett, Clark and Colby, Chicago, 1927. The plan was embodied in a resolution proposed by Senator Borah in the United States Senate, Dec. 12, 1927.

versary of the entrance of the United States into the World War, April 7, 1927, M. Briand, French foreign minister, issued a statement to the Associated Press in which he suggested an agreement for the outlawry of war between France and the United States. The creation of sentiment in the United States following the Briand proposal is a story of much interest in connection with American diplomacy. Drew Pearson and Constantine Brown, in their fascinating account of these activities, refer to Dr. James T. Shotwell of Columbia University and Salmon O. Levinson, a Chicago attorney, as "the two build-up men for the outlawry of war."[1] Mr. Levinson interviewed French officials and used the cable to stimulate interest among influential friends in the United States. Professor Shotwell worked zealously in this country. He secured the influence of Dr. Nicholas Murray Butler, president of Columbia University, who wrote a letter to *The New York Times*, published April 25, which called the attention of the country to the possibilities in the Briand proposal. The public response to the suggestion thereafter was a revelation to Washington. Senator Borah was particularly active in promoting the idea of a treaty. Professor Shotwell and a colleague, Dr. Joseph P. Chamberlain, went so far as to draw up the draft of a treaty to indicate the possible form which such an agreement might take.[2] On June 20, 1927, the French government submitted to the Department of State a proposed treaty renouncing war as an instrument of national policy.[3]

Kellogg's Suggestion That the Treaty Be Multilateral. The Department of State opposed a treaty which would include only France and the United States for the reason that such an agreement would probably be viewed with suspicion by other European powers. If the United States was pledged not to fight France but had made no such pledges to other governments, this country could enter a

[1] *The American Diplomatic Game*, p. 16, Doubleday, Doran & Company, Garden City, N. Y., 1935.

[2] *N.Y. Times*, May 31, 1927.

[3] The texts of the notes are found in Dept. of State, *Treaty for the Renunciation of War*, Govt. Printing Office, Washington, 1933. For various accounts of the negotiations see SHOTWELL, JAMES T., *War as an Instrument of National Policy and Its Renunciation in the Pact of Paris*, Harcourt, Brace & Company, New York, 1929; MILLER, DAVID HUNTER, *The Peace Pact of Paris*, A Study of the Briand-Kellogg Treaty, G. P. Putnam's Sons, New York, 1928; MYERS, DENYS P., *Origin and Conclusion of the Paris Pact*, World Peace Foundation, Boston, 1929; WATKINS, ARTHUR CHARLES, *The Paris Pact*, Harcourt, Brace & Company, New York, 1932.

European conflict in the future only on the side of France. German opinion would be particularly critical of such a bilateral agreement. Mr. Kellogg, therefore, proposed that the agreement should be made multilateral and that it should be signed by all the principal powers of the world.

French Misgivings Regarding a Multilateral Treaty. The French Foreign Office could not endorse without qualifications a general renunciation of war as between all nations, for it feared that such an agreement would nullify all the mutual guarantees for military action against an aggressor that they had so laboriously helped to build up since the World War. Should France be attacked, those nations which had agreed to come to her defense, M. Briand feared, would be prohibited from so doing by the agreement to renounce war. The various mutual guarantees to which France was a party included the Covenant of the League of Nations, the Locarno treaties, and the so-called "treaties guaranteeing neutrality," which were really defensive alliances between France and five countries, to wit: Belgium, Czechoslovakia, Poland, Rumania, and Yugoslavia. M. Briand, therefore, countered with the proposal that the multilateral treaty should renounce "all wars of aggression." This wording would still permit the parties to the mutual guarantees to come to the aid of the victim of aggression. Mr. Kellogg objected to qualifying the agreement in this way, feeling that the strength and simplicity of a sweeping renunciation of war as an instrument of national policy would be destroyed if qualifications were introduced into the text of the treaty.

Senator Borah Shows the Way of Escape. Meanwhile the way out of the difficulty had already been suggested by Senator Borah. In a letter to *The New York Times,* published February 5, 1928, he pointed out that a multilateral treaty need not be inconsistent with the French obligations against aggressor nations. An aggressor by going to war would violate the antiwar pact and would thus release all the signatories from their obligations under the treaty not to resort to military action against the warmaker. The French duty under the treaty with Belgium to assist Belgium against an aggressor nation, to take an example, would not be impaired. "If an attack, nevertheless, is made on Belgium by one of the signatories," he argued, "it would constitute a breach of the multilateral treaty and would thereby *ipso facto* release France and enable her to fulfill her military engagements with Belgium." And further: "Such a universal treaty would put an end to any question of war commitments under the League Covenant or other alliances because the occasion for their exercise could only arise in case of a flagrant breach of the treaty by one or more signatories, and as stated, the legal effects of such a breach would be to free France from alleged restraints." A multilateral treaty would, therefore, not impair the world's machinery for peace.

Following this suggestion, the French government, in a note of March 30, stated that it would be entirely willing to agree to a multilateral treaty and that it would actively attempt to induce the other great powers to sign it, providing it could be assured of the following safeguards: that a breach of the treaty by one signatory would release the other signatories from their obligations toward the offender; that the legitimate right of self-defense would not be impaired; and that previous obligations under the League of Nations Covenant, the Treaties of Locarno, and treaties guaranteeing neutrality should not be prejudiced. The United States felt that this understanding with France was acceptable and the other great powers were accordingly approached by the American government. The Franco-American correspondence, together with a draft treaty, was sent to Great Britain, Germany, Italy, and Japan.

Interpretations. During this period of negotiation with the other powers, Mr. Kellogg delivered an address before the American Society of International Law in which he gave the interpretations that the treaty did not impair the right of self-defense or the obligation of mutual guarantees in the Locarno treaties and certain other agreements. This speech covered the objections raised by France and thereafter the Kellogg interpretations became an integral part of the treaty negotiations. A further addition was made to the interpretations of the treaty by Great Britain. That government asserted, in a note of May 19, that in its pledge to renounce war as an instrument of national policy it could not tolerate any interference with "certain regions of the world the welfare and integrity of which constitute a special and vital interest" for British peace and safety. The protection of these regions against attack is to the British Empire a measure of self-defense. In renouncing war, the British government wished it to be understood that it was not abandoning its freedom of action to prevent interference with these regions. The British statement has been variously interpreted as referring to Egypt or Afghanistan.

With these understandings the treaty negotiations proceeded rapidly. Nine other governments, including the British dominions and India and three French allies, were approached and agreed to the

treaty, thus making fifteen in all who were original signatories.[1]
These fifteen signed the treaty in Paris on August 27, 1928; and, after
the ratifications had been given, the agreement came into effect on
July 24, 1929. Other countries were invited to become parties;
eventually, sixty-three nations accepted the pact.[2] The important
parts of the text of the treaty together with the Kellogg interpretations and the so-called British Monroe Doctrine, are as follows:

PRINCIPAL ARTICLES OF THE MULTILATERAL TREATY FOR THE RENUNCIATION OF WAR

I

The high contracting parties solemnly declare in the names of their
respective peoples that they condemn recourse to war for the solution of
international controversies, and renounce it as an instrument of national
policy in their relations with one another.

II

The high contracting parties agree that the settlement or solution of
all disputes or conflicts of whatever nature or of whatever origin they may
be, which may arise among them, shall never be sought except by pacific
means.[3]

SUMMARY OF THE KELLOGG INTERPRETATIONS

1. *Self-defense.* There is nothing in the American draft of an antiwar
treaty which restricts or impairs in any way the right of self-defense.

2. *The League Covenant.* There is no necessary inconsistency between
the Covenant and the renunciation of war. The Covenant imposes no
affirmative obligation to go to war.[4]

3. *The Treaties of Locarno.* The multilateral pact strengthens the
treaties of Locarno. If any party to the Locarno treaties violates them
by waging war, the other parties to the treaties would immediately be
released from their obligations under the multilateral pact and would be
free to perform their duties under the Locarno treaties.

4. *Treaties of Neutrality.* If a third state attacked the neutralized
state, the guaranteeing state would thereupon be released from its obli-

[1] Australia, Belgium, Canada, Czechoslovakia, France, Germany, Great
Britain, India, Irish Free State, Italy, Japan, New Zealand, Poland, Union of
South Africa, and the United States.

[2] Dept. of State, *Treaty Information Bulletin*, May, 1934, p. 10.

[3] *U.S. Treaty Series*, No. 796.

[4] It would have seemed wiser and more consistent with his other interpretations had Mr. Kellogg admitted that the members of the League, under Article
XVI, might find themselves in a state of war with a country which has resorted
to war in disregard of the Covenant, and that the members of the League would
thereupon be released from all pledges under the pact to the aggressor state.

gations under the multilateral pact and would be free to come to the defense of the neutralized state.

5. *Relations with a Treaty-breaking State.*   As has been pointed out, if a signatory to the multilateral pact should resort to war in violation of the pact the act would thereby automatically release the other parties from their obligations to the treaty-breaking state.

6. *Universality.*   The treaty should come into effect when adhered to by the British, French, German, Italian, Japanese, and the United States governments.   It was the hope of the United States, however, that the treaty should become world-wide in application.

THE BRITISH MONROE DOCTRINE

(Sir Austen Chamberlain, British Secretary of State for Foreign Affairs, to Ambassador Houghton, London, May 19, 1928.)

The language of Article I, as to the renunciation of war as an instrument of national policy, renders it desirable that I should remind your excellency that there are certain regions of the world the welfare and integrity of which constitute a special and vital interest for our peace and safety.   His Majesty's Government have been at pains to make it clear in the past that interference with these regions cannot be suffered.   Their protection against attack is to the British Empire a measure of self-defense.   It must be clearly understood that His Majesty's Government in Great Britain accept the new treaty upon the distinct understanding that it does not prejudice their freedom of action in this respect.

QUESTIONS OF INTERPRETATION

The Renunciation of War.   The pact binds the signatories to abstain from war as an instrument of national policy.   Traditional law placed no such obligation upon a nation.   In the past if nation A made deliberate and unprovoked war upon nation B, it did not violate any legal obligation to nations C and D.   The Pact of Paris created such an obligation as between each party and every other party throughout almost the entire community of nations.   A profound change was thereby brought about in the international legal situation regarding war.

The Obligation against Nonpacific Settlement of Disputes. Article II of the pact stipulates that the settlement of disputes as between the parties shall never be sought except by pacific means. Disputes which cannot be settled by diplomacy must, therefore, be left in abeyance or referred to the usual methods of peaceful adjustment such as judicial settlement, arbitration, mediation, conciliation, or inquiry.   The weakness of the article is that there is no obligation to settle the dispute.   Presumably a quarrel may be left to become aggravated until it arouses emotions too strong to be controlled by a mere paper agreement. The article does, however, give some moral support to the world's machinery for peaceful settlement of disputes.

The World as a Judge of Self-defense. In adding the interpretation that each nation may still go to war in self-defense, Secretary Kellogg did no more than set forth what seemed to be involved in the wording of the agreement. If a nation renounces war merely as an instrument of national policy, it reserves the right to wage wars which are not matters of national policy, *i.e.*, evidently wars waged by a nation in defense of itself or of others against aggression. The pact sets up the world as a judge of a nation's claims of self-defense. If a nation should suddenly and without provocation begin war on another under the plea of self-defense, the act would be met with universal disapproval. This would be true whether the Pact of Paris existed or not. But the pact adds a formal and legal ground for international disapproval. Thus when Japan extended her armed control throughout Manchuria under the excuse of national defense, the world refused bluntly to accept the plea. The refusal of the international community to recognize the state of Manchukuo is equivalent to a verdict of the signatories that Japan violated the Pact of Paris and shows that there are most decided limitations upon the claim of national defense.

The Monroe Doctrine. When the Senate Committee on Foreign Relations reported the Pact of Paris to the Senate, it included the understanding that "the United States regards the Monroe Doctrine as a part of its national security and defense." The committee evidently did not include any of the expansive interpretations of the doctrine and restricted it entirely to national defense. The well-known memorandum by J. Reuben Clark regarding the meaning of the doctrine was presented to the Department of State on December 17, 1928, when the Pact of Paris was still in the hands of the Senate committee. This memorandum, as has been previously pointed out,[1] rejects such expansions of the doctrine as the Roosevelt corollary. The Monroe Doctrine, therefore, under the interpretations which were being made at the time of the recommendations of the Senate committee, is simply a denial of the right of European nations to extend their territories in Latin America. It thus appears that under the committee interpretation the United States would be entitled to wage war only to prevent the seizure of territory in Latin America. With or without the Senate interpretation, this

[1] See p. 56.

would ordinarily not be a violation of the pact. If a European power went to war against a Latin-American nation, the act would in itself be a violation of the Pact of Paris and would release the United States from any obligations toward the European power. The committee's recommendations do not, on the other hand, justify the United States in waging war directly against Latin-American countries under the pretext of enforcing the peace to avoid European intervention. A more difficult question would arise if a European power should attempt to annex territory by the process of manipulation of a Latin-American government. That is, if by some method of influence it should gain control of Latin-American officials and should influence them to cede their territory to the European power, such an action would be a violation of the Monroe Doctrine but not of the Pact of Paris. In such a case, under the committee interpretation, it is possible that the United States would intervene by a preventive war. The committee interpretation would then prove to be a substantial modification of the pact. In such a case, additional machinery for inquiry and adjustment of the dispute would be necessary in order to reach a rational settlement.

The United States and the League under the Pact. Some European observers have considered that the Pact of Paris has drawn the United States into the peace enforcement system of the League of Nations. Thus a French writer on the subject under the caption "Rapprochement of the United States with the League of Nations," declared: "The Kellogg pact is the greatest step which the United States has taken towards Europe since the Peace Conference."[1] The pact, however, contains no reference to the League and makes no suggestion of any kind for enforcement through joint action. The Senate committee interpretation of the pact expressly declared that the agreement did not provide for any sort of sanction and that the pact did not change our position with regard to treaties existing between other nations. When war threatens, the United States, because of its desire to maintain peace, may nevertheless be drawn to some extent toward the League. Individual efforts to prevent war become hazardous and, in the opinion of many students of the question, the only alternative to indifference, and perhaps to giving assistance to an aggressor, is cooperation with other nations for war prevention.

---

[1] BALBAREU, CÉCILE, *Le Pacte de Paris*, p. 98, Librairie Universitaire, Paris, 1929.

CHAPTER XVII

THE PACT OF PARIS: APPLICATION AND WEAKNESS

Within a little more than two years after the proclamation of the Pact of Paris, the agreement was put to two important tests in one of the world's most turbulent storm centers, Manchuria. Chinese population interests and political rights in the land of the Manchus had for some decades been threatened by invading currents of economic and military forces pressing in from Japan and Russia. An economic vacuum in 1900, this area during the next generation was subjected to a romantic development of colonization, railroad building, and industrial evolution. The shifting of political stress due to rapidly changing conditions had placed new strains upon the system of existing legal titles. In the disequilibrium occasioned by unevenness of pressure, it was difficult to solve the resulting problems by purely judicial methods. While the first dispute, that between Russia and China with regard to the railway, was settled upon a basis of the legal *status quo*, it was generally recognized that the second dispute, that between China and Japan, could never have been solved without some modifications of the existing law. The proper function of the Pact of Paris in such a case is to prevent a military settlement and to hold the parties to a readjustment on a rational basis. The third and most recent test of the pact occurred in the Italian-Ethiopian dispute. Italy, like Japan, found the existing system of legal titles oppressive and reached out for more land. The violations of the pact by Japan and Italy have raised the presumption that the renunciation of war cannot succeed without two additional steps: implementation, or organization to restrain an aggressor, and a cooperative policy to make the world's resources more available to cramped but rapidly developing nations.

THE SINO-RUSSIAN DISPUTE

The first attempt at application of the pact was made in the Sino-Russian railroad dispute of 1929. In July of that year difficulty arose over the Chinese Eastern Railway which was being operated jointly by Russians and Chinese under an agreement concluded in 1924. The Manchurian government under Chang

321

Hsueh-liang, claiming that the Russians were misusing their position by attempting to spread communistic propaganda, expelled some 300 Soviet railway officials, including the general manager of the road and the Russian departmental chiefs. After several months of argumentation, the U.S.S.R. resorted to force. A punitive expedition of infantry, artillery, and air forces entered Manchuria. Villages were bombed. The Chinese foreign minister, C. T. Wang, alleged that more than thirty Manchurian towns were raided.[1] China officially protested to the League of Nations and to the governments that had adhered to the Pact of Paris, expressing the hope that the signatories of the pact would "take appropriate steps to stop and punish this deliberate violation."[2]

The United States government took the lead in calling the attention of China and Russia to their obligations under the pact. When the dispute began in July, the United States consulted with the other great-power signatories, Great Britain, France, Germany, Italy, and Japan. After the Russian troop movements in November the negotiations were taken up with renewed energy by Secretary of State Stimson. Mr. Stimson sent a statement to the Chinese government and a similar one to Russia through the French government[3] urging observance of the Pact of Paris. The two parties were asked to abide by the provisions of Article II in which the signatories had agreed that the solution of their disputes would never be sought except by pacific means. The statement called attention to the sanction of international public opinion in the following words:

> The American Government feels that the respect with which China and Russia will hereafter be held in the good opinion of the world will necessarily in great measure depend upon the way in which they carry out these most sacred promises.[4]

The American communication was sent to all the signatories of the pact. A number of the governments, including Great Britain, France, and Italy, informed the United States that they were sending communications of a similar character to the two parties. Altogether there were thirty countries which replied in a manner favorable to the American action.[5]

[1] *N.Y. Times*, Nov. 25, 1929.
[2] *Ibid.*, Nov. 27, 1929.
[3] The United States did not at that time recognize the Russian government.
[4] Dept. of State, *Press Releases*, Dec. 7, 1929, p. 84.
[5] *Ibid.*, pp. 84–87; Dec. 14, 1929, p. 101.

Meanwhile the rapid Russian success made further resistance by the Manchurian forces inadvisable. Negotiations for the reinstatement of Russian officials in the railway administration were carried on between the Soviet representatives and the Chang Hsueh-liang government. The Chinese government was not a party to these negotiations at the beginning but later cabled full authority to Chang to proceed. An agreement was seemingly in process of realization at the time of the publication of the Stimson statements.

The Russian answer to the representations of Mr. Stimson and the other governments was exceedingly gruff. In a memorandum of December 3, 1929, Mr. Litvinoff, Russian commissar for foreign affairs, declared that the note could not be considered as friendly in character and that it was intended to influence the negotiations then in progress. The Soviet government, he stated, could not tolerate any outside pressure of this kind. He feigned surprise that the United States which did not recognize the Soviet government should nevertheless attempt to give it advice.[1]

The negotiations between Russia and the Manchurian government resulted in an agreement for the withdrawal of Russian troops and a return of the railway to the joint administration system provided for in the 1924 agreement. The willingness of Russia to negotiate was regarded by Mr. Stimson as "not the least significant evidence to show that the public opinion of the world is a live factor which can be promptly mobilized and which has become a factor of prime importance in the solution of the problems and controversies which may arise between nations."[2]

Whatever effect the actions of Mr. Stimson had in the solution of the Manchurian controversy, the incident showed the undesirability of action initiated and led by a single nation in settling a dispute between two aroused adversaries. Such intervention is almost certain to be welcomed by the weaker party but resented by the stronger. A more formal method of joint action by a considerable number of powers is necessary if representations are to be made in a safe, dignified, and effective manner.

THE SINO-JAPANESE DISPUTE

The next military action to test the Pact of Paris came likewise in Manchuria in the Japanese invasion which began in 1931. On the

---

[1] *N.Y. Times*, Dec. 4, 1929.
[2] Dept. of State, *Press Releases*, Dec. 7, 1929, p. 88.

night of September 18, 1931, an explosion occurred on the main tracks of the South Manchurian Railway just north of Mukden. The line was slightly damaged. This event was taken by the Japanese as the excuse for launching upon a policy long contemplated in military circles, *i.e.*, the extension of armed occupation beyond the railway zone to the whole of Manchuria. The Manchurian government under Marshal Chang Hsueh-liang was driven from Mukden and later from Manchuria. On March 9, 1932, a government was formerly inaugurated with Henry Pu-yi, heir to the Manchu throne of China, as regent or dictator. The new government was under Japanese protection and declared its independence of China under the name of Manchukuo. On March 1, 1934, a monarchy was established and Pu-yi became Emperor Kang Teh.

Meanwhile, organizations in China proper had started a vigorous boycott against Japanese goods, and Chinese who handled Japanese merchandise were frequently dealt with in a summary manner. The result was a decline of Japanese exports to China. Smarting under the loss of trade and stirred by the frantic appeals of Japanese merchants in China, the Tokyo officials in January, 1932, demanded that the Chinese authorities in Shanghai should suppress the boycott. Finally an attack upon the city was begun. After six weeks of desperate fighting, the defending Nineteenth Route Army was pressed back to a distance about twenty miles from the city.[1]

This series of events, both in Manchuria and in the Shanghai region, created apprehension throughout the world and led to various efforts on the part of the members of the League of Nations and also on the part of the United States to settle the matter. The concern of the United States in the situation was due in the first place to our policy of maintaining the territorial integrity of China, which principle is incorporated in the Nine-Power Treaty signed at Washington in 1922. The American government likewise desired to discourage military action because of a general interest in peace and a particular ambition to maintain the inviolability of the Pact of Paris. The efforts of the United States may be divided into two classes: (1) diplomatic representations by the Department of State

---

[1] An account of the military movements in Shanghai and in Manchuria up until August, 1932, is found in League of Nations, *Appeal of the Chinese Government—Report of the Commission of Enquiry* (C. 663. M. 320. 1932. VII), also published by the Dept. of State, Gov. Printing Office, Washington, 1932, under the title *Manchuria, Report of the Commission of Enquiry Appointed by the League of Nations*.

to the parties in the dispute, and (2) cooperation with the League of Nations.

DIPLOMATIC REPRESENTATIONS TO THE PARTIES

Based partially on the precedents of the Sino-Russian affair, the Department of State proceeded to make diplomatic representations to both the Chinese and the Japanese government. Some of the notes, as will be seen, were outspoken in character. It is quite probable that their strength was due in some measure to the knowledge that the League of Nations was also engaged in making representations.

Remonstrances against Military Operations. Three days after the news of the troop movements had been received in Washington, the Secretary of State handed a memorandum to the Japanese ambassador informing him that the matter was of concern to a considerable number of nations, and that it brought into question the meaning of the Nine-Power Treaty and the Pact of Paris. Mr. Stimson hoped that the orders, which he understood had already been given to restrain the military forces, would be respected and that there would be no further application of force.[1] As the Japanese soldiers swept farther and farther from Mukden and it became apparent that the campaign was to be much more than a local incident, the United States made more emphatic protests. On October 8 the Japanese air forces bombed the city of Chinchow, the new provisional capital of Chang Hsueh-liang. Three days later Secretary Stimson directed the American ambassador in Tokyo to leave with the Japanese Foreign Office a memorandum in which it was stated: "The Secretary of State is at a loss to see what right Japanese military planes had to fly over the town, thereby provoking attack, and to drop bombs. . . . Bombing of an unfortified and unwarned town is one of the most extreme of military actions, deprecated even in time of war."[2]

The Hoover-Stimson Doctrine. In spite of assurances that nothing was further from the thoughts of the Japanese government than to have recourse to war and that they were actuated solely by the necessity of defending themselves and of protecting the South Manchurian Railway, the Japanese military occupation was extended. On January 3 Chinchow, which is more than fifty miles

---

[1] *Conditions in Manchuria*, pp. 4–5, Senate Document No. 55, 72d Cong., 1st Sess.

[2] *Ibid.*, pp. 16–17.

from the railway zone, was taken; and, on January 7 Mr. Stimson sent an identic note to Japan and China which embodied the celebrated Hoover-Stimson doctrine of nonrecognition. This note seems destined to rank with the some of the more important documents in American foreign policy. Regarding the attitude of the United States, Secretary Stimson said that the American government

. . . cannot admit the legality of any situation de facto nor does it intend to recognize any treaty or agreement entered into between those governments, or agents thereof, which may impair the treaty rights of the United States or its citizens in China, including those which relate to the sovereignty, the independence, or the territorial and administrative integrity of the Republic of China, or to the international policy relative to China, commonly known as the open-door policy; and that *it does not intend to recognize any situation, treaty, or agreement which may be brought about by means contrary to the covenants and obligations of the Pact of Paris of August* 27, 1928, to which treaty both China and Japan, as well as the United States, are parties.[1]

The significance of this doctrine of nonrecognition as a first step in the implementation of the Pact of Paris will be referred to later.

COOPERATION WITH THE LEAGUE

It had seemed plain from the Sino-Russian affair that in a serious controversy it is unwise for a single country to attempt individual remonstrances with the parties to the dispute. Had the United States, without diplomatic support from other countries, continued to upbraid Japan for the invasion of Manchuria, the action might easily have involved this country in a bitter international controversy. It was appropriate, therefore, that the American government should have collaborated in no small measure with the League of Nations in the attempt to bring about a pacific settlement of the affair. The isolationist sentiment in the United States, however, prompted the government to proceed with caution. Warm and fulsome rhetoric of cooperation was frequently followed by reticence of action.[2]

Unwillingness to Cooperate in a Boycott. Since 1920 when the League of Nations came into existence the question has recurrently

[1] *Conditions in Manchuria*, p. 54. Author's italics.

[2] For a description of American policy see COOPER, RUSSELL M., *American Consultation in World Affairs for the Preservation of Peace*, pp. 192ff., The Macmillan Company, New York, 1934.

arisen: What would be the attitude of the United States in case the League should seek to subject an aggressor to the severance of all trade and financial relations? There has been apprehension that this country might not only trade with the boycotted nation and thus nullify the League action but that it might also take strong action to set aside any League restrictions which would hamper American commerce. The League showed little disposition to invoke Article XVI, which would have necessitated sanctions against Japan; and this unwillingness was due partly to the fear that lack of American cooperation would thwart any such action. On its part the United States government was reported by press correspondents to be opposed to participation in a boycott. A petition sponsored by Newton D. Baker, former secretary of war, and President A. Lawrence Lowell of Harvard, asking that the United States government should stand ready to cooperate in a boycott instituted by the League to restore peace, received no friendly response at Washington but evoked considerable senatorial opposition. What attitude the United States would have assumed had the League actually invoked Article XVI cannot, of course, be known. Probably this country would have been thrown into a bitter controversy over the issues of isolation and League cooperation, the outcome depending upon the degree of anti-Japanese sentiment existing at the moment.

Support to the League's Diplomatic Remonstrances. The United States expressed wholehearted sympathy for the League's actions in sending notes of protest to Japan and China and on more than one occasion sent notes similar to those of the League Council.[1] Secretary Stimson commended the League as providing tested machinery for the handling of disputes between members and urged the Council to exert all the pressure and authority within its competence.[2]

Presence of an American Representative in or near the Council. Close cooperation between the United States and the League, it would seem, would necessarily include oral consultation between a representative of the American government and the representatives of the leading League powers; and one natural form of such consultation would appear to be participation of the American representative in Council deliberations. In October, 1931, the Council invited the United States to send a representative to its meetings for the purpose

[1] See *Conditions in Manchuria*, pp. 5, 8, 20.
[2] *Ibid.*, p. 14.

of expressing an opinion as to the best method of giving effect to the Pact of Paris. The American representative was not, of course, to act as a member of the Council; but was merely to carry on through personal contact the cooperation which had already been conducted by telegraphic communication.[1] Prentiss Gilbert, American consul in Geneva, was then authorized by the Department of State to participate in the discussions of the Council relative to the application of the pact. In the consideration of any other aspect of the Manchurian situation, Mr. Gilbert was instructed to act only as an observer and auditor. In taking his place with the Council at its October session, Mr. Gilbert explained that he was empowered to confer so that "we may most easily and effectively take common counsel with you" with regard to the relationship of the Pact of Paris and the Manchurian situation.[2]

During the Council's October session the American representative played a minor role, and his remarks were merely of a ceremonial character. The precedent value of his presence seemed at the time, however, to be a matter of considerable consequence. It appeared for a while that a United States-League of Nations cooperative policy for war prevention was in the making. Isolationists in the United States, alarmed at the turn in the procedure, protested to the Department of State.

The next session of the Council was held in Paris on November 16. Instead of sending an American representative to sit with the Council, the Department of State instructed Charles G. Dawes, ambassador to Great Britain, to proceed to Paris so that he might be available for conference with M. Briand and the representatives of other nations gathered there for the meeting. The effects of anti-League protests in the United States were shown in the instructions from the Secretary of State: "It is not expected that you will find it necessary to attend the Council meetings."[3] Mr. Dawes did, however, give some moral support to the Council's decision. When a commission to study the controversy on the spot was proposed by the Council, he issued a statement to the effect that the United States government approved the general plan and that it had urged acquiescence in the proposal upon both China and Japan.[4] On November 26 the Secretary-General of the League suggested to

[1] For the Council's debates regarding the nature of American participation see League of Nations, *Official Journal*, December, 1931, pp. 2322*ff.*

[2] *Ibid.*, pp. 2336–2337; *Conditions in Manchuria*, p. 19.

[3] *Conditions in Manchuria*, p. 38.

[4] *Ibid.*, p. 41.

Mr. Dawes a dispatch of telegrams asking Japan and China not to aggravate the already troublesome situation. The next day the Secretary of State, evidently in consequence of this request, made strong representations to Japan against further troop movements in the Chinchow area. In his communication Mr. Stimson referred specifically to the fact that information regarding proposed Japanese troop movements had come through the president of the Council of the League.[1] Despite this cooperation the failure of the Department of State in November to instruct Ambassador Dawes to sit with the Council was generally regarded as a repudiation of the policy of personal conference with the Council which had been begun in October. The isolationists had won a partial triumph.

Participation in Investigations. Two investigating bodies were set up by the League during the crisis, a commission of inquiry into the general Sino-Japanese question and a special investigating body to report on matters at Shanghai. The general commission was first publicly proposed in a communiqué of the Council of November 25 and the plan was definitely adopted in the Council's resolution of December 10. At the time of its proposal in November it was approved by the United States. On December 10, when the matter was finally adopted by the Council, Mr. Stimson stated: "Such a provision for a neutral commission is in itself an important and constructive step towards an ultimate and fair solution of the intricate problem presented in Manchuria. It means the application with the consent of both China and Japan of modern and enlightened methods of conciliation to the solution of this problem."[2] The body thus created became famous as the Lytton Commission and produced a report upon conditions in Manchuria which stands out as one of the most meritorious of international studies. The commission was composed of five men, nationals of Great Britain, France, Germany, Italy, and the United States. The United States government was consulted in advance of its composition and consented to the appointment of Major General Frank R. McCoy of the United States army.[3] General McCoy was relieved from his military assignment as commander of the Fourth Corps Area to permit him to take part in the investigation.

Another body, the committee for the reporting of information regarding the Shanghai situation, was constituted by the Secretary-

[1] *Ibid.*, p. 42.
[2] *Conditions in Manchuria*, p. 47.
[3] Dept. of State, *Press Releases*, Feb. 13, 1932, p. 135.

General acting under the first clause of Article XV of the Covenant.[1]
The United States, being asked to join in the creation of the committee, replied that it could not appoint an American upon a League
body which would be acting under the provisions of the Covenant.
Because of its interest in the maintenance of peace and treaty rights,
however, the department instructed Consul General Cunningham at
Shanghai to cooperate with the committee in studying and reporting
upon the facts.[2]

Cooperation in the Efforts to Stop the Fighting at Shanghai.
With some 5,000 Americans resident in the International Settlement
the United States had a special reason for attempting to terminate
the hostilities at Shanghai.   As the Japanese attack became immi-
nent late in January, 1932, the United States consulted with Great
Britain as to the possibility of joint action in protecting the International Settlement.   On February 2, 1932, the American government, in concert with Great Britain, drew up hastily a program for a
truce and for troop withdrawals.   The plan received the support
of France, Italy, and Germany; and the president of the Council
associated that body with the proposal when the matter was brought
up at Geneva.   The plan was not immediately accepted but the
endeavor to obtain agreement to a similar proposal was continued
in the Council and later in the Assembly.   The United States gave
its support to these efforts.   Finally on May 5 an arrangement for
the evacuation of Shanghai was signed by Japanese and Chinese
delegates in the presence of representatives of the United States,
Great Britain, France, and Italy.   The agreement called for supervision of the evacuation by a commission of twelve including one
civilian and one military representative from each of the following
governments: China, Japan, the United States, Great Britain,
France, and Italy.[3]

League Cooperation in Supporting the Hoover-Stimson Doctrine.
The doctrine of nonrecognition of any situation, treaty, or agreement entered into by governments in violation of the Nine-Power

[1] This clause provides that, when a party to a dispute has submitted the
matter to the Council under Article XV, the Secretary-General shall make all
necessary arrangements for a full investigation.

[2] Dept. of State, *Press Releases*, Feb. 6, 1932, p. 109; League of Nations,
Official Journal, March, 1932, p. 374.

[3] For the discussions in the Council and Assembly see League of Nations,
Official Journal, March, 1932, pp. 350ff., and Special Supplement No. 101,
I: 25; "The League and Shanghai," *Geneva Special Studies*, May, 1932; MORLEY,
FELIX, *The Society of Nations*, Chapters XII and XIV.   For the text of the
evacuation agreement see *Official Journal*, Special Supplement No. 102, II: 27.

Treaty or the Pact of Paris was announced by the American government, as has been noted, on January 7, 1932.[1] Some weeks later the twelve neutral members of the League Council, that is, the Council members other than Japan and China, took a somewhat similar position. Basing their action on the Covenant, they addressed a note to Japan in which they declared that from the obligations of Article X it appeared to follow "that no infringement of the territorial integrity and no change in the political independence of any Member of the League brought about in disregard of this article ought to be recognized as valid and effectual by the Members of the League of Nations."[2] Secretary Stimson saw at once the value of obtaining the League's support for the doctrine of nonrecognition. In his letter to Senator Borah of February 24 he made a bid for more extended League support. If a position of nonrecognition of situations brought about contrary to the Pact of Paris should be taken by the other governments of the world, he said, a caveat would be placed upon illegal action which would bar any title or right acquired through pressure or treaty violation. This would eventually lead to the restoration to China of rights and titles of which she may have been deprived. The Assembly of the League shortly afterward responded to this suggestion. On March 11 that body with forty-four votes in favor and two abstentions (China and Japan) adopted a notable resolution on the Sino-Japanese dispute which included a proclamation that "it is incumbent upon the Members of the League of Nations not to recognize any situation, treaty, or agreement which may be brought about by means contrary to the Covenant of the League of Nations or to the Pact of Paris."[3] In commenting upon this resolution, Secretary Stimson said:

The action of the Assembly expresses the purpose for peace which is found both in the Pact of Paris and the Covenant of the League of Nations. In this expression all the nations of the world can speak with the same voice. This action will go far toward developing into terms of international law the principles of order and justice which underlie those treaties, and

---

[1] For details concerning the development of the doctrine see HILL, CHESNEY, "Recent Policies of Non-Recognition," *International Conciliation*, No. 293 (October, 1933), p. 12.

[2] *Official Journal*, March, 1932, pp. 383–384.

[3] The reference to the Pact of Paris was a late addition to the resolution, inserted at the suggestion of Sir John Simon because of a desire to join the League efforts as fully as possible with those of the United States. *Official Journal*, Special Supplement No. 101, pp. 82, 87.

the Government of the United States has been glad to cooperate earnestly in this effort.[1]

On February 24, 1933, the Assembly in adopting a report of the Committee of Nineteen restated the doctrine of nonrecognition and applied it specifically to Manchukuo. The report provided that the members of the League would "continue not to recognize this regime either *de jure* or *de facto*."[2]   An advisory committee was created by the Assembly to advise it regarding the problem of nonrecognition. The United States agreed to cooperate in the work of this body without the right to vote.   The committee recommended to the League members a policy of nonrecognition covering seven points[3] which dealt with the exclusion of Manchukuo from international conventions, the nonacceptance of Manchukuoan passports, and the attitude to be taken on questions of postal service, currency, business relations of nationals in Manchuria, the position of consuls, and the application of the Geneva Opium Convention.   While a considerable latitude in intercourse by nationals of nonrecognizing countries is permitted under the committee's recommendations, nevertheless the moral reproach of nonrecognition is still maintained.   Furthermore, a substantial impediment is placed upon the financing of Japanese enterprises in Manchuria owing to the fact that the chief creditor countries are not disposed to favor investments in that area so long as the policy of nonrecognition is maintained.[4]

THE UNITED STATES REMINDS ITALY OF HER OBLIGATIONS AT THE OUTBREAK OF THE WAR WITH ETHIOPIA

In 1935, when it appeared that the Italian government was determined upon the military conquest of Ethiopia, the Ethiopian Emperor asked the United States to examine the means of securing the observance of the Pact of Paris.   The United States then made a series of statements calling attention to the obligation of the parties under the pact.   On July 6 the Ethiopian government was informed that the United States "would be loath to believe" that either party "would resort to other than pacific means as a method of dealing with this controversy or would permit any situation to arise which

[1] Dept. of State, *Press Releases*, Mar. 12, 1932, p. 258.

[2] *Official Journal*, Special Supplement No. 112, p. 76.

[3] MIDDLEBUSH, FREDERICK A., "The Effect of the Non-Recognition of Manchukuo," *American Political Science Review*, XXVIII: 677 (August, 1934).

[4] At the time of writing only Japan and Salvador have recognized Manchukuo.

would be inconsistent with the commitments of the pact."[1] On July 12 the Secretary of State made a public statement in which he asserted that the Pact of Paris was no less binding than when it was entered into and that the "United States and other nations are interested in the maintenance of the pact and sanctity of the international commitments assumed thereby for the promotion and maintenance of peace among the nations of the world."[2] Again another statement from Secretary Hull, released on September 13, declared:

> With good-will toward all nations, the American Government asks of those countries which appear to be contemplating armed hostilities that they weigh most solicitously the declaration and pledge given in the Pact of Paris, which pledge was entered into by all the signatories for the purpose of safeguarding peace and sparing the world the incalculable losses and human suffering that inevitably attend and follow in the wake of wars.[3]

In this case, because of serious threat to the peace of Europe, the League of Nations showed much greater vigor than it had displayed in either of the Manchurian episodes. Encouraged by Great Britain, whose colonial interests were affected, the League bore the brunt of peace enforcement basing its action upon Articles XII and XVI of the Covenant. The effect of the American statements lay merely in the expression of opposition to Italy's warlike designs and the sympathetic position which was thereby assumed with regard to the aims of the League.

THE PROBLEM OF FURTHER IMPLEMENTATION

The Pact of Paris has been tested in three international crises. In the first, the Sino-Russian dispute, a satisfactory solution was achieved, possibly due in part to the pact. In the second, the Sino-Japanese controversy, the pact has failed to accomplish a solution and has done nothing further than to keep the matter open by nonrecognition of Manchukuo and thus to maintain a certain pressure upon the pact violator, *i.e.*, Japan. The pact has in this case been shown to be grossly insufficient. In the third, the Italian-Ethiopian crisis of 1935, the pact was almost lost sight of in the efforts made under the League Covenant. Many students of international affairs have devoted some time to outlining further

---

[1] Dept. of State, *Press Releases*, July 6, 1935, p. 29.
[2] *Ibid.*, July 13, 1935, pp. 53–54.
[3] *Ibid.*, Sept. 14, 1935, p. 196.

plans for providing sanctions, or, as it is called, implementing the pact.

The United States Shows a Willingness to Consider Consultation. The need for international cooperation which has been made apparent in the three disputes above mentioned has already produced some effects upon American policies. In connection with the limitation of armaments European nations have displayed reluctance to reduce armaments without at the same time building up mutual guarantees against aggression. They have desired that the United States should join the world community in guaranteeing action to maintain the peace. The United States delegations at Geneva have, however, refused to make any such pledge. As a compromise this country has offered to join in consultation in case of a threat to the world's peace. The declaration of willingness to consider consultation was first made at the London Naval conference of 1930, but it was later repeated at Geneva. On May 22, 1933, Norman Davis told the Disarmament Conference that the United States was willing "to consult the other states in case of a threat to peace, with a view to averting conflict." Furthermore, in case other states sought to take action against an aggressor and in case the United States should concur with them as to the identity of the aggressor, this country would "refrain from any action tending to defeat such collective effort which these states may thus make to restore peace."[1] In other words the President would, under the conditions set forth, refuse to protect Americans in any efforts they might make to conduct trade with the aggressor nations in opposition to League prohibitions. These promises were contingent upon the adoption of a thoroughgoing disarmament agreement. Mr. Davis was not authorized, however, to promise any action by the United States against an aggressor. Thus, in case a treaty could be obtained, the American government would be willing to consult and to refrain from action which would interfere with joint sanctions but would not be willing to promise participation in the sanctions.[2]

---

[1] Dept. of State, *Press Releases*, May 27, 1933, p. 390. The speech appears in indirect form in League of Nations, *Records of the Conference for the Reduction and Limitation of Armaments, Series B, Minutes of the General Commission,* II: 475, Geneva, 1933.

[2] For this and other pledges regarding consultation see COOPER, *op. cit.,* pp. 71*ff.*, and JESSUP, PHILIP C., *International Security*, pp. 64*ff.*, Council on Foreign Relations, New York, 1935. For a critical view see CRECRAFT, EARL WILLIS, *Freedom of the Seas*, Chapter XXI, D. Appleton-Century Company, Inc., New York, 1935.

On October 2, 1935, when the question of League sanctions against Italy was being discussed, President Roosevelt issued a notable statement to the effect that American citizens who engaged in transactions with either belligerent must take their own risk.[1] In view of the possibility of a League blockade against Italy, a natural inference from this announcement was that the President wished to warn American citizens in advance that they would not be protected as against League sanctions.

The Capper Resolution. A further plan for implementation has been presented in Congress on various occasions by Senator Capper. Late in 1927, before the Pact of Paris had been formulated, the senator drafted a plan for war prevention which aroused wide interest in peace circles. After the Pact of Paris was ratified, he revised the plan; and it was again introduced in the Senate in April, 1932. The revised scheme was in brief as follows:

1. The United States shall not recognize any situation, treaty, or agreement brought about contrary to the pact.

2. When other nations, not parties to a dispute, have in open conference decided that a breach of the pact has been committed and when they have decided not to aid the violator by the export of arms or other supplies of war or not to furnish it financial assistance, and when the President shall have determined that a breach of the pact has occurred, he shall have power to place a ban upon the shipment from the United States to the aggressor of arms or war supplies and upon such financial and commercial transactions with the nationals of the violating country as may in his judgment be used to strengthen or maintain the violation.

3. The President shall be requested to invite a conference of signatories of the pact to frame an agreement which shall define their obligations in case of a violation of the pact.

The proposal has never received favorable Congressional action, but it indicates the drift of informed opinion in certain circles regarding methods of implementation.[2]

Psychological Factors in Connection with Implementation. Any attempt to draft plans for sanctions without consideration of psychological factors is apt to prove impractical. If an attempt were made to apply strong sanctions unbacked by public opinion, the effort would doubtless end in humiliating failure. The synchronizing of the evolution of the pact to the development of opinion is, therefore, necessary to success in this endeavor. But sentiment is undependable and fluctuates in accordance with at least four

[1] See p. 33.
[2] For the action of Congress in passing a different type of embargo resolution, see pp. 31–32.

major influences. In the first place, the willingness to support cooperative sanctions increases with the realization of the horrors of war and decreases as war appears unreal and distant. Strong sentiment for international action to prevent war swept this country in the years 1915–1919 when the disastrous results of armed conflicts were obvious even to the most indifferent. During the years of peace the sentiment has cooled considerably. In the second place, sentiment for cooperation seems to rise with the prosperity of international economic enterprises and to fall during a world depression when international trade dwindles and bonds sold on the international markets go into default. At such times the sentiments of isolation and nationalism are promoted. In the third place, the desire for cooperation at any given moment will be strongly affected by considerations of national policy. If it seems to be in line with nationalistic inclinations that the nation should join with others in order to punish an aggressor, a powerful opinion can be mustered for international cooperation. Thus the French public has been exceedingly warm for joint action to maintain the *status quo* in Europe and somewhat cool regarding cooperation to oppose the projects of Japan in the Far East. The British have been lukewarm as to sanctions against Japan but enthusiastic for League action against Italy in the Ethiopian dispute. The United States, under the spur of hostility to Japan, might conceivably become enthusiastic regarding cooperation in the Far East. In the fourth place, gradual adjustment of the world through education and experience to the necessities of war prevention has brought about a long-time growth of opinion in favor of cooperative sanctions against war which is appreciably stronger today than it was a quarter of a century ago. If this should continue, as one might reasonably expect, the possibility of providing effective sanctions for the preservation of peace may be expected to grow greater with the passage of time.

Direct Prevention of War Is Only Part of the Problem. In conclusion it should be kept in mind that the prevention of war in a fully developed dispute is probably not the most important part of war prevention. In addition there is the work of adjusting international conditions so that reasons for rivalry will be eliminated before they grow to the acute controversial stage. If serious attempts are not made to promote such work as is intended under Article XIX of the Covenant of the League of Nations,[1] there is

---

[1] Article XIX: The Assembly may from time to time advise the reconsideration by Members of the League of treaties which have become inapplicable

good reason to believe that the dissatisfactions of the expanding but underprivileged nations will grow to the point where war-prevention treaties cannot stem the tide. The preventive movement has not thus far developed in the League to the point where specific proposals for American consideration have been considered. Such a movement will require the renunciation of some of the perquisites of nationalism. The readjustment of colonial empires, the further internationalism of mandates, and international understandings concerning raw materials and tariffs must be considered. Will the powers that are now territorially satisfied, including the United States, be willing to adjust themselves to this fuller international life? If not, the nationalist-capitalist philosophy of political conduct may expire in the ruins of its own belligerent system.

---

and the consideration of international conditions whose continuance might endanger the peace of the world.

CHAPTER XVIII

ARMAMENT LIMITATION AND REDUCTION: THE NAVAL TREATIES

THE WASHINGTON CONFERENCE

Background. The attempt to reduce armaments by general international agreement has been seriously undertaken only in recent years. For the acute need of a corrective to the rising costs of armies and navies and to the alarming increase in facilities for mass slaughter has become impressively apparent only with the development of industrialized warfare. In 1899 the First Hague Conference was called by the Russian government for the prime purpose of reaching an agreement to limit armaments. The Russian military position was threatened by the growing armaments of Germany and Austria at a time when Russia was not in a financial position to accept the challenge of an armament race. The first proposal mentioned in the invitation to the conference, therefore, was for an agreement to prevent any increase in armed forces and military budgets. The plan met with strong opposition, particularly from the German delegation; and nothing was accomplished. Armament limitation was not included in the topics enumerated in the Russian invitation to the Second Hague Conference of 1907. The British government, however, feeling the pressure of armament competition from Germany, sought to introduce the subject during the discussion. The United States delegation seconded these efforts, but no results were achieved.[1]

During the early years of the World War the slogan of "preparedness" became popular in the United States. The greatest development from this state of feeling was the naval program of 1916 which provided for a radical increase in the American navy. The central feature of the program was the plan for the construction of sixteen capital ships, consisting of ten battleships, each to be armed with twelve 16-inch guns, and six battle cruisers, each to mount eight 16-inch guns. A large number of cruisers, destroyers,

[1] See *The Reports to the Hague Conferences of 1899 and 1907*, Oxford University Press, 1917; *The Proceedings of the Hague Peace Conferences*, Oxford University Press (5 vols.), New York, 1920–1921; HULL, WILLIAM ISAAC, *The Two Hague Conferences*, Ginn & Company, Boston, 1908.

and submarines were also contemplated. If this program had been completed, it would probably have given to the United States the most powerful navy afloat. The United States would have possessed a capital ship contingent of newer, larger, better protected, and more heavily armed ships than those in the British navy. The debates on the bill were touched here and there with the emotional faith of the sea power theory of history. The United States had risen to be the greatest economic power of all time without a first-rate navy; and in most of the stages of this phenomenal rise it had possessed scarcely any navy at all. But some of the congressmen were more interested in the experience of Athens and Venice. One senator, who counted the residents of a naval base community among his constituents, ignored the evolution of his own country to exclaim: "The rise and fall of nations and empires teach the same lesson—that national safety and national success are inseparable from naval strength and power."[1]

The capital ship portion of the 1916 program was postponed after the entrance of the United States into the World War; but in 1919, the construction of the ships was begun. A strong feeling against the huge program was immediately aroused in naval circles in Japan and Great Britain. The belief that the greatness or even the very existence of Great Britain depended upon naval supremacy was widespread in British conservative and admiralty circles. It could hardly have been expected that the British would consent to see their navy surpassed by a rival power without a strong competitive effort which might have taken the form of naval construction on a huge scale or of further alliance diplomacy to redress the balance of power. The Anglo-Japanese alliance, which had existed since 1902, might have been strengthened to suit the situation. The Japanese government would probably have been willing to bind itself more firmly to its British ally in order to meet the American peril. Japanese sentiment was aroused over the American building program, particularly so since the bulk of American naval strength, the Battle Fleet, had been transferred to the Pacific. The Japanese accordingly plunged into a building program which, if carried out, would have placed an enormous burden upon the finances of the island empire.

In view of the apprehensions which had been aroused by the American construction, a movement was set on foot in this country for a disarmament conference. The Borah amendment to the naval bill of 1921 recommended that a conference should be spon-

[1] *Congressional Record* 53: 10,923 (July 13, 1916).

sored by the United States. Invitations were issued in August, 1921, by President Harding. Considering how closely the situation in Eastern Asia was related to the subject of warships, the scope of the conference was extended to include the Pacific and Far Eastern questions. The five chief naval powers, the United States, Great Britain, Japan, France, and Italy, were brought together to consider the naval question. Four others—China, Holland, Belgium, and Portugal—were invited to join in the discussion of matters regarding the Far East.[1]

The Hughes Program. The outstanding feature of the Washington Conference was a speech made at the opening session by Secretary of State Charles Evans Hughes in which he set forth a plan for drastic reduction in naval armaments. His program contained four proposals:

1. That all capital ship building programs should be abandoned;
2. That further reduction should be made through the scrapping of certain older ships;
3. That, in general, the existing naval strength of the powers should be used as a basis for determining the size of the reduced fleets.
4. That capital ship tonnage ratios should be used in fixing the treaty strength of auxiliary combatant craft.[2]

Secretary Hughes's speech must be counted as one of the landmarks in the field of international cooperation. It appealed to the imagination as well as to the intelligence of the delegates, and all but the last of his four points were written into the final work of the conference.

Capital Ships. The capital ship was defined in the Washington Treaty as a vessel of war, not an aircraft carrier, whose displacement exceeds 10,000 tons or which carries a gun with a caliber exceeding eight inches. This type includes both battleships and battle cruisers. Because of the rapid development of the airplane, capital ships have been regarded by some authorities as of little naval value—the white elephants of the sea. Orthodox American naval officials, however, contend that they are still indispensable in national defense.

Mr. Hughes suggested that capital ship building programs should be abandoned and went further to name a considerable number of older ships which should be scrapped. His plan called for a 10:10:6

---

[1] For the invitation to the conference and suggestions as to the agenda see *Conference on the Limitation of Armament, Washington, November,* 12, 1921–*February* 6, 1922, pp. 4–11, Govt. Printing Office, Washington, 1922.

[2] *Ibid.,* p. 60.

ratio as between the United States, Great Britain, and Japan with the capital ship tonnage to be eventually fixed at 500,000 for the United States and Great Britain and 300,000 for Japan. The Japanese objected to losing one of their latest and finest battleships, the *Mutsu*, and desired to discard an older one instead. To compensate for their retention of this ship the United States was permitted to finish two uncompleted battleships which were to replace two older ships. Great Britain was then permitted to build two new battleships to replace four older ones which were added to the list to be scrapped. These changes necessitated the raising of the tonnage totals, which were fixed at 525,000 for the United States and Great Britain and 315,000 for Japan. France and Italy were each assigned a value of 3.33 in the ratios or a permissible capital ship tonnage of 175,000 each.

The effect of the Washington agreement upon the American 1916 program of 16 capital ships was as follows: One battleship, the *Maryland*, had been completed and was retained. Due to the understanding regarding the *Mutsu* two other battleships, the *West Virginia* and the *Colorado*, were completed. Two battle cruisers, the *Saratoga* and the *Lexington*, were converted into aircraft carriers. All of the other capital ships in the program, *i.e.*, seven uncompleted battleships and four unfinished battle cruisers, were scrapped. In addition the United States destroyed seventeen older capital ships. The British scrapped twenty-four older ships and stopped construction on four which were projected or building. The Japanese dismantled ten older ships and abandoned six upon which some slight work had been done.

The capital ships of the different countries were so varied in individual tonnage and age that it was impossible to pare the fleets immediately to their treaty tonnage. Replacements were to begin in 1931 and from that time on the ships could be built according to standards which would bring each country into line with its precise tonnage allotment. Aircraft carriers were limited according

	Number of capital ships	Capital ship tonnage	Aircraft carrier tonnage
United States	15	525,000	135,000
Great Britain	15	525,000	135,000
Japan	9	315,000	81,000
France	5	175,000	60,000
Italy	5	175,000	60,000

to the 10:10:6 ratio.   France and Italy were in this case each given a value of 4.4.   To recapitulate, by 1942 the capital ship and aircraft carrier strength of the powers was to be limited as shown on page 341.   No capital ship could be larger than 35,000 tons or carry guns of a greater caliber than sixteen inches.[1]

Auxiliary Craft.   The Washington Treaty went no further in tonnage limitation than to restrict capital ships and aircraft carriers. The fourth proposal of Mr. Hughes's program regarding auxiliary combat craft was not carried into effect.   When the question of limiting submarines arose, the French delegation objected to their proposed allotment of about 31,452 tons and blandly announced that the absolute minimum for their country was 90,000 tons.   They counted upon the submarine as a chief weapon in their national defense.   The British delegates, confronted with the possibility of this huge submarine strength near to their coast and remembering the U-boat devastations of the war, refused to consent to any limitation of destroyers and cruisers.   For the great enemy of the submarine is the destroyer, while the antidote to the destroyer is the cruiser.   With the stand of the French delegation on submarines and the natural coolness of the British and most of the naval powers to the reduction of auxiliary craft, the plans for limitation in this field failed.

The Nonfortification Agreement.   The Japanese had shown some alarm at the shift of the American Battle Fleet into the Pacific. They feared that the United States might establish a powerful naval base in the Philippines which would be a menace to their security; and they, therefore, demanded an agreement not to increase insular fortifications in this area.   The plan was resisted by American naval advisers.   The Japanese, however, refused to accept a 60 per cent ratio in capital ships without the agreement on fortifications; and the American delegation finally consented in order to obtain the capital ship ratio.   The treaty provided for the maintenance of the *status quo* in the following possessions:

United States: The Aleutians and islands west of Hawaii, these being particularly Guam and the Philippines.

Great Britain: Islands east of 110 degrees east longitude (east of Singapore) excepting those adjacent to Canada, Australia, and New Zealand.   Hong Kong was the chief base affected.

Japan: Insular possessions outside of Japan proper.[2]

[1] The details concerning the tonnage to be retained and the ships to be scrapped are found in the treaty between the five powers limiting naval armament, *Treaties, etc., of the U.S.*, III: 3100.

[2] Art. XIX.

The effect of this agreement on American policy was to establish the Hawaiian Islands as the farthest western base of naval strength and to make the Philippines exceedingly difficult to defend in case of war with Japan.

The Passing of the Anglo-Japanese Alliance. One of the most important results of the Washington Conference was the dissolution of the Anglo-Japanese alliance. This alliance was formed in 1902, renewed in 1905 and 1911, and could have been denounced by either party in 1921. The British dominions were unfriendly to the alliance which might have brought them into a Pacific war on the side of Japan. The British government felt that the alliance was a liability in that it might have precipitated a death struggle with the United States. About the only common cause to draw Japan and Great Britain together, from the British point of view, was the threat of the American capital ship program. When the United States was willing to abandon that program, the British government became willing to dissolve the alliance. The Japanese were then informed that the alliance was to be terminated. In order to soften the blow to Japan, the Four-Power Treaty was signed by the United States, Great Britain, Japan, and France. It obliges the parties to respect the rights of the parties in their insular possessions in the Pacific and to consult in case of disputes arising from any Pacific question involving these rights which cannot be diplomatically adjusted. If a power, other than these four, should threaten the rights of one of them, the parties will communicate with each other as to the best measures to be taken.[1]

The Washington Treaty is still the subject of controversy in the United States. Did the gains exceed the sacrifices? To answer this question one must balance political imponderables against tons, guns, and fortifications. The sacrifices were the scrapping of most of the 1916 program and the agreement not to increase fortifications in the Philippines. The gains were the reduction of costs, the lessening of naval rivalry, the removal of a cause of conflict, the dissolution of an alliance between two potential enemies of the United States, and the reduction of the strength of our naval rivals. Despite bitter assults on the treaty, it was generally regarded with approval as a bulwark of peace in the Pacific.[2]

[1] *Treaties, etc., of the U.S.*, III: 3094.

[2] For a general description of the conference see BUELL, RAYMOND LESLIE, *The Washington Conference*, D. Appleton & Company, New York, 1922; ICHIHASHI, YAMOTO, *The Washington Conference and After*, Stanford University Press, Stanford University, Calif., 1928.

THE GENEVA CONFERENCE OF 1927

The Crusier Race after 1922.   The failure to agree to the limitation of auxiliary combat vessels proved to be a serious omission in the Washington Treaty.   Checked in the building of capital ships, the powers turned to the construction of the most powerful auxiliary craft, *i.e.*, the cruiser.   Under the treaty, cruisers could be built up to 10,000 tons and could be armed with 8-inch guns.   From 1922 to 1927, inclusive, Great Britain laid down thirteen of these so-called treaty cruisers.   Japan laid down fourteen cruisers of which six were of 10,000 tons.   The United States laid down two and projected six more of the 10,000-ton type.[1]   Accusations between the powers flew thick and fast.   The spirit of naval rivalry mounted and a cruiser race was under way.

To halt this competition, President Coolidge on February 10, 1927, proposed a conference of the five naval powers to be held in Geneva where the nations could be represented by their delegates to the League of Nations Preparatory Commission for the Disarmament Conference.   France and Italy refused the invitation.   When the conference met in June, the representatives of the United States, Great Britain, and Japan were present.

The Stalemate at Geneva.   The Geneva Conference of 1927 was largely a clash of British and American views on cruiser limitation.   Two main differences arose, the first with regard to the amount of cruiser tonnage that should be permitted and the second with regard to the British proposal to divide cruisers into two subcategories and to limit each subcategory separately.

Concerning the amount of cruiser tonnage to be permitted, the British delegates asked for some seventy cruisers.[2]   The British plan, it was estimated, called for some 426,000 tons of cruisers.[3]   The American proposal, on the other hand, would have restricted the United States and Great Britain each to between 250,000 and 300,000 tons with an allotment for Japan of between 150,000 and 180,000 tons.[4]   The difference of more than 100,000 tons between the British and American proposals stood in the way of the success of the conference.

The British desired also to divide cruisers into two subcategories in order to limit strictly the larger type of cruiser mounting 8-inch

---

[1] See WILLIAMS, *The United States and Disarmament*, pp. 161–162.

[2] *Records of the Conference for the Limitation of Naval Armament Held at Geneva from June 20 to August 4, 1927*, p. 29, Geneva, 1927.

[3] *Ibid.*, p. 44.

[4] *Ibid.*, p. 20.

guns. They proposed two subcategories: one of not more than 7,500 tons, mounting guns of not more than 6 inches, and a larger type with a maximum of 10,000 tons, mounting guns of a maximum caliber of 8 inches. The large subcategory was to be strictly limited. The United States did not desire to divide cruisers into two subcategories but contended that each power should be entitled to construct its entire allotment of cruisers in whatever sizes it should choose under the Washington Treaty limits.

The British reasons for insisting on a division of cruisers were as follows: (1) For trade protection purposes it is better for the British to construct a large number of smaller cruisers than for them to build all of their cruisers of the 10,000-ton type. Their numerous naval bases located at convenient points make it possible for the British government to use the smaller cruisers despite their shorter cruising radius. If they should construct many small cruisers, however, while the United States should build only the 10,000-ton vessels, the British would be at a disadvantage because the 10,000-ton 8-inch gun cruiser is estimated to have a combat superiority over a 7,500-ton 6-inch gun ship out of proportion to the difference in tonnage.[1] The British desired, therefore, to place strict limitations upon the 10,000-ton, 8-inch cruiser. (2) A large number of British merchant ships are built so that they can be converted into cruisers on the outbreak of war. These ships can mount 6-inch guns. While they might give battle to a 6-inch gun cruiser, they would probably fall easy prey to 8-inch gun ships. At the time of the Geneva Conference, the American delegation stated that the British merchant shipping which could be thus converted totaled 888,000 tons while the United States had but 188,000 tons.[2]

The American reasons for refusing to agree with the British were: (1) The distance between American bases was so great that large cruisers with a longer cruising radius were desired.[3] (2) The preponderance of British merchant shipping which was convertible into 6-inch gun cruisers made it necessary that the United States should have a large number of 8-inch gun cruisers. Therefore the United States stood fast for the right to build all of its cruiser tonnage in the larger types should it so desire. The difference in the views of the two governments could not be adjusted and the conference failed to arrive at a treaty.

[1] *Ibid.*, p. 28.
[2] *Ibid.*, p. 43.
[3] *Ibid.*

THE LONDON CONFERENCE

Clearing Away the Difficulties. The impossibility of coming to an agreement on cruisers by measuring the tons of such vessels as were desired by Great Britain against the tons of ships preferred by the United States made it advisable that some further standards of measurement than tonnage should be introduced which would more accurately compare the combat power of two dissimilar ships. It was felt by many students of the question that gun power should also be taken into consideration. Others would have added the factors of speed and age. On April 27, 1929, Hugh Gibson, speaking in the League of Nations Preparatory Commission for the Disarmament Conference, proposed a system of equivalent naval values which would take into consideration other factors than tonnage. One of these was gun power.[1] With this concession made by the Hoover administration, which was well disposed toward the disarmament movement, and with the coming into power of a Labor government in Great Britain following the elections of May, 1929, a better atmosphere for a disarmament conference was created. The British government announced that it could get along with fifty cruisers, thus dropping twenty cruisers from the irreducible minimum which it had announced at Geneva. After some preliminary negotiations, including a visit to the United States by the eloquent Ramsay MacDonald, the British government issued invitations for a new naval conference which met in London on January 21, 1930.

Capital Ships Further Limited. The London Treaty provided for further reduction[2] of capital ship strength below the terms of the Washington Treaty; and the powers agreed not to lay down any new capital ships until 1937, thus postponing for six years the replacements contemplated by the Washington Treaty.[3] The postponement of new construction has operated as a substantial reduction of the capital ship strength of the powers inasmuch as during this period of six years a large proportion of the capital ship tonnage in

[1] *Documents of the Preparatory Commission for the Disarmament Conference, Minutes of the Sixth Session* (First Part) (C. 195. M. 74. 1929. IX), p. 57.

[2] For the work of the conference see Dept. of State, *Proceedings of the London Naval Conference of 1930 and Supplementary Documents*, Govt. Printing Office, Washington, 1931, and British Foreign Office, *Documents of the London Naval Conference*, 1930, H. M. Stationery Office, London, 1930.

[3] Article I of the London Naval Treaty of 1930. The French and Italian governments had been permitted to lay down certain ships in 1927 and 1929. The right was not exercised, but the privilege was to be retained under the London Treaty.

each of the navies has been growing obsolete. In addition to delaying the date of replacements the parties agreed upon an immediate reduction through the scrapping of existing ships by Great Britain, the United States, and Japan. Great Britain agreed to scrap five capital ships, the United States, three, and Japan, one.[1] This immediate reduction brought the respective navies to a condition more nearly approximating a true 10:10:6 ratio. The effect upon the capital ship strength of the three powers may be shown by the following table:

Country	Capital ships before the London Treaty		Capital ships after* the London Treaty	
	No.	Tonnage	No.	Tonnage
United States.............	18	532,400	15	462,400
Great Britain................	20	608,650	15	474,750
Japan.......................	10	292,400	9	266,070

* Tonnage figures taken from *Treaty on the Limitation of Naval Armaments*, Hearings before the Senate Committee on Foreign Relations, p. 23, Govt. Printing Office, Washington, 1930.

Cruisers. The London Treaty accepted the principle of equivalent naval values to the extent that it regarded a certain tonnage of cruisers mounting 8-inch guns as somewhat higher in its combat value than a similar tonnage of cruisers mounting smaller guns. Cruisers were divided into two subcategories based upon gun calibers rather than tonnage. The subcategories were (a) those with guns of more than 6.1 inches in caliber, and (b) those with guns of 6.1 inches in caliber or less. The limitations for the three principal naval powers were as follows:

Country	Subcategory (a)	Subcategory (b)	Total*
United States................	180,000	143,500	323,500
Great Britain................	146,800	192,200	339,000
Japan.......................	108,400	100,450	208,850

* Art. XVI. The United States was, however, restricted as to its subcategory (a) cruisers in that the last three of these vessels could not be laid down until 1933, 1934, and 1935 and could not be completed before 1936, 1937, and 1938 respectively.

By an examination of the table it can be seen that the United States was given a greater tonnage in the large-gun cruisers and the British, by way of compensation, were given a sufficiently greater tonnage in

[1] Art. II.

the smaller-gun class to offset the combat power of the large guns. For an excess of 33,200 tons on the part of the United States in the large-gun class, Great Britain was given an excess of 48,700 tons in the small-gun class. In this calculation a certain amount of tonnage in subcategory (a) cruisers has a value equal to 1.467 times that of the same tonnage in subcategory (b) cruisers. The United States was given the option, which it did not accept, of limiting its cruisers in subcategory (a) to 150,000 tons. To compensate for this, the United States could then build 15,166 tons of subcategory (b) vessels for each of the three subcategory (a) vessels which it failed to build. The figure 15,166 was purely an arbitrary sum to give the United States and Great Britain an equal cruiser tonnage should the United States choose this option.

Destroyers and Submarines. The destroyer tonnage was limited for the three largest navies as follows: United States, 150,000 tons; Great Britain, 150,000 tons; and Japan, 105,500 tons. The United States had held a substantial lead in destroyer tonnage because this country had specialized in destroyer construction during the World War. This tonnage was becoming obsolete and the American advantage could not have been maintained without considerable new construction. The tonnage of 150,000 which was agreed to in the treaty was little more than half of the 290,304 tons which this country possessed at the time the conference met.

The three powers agreed to equality in submarines with a tonnage for each of 52,700. Japan made a special effort to obtain a position of equality in this class because of the great emphasis placed upon submarines for defensive purposes. The Japanese had a large submarine force of 77,842 tons built and building at the time the conference met which they were hesitant to reduce drastically. They finally agreed to accept the treaty limitations in return for a position of equality.

Ratios. The United States had followed the policy of securing the 10:10:6 ratio as between the three powers. After the treaty this country did not have an equal tonnage with Great Britain and thus the plan for a 10:10 ratio in tonnage was not quite achieved. The United States chose the alternative of a lower total cruiser tonnage in order that it might have a stronger force of subcategory (a) cruisers. In combat power the two navies were reckoned by the naval experts of the American delegation to be substantially equal.

The problem of the ratio with Japan has proved to be a much more difficult matter than that with Great Britain. At the Washington Conference a 10:6 ratio was accepted between the two for capital ships and aircraft carriers. The ratio was made possible, despite the opposition of naval interests in Japan, by the agreement not to increase the fortifications in the Philippines. A larger ratio has been insistently demanded since that time by the Japanese naval groups. In the London Conference the ratio was increased somewhat in certain categories of vessels, and in submarines the Japanese were given equality with the United States. The Japanese are not satisfied with that ratio and, as will be seen, have given notice of the termination of the whole system of ratios of the naval treaties. The ratios between the three powers as fixed by the Washington and London treaties were as follows:

	United States	Great Britain	Japan
Capital ships.................	10	10	6
Aircraft carriers...............	10	10	6
Cruisers, subcategory (a)*.......	10	8.1	6
Cruisers, subcategory (b)........	10	13.4	7
Destroyers...................	10	10	7
Submarines..................	10	10	10

* With regard to the ratio in subcategory (a) cruisers we must remember that three American cruisers cannot be completed before the years 1936, 1937, and 1938. France and Italy signed part of the treaty but did not accept limitations with regard to their cruisers, destroyers, and submarines.

THE APPROACHING END OF THE TREATIES

Provisions for the Termination of the Treaties. By the terms of the Washington Treaty that agreement is to remain in force until the end of 1936 after which time it can be terminated upon two years' notice. This notice has already been given by Japan. The principal armament limitation provisions of the London Treaty expire automatically at the end of 1936. The treaty, looking forward to its own end, made provision for a naval conference to be held in the year 1935 in order to arrange a replacement agreement.

Japan's Dissatisfaction with the Treaties. The militaristic government of Japan has for several years been dissatisfied with the inferior naval ratios allotted to that country. Conversations were held in London during 1934 between the United States, Great Britain, and Japan with the hope that an agreement might be reached which would make possible a successful conference in 1935. At these meetings the Japanese made it clear that they desired equality in naval strength. They proposed that if this were granted they would be willing to agree to a reduction in the tonnage of capital ships and aircraft carriers which they deemed to be aggressive types of vessels. They desired freedom to construct defensive types, as they called them, such as smaller cruisers and submarines, with the sole restriction that they should observe the tonnage limits which might be set for the navy as a whole.[1] The United States refused to concede the Japanese demands and countered with a proposal of equality of security. Since this country has two important coast lines as well as oversea possessions to defend, the superiority which is allowed by the Washington and London treaties was alleged to be necessary in order to give equality in security with Japan which can concentrate her entire navy in the defense of a relatively small area. The United States, therefore, proposed the maintenance of the existing treaty ratios although some reductions in tonnage were suggested.[2] The British government offered a compromise by which the Japanese would be given nominal equality coupled with an informal gentlemen's agreement that they would not build above their Washington and London treaty ratios. But the Japanese, not content with the shell of mere prestige, refused the suggestion.

On December 29, 1934, the Japanese government gave notice of the termination of the Washington Treaty, thus preparing for the end of the agreement on December 31, 1936. The stability in armaments which has been maintained in the Pacific under the two treaties will, therefore, come to an end unless some substitute agreement can be arrived at; and January 1, 1937, looms ahead as an ominous date in the affairs of the Pacific. Suspicions and temptations to armament races and alliances will then be rampant. The United States will be confronted by three alternatives: (1) This country might build a great navy sufficient to contest the supremacy of the Western Pacific with Japan, thus hazarding all the dangers, responsibilities, and wastes of an oversea military policy. (2) The United States might join with Great Britain in a naval bloc which would overshadow the power of Japan without the necessity of expensive building, but such an alliance is apt to prove embarrassing

---

[1] This is called the principle of "global" limitation as opposed to limitation by categories.

[2] For Norman Davis's statement of the American position in a public address of Dec. 6, 1934, see Dept. of State, Press Releases, Dec. 8, 1934, p. 331. For the views of leading naval authorities of the three powers, Sir Herbert W. Richmond, Admiral William V. Pratt, and Admiral Kichisaburo Nomura, see Foreign Affairs, XIII: 45 (October, 1934), XIII: 196 (January, 1935), and XIII: 409 (April, 1935).

inasmuch as the British have many aims in Asia which this country does not share. Some kind of an understanding with Great Britain seems necessary, however, for a bitter Anglo-American rivalry regarding naval matters might well prove to be disastrous. (3) The American policy might be based on the strict principle of national defense, maintaining such armaments as will give this country a satisfactory margin of security against attack. The last of the alternatives, coupled with a careful treatment of Anglo-American relations, would seem to be wise so far as the essential welfare of the American people is concerned.

The Three-power Treaty of 1936. The naval conference which had been provided for in the London treaty met in London in 1935. The Japanese delegation withdrew in the middle of the conference, and the limitation system provided for in the two naval treaties could not be saved. A treaty providing for mild qualitative limitations was, however, signed by the United States, Great Britain, and France in March, 1936, and awaits ratification. By this agreement capital ships are to be limited to 35,000 tons and to gun calibers of 14 inches. The caliber limitation must, however, be agreed to by Japan and Italy to become effective. Aircraft carriers are to be limited to 23,000 tons and submarines to 2,000 tons. Cruisers above 8,000 tons or with guns of more than 6.1 inches are not to be built during the life of the treaty; and small capital ships, that is those of less than 17,500 tons, are not to be constructed. Information as to building programs is to be exchanged. The agreement is to extend until January 1, 1943; but escape clauses are provided in case the national security of the signatories is jeopardized. In addition to signing the treaty the United States and Great Britain exchanged assurances opposing competitive building and reaffirming the principle of parity as between the two nations.

CHAPTER XIX

ARMAMENT LIMITATION: ATTEMPTS MADE AT GENEVA

THE LEAGUE'S PROBLEM

Pledges in the Treaty of Versailles and the United States Treaty with Germany of 1921. The arms question has not only been one of the most difficult with which the League of Nations has been confronted, but it has also been one in which the demand for a solution has been urgent and the dangers of inaction most menacing. Disaster has loomed in the path of failure. The idealism which governments were forced by circumstances to avow to their people during the war found a partial expression at the end of the conflict in a demand that the vast and expensive armaments of the powers should be substantially reduced. The story is told elsewhere[1] of the development of Point Four of President Wilson's famous Fourteen Points into the arms reduction pledge in Article VIII of the Covenant, which reads:

> The Members of the League recognize that the maintenance of peace requires the reduction of armaments to the lowest point consistent with national safety and the enforcement by common action of international obligations.

However indefinite this promise may be, it is certainly an agreement for substantial reduction.

In addition to the clause in the Covenant the preamble of Part V of the Treaty of Versailles, which provided for the wholesale reduction of German armaments, reads as follows:

> In order to render possible the initiation of a general limitation of the armaments of all nations, Germany undertakes strictly to observe the military, naval and air clauses which follow.

The United States, although not a party to the Treaty of Versailles, was involved in the disarmament pledges through President Wilson's Point Four and through the fact that this

[1] See p. 252.

government entered into a separate treaty with Germany in 1921 which gave to the United States the rights and advantages of certain parts of the Treaty of Versailles including Part V. The United States must avail itself of these rights "in a manner consistent with the rights accorded to Germany under such provisions."[1]

The Violation of the Treaty Pledges. Within a few years after the war it became apparent that Germany could not be kept indefinitely in a disarmed condition unless the other nations should comply materially with their promises. The probability that Germany would refuse to endure her restrictions unless progress in reduction should be achieved by other nations made the disarmament work of the League a matter of vital importance to the peace of the world.

In the period of demobilization following the Armistice the belligerents reduced their huge wartime military forces, but most of them retained armaments which were somewhat more expensive and far more destructive in their possibilities than those which they possessed at the outbreak of the World War. Expenditures on armaments shortly after this initial reduction resumed their upward trend. The result was that annual costs were kept above the pre-war level. While the national defense expenditures for the seven great powers amounted to $2,154,000,000 in 1913, they totaled $2,958,800,000 in 1930.[2] The greatest increase occurred in the case of the United States and Japan, the United States having risen from fifth to first place in money spent. The increase in the expenditures of the seven governments amounted to 37 per cent. When the rise in prices is taken into consideration the real increase was not in itself of great significance except that the war to end wars has grossly failed to accomplish the purposes set forth by the Allied leaders. Two additional comments may, however, be made regarding it: In the first place, the increase in the destructive power of armaments was much greater than the increase in costs, owing particularly to the development of chemical and aerial weapons. In the second place, the fact that Germany's military budget was reduced while those of other countries were increased brought about a dangerous lack of equilibrium and a condition of jealousy, suspicion, and frustrated nationalism in Germany which augured ill for world harmony. Since 1930 the expenditures of the powers have

---

[1] *Treaties, etc., of the U.S.*, III: 2598.

[2] STONE, WILLIAM T., "The Burden of Armaments," *Foreign Policy Reports*, Vol. VII, No. 20 (Dec. 9, 1931), p. 368.

been increasing, particularly in the cases of Japan, Russia, Germany, and the United States.[1]

The Machinery of the League.   When the framers of the Covenant in 1919 gave their attention to the task of armament reduction, they had little idea of the complexities and difficulties which lurked ahead.   They provided for a permanent commission which was to advise the Council on military problems.[2]   This body, the Permanent Advisory Commission as it is called, was constituted of three representatives—an army, a navy, and an air expert—from each member of the Council.   The framers of the Covenant intended that the Council, with the advice of the P.A.C., should formulate plans for reduction of armaments, which should be submitted for the consideration of the several governments.   The task was soon found to be far too intricate to be settled in such a manner, and additional machinery for the consideration of the problem was set up.

The first additional body was the Temporary Mixed Commission which was designed to add the civilian view to that of the P.A.C., which body, being loaded with military experts, had been unable to wax sympathetic regarding disarmament.   The T.M.C., consisting of six military experts and sixteen civilians, considered some schemes of direct disarmament but they came to nothing.   The T.M.C. likewise suggested action for indirect disarmament, *i.e.*, the building of machinery for peace and mutual guarantee against aggression for the purpose of creating a greater feeling of security among the nations.   If fears of aggression could be reduced in this way, it was expected that the nations would be much more willing to reduce armaments.   Following a plan prepared by Lord Robert Cecil, the T.M.C. proposed a convention to the Assembly which was drawn up in formal shape in that body as the Draft Treaty of Mutual Assistance of 1923.   The treaty failed of acceptance but was followed by the Protocol of Arbitration, Security, and Disarmament which was drawn up in the Assembly the following year.   The protocol, like the draft treaty, was designed to give security against aggression. It also failed of acceptance, but some of its principles were given a regional application the following year in the Locarno treaty for the mutual guarantee of the Franco-German frontier.

The T.M.C. reported to the Assembly in 1924 and then went out of existence.   In 1925 the Council of the League established the

---

[1] STONE, WILLIAM T., and DAVID H. POPPER, "The Increasing Burden of Armaments," *Foreign Policy Reports*, Vol. X, No. 17 (Oct. 24, 1934), pp. 222–223.

[2] Art. IX of the Covenant.

Preparatory Commission for the Disarmament Conference, which met in 1926. For five years the commission attempted to bring together the various conflicting views regarding disarmament and to construct a provisional draft of a treaty which would make it possible to call a disarmament conference with some hope of success.

The United States entered the League disarmament movement during this period and was represented at the various sessions of the Preparatory Commission. American delegates played an important part in the deliberations of the commission. In 1930 the P.C. hastened its labors and was able to bring the various national views together sufficiently to report a draft convention, which document was, however, subject to reservations by one or more governments in almost every one of its articles. On February 2, 1932, the Conference for the Limitation and Reduction of Armaments convened and held sessions until July 23 of that year. The general commission of the conference, comprising one representative of each delegation, continued to meet from time to time during 1932, 1933, and 1934. Just previous to its meeting in October, 1933, the German government announced its withdrawal from the conference.[1] The commission, faced with this crisis, met on October 16, 1933, adjourned until October 26, and then again adjourned until May 29, 1934. The 1934 session adjourned on June 11 and neither the conference nor the general commission has met since. There have been, however, some meetings of the bureau of the conference and of some of the committees.[2]

The chief reason for the breakdown of the disarmament discussions has been the fear of war in Europe. When the depression and stoppage of loans reduced Germany to a critical condition, the Hitler movement came as a desperate resort of frantic nationalism. With the Nazis in power Germany was no longer willing to wait for the fulfillment of the Versailles pledges of disarmament. Withdrawal from the League and from the Disarmament Conference followed. On March 16, 1935, Herr Hitler gave notice of the

---

[1] The German government had previously withdrawn in 1932 but had been brought back into the conference after some persuasion.

[2] Regarding the work of the League during this period see for secondary sources BAKER, PHILIP J. NOEL, *Disarmament*, Hogarth Press, London, 1926; MADARIAGA, SALVADOR DE, *Disarmament*, Coward-McCann, Inc., New York, 1929; MYERS, DENYS P., *World Disarmament, Its Problems and Prospects*, World Peace Foundation, Boston, 1932. For primary sources, see League of Nations *Official Journal, Records of the Assembly, Documents of the Preparatory Commission for the Disarmament Conference*, and *Records of the Conference*. More specific citations to these documents are found in the following pages.

abrogation of the disarmament clauses of the Treaty of Versailles by announcing that the German army had been increased by law to thirty-six divisions or about five times the strength of 100,000 soldiers permitted under the treaty.   Since that date the machinery of preparation for disarmament has been in a state of paralysis.

AMERICAN DISARMAMENT POLICIES AT GENEVA

Although little has been accomplished in the League disarmament conferences beyond preliminary discussion, the attitude of the United States in these meetings is of importance in a consideration of American foreign policy.   In the Preparatory Commission for the Disarmament Conference, at the conference itself, and in the general commission and bureau of the conference, the United States has contended for certain types of arms reduction and has urged certain principles.   Compromise has seemed to be essential on several matters and throughout the discussion a drift in American attitudes toward closer cooperation can be clearly discerned.   The trend has been toward a mild cooperation with regard to the prevention of war, toward an agreement for supervision, and toward a willingness to admit certain Continental ideas regarding disarmament, such, for example, as the existence of unrestricted reserves outside of the legal effectives.

The Extent of Reduction.   The American position at Geneva has been that prompt and substantial reduction in armaments is highly desirable not only to bring relief to an overtaxed world but also to prevent a violent collapse of the postwar system built upon the treaties that ended the war.   The United States was not willing, however, to support the Russian plan for immediate, complete, and general disarmament to a police basis which was introduced in the Fifth Session of the Preparatory Commission in 1928.   At that time the plan was opposed by the delegates of practically all the other powers.   The French, in particular, were unable to agree with the Russian proposal because it ran contrary to their thesis that security was necessary prior to disarmament. Mr. Gibson, the American delegate, refused also to join with the Soviets against the opposition of the capitalist world.[1]

The desires of the United States for direct disarmament finally crystallized in a policy of attempting to secure a reduction of armaments to a *defense* standard.   The Hoover plan, which was

---

[1] For this discussion see League of Nations, *Documents of the Preparatory Commission for the Disarmament Conference, Minutes of the Fifth Session* (C. 165. M. 50. 1928. IX), pp. 239, 258.

presented as an instruction to the American delegates to the conference on June 22, 1932, set forth as its first principle that under the Briand-Kellogg Pact the nations of the world are agreed to use their arms solely for defense.[1] His plan for abolishing offensive weapons (qualitative disarmament) and reducing military establishments (quantitative disarmament) will be mentioned later. President Roosevelt, in his dramatic message sent to the sovereigns and presidents of the nations participating in the World Economic Conference and the Disarmament Conference on May 16, 1933, elaborated on the policy of reduction to a defense basis as follows:

> If all nations will agree wholly to eliminate from possession and use the weapons which make possible a successful attack, defenses automatically will become impregnable, and the frontiers and independence of every nation will become secure.
>
> The ultimate objective of the Disarmament Conference must be the complete elimination of all offensive weapons. The immediate objective is a substantial reduction of some of these weapons and the elimination of many others.[2]

And on May 22, 1933, Norman Davis explained the aims of the United States to the conference in terms of mutual reduction to a police basis, an aim which does not seem to differ greatly from the intent of the Russian proposal of 1928. Mr. Davis said:

> As regards the level of armaments, we are prepared to go as far as the other states in the way of reduction. We feel that the ultimate objective should be to reduce armaments approximately to the level established by the peace treaties; that is, to bring armaments as soon as possible through successive stages down to the basis of a domestic police force.[3]

Specific Proposals for Reduction toward a Defense Basis. The Hoover plan of June 22, 1932, proposed the abolition of tanks, chemical warfare, large mobile guns, bombing planes, and the prohibition of air bombardment. The strength of the land forces of each country over and above the police component was to be reduced. The police component was defined as the strength required for the maintenance of internal order and was to be

[1] Dept. of State, *Press Releases*, June 25, 1932, p. 593; League of Nations, *Records of the Conference for the Reduction and Limitation of Armaments*, Series B, I: 122, Geneva, 1932. Also the text is given in League of Nations, *Conference for the Reduction and Limitation of Armaments, Conference Documents*, I: 259, Geneva, 1932.

[2] Dept. of State, *Press Releases*, May 20, 1933, p. 352.

[3] *Ibid.*, May 27, 1933, p. 389; *Records of the Conference, Series B., Minutes of the General Commission*, II: 475, Geneva, 1933.

calculated upon the basis of the forces allowed to Germany and the other disarmed states. The strength of the land forces over and above this component was to be diminished by one-third. The number and tonnage of battleships and submarines were to be reduced by one-third. No nation was to retain more than 35,000 tons of submarines. The number and tonnage of aircraft carriers, cruisers, and destroyers were to be cut by one-fourth. The plan received much warm commendation at the conference but was not adopted. It did, however, have its effects upon the MacDonald plan for arms reduction, which was presented later and was supported by the United States.

War Potential. At the commencement of the work of the Preparatory Commission the question arose as to whether the war potential of the various countries should be considered. Plans for modern warfare include the mobilization of much peacetime industrial, commercial, and financial equipment. These are military accessories of the greatest importance; but, as they are the framework of a nation's economic life, no plan for limitation can, of course, be contemplated. Certain countries, such as, France, Italy, Japan, Belgium, Czechoslovakia, Poland, Rumania, and Yugoslavia, which were strong in armaments but less strong in potential, contended that in the fixing of armament limitations the potential should be counted. Other countries, in which the industrial and commercial resources were relatively stronger than the immediate armaments, naturally objected to a consideration of potential. The United States, Great Britain, and Germany were the principal nations of this class. Chile, Finland, the Netherlands, Spain, and Sweden took a similar view. The United States put forth the argument that war potential could hardly be considered as it could not be converted into active armament without long delay. Although this country was at war for nineteen months following April, 1917, only four cannon produced in the United States reached the front before the Armistice.[1] As no agreement on the subject was possible, the matter of war potential was left out of consideration in the draft treaty drawn up by the Preparatory Commission.

[1] Preparatory Commission for the Disarmament Conference, *Report of Subcommission A* (C. 739. M. 278. 1926. IX), p. 20. For a full discussion of the armament lag, that is, of the length of the period which must pass before armaments can be manufactured and assembled after the outbreak of war, see LEFEBURE, VICTOR, *Scientific Disarmament*, The Macmillan Company, New York, 1931.

Budgetary Limitation. The restriction of expenditures has frequently been proposed as one method of limitation of armaments. The reasons are twofold. In the first place, such a limitation would be a relief to the taxpayers; and, in the second place, it would afford a general method of restricting national armaments which might be otherwise difficult to limit by specific measures. Where two national armament systems are dissimilar, one being strong in one kind of arms such as aircraft and the other in a different type such as artillery or warships, it is difficult to set a specific standard of limitation which will be acceptable to both or which will apply with equal justice to both. Budgetary limitation would set a limit without the necessity of stating what particular restrictions were to be placed on each branch of armaments.

The United States at first objected to budgetary limitation because the costs of armaments are higher in this country than abroad. Construction is more expensive and the pay and upkeep per man are greater than in the conscript armies of Europe. The American objection was originally based on the supposition that this country would be limited by the same expense standards as other signatories. It was made clear in the Preparatory Commission, however, that budgetary limitation was not designed to limit one country in comparison with another but in comparison with its own previous expenditures.[1] Another reason behind the American opposition to budgetary limitation is that this country leads the world in national wealth and potential public revenues. Through its ability to spend more, the United States may be able to build better armaments within treaty limitations than its rivals.

On February 9, 1932, shortly after the opening of the Disarmament Conference, Mr. Gibson made certain concessions to budgetary limitation as follows:

We are prepared to consider a limitation of expenditure on material as a complementary method to direct limitation, feeling that it may prove useful to prevent a qualitative race if and when quantitative limitation has been made effective.[2]

---

[1] League of Nations, Preparatory Commission for the Disarmament Conference, *Report by the Committee of Experts on Budgetary Questions* (C. 182. M. 69. 1931. IX), p. 26, Geneva, 1931.

[2] *Records of the Conference for the Reduction and Limitation of Armaments, Series A*, I: 66, Geneva, 1932.

This applied only to limitation on expenditures on material. As to a general limitation of armament expenditures, however, the United States refused to consider the matter. Mr. Gibson was quoted as informing the conference on July 20, 1932, as follows:

Global limitation [of expenditures] had been consistently opposed by the United States Government as applied to itself, since it considered that such a method was unfair to a nation like the United States, which had already drastically reduced its armaments; his Government has made clear that it could not accept such a method for itself.[1]

Thus the United States, which spends more than any other nation on armaments, has been reluctant to give up the advantage of its long purse in the armaments race.

International Supervision. Probably no more striking change has been registered in the American attitude toward disarmament at Geneva than that with regard to the acceptance of the principle of supervision for the purpose of carrying out the terms of an arms convention. The United States, in the beginning, was stanchly opposed to supervision. This country did not desire that any foreign military officials should have the jurisdiction to ascertain the state of American armaments. Furthermore, a supervision plan must inevitably be linked with the League of Nations. American antipathies to the League increased the objections to supervision. In the Third Session of the Preparatory Commission Mr. Gibson did not mince words when he said that supervision was unacceptable. He stated:

In the course of the discussions in the Preparatory Commission and its Sub-Commissions, it has been repeatedly made clear that any Convention, in order to be acceptable to my Government, must take full account of the fact that it cannot accept the jurisdiction of the League, and, further, that it is not in a position to subscribe to international agreements based on supervision and control.[2]

The drift of the United States toward international cooperation is illustrated by the manner in which its attitude has gradually changed on this point. In the draft convention, drawn up in 1930, the United States accepted a plan for supervision which did not mention the League so far as its composition was concerned. The supervising commission was, however, to be set up at the seat of the League, was to be summoned for its first meeting by the Secre-

[1] *Records of the Conference, Series B*, I: 163.
[2] *Minutes of the Third Session* (C. 310. M. 109. 1927. IX), p. 273.

tary-General of the League, and was to receive its information from the signatories of the convention through the Secretary-General.[1]

The agreement of the United States to the principle of supervision in the draft convention represented the beginning of a more cooperative attitude. As the feeling between France and Germany over armaments grew more tense it became apparent that supervision was absolutely necessary if the controversy were to be solved. France would not accept a treaty knowing that Germany might build up large armaments without detection. The United States, in its desire to solve this difficulty, expressed more clearly its approval of supervision. In his address before the general commission of the Disarmament Conference on May 22, 1933, Mr. Davis supported the idea with enthusiasm. He said:

> Finally, we believe that a system of adequate supervision should be formulated to insure the effective and faithful carrying out of any measure of disarmament. We are prepared to assist in this formulation and to participate in this supervision. We are heartily in sympathy with the idea that means of effective, automatic, and continuous supervision should be found whereby nations will be able to rest assured that as long as they respect their obligations with regard to armaments the corresponding obligations of their neighbors will be carried out in the same scrupulous manner.[2]

In November, 1934, the United States delegation presented to the bureau of the Disarmament Conference a plan for the regulation of the manufacture and traffic in arms which contained proposals for a Permanent Disarmament Commission with powers of publicity and investigation.[3] Thus, on the matter of supervision, the United States has progressed from strong opposition to acquiescence and then to hearty support.

Naval Disarmament. The question of limitation of naval armaments has been dealt with in the Washington and London conferences. The matter has also arisen at Geneva for two reasons: (1) minor naval countries which are not parties to the Washington and London treaties have been represented in the League conferences; and (2) the Continental view of disarmament is that the movement must involve simultaneously all major armament

[1] Part VI of the Draft Convention drawn up by the Preparatory Commission in 1930.

[2] Dept. of State, *Press Releases*, May 27, 1933, p. 390; *Records of the Conference, Series B., Minutes of the General Commission*, II: 475.

[3] See pp. 381–382.

questions. Such countries as France, representing the European view, have continually emphasized that the matter of naval forces must be dealt with in the general consideration of armaments.

One of the first questions to arise concerning naval armaments was whether disarmament should proceed by the category method or by global limitation. The category method would fix definite tonnage figures for each of the naval categories, *i.e.*, capital ships, aircraft carriers, cruisers, destroyers, and submarines. Under the global system a total tonnage figure would be given for each power which could then adjust in its own way the tonnage figures for the various categories, keeping, of course, within its general tonnage allotment. The large naval powers preferred limitation by categories so that a stability would be maintained in each class of ships.[1] The smaller powers desired global or total tonnage limitation without specification as to categories. This would permit them to concentrate their construction upon any one category.[2]

The United States, as one of the great naval powers, argued strongly for the category system of limitation. After considerable discussion, however, the American delegation agreed to accept as the basis of discussion a compromise by which warships were to be limited in tonnage for each category, subject to the proviso that transfers of tonnage could be made from one category to another upon formal notice. The transfers were, however, to be limited in amounts.[3]

Attempts have been made at Geneva to restrict the size of warships, particularly capital ships and cruisers. The Washington Treaty limits capital ships to 35,000 tons and to guns of 16 inches. Practically all the powers except the United States have expressed a desire or a willingness to reduce the maximum size of these ships. American naval men have tenaciously contended that large ships are necessary for this country. The United States, almost the last friend of the large battleship, is able to build these expensive monsters with greater ease than other countries.

Limitation of Land Material. The Continental states of the French group, with their large conscript reserves, have opposed

---

[1] The Japanese changed their attitude somewhat on this question in 1934. See p. 350.

[2] For this dispute see *Report of Subcommission A*, pp. 53, 128; Preparatory Commission, *Minutes of the Third Session*, pp. 163*ff.*

[3] See Preparatory Commission, *Minutes of the Sixth Session (First Part)* (C. 195. M. 74. 1929. IX), p. 56. This compromise was included in the draft convention of 1930, Chapter B, Table 3.

the limitation of land material. They have feared that such limitation would deprive them of the immense stocks of arms which are necessary to equip their huge armies in case of mobilization. The German[1] and Russian delegations have led the fight for a strict limitation of land material. The United States has, in the main, adhered to the limitation group. In the final session of the Preparatory Commission, the United States voted for direct limitation; and later, as has been pointed out, the delegation showed a willingness to accept also a plan for budgetary limitation of such armaments. The United States, in supporting the Hoover and MacDonald plans, has also urged the abolition of certain kinds of material which are said to be "offensive" in character.

Reserves. The American military policy, under which a small professional army is recruited by voluntary enlistments and is supported by the national guard and a skeleton reserve, is in sharp contrast to the conscription systems of Continental Europe. The European plans provide not only for large standing armies but also for large reserves of partly trained soldiers which can be mobilized on short notice. The able-bodied young men in those countries must spend a certain period in the army and then take their places in the reserves. At the beginning of the discussions in the Preparatory Commission at Geneva the American delegates supported the proposal to limit the number of trained reserves. As can be readily imagined, the French group opposed such limitation. In the sixth session of the commission the United States, in the interests of compromise and harmony, expressed a willingness to withdraw its demand for the limitation of reserves.[2]

Methods and Material of Aerial Warfare. In Europe the threat of aerial attack is a real and terrible danger. The annual maneuvers of the various countries include large-scale aircraft and antiaircraft demonstrations, and the public is instructed in gas defense. Should another desperate world war occur, it would probably be far more devastating than the last because of the improvements in aircraft design and the increase in the number of planes. It is further probable that the distinction between civil and military populations would be disregarded and that wholesale slaughter of men, women, and children in the large cities and centers of commerce and industry would result.

---

[1] This policy was followed by the German government so long as it felt bound by the Versailles restrictions.

[2] *Minutes of the Sixth Session (First Part)*, p. 114.

In order to humanize future wars, a plan to abolish aerial bombardment was proposed in the Preparatory Commission by the German delegation.[1] The French delegates opposed such a prohibition. The United States joined in opposition at that time because the proposal would have introduced an exceedingly complicated problem at an inopportune time. Later, in the Hoover proposal, the United States advocated the prohibition of all bombardment from the air and the abolition of all bombing planes. "This," said President Hoover, "will do away with the military types of planes capable of attacks upon civilian populations." The British plan, which received the support of the United States, went further. It not only suggested the abolition of bombing from the air and a direct limitation of planes but also proposed that a Permanent Disarmament Commission should work out a scheme for "the complete abolition of military and naval aircraft." This abolition, however, was to be dependent on the effective supervision of civil aviation to prevent its misuse for military purposes.

The Control of Civil Aviation. This latter suggestion brings up one of the most difficult matters in connection with the arms question, that is, the provision of assurance that if military planes are limited the countries with large civil aviation industries will not convert them to military use and thereby gain an overwhelming arms superiority. It would, of course, be both impossible and undesirable to restrict the rapidly expanding civil aviation industry. Because of its great potential military value, however, the countries which do not possess an important civil aviation industry desire that it should in some way be prevented from becoming available for military purposes. France, with a strong force of military planes and a weak civil aviation industry, showed in the discussions a strong aversion to limiting military planes unless some guarantee against civil planes could be had. Germany, on the other hand, which was forbidden to possess military planes but which had a well-developed system of aerial transportation, naturally opposed any regulation of civil aviation. The United States, which likewise possessed a large and rapidly growing civil aviation industry, took sides with Germany. At first this country opposed in a categorical manner the consideration of civil aviation.[2] When the draft treaty was completed in 1930, it contained some proposals of limitation, however, which stipulated that military features should not be

[1] *Ibid.*, p. 85.

[2] Preparatory Commission, *Minutes of the Third Session*, p. 110.

embodied in civil aircraft, that civil aviation companies should not be required to employ personnel specifically trained for military purposes, that the parties to the treaty should not subsidize air lines principally established for military ends, and that they should undertake to encourage economic agreements between civil aviation in the different countries. The United States signed the treaty without reservations as to these rather weak stipulations. The last provision as to the encouragement of economic agreements between civil aviation in the different countries would probably accomplish little; but the principle behind it, *i.e.*, the internationalization of civil aviation, is, in the minds of many who have studied the difficulties of the question, the best approach to a solution of the baffling problem.

The Prohibition of Chemical Warfare. Another proposal for the protection of civil populations in future wars is to prohibit chemical and bacteriological warfare. The United States signed treaties forbidding this kind of warfare in 1922 at the Washington Conference and in 1925 at the Geneva Traffic in Arms Conference. The first of these treaties failed to become effective through the failure of France to ratify it, and the second failed largely because of the unwillingness of the United States Senate to consent to its ratification. That the executive branch of the American government is committed to the idea, however, is shown by the fact that this government has not only signed the two treaties above mentioned but has affixed its signature also to the draft treaty of 1930 which would have prohibited the use of poison gas. The Hoover plan of 1932 reiterated the desire for the abolition of chemical warfare; and the MacDonald plan of 1933, which was supported by the United States, contained a similar stipulation.

Publicity. The clause in Article VIII of the Covenant of the League of Nations binding the members to exchange "full and frank information as to the scale of their armaments, their military, naval, and air programs, and the condition of such of their industries as are adaptable to warlike purposes" is American in origin.[1] The principle has been put into partial operation in the annual publication by the League of the *Armaments Year Book*. Some statistics are withheld by many governments, such as the figures for land material in both service and reserve. The United States has been a consistent advocate of full publicity. Provisions were made in the draft treaty of 1930 for publicity for most items but information regarding land and air material was not included.

[1] See p. 252.

The United States Has Swerved toward Indirect Disarmament.
The American government at first gave no indication of joining in
cooperative plans for security which would make reductions in armaments possible. In the latter part of the Coolidge administration
and during the terms of President Hoover and President Roosevelt,
the United States has moved slowly and very cautiously toward
the world system of security. The measures approved during this
time are discussed elsewhere, but they should be briefly recapitu-
lated here as they have played no small part in our relationship to
the disarmament movement. The Pact of Paris and the Hoover-
Stimson doctrine enforcing the pact were largely American in origin
and were advocated without reference to the disarmament conference. The promise to consult, the willingness to agree not
to interfere with cooperative action of other countries in punishing
an aggressor should we agree as to the identity of the aggressor, the
willingness to agree to supervision, and the proposal of a nonaggression pact were all substantial changes in American policy
brought about because of American desire to contribute to the
success of the limitation of armaments.

CHAPTER XX

THE CONTROL OF THE ARMS TRAFFIC

THE NEED OF INTERNATIONAL CONTROL

Closely connected with disarmament is the matter of control of the traffic in arms. Considering the enormous destructiveness of modern implements of warfare, it seems clear that from the standpoint of civilization the distribution of such weapons over the face of the earth should be subject to intelligent supervision. Again, considering the strength of national rivalries for supremacy in arms production, it would appear to be logical that such control cannot be instituted by individual nations but that it must be international and cooperative in character. The obstacles against the acceptance by the community of nations of these obvious conclusions are serious. War dangers, both real and imagined, make it difficult to take action for the weakening or reduction of the arms and munitions factories, which are such an important part of armament potential. The arms industry, operating upon a profit basis, is full of energy in seeking markets for the sale of the instruments of death. Its agents and lobbyists gather at the capitals of all nations, searching for contracts, opposing restrictive legislation, and sometimes promoting conditions which lead to war.

An excellent illustration of the promiscuous and nonnational nature of the arms maker is seen in the cosmopolitan career of the great inventor of machine guns, Hiram Stevens Maxim. Maxim was born in the United States and learned the trade of the machinist. At one time while on a business trip to Europe he was advised: "If you wish to make a pile of money, invent something which will enable these Europeans to cut each other's throats with greater facility."[1] Maxim remained in Europe and perfected his machine gun which reloads and fires from the energy of its own recoil. He became a British subject and was knighted for his achievement. He sold his patents internationally to all buyers. According to Maxim's claim this revolutionary weapon was responsible for the deaths of two-thirds of the Japanese killed in the Russo-Japanese

[1] Quoted from LEFEBURE, VICTOR, *Scientific Disarmament*, p. 175, The Macmillan Company, New York, 1931.

367

War. The gun was sold to Spain prior to the Spanish-American War and was also used to some extent by the Boers against the British. At the outbreak of the World War Germany possessed about 50,000 of the guns. Major Lefebure states that the Maxim gun was responsible for the deaths of hundreds of thousands of British soldiers. To make realistic the effect of the inventor's handiwork, he quotes the description of a bloody shambles in a barbed-wire entanglement along a hillside where a division had twice been hurled back by hidden machine guns and where khaki-clad English boys lay thick as "flies on a fly-paper."[1] Thousands of Americans were likewise slain by this same invention. Thus a profit-seeking, expatriated American and knighted British subject produced the means to destroy both Englishmen and Americans. The weapons which were the product of his genius desolated the homes of Japanese, Russians, Serbs, Rumanians, and others whose connection with his automatic gun had never entered his mind when he was demonstrating its accuracy and rapidity of fire before generals, princes, and emperors.

The promiscuity and uncontrollability of the arms traffic have created a most menacing situation in the modern world. The character of the trade was well summarized by a critic of the arms business, George Seldes, when he said:

> The Harveys, Zaharoffs, Schneiders, Krupps, Vickers and Armstrongs, it is all too evident, had no thought but profit when they cooperated in arming the world, when they exchanged patents and secrets, when they spurred nations, including their own, into the armaments race.[2]

The Munitions Investigation of 1934–1936. One of the most useful services rendered in connection with the discussion of the arms traffic was the recent investigation of the munitions industry by the special committee of the United States Senate. Much of the sham of patriotism and idealism was stripped away from the business, and the way in which private profits have stirred an uncontrolled business to promote the slaughter of human beings was laid bare. The committee, under the chairmanship of Senator Gerald P. Nye, held its sessions from 1934 until 1936. The hearings brought forth a great wealth of evidence to illustrate the

---

[1] For a discussion of the machine gun and its effects see LEFEBURE, *op. cit.;* MAXIM, SIR HIRAM S., *My Life*, McBride, Nast & Company, New York, 1915; ENGELBRECHT, H. C., and F. C. HANIGHEN, *Merchants of Death*, pp. 85*ff.*, Dodd, Mead & Company, New York, 1934.

[2] *Iron, Blood and Profits*, p. 27, Harper & Brothers, New York, 1934.

well-known characteristics of the armaments industry.[1] The testimony emphasized that:

1. The armament firms have wielded an influence on national policies through the promotion of armament appropriations and through opposition to arms embargoes and disarmament. Embargoes have been circumvented. Bribery has sometimes been resorted to. Lobbies have been maintained.

2. The munitions business is international in character. Patents and sales agreements have been entered into between the industries of different countries. Profits have been divided. Armament races between friendly nations have been stimulated and munitions have been sold simultaneously to both sides in times of war.[2]

AIMS AND METHODS OF CONTROL

Objects. Before coming to a detailed study of the action of the United States upon various international proposals, some of the principles which affect the problem are deserving of mention. There have been three main reasons for the control of the arms traffic:

1. Regulation has been sought to prevent disorders and revolutions in colonies, mandates, protectorates, spheres of influence, and other backward areas in which the powers have a particular interest. Efforts have been made to subject the traffic in these areas and adjacent territories to special regulation in order to prevent arms from falling into the hands of revolutionists and malcontents. The European powers have been most interested in stopping the traffic in Africa. The United States has been indifferent about Africa but anxious and zealous to keep arms shipments from revolutionists in the Caribbean and Central America.

2. The attempt to draft a thoroughgoing disarmament treaty brings up the necessity of limiting and supervising the quantity of war material in each country. To do this effectively, the manufacture and imports of war material from year to year must be known to the supervising body and must be kept under strict control by each government which has obligations to perform under the disarmament treaty.

3. Various movements are also under way to control the shipment of arms from neutral countries during times of war. There are two distinct theories controlling these proposals. In the first place, the view has been strongly advanced that neutral nations

[1] See the report of the hearings, published under the title *Munitions Industry.*

[2] See Stone, William T., "The Munitions Industry, An Analysis of the Senate Investigation, September 4–21, 1934," *Foreign Policy Reports*, Vol. X, No. 20 (rev. ed.) (Jan. 21, 1935).

should not export arms to either of the belligerents.   The laws of neutrality should be so extended, according to this view, that the shipment of arms by private individuals or corporations in neutral countries would be regarded as an unneutral act, just as the shipment of arms by neutral *governments* has long been held to be unneutral.   In the second place, there has been a movement afoot since the World War to enforce the world's treaty obligations against war by designating the aggressor nation in case of conflict and by placing an embargo against shipments to that nation, while, at the same time, permitting shipments to the other belligerent, that is, to the victim of the aggression.

Methods.   The methods of control which have been proposed in the numerous conferences held upon the subject have been the following:

1. *Control over Manufacturing.*   In order that governments may successfully trace imports, exports, and sales, and enforce treaty obligations, the unrestricted and secret manufacture of arms must be prevented.   If a free and unlimited system of production should prevail, it would be impossible for the government adequately to prevent the activities of illicit gunrunners.   Two general plans to control manufacturing have been suggested.   (*a*) The extreme measure of abolishing the private manufacture of arms has been advocated.   A governmental monopoly on arms production would not only eliminate the profit motive from the business but would also place the state in full control of arms shipments from the beginning.   Woodrow Wilson, probably sickened by defending the legality of the American trade from 1914 to 1917, proposed the abolition of private manufacture in his drafts of the Covenant of the League of Nations.[1]   The Paris Conference, however, rejected the plan and substituted in the Covenant (Article VIII) a statement that private manufacture "is open to grave objections."   The Council of the League of Nations was given the duty of advising as to how the evils of the system could be prevented.   (*b*) A less drastic plan, which has been the center of discussion in the postwar conferences, is that of license and publicity.   The plans to achieve this have generally provided that any private companies which manufacture arms must be licensed by the governments.   Figures are to be made public regarding the quantity of arms manufactured and stocks of arms.   It has been suggested that holders of licenses should not be in a position to influence the policies of newspapers

[1] See p. 253.

and that a director or manager of a munitions company should not be a member of a legislature.[1]

2. *Control over Traffic.* A principal feature of projects for traffic restriction is the right of the government of the exporting state to be informed of shipments and to pass upon their legitimacy. The license to export, according to what seems to be the consensus of expert opinion, should be signed or endorsed by an official of the government of the exporting country. The government of the importing country should also have control of shipments. Export licenses should be issues only upon authorization of the importing government and shipments should be made only to the government of the importing country or to associations or individuals approved by it. Full publicity concerning the shipments ought to be made through an international body which would receive its data from both the governments of the exporting and importing countries. In the case of restricted zones further regulations have been projected. The rule regarding African traffic, for example, provides that imports shall take place only through designated ports and that imported arms shall be deposited in publicly controlled warehouses.

CHANGES IN AMERICAN POLICY

Influences against Cooperation. In the United States large and influential industries have exerted pressures against control. This country has been one of the foremost of the arms and munitions exporting nations. In the period of American neutrality during the World War American firms were busy supplying the Allies with munitions. The export of explosives, which amounted to $6,272,197 during the last prewar year ending June 30, 1914, rose to $802,789,327 for the year ending June 30, 1917. In other words, in three years the export business in explosives as measured in dollars and cents was multiplied 128 times. The export of firearms increased from $3,442,297 to $95,470,009 during the same period. Forty per cent of the propellent powder used by the Allies during the World War was supplied by the E. I. Du Pont de Nemours Powder Company of Wilmington, Del.[2] The published earnings of the Du Pont company went up from $4,997,772.55 in 1914 to

[1] League of Nations, *Report of Temporary Mixed Commission for the Reduction of Armaments,* July 30, 1924 (A. 16. 1924. IX), p. 22.

[2] *Munitions Industry,* Part 5, p. 1038. See also *Encyclopaedia Britannica* (14th ed.), 7: 748, article on E. I. Du Pont de Nemours & Company by Lammot Du Pont.

$82,107,692.55 in 1916.[1] The company declared 100 per cent
dividends in 1916;[2] and, when Congress passed an act to collect a
12½ per cent tax on these swollen earnings of the death traffic,
the president of the corporation deplored the fact that "the United
States government has made our stockholders victims of excessive
taxation."[3]

For the years from 1920 to 1930 inclusive the United States
ranked second in the export of arms and ammunition. The
figures for the exports of the principal manufacturing countries
during these eleven years were as follows:

Great Britain	$179,729,000
United States	155,510,100
France	124,638,900
Czechoslovakia	29,825,600*

* STONE, WILLIAM T., "International Traffic in Arms and Ammunition," *Foreign Policy
Reports*, Vol. IX, No. 12 (Aug. 16, 1933), p. 139.

The firearms industry, largely centered in Connecticut, has been
a strong factor in persuading the United States government to
abstain from controlling the exports of arms. The Winchester
Repeating Arms Company, Colt's Patent Fire Arms Manufacturing
Company, and the Remington Arms Company have all lobbied
against control and have been assisted in their opposition by
Connecticut congressmen. In recent years the airplane industry
and the chemical manufacturing companies have come to their aid.
The War and Navy departments have also presented views in
opposition to control arguing from the principle that, as the United
States depends upon private companies for munitions in times of
war, any action which would tend to injure the munitions industry
would be detrimental to national defense.[4]

In the decade of the 1920's, particularly during the reaction of
the Harding administration against the League of Nations, the
United States refused to participate in the movement to regulate
the arms business. This country did not desire to supervise arms

[1] *Munitions Industry*, Part 5, p. 1278.

[2] *Ibid.*, Part 5, p. 1039.

[3] *N.Y. Times*, Feb. 14, 1917; *Munitions Industry*, Part 5, p. 1044.

[4] Statements opposing restrictions on exports made by representatives of
these various industries and also by representatives of the War and Navy
departments will be found in the Hearings before the Committee on Foreign
Affairs, House of Representatives, on the *Exportation of Arms, Munitions or
Implements of War to Belligerent Nations*, Govt. Printing Office, Washington,
1929, and a similar hearing on the *Exportation of Arms or Munitions of War*,
Govt. Printing Office, Washington, 1933.

manufacture and continually explained that it was constitutionally impossible for the Federal government to deal with manufacturing. As for the attempt to regulate international *commerce* in arms, much fault was found with all the proposed treaties. Extraordinary concern was shown for the plight of countries which did not manufacture arms but which were dependent upon imports. These, it was contended, should not be unduly handicapped in their national defense requirements. The United States, furthermore, let it be known that this country would not associate with any international control group set up in connection with the League of Nations.

The Drift toward Cooperation. Strong forces which pressed the United States in the direction of international governmental action gradually brought about a substantial change in American policy. As the decade of the 1920's dragged along, it was found convenient that this country should be associated with League action in many fields, such as drug control, economic matters, and disarmament. The League lost much of its terror in American politics. The societies which were interested in peace and which numbered millions of members upon their lists made a special attack upon the arms industry. It took, in their eyes, the form of a personal devil, embodying all the evils of the war system. The government gradually accepted the principle of control. By 1933 the policy of the United States was strikingly different from that which had been adhered to in the administration of Warren G. Harding. The constitutionality and desirability of the control of arms manufacture was now admitted. This country was now willing to accept an overseeing body which had some connection with the League of Nations. In other words, the principles of governmental control and international supervision had triumphed over *laissez faire* and isolation. The detailed steps in this significant evolution of attitude are set forth in the following pages.

CONFERENCES AND TREATIES

Brussels, 1890. In 1890 the United States signed and in 1892 ratified the General Act of the Brussels Conference for the Repression of the African Slave Trade. One portion of the act dealt with the traffic in arms. A large prohibited zone was marked out in Africa between the twentieth parallel of north latitude and the twenty-second parallel of south latitude, extending from the Atlantic to the Indian Ocean and comprising the greater part of the continent. The traffic in arms in this zone was placed under governmental control. Modern rifles and ammunition, it was provided, must be placed in publicly controlled warehouses and could be withdrawn only for governmental or restricted private use. Only flintlocks, unrifled guns, and common gunpowder could be bought and sold privately.[1] The exception gave the natives a supply of old-fashioned arms for hunting and for protection against animals. This convention was not entirely successful. The traffic in the old-fashioned rifles was considerable and there was some gunrunning in the more modern firearms, particularly through Ethiopia which was not a party to the act.[2] Attempts were made to obtain a more effective treaty, covering a larger zone and placing control in the hands of international bureaus; but the efforts failed.[3] The United States had no particular concern in the arms control part of the convention as a political matter but was sympathetic to the movement to prevent the sale of arms for the equipment of slave raiders. The Italian government in 1895, shortly before the Battle of Adowa, requested the United States to prohibit the introduction of arms into Ethiopia.[4] Congress, however, did not pass the legislation necessary to enforce the terms of the convention as against American citizens although the treaty pledged this country to enact legislation and such action had been recommended to Congress by the President.

Saint-Germain, 1919. Following the World War a serious situation with regard to the arms traffic was threatened. A condition of unrest prevailed in many dependent territories. Large surplus stocks of arms and ammunition existed in European and American commercial centers. Governments and private manufacturers alike were ready to sell consignments in various parts of the world. The victorious Allies, who hoped to maintain the new world order, were anxious to place the arms traffic under restriction because of its threat to the tranquillity of colonies and mandates. A new treaty for arms control was accordingly signed at Saint-Germain-en-Laye in 1919.[5]

[1] Arts. VIII–XIV, *Treaties, etc., of the U.S.*, II: 1970–1973.

[2] BEER, GEORGE LOUIS, *African Questions at the Paris Peace Conference*, p. 235, The Macmillan Company, New York, 1923.

[3] A drastic protocol was in effect between certain of the powers from 1908 to 1912. KEITH, ARTHUR BERRIEDALE, *The Belgian Congo and the Berlin Act*, pp. 216–217, Oxford University Press, 1919.

[4] *Foreign Relations*, 1895, Part II, p. 960. See also *Moore's Digest*, II: 470–472.

[5] The text is published in *Treaties, etc., of the U.S.*, III: 3752.

The Saint-Germain convention was much broader than that of Brussels and provided that the export of certain types of weapons, including artillery, small arms, and ammunition, should be prohibited except that the governments could issue licenses for export to meet their own requirements or those of any of the high contracting parties. It did not permit the licensing of shipments to governments not parties to the treaty. A Central International Office was to be set up under the control of the League of Nations. The central office was given the duty to collect all documents exchanged by the high contracting parties with regard to the trade in arms. Prohibited zones were established in (1) the whole of Africa, except Algeria, Libya, and the Union of South Africa; (2) Transcaucasia, Persia, Gwadar, the Arabian Peninsula, and such continental parts of Asia as were included in the Turkish Empire on August 4, 1914; and (3) a maritime zone including the Red Sea, the Gulf of Aden, the Persian Gulf, and the Sea of Oman. No arms could be sent into the prohibited zones without special license. A system of public warehouses, similar to that in the Brussels act, was likewise provided for.

American Objections to the Saint-Germain Treaty. The United States signed the treaty; but, with the coming of the Harding administration, ratification was refused. After two requests had been made by the president of the Council of the League of Nations to ascertain the objections of the United States, the Secretary of State replied in a letter of November 12, 1923, summarizing his opposition to the convention. As the objections seem to be typical of the attitude of the United States toward arms control in the immediate post-Wilson period, the letter is herewith quoted at some length, as follows:

After a careful examination of the terms of the Convention, it has been decided that the objections found thereto render impossible ratification by this Government.

While the application of the Convention to certain designated areas or zones, extending in effect the Brussels Convention, may fulfill a useful object, the plan of the present Convention is much broader. The distinctive feature of this plan is not a provision for a general limitation of armament but the creation of a system of control by the signatory Powers of the traffic in arms and munitions, these signatory Powers being left free not only to meet their own requirements in the territories subject to their jurisdiction but also to provide for supplying each other with arms and munitions to the full extent that they may see fit.

There is particular objection to the provisions by which the contracting parties would be prohibited from selling arms and ammunitions to States not parties to the Convention. By such provisions this Government would be required to prevent shipment of military supplies to such Latin American countries as have not signed or adhered to the Convention, however desirable it might be to permit such shipments, merely because they are not signatory Powers and might not desire to adhere to the Convention.[1]

It should be observed also that the acceptance by the United States of an agreement of the nature and scope of the Convention of Saint-Germain would call for the enactment of legislation to make it operative and particularly for the imposition of penalties applicable to private arms producing concerns as a means of establishing an effective control. *This Government is not in a position to undertake the enactment of such legislation.*

Finally, it may be observed that the *provisions of the Convention relating to the League of Nations are so intertwined with the whole Convention as to make it impracticable for this Government to ratify, in view of the fact that it is not a Member of the League of Nations.*[2]

The position of the United States regarding the arms traffic as above expressed is to be contrasted with that regarding the drug traffic which was being set forth at the same time. With regard to drugs the United States was not a producer of raw opium but was a principal victim of the traffic in opium derivatives. This country was, therefore, the outstanding advocate of drug control. With regard to arms a contrary situation existed. The United States was a great producer, but not an immediate victim of the sort of traffic which the Saint-Germain convention sought to prevent. The American government, owing to this contrast in motives, found that it could constitutionally control drug manufacturers in this country but could not lay a hand on arms manufacturers. The reasons for the rejection of the convention can be summarized as lack of practical interest, the pressure of arms companies, the desire to sell arms to Latin-American governments for use against revolutionists, constitutional objections to the regulation of manufacturers, and an unwillingness to associate with the League of Nations.

Geneva, 1925. After 1919 the League of Nations took up the work of attempting to control the arms traffic and the problem was turned over to the Temporary Mixed Commission. Since it was generally admitted that the refusal of the United States, a

---

[1] On several occasions the United States government has itself sold arms to Latin-American countries to defeat revolutionists, *i.e.*, to Cuba, 1917, to Mexico, 1924, and to Nicaragua, 1927.

[2] League of Nations, *Conference for the Control of the International Trade in Arms, Munitions and Implements of War* (C. 758. M. 258, 1924 IX), p. 13. The italics are the author's.

chief arms manufacturer, to ratify the Saint-Germain convention had made it impossible for other countries to regulate the international traffic, the League made efforts to bring the United States into a conference in which an acceptable convention could be agreed upon by all parties. The American minister to Switzerland —at first Joseph C. Grew and later Hugh S. Gibson—acted in the capacity of observer during some of the sessions of the T.M.C. Finally a draft convention was drawn up which was submitted to a general conference of delegates at Geneva in 1925, known as the International Conference for the Supervision of the International Trade in Arms and Munitions.

The American Position at Geneva. The attitude of the American delegates to the 1925 conference, Congressman Theodore E. Burton and Minister Hugh S. Gibson, was, in general, one of cooperation in seeking a convention to regulate traffic in arms through export licenses and through publicity by the governments. They refused to accept, however, some of the most important projects for regulation. They further refused to consider the regulation of manufacturing. Previously, during the sessions of the T.M.C., it had been made clear that the American observers were there to discuss traffic and not manufacturing.[1] At the Geneva conference Mr. Burton argued against a proposal, favored by some of the nonproducing countries, that the convention regarding traffic should not go into effect until a convention on manufacturing should be adopted. He praised the system of private manufacture as a flexible one which could expand in war and contract in peace. He said that the American delegation had come to Geneva with the understanding, gained in the discussions of the T.M.C., that traffic was to be considered entirely separately from manufacture.[2] On various occasions the American delegation set forth the basic contention that the private manufacture of arms was important to the national defense of the United States and that the legitimate interests of the industry must be protected.[3] The United States did, however, argue for publicity regarding the statistics of manufacture and traffic. The American delegation pointed out that this country already published production statistics.[4]

[1] *Conference for the Control of the International Trade in Arms, etc.*, p. 47.

[2] League of Nations, *Proceedings of the Conference for the Supervision of the International Trade in Arms and Ammunition and in Implements of War* (A. 13. 1925. IX), p. 251.

[3] *Ibid.*, pp. 282, 653.

[4] *Ibid.*, p. 299.

A proposal to create an international office to be placed under the supervision of the League of Nations was again opposed by the United States.[1] Congressman Burton submitted a plan for an independent international office to be constituted of representatives nominated by certain enumerated powers. As the members of the League of Nations represented at the conference objected to a central office which was outside of the League, no office could be agreed upon. After this important feature was eliminated from the convention, the much less satisfactory plan of separate publicity by each signatory power was provided in its place.

Terms of the 1925 Convention. The convention as finally agreed upon classified arms into five categories: (1) arms, ammunition, and implements of war exclusively designed for warfare; (2) arms and ammunition capable of use for both military and other purposes; (3) war vessels and their armaments; (4) aircraft and aircraft engines; and (5) gunpowder and explosives, except common black gunpowder; arms and ammunition without military value.

According to the terms of the treaty the parties agree not to permit the export of articles in category 1 unless for the direct supply of the government of the importing state or, with the consent of the government, to a public authority subordinate to it. The governments to which arms may be shipped are not limited to parties to the treaty, and one of the objections of the United States to the Saint-Germain convention is thus eliminated. In certain cases, with the consent of the government, shipments may also be permitted to private arms manufacturers or private associations. The authorities of the exporting state must issue a license for the exportation or approve an export declaration. In either case the document shall contain the names and addresses of the exporters and importers and a description of the articles shipped. Shipments in this category also require an order signed or endorsed by a representative of the importing state which must be presented to the authorities of the exporting state before the issuance of the export authorization. The parties to the treaty agree to publish quarterly statistics of their foreign trade in the articles of categories 1 and 2.

Articles of category 2 also require an export license or an export declaration approved by the government of the exporting state. If the laws of the importing government require it, an endorsement must be obtained from an agent of the importing country before the export may take place. Whenever on account of the size or

[1] *Ibid.*, p. 223.

destination of the shipment it appears that it is destined for war
purposes, the provisions regarding category 1 will be put into effect.
Shipments will not then be permitted except to governments or
authorized associations and an endorsement of the government
of the importing country will be compulsory. Publicity of construction is the chief requirement for category 3. Articles in categories 4
and 5 may be exported without restriction except with regard to
the prohibitions and regulations for special zones.

Special zones are set aside for particular regulation. One of
these includes the African continent with the exception of Egypt,
Libya, Tunisia, Algeria, the Spanish possessions in North Africa,
Ethiopia, the Union of South Africa with its mandated territory, and Southern Rhodesia. Another covers the Arabian peninsula, Gwadar, Syria, and Lebanon, Palestine and Transjordan, and
Iraq. A third zone includes a maritime district embracing the Red
Sea, the Gulf of Aden, the Persian Gulf, and the Gulf of Oman.
The zones are designed to protect Africa and the Class A mandates
from the gunrunner and to buttress the African zone by guarding
against the arms dealer in Arabia and adjacent waters. In these
areas a strict system of control is used for articles in categories 1, 2,
4, and 5. Export licenses or declarations are required. The parties
to the convention which have jurisdiction over the territories in the
zones agree to prohibit importation except upon authorization
of the officials of the territory. Authorized importations shall take
place only through certain ports or other places to be designated
by the authorities of the importing country. Whether such arms
are sent to territories which are under the jurisdiction of parties
to the treaty or not, the government of the exporting country must
be satisfied of the lawfulness of the intended use.[1]

Ratification by the United States. The Hoover and Roosevelt
administrations made special efforts to secure senatorial consent to
ratification. In 1933 President Hoover sent a special message to
the Senate urging favorable action by that body, but there was no
response. In 1934 the problem was attacked with new energy
by the leaders of the Democratic administration. Secretary Hull
urged the Committee on Foreign Relations to report the treaty
favorably. He felt that ratification by the United States would be
an important contribution to world peace.[2] President Roosevelt

---

[1] For the text of the convention see HUDSON, MANLEY O., *International
Legislation*, III: 1634, Carnegie Endowment for International Peace, Washington, 1931.

[2] Dept. of State, *Press Releases*, May, 19, 1934, pp. 291–293.

shortly afterward sent a special message to the Senate in which he set forth that the ratification of the convention, which had been too long delayed, would be a concrete indication of the willingness of the American people to deal with the abuses of the arms traffic. He concluded his message with these words:

The peoples of many countries are being taxed to the point of poverty and starvation in order to enable governments to engage in a mad race in armament which, if permitted to continue, may well result in war. This grave menace to the peace of the world is due in no small measure to the uncontrolled activities of the manufacturers and merchants of engines of destruction, and it must be met by the concerted action of the peoples of all nations.[1]

The Senate finally approved the treaty subject to the reservation that the agreement was not to come into force for the United States until it had likewise come into force for nine other specified powers.[2]

The United States Adopts the Principle of the Control of Manufacture. Meanwhile the policy of the United States has been undergoing a gradual evolution in the direction of closer cooperation in the control of arms manufacture. In the early stages of arms traffic discussion the American government, on several occasions, made official reservations regarding its constitutional inability to control the manufacture of arms. Thus, in 1929, a comment was inserted in the draft convention on arms manufacture prepared by a special commission of the Council as follows:

The delegation of the United States of America recalled its declaration of principle made previously to the effect that its Government is powerless to prescribe or enforce a prohibition or a system of licenses upon private manufacture, which takes place under the jurisdiction of the States which form the United States of America.[3]

This continued to be the American position until 1932. Those who drafted the instructions of our delegates at Geneva were evidently indulging in wishful thinking along the lines of strict construction of the Constitution. When it is considered how far the Federal government has been permitted to invade the field of the drug traffic under treaties and tax measures and how far it has gone in the regulation of other matters under the treaty power,[4] it would

---

[1] *Ibid.*, p. 294.

[2] *Treaty Information Bulletin*, June, 1935, p. 8.

[3] League of Nations, *Reduction of Armaments—Supervision of the Private Manufacture and Publicity of the Manufacture of Arms and Ammunition and of Implements of War* (A. 30. 1929. IX), p. 7, Geneva, 1929.

[4] See, for example, Missouri *v.* Holland, 252 U.S. 416.

seem to be an easy constitutional proposition that arms manufacturing as well as traffic could be regulated by Congress in the enforcement of treaties.

Late in 1932 the United States changed its position. On November 14 Secretary Stimson admitted that the American government doubtless possessed the constitutional power to regulate the manufacture of arms although this did not necessarily mean that the supervision of manufacturing would be accepted.[1] On November 18 Hugh Wilson declared to the bureau of the Disarmament Conference that the United States would consider favorably provisions for the control of private manufacture provided that state manufacture should also be supervised and that such control should be accompanied by a convention for the substantial reduction of armaments.[2] The way was thus cleared. On June 15, 1934, the United States presented to the subcommittee on the manufacture of arms a plan for arms control which went beyond any which the committee had yet been willing to adopt. This plan was attributed to President Roosevelt.

The United States Submits a Draft Convention. On November 20, 1934, shortly after the first revelations of the munitions investigation in Washington, the American delegation submitted to the bureau of the Disarmament Conference the draft of a convention of an advanced type for the regulation and control of the manufacture of and trade in arms. A brief summary of some of the provisions of the proposal is as follows:

The high contracting parties assume entire responsibility for the manufacture of and trade in arms within their territories. They undertake to enact the necessary legal provisions to insure in the strictest manner the inspection and supervision of such manufacture and trade.

Licenses are required for private manufacture, the term of the license to be not more than five years renewable upon the decision of the government.[3]

Licenses are required for the export and import of arms.

---

[1] *N.Y. Times*, Nov. 15, 1932.

[2] League of Nations, *Records of the Conference for the Reduction and Limitation of Armaments, Series C, Minutes of the Bureau*, I: 100; HUDSON, MANLEY O., *International Regulation of Trade in and Manufacture of Arms and Ammunition* (Report submitted to the Special Committee of the U.S. Senate), p. 51, Govt. Printing Office, Washington, 1935; DREXEL, CONSTANCE, "Armament Manufacture and Trade," p. 549, *International Conciliation*, No. 295 (December, 1933).

[3] Such licenses are now required in the United States under the Neutrality Resolution of 1935. See p. 32.

A Permanent Disarmament Commission shall be set up at the seat of the League of Nations to be composed of the representatives of the governments of the high contracting parties. The Secretary-General of the League of Nations shall provide the Secretariat of the commission.

The high contracting parties shall send to the commission a list of state establishments capable of manufacturing arms, copies of all licenses to private manufacturers, a list of orders received by the state and licensed establishments, a statement of all manufactures effected, and copies of all import and export licenses.

The commission shall examine the information, establish a system of publicity, set up a permanent and automatic system of inspection and cause special investigations to be made.[1]

The policy of the United States has thus been distinctly changed from the isolationist and individualistic stand of the Harding administration to the cooperative and regulative attitude of Hoover and Roosevelt.

THE ABOLITION OF THE NEUTRAL MUNITIONS TRADE

Attempts to Stop Traffic with Both Belligerents.   When nations go to war, a rich field is opened up to the arms merchants in such neutral countries as are able to maintain their trade relations with one or both belligerents.   International law has not thus far placed any obligation upon the neutral government to stop its citizens from engaging in this species of business.   Whatever the lawbooks may say on the subject, the people of the belligerent nation whose soldiers have been slain by neutral munitions will naturally feel indignation toward the country which is to a real extent the source of their misfortune.   James Russell Lowell voiced this feeling toward Great Britain during the Civil War in the following lines:

> You wonder why we're hot, John?
> Your marks wuz on the guns,
> The neutral guns, thet shot, John,
> Our brothers an' our sons.

During the World War the United States became the greatest neutral source of arms and munitions that the world has ever seen. Millions of rifles and hundreds of thousands of tons of explosives were sold to the Allies at high prices by American arms and powder firms.   Repeated protests were made to the United States by the Central Powers; but this country stood firm, basing its position upon traditional international law.   In a public circular issued

[1] Text from Dept. of State, *Press Releases*, Dec. 22, 1934, p. 391.

on October 15, 1914, Secretary Bryan stated the attitude of the American government as follows:

> In the first place it should be understood that, generally speaking, a citizen of the United States can sell to a belligerent government or its agent any article of commerce which he pleases. He is not prohibited from doing this by any rule of international law, by any treaty provisions, or by any statute of the United States. It makes no difference whether the articles sold are exclusively for war purposes, such as firearms, explosives, etc., or are foodstuffs, clothing, horses, etc., for the use of the army or navy of the belligerent.
>
> Furthermore, a neutral government is not compelled by international law, by treaty, or by statute to prevent these sales to a belligerent. Such sales, therefore, by American citizens do not in the least affect the neutrality of the United States.[1]

This position was maintained until the end of American neutrality.

There are now good reasons for believing that the old doctrines of international law are obsolete, and that the modern world situation in which such tremendous damage may be indirectly inflicted by private citizens in neutral countries upon belligerents calls for new principles of arms control. In the first place, a munitions-manufacturing nation which supplies a belligerent with arms is, regardless of legal concepts, actively participating in war on the side of the favored belligerent. It is a commonplace of wartime policy that the belligerent citizen in the munitions plant is performing as great a service to his country as is the soldier in the trenches. The neutral munitions maker is performing this identical service. During the period of American neutrality in the World War some of the best officers of the Allies served their countries not on the front but in the munitions plants of the United States where they were directing neutral Americans in providing the means for blowing up German divisions. In the second place, a view has received wide acceptance since 1917 that close trade relations between a neutral and a belligerent are of little value to the neutral because of the difficulty in obtaining ultimate payment for goods. Finally the tendency of such commercial intimacy may well be to draw the neutral into the war on the side of its best customers, an exceedingly disastrous outcome for a commercial enterprise from the standpoint of the nation as a whole.

For these various reasons it seems inconsistent with true neutrality to permit this trade. During the bloody Chaco dispute

[1] *Foreign Relations*, 1914 (Supplement), p. 574.

in 1934 Congress passed a resolution authorizing the President to stop the sale of arms or munitions of war in the United States to the belligerents.   The resolution was requested by the Department of State after a report from a League of Nations committee had asserted that the sanguinary character of the war was largely due to the importation of munitions.   In his letter of request, which was addressed to the chairman of the House Committee on Foreign Affairs, Secretary Hull declared:

> I have reason to believe, however, that the arms producing nations of the world will find it possible to join in this movement, and that the selfish interests of manufacturers and merchants of arms and munitions will not be permitted to stand in the way of concerted action sponsored by the enlightened opinion of the world.[1]

The resolution was passed by both houses without a dissenting vote and was approved by the President on May 28.   On the same day President Roosevelt issued a proclamation putting the prohibition into effect.[2]

The Regulations of 1935.   The principle of the embargo as against both belligerents was embodied as a general policy in the Neutrality Resolution of 1935 which has been described.[3]   It was provided that arms, ammunition, and implements of war could not be shipped to belligerents in time of war and that licenses must be obtained for the import and export of these articles in peacetime commerce.   The term "arms, ammunition, and implements of war" is susceptible of various interpretations.   According to some views it might be expanded to include the whole list of contraband goods.   When the President came to apply the term in the administration of the law, however, he used it in a more restricted sense.   His proclamation of September 25, 1935, in which he set forth the list of articles for the import and export of which licenses were to be required mentioned only six categories and the same definition was employed in the proclamation of October 5, 1935, placing the embargo into effect as against Italy and Ethiopia.   The list of articles is as follows:

1. Rifles using ammunition in excess of cal. 26.5, machine guns, artillery; ammunition for the above-mentioned weapons; grenades, bombs, torpedoes, and mines; tanks, military armored vehicles, and armored trains.
2. War vessels.

[1] Dept. of State, *Press Releases*, May 26, 1934, p. 303
[2] *Ibid.*, June 2, 1934, p. 327.
[3] See pp. 31–32.

3. Aircraft designed, adapted, or intended for aerial combat or bombing.

4. Revolvers and automatic pistols of a weight in excess of 1 pound 6 ounces using ammunition in excess of cal. 26.5 and ammunition therefor.

5. Aircraft other than those in category 3.

6. Livens projectors and flame throwers; mustard gas, lewisite, and certain other chemicals.[1]

PROHIBITION OF ARMS SHIPMENTS TO REVOLUTIONISTS AND GOVERNMENTS UNDER OUR DISPLEASURE IN LATIN AMERICA

The Resolutions of 1912 and 1922. One remaining aspect of the arms traffic, the national policy of the United States in controlling arms shipments to Latin-American countries, remains to be described in order to complete the entire picture. The United States, although somewhat indifferent regarding the control of arms shipments to Africa, has been quite alive to the need for curbing the traffic in regions which are vital to its own interests. Thus Congress has passed statutes to prohibit the sale of firearms within any district or country in our territories occupied by uncivilized or hostile Indians,[2] and to aboriginal natives in certain islands of the Pacific.[3] The most notable legislation of this type has been that to control the shipment of arms to Latin-American countries during times of revolution. The first action to check this traffic was taken in 1912 during the Mexican revolution. American property in Mexico was threatened by violence, and the United States was engaged in making severe demands that the interests of its citizens should be protected. At the same time the export of arms across the border supplied the revolutionists with the implements which enabled them to carry on the work of destruction. American munitions manufacturers were nullifying the efforts of the Department of State. The incongruity of the situation was recognized by Congress which passed the resolution of 1912 authorizing the President, in case of domestic violence in any American country which was promoted by arms procured from the United States, to forbid the export of arms to that country except under such limitations as he should prescribe.[4] In 1922 the resolution was repassed. This time, in addition to American countries, it included countries in which the United States exercised extraterritorial jurisdiction, meaning specifically China. The text of the 1922 resolution reads as follows:

[1] Dept. of State, *Press Releases*, Oct. 5, 1935, pp. 251–253.

[2] *U.S. Compiled Statutes*, 1916, §4133.

[3] *Ibid.*, §10,481.

[4] 37 *U.S. Statutes at Large*, 630.

That whenever the President finds that in any American country, or in any country in which the United States exercises extraterritorial juris- diction, conditions of domestic violence exist, which are or may be pro- moted by the use of arms or munitions of war procured from the United States, and makes proclamation thereof, it shall be unlawful to export, except under such limitations and exceptions as the President prescribes, any arms or munitions of war from any place in the United States to such country until otherwise ordered by the President or by Congress.[1]

It will be observed that the resolution gives great discretion to the President by providing that the embargo shall be imposed "under such limitations and exceptions as the President prescribes." Thus it may be possible for the President to discourage all fighting by imposing the ban against shipments to either faction. Again, and this was the action probably contemplated by Congress, he may permit shipments to the government while prohibiting them to the revolutionists. Or should he desire to overthrow a govern- ment which is not favorably disposed toward United States policies, he may permit arms shipments without restriction. The latter action was taken in 1914 when the Wilson administration, desiring to overthrow the Huerta government in Mexico, lifted a previously imposed ban upon arms shipments for the express purpose of promoting a civil war in Mexico.[2] The Huerta government was shortly afterward overthrown.

The Application of the Embargo to Nicaragua. Probably the outstanding instance of the use of arms control to suppress an alleged revolution occurred in 1926–1927 in Nicaragua when the United States was endeavoring to suppress the Sacasa movement to gain control of the government. An embargo was placed upon arms shipments from the United States to the Sacasa forces, but freedom was allowed for shipments to the favored Diaz faction which was in control of the government. American marines seized a quantity of arms in the hands of Sacasa forces for the purpose of determining whether or not they had come from the United States. When it was found that they were not of United States origin, they were conveniently "lost" in the river. The United States government, furthermore, sold to Diaz from public supplies some 3,000 Krag rifles, 200 Browning machine guns, and 3,000,000 rounds of ammunition; while New York bankers, with the acquiescence if not request of the Department of State, furnished

[1] 42 *U.S. Statutes at Large,* 361.
[2] *Foreign Relations,* 1914, pp. 446–448.

the money with which the purchase was made.[1] Finally, under threats of active intervention by the United States marines, the revolutionary forces were induced to surrender their arms in exchange for a compensation of $10 per rifle.[2]

The Case of Brazil. At the Sixth International Conference of American States (1928) the United States signed a convention on the Rights and Duties of States in the Event of Civil Strife under which the parties agreed in the event of revolution:

To forbid the traffic in arms and war material, except when intended for the government, while the belligerency of the rebels has not been recognized, in which latter case the rules of neutrality shall be applied.

The attempt to carry out this pledge by President Hoover in the case of the revolution in Brazil in 1930 proved not altogether happy. On October 22 an arms embargo was proclaimed against the rebels in accordance with the convention of 1928 and under the resolution of 1922. Two days later the government fell. The United States offended the *de facto* government by this untimely and futile embargo.[3]

The areas against which the arms embargoes have been imposed by the United States under the resolutions of 1912 and 1922 are as follows:

Mexico, 1912, 1915, 1924.
China, 1922.
Honduras, 1924.
Cuba, 1924, 1934.
Nicaragua, 1926.
Brazil, 1930.[4]

German Munitions and the Occupation of Veracruz. The attempt to prevent the landing of a supply of foreign munitions in Mexico had much to do with one of the most widely criticized interventions of the United States. At 9 P.M. on April 20, 1914, in the midst of the controversy with Huerta over a salute to the American flag following the Tampico incident, the American consul

---

[1] *N.Y. Times*, Mar. 10, 1927; Dept. of State, *Press Releases*, Mar. 23, 1927; WILLIAMS, *Economic Foreign Policy of the United States*, p. 150.

[2] Cox, ISAAC JOSLIN, *Nicaragua and the United States*, 1909–1927, p. 800, World Peace Foundation, Boston, 1927.

[3] For Secretary Stimson's explanation of this incident see his address on "The United States and the Other American Republics," p. 13, Publications of the Department of State, *Latin American Series*, No. 4.

[4] Dept. of State, *Press Releases*, June 30, 1934, p. 455.

at Veracruz cabled the Department of State that a German steamer with 200 machine guns and 15,000,000 cartridges was expected to discharge its cargo at the Veracruz docks the next morning. Called from his bed shortly after 2:30 A.M. on the morning of April 21, President Wilson gave orders that the Veracruz customhouse should be seized and that the delivery of the arms and ammunition should be prevented.[1]

Seeking International Cooperation to Control Shipments to Latin America. While European governments with interests in Africa began in the latter part of the nineteenth century to promote international agreements for arms control in the Dark Continent, the United States has made no effort to obtain a thoroughgoing convention with regard to Latin-American arms commerce. Some sporadic attempts have been made to enlist the cooperation of particular governments in special cases. When in 1914 the United States requested Austria-Hungary to prevent arms shipments into Mexico, the Austrian government refused on the ground that the arms manufacturers were "very jealous of their rights." It is quite probable that the outbreak of the World War stopped the shipment of large supplies of Austrian arms. Rifles manufactured for Mexico were found lying on European battlefields.[2] Shortly afterward the American munitions makers, also very jealous of their rights, were engaged in shipping arms to be used against Austria and her allies.

The American government has met with greater success in the attempts to persuade or compel the governments in and adjacent to the Caribbean region to join in the restriction of arms shipments. In 1914 the United States strongly protested the shipment of arms from Haiti to revolutionists in Santo Domingo.[3] In the following year representations were made to the Dominican Republic to stop the shipment of arms to Haiti.[4] In 1916 the United States solicited the aid of Guatemala and Salvador in prohibiting the export of arms to Mexico.[5] During the Nicaraguan revolution of 1926–1927 the Department of State asked Costa Rica, Honduras, Salvador, Guatemala, and Mexico to prevent arms shipments to

---

[1] *Foreign Relations*, 1914, p. 477; TUMULTY, JOSEPH P., *Woodrow Wilson as I Knew Him*, p. 151, Doubleday, Page & Company, Garden City, N.Y., 1921.

[2] Reference to this situation is made in a dispatch from the United States ambassador in Vienna, *Foreign Relations*, 1915 (Supplement), p. 789.

[3] *Foreign Relations*, 1914, p. 238.

[4] *Ibid.*, 1915, p. 488.

[5] *Ibid.*, 1916, p. 794.

Nicaragua.[1] The failure of Mexico to comply with the request of the United States gave rise to strong condemnatory public statements from Washington.[2]

The Need of an International Convention. The single policy of the United States with regard to arms control in Latin America has not been entirely satisfactory and has given rise to several unfortunate incidents. The United States has in this matter an added reason for advocating the universal adoption of an international convention such as that suggested in 1934 at Geneva. If the whole world community could be induced to adhere to the convention, the traffic would be under control with regard to exports into Latin America from all countries. The shipment to revolutionary factions would be prevented by the provision that exports shall be for the direct supply of the importing state. Furthermore, as a more satisfactory means of enforcement than the diplomatic protests of the United States acting alone, the convention would introduce the principle of international supervision.

---

[1] President Coolidge's message to Congress of Jan. 10, 1927, *Congressional Record*, 68: 1324.

[2] *N.Y. Times*, Nov. 18, 1926.

PART IV
CONDUCT AND MACHINERY
CHAPTER XXI

THE GENERAL CONTROL OF FOREIGN RELATIONS: THE PRESIDENT, CONGRESS, THE PUBLIC

THE LEGISLATIVE-EXECUTIVE STRUGGLE FOR POWER

The shift of power from the legislative to the executive branch of government, largely in disregard of the intent of the framers of the Constitution, has been one of the most notable developments in American constitutional practice. The authors of our first state constitutions and of the Articles of Confederation revolted against the domination of the executive because of the highhanded practices of colonial governors. They bestowed practically all political power upon the legislature. The Constitutional Convention of 1787, however, created an executive branch of the national government and vested in it a considerable number of functions. Since that time the demands of practical government, which are not always respectful of written documents, have compelled the growth of many extralegal practices which have further enlarged the power of the executive. This development in national government is paralleled in a large measure by similar movements in state and local government.

Since the World War the strengthening of the executive branch has been a characteristic of government in many parts of the world. Parliaments have been denuded of their independent functions and have become rubber stamps for dictators. In the United States legislators have stubbornly resisted the movement. The idealistic desire to preserve this country as one of the last favored areas of liberal parliamentarianism has increased the legislative morale. But the necessity of action in a highly complicated civilization, particularly in times of crisis, has given power to the executive. The vastly increased duties of government have made it impossible that the details of politics in each of its many specialized fields can be comprehended by a body devoted to the general task of legislation. Congress can only be superficially aware of the multitude of facts that bear on the political problem, and is not, therefore, prepared to assume the initiative in piloting the ship of state through hazardous waters over an unknown course. A few years ago when certain civic organizations in an Eastern state asked a senator to state his position upon the World Court, he replied that he had not investigated the subject sufficiently to make up his mind. American membership had, however, been an important issue before the Senate for some years during which time the statesman in question had been a respected member of that body.

In a world where governmental action is necessary as events shift from crisis to crisis, the attitude of the legislature must too often be one of delay because of unpreparedness to act. Through well-organized lobbies the special interests turn this inertia to their advantage. Obstruction and paralysis of legislative initiative are the result. The positive formulation of policy has, therefore, passed in a large measure from Congress; and the drafting of measures is now frequently a function exercised by the executive. An authoritative writer on American government has described the change in the President's position as follows: "It is not easy to find a single aspect of the President's office which has worked out as it was originally intended. The limits and restrictions placed on him have proven vain, the powers originally given him have grown steadily with the increasing work of government, and the attitude of the people has become one of dependence rather than distrust. . . . If the men of 1787 could see the executive office as it is today, they would not recognize their handiwork."[1]

The legislature is nevertheless still regarded in the United States as an indispensable critic. The executive works with speed, frequently in secret. The bureaucrat oftentimes becomes sentimentally attached to his own policies. It is essential that a forum should be kept open in which objections may be vigorously raised. If the legislature has lost much of its leadership, its functions of criticism and negation are more important than ever, because the amount of governmental power exercised by the executive which calls for supervision and review is greater than in previous periods of our history. And it should be noted that the powers of checking the executive, while less than they were intended to be by the Constitution, are still considerably greater than those of the legislatures of most other countries.

CONSTITUTIONAL DEVELOPMENT OF FOREIGN POLICY CONTROL

Before the Constitution. During the Revolution and under the Confederation the control of American diplomacy was in the

[1] Young, James T., *The New American Government and Its Work*, pp. 84–85 (3d ed.), The Macmillan Company, New York, 1933.

hands of Congress. A Committee of Secret Correspondence was created in 1775 to communicate with agents of the colonies established abroad. In 1777 this body was superseded by the Committee for Foreign Affairs. Thomas Paine was chosen secretary of the committee at a salary of $70 per month. Congress retained control and at times appointed special committees to consider particular matters in the field of foreign relations. The result was chaos. Accordingly in 1781 a Department of Foreign Affairs was created "as a remedy against the fluctuation, the delay and indecision to which the present mode of managing our foreign affairs must be exposed."[1] The secretary of the department was under the control of the legislative branch. He was to transmit such communications as Congress should request. It was his duty to obtain information of the state of affairs abroad and lay the same before Congress. Congress continued to appoint special committees to consider particular diplomatic communications. The secretary was still prevented from carrying on correspondence with that promptness which is necessary in effective diplomacy. The first secretary, Robert Livingston, was treated as little more than a clerk.[2] John Jay, who succeeded to the post in 1784, raised the prestige of the office; but Congress, much to Jay's dissatisfaction, continued to demand the right to scrutinize all proposals regarding foreign affairs. Jay complained that legislators could not keep secrets and that the submission of correspondence to Congress was a serious handicap.[3]

Provisions of the Constitution. The members of the Constitutional Convention of 1787 had no clear intention to give to the executive branch the management of foreign affairs. It seems to have been generally assumed at the outset that either Congress or the Senate would retain control.[4] As the work of building the Constitution proceeded in the convention, the necessity of a stronger executive became apparent. Even to the end of their labors at Philadelphia, however, the delegates evidently did not intend to shift the general control of foreign relations to the President. The

---

[1] Report of Committee of Congress, *Journals of the Continental Congress,* XIX: 43. For the development of the methods of control previous to the Constitution see HUNT, GAILLARD, *The Department of State of the United States,* Chapters I, II, and III, Yale University Press, New Haven, 1914, and WRISTON, HENRY MERRITT, *Executive Agents in American Foreign Relations,* Chapter I, Johns Hopkins Press, Baltimore, 1929.

[2] WRISTON, *op. cit.,* p. 20.

[3] *Ibid.,* p. 23.

[4] *Ibid.,* p. 37.

Constitution mentions only a few of the many aspects of foreign affairs. The document provides:

Art. I, Sec. 8, Clause 11: Congress shall have the power "to declare war."

Art. II, Sec. 2, Clause 2: The President "shall have power, by and with the advice and consent of the Senate, to make treaties, provided two-thirds of the Senators present concur."

Art. II, Sec. 2, Clause 2: The President "shall nominate and by and with the advice and consent of the Senate shall appoint ambassadors, other public ministers and consuls."

Art. II, Sec. 3: The President "shall receive ambassadors and other public ministers."

There are also a number of provisions which affect in an indirect but important way the conduct of foreign relations, such, for example, as the power of Congress regarding the appropriation of money; the raising of revenue; the regulation of commerce with foreign nations, including the control of immigration; and the power of the President as commander in chief of the army and navy. Altogether these provisions touch but a fraction of the problems which are presented in international affairs.

Constitutional Practice Has Given Power to the President. As the Constitution says little about foreign affairs, it has been left to custom to work out practical rules on the subject. The handling of the great mass of diplomatic detail is by its nature an executive function. The grasp of the subject on the part of administrative officers and their ability to act quickly give them an enormous advantage over the legislature. The greater part of the work of diplomacy has, therefore, inevitably gravitated into the executive department despite the theories that may have existed at the time of the formation of the Constitution.

How far practice has gone in shifting powers to the executive may be seen from the fact that of the four constitutional provisions above quoted, the first three, concerning declarations of war, treaties, and diplomatic appointments, have been materially altered by usage from their originally intended meaning. In each of these provisions, as will be seen, the President has gained power beyond and contrary to the letter of the Constitution. Furthermore, the President has acquired by usage a number of powers which are not mentioned in the Constitution. Some of these are: the function of diplomatic communication, recognition, the making of certain decisions concerning neutrality, and the determination of national policies in general.

Helvidius versus Pacificus. The debate over the relative powers of Congress and the President broke out a few years after the Constitution was put into operation. In 1793 President Washington issued a proclamation of neutrality with respect to the war between Great Britain and France. The sympathizers of France, many of whom felt that the proclamation was contrary to the treaty of alliance of 1778, objected to the President's action as beyond his constitutional authority. Hamilton, writing under the pseudonym Pacificus, defended the right of the President to issue the proclamation. He pointed out that the executive power is vested in the President. As the declaration of neutrality and determination of the obligation of treaties are executive functions, he argued, they clearly belong to the President. Hamilton went on to show that the conduct of foreign affairs is in many other ways executive in character.

His doctrines were probably shocking to many who remembered the full control that had been exercised by Congress over such matters previous to the Constitution. Jefferson urged Madison: " . . . take up your pen, select the most striking heresies, and cut him to pieces in face of the public."[1] Madison, adopting the pen name, Helvidius, attacked Hamilton's position in a series of articles. He contended that, as the power of declaration of war is given to Congress, the power of deciding whether we are to remain out of a war belongs to the same body. He attacked the contention that the conduct of foreign affairs is an executive function.

It is impossible to demonstrate from the fragmentary references in the Constitution to foreign affairs what was the intent of the framers as to the specific power to declare neutrality. Madison may have been correct from the traditional and legal point of view. Ignoring the provisions of the Constitution and viewing the matter from the standpoint of practical statesmanship, however, most of the argument seems to have been on the side of Hamilton.

PRESIDENTIAL INITIATIVE IN THE DETERMINATION OF FOREIGN POLICY

As shifting events bring new problems in foreign policy and make advisable a reconsideration of the American attitude toward world affairs, it is usually the executive branch alone which has sufficient grasp of new developments to be aware of the necessity

---

[1] An account of this dispute is found in CORWIN, EDWARD S., *The President's Control of Foreign Relations*, Chapter I, Princeton University Press, Princeton, 1917.

of change or sufficient unity of action to present a well-defined project for diplomatic readjustment. Furthermore, the development of constitutional practice has armed the President with a considerable number of specific powers which make it possible for him within a certain scope to carry out policies without the necessity of resorting to Congress for aid. It is for these reasons that new policies almost invariably arise from the executive branch.

The policy of aloofness from European affairs came from a series of executive pronouncements which included: the neutrality proclamation of 1793, Washington's admonition against permanent alliances in his Farewell Address of 1796, and Jefferson's warning against entangling alliances in his first inaugural address in 1801. More recent actions by the United States which seem to be a modification of the isolation policy and which have drawn the United States into political contact with Europe have been taken also on the initiative of the executive. Thus American participation in the Algeciras Conference of 1906 was brought about by the decision of President Theodore Roosevelt. The gradually increasing cooperation between the United States and the League of Nations since 1921 has been due with little exception to the determinations of the executive. Another policy, the Monroe Doctrine, was formulated in cabinet discussions and made public in President Monroe's message of December, 1823. The doctrine as a general policy received no official support by Congress until 1899 when the Senate attached a reservation to the Hague Convention of that year to protect the policy, although the doctrine was not then referred to by name.[1] The various expansions of the Monroe Doctrine took place by executive announcement.[2] The Roosevelt corollary to the doctrine, as the name implies, was originated by the President. The Roosevelt corollary was later cut away from the doctrine by executive interpretation during the Hoover administration. A third major policy, the open door in China, originated formally in the Hay notes of 1899. The policy was supplemented by executive agreements and diplomatic representations as well as by the Nine-Power Treaty of Washington of 1922, all of which were initiated by the executive. The doctrine of the freedom of the seas originated in executive attempts to protect American

[1] WRIGHT, QUINCY, *The Control of American Foreign Relations*, p. 283, The Macmillan Company, New York, 1922.

[2] Except in the unusual case of the Senate resolution regarding Magdalena Bay.

neutral commerce, and it was greatly contracted in 1935 by executive warnings against dealing with belligerents.

CONGRESSIONAL INABILITY TO INITIATE POLICIES

The houses of Congress have attempted on several occasions to outline American policies by resolution. In 1864, while the Department of State was engaged in correspondence with the French government over the operations of French troops in Mexico, the House of Representatives was evidently impatient and passed a resolution by unanimous vote voicing its disapproval of the overthrow of the Mexican republic. The resolution stated that it did not accord with the policy of the United States to acknowledge a monarchical government erected on the ruins of an American republican government under the auspices of a European power. Secretary of State Seward, fearing a rupture with France, informed the French government through the American minister in Paris that the matter was for the executive to decide and that the action of the House was not taken upon any suggestion of the President.[1]

The Senate in 1912 attempted to extend the scope of the Monroe Doctrine by a Senate resolution. A Japanese company, it was reported, had been negotiating for land for coaling purposes at Magdalena Bay in Lower California. Senator Lodge thereupon introduced a resolution protesting against the control of places of strategic importance to the United States in the American continents by quasi-political non-American corporations. The resolution was an attempt to amplify a previously developed executive policy, the Monroe Doctrine. Should a similar occasion arise in the future, it is not unlikely that the executive attitude would be considerably affected by the Senate resolution.

Congressional declarations of this character are taken as expressions of legislative opinion. They may be accorded considerable weight but, as was shown in the case of the House action in 1864, the recommendations are not necessarily accepted by the President. In 1927 a resolution favoring arbitration of the oil dispute with Mexico was passed by the Senate but was disregarded by the President. In the Shipping Act of 1920 Congress directed the President to denounce all commercial treaties which gave to foreign countries the rights of national treatment, *i.e.*, the same treatment as accorded to

---

[1] *Moore's Digest*, VI: 496–497; MATHEWS, JOHN MABRY, *American Foreign Relations, Conduct and Policies*, pp. 227–228, Century Company, New York, 1928. The House measure was a joint resolution which was not concurred in by the Senate.

Americans, with regard to customs duties and tonnage dues levied at American ports. Presidents Wilson, Harding, and Coolidge, in turn, refused to do this. The words of rejection used by President Harding in his message of December 6, 1921, should at least be of interest to students of diplomatic finesse: "I invite your tolerance of noncompliance."[1]

Congressional Instructions to Diplomats. Through attaching diplomatic instructions to appropriation measures, Congress has in recent years made several attempts to fix policies. The opportunity to do this has arisen when the President in advance of an international conference has requested of Congress the funds to pay the expenses of the American delegation. In 1924 an appropriation act providing funds for the attendance of delegates at the International Opium Conference at Geneva was thus passed by Congress. The act provided further that the American delegation should sign no agreement which did not fulfill the conditions necessary for the suppression of the traffic in habit-forming narcotic drugs as set forth in the preamble, to wit, that there should be no surplus of raw opium available for nonmedical and nonscientific purposes. When the American delegation found at Geneva that a treaty providing for such a limitation of raw opium was not attainable, it withdrew from the conference. The instructions of Congress were fully observed. But this case is unique in that Stephen G. Porter, chairman of the House Committee on Foreign Affairs and author of the policy incorporated in the appropriation act, was also the head of the American delegation. He not only originated the instructions but was appointed to carry them out. The principle of the instructions, however, was not followed in the successful conference of 1931.

Under other circumstances it is doubtful if Congressional instructions need be regarded as binding upon the executive and his appointed delegates. In fact it would appear that the Congressional instruction of delegates, should it become an established custom, would frequently result in a breakdown of international negotiations. Congress is not in touch with the diplomatic situation. Instructions would probably be framed with regard to their domestic

[1] In one dispute over a matter of policy, the character of the embargo which should be placed upon the shipment of munitions during neutrality, the advantage has rested, for the time being at least, with Congress. For some years the President has requested the power of an optional embargo which would leave it within his discretion to apply the prohibition against shipments to one or both belligerents. In the Neutrality Resolution of 1935, however, Congress enacted a rule for an embargo to be applied against both belligerents alike. See pp. 31-32. This part of the resolution expires on May 1, 1937.

political effect, and might well be impossible to carry out, as was the case at the opium conference. A further illustration of impractical instructions set down by Congress, this time in directing an executive agreement, may be seen in the stipulations for the negotiation of the refunding or conversion of the inter-Allied indebtedness. Congress attempted to bind the World War Foreign Debt Commission in its negotiations to certain impossible terms. No part of the indebtedness was to be canceled, the interest was not to exceed 4¼ per cent, and the time of the payment was not to be extended beyond twenty-five years. It was provided that the refunding arrangements thus negotiated would go into effect upon the approval of the President; but the conditions prescribed by Congress could not be fulfilled. They were violated in every debt-funding agreement that was negotiated. Accordingly each agreement had to be returned to Congress for special ratification. It was only the disregard of Congressional instructions by the commission that made progress possible. Successful diplomacy often requires flexibility in instructions to conform to shifts in the process of bargaining. It necessitates a thorough knowledge of the points of view and problems of other governments involved. The conduct of negotiations through Congressional instruction cannot meet these requirements.

Congress and International Conferences. Probably the outstanding development of diplomatic procedure since the World War has been the rise of the conference method of diplomacy.[1] The need for cooperation to regularize the details of international life through treaties has multiplied rapidly within the last few decades, and the necessity of accomplishing a greater volume of work has led to the common use of the wholesale diplomacy of the conference. "Of all the achievements of the past hundred years," said John Bassett Moore, "the thing that is most remarkable, in the domain of international relations, has been the modification and improvement of international law by what may be called acts of international legislation."[2]

Congress has attempted to place a severe restriction upon the power of the President to participate in negotiation by the conference method. In 1913 a rider was attached to the general deficiency appropriation bill providing that "the Executive shall not

---

[1] For the number of conferences in which the United States has participated in recent years, see p. 19, note 2.

[2] Quoted in HUDSON, MANLEY O., *Progress in International Organization*, p. 77.

extend or accept any invitation to participate in any international congress, conference, or like event, without first having specific authority of law to do so." The sending of an imposing group of delegates and experts to an international conference is an enterprise which costs more than the President would ordinarily wish to spend from the contingent fund. An appropriation is desirable. The holding of conferences in this country also involves expenditures for the accommodations customarily furnished by the host country. Furthermore, attendance at certain conferences held under the auspices of the League of Nations has been followed by appropriations to pay the share of the United States in the special expenses incident to the holding of the conference. Thus it might at first seem that Congress is within its rights in seeking to control a matter where expenditure is involved. On the other hand, most authorities contend that the 1913 provision is not binding on the President. The principal purpose of a conference is ordinarily to draw up an international agreement. Congress cannot well restrict the President with regard to one of the powers with which he is most clearly endowed by practice, *i.e.*, that of treaty negotiation. President Wilson stated that the provision of the act was "utterly futile" and in excess of the power of Congress. Should the President on his own initiative send representatives to an international conference and should he pay them from the contingent fund, there is nothing that Congress could do, except that the Senate might attempt to defend Congressional prestige by refusing its consent to any treaties that might be drawn up.

The practice since 1913 has not been entirely consistent. The President has sought Congressional consent for the holding of conferences in the United States. He has also asked for consent and for appropriations previous to the sending of delegates to a number of conferences, the majority of them unimportant and technical. With regard to most politically important conferences, however, and to the majority of other meetings, the President has paid little heed to the 1913 law. He has been represented at a number of conferences by persons in the diplomatic service who have been assigned to attend as representatives of the United States. In some cases where large appropriations have been necessary for the sending of delegates and experts he has committed the United States to attendance before asking for appropriations. Thus he accepted the invitation to the London Naval Conference of 1930 almost immediately after it was extended and at a time when Congress was

not in session.   The United States was committed to attendance at
the League of Nations Disarmament Conference of 1932 several
years before Congress was consulted.   In both cases Congress
obligingly granted a sufficient appropriation to send the necessary
representation.[1]   The essential power of the President has thus not
been substantially impaired by practice.   As a matter of practical
government it would be difficult for Congress to pass intelligently
upon the question of representation in each of fifty conferences and
other international meetings per year.

POWERS OF CONGRESS TO CHECK AND CRITICIZE

The Power of Investigation.   Although executive initiative is
necessary, the policies of diplomatic experts, conducted in secret,
are apt at times to be carried to logical or sentimental extremes.
Powerful interests may sometimes influence governmental action
for their own benefit contrary to the requirements of the general
welfare.   As no party in power wishes to give ammunition to its
political opponents, the force of necessity compels the administration at times to conceal the details of a foreign policy that might be
unpopular.   For these reasons a Congressional or senatorial
investigation may well prove to be a wholesome influence in casting
light upon a concealed negotiation in matters where the public
safety cannot be endangered.

Secrecy in American Diplomacy.   A great deal of American
diplomacy has been conducted unknown to the public or even to
members of Congress.   The series of annual volumes known as
Foreign Relations of the United States is probably the most valuable
of all Department of State publications.   It discloses much of the
details of negotiations although it omits some materials of a delicate
character.[2]   At one time these volumes were promptly issued.
For some years previous to 1880 the volume for each year was
published immediately after the President's message to Congress

---

[1] For a discussion of the general question see WRISTON, *op. cit.*, pp. 128*ff.*;
MATHEWS, *op. cit.*, pp. 342*ff.*; LAY, TRACY HOLLINGSWORTH, *The Foreign
Service of the United States*, pp. 57–58, Prentice-Hall, Inc., New York, 1925.

[2] Secretary of State Kellogg's statement of principles for the editing of this
publication are found in *Foreign Relations*, 1914 (Supplement), p. iii.   Other
publications of the department which are exceedingly convenient to students
are the *Press Releases*, the *Treaty Series*, the *Executive Agreement Series*, and the
Treaty Information Bulletin.   These publications place in accurate and citable
form much current information.   They seldom go into complete detail, however, regarding disputes in which the policy of the United States might be open
to criticism at home.

early in December. Thus the year of publication was the same as that of most of the correspondence which it contained. From 1881 to 1905 the volume was published in the year following that of the correspondence. From that time on the delay grew greater. By 1911 the material was held for seven years before publication. The volume containing the correspondence for 1917 was published in 1926, and since then the volumes have been issued for only three additional years. The years following 1917 witnessed the unparalleled export of American capital and a great stiffening of American policies in the protection of the investments and speculations of United States citizens. But the volumes of *Foreign Relations* which would have set forth these policies have not been published beyond 1920, and thus are now fifteen years behind the facts.[1] Failure of the department to obtain appropriations is sometimes given as the reason why this valuable publication has been retarded. Whatever the explanation, the result has been that, owing to the lack of the information which the series should have supplied, a large part of American creditor diplomacy has never been revealed. When the volumes for the important years from 1920 to 1930 are published, all books which deal with this field of American foreign relations will doubtless become obsolete.

The Haitian Investigation. The lack of prompt publication of diplomatic matters makes it essential that Congress should be prepared to investigate when the occasion demands and when the national safety will not be jeopardized by publicity. An excellent illustration of the manner in which a legislative inquiry has shed light on unrevealed matters is found in the examination of the occupation of Haiti and Santo Domingo conducted by a select committee of the United States Senate in 1921–1922. The investigation revealed many facts which had previously not been suspected even by the members of the Senate. The actual occurrences in Haiti from 1915 to 1921 were shown to be inadequately and sometimes inaccurately reported in American newspaper accounts

---

[1] There have been, however, a number of volumes issued in recent years which are supplementary to previous volumes. For a criticism of the department publication policy see HUDSON, MANLEY O., "The Department of State and the Teaching of International Law and International Relations," *Proceedings of the Third Conference of Teachers of International Law*, p. 170, Carnegie Endowment for International Peace, Washington, 1928. For an explanation of the publication policy of the department see WYNNE, EDWARD C., "Publications and Available Documents of the Department of State," *Proceedings of the Fifth Conference of Teachers of International Law and Related Subjects*, p. 138, Carnegie Endowment for International Peace, Washington, 1933.

based on dispatches from Washington. The following columns present a contrast between some items of news regarding the negotiation of the Treaty of 1915 with Haiti as published in *The New York Times* and the events as found in the evidence presented to the Senate Committee.[1]

ACCOUNTS TAKEN FROM THE NEW YORK TIMES

ACCOUNTS TAKEN FROM TESTIMONY BEFORE THE SENATE COMMITTEE

On July 28, 1915, the United States marines entered Port au Prince following the killing of President Guillaume Sam. These occurrences were freely reported. A convention for customs control was then sought by the United States.

In view of the approaching election of a new President by the National Assembly, the U.S. Marines occupied the National Assembly room. Capt. Beach was quoted as stating that he "would protect the liberty of the election and repress any attempt at disorder." Port au Prince dispatch of Aug. 11, published Aug. 12.

On Aug. 12 Sudre Dartiguenave was elected President under American influence. He was "about the only politician in Haiti who was willing to accept office as President and father the American demands." From a letter of Brig. Gen. Eli K. Cole, *Inquiry*, p. 1784. The demands mentioned refer to the proposed customs control treaty.

Project of treaty presented on Aug. 14. Haitian government replied that rather than accept it without modification they would resign in a body. *Inquiry*, p. 8.

A Port au Prince dispatch of Aug. 24 carried the news that the Haitian legislature was hostile to the proposed convention. Published Aug. 25. This dispatch, as can be seen, was more realistic than those which came from official sources in Washington. Port au Prince reports from this time on seem to have been largely suppressed.

(It should be interpolated that Secretary Lansing on Aug. 24 took the position that if the treaty were not immediately ratified this country should consider establishing a military government until "honest" elections could be held or permitting the government to pass to some more willing faction. *Foreign Relations*, 1915, p. 438.)

---

[1] *The New York Times* is selected because of its outstanding position among American newspapers in the publication of foreign news. The value of its index in checking news stories likewise makes it convenient for this purpose. The information from the Senate hearings is taken from *Inquiry into Occupation and Administration of Haiti and Santo Domingo*, Hearings before a Select Committee of the United States Senate, Govt. Printing Office, Washington, 1922, cited as *Inquiry*.

"The initiative for this convention, it was learned today, came from Haitian leaders." Washington dispatch of Aug. 25, published Aug. 26.

"The United States Government is willing to wait a reasonable time for the Haitians to act." Washington dispatch of Aug. 26, published Aug. 27.

"President Dartiguenave and a majority of the Haitian Congress are favorable to the treaty. The principal opposition comes from revolutionary leaders and men identified with them in the Haitian Congress." Washington dispatch of Aug. 27, published Aug. 28.

The Haitian customhouses were meanwhile being taken over and money formerly available for governmental purposes was for a time withheld. Secrecy of troop movements in occupying customhouses had been deemed "extremely important" because of treaty negotiations. Admiral Caperton, *Inquiry*, p. 335.

Sept. 8. Admiral Caperton stated that a situation more favorable to the treaty had been brought about by "exercising military pressure at propitious moments in negotiations." *Inquiry*, p. 353.

On Sept. 16, 1915, the treaty was signed. The approval of both chambers of the Haitian Congress then became necessary.

The announcement of signature of the treaty and of the consequent recognition of the Haitian government by the United States was made in a Washington dispatch of Sept. 17, published Sept. 18. Ratification of Haitian Congress by Sept. 18 was expected by Secretary Lansing. "Ratification of the treaty by the Haitian Parliament will not be deferred. Haitian approval of the new arrangement is general, and no objection has been made to the establishment on the island of a modified protectorate," Editorial, Sept. 19.

Sept. 24. Unsigned Haitian bank notes to the amount of 500,000 gourdes were seized by the United

States. They were signed and were to be turned over to the Haitian government upon ratification of the treaty. *Inquiry*, pp. 378–380.

Oct. 3. Chargé Davis: "I told the President that, as before stated, funds would be immediately available upon ratification of the treaty." *Inquiry*, p. 381.

On Oct. 6 the Chamber of Deputies approved the treaty subject to interpretative resolutions which, however, were later ignored by the United States. Approval by the Senate was still necessary.

Oct. 19. Admiral Caperton authorized the payment of $35,000 from customs funds for current salaries of senators and deputies, but back salaries were not to be paid until the ratification of the treaty. *Inquiry*, pp. 387, 638.

Nov. 3. Admiral Caperton stated that Captain Beach had interviewed members of the Haitian Senate treaty committee and had earnestly and forcefully presented arguments for the ratification of the treaty. *Inquiry*, p. 391.

Nov. 5. The Senate committee brought in an adverse report upon the treaty. *Inquiry*, p. 392.

Evidently no news was given out at Washington regarding the steps taken to influence the vote of the Haitian Senate. At least the author could find no dispatches in the *Times* upon the subject.

Nov. 8. An American warship was ordered to bring from Cap Haitien to Port au Prince a Haitian who was to be elected senator to fill a vacancy and who was favorable to the treaty. *Inquiry*, p. 393.

Nov. 11. Admiral Caperton addressed the President and his cabinet in part as follows: " . . . I am confident if the treaty fails of ratification that my government has the intention to retain control in Haiti until the desired end is accomplished and that it will forthwith proceed to the complete pacification of Haiti so as to insure internal tranquility necessary to such development of the country and its industry as will afford relief to the starving populace now unemployed." *Inquiry*, p. 394.

The Senate voted favorably and the treaty was ratified on Nov. 11.

News of ratification was contained in dispatches of Nov. 12 from both Port au Prince and Washington. Published Nov. 13.

A similar lack of news existed regarding other matters brought out in the investigation, such as the dissolution of the Haitian National Assembly and the amendment of the Haitian Constitution in accordance with the desires of the forces of occupation.

THE POWER OF CONGRESS TO CONTROL COMMERCE

Congress is given the power in the Constitution to regulate commerce with foreign nations,[1] and thus far the executive has made but few inroads into that field. In certain respects, however, the control of commerce is in other countries almost universally recognized to be a diplomatic matter; and large powers of direction are usually placed in the hands of the executive for commercial bargaining purposes. The making of reciprocity arrangements by the United States can be carried on constitutionally through the treaty power. Treaty making for this purpose, however, is an almost impossible task inasmuch as the special interests which are opposed to any tariff reduction can nearly always muster a sufficient minority to block a treaty in the Senate even if the majority of senators are clearly favorable to such arrangements. Accordingly if reciprocity agreements are a desirable thing, other means than the making of treaties must be used. A plan, which has sometimes been tried and which is put into practice by the Trade Agreements Act of 1934, is a grant of power by Congress to the President to enter into reciprocal tariff-reducing compacts with other countries by means of executive agreements. This places the function of concluding reciprocity arrangements in the hands of the President alone and transfers the power of fixing tariffs to some extent from the field of legislation to that of diplomacy.[2]

[1] Art. I, Sec. 8, Clause 3.
[2] See p. 175.

PUBLIC OPINION

Popular sentiment has long been a force to be reckoned with in the conduct of foreign relations. Skeptics have had ample grounds for scoffing at it owing to the fact that, although there have been great demonstrations of opinion in behalf of such principles as peace and disarmament, the results have usually been slight. Granting the general ineffectiveness of popular opinion in this field, however, there can be little question that the part played by the public is on the increase. The facilities for the spread of information have made it possible that the public should be better informed than in centuries past. The growth in size of international transactions has made diplomacy a matter of greater importance to the citizen than it was during the period when the participation of the United States in world affairs was relatively slight.

Machinery for the spread of ideas has thrown more light upon foreign relations than was previously possible. As has been mentioned in Chapter I, more than six months elapsed after the signature of the Jay Treaty before it was published in the United States. In recent years international agreements many times longer than the Jay Treaty have frequently been published in the press on the day following their signature. The public has thus been able to read the full text of conventions drawn up at Washington, Geneva, London, or Paris within twenty-four hours after they have been signed. The newspapers publish a far greater amount of material on foreign affairs than in the days of isolation. They have developed an army of correspondents, trained in world affairs, whose function it is to seek out and report the news regarding important international events. The way in which the professional interest of the journalist furthers the cause of popular enlightenment is shown by the stand of the American correspondents at Paris in 1919. During the Peace Conference they presented a resolution to President Wilson which read: " . . . we vigorously protest, on behalf of the American press representatives, against what we have reason to regard as gag rule; and in common with the action of our British colleagues, who have laid their case before the Prime Minister, we appeal to you for relief from this intolerable condition."[1] Radio programs from Washington stress international affairs while broadcasts from European capitals serve to call some attention to world conditions. Nonofficial groups, such as the Carnegie Endowment for Inter-

---

[1] BAKER, RAY STANNARD, *Woodrow Wilson and World Settlement*, I: 141.

national Peace, the Foreign Policy Association, the Council on Foreign Relations, and the World Peace Foundation, are interested in the scientific study of international relations, while some hundreds of church and civic organizations sponsor particular ideas of international character. It is largely through these organizations that public opinion operates. The multiplication of courses in the college curriculum has helped to make a generation of students conscious of the importance of international questions. And the development of a large number of teachers of specialized subjects dealing with world affairs has added another group which is anxious that the secrets of diplomacy shall be more freely revealed.[1] The increasing use of the conference method of diplomacy has done much for the promotion of interest in international questions. International conferences are conducted in a large part in public; and, in some of them, all or a part of the proceedings are broadcast.

It would be a serious mistake to conclude from all this that the general public possesses a grasp of diplomatic problems. The great majority are completely out of touch with all but a few of the simplest facts, while unfounded popular prejudices on foreign questions flourish luxuriantly. Furthermore, the nature of diplomacy is such that it must be conducted by a few experts, competent to make compromises and shift positions from day to day in order to procure the greatest benefits for this government. The public, of course, does not have the knowledge and the singleness of decision necessary to carry on or control intricate negotiations. Well-informed group leaders, however, frequently act to advise or persuade governmental action on important matters and have at times a determining influence. This is due to the fact that many civic organizations have developed a competent set of experts in foreign relations who have in addition to their expertness the point of view of a considerable portion of the public.

The Beginnings of the Pact of Paris. Elsewhere the story is told of the origin of the Pact of Paris through the representations of public-spirited citizens, but the case may be appropriately summarized here as one of the outstanding instances in which public sentiment has produced an effective outcome.

1. The pact originated in the Briand statement to the American public given out through the representatives of the Associated Press in Paris on April 7, 1927.

[1] See the proceedings of the conferences of teachers of International Law, as cited on p. 401.

2. Certain individuals were active in promoting the plan for a treaty, Dr. James T. Shotwell, Salmon O. Levinson, Dr. Nicholas Murray Butler, and Senator Borah deserving particular mention.   The news value or diplomatic importance of the suggestion was not recognized until Dr. Butler called attention to the salient points in the Briand message by a letter published in *The New York Times* on April 25, 1927.   The response which the Briand offer received from the press and public of the United States, following this letter, gave an electric impulse to the project.

3. The French government presented a draft treaty to Washington on June 20, 1927, after which the United States government was silent for more than six months.   During this time, however, the friends of peace continued to carry on a public campaign to arouse interest in the proposal.

4. On December 28 the Department of State took up the negotiations and from that time on worked out the details of the treaty through correspondence with the French government.   In this complicated negotiation, which brought out a strong contrast between the peace policies of the two countries, the details were ably handled by the Department of State and public opinion could exert but little influence.   It did, however, provide the pressure without which the department would probably have failed to act.[1]

[1] See pp. 313–317 for a more detailed account of the formulation of the pact.

CHAPTER XXII

PARTICULAR POWERS IN THE CONDUCT OF DIPLOMACY

An examination of the particular powers exercised in the conduct of diplomacy shows the strength of the tendency toward executive control. In a few particulars, such as the formation of commercial policy and the setting up of the machinery for the conduct of foreign affairs, Congress has, for the most part, held to its constitutional functions. But in the operation of the machinery after it is set up, the powers of government have, generally speaking, flowed toward the executive in a strong and persistent tide. The reason for this is obvious. The administrator is permanently on the job and ready to act. Today the Department of State is an effective and elaborate machine consisting of more than one hundred officials, including Foreign Service officers on departmental assignment. The members of this large staff are well trained and many of them are highly expert. The power of the executive to command such an extensive mechanism and to derive information and prompt advice from it gives him a great advantage over Congress. For Congress is ponderous, not so fully informed as the administration, and it is only intermittently in session. The advantage of the administrator over the legislator in dealing with the current diplomatic problems which are brought each day by telegraphic dispatches from all parts of the world has played a large part in determining the procedure in this field, even sometimes in direct opposition to the expectations of the forefathers as set forth in the Constitution.

THE CONTROL OF DIPLOMATIC COMMUNICATION

When the Secretary for Foreign Affairs conducted the diplomatic correspondence of the Confederation under the watchful eye of Congress he found himself embarrassed and handicapped by legislative domination. The Confederation statesmen, in their passion for legislatures, had placed what was essentially an executive function under the control of Congress. The Constitution, which went into effect in 1789, said nothing as to who should control diplomatic communication. In the association of the Senate with the President in treaty making, the framers probably intended that that body should join with him in shaping correspondence with foreign governments, since treaties were regarded as the most important subject of communication. In the Act of July 27, 1789, creating the Department of Foreign Affairs, it was provided that the secretary should perform such duties as should be entrusted to him by the President, "agreeable to the constitution," relative to correspondence, etc. It is the opinion of Wriston that the sponsors of the legislation expected that the diplomatic instructions which were to be drafted by the secretary would be subject to the approval of the Senate.[1] The practice which arose out of the early experience of the President and Senate, however, reformed the Constitution in this respect. The Senate lost its intended participation in the preliminary negotiation of treaties. Accordingly such communication as was carried on in the bargaining period prior to the signature of treaties was soon left entirely in the hands of the executive. In other ways the practice of sole executive control was quickly fixed. In 1793 M. Gênet, the French minister, requested an exequatur for a consul, the commission being addressed to "The Congress of the United States." Secretary of State Jefferson returned the document with the explanation that the President would issue no exequatur unless the commission were addressed to the President, who, he informed Gênet, is the only channel of communication between the United States and foreign nations.[2]

The early precedents have been consistently followed, and the power to conduct communications has thus been given exclusively to the President. In case Congress should seek to send a message to a foreign government, it would be possible, should the President consent, to convey it through diplomatic channels. But such transmission would not be obligatory upon the President. In 1877 President Grant vetoed two resolutions of Congress which called upon the Secretary of State to acknowledge the receipt of congratulatory messages regarding the Centennial Exposition of 1876. His reason for the veto was that he regarded himself as the constitutional organ of communication with foreign states.[3] The resolutions were not repassed over the veto. If they had been so repassed, says Mathews, it is doubtful if there would have been any legal means of compelling their transmission through the President or the Secretary of State.[4]

[1] *Op. cit.*, p. 115.
[2] *Moore's Digest*, IV: 680.
[3] WRIGHT, *op. cit.*, p. 30.
[4] *Op. cit.*, p. 238.

RECOGNITION

The power of recognizing new governments and new states is not mentioned in the Constitution. The President is assigned the function of receiving ambassadors and other public ministers and he is given the authority to appoint such officers with the advice and consent of the Senate. Whether it was the intent of the framers that these provisions should vest in the President the right to determine what states and governments should be recognized is at least extremely doubtful. Probably they had not even considered the matter. Madison, arguing for a legislative control of foreign affairs in the Pacificus-Helvidius dispute, contended that the clause regarding the reception of diplomats made the President responsible for the ceremony of admitting public ministers, of examining their credentials, and of authenticating their titles, but that it could not be expanded into an authorization to determine whether or not an existing government ought to be recognized.[1] Regardless of the design or lack of design of the framers of the Constitution, practice came in time to bestow the power upon the executive, although there have been, as will be seen, several cases of the recognition of new states in which Congress has cooperated.

Congressional Interest in the Recognition of New States. The recognition of new *governments* seldom raises an issue of major international importance. Minor diplomatic irritations have frequently arisen from refusal of recognition, but these have almost always concerned our relations with small countries; and even in cases of stronger countries such refusal can hardly produce anything more serious than a sense of offended dignity on the part of the other government. The decision to extend recognition to a newly established government can ordinarily give no serious offense, as those who might resent the action have been overthrown. Decisions as to recognitions of new governments have become matters for the executive alone. But the question of the recognition of new *states* has on several occasions threatened to involve the United States in serious controversies with other powers. Premature recognition of a revolting territory as an independent state is almost certain to arouse the bitter resentment of the parent country. Issues of war and peace may be raised. In such cases the executive has sometimes been inclined to rely upon Congress for support. Some members of Congress, in their turn, have made insistent demands that Congress should have something to say in a

[1] CORWIN, *op. cit.*, pp. 24–25.

matter which is of such a serious character.   During the revolt of
the Spanish colonies in South America, Henry Clay contended that
Congress had a concurrent right of recognition.[1]   In 1896, during
the discussion of Cuban independence, Senator Bacon introduced a
resolution, which failed to pass, declaring that recognition is
exclusively for the determination of Congress.[2]

**Presidential Reliance upon Congress in Certain Recognitions of
a Serious Character.**   While members of Congress have not been
able to establish any Congressional rights of recognition, the executive has nevertheless leaned heavily upon that body in various cases.
Prior to the recognition of the independence of the revolted Spanish
colonies, President Monroe asked for and obtained from Congress
an appropriation with which to send such diplomatic missions to the
new states as he might deem proper.   Armed with the sanction of
Congress he then proceeded to recognize Colombia by the reception
of a chargé d'affaires.   Other South American states were recognized
in turn, some by the appointment of diplomatic representatives
and others by the reception of such representatives.   In 1836, when
the question of the recognition of Texas had raised serious issues
between the United States and Mexico, resolutions were passed by
both houses to the effect that recognition should be given whenever
Texas should set up a civil government capable of fulfilling the duties
of an independent state.   The preamble of the House resolution
suggested that the expediency of recognition should be left to
Congress.   President Jackson in a message to Congress stated that
he was disposed to agree with this view on grounds of expediency,
although he left open the question of constitutional right.   As the
recognition of Texas would be apt to lead to war, he felt that the
question of recognition should be decided after a previous understanding with Congress, which body possessed the power of declaring
war and of making provision for carrying it on.[3]   Congress then, by
act of March 3, 1837, appropriated money for the sending of a
diplomatic representative whenever the President, having received
evidence that Texas was an independent state, should deem it
expedient to appoint a minister.   Four days later, President Van
Buren, having just been inaugurated, granted recognition by
appointing a chargé d'affaires to carry on diplomatic relations with
the Texas government.[4]   In 1849, when a special agent was sent to

[1] CORWIN, *op. cit.*, p. 76.
[2] MATHEWS, *op. cit.*, pp. 384–385.
[3] *Moore's Digest*, I: 99.
[4] *Ibid.*, I: 101.

investigate the possibilities of recognizing the independence of Hungary, the Secretary of State instructed him: "Should the new government prove to be in your opinion firm and stable, the President will cheerfully recommend to Congress, at their next session, the recognition of Hungary."[1]

The Case of Cuba. Further evidence to support the view that dangerous international complications caused by the recognition of a revolting community are apt to incline the President to rely upon Congress may be found in the case of Cuba. On April 19, 1898, Congress passed a joint resolution declaring that the Cuban people "are and of right ought to be, free and independent." The resolution also demanded the withdrawal of Spain from the island and directed the President to use the armed forces of the United States to carry the resolutions into effect. The measure was approved by the President on the following day. This resolution has proved a puzzle to writers on international law, and deserves examination. It makes no provision for recognition of the *government* of Cuba. An early draft provided for the recognition of the "Republic of Cuba as the true and lawful government of that island" but this provision was stricken from the resolution on final passage. The omission was in accord with the wishes of the President as expressed in his message of April 11.[2] The resolution in recognizing the people of Cuba but not their government must have meant that the Cuban community was to be regarded as in a condition of unorganized and chaotic independence. This sort of recognition does not coincide with any classification in the lawbooks. It was nevertheless one of the most important recognitions, if it may be called so, ever announced by the American government.

The participation of Congress in the recognition of Cuba did not stop with the joint resolution. When hostilities were concluded and the time for the withdrawal of American troops arrived, Congress affixed a rider to the army appropriation bill of 1901 setting the conditions for recognition of the Cuban government. The act directed the President to "leave the government and control of the island of Cuba to its people" so soon as a government should be established under a constitution which should include certain stipulations for American control. These provisions, which were known as the Platt Amendment, were drafted for the most part by Secretary of War Root. They were discussed by the McKinley cabinet and were then turned over to Senator Platt for introduction

---

[1] *Ibid.*, I: 218.

[2] The documents are contained in *Moore's Digest*, VI: 211–239.

in Congress.[1] After passage they were appended to the Cuban constitution.[2] Formal recognition of the Cuban government took place in 1902 when the first president of Cuba was inaugurated. Thus there was collaboration between the President and Congress both with regard to the recognition of the independence of the Cuban community in 1898 and with regard to the conditions preliminary to the recognition of the Cuban government in 1902.

Methods of Recognition. In most cases of recognition the President takes action without the cooperation of Congress and even in the exceptional cases of Congressional cooperation he performs the act of recognition.[3] The methods used in recognizing both new states and new governments have been as follows:[4]

1. The reception of the accredited diplomatic representatives of the new state or government opens up a channel for full diplomatic relations. This is said by Mathews to be the customary, regular, and most proper method of giving recognition, inasmuch as the application for recognition should come from the new state or government.[5] The first act of recognition of a new government performed by the United States was the reception of Citizen Gênet, who came to this country as minister from the republican government of France in 1793.

2. The appointment of a diplomatic representative to a new government or state is also a frequently used method of opening diplomatic relations. Sometimes by this procedure the consent of Congress has been obtained in advance through the passing of an appropriation for the expense of the diplomatic mission. In other cases the Senate has given an advance approval by agreeing to the appointment. It is not necessary, however, that either of these actions be taken by the legislative bodies.

3. The issuance of an exequatur to a consul commissioned by the government desiring to be recognized is a third method of granting recognition.

The recognitions given to the revolted colonies of Spain give ample illustration of each of these three forms. In the first series of recognitions, extending from 1822 to 1826, recognition was given by the reception of diplomatic representatives from the new states[6]

---

[1] LATANÉ, *The United States and Latin America*, p. 139.

[2] They were later embodied in the Treaty of 1903 between the two countries.

[3] Except in the case of the anomalous resolution of 1898 regarding Cuba.

[4] For a summary of recognition methods see *Foreign Relations*, 1913, p. 102.

[5] *Op. cit.*, p. 387.

[6] As in the cases of Colombia, Brazil, and the Federation of Central American States.

or by the appointment of diplomatic representatives to them.[1] In a series of recognitions from 1835 to 1853, after additional states had been formed from the splitting up of states already recognized, some of the new states were recognized by the granting of exequaturs to their consuls.[2]

4. A common method of recognition of a new government following a revolution is to instruct the American diplomatic representative who was accredited to the former government to enter into relations with the newly established government.

5. On some occasions, when the change in the form of government has been particularly notable, a more formal step has been taken by instructing the American diplomat at the foreign capital in question to deliver a public pronouncement of recognition at such time as the new government shall be sufficiently organized.[3] Following the Chinese Revolution of 1911, the American chargé, Edward T. Williams, was instructed to await the organization of the National Assembly as evidenced by the election of its officers, at which time he was to deliver a message of recognition to the President. This was done on May 2, 1913, amidst elaborate ceremonies at the presidential palace.[4]

6. The completion of a treaty made directly with a new government or state would, of course, constitute recognition; and, in fact, recognition ordinarily would take place as soon as the diplomat should be appointed for the purpose of negotiating the treaty. Such a treaty may be negotiated without the formal appointment of a diplomat, however, by an ambassador or minister stationed at the capital of a third power. The granting of the full power to negotiate is in such case the act of recognition. Thus, in 1837, the United States recognized Greece, when the American minister at London was empowered to negotiate a treaty of commerce with the Greek minister at that capital.[5]

7. Finally a simple method of recognition is by a note or letter from the President to an official or diplomatic representative of the new government or state specifically declaring that recognition is extended. The United States recognized the German Empire by a

[1] As in the cases of Buenos Aires (Argentine Republic), Chile, Mexico, and Peru.

[2] As in the cases of Venezuela, New Granada, Uruguay, and Guatemala.

[3] For the case of the Portuguese Republic see *Foreign Relations*, 1911, pp. 689*ff.*

[4] *Foreign Relations*, 1913, pp. 109–110, 115, 117.

[5] *Moore's Digest*, I: 112. See also *ibid.*, pp. 90, 91, 92, and 116, for the cases of Ecuador, Paraguay, Salvador, and Liberia.

letter from the President to the Emperor.[1]   The recognition of the
Soviet government by the United States in 1933 was preceded by
negotiations at Washington between Maxim Litvinoff, the Russian
commissar for foreign affairs, and United States officials including
Secretary Hull and President Roosevelt.   After the outstanding
causes of disagreement were sufficiently adjusted, President Roosevelt recognized the Soviet government in the following note to
Litvinoff on November 16, 1933:

> I am very happy to inform you that as a result of our conservations the
> Government of the United States has decided to establish normal diplo-
> matic relations with the Government of the Union of Soviet Socialist
> Republics and to exchange ambassadors.
>
> I trust that the relations now established between our peoples may
> forever remain normal and friendly, and that our nations henceforth may
> cooperate for their mutual benefit and for the preservation of the peace of
> the world.[2]

Recognition a Weapon in the President's Hands.   The power of
recognition has at times proved to be an effective implement of
diplomacy in the hands of the President.   In exceptional cases
with regard to weak countries the withholding of recognition has
upset disapproved governments while premature recognition has
sometimes held in power governments which were otherwise not
capable of surviving.[3]   The refusal to recognize any treaty, situation, or agreement brought about contrary to the Pact of Paris,
known as the Stimson or Hoover-Stimson doctrine, has become a
policy of the United States which may have possibilities in restraining aggression.   Thus the refusal to recognize the State of
Manchukuo because of its creation by acts of violence has been
something of an impediment to the Manchurian policy of Japan.[4]

POWER IN RELATION TO NEUTRALITY

Neutrality Proclamations.   The question as to which agency of
the American government shall declare American neutrality and
enforce the duties of neutrality upon American citizens in case of a
war between two other powers is one which is not settled by the
words of the Constitution.   An allusion has already been made to
the difference of opinion on this matter in 1793.   At the time of the

[1] *Ibid.*, I: 137.
[2] Dept. of State, *Establishment of Diplomatic Relations with the Union of Soviet Socialist Republics*, p. 4, Govt. Printing Office, Washington, 1933.
[3] See pp. 63, 68, 74.
[4] See p. 332.

outbreak of war in Europe in that year President Washington announced that the interests of the United States required this country to pursue a friendly and impartial course toward the belligerents. Washington's declaration intentionally avoided the use of the term "neutrality," but it was nevertheless a proclamation of neutrality in substance and is commonly referred to as such. Washington warned American citizens under pain of punishment not to aid nor to abet the belligerents in violation of international law, and stated that citizens acting in that manner would not receive the protection of the United States. At that time there were no United States statutes defining specific offenses against neutrality or providing punishment for them. The President relied upon the hope that the courts would punish violations of the proclamation as offenses against the law of nations or as breaches of the treaties of peace existing between the United States and the principal belligerents.[1] As the law of nations and the peace treaties constituted an indefinite and imperfect system of law for the enforcement of neutrality, President Washington asked Congress to supplement them by legislation. Congress, in response, passed the Neutrality Act of 1794. The law was revised and strengthened in 1818[2] and additional provisions have been added by subsequent legislation. The statutes set forth a number of acts which are declared to be contrary to the obligations of the United States toward nations with which we are at peace,[3] and penalties are imposed for the commission of these acts within the territory of the United States. Congress has thus determined the matter of neutral duties on the part of citizens or residents within the United States. The decision as to the existence of war and consequently as to the times at which the neutrality statutes shall be effective has by custom been left to the executive.[4] Upon the outbreak of war between other countries the President issues a proclamation of neutrality.[5]

The President's Option Regarding the Protection of So-called Neutral Rights. The enforcement of the *rights* of American citizens, that is, the protection of their lives and property against illegal acts of the belligerents, is a matter for the executive department. Such doctrines of commerce protection as those loosely described

[1] For the text of the proclamation and for comments upon it see *Moore's Digest*, VII: 1002*ff*.

[2] FENWICK, *The Neutrality Laws of the United States*.

[3] See p. 27.

[4] A grant of this power is found also in the Neutrality Resolution of 1935.

[5] For an example see *Moore's Digest*, VII: 1007.

by the term "the freedom of the seas" have been built up through protests made by the executive against the actions of warring states that have been deemed to infringe the rights of American citizens.[1] The attempt to enforce these so-called rights has brought the United States into European wars on two occasions.

In recent years a strong attack has been made upon the doctrine of neutral rights. The theory has developed that the prevention of war requires an international organization to enforce sanctions against aggressor nations. Should a nation begin war in violation of the obligations of nations in such an organization, the act of the transgressing nation would be an offense against the international community. In such a situation third nations would not be expected to be impartial in attitude but would be under obligation to maintain international security by supporting the victim of the aggression. Should such an organization as the League of Nations attempt to shut off all foreign trade with the aggressor, the question would arise as to whether the United States would acquiesce or would combat the League action by diplomatic or naval means. Acquiescence of the United States in the stoppage of trade could be accomplished by the decision of the President who has always had the discretion of determining to what extent American neutral rights should be defended or to what extent American property abroad should be protected. When the matter was discussed at Geneva in 1933, President Roosevelt felt that the decision on this question lay within his power, as is evidenced by the declaration of American policy made by Norman Davis before the General Commission of the Disarmament Conference on May 22, 1933.[2]

WAR AND MILITARY SANCTIONS

The Power of Deciding upon War. The Constitution gives to Congress the power "to declare war." Nothing could be more clear than the intention of the framers to vest this authority in Congress; but their wishes have here again been neglected because of the realities of politics. The way in which practice has transferred the decision of entering a war from Congress to the executive illustrates more strikingly than any other instance the impossibility of confining the procedure of government to the written words of a

[1] For diplomatic protests made to protect American neutral rights see *Moore's Digest*, Vol. VII, *passim;* SAVAGE, *op. cit.*, and also the supplements of *Foreign Relations* for 1914, 1915, and 1916.

[2] See p. 334. See also the declaration of President Roosevelt of **Oct. 5,** 1935, which warned against transactions with belligerents, *supra*, p. 33.

rigid constitution if the provisions of that constitution violate the principles of an effective allocation of power.

The declaration of war by Congress has almost invariably been brought about on the initiative of the President and by his request. The President has the ability through his various executive powers to bring the nation so far along the road leading to war that Congress can have no alternative but to grant, at the President's request, the desired declaration. The presidential campaign of 1916 revealed a widespread popular belief that the President has the decision in the question of war or peace. Woodrow Wilson was elected president after his party had made wide use of the slogan: "He kept us out of war." The attitude of the President changed, however, when on January 31, 1917, the German government announced a policy of indiscriminate submarine sinkings in the proscribed zone. The German ambassador was given his passports. The President asked authority from Congress to arm American merchantmen; but the request was not granted owing to a filibuster in the Senate. The President then, by executive order, proceeded with the arming of the ships. He directed that the famous and fantastic Zimmermann note regarding a German-Mexican alliance should be made public. He called Congress in special session on April 2 and delivered a message asking for a declaration of war. The declaration came on April 6 as an almost automatic answer to the President's request.

In all cases in which Congress has passed a resolution declaring war, the wording of the declaration has indicated that the beginning of hostilities is not a matter of Congressional discretion but that the war has already been started before the declaration has been passed.[1] The declarations have merely recognized that war exists. The declaration of war against Mexico read: "by the acts of the Republic of Mexico, a state of war exists between that government and the United States."[2] Furthermore, the President may carry on *de facto* wars without a declaration by Congress.[3]

The Termination of War. A question arose at the end of the World War as to the constitutional methods of proclaiming a legal end to the status of war. The most common method is by treaty of peace in which the Senate has a veto over the acts of the Presi-

---

[1] CORWIN, *op. cit.*, pp. 140–141; WRIGHT, *op. cit.*, p. 286.

[2] The method of stating that war already exists owing to the action of the enemy has been adopted by Congress partially, at least, to obtain a psychological advantage by proclaiming to the world that the United States is the victim of an aggression.

[3] See p. 420.

dent. The Senate is at a certain disadvantage, however, because the conditions of the armistice which precedes the treaty are set by a military agreement. The Senate may find accordingly that the final terms have already been fixed to a large extent by the President as commander in chief of the army and navy. The failure of the Senate to approve the Treaty of Versailles caused constitutional lawyers to look for some method other than a treaty of peace for bringing a legal end to hostilities. A resolution, repealing the declaration of war, was passed in May, 1920, but was vetoed by President Wilson. A similar resolution was passed in April, 1921, and was approved by President Harding. This resolution signified in that particular instance the victory of Congress over the peace policy of President Wilson.[1]

The Diplomatic Power of the President as Commander in Chief of the Army and Navy. The President, aside from the great military responsibilities in wartime which he assumes as commander in chief of the army and navy, has a considerable power during times of peace in fixing and supporting American policies by armed force. Troop movements, precipitating what amount to *de facto* wars, may be ordered without Congressional declarations, as in the case of the allied relief expedition in China in 1900 and in the occupations of Haiti in 1915 and Santo Domingo in 1916. The efficiency of force in achieving diplomatic ends is particularly to be seen in the relations of the United States with the smaller countries in the American sphere, countries which are so incapable of effective resistance that naval expeditions may be used against them without bringing about a declared state of war. The policies of the United States throughout the Caribbean have been molded by the President partly through his ability to move naval vessels and troops to support his policies. Favored governments have sometimes been maintained and disapproved governments have been upset by displays of force. These policies have been abandoned by the present Roosevelt administration. In conducting normal relations with stronger and more stable countries which are able to offer substantial resist-

[1] Other methods of announcing the termination of war are: a decree of annexation following a war of subjugation; simple termination of hostilities unmarked by legal act, in which case the courts are forced to fix the date from the facts; and a proclamation by the President that the war is ended. The latter is the method often referred to as having marked the end of the Civil War. Whether it could be used in proclaiming the end of a foreign war is a matter of doubt. For a discussion of termination of war see FENWICK, *International Law*, Chapter 33; MATHEWS, *op. cit.*, Chapter 17; WRIGHT, *op. cit.*, pp. 290*ff*.

ance the presidents have found no appropriate field for the use of military force as an adjunct of diplomacy.

THE APPOINTMENT OF DIPLOMATIC AGENTS

The Constitution states that the President "shall nominate, and by and with the advice and consent of the Senate shall appoint ambassadors, other public ministers and consuls." There is no hint in the Constitution that there may exist diplomatic agents in addition to ambassadors and other public ministers and that the appointment of these other agents may be made by the President alone. Practice has informally amended the written document, however, and has supplied the President with this power.

With regard to the custom of senatorial approval the diplomatic representatives of the United States may be classified as follows:

(1) *Ambassadors and Ministers Serving as Regular Chiefs of Missions.* The names of officials in this class are submitted to the Senate for approval which is given as a routine matter. Appointments may be made without such approval during a recess of the Senate. Recess appointees hold until the end of the following session of Congress.

(2) *Foreign Service Officers.* Foreign Service appointments are also approved by the Senate. Nominations to the Foreign Service are determined by examination and neither the President nor the Senate is supposed to exercise any discretion regarding them. This arrangement was put into effect by the cooperation of Congress and the President by the Acts of Congress of 1906, 1915, 1924, and 1931, and by executive orders in pursuance of these acts.

(3) *Agents Appointed for Special Diplomatic Work.* In the case of special diplomatic missions nominations have sometimes been presented for approval but the great weight of practice has been to fill the positions by appointment without submitting the names to the Senate.[1] The practice by which the President took over the whole task of negotiating treaties had much to do with the development of the power of appointment of negotiators without senatorial confirmation for the purpose of constructing the draft agreement. In a minority report of a House committee made in 1919, it was pointed out that from five hundred to six hundred appointments of special negotiators had been made without sub-

---

[1] For illustrations of the appointment of executive agents outside the field of diplomacy see WRISTON, *op. cit.*, pp. 124–126.

mission of the names to the Senate while in not more than thirty-five cases had the names been submitted.[1]

Objections Made by Senators to Appointment of Special Diplomats without Senatorial Confirmation. The failure of the President to send the names of the negotiators to the Senate has in the past, as may be imagined, called forth some lively objections from opposition senators and from those who have sought to guard the senatorial prerogatives. Thus in 1831, when President Jackson sent a special mission to Turkey and failed to submit the names of the appointees to the Senate, he was reproached by Senator Tazewell for exceeding his constitutional authority. After quoting the appropriate clauses of Article II of the Constitution, the senator proceeded:

Hence, it is obvious, that, although the Executive power is vested in the President alone, he is expressly inhibited from making treaties, (if indeed that is an Executive power,) or appointing to any office of the United States, (which certainly is such,) without the advice and consent of the Senate. But the officers in question never have been nominated to the Senate, nor has this body advised or consented to their appointment in any way; therefore, the act of the President in conferring these appointments without the concurrence of the Senate can derive no sanction or support from this part of the Constitution.[2]

While the arguments of the senator may bear much weight when judged from a strictly legal standpoint, yet the overwhelming demand made upon the President to conduct diplomatic negotiations without undue delay together with a sympathetic understanding of his position by Congress has led to a sensible practice which seems to be at variance with the written Constitution. Wriston, after a thorough consideration of Congressional opinion on the constitutional question, comes to the conclusion that senators have seldom raised objections except when political bias has also been present, and that protests in Congress have now practically ceased.[3]

The Contingent Fund. Congress could probably block the use of unconfirmed agents without much difficulty by refusing to appropriate money to pay their salaries or expenses. Diplomatic negotiation is such a delicate and important matter, however, that Congress has not felt justified in withholding funds. It has rather placed at the

[1] House Report, No. 387, 66th Cong., 1st Sess., Part 2, p. 5; MATHEWS, *op. cit.*, p. 331, note 1.

[2] *Benton's Abridgment of the Debates of Congress*, XI: 199 (Feb. 22, 1831), quoted in CORWIN, *op. cit.*, p. 60.

[3] *Op. cit.*, Chapter 4.

disposal of the President a "secret" or "contingent" fund which is a sum of money to be drawn upon by the executive for the conduct of diplomatic business and which need not be fully accounted for. A certificate of the Secretary of State, specifying the items where there is no objection to making them public and setting forth only the total amount of the expenditures in cases in which he does not deem it advisable to be explicit, is regarded as a sufficient accounting. From the contingent fund the President may pay his special agents without referring the matter to Congress.[1]

Practice Alters the Constitution. The extent to which the practice of appointment of special diplomats ignores the wording of the Constitution may be shown by a little further examination. The Constitution says that senatorial approval shall be obtained in the appointment of "ambassadors, other public ministers, and consuls." Nothing is said about diplomatic representatives which do not bear the rank of ambassador or minister. An opinion by Attorney General Cushing, however, in explaining Article II, Section 3, regarding the reception of "ambassadors and other public ministers," states that these terms include "all possible diplomatic agents which any foreign power may accredit to the United States."[2] If this is so, the appointment of any accredited diplomat should, according to technical law, be concurred in by the Senate.

Furthermore, the President in recent years has made appointments without senatorial approval of special agents which have been given specifically the ranks of ambassador and minister. The first instance of such an appointment was that of Whitelaw Reid who was sent as ambassador extraordinary on special mission to congratulate Queen Victoria on the sixtieth anniversary of her accession to the throne. Reid was thus placed upon an even footing with the representatives of the sovereigns of Europe, all of whom held the rank of ambassador. The Senate, however, was not called upon to confirm his appointment. Representatives to political conferences have also been appointed with ambassadorial and ministerial rank without senatorial confirmation. In 1907 the American delegation to the Second Hague Conference consisted of Joseph H. Choate, Horace Porter, and Uriah M. Rose, who were ambassadors extraordinary, and Brigadier General Davis, Rear Admiral Sperry, and William I. Buchanan, who were ministers plenipotentiary. The ambassadorial rank was given to the four American delegates to the Washington Conference, two of these being also United States

[1] LAY, *op. cit*; p. 46.
[2] *Opinions of Attorneys General*, VII: 209.

senators. The Senate, it seems, now raises no objection to the appointment of such representatives by presidential action alone.[1]

The Designation of Diplomatic Grades. One instance in which the power of Congress has grown at the expense of that of the President is in the designation of the diplomatic grades of American chiefs of mission in foreign capitals. In the beginning this matter was left entirely in the hands of the President who was guided by a system of diplomatic grades based on the common usage of other nations as expressed in the rules of the Congress of Vienna (1815) and of the Congress of Aix-la-Chapelle (1818). The President continued to determine the grades of American diplomats until 1855, using ordinarily those of minister, minister resident, and chargé d'affaires. In 1855 Congress invaded the field of executive discretion and enacted that the President should appoint representatives of the grade of envoy extraordinary and minister plenipotentiary to certain designated countries. In 1893 Congress authorized the President to appoint ambassadors to such countries as he should find were, or were about to be, represented by ambassadors to the United States. In 1909 another act forbade the President to create ambassadorships without Congressional authorization. According to an opinion of the Attorney General, rendered in 1855, such legislation is recommendatory only and does not limit the President to appointments in the grades indicated.[2] Despite this opinion the terms of the act have been followed by the President; and, by the weight of practice, Congress has gained a distinct advantage in the matter of the designation of grades.[3]

Probably the designation of grades is not of much importance in the control of foreign relations. The shift of this power to Congress illustrates a principle that is evidenced in other aspects of national administration, *i.e.*, that Congress is best situated to shape machinery while the President tends to gain control over the machinery after it is set up.

---

[1] WRISTON, *op. cit.*, pp. 194–200. The appointment of senators to negotiate international agreements is discussed in the following chapter as a practice designed to offset the difficult provisions of the Constitution regarding treaties.

[2] *Opinions of Attorneys General*, VII: 195.

[3] CORWIN, *op. cit.*, pp. 66*ff.*; MATHEWS, *op. cit.*, pp. 318–321; WRIGHT, *op. cit.*, pp. 324–325; LAY, *op. cit.*, pp. 58–61.

CHAPTER XXIII

TREATIES AND EXECUTIVE AGREEMENTS

The procedure by which the American government enters into international agreements is a matter of no small importance as it determines the ease or difficulty with which the United States may follow the path of world cooperation. The formal method set forth in the Constitution is often a matter of embarassment to the executive. The approval of the Senate is not always easy to obtain. Even where the Senate desires to cooperate, its confirming will cannot always be made effective because, under the two-thirds rule, a minority of one-third plus one has the power to block treaties. There has been much opinion that the formal requirements for treaty making are too difficult under modern conditions. Modifications have already been introduced by practice in order to elude the written constitution and to give greater ease in the completion of agreements. Perhaps, in the future, further modifications will take place; for it may be taken as a principle of government that written forms cannot permanently obstruct the natural course of political development.

I. TREATIES

There are five stages in the process of making treaties in the United States:

1. *Preliminary Negotiation and Signature.* The drawing up and the signing of the treaty under American practice are functions of the executive. These duties may be performed by the President himself; but in practice they are transacted by the Secretary of State, a regular ambassador or minister abroad, or an agent or commission especially appointed for the task.

2. *Action of the Senate.* The signed treaty is placed before the Senate which may advise or refuse to advise ratification. A two-thirds vote is necessary for affirmative action. The Senate may also attach amendments or reservations to the treaty which become effective only after acceptance by the other party or parties.

3. *Ratification.* Ratification is the act of the President. He signs an instrument of ratification which is attested by the Secretary

of State and is attached to the treaty. The great seal of the United States is then impressed upon the document.

4. *Exchange of Ratifications.* The United States keeps a counterpart of the treaty and delivers to the other government the copy which bears the due evidence of ratification. A plenipotentiary with full powers performs the act of delivery and receives in return a copy with the ratification and seal of the other government.

5. *Proclamation.* The President then proclaims the treaty, giving notice to the public of its terms and of the fact of its ratification. The treaty takes effect as the law of the land controlling private rights in the United States at the time of its proclamation. As affecting the rights of the signatory governments it becomes binding upon exchange of ratifications although it sometimes takes retroactive effect from the time of signature.

The principal work of treaty making in the United States is in the negotiation and in the action by the Senate. In any discussion of treaty procedure it is necessary to consider some of the problems which arise in these stages.

Preliminary Negotiation

Washington Alters the Constitution. The Constitution states that treaties shall be made by the President by and with the advice and consent of the Senate, provided two-thirds of the Senators present concur. No separate provision is made for the negotiation of the treaty or for the subsequent steps. The intention of the framers, so far as can be ascertained from the remarks of the delegates or from an examination of the previously accepted meaning of the words "by and with the advice and consent of" as used in connection with colonial legislation, was that the President should act in personal conference with the Senate, the latter being a sort of council.[1] President Washington in the beginning attempted to negotiate treaties with the close cooperation of the Senate, and formally stated that oral communication with that body seemed "indispensably necessary" in all matters respecting treaties. The discussion of the terms of treaties by written communications, he thought, "would be tedious without being satisfactory."[2] On

---

[1] See Wriston, *op. cit.*, pp. 61*ff.* Crandall also states that it was the clear intention of the framers that the President should consult with the Senate prior to the opening of negotiations. Crandall, Samuel B., *Treaties, Their Making and Enforcement* (2d ed.), p. 70, John Byrne & Company, Washington, 1916.

[2] *The Writings of George Washington*, X: 484, Jared Sparks, editor, Russell, Shattuck, and Williams, Boston, 1836.

August 22, 1789, President Washington went to the Senate chamber accompanied by General Knox, Secretary of War, for the purpose of discussing a proposed treaty with the Southern Indians. He asked that the Senate give an answer in the affirmative or negative to seven specific propositions. The Senate was not willing to make a decision immediately and postponed the matter till the next legislative day, at which time it accepted only part of the proposals. The Senate's unwillingness to discuss the matter caused President Washington finally to withdraw from the Senate chamber with a discontented air; and, according to John Quincy Adams, "he said he would be dammed if he ever went there again."[1] And no president has gone into the Senate chamber to seek advice on the negotiation of treaties from that day to this. For some time after this occurrence Washington persisted in asking the opinion of the Senate prior to the negotiation of treaties, using the medium of the written message. He finally abandoned such communications, however, and since that time correspondence with the Senate on proposed treaties has occurred only in exceptional cases.[2] The reason for the development of the practice of drawing up treaties through administrative officers is that the executive is the only branch competent for the work of negotiation. Howard Lee McBain appropriately points out the difficulties which would be encountered in the negotiation of treaties by legislatures in the following words: "Multitudinous minds do not readily meet at such long range. Contracts are more easily drafted by a few persons around a table."[3] And such stubborn characteristics of political procedure are of greater importance than the intent of the framers of the Constitution.

Agents of Negotiation. According to practice a treaty is drawn up and signed before it is presented to the Senate. As has been stated, various agencies are employed by the President in the negotiations. Woodrow Wilson's role in the Peace Conference in Paris presents an unusual case. In that instance the President personally participated in the actual negotiation and signature of the treaty acting "in his own name and by his own proper author-

[1] *Memoirs of John Quincy Adams*, VI: 427, J. B. Lippincott & Company, Philadelphia, 1875; see also, MACLAY, WILLIAM, *Sketches of Debate in the First Senate of the United States*, p. 122, Lane S. Hart, Harrisburg, Pa., 1880; FLEMING, DENNA FRANK, *The Treaty Veto of the American Senate*, pp. 16ff., G. P. Putnam's Sons, New York, 1930.

[2] CRANDALL, *op. cit.*, pp. 68–72.

[3] *The Living Constitution*, pp. 194–195. The Macmillan Company, New York, 1928.

ity." He was assisted by four commissioners plenipotentiary appointed by him to represent the United States. President Wilson was, however, the principal American negotiator and had no small part in determining the content of the Treaty of Versailles. In normal cases the negotiations are conducted by the Secretary of State or by some diplomatic officer. If the treaty is made in Washington, it is customary for the Secretary of State to sign for the United States although various officials of the department participate in the bargaining and in the drafting of the document. Examples of treaties drawn up in Washington bearing the name of secretaries of state as negotiators are the Hay-Pauncefote Treaty of 1901 and the Bryan-Chamorro Treaty of 1914. If the treaty is negotiated in the capital of another power, the interests of the United States are cared for by the American embassy or legation in that city or by one or more special diplomatic representatives appointed for the particular purpose, acting in any case under instructions from Washington. In recent years, with the increase in the use of international conferences, there has been a growth in the number of treaties negotiated by missions of four or five or more special diplomats.

Consultation with Individual Senators. While it has long ceased to be the custom for the President to consult the Senate formally before or during negotiations, he has frequently conferred with individual senators. Thus, when in February, 1919, President Wilson returned to the United States in the midst of the negotiations of the Treaty of Versailles, he met with the members of the Senate Committee on Foreign Relations and the House Committee on Foreign Affairs. The President made a statement regarding the tentative agreement reached in Paris. Some of the senators criticized the proposed treaty, particularly the provisions of the Covenant of the League of Nations. On his return to Paris President Wilson obtained several amendments to the Covenant for the purpose of satisfying the objections of the senators.

The Use of Senators as Agents of Negotiation. Another method of cooperation with the Senate which has now become a regular part of constitutional practice is that of appointing senators as diplomatic representatives to aid in the negotiation of treaties at international conferences. The principal purposes in making use of Senate members in this way are to obtain the assistance of able men and to be assured in advance of the favorable attitude of influential and thoroughly informed members of the Senate in order to prepare the way for an affirmative vote on the treaty. The two-thirds requirement for passage is difficult to comply with and has sometimes interfered with the intelligent direction of international affairs. The extralegal device of using senators as negotiators in order to weaken the unusual power of a Senate minority has, therefore, seemed justifiable.

The wording of the Constitution appears to raise some difficulty to the use of senators in this way. Article I, Section 6, Clause 2 states that "no person holding any office under the United States shall be a member of either house during his continuance in office." The purpose of the clause was to make a sharp distinction between the executive and legislative branches and to prevent any person from holding positions in both. The question arises: Is membership upon a special diplomatic mission to be considered an "office" in the meaning of the Constitution? Since the work to be performed is executive in character and since the position sometimes carries with it a diplomatic grade, there is good reason to believe that such appointments do violate the letter of the Constitution.[1] This seems to have been the view of the earlier statesmen. In 1814 when President Madison appointed Senator Bayard and Speaker of the House Henry Clay upon the commission to negotiate a treaty of peace with Great Britain, the two men evidently considered that the new positions conflicted with their legislative status and resigned their membership in Congress. As late as 1898, after President McKinley had made eight or ten appointments of this sort, considerable opposition developed in the upper house. The important Judiciary Committee of the Senate was almost unanimous in its opposition to the practice. Senator Hoar was instructed to protest to the President against such appointments. Some years later Senator Hoar, in describing his interview with the President, stated that Mr. McKinley had said that "he was aware of the objections; that he had come to feel them very strongly; and while he did not say in terms that he would not make another appointment of the same kind, he conveyed to me, and I am sure meant to convey to me, an assurance that it would not occur again."[2]

Regardless of objections the practice of appointing senators upon these missions has in recent years been resorted to in the case of

[1] Lindsay Rogers comments regarding the practice: "only by logomachy can it be said that there has been no violation of the clause of the Constitution forbidding Senators and Representatives from holding offices under the United States." *The American Senate*, p. 66, Alfred A. Knopf, New York, 1926.

[2] *Congressional Record*, 36: 2698 (Feb. 26, 1903). See also MATHEWS, *op. cit.*, pp. 327–329.

important conferences with a fair degree of regularity. Possibly the deadlock between President Wilson and the Senate over the Treaty of Versailles may have had something to do with the change. In the case of that treaty the power of the minority in the Senate motivated partly by political reasons was strikingly emphasized. The statement has frequently been made that if President Wilson had taken some senators with him to Paris, the difficulty would have been greatly reduced. At any rate, when in 1921 President Harding selected four delegates to represent the United States at the Washington Conference, he named among them Senators Lodge and Underwood, who were respectively the majority and minority leaders of the Senate.[1] The appointment of the two senators seemed to arouse no material opposition. President Harding had no doubts as to the appropriateness of the appointments. Regarding the selection of Lodge he wrote: "You can understand how . . . naturally I have turned to the Chairman of the Foreign Relations Committee of the Senate for a member of the delegation."[2] The wisdom of the choice appeared later when the support of both the senators and their associates was instrumental in securing prompt approval by the Senate of the conference treaties.

At the London Conference in 1930 the United States was represented by a strong delegation which included Senators Reed of Pennsylvania and Robinson of Arkansas. The appointment of the senators was a further demonstration of the wisdom of the practice from the standpoint of the executive. During the hot summer months of 1930, when the treaty was considered in a special session of the Senate, the work of these two senators was outstanding in defense of the treaty. Senator Reed, in particular, by his unusual ability as an advocate and by his knowledge of the details of armaments confounded the enemies of the treaty in the committee room. On the floor of the Senate he distinguished himself by the manner in which he withstood the attacks of the treaty opponents. The advantage of this strategy is emphasized by the fact that Senator Reed, a World War Veteran, had been considered in advance by some observers as one likely to be critical of armament limitation. In 1933 Senators Pittman and Couzens were appointed on the delegation to the World Economic Conference at London.

The appointment of members of the House of Representatives as delegates to international conferences in which treaties are to be

[1] POOLE, DeWITT CLINTON, *The Conduct of Foreign Relations under Democratic Conditions*, p. 69, Yale University Press, New Haven, 1924.

[2] Letter to Lamar Jeffers, *N.Y. Times*, Sept. 9, 1921.

considered which may later require legislation to put them into effect has been employed in recent years. Stephen G. Porter was a delegate to the Second Opium Conference at Geneva in 1924–1925. Theodore Burton represented this country at the Traffic in Arms Conference at Geneva in 1925. At the World Economic Conference at London in 1933 the American delegation included Congressmen McReynolds and Morrison.

ACTION OF THE SENATE

Form of Action. Contrary to popular terminology the Senate does not ratify treaties. In correct and technical language the ratification is performed by the President after the Senate has acted. The Senate merely advises ratification. When the treaty reaches the Senate it is referred to the powerful Committee on Foreign Relations. The committee may hold hearings upon it. It may then fail to act (generally an effective method of killing a treaty) or it may report adversely. If the committee is favorably inclined, it will make a report recommending that the Senate should advise the ratification of the treaty as it stands, or that it should advise the ratification with certain amendments or reservations. The committee may take still another form of action, as it did with regard to the Pact of Paris, *i.e.*, report the treaty favorably but at the same time pass an interpretative resolution intended to make more certain the attitude of the committee as to the obligations to be assumed.

When the treaty reaches the floor of the Senate it is discussed in either executive or open session. The custom up to the time of the World War was to consider treaties in secret. Such was undoubtedly the intention of many of the framers of the Constitution, as the possibility of secrecy in connection with the small size of the Senate was mentioned in the Convention of 1787. A Senate rule adopted in 1800 provided that treaties should be kept secret until a resolution should remove the injunction of secrecy.[1] With the growth in size of the Senate the rule of secrecy became difficult to enforce and leaks became numerous. Meanwhile the demand for open diplomacy was growing. The treaty of 1888 on the question of the Canadian fisheries and some of the arbitration treaties of 1911 were discussed in open session. The Treaty of Versailles was likewise debated in 1919 and 1920 in open session. Since that time practically all the treaties have been considered openly.

[1] CRANDALL, *op. cit.*, p. 84.

Amendments or Reservations.   Amendments or reservations to treaties by the Senate may be attached by a majority vote.   The practice of the Senate in thus adding amendments began as early as the Jay Treaty of 1794 and it has become relatively common in recent years.   A study of the amending of treaties, extending into the year 1928, shows that, of 725 treaties approved by the Senate and later proclaimed, 101 were amended.[1]   When the amendment is attached to the treaty, the revised agreement must receive a two-thirds vote for approval.   It then goes to the President.   Sometimes the amendment has been so out of line with the purpose of the President's negotiation that he has dropped the treaty and the Senate's revisions have never been submitted to the other party for acceptance.   If the President should submit the revised draft, the other government may reject it.   In fifty-one cases treaties amended by the Senate have failed, either because the President has been unwilling to proceed with the matter or because of rejection by the other party.[2]

Some writers take the position that the affixing of amendments to a treaty by the Senate is an exceedingly defective method of negotiation.   The President through his agents gives careful study to the needs of the United States and to the best possible bargain which this country can obtain.   The draft agreement is accepted by both parties and signed.   After this the Senate, often without much consideration, attaches amendments, changing items which have been agreed upon or adding others.   This procedure is apt to appear to the foreign government as a disagreeable ultimatum.[3] In several instances the other party has refused to go ahead with the treaty because of opposition in principle to this method of conducting international business.[4]

The Two-thirds Vote Has Become a Difficult Requirement. The final approval of the Senate to treaties whether amended or not must be given by a two-thirds vote of the members present.   The difficulty of obtaining such an unusual majority has aroused much opposition to the requirement.   Secretary Hay called it "the irreparable mistake of our Constitution."[5]   A declaration of war requires a less difficult vote than does the act of approving a treaty of

---

[1] DANGERFIELD, ROYDEN J., *In Defense of the Senate, A Study in Treaty Making*, p. 171, University of Oklahoma Press, Norman, Okla., 1933.

[2] *Ibid.*, p. 185.

[3] McBAIN, *op. cit.*, pp. 196–197.

[4] FLEMING, *op. cit.*, pp. 39*ff.*

[5] THAYER, WILLIAM ROSCOE, *The Life and Letters of John Hay*, II: 219.

peace. Some of the objections to the two-thirds provision arise from the fact that conditions have been greatly altered in several respects since the Constitution was framed. Some of these changes are:

1. The Senate is now more than three times the size of the first Senate of the United States. One of the reasons for not including the House of Representatives in the treaty-making power was the greater number of its members, but the Senate is now larger than was the House in 1789. The size of the Senate makes obstruction easier than was previously the case.

2. The rise of the party system has changed the nature of the Senate's consultation on treaties. The party system was not anticipated by the majority of the framers of the Constitution. They expected that the Senate would sit as a homogeneous body devoted to the interests of the nation. But party policies and party antagonisms have had much to do with the votes on many treaties, as was the case when a number of Republicans for party reasons opposed the Treaty of Versailles. If the vote follows strict party lines, it is almost impossible to obtain a two-thirds majority. In recent years, except in the present 74th Congress, no party has commanded that many votes. The administration party by itself has ordinarily been unable to carry out a treaty policy; and the two-thirds clause must be regarded as in conflict with the theory of party government.

3. The United States is now much nearer to other nations in travel and communication than in Washington's administration and the volume of our international commerce has been vastly increased. The need for treaties to give a more secure status to American interests as well as to provide for the amicable adjustment of disputes that are certain to arise regarding them has consequently increased far beyond the anticipations of the fathers. The two-thirds provision, based on the theory that treaties are to be viewed with suspicion, is unduly obstructive at a time when international legislation has become desirable in order to escape many irritations that arise in dealings between nations.

The Treaty Veto in Practice. Judging from the treaties that have been defeated in the Senate and from the attitude of senators by and large, there are certain generalizations that we can make concerning the effect of the treaty veto upon American policy.

In the first place, the Senate is more suspicious in dealing with the great powers than is the President. The effect of the two-thirds rule has been to accentuate the effects of antiforeign suspicions. There have been some rare occasions on which the Senate has been anxious to take steps in the direction of closer and more friendly international relations with strong countries where at the same time the President has been unwilling. On the other hand, in a much greater number of cases presidential plans for closer cooperation have been defeated. Senators are not so intimately in touch with international affairs as is the executive and are not in such an advantageous position to see how American interests may be advanced or to perceive how threatened injuries may be avoided by international legislation. Small local objections loom large in the senatorial mind. The nationalistic view has been shown by the defeat through rejection or emasculation of such agreements as the Slave Trade Treaty with Great Britain signed in 1824; the Johnson-Clarendon Treaty for the settlement of the Alabama claims in 1869 (although a subsequent treaty was approved in 1871); the Canadian Fisheries Treaty in 1888; the arbitration treaties in 1897, 1904, and 1911; the Treaty of Versailles of 1919; the St. Lawrence Waterways Treaty defeated in 1934; and the Protocol of the World Court defeated in 1935.

In the second place, the Senate operating under the two-thirds rule has been less imperialistic in dealing with small and weak countries than has the President. This is probably due to the fact that the President has been in closer touch with international investment interests which have sometimes urged strong action upon him. Treaties drawn up by the President to annex foreign territory or to bring other nations more strictly under American control have in several cases been blocked by the Senate. In 1860 two treaties giving the United States unusual opportunities for controlling Mexico were before the Senate. One would have granted to the United States the right to transport goods and troops on certain Mexican highways and to use force if necessary to protect goods and persons in transit. The other would have made it obligatory upon Mexico to seek the aid of the United States in maintaining treaty stipulations or to provide for the safety of American citizens. The costs of American aid were to be paid by Mexico. The first of these treaties was defeated by a vote of 18 for and 27 against and the second never came to a vote.[1] Republican opposition to the treaties was based to a great extent on opposition to imperialism, partly because of principle but more because of the fear of the creation of slave states. In 1870 President Grant

[1] HOLT, W. STULL, *Treaties Defeated by the Senate*, pp. 92–96, Johns Hopkins Press, Baltimore, 1933.

pressed the Senate to approve a treaty for the annexation of the Dominican Republic, but anti-imperialists, such as Sumner and Schurz, attacked it vigorously. The treaty failed by a vote of 28 to 28. A treaty for the purchase of the Virgin Islands for $7,500,000, negotiated in 1867, was rejected by the Committee on Foreign Relations and did not come to a vote in the Senate although another treaty to purchase the islands for $25,000,000 was approved in 1916. A treaty which was to give the United States financial control over the Dominican Republic in 1905 failed to come to a vote and President Roosevelt proceeded under an executive agreement. In 1907, however, a treaty to the same effect was approved. Treaties to bring Nicaragua and Honduras under American financial control were presented to the Senate in 1911 and their approval was strongly urged by President Taft. The Senate failed, however, to approve them. The Treaty of Paris of 1898, which provided for annexation of the Philippines, was strongly opposed in the Senate and probably would have been defeated had not the Democrats preferred to raise a party issue of imperialism in the 1900 campaign. William Jennings Bryan advised Democrats to support the treaty. The question was then carried before the people.[1]

In the third place, the two-thirds rule in the Senate magnifies the power of special interests which may be opposed to a certain treaty, giving them an opportunity for obstruction much greater than that which they would have under a majority-vote rule.[2] In 1876 the American claimants in the Benjamin Weil and La Abra Silver Mine cases were awarded $479,975.95 and $672,070.99 respectively in claims against the Mexican government. Perjury had been used in establishing these claims. On suspicion of fraud President Arthur suspended payment of money to the claimants and prepared a convention to reopen the case. The friends of the claimants were able to obtain twenty votes in the Senate against the treaty as compared with thirty-four in favor of it and the agreement failed of adoption. Later the injustice to Mexico was corrected by returning the undistributed money and appropriating funds to repay Mexico for that already spent. This was done by an act of Congress, however, and not by treaty.[3] The Treaty of 1904 between the United States and Cuba, by which the United States relinquished all

---

[1] For evidence as to Bryan's motives see Curti, *Bryan and World Peace*, pp. 121*ff.*

[2] Rogers, *op. cit.*, pp. 71–72; Holt, *op. cit.*, pp. 287–288.

[3] *Moore's Digest*, VII: 63–68; Fleming, *op. cit.*, pp. 57–58.

title to the Isle of Pines, was before the Senate for twenty-one years.[1]
Some American land speculators who felt that the value of their
purchases would be enhanced under the American flag opposed the
treaty and were able to obtain support from a few senators. This
was sufficient in the press of business to prevent the United States
from ratifying the agreement for over two decades.[2] Probably the
best illustrations of the power of special interests to block treaties
under the two-thirds rule are to be found in the defeat of reciprocity
treaties.   Three such treaties have been approved, but some sixteen
that have been negotiated failed of ratification.   Fourteen of
these were never acted upon by the Senate and two were rejected.[3]
Denna F. Fleming, in writing of the reasons for the defeat of
reciprocity treaties, particularly mentions the opposition of sec-
tional and occupational interests as well as political factors in the
Senate.[4]

Royden J. Dangerfield, basing his opinion on a detailed statistical
study of Senate action on treaties, states that including two doubtful cases only seven treaties have been defeated finally by the
existence of the two-thirds rule.   That is, there have been only
seven rejected treaties which have received more than a majority
and less than a two-thirds vote.   Several other rejected treaties
have not even received a majority vote and would doubtless have
failed even if the two-thirds rule had not been in effect.   Furthermore, Professor Dangerfield contends, since amendments are
adopted by a majority vote, the two-thirds rule cannot be held
responsible for forcing alterations in the 152 treaties that were
amended in the Senate.   Their fate would not have been seriously
altered, he says, if the two-thirds rule had been abolished.[5] This

---

[1] An identical treaty had also been before the Senate in 1903.

[2] Senate Document 166, 68th Cong., 2d Sess.; JENKS, LELAND HAMILTON,
Our Cuban Colony, p. 144, Vanguard Press, New York, 1928; DANGERFIELD,
op. cit., pp. 137–142; WILLIAMS, BENJ. H., "The Isle of Pines Treaty," *Foreign
Affairs*, III: 689 (July, 1925).   The treaty was evidently in accord with international justice.   It was also a part of a bargain by which the United States
acquired a lease of Guantánamo.   The lease was acquired by executive agreement which went into effect immediately in 1904.

[3] DANGERFIELD, *op. cit.*, p. 259.

[4] *Op. cit.*, p. 75.   See also U.S. Tariff Commission, *Reciprocity and Commercial Treaties*, p. 222, Govt. Printing Office, Washington, 1919.

[5] *Op. cit.*, pp. 310–312.   See also McCLENDON, R. EARL, "The Two-Thirds
Rule in Senate Action upon Treaties, 1789–1901," *American Journal of Inter-
national Law*, XXVI: 37 (January, 1932).   For an article criticizing the two-
thirds rule as an obstacle to American peace policies see FLEMING, DENNA
FRANK, "The Role of the Senate in Treaty-Making: A Survey of Four
Decades," *American Political Science Review*, XXVIII: 583 (August, 1934).

study deals with the treaties signed on the part of the United States down to February 6, 1928. Since that time one of the most notable of all senatorial rejections which can be traced to the two-thirds rule has occurred, *i.e.*, the rejection of the World Court Protocol in 1935 by the vote of 52 for as against 36 in opposition.

The statistical method does not entirely measure the effects of the two-thirds rule as, indeed, Dangerfield points out. It fails to make clear to what extent the rule has discouraged the friends of treaties from pressing them when a majority vote is possible but when a two-thirds vote is out of the question. In the words of one well-informed observer:

> The record does not show from what wise and helpful measures our Presidents and Secretaries of State have been estopped by perhaps unfounded fear of what a single Senator might do, nor is it clear into what brusque and harmful actions the bogey on Capitol Hill has frightened them. I am sure that both misfortunes have befallen frequently.[1]

The study referred to above shows that 47 treaties were not acted upon by the Senate at all. A goodly number of these, we may assume, were left to repose in their senatorial grave because of the lack of vigor on the part of their sponsors in prosecuting a hopeless task. And there is, after all, good reason to charge the two-thirds rule with some responsibility for the practice of amending treaties in order to eliminate such provisions as may be opposed by small groups of senators. For with the requirement of an extraordinary majority the necessity of appeasing the feelings and prejudices of minorities in the Senate is greatly increased.

The serious irritation which our difficult constitutional requirements for treaties may cause can be indicated somewhat by the impatient attitude which this country has sometimes taken toward the treaty machinery of other countries, even where such machinery has been partially copied from our own Constitution. With regard to a treaty negotiated with Mexico in 1826 the Secretary of State instructed the American chargé to protest to the Mexican government concerning the spirit of procrastination which could not be "ascribed to any motives consistent with a friendly disposition towards the United States." He complained also of the action of the committee of foreign affairs in recommending amendments apparently to defeat the agreement.[2] The resentment of President

[1] POOLE, DEWITT CLINTON, "Cooperation Abroad through Organization at Home," *Annals of the American Academy of Political and Social Science,* CLVI: 137 (July, 1931).

[2] HOLT, *op. cit.*, p. 54.

Roosevelt toward Colombia for failure to approve the Hay-Herran Treaty of 1903 has been referred to.[1] Mr. Roosevelt described the refusal of the Colombian Senate to approve the treaty as a breach of an obligation to the United States. He declared that: "the Colombian Government peremptorily and offensively refused thus to do its part."[2]

Devices for Mitigating or Evading the Two-thirds Rule. It has been necessary to review the objections to treaty procedure in order that the reasons for certain constitutional developments may be made clear. Various practices have naturally arisen for the purpose of surmounting or avoiding the obstacles in the paths of treaties. One of these has already been considered, *i.e.*, the appointing of senators upon delegations to negotiate treaties so that their assistance may be counted on later in obtaining the approval of the Senate.

A second device is the substitution of the joint action of both houses of Congress for a treaty. The treaty with the Republic of Texas providing for annexation, which was signed in 1844, was defeated in the Senate. Texas was annexed the following year by a joint resolution of Congress. The method of joint resolution was also followed in 1898 in the annexation of Hawaii. Two treaties for this purpose which had been negotiated had not been approved. When in 1911 the United States attempted to make a reciprocity arrangement with Canada, the form of action agreed upon was concurrent legislation in the two countries instead of treaty. The reciprocity bill consequently introduced passed both houses of Congress, the vote in the Senate being 53 to 27. As can be seen, this vote would have been a defeat for a treaty. In 1934, when the Roosevelt administration decided upon entrance into the International Labor Organization, concurrent action by the houses was decided upon in preference to the ratification of the relevant part of the Treaty of Versailles, which seemed to have been the method intended by the creators of the treaty. Accordingly the joint resolution of June, 1934, authorized the President to accept membership, an action which he took in August of the same year.

A third and more important device for sidestepping the two-thirds vote requirement and, in fact, of avoiding any action by the Senate at all, is the executive agreement, which will be discussed at some length in the following pages. Altogether the growth of these devices is a hopeful sign of flexibility. If the difficulty of the

[1] See p. 63.

[2] In Annual Message of Dec. 7, 1903, *Moore's Digest*, III: 53.

requirements for treaty making cannot be reduced or circumvented, the effects upon the nation may well be serious when a situation arises in which international action is necessary to advance the national interests but is opposed by a sufficient Senate minority.

II. EXECUTIVE AGREEMENTS

While the Constitution makes no provision for international compacts which do not receive the consent of the Senate, there are, nevertheless, many matters which in practice are adjusted by simple agreements between the executive of the United States and the governments of foreign countries. In matters where the engagement places no obligation upon the United States beyond that which can be performed by the President alone, it seems that executive agreements can be used without particular constitutional friction. A large number of minor diplomatic transactions cannot wait for the ponderous action of the upper house without seriously hampering the work of the Department of State. In some matters of policy which are under the control of the President, and where it may not seem desirable to submit the question to the deliberate consideration of the Senate, executive agreements in line with American desires are the simplest and most satisfactory solutions. There are, furthermore, some urgent international transactions which cannot be performed by treaty because of the impossibility of obtaining the consent of two-thirds of the Senate due to the blocking power of minority interests. In other cases secrecy has been considered of such importance that the Senate has been disregarded and executive agreements have been made.

An executive agreement may be defined as an international understanding with a foreign government entered into by the executive without the consent of the Senate. Unless made under the authorization of Congress, it is not the law of the land. Without Congressional authorization the agreement depends only upon the good faith and power of the executive. But executive agreements are sometimes of greater importance than treaties and for practical purposes they are ordinarily just as binding. In these days of high-pressure international business, since the volume of diplomatic transactions has reached an unprecedented level, the executive agreement is an invaluable part of American diplomatic machinery.

There are two main classes into which these agreements fall: those made by the President on his own authority, and those made by him upon authorization of Congress.

AGREEMENTS MADE BY THE PRESIDENT UPON HIS OWN AUTHORITY

Agreements Committing the Parties to General Principles of Policy. Since the executive department ordinarily outlines foreign policy, it seems quite possible for that branch to enter into agreements in most matters with other governments fixing the general course of mutual action. In any case it should always be understood by the other government that if the policy promised by the President requires some act of Congress to make it effective there is a possibility that the President cannot carry it out. All that he pledges is the good faith of the executive department.

A case illustrating this point was the remarkable executive agreement or understanding between the United States and Japan made in 1905.[1] The agreement was in the form of a conversation, a memorandum of which was retained by each government. The conversation took place between Count Katsura and a personal representative of President Roosevelt. Count Katsura stated that Japan had no aggressive designs regarding the Philippines. The American diplomat stated "that it was difficult, indeed impossible, for the President of the United States of America to enter even to any understanding amounting in effect to a confidential informal agreement, without the consent of the Senate, but that he felt sure that without any agreement at all the people of the United States was [sic] so fully in accord with the people of Japan and Great Britain in the maintenance of peace in the Far East that whatever occasion arose appropriate action of the Government of the United States, in conjunction with Japan and Great Britain, for such a purpose could be counted on by them quite as confidently as if the United States were under treaty obligation to take [it]." Despite the guarded promise of the United States this conversation was evidently regarded by President Roosevelt as committing this country to cooperation with Great Britain and Japan in the Pacific.

A number of executive agreements have been entered into regarding the open door in China. The Hay Open-Door Notes of 1899, which were sent to the powers holding spheres of interest or leased territory in China, brought about general acceptance of the principle that no discriminations would be made in such areas with regard to tariffs, harbor dues, and railroad rates. This country had

[1] DENNETT, TYLER, *Roosevelt and the Russo-Japanese War*, pp. 112–114, Doubleday, Page & Company, Garden City, N.Y., 1925. See also an article by the same author, "President Roosevelt's Secret Pact with Japan," *Current History*, XXI: 15 (October, 1924).

no spheres of interest or leased territories in China and the agreement placed no obligations upon the United States aside from a general tacit pledge as to future attitudes. The Root-Takahira agreement of 1908 between the United States and Japan reaffirmed the open-door principle. The Lansing-Ishii agreement of 1917, while restating the doctrine of the territorial integrity of China and the open door, recognized that Japan had special interests in China. This agreement was canceled by an exchange of notes in 1923. The obligations of the United States under the open-door agreements were of the kind that could be carried out by the executive alone since they dealt with matters of diplomatic policy which did not require Congressional legislation.

Agreements for the Control of the Customhouses of Weaker Nations. Since agreements providing for customs control by Americans in weaker countries have been quite commonly regarded as imperialistic in nature, such treaties have sometimes met with searching criticism in the Senate. In some cases, therefore, the arrangements have been concluded by executive agreement. In 1905 a treaty providing for customs collection by an American official was signed with the Dominican Republic. The Senate debated the treaty but adjourned without acting upon it. President Roosevelt thereupon put the plan into operation by an executive agreement with the Dominican government. In the words of President Roosevelt: "I went ahead and administered the proposed treaty anyhow, considering it as a simple agreement on the part of the Executive which would be converted into a treaty whenever the Senate acted."[1] Here again the agreement was of such a character that all of the obligations which it placed upon the United States, such as the protection of the collecting officer, could be performed by the President as commander in chief of the army and navy. Two years later a treaty providing for the collectorship was approved by the Senate.

Another case of an executive agreement for customs control occurred in 1911 and 1912 with regard to Liberia. An arrangement had been made for an international loan which was to be guaranteed by a four-power customs control. Possibly fearing to place the plan before the Senate, the Department of State negotiated the agreement with Great Britain, France, and Germany without putting it into treaty form.[2] Treaties for customs control with

[1] *Theodore Roosevelt, An Autobiography*, p. 511, Charles Scribner's Sons, New York, 1920.

[2] *Foreign Relations*, 1911, pp. 342*ff.*; 1912, pp. 667*ff.*

Honduras and Nicaragua were drawn up in 1911 but these were defeated by the Senate. In the case of Nicaragua, however, an agreement between American bankers and the Nicaraguan government was concluded to provide for customs control. The Department of State was not a party to the agreement, but it gave advice regarding the terms of the contract and formally approved the nominee of the bankers for the post of collector-general.[1]

Most-Favored-Nation Agreements. During the Harding-Coolidge-Hoover administrations the policy of the United States was to obtain agreements to unconditional most-favored-nation treatment. The American government at that time employed the single-schedule, equal-treatment tariff which gave no advantage to any country except Cuba. A number of treaties providing for most-favored-nation treatment were negotiated and approved by the Senate. In addition more than a dozen agreements for most-favored-nation treatment were arranged by simple exchanges of notes. As can be seen, such agreements could readily be made by the executive as they involved no conflict with Congressional tariff policy. The President was armed by the Tariff Act of 1922 with the authority to raise tariffs or place embargoes against other countries which discriminated against American goods. As the only probability of discrimination against other countries was through the exercise of the power by the President, he was fully able to give guarantees against such action.

Agreements by the President as Commander in Chief of the Army and Navy. The President's power of making agreements is particularly complete regarding movements of troops, such as the withdrawal of the armed forces following military interventions or wars. Not only is the need of promptness of action great in such matters, but the obligations which the United States assumes are ordinarily those which the President can carry out alone through his control of the army and navy. Armistice agreements are of this character. Some of the principal provisions that were written into the treaty of peace with Spain were first formulated in a preliminary protocol of August 12, 1898.[2] The treaty of peace was not signed till four months later. Following the armed intervention of the powers in China during the Boxer rebellion of 1900, a protocol was drawn up to fix the terms of settlement with China. The protocol dealt with such matters as the amount of the total indemnity, the assignment of revenues to provide for payment, and the

[1] *Ibid.*, 1912, 1080.

[2] *Treaties, etc., of the U.S.*, II: 1688.

razing of the Taku forts.[1] Several agreements of a somewhat different character have been made with Mexico permitting the reciprocal crossing of the boundary line by troops of the two countries when in close pursuit of bands of savage Indians.[2]

Protocols for Special Arbitration, Made with or without Treaty Authorization. With regard to the possibility of independent executive action in drawing up a *compromis* or special agreement for arbitration, disputes are of two general kinds: those which fix the responsibility of foreign governments and involve no liability on the part of the United States, and those which involve a claim against the United States. In the first class it seems that a special agreement to arbitrate can be arranged by the executive alone without undue friction with Congress or the Senate. An exchange of notes, for example, is a recognized form of *compromis*.[3] When an American citizen undertakes to press a claim against another government through the Department of State, he places the matter in the discretion of the department which "will take such action, if any, as may be deemed appropriate and opportune, considering the foreign relations of the United States and the circumstances of the case."[4] It would then seem to be a matter for the judgment of the department as to whether the claim should be subjected to arbitration or to any other reasonable process of ascertaining its validity. The department can, if it should deem best, bring pressure to bear upon the claimant through its power to refuse to proceed with the matter unless it is submitted to arbitration. When arbitration has been decided upon, the practice has been at times to submit the *compromis* in treaty form to the Senate and at other times to proceed with the matter under a simple executive agreement. A number of such agreements can be found scattered through the volumes of *Treaties, Conventions, International Acts, Protocols, and Agreements between the United States and Other Powers*.[5] The submission of claims *against* the United States to arbitration by simple executive agreement is, on the other hand, a procedure of more doubtful expediency, for in such cases a resort must be had to Congress for

[1] *Ibid.*, II: 2006.

[2] *Ibid.*, I: 1144, 1170, 1177.

[3] RALSTON, *The Law and Procedure of International Tribunals* (rev. ed.), p. 5.

[4] Dept. of State, *General Instructions for Claimants*, Oct. 1, 1924 (rev.).

[5] Such for example as the exchange of notes in 1871 with Spain for the arbitration of claims of American citizens growing out of a Cuban insurrection (II: 1661) and the protocol regarding the Benner claims against Brazil in 1902 (I: 152). See also *Executive Agreement Series*, No. 33, for the arbitration arrangement with Egypt regarding the claim of George J. Salem.

an appropriation with which to pay the claims should any be awarded. The practice in such cases is ordinarily to draw up the *compromis* as a formal treaty.

The Senate in acting upon general treaties of arbitration has ordinarily shown an aversion to permitting arbitrations conducted under a *compromis* in the form of a simple executive agreement. On two occasions, in 1905 and 1912, treaties of general arbitration have been dropped by the President because the Senate has insisted on amending them so as to compel the submission of the *compromis* to that body for confirmation by a two-thirds vote. Presidents Roosevelt and Taft in the two cases mentioned complained against the amendment as a practical fraud upon the other contracting party inasmuch as an additional treaty would be required each time the occasion for arbitration should arise. This, said President Roosevelt, would be no gain but rather a loss for arbitration. For without such a treaty it had previously been possible to submit some cases to arbitration by simple executive agreement. The Root arbitration treaties of 1908–1909 required submission of the *compromis* to the Senate. The Root treaties are now generally replaced by the Kellogg arbitration treaties which also require the submission of the *compromis* to the Senate. In 1929 the United States signed the Pan American Arbitration Treaty which omitted the requirement that the *compromis* should be approved by the Senate. The Senate, however, added by reservation the stipulation that the *compromis* must be concluded in treaty form.

In some cases the Senate has consented to the ratification of treaties on other subjects than arbitration which, however, contain clauses of arbitration regarding disputes which may arise as to the interpretation or application of the particular treaty. Arbitration over such disputes evidently does not require a special *compromis* agreed to by the Senate. In the treaty of 1924 with Great Britain for the prevention of smuggling of intoxicating liquor a provision was made in Article IV for the arbitration of certain claims under the treaty.[1] Nothing was said about submission of the *compromis* to the Senate. Accordingly when the dispute with Canada over the sinking of the *I'm Alone* arose in 1929, the controversy was submitted to arbitration by a special agreement without the consent of the Senate. This case, it will be observed, involved a claim against the United States and is, therefore, an extreme instance of the submission of a controversy to arbitration by executive agreement.

---

[1] *U.S. Treaty Series*, No. 685.

The United States has joined in several multilateral conventions containing similar agreements to arbitrate disputes regarding the interpretation or application of the convention and specifically describing the tribunal to be employed. The Pan American Convention for Commercial Aviation of 1928[1] (Article 36), the International Radio Telegraph Convention of 1927[2] (Article 20), the Convention on the Abolition of Import and Export Prohibitions and Restrictions of 1927[3] (Article 8), and the Convention on Narcotic Drugs of 1931[4] (Article 25) belong to this number. In addition the United States is a party to several other treaties which provide for abitration with regard to their terms but which do not prescribe a particular tribunal.[5] Should arbitration be arranged by executive agreement under any of these treaties and should the United States be adjudged liable to pay a sum of money, it would seem that Congress would be morally obligated to provide the appropriation.

Other Agreements Which May Require Subsequent Acts of Congress. Although most executive agreements are such as the President can carry out without the cooperation of Congress, there have been a few additional examples of such agreements which, like those for arbitrating claims against the United States, may require subsequent legislation. In these cases the President runs the hazard of being unable to obtain action from Congress. He should, therefore, be sure of Congressional support in advance. In 1830 the United States and Great Britain entered into an agreement by which Horseshoe Reef, situated in the Niagara River, was ceded to this country in return for a promise to maintain a lighthouse upon the reef and a pledge not to erect fortifications.[6] The President could not, of course, fulfill the promise to erect the lighthouse without an appropriation. Congress had already passed an appropriation for the erection of a lighthouse on American territory, but on making a survey it had been found that the best place for the lighthouse was on Horseshoe Reef. After the agreement to transfer the reef to the United States had been made, Congress provided the necessary appropriation.[7] In 1903 the United States

---

[1] *Ibid.*, No. 840.
[2] *Ibid.*, No. 767.
[3] *Ibid.*, No. 811. The United States has withdrawn from this convention.
[4] *Ibid.*, No. 863.
[5] See, for example, *ibid.*, Nos. 751, 754, and 877.
[6] *Treaties, etc., of the U.S.*, I: 663.
[7] *Moore's Digest*, V: 215; FOSTER, *The Practice of Diplomacy*, p. 319.

by executive agreement with Cuba obtained a lease of naval or coaling stations in Guantánamo and Bahia Honda. The United States agreed to pay $2,000 per year and to furnish Cuba the funds necessary to acquire all private lands within the areas.[1] The agreement was, however, in pursuance of the policy set forth in the Platt Amendment which had been enacted by Congress in 1901. After the 1903 agreement Congress granted the necessary appropriations.

Agreements under Legislative Authorization

One of the best-known executive agreements ever entered into by the United States was the Rush-Bagot agreement in 1817. In 1815 Congress authorized the President to reduce the naval forces upon the Great Lakes in his discretion. By an exchange of notes two years later the United States and Great Britain agreed that their naval forces on the lakes should be limited to one vessel of not more than 100 tons armed with one eighteen-pound cannon on Lake Ontario, two similar vessels on the upper lakes, and one on Lake Champlain.[2] The Secretary of the Navy then issued orders to carry out the agreement by the transfer and reduction of naval forces to the prescribed strength. One year later the Senate advised the ratification of the agreement. The matter was submitted to the Senate for the sake of policy and propriety. Ratifications were not exchanged as in the case of treaties, and it does not appear that the consent of the Senate was necessary to the validity of the arrangement as the President was authorized to put it into effect without such consent. In fact the orders for naval reduction had been given immediately after the conclusion of the agreement and a year before it had been acted upon by the Senate.[3]

Postal, Trademark, and Copyright Agreements. Certain laws of Congress have authorized the President to make agreements with other governments which, when they have been duly consummated, have had the force of law. The statutes of the United States since 1792 have authorized the Postmaster General to make agreements with foreign postal authorities for reciprocal receipt and delivery of mail. In the act of 1872 the Postmaster General was authorized to make treaties and conventions "by and with the advice and consent of the President." A large number of

---

[1] *Treaties, etc., of the U.S.*, I: 360.

[2] *Ibid.*, I: 628.

[3] Report of John W. Foster, Secretary of State, reprinted in *Limitation of Armament on the Great Lakes*, Carnegie Endowment for International Peace, Washington, 1914.

agreements have been made under this authorization with individual countries, and the President has also participated in multilateral agreements, including the exceedingly important conventions of the Universal Postal Union,[1] the establishment of which, says a writer on international organization, "made a tremendous breach in the wall of national sovereignty."[2] By law also the United States extends national treatment to a foreigner in matters of trademark and copyright when the country of the foreigner in question extends national treatment to American citizens. The question as to whether national treatment is given to American citizens in the foreign country is decided by the President. Accordingly the executive has frequently entered into understandings with other governments for reciprocal national treatment in these matters. Sometimes these understandings have been submitted to the Senate for approval as treaties and at other times they have taken the form of a simple exchange of notes.[3]

Agreements for Commercial Reciprocity. Congress on several occasions has sought to make the treatment of the commerce and shipping of particular nations contingent upon the treatment accorded by those nations to the commerce and shipping of the United States. Statutes have given to the President the power to determine whether or when each foreign nation shall be accorded favorable treatment under the American law. In 1815 Congress repealed discriminating duties against the ships of any country which should be found not to discriminate against the shipping of the United States. The act left it to the President to determine which nations should be entitled to these benefits. Similar acts relating to shipping and commerce were passed in 1824, 1828, 1886, 1888, and 1897.[4] Under these acts the President has entered into various arrangements with foreign countries for the removal of their discriminations against American commerce. When satisfied that this has been accomplished he has reduced the duties against the vessels and produce of those countries by proclamation. In some cases the arrangements were made by formal treaty and in others by an exchange of notes or similar informal method.

[1] CRANDALL, *op. cit.*, pp. 131–133.

[2] VINACKE, *International Organization*, p. 405.

[3] Examples of these are found in *Treaties, etc., of the U.S.* It seems that agreements regarding trademarks have generally been referred to the Senate excepting those agreements regarding trademark protection in third countries where extraterritoriality has existed, as in China and Morocco. Such arrangements have usually been accomplished by exchanges of notes.

[4] CRANDALL, *op. cit.*, p. 121.

Under the Tariff Act of 1890 Congress placed sugar, coffee, and certain other commodities on the free list, but gave to the President the power to impose duties upon them when coming from countries which in the opinion of the President were placing reciprocally unequal and unreasonable duties on American products in view of the free introduction of sugar, etc., into the United States. Secretary of State Blaine then called on an experienced diplomat, John W. Foster, to supervise the negotiation of agreements to reduce tariffs charged on American goods in sugar- and coffee-producing countries. Notes were addressed to the diplomats in Washington who represented the governments with which agreements were desired. The Brazilian minister was first to respond and an agreement was soon formulated admitting certain American products free in Brazil. The next approach was made to Spain for agreements regarding Cuba and Puerto Rico. Mr. Foster went to Cuba to interview planters, sugar exporters, and the governor general. He stirred up considerable sentiment favorable to an agreement which resulted in strong representations from Havana to Madrid. Mr. Foster then journeyed to Spain and arranged an agreement.[1] Ten such agreements were negotiated. In three cases agreements could not be made and penalty tariffs were imposed upon sugar, coffee, etc., of the recalcitrant country.[2] The agreements were terminated when Congress repealed the bargaining powers in 1894. In 1897 another tariff act gave like powers to the President with regard to a somewhat similar list of commodities. It furthermore empowered him to reduce the rates on a list of imports, principally wines, for the purpose of obtaining concessions. John A. Kasson was employed to conduct negotiations under this law and a number of agreements were entered into to obtain lower tariff rates abroad for American goods.[3] These acts were attacked as an unconstitutional delegation of legislative power by Congress, but they were upheld by the Supreme Court.[4]

The Trades Agreements Act of 1934 and some of the reciprocity arrangements made under it are discussed elsewhere.[5] The act passed the Senate by a vote of 57 to 33 which would have been

[1] FOSTER, JOHN W., *Diplomatic Memoirs*, II: 6*ff.*, Houghton Mifflin Company, Boston, 1909.

[2] See p. 169.

[3] See *Treaties, etc., of the U.S.*, I: 542, 547, for the commercial agreements with France.

[4] Field *v.* Clark, 143 U.S. 649.

[5] See pp. 175–178.

insufficient for the approval of a treaty. Thus the two-thirds rule was circumvented.

Recent Executive Agreements Regarding Shipping and Air Navigation under the Authority of Statute. The increasing contacts between the United States and other countries in shipping and aerial navigation have made necessary various kinds of agreements reducing the impediments of national fiscal and administrative requirements. The *Executive Agreement Series* contains examples of several arrangements of this sort. Among such agreements are those dealing with relief from double income taxes on shipping profits, authorized under the provisions of the Revenue Act of 1924;[1] the reciprocal recognition of load line certificates previous to the coming into effect of the International Load Line Convention of 1930, based on the Load Line Act of 1929;[2] the reciprocal agreements regarding air navigation, under the authority of the Air Commerce Act of 1926;[3] and the reciprocal recognition of certificates of air-worthiness for imported aircraft, made also under the Air Commerce Act of 1926.[4]

[1] *Executive Agreement Series*, Nos. 3, 4, 6, 7, 10–17, and 56.
[2] *Ibid.*, Nos. 25, 27, 29, 30, 31, 35, 36, 40, and 42.
[3] *Ibid.*, Nos. 24, 38, 47, 50, 54, 58, and 76.
[4] *Ibid.*, Nos. 39, 43, 49, 52, and 69.

CHAPTER XXIV

THE MACHINERY OF AMERICAN FOREIGN RELATIONS: DEPARTMENT OF STATE, DIPLOMATIC REPRESENTATIVES, FOREIGN SERVICE

THE DEPARTMENT OF STATE

Double Character of the Department. In most governments the department which has charge of the conduct of diplomacy is called the foreign office or the ministry of foreign affairs. The reason for the use of the less descriptive name of the Department of State to describe the corresponding office in the United States lies in the evolution of American administration during the first year under the Constitution. A department of foreign affairs had existed during the Confederation. After the Constitution went into effect, a department of the same name was speedily created by act of July 27, 1789; but under this designation it lasted less than two months. The suggestion was made that a separate department of home affairs with numerous domestic secretarial duties, such as the custody and publication of the laws of Congress, should be created; but the proposal was rejected because of the fear of a too-rapid multiplication of departments. Accordingly these duties were given to the Department of Foreign Affairs and the name was changed to the Department of State. Various functions once vested in this department have since been transferred to the Department of the Interior, such as the issuance of letters patent. The double character of the department, however, still remains, as can readily be seen by the brief description of its functions under the dual classification (1) diplomatic and (2) domestic, which follows:

1. The Secretary of State is given the duty of correspondence with the diplomats and consuls of the United States and with foreign diplomats accredited to the United States. He conducts negotiations relating to the foreign affairs of this country. These duties will be described more fully in the following pages.

2. He is the medium of correspondence between the President and the state governors; he has the custody of the seal of the United States which he affixes to state documents; he is the custodian of treaties and laws of the United States and provides for their publication; and he issues passports.

450

THE SECRETARIES

The Secretary of State is regarded as first in rank among the departmental heads. Much has been written about the relative influence of the Secretary and the President in the formation of foreign policy, and it is generally agreed that this depends largely upon the force of character and personal influence of the two. Under McKinley, John Hay exercised much authority in policy formation. Thus we speak of the Hay Open-Door Notes. Under Roosevelt, however, he was overshadowed. The actions of the United States in Panama, for example, are ascribed to Roosevelt, who said with regard to the Canal Zone, "I took it." William Jennings Bryan accepted presidental leadership with qualifications. His differences with the President over the *Lusitania* affair led to his resignation. After Wilson was rid of Bryan, he dominated the Department of State. Charles Evans Hughes was a strong Secretary under both Harding and Coolidge, as was Stimson under Hoover. Secretary Hull at the opening of the administration of Franklin Roosevelt labored under a handicap. Raymond Moley, who was assistant secretary of state, seemed to have the confidence of the President to a greater degree than did his chief. It was common talk in Washington that Mr. Moley was out of sympathy with the policies of Mr. Hull. Hull, however, by dint of ability and energy fought his way to an independent and influential position in the administration. Moley resigned, and the Secretary of State became to a large extent the master of his own realm.

The Secretary of State concerns himself with only the more important matters of treaty negotiation, policy formation, and departmental administration, delegating as much of the less important work as he can to his subordinates. He holds daily press conferences. A new field of activity, that of conference diplomacy, has been opened to the Secretary in the years since the war. In Europe the foreign minister has found one of his chief functions to be that of participation in the Council and Assembly meetings of the League of Nations and in other important international gatherings. So in this country some of the recent secretaries of state have taken a foremost part in international conferences. The powerful efforts of Hughes at the Washington Conference of 1921–1922, the determined work of Stimson at the London Naval Conference of 1930, and the gracious impression created by Hull at the Seventh International Conference of American States at Montevideo in 1933 have been outstanding. Certainly the ability of the Secretary to formulate and procure the adoption of policies of common interest at such gatherings should now be taken into consideration in appointments to the position.

The principal assistant of the Secretary of State is the undersecretary of state. He aids in the formulation and execution of foreign policies. He becomes acting secretary of state during the absence of the Secretary.[1] There are four assistant secretaries of state. One is charged with the general administration of the department and the foreign service and with supervision of matters relating to personnel and management. The other three are given such supervision over matters of political and economic policy as may be assigned by the Secretary of State. The tendency is to withdraw the offices of undersecretary and the assistant secretaries to a large extent from politics. The present undersecretary, William Phillips, has had a long career service in diplomatic posts abroad and also in the administration of the Department of State. Assistant Secretary Wilbur J. Carr has had a continuous service in the Department of State for a third of a century. Assistant Secretary Sumner Welles is a career man with important diplomatic service in the field. Assistant Secretary Francis B. Sayre is a lawyer, a former teacher of government, and has seen service as adviser in foreign affairs to the government of Siam. Assistant Secretary R. Walton Moore is a lawyer and a former member of Congress. In addition to the assistant secretaries the Secretary of State has a special assistant, chosen without senatorial confirmation, who works under the sole direction of the Secretary and who is independent of the other officers of the department.

A perspective of the general work of the department may be obtained from the following sketch of departmental offices, divisions, and bureaus.

ORGANS OF ADVICE AND RESEARCH

The legal adviser drafts and interprets treaties; handles diplomatic claims of American citizens against foreign governments and deals with claims of foreigners against the United States. He appears before international tribunals on behalf of the United

---

[1] The account of the various divisions and officers of the department is taken rather freely from the publications of the department, particularly *The Department of State of the United States*, prepared in the Office of the Historical Adviser, Govt. Printing Office, Washington, 1933, and the *Register of the Department of State*. The *Congressional Directory* contains a similar account of departmental organization and functions.

States. He advises the department with regard to questions of international law in general. There are at present twenty-three assistants to the legal adviser. Members of the staff act at times as commissioners, counsel, or agents in cases of international arbitrations in which the United States is a party. Members of the staff are sometimes sent to international conferences as delegates or advisers.

The economic adviser makes recommendations on questions of general economic policy, maintains liaison with the various economic bureaus in other departments, and handles economic cases which have no regional character or which overlap geographical divisions.

The Division of Trade Agreements carries out the work of the Department of State with reference to the Trade Agreements Act of 1934.

The historical adviser gives advice on historical and constitutional questions and matters of current policy. He is charged with editing and compiling the treaties of the United States and certain other documents. He has custody of the archives of the department up to August 15, 1906.

The Division of Research and Publication edits and compiles such publications as *Foreign Relations of the United States*, the statutes, executive orders, proclamations, and all departmental publications not edited by the historical adviser. It has supervision of the library of the department.

The Treaty Division assists, when requested, in the drafting of treaties. It maintains a set of treaties and other international agreements to which the United States is a party and likewise of those to which it is not a party. It recommends such action as may be required to obtain the fulfillment of treaty obligations by the other parties and also such as will fulfill the obligations of the United States by legislative or administrative acts.

The Division of Current Information prepares news items for the press, distributes daily press summaries and special articles to officials of the department and the foreign service, and furnishes them with copies of texts and general information on foreign relations.

Geographical Divisions

Six geographical divisions have been created within the department to correspond to the main regions of American diplomatic interest. The chief of each is chosen for his familiarity with the particular region of his division where he has generally had diplomatic, consular, or other experience. Specialization and expertness in the handling of regional problems are thus promoted. A short summary of the experience of each chief in the particular geographic area or adjacent region is here given in order to convey some notion of the type of regional specialist employed by the department in this capacity. The divisions with the chiefs are as follows:

Division of Far Eastern Affairs. Stanley K. Hornbeck, chief, is a political scientist who has had teaching experience in China and is a writer on Far Eastern politics. He served as adviser on Far Eastern questions to the American Commission to Negotiate Peace, 1919, to the Washington Conference, 1921, and to the special conference on Chinese customs tariffs, 1925.

Division of Latin-American Affairs. Laurence Duggan, chief, is a product of the Department of State rather than of the field service. He has had experience as a divisional assistant and as assistant chief of the Latin-American division.

Division of Western European Affairs. James C. Dunn, chief, has had diplomatic experience at Berne, Madrid, Brussels, London, and various other places. He has been connected with the American delegations at several international gatherings, such as the General Disarmament Conference, Geneva, 1932, and the International Monetary and Economic Conference, London, 1933.

Division of Near Eastern Affairs. Wallace Murray, chief, has had diplomatic experience in Budapest and Teheran; and he was sent in 1929 upon a special mission to the Near East.

Division of Mexican Affairs. Edward L. Reed, chief, has had diplomatic experience in Buenos Aires, Panama, Havana, and in various European capitals. He was a member of the United States-Panama Commission, 1924–1926.

Division of Eastern European Affairs. Robert F. Kelley, chief, has had experience as assistant military attaché at Copenhagen and Helingfors and as a military observer in the Baltic provinces. He has likewise had consular experience.[1]

The common procedure in policy formation generally leads through the office of one of these divisions. When a cablegram arrives which demands a decision as to policy in any section of the world it is decoded and sent to the proper geographical division. The division chief usually discusses the problem with subordinates in the division and then takes the matter up with the assistant secretary who has supervision over policies in that area. If a legal question is involved, the office of the legal adviser is consulted or,

[1] The data regarding the division chiefs are taken mostly from the *Register of the Department of State*, Govt. Printing Office, Washington, 1935.

if the decision cuts across economic lines, the economic adviser is approached. Perhaps the assistant secretary confers with the undersecretary. The proper instruction to the diplomat in the field or the note to the foreign diplomat in Washington is then drafted under the direction of the assistant secretary or division chief and presented to the Secretary of State for signature. The Secretary of State or, in his absence, the acting secretary signs all notes and instructions which go out from the department.[1]

SUPERVISION OF FOREIGN SERVICE PERSONNEL

The Board of Foreign Service Personnel passes upon the professional fortunes of the Foreign Service officers of the United States. The board makes recommendations to the Secretary of State regarding the efficiency of Foreign Service officers, promotion in the Foreign Service, promotion of Foreign Service officers to the grade of minister, transfers of Department of State employes to the Foreign Service, assignments to posts, transfers from one branch of the service to the other, and disciplinary action. Working under the board, the *Division of Foreign Service Personnel* discusses with Foreign Service officers ways for the improvement of their work. It has charge of the personnel records of the Foreign Service. The division also interviews prospective candidates for the Foreign Service and attends to the details connected with the Foreign Service examinations. *The Board of Examiners for the Foreign Service* formulates rules for and holds examinations to test fitness for appointment to the Foreign Service.

A *Foreign Service Officers' Training School* is maintained for the instruction of new appointees to the Foreign Service. After passing the examinations for entrance into the service, the successful candidates are commissioned to the unclassified service and after a probationary period in the field they are assigned to the school. The school is under the direction of a *Foreign Service Officers' Training School Board*. The director is a Foreign Service officer who is assigned to the department for this work.

The Division of Foreign Service Administration is charged with the routine administration of the Foreign Service, including matters relating to general instructions of diplomatic and consular officers,

---

[1] STONE, WILLIAM T., "The Administration of the Department of State," Foreign Policy Association, *Information Service*, Vol. IV, Special Supplement No. 3 (February, 1929), p. 9; NORTON, HENRY KITTREDGE, "Foreign Office Organization," *Annals of the American Academy of Political and Social Science*, Vol. CXLIII, Supplement (May, 1929), pp. 21–24.

the diplomatic pouch service between the United States and foreign countries, appropriations and expenditures, rentals, equipment, and the noncommercial work of consular officers, such as is connected with immigration, quarantine, and notarial acts.

The Consular Commercial Office drafts correspondence on consular trade promotion and commercial activity in general. It passes upon the quality of commercial and economic reports and distributes economic data to the Department of Commerce and other appropriate governmental and nongovernmental agencies.

The Visa Division supervises the administration of the immigration laws insofar as they concern the Department of State and its officers in the field.

The Foreign Service Buildings Office supervises matters relating to the housing of diplomatic and consular establishments abroad and the protection of United States properties used for that purpose. The division has charge, subject to the approval of the departmental budget officer, of programs of expenditures for purchase, construction, and furnishing of such housing facilities.

DEPARTMENTAL ADMINISTRATION, CEREMONIALS, AND MISCELLANEOUS

The chief clerk and administrative assistant supervises the clerical personnel of the department and has oversight regarding such matters as property, expenditures for salaries and contingent expenses, and office space. He is the custodian of the great seal of the United States and of the seal of the department.

The Division of Protocol and Conferences provides for the presentation of foreign ambassadors and ministers to the President and conducts the correspondence regarding the acceptability to the United States of foreign ambassadors and ministers and of American ambassadors and ministers to foreign governments. It is charged with arrangements for ceremonials and for international conferences in which the United States is to participate at home or abroad.

The Division of Communications and Records is charged with the dispatch and receipt of all telegraphic correspondence of the department, the encoding and decoding of messages, the building of codes and ciphers, the custody of and conduct of research in the archives subsequent to 1906, and the maintenance of a record of precedents of policy and procedure.

The Office of Coordination and Review inspects all outgoing correspondence, coordinates the correspondence of the several branches of the department for consideration and initialing before signing, dispatches the mail, and certifies copies for the record.

The Passport Division passes upon applications of American citizens for passports. The division conducts correspondence regarding citizenship, passports, registration, and the right to protection of citizens abroad.

Two subdivisions of the department, the *Bureau of Accounts* and the *Translating Bureau*, perform such administrative and ministerial functions as are indicated by their names.

DIPLOMATIC REPRESENTATIVES

There are four principal grades used in the regular diplomatic representation of the United States in foreign capitals: those of ambassador, minister, minister resident, and chargé d'affaires. In addition to these four there is the minor grade of diplomatic agent, and on frequent occasions special representatives of varying rank are appointed for temporary missions.

Ambassadors are diplomatic representatives of the highest rank, the full title being ambassador extraordinary and plenipotentiary. The ambassador has been traditionally regarded as the personal representative of his sovereign and has the distinctive right of audience with the head of the state to which he is accredited. In former days this right was of some importance; but, since in the postwar world decisions are not often made by the titular sovereign, the right of access to the monarch has lost its former meaning. The United States, during the first century of its existence under the Constitution, sent no ambassadors, since that rank seemed to the democratically inclined statesmen of the New World to be tainted with the flavor of monarchy. The ambassadorial grade also carried the disadvantage of greater expense. American ministers were under a handicap in foreign capitals, however, as compared with the ambassadors of other countries who outranked them in all ceremonials and had the right of personal audience. In 1893 Congress provided that the President might, in his discretion, send ambassadors to foreign governments which were represented or were about to be represented in the United States by ambassadors. From time to time Congress has passed acts authorizing the sending of ambassadors to additional countries until the United States maintains embassies at seventeen capitals. It is difficult to derive from these seventeen instances any single rule as to which countries are to be selected for the establishment of embassies. The rule of reciprocity, set forth in the 1893 act, is observed, *i.e.*, ambassadors

are sent in each case to governments which likewise send ambassadors to the United States. But frequently in adding new countries
to the list the United States has taken the initiative and has selected
the countries with which the ambassadors are to be exchanged.
The seventeen governments may be generally classified as follows:
the great powers;[1] a secondary list of important powers, including
three in Europe and two in Asia;[2] and six outstanding countries of
Latin America.[3] Political importance and the closeness of diplomatic relations with the United States seem to be the principles
which determine the choice for the ambassadorial exchange,
although as can be seen by an inspection of the list there are one or
two cases, such as Belgium and Peru, which are dubious applications of either principle. The salary of the ambassador is $17,500
per year.

Ministers, i.e., envoys extraordinary and ministers plenipotentiary, are normally sent to all governments except the seventeen
above referred to and except three others to which officers of lesser
diplomatic grades are accredited. At present diplomats of the
grade of minister are normally accredited to forty-one governments,[4]
including three members of the British Commonwealth of Nations,
Canada, South Africa, and Ireland. The salary of American
ministers is $10,000 in all countries except the Netherlands, in
which case it is $12,000.

Ministers resident constitute a lower diplomatic grade which
was especially created by the powers at the Congress of Aix-la-
Chapelle in 1818 for convenience in providing subordinate rank
for minor countries. The United States sends ministers resident
to Iraq and Ethiopia. Foreign Service officers are used in these
positions.

Chargés d'Affaires. The three grades of diplomatic officers
above named are accredited by the President of the United States
to the head of the state to which they are sent. The chargé
d'affaires is a lower officer who is accredited by the Secretary of
State to the foreign minister of the other government. The chargé
d'affaires *ad interim* is an officer who takes charge of the embassy
or legation during the temporary absence of the chief or during a

---

[1] Great Britain, France, Italy, Germany, Russia, and Japan.

[2] Spain, Poland, Belgium, Turkey, and China.

[3] Argentina, Brazil, Chile, Mexico, Cuba, and Peru.

[4] In some cases, one diplomatic officer serves to represent the United States
in more than one country. The ambassador to Belgium acts as the minister
to Luxemburg; and one legation serves for Estonia, Latvia, and Lithuania.

temporary vacancy in the post of ambassador or minister. It is in this capacity that the grade is used by the United States. The position is filled by the highest ranking Foreign Service officer at the particular capital.

Diplomatic Agent. A Foreign Service officer with the rank of diplomatic agent represents the United States in the French protectorate of Morocco.

Career Men in Diplomatic Posts. Until recently American ambassadors and ministers have been chosen from civil life, usually without previous diplomatic experience. Political service was frequently rewarded with such appointments. Wealth was often a desirable attribute, owing to the inadequacy of the salary. Literary distinction was also given consideration. Within recent years, however, since the development of the career service, a growing number of appointments have been made from among those who are, or at one time have been, members of the Foreign Service or who have been connected with the Department of State.

The fifty-seven chiefs of mission who were accredited to sixty-one foreign governments as listed in the *Register of the Department of State* for July 1, 1935, may be classified as follows:

DIPLOMATIC OFFICERS CLASSIFIED AS TO CAREER AND NONCAREER CHARACTER

Officers	Officers without previous career experience	Officers with previous career experience[1]	Officers retaining their status as Foreign Service officers	Total
Ambassadors........	8	9	..	17
Ministers..........	18	17	..	35
Ministers resident...	..	..	1	1
Chargés d'affaires[2]...	..	..	3	3
Diplomatic agents...	..	..	1	1
Total.............	26	26	5	57

[1] Includes former Foreign Service officers (18), former career diplomats whose service antedated July 1, 1924, and who were never, therefore, classified as Foreign Service officers (7), and one officer who served in the Department of State but not in the career diplomatic service abroad.

[2] The chargés d'affaires at the time of compiling this table were serving in Albania and Paraguay, countries to which ministers are normally accredited, and in Ethiopia, to which a minister resident is normally sent.

THE FOREIGN SERVICE

Below the grade of minister plenipotentiary are the Foreign Service officers on assignment as ministers resident, diplomatic agents, counselors of embassy and legation, secretaries, consuls general, consuls, and vice-consuls. These officers have long been regarded as more permanent in status than the ambassadors and ministers. In 1906 the consular service was placed on a merit basis, while the permanent diplomatic service obtained a similar status in 1909. The most important measure dealing with the qualifications of these officials is the Rogers Act of 1924. Until 1924 the consular and permanent diplomatic services were separate. Admission to each was by examination. The examination for admission to the diplomatic service dealt with one or two modern languages, international law, history of the United States, and diplomatic usage. The consular examination was roughly similar. It did not require diplomatic usage, however, but stressed political and commercial geography. Once the candidate was admitted into either service there was no method by which he could be transferred to the other without examination; and, unless the exigencies of the service demanded, he was to have no preference in appointment after having taken the examination.[1] The salaries in the diplomatic branch were comparatively low, the range being from $2,500 to $4,000.[2] Salaries in the consular service were much higher, rising to $8,000 and in two exceptional cases to $12,000.

The Rogers Act. Under the Rogers Act of 1924 and subsequent legislation, the two services are merged for personnel purposes into the Foreign Service of the United States. One examination now is held instead of two. The examination consists of two parts: a written test held in various cities under the supervision of the Civil Service Commission and an oral interview before the Board of Examiners in Washington. Regarding the nature of the examinations the Department of State pamphlet, *The American Foreign Service*,[3] says:

The examinations shall be both written and oral, except that American clerks and employees in the Foreign Service who have rendered satisfactory service in such capacities for the five years immediately preceding application for appointment as Foreign Service officers shall be exempted from the written examinations prescribed for other candidates. The written examination will include the subjects prescribed by the President, to wit:

---

[1] Executive order, Nov. 26, 1909, quoted in LAY, *op. cit.*, p. 246, note 20.

[2] LAY, *op. cit.*, p. 237; *Foreign Service of the United States*, Hearings before the House Committee on Foreign Affairs, January, 1924, p. 23, Govt. Printing Office, Washington, 1924.

[3] Pp. 30–31, Govt. Printing Office, Washington, 1932.

Elements of international, maritime, and commercial law; arithmetic as used in commercial statistics, tariff calculations, exchange, and simple accounting; modern languages (French, Spanish, or German is required, and a candidate may offer, in the oral test, in addition to one of these any languages with which he may be familiar); elementary economics, including the natural, industrial, and commercial resources of the United States; political and commercial geography; American history, government, and institutions since 1776; and history of Europe, Latin America, and the Far East since 1776. Candidates will also be examined in political economy, and they will be rated in English, composition, grammar, punctuation, spelling, and penmanship as shown by their replies to questions in the written examination.

The oral examination will be designed to ascertain the physical, mental, and temperamental qualifications of candidates for the proper performance of the duties of the Foreign Service; their character, ability, address, judgment, fitness, general education, culture, contemporary information, experience, and business ability. In this part of the examination the applications previously filed, together with all other available information concerning the candidates, will be utilized in ascertaining the pertinent facts.

A candidate passing the examination is placed upon an eligible list. He is appointed to the unclassified rank of the service in order of marks as, and if, vacancies occur. After appointment the officer is given a probationary status in the field for preliminary training and is then assigned to the Department of State for a course of instruction in the Foreign Service Officers' Training School. Following the work in the school an assignment is made to duty as vice-consul. The officer may later be assigned to either a diplomatic or a consular post, or, as is frequently the case, to a post which includes both consular and diplomatic functions.

Under the Rogers Act there were nine classes of Foreign Service officers in addition to the unclassified service. Under an act passed in 1931 the ninth class was eliminated. The classes with their salaries as provided under the Act of 1931 are as follows:

Class 1	$9,000 to $10,000
Class 2	8,000 to 8,900
Class 3	7,000 to 7,900
Class 4	6,000 to 6,900
Class 5	5,000 to 5,900
Class 6	4,500 to 4,900
Class 7	4,000 to 4,400
Class 8	3,500 to 3,900
Unclassified	2,500 to 3,400*

* Salaries are at times supplemented by additional sums to allow for the depreciation of the dollar abroad.

Promotions are made according to merit upon the recommendations of the Board of Foreign Service Personnel.[1] As has been stated above, a Foreign Service officer may be assigned to duty as minister resident, chargé d'affaires, or diplomatic agent without loss of grade.

There are in consular work outside of the Foreign Service two kinds of officials, noncareer vice-consuls, who are appointed without examination and who are ineligible for promotion, and consular agents, who are appointed to minor and remote posts. These latter need not be American citizens. They receive one-half of the fees collected but not more than $1,000 per year. There are consular agents serving at various posts in some fourteen countries at the present time.

DIPLOMATIC FUNCTIONS

The Diplomat as the Channel of Communications. In presenting matters for the consideration of other governments through American embassies or legations abroad, the department sends to the diplomat what is called an "instruction." The diplomat is expected to communicate the instruction to the Foreign Office of the other government by a "note" or a "conversation," and to report the result to the department in a "dispatch." The communication of the instruction is supposed to be performed without changing its substance. Should the diplomat vary from its terms materially he would be open to censure or dismissal.

Sometimes it has happened that the diplomat, being in the possession of firsthand knowledge of the foreign situation, has viewed a particular controversy from a different point of view from that of the officials in Washington. Charles Francis Adams, who represented the United States in London during the trying times of the Civil War, once made a departure from his instructions which was justified by later events. He was instructed to inform Great Britain that if the rulings of the British government with regard to Confederate cruisers should be maintained, the United States might instruct its naval officers to pursue the Confederate vessels into British ports. Adams, however, assumed the responsibility of acting upon his own judgment and refused to communicate this drastic threat, which, he feared, would have involved the two countries in war. Removed from the fiery nationalism of wartime

[1] For general information on the Foreign Service see the pamphlet issued by the Department of State, *The American Foreign Service*, above cited.

America, he was better able to decide than was Seward the question of American interest.[1] Such procedure under a disciplined diplomatic system is exceedingly rare. Should ministers or ambassadors abroad frequently substitute their own opinions for those of the department, there could be no unity or continuity of policy. Furthermore, those in Washington must be regarded as better able to determine the wisdom of a particular policy from the standpoint of the United States. When the question of British negligence with regard to Confederate commerce destroyers was being negotiated after the Civil War, John Motley, the historian, was minister to Great Britain. Senator Sumner, who had more extreme views on the matter of British liability than did the administration, had been influential in obtaining Motley's appointment. President Grant later charged that Motley had been influenced in the performance of his duties by Sumner's views. In one instruction to Motley the Department of State in a dignified manner set forth its opposition to a British proposal for the selection of the umpire on the arbitration tribunal by lot. The instruction read: "It might, indeed, well have occurred in the event of selection by lot of the arbitrator or umpire in different cases, involving, however, precisely the same principles, that different awards, resting upon antagonistic principles, might have been made." Motley could not resist the temptation to color the language of the department, and reported: "I called his lordship's attention to your very judicious suggestion that the throwing of the dice for umpires might bring about opposite decisions," etc. Secretary Fish avowed that he had said nothing about the "throwing of dice." Years afterward President Grant, in a letter to the New York *Herald* stated: "Mr. Motley, instead of obeying his explicit instructions, deliberately fell in line with Sumner and thus added insult to the previous injury." The negotiations regarding the claims against Great Britain were transferred to Washington where they were conducted by the Department of State with the British minister. Later, when the administration had broken openly with Sumner, Mr. Motley's resignation was requested; and when he refused to resign he was recalled.[2]

In recent decades the diplomat has been closely restricted in communicating his instructions, and he ordinarily presents to the

[1] ADAMS, CHARLES FRANCIS, *Charles Francis Adams*, pp. 337–338, Houghton Mifflin Company, Boston, 1900.

[2] HOLMES, OLIVER WENDELL, *John Lothrop Motley, A Memoir*, pp. 155*ff*., Houghton Mifflin Company, Boston, 1889.

Foreign Office a verbatim repetition of the department's telegram.[1]
Examples of the instruction, the note, and the dispatch are herewith
set forth from a case occurring in 1915 with reference to the release
from military service of a citizen of the United States who was the
son of a naturalized American citizen of Italian birth.[2]

INSTRUCTION OF THE SECRETARY OF STATE AD INTERIM TO THE UNITED
STATES AMBASSADOR TO ITALY
Telegram

Department of State,
Washington, June 14, 1915.

261. Your 321, June 10.   Inform Italian Government Ugo Da Prato
has been residing in Italy temporarily to study architecture.   His father,
Antonio Da Prato, has been there representing his firm, A Da Prato Company of Boston, dealers in marble and works of art, and also preparing
exhibit of company for Panama Exposition.   As his stay in Italy has been
in the interest of trade and commerce between that country and the
United States, it seems manifestly unreasonable to apply to him the provision of Italian law mentioned in your telegram.   For this reason and
because Uga Da Prato was born an American citizen and evidently had no
intention to resume Italian nationality, it is earnestly hoped latter will be
speedily released.

LANSING

DISPATCH OF AMBASSADOR PAGE TO THE SECRETARY OF STATE AD INTERIM

American Embassy,
No. 318]   Rome, June 17, 1915.

Sir: Referring to the Department's telegram No. 254 of June 9 and
telegram No. 261 of June 14 in regard to the detention by the military
authorities of Uga Da Prato, I have the honor to enclose herewith a copy
of my last note to the Foreign Office upon the subject, which I have handed
personally to the Foreign Office yesterday afternoon.

. . . .

Recognizing the importance of the principle on which this case is based,
I took occasion to discuss again with the Minister for Foreign Affairs, the
entire subject of the detention in Italy of native-born American citizens,
born after the naturalization of their father.

[1] HUNT, GAILLARD, "The Department of State," *Harper's Magazine*,
CXXXIII: 525 (September, 1916).   An executive order of March 8, 1927,
provides that diplomatic officers "owe implicit and immediate obedience to
the department's instructions."   FELLER, A. H., and MANLEY O. HUDSON, *A
Collection of the Diplomatic and Consular Laws and Regulations of Various
Countries*, II: 1254, Carnegie Endowment for International Peace, Washington,
1933.

[2] *Foreign Relations*, 1915, pp. 565ff.

I impressed on him the fact that it has, for more than a hundred years, been a traditional principle of the United States to protect its citizens, and that it was one which he would, I felt sure, recognize as impossible to be waived. He promised to have the question studied carefully at once.

. . . .

THOMAS NELSON PAGE

[Inclosure 2]

NOTE OF AMBASSADOR PAGE TO THE ITALIAN MINISTER FOR FOREIGN AFFAIRS

American Embassy,
Rome, June 16, 1915.

EXCELLENCY: With reference to my note No. 557 of June 11 and to our previous correspondence on the subject of the detention in Italy by the military authorities of Mario Uga Da Prato, a native born American citizen, born after his parents had become duly naturalized American citizens, I have the honor to inform your excellency that I have just received from my Government the following telegram, expressive of the great interest which is taken by my Government in the case:

[Quotes Department's telegram 261 of June 14.]

Your Excellency will appreciate the point raised by my Government, namely, that the father's residence in Italy has been in the interest of trade and commerce between Italy and the United States and not, as has apparently been considered by the Royal Italian Ministry of War, by reason of a permanent change of residence.

Consequently, it would certainly seem that the Law No. 555 of June 12, 1912, which was quoted in your excellency's note of May 4, No. 25019/101, should not be applied in this case.

In fact, this case and the few other cases of native-born American citizens—born, like this youth, after their parents became American citizens—rest on a principle which is, I believe, recognized by Italy and by all other powers; and I feel confident that when the fact shall be realized, your excellency's Government will appreciate the earnestness with which the case is now presented, and the sanctity of the principle involved.

I therefore hope that your excellency will enable me to send a favorable telegraphic reply to my Government at the earliest possible moment.

Accept, etc.

THOMAS NELSON PAGE[1]

Frequently when the Department of State wishes to communicate with another government, different channels are selected. The Secretary sends a note to the diplomatic representative of that

---

[1] After further negotiation it was reported to the American embassy on Aug. 24 that Da Prato had been released.

country in Washington who advises his government in a dispatch. The answer then comes back through an instruction which is transmitted to the Department of State in a note. Various factors of diplomatic strategy determine whether the initial communication to the other government is to take place in the foreign capital or in Washington.

The Diplomat as the Source of Information. The speed and ease of communication enable the department to hold the diplomat under control and to restrict his initiative, on the one hand, but, on the other, they enlarge his functions in providing better facilities with which he can keep the department informed as to significant events in the foreign capital. The advice of the diplomat supplemented by information dispatched to Washington often determines the policy of the Department of State. Reference to the volumes of *Foreign Relations of the United States* will reveal a multitude of dispatches from our diplomatic representatives abroad, shedding light on commercial, sociological, and political conditions and on such aspects of public opinion as affect our interests and policies. Thus, to take an important illustration, during the American Civil War when French troops occupied Mexico, Mr. Dayton, the American minister in France, supplied valuable material as to the French sentiment concerning the occupation and also regarding the intention of the French to withdraw at an early opportunity. While Mr. Dayton was not entirely correct in his estimate of French policy, he did help to put the administration at rest regarding some of the exaggerated rumours current in the United States.[1] Such information enabled the department to adopt the wise course of dignified protest coupled with watchful waiting until the withdrawal was accomplished. Without this information it is not unlikely that the American government would have become so impatient with France that a serious quarrel between the two governments would have resulted.

During the World War, while the United States was still a neutral, Walter Hines Page performed a service to this country by his continual advice that the United States should not insist uncompromisingly on what it regarded as its neutral rights, *i.e.*, the freedom of trade in certain raw materials as set forth in the unratified Declaration of London of 1909. England, he said, would not give way before American demands far enough to permit war materials to enter Germany. In dispatches and personal

---

[1] See *Foreign Relations*, 1862, p. 385; 1863, Part II, pp. 711, 716.

letters to President Wilson he energetically represented the attitude of the British government and advised against pressing the matter too hard. "England," he said, "will risk a serious quarrel or even hostilities with us rather than yield. You may look upon this as the final word."[1]

In one respect the reports of diplomats from abroad have not always proved to be trustworthy, *i.e.*, regarding popular movements directed against the existing government. The ambassador or minister is often unable to discount sufficiently the influence upon his opinions of the small circle of government officials with which he is constantly in contact. Thus the dispatches of Ambassador Francis regarding the Bolshevist chances of success in Russia in 1917 were a most inaccurate judgment of the possibilities of the movement. At one time he reported to the Department of State:

> Rodzyanko, Guchkov and Japanese Ambassador who visited the Embassy this afternoon separately by appointment each expressed confidential opinion that in contest between Government and Soviet latter will succeed. I disagreed as believe Government will command loyalty of decided majority of army. Minister for Foreign Affairs just left Embassy says test of strength with Soviet will result in decided victory of Government and I so believe.[2]

In 1930, during the revolutionary movement in Brazil, the Department of State was evidently badly informed regarding the relative strength of the Brazilian government and the revolutionary forces. On October 22 President Hoover proclaimed an arms embargo against the revolutionists. Two days later the government fell into the hands of the rebels, a development which created an embarrassing situation for the United States.

Protection of American Citizens and Promotion of Their Interests. In countries which are subject to domestic violence or in which the attitude toward foreigners is unfavorable, the American embassy or legation is frequently called upon to make representations to the government calling for greater zeal on the part of officials in extending protection. Thus an important task of the American ministers to China for many years has been the seeking of better protection for American missionaries. The history of the embassy in Mexico City for the decade following

---

[1] HENDRICK, BURTON J., *The Life and Letters of Walter H. Page*, I: 371, Doubleday, Page & Company, Garden City, N.Y., 1922.

[2] The dispatch was sent Sept. 16, 1917, two months before the fall of the government. *Foreign Relations*, 1918 (Russia I), p. 192.

the revolution of 1910 was largely one of protection of American citizens and property against the violence of revolutionary factions. Much of this work is done under special instructions from Washington, but the diplomat must also be ready to respond promptly to reasonable requests made by citizens at the embassy or legation. The general instructions read that the diplomatic officers should protect American citizens before the local authorities in all cases in which they may be injured or oppressed, but their efforts should not be exerted in behalf of those who have been guilty of an infraction of the law.[1]

American businessmen seeking to obtain concessions or to bid on contracts frequently make use of the embassy or legation. Hugh Gibson once testified that the governmental control of business has made diplomatic assistance necessary. He said:

Business, in Europe especially, is to an almost unbelievable extent either in the hands of the various governments, supported by governmental subvention, or subject to some form of government control. In such conditions the individual business man can no longer shift for himself. He must have help at every step.[2]

Mr. Gibson stated that greater reliance is being placed upon the aid of the diplomats and recommended that the American businessman should come to the embassy for advice and assistance in obtaining introductions and in drawing up bids and contracts.

Miscellaneous Functions. Under authorization of the Department of State the ambassador or minister may issue passports to American citizens abroad. The power is also sometimes delegated by the department to consular officers. One function which has obtained an amount of publicity out of proportion to its importance is that of obtaining introductions at court for socially ambitious women. A special type of assistance was rendered when at the outbreak of the World War, because the banks stopped payment on travelers' checks, many Americans were stranded in Europe without means to obtain money. They became panic-stricken. The United States sent gold to Europe on a battleship. Relatives and friends of the stranded tourists deposited funds with the United States Treasury; the names and amounts were telegraphed to American embassies and legations; and the American ambassadors and ministers issued drafts, which were honored by selected banks

---

[1] FELLER and HUDSON, II: 1269.

[2] *Foreign Service of the United States*, Hearings, above cited, p. 42.

with which the gold had been deposited.[1] An experienced diplomatic secretary has described the day to day routine of dealing with American tourists as follows:

A great number of traveling Americans look on a legation as a sort of tourist bureau. They come in all the time to ask about the hours trains leave, how much they ought to pay at the hotel and whether this place and another one are considered healthy at that season. Almost every day a passport has to be renewed or visa given. Then there are numerous cases of people getting in trouble, losing their money and falling into all sort of difficulties, some even going so far as to have themselves locked up in prison for neglecting to observe obvious laws of any country.[2]

Social life and ceremonials take up a considerable part of the diplomat's time. These matters are important in that it is necessary to be on terms of acquaintance and good feeling with the official circle in the capital. On the other hand, after a period spent in the charming social environment of a particular country, there is a danger that the diplomat will lose the American point of view and that he will be in need of re-Americanization. Walter Hines Page was severely criticized for his extreme sympathy with the British point of view during the World War. As a corrective to undue foreign influence, ambassadors and ministers are given a sixty-day leave each year plus traveling time in case they visit the United States. Foreign Service officers may be granted similar leaves by the Secretary of State[3] or may be assigned to the Department of State for a period of not more than three years unless the public interests demand further service. The assignment may then be extended for not more than one year.

The delivery of public addresses is a part of the routine of the ambassador. Such speeches are ordinarily confined to noncontroversial subjects, and when this rule is departed from the diplomat may find himself the center of undesired publicity. In a public speech in London in 1921 Ambassador George Harvey referred to the League of Nations and stated that the United States under the Republican administration would not "have anything whatsoever to do with the League or with any commission or committee appointed by it or responsible to it, directly or indirectly, openly,

[1] RICHARDSON, NORVAL, *My Diplomatic Education*, pp. 130*ff.*, Dodd, Mead & Company, New York, 1923.

[2] *Ibid.*, p. 37.

[3] Appropriations for traveling expenses to the United States, however, have not been adequate.

or furtively."[1] For this personal and factional view (which proved to be an extremely inaccurate prediction) Ambassador Harvey was subjected to some criticism abroad and to much denunciation and ridicule by members of Congress at home. His later public remarks were less controversial in character, one subsequent address being devoted to a discussion of the subject: "Have Women Souls?"[2] Better fitted to the function of the diplomat are addresses on such subjects as progress in education, the need of improved agriculture, or the contributions to learning of the distinguished scholars of bygone centuries. Speeches of a dignified character made upon important ceremonial occasions or before significant groups are often a distinct contribution to international good will. The executive order of March 8, 1927, states that diplomats "should be careful not to allude in any public address to political issues pending in the United States or elsewhere."[3]

CONSULAR FUNCTIONS

While the diplomat is stationed at the foreign capital and deals with national officials, the consular officers are stationed at important commercial cities. Their jurisdiction is restricted to consular districts and they deal largely with local authorities. The diplomat is concerned with general policies of national character while the consul deals to a great extent with matters which primarily affect particular individuals. It should be noted that there are distinct exceptions to these generalizations. The functions of the consul are of varied character.

Functions in Connection with American Shipping. The most important reason for the existence of consular establishments in the early history of this country was the supervision of several vital matters relating to American shipping. These duties still rank high in the consular functions at seaboard cities. When an American ship arrives in port, the ship's papers, including the ship's register, the crew list, and the shipping articles, are delivered to the consul. These papers are retained during the ship's stay in port and are returned to the master after he produces the ship's clearance signed by the port authorities and satisfies the consul that the

[1] *N.Y. Times*, May 20, 1921.

[2] Mrs. W. H. Felton, at that time the only woman member of the United States Senate, declared regarding this speech, however, that "Ambassador Harvey would do well to talk plain common sense and less of buncombe." *N.Y. Times*, Oct. 26, 1922.

[3] FELLER and HUDSON, II: 1276.

obligations toward the crew have been discharged. The consul supervises the shipping and discharging of seamen on American vessels, and furnishes relief to destitute American seamen. He is authorized to settle disputes between masters and crews, to investigate mutinies on American vessels on the high seas, and to render assistance to American vessels in distress. In the absence of the master he may take charge of wrecks and cargoes.[1]

Functions in Connection with Cargoes and Passengers Bound to the United States. The consul aids in the enforcement of customs and port laws in the United States in various ways. Cargoes of a greater value than $100 are certified or invoiced by him for the purpose of assisting the American customs authorities to evaluate the goods. Passenger vessels destined for the United States must receive a bill of health from the consul, the document being required to prevent the carrying to this country of epidemic diseases. At important ports medical officers are employed to make inspections previous to granting bills of health. Foreigners bound for the United States receive passport visas at the American consulates. Cooperation in enforcing the quota provisions of the immigration law is required of the consular officers, and immigrants to the United States receive a quota visa at the American consulate in their district. Monthly reports are made to the principal quota officer regarding the number of quota visas.

Functions Relating to Commerce Promotion. Within the past two or three decades the commerce promotion work of the consular establishments has become their most important function. John W. Davis, former ambassador to Great Britain, once described the consular service as "the spearhead of the country's trade."[2] Reports are rendered for the benefit of American exporters showing the condition of foreign markets with regard to particular commodities. A large number of letters are sent to persons or houses in the United States in answer to requests for information on tariffs, freight rates, advertising rates, the possibility of markets for particular articles, and foreign competition in the field. Traveling representatives of American houses who call at the consulates are given like assistance. The consular officers aid in making the proper connections between the exporters and such local firms in the district as are thought to be competent to handle the American products. Sometimes the consul is called in to attempt the settle-

---

[1] For the duties of consuls see FELLER and HUDSON, II: 1225*ff*.

[2] *Foreign Service of the United States*, Hearings, p. 205.

ment out of court of commercial disputes between American business houses and their local agents.

Notarial and Judicial Functions. The consul is invested with powers to execute legal documents, such as income tax returns, and to take depositions. It is his duty to take charge of the estate of an American citizen dying abroad if no relatives or legal representative are present, to preserve the effects, and to represent the estate before local courts should there be property under the jurisdiction of the courts. In countries where the system of extraterritoriality exists, such as China, American consuls act as judicial officers in trying offenses against American citizens or in hearing civil cases brought against them. In China the consular officers have had this power since 1844. In 1906, however, the United States Court for China was created to take jurisdiction in civil cases in which the property involved exceeds $500 in value and in criminal cases where the penalty may exceed $100 fine or sixty days in jail. This leaves to the consular officers the minor civil and criminal cases against American citizens.

Registration and Protection of Citizens. Each consulate keeps a register of all American citizens residing within the district. The births of children of American parentage are likewise recorded, and a registry of deaths is kept. The consul is expected to protect American citizens in all privileges provided by law or treaty. He should intercede with the authorities where citizens are illegally oppressed, and he is required to maintain and promote their rightful interests.

The Value of American Consular Officers to the Foreign Government. American consular representatives are maintained abroad primarily in the interests of the American government. Since the advantages of trade are reciprocal, their services are also of considerable value to the foreign community. It is for this reason that governments grant exequaturs to foreign consuls. An exequatur is the warrant or permission given to the foreign consul to exercise his consular rights and duties within the jurisdiction of the government granting the exequatur. An illustration of the value of the consul to the foreign community is shown by the Newcastle case of 1922. The American consul and vice-consul at Newcastle-on-Tyne in England were accused of refusing to grant visas to British subjects sailing to the United States unless they should agree to travel on American lines. This charge was denied and was evidently groundless. An investigation by the United States vindicated the American consular officials. The British government, nevertheless, revoked the exequaturs of the two officers. The consulate was then closed. This action resulted in a considerable blow to local business. A newspaper dispatch from Newcastle gave the following description of resulting conditions:

Newcastle shipping and business circles today are in a state bordering on consternation owing to the closing of the American Consulate. Numerous ships of various nationalities are already held up, lacking consular bills of health. Shipments of merchandise for the United States cannot go forward without consular invoices, and many persons desiring to travel to America are clamoring for visas, which under the regulations must be obtained from the Consul in the district in which they reside.[1]

An order requiring consular invoices to be obtained at Hull resulted in the diversion of shipping to that rival port. Civic organizations in Newcastle appealed to their government and continued to seek redress until the consulate was reopened.

THE VALUE OF THE SERVICES

The Department of State and the Foreign Service have stood out among the subdivisions of the executive branch as exemplifying the merit principle in administration. It is well that the principle should be thoroughly applied in these important services for in them the United States must place much reliance for the maintenance of friendly relations with the world. These services are the road builders along the way of peace. Training and proficiency is particularly necessary in a field in which every decade brings fresh problems of a technical and dangerous character. The lay administrator, lacking perspective and intimate knowledge, is apt here to fall back too freely upon broad sentimentalities handed down from previous generations. The part which the United States is to play in this unifying and hazardous world will be determined not only by policymakers in the White House and the halls of Congress but also by hundreds of men engaged in the day to day routine of the Department of State and of the embassies, legations, and consulates spread over the earth. The wise and discriminating protection of citizens, treaty making, arbitration, legislative preparations in committees and conferences, the administrative work of international commissions, and many other aspects of international contact, all depend upon a well-trained personnel which can give advice and apply policies wisely in conformity with the public interest.

[1] *N.Y. Times*, Sept. 2, 1922.

The work of diplomacy of the United States has grown so rapidly and has attained a significance so vast that the conception of Congress as expressed through appropriations has not kept pace with the facts. The conduct of peaceful international relations is relatively inexpensive. The expenditure for the construction of one large cruiser in our navy is equal to the entire budget of the League of Nations for more than two years. The cost to the United States of one day's participation in the World War is equivalent to the net cost of the Department of State and the Foreign Service for about eight years. In the present fiscal year, that for 1935–1936, the appropriations for the Department of State are given in the President's budget message as $15,958,565 while those for national defense total $829,329,901. In the estimates for 1936–1937 the Department of State is allotted $15,348,652[1] as compared with $920,894,697 for national defense.[2] A comparison of expenditures for these purposes may be open to the criticism that it is a contrast of the costs of utterly dissimilar things. But it can be well argued that the dangers to the national safety may be as great from unwise diplomacy as from the lack of military preparedness. And since an additional expenditure of relatively small sums can be productive of large returns, it is particularly desirable that the funds should be adequate to keep the services fit to perform their greatly expanded duties.

Some of the important needs of the services which cannot be met under present budgets may be briefly summarized. Additional personnel is necessary to meet the growing burden of work which has arisen from the rapid extension of American interests abroad. The economy movement which came with the depression resulted in the reduction of the staff of the Department of State, which lost almost a hundred people, and of the Foreign Service, which was reduced by a somewhat similar number of officers. Meanwhile these services have been confronted with increased work, and today they are decidedly understaffed. The quality of the Foreign Service should be improved through admissions into the lower ranks and through more frequent promotions in deserved cases. While a law was passed in 1931 providing for automatic promotions it did not go into effect until 1934. The Foreign Service has consequently shown a heavier loading than desirable in the unclassified

---

[1] Of these annual amounts more than $3,000,000 will be covered by fees.

[2] *Message of the President of the United States Transmitting the Budget for the Service of the Fiscal Year Ending June* 30, 1937, pp. 457, 493, 575, Govt. Printing Office, Washington, 1936.

group and lower classes and a lighter loading in the higher classes.[1]
Adequate funds should be allotted for transportation to the United
States of officers on leave from distant posts for purposes of renew-
ing contacts with conditions in this country.[2] The provision of
expenses for entertainment and other necessary costs of social intercourse for acquiring friendly contacts in foreign capitals is essential
to a smoothly working and effective diplomacy. Congress now
makes no contribution for these purposes. A more generous
appropriation for the Department of State would hold in the service
men of high quality and would attract others to the department.
There are many other needs which must wait upon more adequate
funds as, for example, the previously mentioned requirement of
publishing more rapidly the volumes of *Foreign Relations of the
United States*. The Department of State has been continually
confronted with unexpected duties thrust upon it by forces outside
of its control; and, when emergencies arise which must be met, the
normal work of the department suffers.[3]

[1] *Department of State Appropriation Bill for* 1936, Hearings before Subcommittee of the House Committee on Appropriations, p. 109, Govt. Printing
Office, Washington, 1935.

[2] *Ibid.,* p. 120.

[3] For a discussion of the needs of the Department of State, see STONE, "The
Administration of the Department of State," and NORTON, "Foreign Office
Organization," both previously cited in this chapter; POOLE, DEWITT CLINTON,
"Cooperation Abroad through Organization at Home," *Annals of the American
Academy of Political and Social Science*, CLVI: 138 (July, 1931).

CHAPTER XXV

CONCLUSION: CHANGING TIMES, CHANGING POLICIES

The alterations made in American foreign policies during the past quarter of a century have been more numerous than is generally realized. A glance back upon the subjects considered in this volume will reveal a surprising number of innovations. Most of them are along the line of greater international cooperation and show a determination to renounce forceful methods. Some of the more important of the changes made in this direction have been:

Cooperation in many matters with a great world organization, the League of Nations, and the acceptance of the conference method as a normal and frequently employed procedure in world affairs.

The renunciation of war as an instrument of national policy.

The retreat from imperialism.

The willingness to submit questions of armament limitation to international discussion.

The willingness to subject the arms traffic to international supervision.

The weakening of the doctrine of the freedom of the seas through the evident determination not to support American merchants in their efforts to make profits out of the wars of other nations.

If the swing toward the policies of peace and cooperation has not been sufficient to satisfy the champions of peace, it nevertheless represents a considerable departure from prewar policies.

On the other hand, there are certain indications in the American political situation that show the possibilities of the employment of force. Perhaps of no alarming significance is the failure to join the World Court, a failure which detracts from a generally good record in peaceful settlement of disputes, but which has been due to the difficulty of our treaty machinery more than to any fundamental lack of cooperative intention in the American government. A more serious manifestation of what may be a subconscious and latent tendency to employ force as an instrument of policy is to be seen in the phenomenal growth of the expenditures for national defense. For no persons, not even those who are asking for the defense appropriations, can tell for what purpose the armaments are to be employed.

American diplomacy will continue to evolve. The policies of any government in this kaleidoscopic world must be continually subject to ruthless revision if the interests of the people of the nation are to be served. No better illustration of the realistic revision of an old and sentiment-enshrouded doctrine can be cited than the modification in 1935 of the ancient slogan, the freedom of the seas, by a saner and more economical interpretation of neutrality. But the changes of the past quarter century do not represent the arrival at ultimate goals. Nothing is ultimate. No sooner are we acquainted with the positions so recently reached than we must look forward along the direction of our drift to prepare ourselves for new scenes and to become acquainted with new concepts. Where will we be in another quarter century? An ever-recurring creditor balance, almost inevitable in the accounting of a great industrial and financial power, will doubtless have driven this country into closer relations with the world. Whether the predominant characteristic of our closer relations will be peaceful cooperation or aggressive expansion—that we shall leave to the soothsayers to foretell and to the future to disclose.

BIBLIOGRAPHY

The following list of books, documents, and periodicals is in no sense exhaustive. The volumes mentioned represent most of the principal sources which the author has consulted. In some fields, like that of regional policy, it is impossible to set forth more than a small proportion of the worth-while books. The literature of pamphlets and magazine articles is so vast that no attempt is made to refer to it further than by citations in the main body of the book.

General References

ADAMS, RANDOLPH GREENFIELD, *A History of the Foreign Policy of the United States*, The Macmillan Company, New York, 1924.

American Journal of International Law, The.

American Political Science Review, The.

Annals of the American Academy of Political and Social Science.

BEARD, CHARLES A., *The Idea of National Interest, An Analytical Study in American Foreign Policy*, The Macmillan Company, New York, 1934.

BEMIS, SAMUEL FLAGG, *The Diplomacy of the American Revolution*, D. Appleton-Century Company, New York, 1935.

———, *Jay's Treaty, A Study in Commerce and Diplomacy*, The Macmillan Company, New York, 1923.

BLAKESLEE, GEORGE H., *The Recent Foreign Policy of the United States*, Abingdon Press, New York, 1925.

BUELL, RAYMOND LESLIE, *International Relations* (rev. ed.), Henry Holt & Company, New York, 1929.

Congressional Record.

COUNCIL ON FOREIGN RELATIONS, *Survey of American Foreign Relations* (a series of 4 vols. edited by Charles P. Howland), Yale University Press, 1928–1931.

———, *The United States in World Affairs* (a series of annual volumes beginning in 1931). The editors have been Walter Lippmann, William O. Scroggs, and Whitney H. Shepardson. Harper & Brothers, New York.

Current History Magazine.

DEALEY, JAMES QUAYLE, *Foreign Policies of the United States, Their Bases and Development*, Ginn & Company, Boston, 1926.

DEPARTMENT OF STATE, *Executive Agreement Series.* The series began in 1929.

———, *Press Releases*, issued weekly.

———, *Treaty Information Bulletin*, a monthly publication.

———, *Treaty Series*, Treaties of the United States issued serially from 1923 to date. Cited as *U.S. Treaty Series.*

EAGLETON, CLYDE C., *International Government*, Ronald Press Company, New York, 1932.

FENWICK, CHARLES G., *International Law* (rev. ed.), D. Appleton-Century Company, New York, 1934.

————, *The Neutrality Laws of the United States*, Carnegie Endowment for International Peace, Washington, 1913.

FISH, CARL RUSSELL, *American Diplomacy* (3d ed.), Henry Holt & Company, New York, 1919.

Foreign Affairs (New York).

FOREIGN POLICY ASSOCIATION, *Foreign Policy Reports*, issued biweekly. Until 1931 these were issued under the title *Information Service*.

Foreign Relations of the United States, Papers Relating to, an annual publication. Issued from 1861 to 1869 under the title *Diplomatic Correspondence of the United States*. The latest volumes are for 1920. Cited as *Foreign Relations*.

FOSTER, JOHN W., *A Century of American Diplomacy*, Houghton Mifflin Company, Boston, 1900.

GARNER, JAMES WILFORD, *American Foreign Policies*, New York University Press, New York, 1928.

HARLEY, JOHN EUGENE, *Documentary Textbook on International Relations*, Suttonhouse, Los Angeles, 1934.

HILL, NORMAN L., *International Administration*, McGraw-Hill Book Company, New York, 1931.

HODGES, CHARLES, *The Background of International Relations*, John Wiley & Sons, Inc., New York, 1931.

HUDSON, MANLEY O., *International Legislation* (4 vols.), Carnegie Endowment for International Peace, Washington, 1931.

HYDE, CHARLES CHENEY, *International Law Chiefly as Interpreted and Applied by the United States* (2 vols.), Little, Brown & Company, Boston, 1922.

International Conciliation, pamphlets issued monthly by the Carnegie Endowment for International Peace, New York.

JONES, ROBERT L., *History of the Foreign Policy of the United States*, G. P. Putnam's Sons, New York, 1933.

Journal of Political Economy.

LATANÉ, JOHN HOLLADAY, *A History of American Foreign Policy*, Doubleday, Page & Company, Garden City, N.Y., 1927.

LAUTERPACHT, H., *The Function of Law in the International Community*, Oxford at the Clarendon Press, 1933.

League of Nations, *Treaty Series*, a publication of treaties and engagements registered with the Secretariat of the League.

MOON, PARKER THOMAS, *Imperialism and World Politics*, The Macmillan Company, New York, 1926.

————, *Syllabus on International Relations*, The Macmillan Company, New York, 1925.

MOORE, JOHN BASSETT, *A Digest of International Law* (8 vols.), Govt. Printing Office, Washington, 1906. Cited as *Moore's Digest*.

————, *The Principles of American Diplomacy*, Harper & Brothers, New York, 1918.

MOWER, EDMUND C., *International Government*, D. C. Heath & Company, Boston, 1931.

MOWRER, PAUL SCOTT, *Our Foreign Affairs*, E. P. Dutton & Company, New York, 1924.

New York Times, The.

Political Science Quarterly.

POTTER, PITMAN B., *An Introduction to the Study of International Organization* (rev. ed.), Century Company, New York, 1925.

——, *A Manual Digest of Common International Law*, Harper & Brothers, New York, 1932.

——, *This World of Nations, Foundations, Institutions, Practices*, The Macmillan Company, New York, 1929.

Proceedings of the American Society of International Law.

Proceedings of the Conferences of Teachers of International Law and Related Subjects, Carnegie Endowment for International Peace, Washington. There have been five conferences.

RICHARDSON, JAMES D., *The Messages and Papers of the Presidents* (10 vols.), Govt. Printing Office, Washington, 1896–1899.

SAVAGE, CARLTON, *Policy of the United States toward Maritime Commerce in War*, Govt. Printing Office, Washington, 1934.

SCHUMAN, FREDERICK L., *International Politics, An Introduction to the Western State System*, McGraw-Hill Book Company, New York, 1933.

SEARS, LOUIS MARTIN, *A History of American Foreign Relations*, Thomas Y. Crowell Company, New York, 1927.

SIMONDS, FRANK H., and EMENY, BROOKS, *The Great Powers in World Politics*, American Book Company, New York, 1935.

STOWELL, ELLERY C., *International Law*, Henry Holt & Company, New York, 1931.

TOYNBEE, ARNOLD J., *Survey of International Affairs*, an annual publication for the Royal Institute of International Affairs, Oxford University Press, London.

Treaties and Other International Acts of the United States of America (4 vols. thus far published bring the collection up to 1846), Hunter Miller, editor, Govt. Printing Office, Washington.

Treaties, Conventions, International Acts, Protocols and Agreements between the United States and Other Powers (3 vols.), Govt. Printing Office, Washington. The first two volumes are for the years 1776 to 1909. Vol. 3 is for 1910 to 1923. Cited, *Treaties, etc., of the U.S.*

VINACKE, HAROLD M., *International Organization*, F. S. Crofts & Company, New York, 1934.

Regional—Latin America

ALVAREZ, ALEJANDRO, *The Monroe Doctrine*, Oxford University Press, New York, 1924.

BEALS, CARLETON, *The Crime of Cuba*, J. B. Lippincott Company, Philadelphia, 1933.

Bulletin of the Pan American Union.

CALLAHAN, JAMES MORTON, *American Foreign Policy in Mexican Relations*, The Macmillan Company, New York, 1932.

CHASE, STUART, *Mexico, A Study of Two Americas*, The Macmillan Company, New York, 1931.

CLARK, J. REUBEN, *Memorandum on the Monroe Doctrine*, Govt. Printing Office, Washington, 1930.

CLEVEN, N. ANDREW N., *Readings in Hispanic American History*, Ginn & Company, Boston, 1927.

COX, ISAAC JOSLIN, *Nicaragua and the United States, 1909–1927*, World Peace Foundation, Boston, 1927.

DENNETT, TYLER, *John Hay, from Poetry to Politics*, Dodd, Mead & Company, New York, 1934.

DUNN, FREDERICK SHERWOOD, *The Diplomatic Protection of Americans in Mexico*, Columbia University Press, New York, 1933.

FITZGIBBON, RUSSELL H., *Cuba and the United States, 1900–1935*, George Banta Publishing Co., Menasha, Wis., 1935.

GRUENING, ERNEST, *Mexico and Its Heritage*, Century Company, New York 1928.

GUGGENHEIM, HARRY F., *The United States and Cuba, A Study in International Relations*, The Macmillan Company, New York, 1934.

HACKETT, CHARLES WILSON, *The Mexican Revolution and the United States, 1910–1926*, World Peace Foundation, Boston, 1926.

HILL, HOWARD C., *Roosevelt and the Caribbean*, University of Chicago Press, Chicago, 1927.

HUGHES, CHARLES EVANS, *Our Relations to the Nations of the Western Hemisphere*, Princeton University Press, Princeton, 1928.

International American Conference (4 vols.), Govt. Printing Office, Washington, 1890.

Inquiry into Occupation and Administration of Haiti and Santo Domingo, Hearings before a select committee of the U.S. Senate, 1921–1922, Govt. Printing Office, Washington, 1922.

Investigation of Mexican Affairs, Hearings before the Senate Committee on Foreign Relations, 1919–1920, Govt. Printing Office, Washington, 1920.

JENKS, LELAND H., *Our Cuban Colony*, Vanguard Press, New York, 1928.

JOHNSON, EMORY R., *The Panama Canal and Commerce*, D. Appleton & Company, New York, 1916.

JONES, CHESTER LLOYD, *Caribbean Backgrounds and Prospects*, D. Appleton & Company, New York, 1931.

——, *Caribbean Interests of the United States*, D. Appleton & Company, New York, 1919.

JONES, CHESTER LLOYD, HENRY KITTREDGE NORTON, and PARKER THOMAS MOON, *The United States and the Caribbean*, University of Chicago Press, Chicago, 1929.

KNIGHT, MELVIN M., *The Americans in Santo Domingo*, Vanguard Press, New York, 1928.

LATANÉ, JOHN HOLLADAY, *The United States and Latin America*, Doubleday, Page & Company, Garden City, N.Y., 1921.

LOCKEY, JOSEPH BYRNE, *Pan-Americanism, Its Beginnings*, The Macmillan Company, New York, 1926.

MARSH, MARGARET A., *The Bankers in Bolivia*, Vanguard Press, New York, 1928.

MILLSPAUGH, ARTHUR C., *Haiti under American Control, 1915–1930*, World Peace Foundation, Boston, 1931.

MUNRO, DANA G., *The Five Republics of Central America*, Oxford University Press, New York, 1918.

——, *The United States and the Caribbean Area*, World Peace Foundation, Boston, 1934.

NERVAL, GASTON, *Autopsy of the Monroe Doctrine*, The Macmillan Company, New York, 1934.

PERKINS, DEXTER, *The Monroe Doctrine*, 1823–1826, Harvard University Press, Cambridge, 1927.

——, *The Monroe Doctrine*, 1826–1867, Johns Hopkins Press, Baltimore, 1933.

PRINGLE, HENRY F., *Theodore Roosevelt, A Biography*, Harcourt, Brace & Company, New York, 1931.

Problems of the New Cuba, Foreign Policy Association, New York, 1935.

Proceedings of the International Conference of American States on Conciliation and Arbitration, Washington, December 10, 1928–January 5, 1929, Govt. Printing Office, Washington, 1929.

Report of the Delegates of the United States of America to the Fifth International Conference of American States, Govt. Printing Office, Washington, 1924, and similar reports for the sixth and seventh conferences.

RIPPY, J. FRED, *The Capitalists and Colombia*, Vanguard Press, New York, 1931.

——, *Historical Eevolution of Hispanic America*, F. S. Crofts & Company, New York, 1932.

——, *Latin America in World Politics, An Outline Survey*, Alfred A. Knopf, New York, 1928.

ROBERTSON, WILLIAM SPENCE, *Hispanic-American Relations with the United States*, Oxford University Press, New York, 1923.

SCOTT, JAMES BROWN, *International Conferences of American States, 1889–1928*, Oxford University Press, New York, 1931.

STUART, GRAHAM H., *Latin America and the United States* (2d ed.), Century Company, New York, 1928.

TANNENBAUM, FRANK, *The Mexican Agrarian Revolution*, The Macmillan Company, New York, 1929.

THAYER, WILLIAM ROSCOE, *The Life and Letters of John Hay* (2 vols.), Houghton Mifflin Company, Boston, 1915.

Theodore Roosevelt, An Autobiography, Charles Scribner's Sons, New York, 1920.

THOMAS, DAVID Y., *One Hundred Years of the Monroe Doctrine*, The Macmillan Company, New York, 1923.

WEINBERG, ALBERT K., *Manifest Destiny, A Study of Nationalist Expansionism in American History*, Johns Hopkins Press, Baltimore, 1935.

China and the Philippines

Annual Report of the Governor General of the Philippine Islands.

BARROWS, DAVID P., *A History of the Philippines*, American Book Company, New York, 1905.

BAU, MINGCHIEN JOSHUA, *The Open Door Doctrine*, The Macmillan Company, New York, 1923.

BLAKESLEE, GEORGE H., *The Pacific Area*, World Peace Foundation, Boston, 1929.

CALLAHAN, JAMES MORTON, *American Relations in the Pacific and the Far East, 1784–1900*, Johns Hopkins Press, Baltimore, 1901.

The China Year Book. 1933, North-China News and Herald Ltd., Shanghai, 1933.

CLARK, GROVER, *Economic Rivalries in China*, Yale University Press, New Haven, 1932.

——, *The Great Wall Crumbles*, The Macmillan Company, New York, 1935.

CROLY, HERBERT, *Willard Straight*, The Macmillan Company, New York, 1925.

DENNETT, TYLER, *Americans in Eastern Asia*, The Macmillan Company, New York, 1922.

——, *Roosevelt and the Russo-Japanese War*, Doubleday, Page & Company, Garden City, N.Y., 1925.

FOSTER, JOHN W., *American Diplomacy in the Orient*, Houghton Mifflin Company, Boston, 1903.

FORBES, W. CAMERON, *The Philippine Islands* (2 vols.), Houghton Mifflin Company, Boston, 1928.

HARRIS, NORMAN DWIGHT, *Europe and the East*, Houghton Mifflin Company, Boston, 1926.

HARRISON, FRANCIS BURTON, *The Corner-Stone of Philippine Independence*, Century Company, New York, 1922.

HAWES, HARRY B., *Philippine Uncertainty*, Century Company, New York, 1932.

HOLCOMBE, ARTHUR N., *The Chinese Revolution, A Phase in the Regeneration of a World Power*, Harvard University Press, Cambridge, 1931.

HORNBECK, STANLEY K., *China Today: Political*, World Peace Foundation, Boston, 1927.

——, *Contemporary Politics in the Far East*, D. Appleton & Company, New York, 1916.

Independence for the Philippine Islands, Hearings before the Committee on Insular Affairs, House of Representatives, Govt. Printing Office, Washington, 1932.

LATOURETTE, KENNETH SCOTT, *The Development of China* (rev. ed.), Houghton Mifflin Company, Boston, 1920.

MACMURRAY, JOHN V. A., *Treaties and Agreements with and Concerning China* (2 vols.), Oxford University Press, New York, 1921.

MORLEY, FELIX, *Our Far Eastern Assignment*, Association Press, New York, 1926.

MONROE, PAUL, *China: A Nation in Evolution*, The Macmillan Company, New York, 1928.

MORSE, HOSEA BALLOU, and HARLEY FARNSWORTH MCNAIR, *Far Eastern International Relations*, Houghton Mifflin Company, Boston, 1931.

NORTON, HENRY KITTREDGE, *China and the Powers*, John Day Company, New York, 1927.

REMER, C. F., *Foreign Investments in China*, The Macmillan Company, New York, 1933.

Report of the Commission on Extraterritoriality in China, Govt. Printing Office, Washington, 1926.

REYES, JOSÉ S., *Legislative History of America's Economic Policy toward the Philippines*, Columbia University Studies in History, Economics, and Public Law, Vol. 106, No. 2.

SOKOLSKY, GEORGE E., *The Tinderbox of Asia*, Doubleday, Doran & Company, Garden City, N.Y., 1932.

T'ANG LEANG-LI, *China in Revolt*, Noel Douglas, London, 1927.

TREAT, PAYSON J., *The Far East*, Harper & Brothers, New York, 1928.

VINACKE, HAROLD M., *A History of the Far East in Modern Time* Knopf, New York, 1928.

WARE, EDITH E., *Business and Politics in the Far East*, Yale Univer New Haven, 1932.

WILLIAMS, EDWARD THOMAS, *China, Yesterday and Today*, Thomas Y Company, New York, 1923.

WILLIAMS, S. WELLS, *The Middle Kingdom*, Charles Scribner's Sons, Ne 1898.

WILLOUGHBY, WESTEL W., *Foreign Rights and Interests in China*, (re 2 vols.), Johns Hopkins Press, Baltimore, 1927.

WORCESTER, DEAN C., *The Philippines, Past and Present* (2 vols.), The millan Company, New York, 1914.

YOUNG, C. WALTER, *Japan's Special Position in Manchuria*, Johns Ho Press, Baltimore, 1931.

Economic

ANGELL, JAMES W., *Financial Foreign Policy of the United States*, a report t the Second International Studies Conference on The State and Economi Life, London, May 29 to June 2, 1933, published in New York, 1933.

BEARD, CHARLES A., *The Open Door at Home*, The Macmillan Company, New York, 1935.

BORCHARD, EDWIN H., *The Diplomatic Protection of Citizens Abroad*, Banks Law Publishing Co., New York, 1915.

BUELL, RAYMOND LESLIE, *The Native Problem in Africa* (2 vols.), The Macmillan Company, New York, 1928.

BUREAU OF FOREIGN AND DOMESTIC COMMERCE, DEPT. OF COMMERCE, *The Balance of International Payments of the United States*, an annual publication, Govt. Printing Office, Washington.

———, *Commerce Reports*.

CULBERTSON, WILLIAM SMITH, *International Economic Policies*, D. Appleton & Company, New York, 1925.

DEPARTMENT OF STATE, *Annual Reports of the American High Commissioner at Port au Prince, Haiti*, Govt. Printing Office, Washington.

———, *Liberia, Documents Relating to the Plan of Assistance Proposed by the League of Nations*, Govt. Printing Office, Washington, 1933.

———, *Right to Protect Citizens in Foreign Countries by Landing Forces* (3d rev. ed. with supplemental appendix up to 1933), Govt. Printing Office, Washington, 1934.

DAVENPORT, E. H., and SIDNEY RUSSELL COOKE, *The Oil Trusts and Anglo-American Relations*, The Macmillan Company, New York, 1924.

DENNY, LUDWELL, *We Fight for Oil*, Alfred A. Knopf, New York, 1928.

DONALDSON, JOHN, *International Economic Relations*, Longmans, Green & Company, New York, 1928.

DUNN, ROBERT W., *American Foreign Investments*, B. W. Huebsch and the Viking Press, New York, 1926.

FISCHER, LOUIS, *Oil Imperialism*, International Publishers, New York, 1926.

FISK, GEORGE MYGATT, and PAUL SKEELS PIERCE, *International Commercial Policies*, The Macmillan Company, New York, 1923.

FOREIGN BONDHOLDERS PROTECTIVE COUNCIL, INC., *Annual Report, 1934*.

International Economic Relations, Report of the Commission of Inquiry into National Policy in International Economic Relations, University of Minnesota Press, Minneapolis, 1934.

ISE, JOHN, *The United States Oil Policy,* Yale University Press, New Haven, 1926.

LEAGUE OF NATIONS, *Journal of the Monetary and Economic Conference,* 1933.

——, *Proceedings of the International Conference for the Abolition of Import and Export Prohibitions and Restrictions, Geneva, October 17th to November 8th,* 1927 (C. 21. M. 12. 1928. II).

——, *Reports and Proceedings of the World Economic Conference, Held at Geneva, May 4th to 23rd,* 1927 (C. 356. M. 129. 1927. II).

——, *World Economic Survey,* an annual publication of the League's Economic Intelligence Service.

MCCLURE, WALLACE, *A New American Commercial Policy as Evidenced by Section 317 of the Tariff Act of* 1922, Columbia University Studies in History, Economics and Public Law, Vol. 114, No. 2.

——, *World Prosperity as Sought through the Economic Work of the League of Nations,* The Macmillan Company, New York, 1933.

MOULTON, HAROLD G., and LEO PASVOLSKY, *War Debts and World Prosperity,* Brookings Institution, Washington, 1932.

NEARING, SCOTT, and JOSEPH FREEMAN, *Dollar Diplomacy,* B. W. Huebsch and the Viking Press, New York, 1925.

NOYES, ALEXANDER D., *The War Period of American Finance,* 1908–1925, G. P. Putnam's Sons, New York, 1926.

Reports of the Dominican Customs Receivership, by fiscal periods, Govt. Printing Office, Washington.

Sale of Government Bonds or Securities in the United States, Hearings before the Senate Committee on Finance, 1931–1932, Govt. Printing Office, Washington, 1932.

SAYRE, FRANCIS BOWES, *America Must Act,* World Peace Foundation, Boston, 1936.

STALEY, EUGENE, *War and the Private Investor,* Doubleday, Doran & Company, New York, 1935.

TAYLOR, ALONZO E., *The New Deal and Foreign Trade,* The Macmillan Company, New York, 1935.

TRAMERYE, PIERRE L'ESPAGNOL DE LA, *The World Struggle for Oil,* Alfred A. Knopf, New York, 1924.

U.S. TARIFF COMMISSION, *Colonial Tariff Policies* (2d ed.), Govt. Printing Office, Washington, 1922.

——, *Reciprocity and Commercial Treaties,* Govt. Printing Office, Washington, 1919.

YOUNG, JAMES C., *Liberia Rediscovered,* Doubleday, Doran & Company, Garden City, N.Y., 1934.

WILLIAMS, BENJAMIN H., *Economic Foreign Policy of the United States,* McGraw-Hill Book Company, New York, 1929.

Peace and World Organization

Arbitration and the United States, World Peace Foundation, Boston, 1926.

BAKER, RAY STANNARD, *Woodrow Wilson and World Settlement* (3 vols.), Doubleday, Page & Company, Garden City, N.Y., 1922.

BERDAHL, CLARENCE A., *The Policy of the United States with Respect to the League of Nations*, Graduate Institute of International Studies, Geneva, 1932.

BOECKEL, FLORENCE BREWER, *Between War and Peace*, The Macmillan Company, New York, 1928.

Boycotts and Peace, A Report by the Committee on Economic Sanctions, edited by Evans Clark, Harper & Brothers, New York, 1932.

BRADLEY, PHILLIPS, *Can We Stay Out of War?* W. W. Norton & Company, New York, 1936.

BUELL, RAYMOND LESLIE, *The International Opium Conferences*, World Peace Foundation, Boston, 1925.

BUSTAMANTE, ANTONIO SANCHEZ DE, *The World Court* (translated), The Macmillan Company, New York, 1925.

COLEGROVE, KENNETH W., *International Control of Aviation*, World Peace Foundation, Boston, 1930.

Conditions in Manchuria, Senate Document 55, 72nd Cong., 1st Sess.

COOPER, RUSSELL M., *American Consultation in World Affairs*, The Macmillan Company, New York, 1934.

CRECRAFT, EARL WILLIS, *Freedom of the Seas*, D. Appleton-Century Company, New York, 1935.

CURTI, MERLE EUGENE, *The American Peace Crusade*, 1815–1861, Duke University Press, Durham, N. C., 1924.

———, *Bryan and World Peace*, Smith College Studies in History, Vol. XVI, Nos. 3 and 4.

DEPARTMENT OF STATE, *American Delegations to International Conferences, Congresses and Expositions*, an annual publication.

———, *Manchuria, Report by the Commission of Inquiry Appointed by the League of Nations*, Govt. Printing Office, Washington, 1932.

———, *Report of the International Commission of Inquiry into the Exchange of Slavery and Forced Labor in the Republic of Liberia*, Govt. Printing Office, Washington, 1931.

———, *Treaty for the Renunciation of War*, Govt. Printing Office, Washington, 1933.

Development of the League of Nations Idea, Documents and Correspondence of Theodore Marburg, edited by John H. Latané (2 vols.), The Macmillan Company, New York, 1932.

DEWOLF, FRANCIS COLT, *General Synopsis of Treaties of Arbitration, Conciliation, Judicial Settlement, Security and Disarmament, Actually in Force between Countries Invited to the Disarmament Conference*, Carnegie Endowment for International Peace, Washington, 1933.

DULLES, ALLEN W., and HAMILTON FISH ARMSTRONG, *Can We Be Neutral?* Harper & Brothers, New York, 1936.

EISENLOHR, L. E. S., *International Narcotics Control*, G. Allen and Unwin Ltd., London, 1934.

FACHIRI, ALEXANDER P., *The Permanent Court of International Justice* (2d ed.), Oxford University Press, London, 1932.

FLEMING, DENNA FRANK, *The United States and the League of Nations*, 1918–1920, G. P. Putnam's Sons, New York, 1932.

FOLEY, HAMILTON, *Woodrow Wilson's Case for the League of Nations*, Princeton University Press, Princeton, 1923.

Geneva Special Studies, a series published by the Geneva Research Center, Geneva, Switzerland.

The Hague Court Reports, James Brown Scott, editor, Oxford University Press, New York, 1916. A second series was published in 1932.

HOUSTON, DAVID F., *Eight Years with Wilson's Cabinet* (2 vols.), Doubleday, Page & Company, Garden City, N.Y., 1926.

HUBBARD, URSULA P., "The Cooperation of the United States with the League of Nations and with the International Labour Organization," *International Conciliation*, No. 274 (November, 1931).

HUDSON, MANLEY O., *American Cooperation with the League of Nations*, World Peace Foundation, Boston, 1924.

———, *By Pacific Means, the Implementation of Article Two of the Pact of Paris*, Yale University Press, New Haven, 1935.

———, *The Permanent Court of International Justice*, The Macmillan Company, New York, 1934.

———, *Progress in International Organization*, Stanford University Press, Stanford University, Calif., 1932.

International Labour Conference, annual reports of the sessions, International Labour Organization, Geneva.

The Intimate Papers of Colonel House, edited by Charles Seymour (4 vols.), Houghton Mifflin Company, Boston, 1926–1928.

JESSUP, PHILIP C., *International Security*, Council on Foreign Relations, New York, 1935.

LASSWELL, HAROLD D., *World Politics and Personal Security*, Whittlesey House, McGraw-Hill Book Company, New York, 1935.

LODGE, HENRY CABOT, *The Senate and the League of Nations*, Charles Scribner's Sons, New York, 1925.

LEAGUE OF NATIONS, *Appeal by the Chinese Government—Report of the Commission of Inquiry* (C. 663. M. 320. 1932. VII).

———, *Official Journal*.

———, *Records of the Conference for the Limitation of the Manufacture of Narcotic Drugs, Geneva, May 27th to July 13th*, 1931 (C. 509. M. 214. 1931. XI).

———, *Records of the Second Opium Conference, Geneva, November 17th, 1924–February 19th*, 1925 (C. 760. M. 260. 1924. XI).

———, *Report of the International Commission of Inquiry in Liberia* (C. 658. M. 272. 1930. VI).

League to Enforce Peace, American Branch, Published by the League to Enforce Peace, New York, 1915.

MARTIN, CHARLES E., *The Politics of Peace*, Stanford University Press, Stanford University, Calif., 1929.

MILLER, DAVID HUNTER, *The Drafting of the Covenant* (2 vols.), G. P. Putnam's Sons, New York, 1928.

———. *The Peace Pact of Paris, A Study of the Briand-Kellogg Treaty*, G. P. Putnam's Sons, New York, 1928.

MILLIS, WALTER, *Road to War*, Houghton Mifflin Company, Boston, 1935.

MOORE, JOHN BASSETT, *History and Digest of the Arbitrations to Which the United States Has Been a Party*, Govt. Printing Office, Washington, 1898.

———, *International Adjudications*, Modern Series (6 vols. published), Oxford University Press, New York.

MORLEY, FELIX, *A Society of Nations*, Brookings Institution, Washington, 1932.

MORRISON, CHARLES CLAYTON, *The Outlawry of War*, Willett, Clark and Colby, Chicago, 1927.

MYERS, DENYS P., *Origin and Conclusion of the Paris Pact*, World Peace Foundation, Boston, 1929.

NOBLE, GEORGE BERNARD, *Politics and Opinions at Paris, 1919*, The Macmillan Company, New York, 1935.

PAGE, KIRBY, *National Defense, A Study of the Origins, Results and Prevention of War*, Farrar and Rinehart, New York, 1931.

PEARSON, DREW, and CONSTANTINE BROWN, *The American Diplomatic Game*, Doubleday, Doran & Company, Garden City, N.Y., 1935.

PHELPS, CHRISTINA, *The Anglo-American Peace Movement in the Mid-Nineteenth Century*, Columbia University Press, New York, 1930.

The Public Papers of Woodrow Wilson, edited by Ray Stannard Baker and William E. Dodd (3 vols.), Harper & Brothers, New York, 1926.

RALSTON, JACKSON, *The Law and Procedure of International Arbitration* (rev. ed.), Stanford University Press, Stanford University, Calif., 1926.

Report of the United States Delegation at the International Labor Conference, Geneva, June 1933, to the Secretary of Labor, Govt. Printing Office, Washington, 1934.

SCHMECKEBIER, LAURENCE F., *International Organizations in Which the United States Participates*, Brookings Institution, Washington, 1935.

SEYMOUR, CHARLES, *American Neutrality, 1914–1917*, Yale University Press, New Haven, 1935.

SHOTWELL, JAMES T., *The Origins of the International Labour Organization* (2 vols.), Columbia University Press, New York, 1934.

———, *War as an Instrument of National Policy and Its Renunciation in the Pact of Paris*, Harcourt, Brace & Company, New York, 1929.

STRATTON, GEORGE MALCOLM, *International Delusions*, Houghton Mifflin Company, Boston, 1936.

Taft Papers on League of Nations, edited by Theodore Marburg and Horace E. Flack, The Macmillan Company, New York, 1920.

TAYLER, WILLIAM LONSDALE, *Federal States and Labor Treaties, Relations of Federal States to the International Labor Organization*, New York, 1935.

Towards an Enduring Peace, A Symposium of Peace Proposals and Programs, 1914–1916, compiled by Randolph S. Bourne, American Association for International Conciliation, New York (no date given).

TUMULTY, JOSEPH, *Woodrow Wilson as I Knew Him*, Doubleday, Page and Co., Garden City, N.Y., 1921.

WATKINS, ARTHUR CHARLES, *The Paris Pact*, Harcourt, Brace & Company, New York, 1932.

WILLOUGHBY, WESTEL WOODBURY, *Opium as an International Problem, the Geneva Conferences*, John Hopkins Press, Baltimore, 1925.

WILSON, FLORENCE, *The Origin of the League Covenant*, Hogarth Press, London, 1928.

WILSON, FRANCIS GRAHAM, *Labor in the League System*, Stanford University Press, Stanford University, Calif., 1934.

Arms and Arms Traffic

BAKER, PHILIP J. NOEL, *Disarmament*, Hogarth Press, London, 1926.

BEER, GEORGE LOUIS, *African Questions at the Paris Peace Conference*, The Macmillan Company, New York, 1923.

BUELL, RAYMOND LESLIE, *The Washington Conference*, D. Appleton & Company, New York, 1922.

Conference on the Limitation of Armament, Washington, November 12, 1921–*February* 6, 1922, Govt. Printing Office, Washington, 1922.

Documents of the London Naval Conference, 1930, H. M. Stationery Office, London, 1931.

ENGELBRECHT, H. C., and F. C. HANIGHEN, *Merchants of Death*, Dodd, Mead & Company, New York, 1934.

Exportation of Arms, Munitions, or Implements of War to Belligerent Nations, Hearings before the House Committee on Foreign Affairs, 1928, Govt. Printing Office, Washington, 1929.

Exportation of Arms or Munitions of War, Hearings before the House Committee on Foreign Affairs, 1933, Govt. Printing Office, Washington, 1933.

HULL, WILLIAM ISAAC, *The Two Hague Conferences*, Ginn & Company, Boston, 1908.

HUDSON, MANLEY O., *International Regulation of Trade in and Manufacture of Arms and Ammunition* (Report submitted to the Special Committee of the United States Senate Investigating the Munitions Industry), Govt. Printing Office, Washington, 1935.

ICHIHASHI, YAMOTO, *The Washington Conference and After*, Stanford University Press, Stanford University, Calif., 1928.

KEITH, ARTHUR BERRIEDALE, *The Belgian Congo and the Berlin Act*, Clarendon Press, Oxford, 1919.

LEAGUE OF NATIONS, *Armaments Year Book.*

———, *Conference for the Control of the International Trade in Arms, Munitions and Implements of War* (C. 758. M. 258. 1924. IX.).

———, *Conference for the Reduction and Limitation of Armaments, Conference Documents*, 1932.

———, *Documents of the Preparatory Commission for the Disarmament Conference*, minutes of the sessions, etc., 1926–1931.

———, *Proceedings of the Conference for the Supervision of the International Trade in Arms and Ammunition and in Implements of War* (A. 13. 1925. IX.).

———, *Records of the Conference for the Reduction and Limitation of Armaments,* 1932—

   Series A., Verbatim Records of Plenary Meetings.

   Series B., Minutes of the General Commission.

   Series C., Minutes of the Bureau.

LEFEBURE, VICTOR, *Scientific Disarmament*, The Macmillan Company, New York, 1931.

Limitation of Armament on the Great Lakes (Report of John W. Foster, Secretary of State, reprinted), Carnegie Endowment for International Peace, Washington, 1914.

MADARIAGA, SALVADOR DE, *Disarmament*, Coward-McCann, Inc., New York, 1929.

MAXIM, SIR HIRAM S., *My Life*, McBride, Nast & Company, New York, 1915.

Munitions Industry, Hearings before the Special Committee Investigating the Munitions Industry, U.S. Senate, 1934–1936, Govt. Printing Office, Washington, 1934–1936.

MYERS, DENYS P., *World Disarmament, Its Problems and Prospects*, World Peace Foundation, Boston, 1932.

The Proceedings of the Hague Peace Conferences (5 vols.), Oxford University Press, New York, 1920–1921.

Proceedings of the London Naval Conference of 1930 and Supplementary Documents, Govt. Printing Office, Washington, 1931.

Records of the Conference for the Limitation of Naval Armament Held at Geneva from June 20 to August 4, 1927, Geneva, 1927.

The Reports to the Hague Conferences of 1899 and 1907, Oxford at the Clarendon Press, London, 1917.

SELDES, GEORGE, *Iron, Blood and Profits*, Harper & Brothers, New York, 1934.

Treaty on the Limitation of Naval Armaments, Hearings before the Senate Committee on Foreign Relations, 1930, Govt. Printing Office, Washington, 1930.

WILLIAMS, BENJAMIN H., *The United States and Disarmament*, Whittlesey House, McGraw-Hill Book Company, New York, 1931.

Practice

ADAMS, CHARLES FRANCIS, *Charles Francis Adams*, Houghton Mifflin Company, Boston, 1900.

CORWIN, EDWARD S., *The President's Control of Foreign Relations*, Princeton University Press, Princeton, 1917.

CRANDALL, SAMUEL B., *Treaties, Their Making and Enforcement* (2d ed.), John Byrne & Company, Washington, 1916.

DANGERFIELD, ROYDEN J., *In Defense of the Senate, A Study in Treaty Making*, University of Oklahoma Press, Norman, Okla., 1933.

DEPARTMENT OF STATE, *The American Foreign Service*, Govt. Printing Office, Washington, 1932.

———, *The Department of State of the United States*, Govt. Printing Office, Washington, 1933.

———, *Register of the Department of State*, an annual publication.

Department of State Appropriation Bill for 1936, Hearings before Subcommittee of the House Committee on Appropriations, 1935, Govt. Printing Office, Washington, 1935.

FELLER, A. H., and MANLEY O. HUDSON, *A Collection of the Diplomatic and Consular Laws and Regulations of Various Countries* (2 vols.), Carnegie Endowment for International Peace, Washington, 1933.

FLEMING, DENNA FRANK, *The Treaty Veto of the American Senate*, G. P. Putnam's Sons, New York, 1930.

FOSTER, JOHN WATSON, *Diplomatic Memoirs* (2 vols.), Houghton Mifflin Company, Boston, 1909.

———, *The Practice of Diplomacy*, Houghton Mifflin Company, Boston, 1906.

Foreign Service of the United States, Hearings before the House Committee on Foreign Affairs, 1924, Govt. Printing Office, Washington, 1924.

HENDRICK, BURTON J., *The Life and Letters of Walter H. Page* (3 vols.), Doubleday, Page & Company, Garden City, N.Y., 1922–1925.

HOLT, W. STULL, *Treaties Defeated by the Senate*, Johns Hopkins Press, Baltimore, 1933.

HUNT, GAILLARD, *The Department of State of the United States*, Yale University Press, New Haven, 1914.

LAY, TRACY HOLLINGSWORTH, *The Foreign Service of the United States*, Prentice-Hall, Inc., New York, 1925.

MATHEWS, JOHN MABRY, *American Foreign Relations*, Century Company, New York, 1928.

POOLE, DEWITT C., *The Conduct of Foreign Relations under Modern Democratic Conditions*, Yale University Press, New Haven, 1924.

RICHARDSON, NORVAL, *My Diplomatic Education*, Dodd, Mead & Company, New York, 1923.

ROGERS, LINDSAY, *The American Senate*, Alfred A. Knopf, New York, 1926.

WRIGHT, QUINCY, *The Control of American Foreign Relations*, The Macmillan Company, New York, 1922.

WRISTON, HENRY MERRITT, *Executive Agents in American Foreign Relations*, Johns Hopkins Press, Baltimore, 1929.

INDEX